Alphabetical List of the Elements

Element	Symbol	Atomic Number	Atomic Mass	Element	Symbol	Atomic Number	Atomic Mass	Element	Symbol	Atomic Number	Atomic Mass
Actinium	Ac	89	(227)	Gold	Au	79	196.96655	Praseodymium	Pr	59	140.90765
Aluminum	Al	13	26.981538	Hafnium	Hf	72	178.49	Promethium	Pm	61	(145)
Americium	Am	95	(243)	Hassium	Hs	108	(269)	Protactinium	Pa	91	231.03588
Antimony	Sb	51	121.760	Helium	He	2	4.002602	Radium	Ra	88	(226)
Argon	Ar	18	39.948	Holmium	Ho	67	164.93032	Radon	Rn	86	(222)
Arsenic	As	33	74.92160	Hydrogen	H	1	1.00794	Rhenium	Re	75	186.207
Astatine	At	85	(210)	Indium	In	49	114.818	Rhodium	Rh	45	102.90550
Barium	Ba	56	137.327	Iodine	I	53	126.90447	Rubidium	Rb	37	85.4678
Berkelium	Bk	97	(247)	Iridium	Ir	77	192.217	Ruthenium	Ru	44	101.07
Beryllium	Be	4	9.012182	Iron	Fe	26	55.845	Rutherfordium	Rf	104	(261)
Bismuth	Bi	83	208.98038	Krypton	Kr	36	83.798	Samarium	Sm	62	150.36
Bohrium	Bh	107	(264)	Lanthanum	La	57	138.9055	Scandium	Sc	21	44.955910
Boron	B	5	10.811	Lawrencium	Lr	103	(262)	Seaborgium	Sg	106	(266)
Bromine	Br	35	79.904	Lead	Pb	82	207.2	Selenium	Se	34	78.96
Cadmium	Cd	48	112.411	Lithium	Li	3	6.941	Silicon	Si	14	28.0855
Calcium	Ca	20	40.078	Lutetium	Lu	71	174.967	Silver	Ag	47	107.8682
Californium	Cf	98	(251)	Magnesium	Mg	12	24.3050	Sodium	Na	11	22.989770
Carbon	C	6	12.0107	Manganese	Mn	25	54.938049	Strontium	Sr	38	87.62
Cerium	Ce	58	140.116	Meitnerium	Mt	109	(268)	Sulfur	S	16	32.065
Cesium	Cs	55	132.90545	Mendelevium	Md	101	(258)	Tantalum	Ta	73	180.9479
Chlorine	Cl	17	35.453	Mercury	Hg	80	200.59	Technetium	Tc	43	(98)
Chromium	Cr	24	51.9961	Molybdenum	Mo	42	95.94	Tellurium	Te	52	127.60
Cobalt	Co	27	58.933200	Neodymium	Nd	60	144.24	Terbium	Tb	65	158.92534
Copper	Cu	29	63.546	Neon	Ne	10	20.1797	Thallium	Tl	81	204.3833
Curium	Cm	96	(247)	Neptunium	Np	93	(237)	Thorium	Th	90	232.0381
Darmstadtium	Ds	110	(281)	Nickel	Ni	28	58.6934	Thulium	Tm	69	168.93421
Dubnium	Db	105	(262)	Niobium	Nb	41	92.90638	Tin	Sn	50	118.710
Dysprosium	Dy	66	162.500	Nitrogen	N	7	14.0067	Titanium	Ti	22	47.867
Einsteinium	Es	99	(252)	Nobelium	No	102	(259)	Tungsten	W	74	183.84
Erbium	Er	68	167.269	Osmium	Os	76	190.23	Uranium	U	92	238.02891
Europium	Eu	63	151.964	Oxygen	O	8	15.9994	Vanadium	V	23	50.9415
Fermium	Fm	100	(257)	Palladium	Pd	46	106.42	Xenon	Xe	54	131.293
Fluorine	F	9	18.9984032	Phosphorus	P	15	30.973761	Ytterbium	Yb	70	173.04
Francium	Fr	87	(223)	Platinum	Pt	78	195.078	Yttrium	Y	39	88.90585
Gadolinium	Gd	64	157.25	Plutonium	Pu	94	(244)	Zinc	Zn	30	65.409
Gallium	Ga	31	69.723	Polonium	Po	84	(209)	Zirconium	Zr	40	91.224
Germanium	Ge	32	72.64	Potassium	K	19	39.0983				

Numbers in parentheses indicate estimates of the atomic mass based on the longest-lived isotopes.

Chemistry: The Practical Science

Volume Two

Selected Chapters
Custom Version for Michigan State University

Paul Kelter
University of Illinois, Urbana-Champaign

Michael Mosher
University of Nebraska at Kearney

Andrew Scott
Perth College, UHI Millennium Institute

Contributing Writer:

Charles William McLaughlin
University of Nebraska at Lincoln

HOUGHTON MIFFLIN COMPANY   BOSTON   NEW YORK

CHEMISTRY: THE PRACTICAL SCIENCE
by Paul Kelter, Michael Mosher, and Andrew Scott
Copyright © 2008 by Houghton Mifflin Company. All rights reserved.

Publisher: Charles Hartford
Development Editor: Rebecca Berady Schwartz
Assistant Editors: Amy Galvin, Liz Hogan
Editorial Assistant: Henry Cheek
Project Editor: Andrea Cava
Senior Art and Design Coordinator: Jill Haber
Senior Photo Editor: Jennifer Meyer Dare
Composition Buyer: Chuck Dutton
Senior Manufacturing Buyer: Karen B. Fawcett
Marketing Manager: Laura McGinn
Marketing Assistant: Kris Bishop

Credits appear on pages A49–A52, which are considered an extension of the copyright page.

GENERAL CHEMISTRY
by Darrell D. Ebbing, Steven D. Gammon
Copyright © 2008 by Houghton Mifflin Company. All rights reserved.

Publisher: Charles Hartford
Senior Marketing Manager: Laura McGinn
Marketing Assistant: Kris Bishop
Development Editor: Kate Heinle
Editorial Assistant: Amy Galvin
Project Editor: Nan Lewis-Schulz
Editorial Assistant: Katherine Roz
Senior Production/Design Coordinator: Jill Haber
Composition Buyer: Chuck Dutton

Warning: This book contains descriptions of chemical reactions and photographs of experiments that are potentially dangerous and harmful if undertaken without proper supervision, equipment, and safety precautions. **DO NOT** attempt to perform these experiments relying solely on the information presented in this text.

Photo credits: A list of credits precedes the index.

Custom Publishing Editor: Dan Luciano
Custom Publishing Production Manager: Christina Battista
Project Coordinator: Janell Sims

Cover Designer: Emily Quillen
Cover Image: PhotoDisc

This book contains select works from existing Houghton Mifflin Company resources and was produced by Houghton Mifflin Custom Publishing for collegiate use. As such, those adopting and/or contributing to this work are responsible for editorial content, accuracy, continuity and completeness.

Printed in the United States of America.

ISBN-13: 978-0-618-99035-1
ISBN-10: 0-618-99035-6
1025947

2 3 4 5 6 7 8 9 – BR– 09 08 07

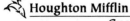

Houghton Mifflin
Custom Publishing

222 Berkeley Street • Boston, MA 02116

Address all correspondence and order information to the above address.

Brief Contents

Chapter 17

Acids and Bases   717

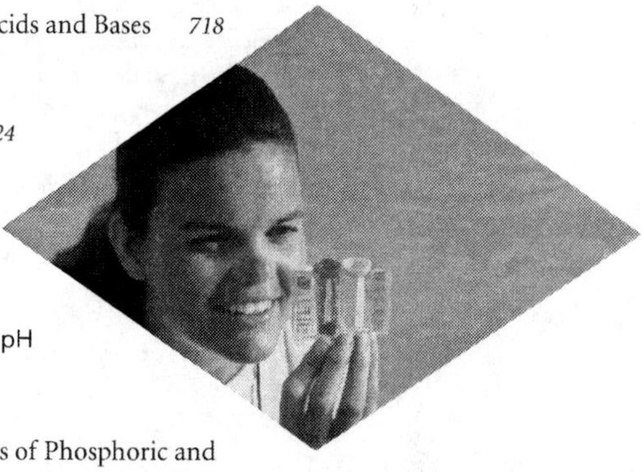

Chapter 18

Applications of Aqueous Equilibria   765

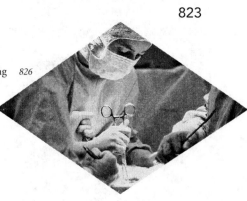

Chapter 21

Nuclear Chemistry   900

Chapter 22

Chemistry of the Main-Group Elements   934

Appendixes

Preface

To the Instructor

We are excited to be presenting you with a different kind of textbook—one that is written from the standpoint of *how chemists really teach in the twenty-first century*. It is our aim to complement your teaching style by giving your students a teacher's viewpoint in print. This book is about the questions we ask when we teach chemistry. It focuses on the "big ideas" of chemistry that we, as chemists, found so appealing that we chose a career in this field. For example, we explore the periodic table, the energy exchanges that accompany all chemical changes, the ideas of quantum mechanics (science is about probability, not perfection), and how we can use Le Châtelier's principle to control the extent of chemical reactions. These are just some of the ideas we want students to grasp deeply when we say, "*Here's what it means to think like a chemist.*"

A Framework of Interwoven Applications

In addition to our commitment to sharing the big ideas that define science in general and chemistry in particular, we write from the belief that chemistry is vitally important to the world in which we live. In this text, we present chemistry in the context of how it is related to our everyday lives by interweaving the concepts of chemistry with their uses in the chemical industry, the human body, and the environment. For example, a discussion of the energy changes that occur in chemical reactions is entwined with how these concepts are used in the U.S. space shuttle program. The discussion of kinetics is applied to the fate of pesticides in the environment. We view chemistry's applications in society as fundamentally good, and we note that when the use of chemistry has led to unfortunate consequences (especially for the environment), chemistry has also been used to clean up the mess. This focus on the *vital role* that the ideas and practice of chemistry have in our day-to-day lives is written into the storyline of the text. We mean it when we say that this textbook is *applications-based*.

An Interrogative Style

In our classrooms, we enjoy raising questions with our students, both because we like to hear their ideas and because raising questions is a key characteristic that defines the curious minds of scientists. We wrote our textbook to reflect an interrogative style, in which questions addressed to the student—often the same questions we ask in our own lectures—begin various topics. This approach involves students in the discussion, encourages them to pose questions about their world, and nurtures their curiosity about science and how it applies to society. This approach recurs throughout every chapter, as we continue to engage the student in what is most fundamental to practicing scientists: questioning the world around them.

Problem-Solving Approach

Our discussions are geared to science majors and unfold in the context of how they and their classmates will need to apply chemistry to their lives to solve problems. Our approach to problem solving helps students think critically by encouraging them to ask the right questions and frame them in such a way as to solve a problem effectively. Then, once the problem is solved, the text guides students in evaluating whether their answers make sense. The in-chapter *Exercises* include worked-out *Solutions* and are framed with a variety of pedagogical aids.

- *First Thoughts* engage the student.
- Worked-out *Solutions* guide the student step-by-step through the problem.
- *Further Insights* extend the concept.
- *Practice Problems* give students additional problems, to which answers are provided at the back of the book.
- The *list of corresponding end-of-chapter problems* at the end of each *Exercise* directs students to more practice.

These *Exercises* demonstrate how scientists think about problems and show how we work through a problem to arrive at an answer by asking questions.

Chapter Organization

Chapter 12 (Carbon) and Chapter 13 (Modern Materials) are strategically placed in the middle of this text for many reasons. The theme of the organic chapter (structure changes lead to changes in function and properties) logically follows the introduction of the topics on structural bonding models. The materials chapter logically follows the sequence of chapters on gases (Chapter 10) and liquids (Chapter 11). In addition, the placement of these chapters at the end of a typical semester of undergraduate chemistry allows the instructor the opportunity to end the semester on these applied topics of chemistry. The topical order is flexible, and these chapters can easily be taught in a different sequence than represented in the textbook.

The Bottom Line

Our applications-based and interrogative approach has resulted in a book that *students will actually read* and that reflects how *teachers really teach*. Here, then, as we say at the end of every chapter in the text, is *The Bottom Line*—in this case, a concise list of the main features of the textbook:

- **Applications** of chemistry are interwoven within the concepts of chemistry. Students often ask "Why do I need to know this?," so we have shown, at every opportunity, how chemistry is a part of our world.

- An **interrogative style** encourages students to be inquisitive about their world both locally and globally and involves them in discussing and learning concepts that are important to chemistry.

- Our **problem-solving approach** helps students to first think about a problem, to next approach the problem in a logical manner in order to arrive at a solution efficiently, and then to think beyond the calculation to uncover related information about the concepts that are being explored.

- A practical, **student-friendly pedagogy** includes writing that involves students and offers many opportunities for review (such as in the *Here's What We Know So Far* sections and *The Bottom Line* summaries). In addition, **visually engaging illustrations** clearly represent concepts for students and illustrate the vital connection of the world of the atom to the world in which we live.

- A **dynamic, contemporary art program** appeals to today's students, who expect exciting and visually appealing graphics. This program features molecular-level illustrations of key concepts to help students connect microscale activity to macroscale phenomena. In addition, electrostatic potential maps use vibrant color to show how electron density changes across a molecule.

■ **Technology and print resources** accommodate a variety of student learning styles and help instructors more easily manage homework by creating assignable activities that can be graded automatically in an online environment.

We hope that you and your students will enjoy reading and working with this textbook as much as we enjoyed writing it.

To the Student

Please allow us, for a moment, to share with you what happens on the first day of class in our own first-year chemistry classrooms. Often, we spend some time meeting as many of you as we can—beginning to know your names, learning your majors, and finding out why you have enrolled in our chemistry course. We then tell a few stories about ourselves, because part of studying together is seeing each other's very human side. During the entire year, we attempt to learn more about each other in order to make this new and exciting journey into chemistry a shared trip—where we ask each other questions, find answers, make connections, and discover why this wonderful subject is so useful for us to understand. By the same token, insofar as it is possible to share a bit of ourselves and our own sense of the beauty of this subject, we have tried to do so in this textbook.

In many ways, our presentation of material in this book is quite similar to the way we teach in class. We will share with you the big ideas of chemistry, and, because we all want to know "why we need to know this," we will discuss how the concepts of chemistry are applied to real-world issues, such as manufacturing processes, the blastoff of a rocket, the interaction of pharmaceuticals with the blood, and the age of life itself. We will then ask questions that lead to an explanation of how we know these things.

Our book has two overriding goals. The first is to help you appreciate the depth and breadth of chemistry. The second goal is to encourage you to make connections between concepts in chemistry and the world in which we live. "How do we know?" is one of the most vital questions, no matter what your field of study. In chemistry, we often say that asking good, focused questions is vital to "thinking like a chemist." *Knowing how to know* and *wanting to know* are two essential traits of successful, independent learning that not only are crucial to your study of chemistry but also will really pay off for a lifetime.

As you read this book (and we do believe that it can be read as a wonderful story of chemistry), look for the places where we raise questions. Ask yourself why we raise each question at the point where we do. What is the key idea? Why is this useful to know? What can I now figure out that I was not able to before? What connections can I make? What have I learned?

It is true that chemistry can be quite challenging and that persistence is necessary. Daily reading and study are the keys, and making a serious investment with your heart as well as your head will pay off in an understanding of chemistry as well as in the enjoyment of learning. If this book enhances your desire to learn more about the world around you, then we've been successful—and so have you.

These are the very things that we say to our own students. And then, together, we start doing chemistry. Let's go!

Paul Kelter
Michael Mosher
Andrew Scott

Features of the Text

Feature	Purpose	Example	What Is It?
Integrated applications Application CHEMICAL ENCOUNTERS: Energy Choices	To demonstrate why students need to know each concept	See page 197.	■ An application opens each chapter. ■ *Chemical Encounters* present major applications that are emphasized as themes and listed in the Table of Contents and chapter outlines. ■ Application icons highlight major applications in the text narrative.
Key questions within the chapter about energy: **What is energy?** uttle store energy and release it hin molecules and compounds?	To model the interrogative approach in chemistry and to encourage students to think critically	See page 168.	■ Important questions are highlighted throughout the text.
Exercises within the chapter EXERCISE 5.3 The First Law of Thermodynamics Calculate the change in the energy of a system if 51.	To help students think critically about questions and practice solving problems in chemistry	See page 178.	Features of in-chapter *Exercises:* ■ *First Thoughts* engage the student. ■ Worked-out *Solutions* are shown. ■ *Further Insights* extend the concept. ■ Additional *Practice* problems are provided. ■ Corresponding end-of-chapter problems are listed.
Here's What We Know So Far **The Bottom Line**	To provide multiple opportunities for student review throughout each chapter	See pages 175 and 186. See page 200.	■ Key concepts are reviewed in bulleted lists throughout the chapter. ■ Important concepts are summarized at the end of each chapter.
Boxed features	To provide detailed applications of chemistry concepts outside of the flow of the text discussion	See page 14. See page 62. See page 116.	■ *How Do We Know?* features demonstrate the use of key chemical concepts in medicine, research, and other applications. ■ *NanoWorld / MacroWorld* essays focus on how the interactions at the molecular level translate into explanations of chemistry at the macro level. ■ *Issues and Controversies* essays explore current, controversial topics related to science.

Feature	Purpose	Example	What Is It?
Illustrations and photos 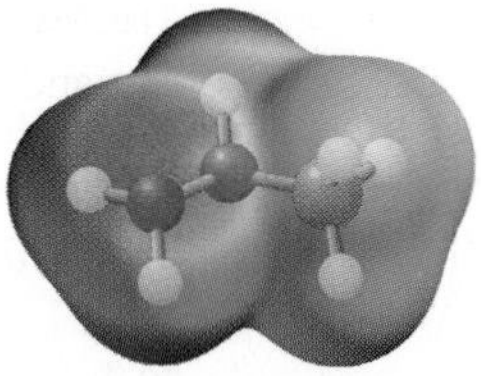 Methylhydrazine	To engage visual learners, help clarify key concepts, offer examples of real-world applications, and demonstrate the connections between the macroworld and the microworld	See page 195.	■ Art and photos appear throughout each chapter and within end-of-chapter problems.
End-of-chapter problems	To promote student review and comprehension of material To provide instructors with numerous ways to meet student and course needs	See pages 118–123.	Features of end-of-chapter problems: ■ *Skill Review* helps students practice applying specific concepts via paired problems. ■ *Chemical Applications and Practices* provide paired problems within the context of the real world. ■ *Comprehensive Problems* test students' mastery of concepts in the chapter. ■ *Thinking Beyond the Calculation* provides rigorous, cumulative, and conceptual problems based on multiple concepts.
Appendixes	To provide students with a ready source of useful data in chemistry To provide instructors with data that can be used to construct problems that meet specific course needs	See page A1.	■ Eight appendixes appear at the back of the book.

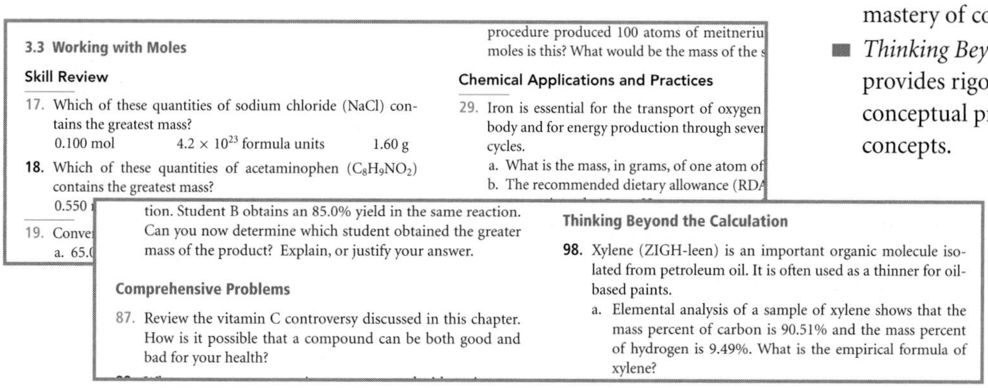

3.3 Working with Moles

Skill Review

17. Which of these quantities of sodium chloride (NaCl) contains the greatest mass?
   0.100 mol 4.2×10^{23} formula units   1.60 g
18. Which of these quantities of acetaminophen ($C_8H_9NO_2$) contains the greatest mass?
   0.550
19. Conve
   a. 65.0

procedure produced 100 atoms of meitneriu moles is this? What would be the mass of the s

Chemical Applications and Practices

29. Iron is essential for the transport of oxygen body and for energy production through sever cycles.
   a. What is the mass, in grams, of one atom of
   b. The recommended dietary allowance (RDA

tion. Student B obtains an 85.0% yield in the same reaction. Can you now determine which student obtained the greater mass of the product? Explain, or justify your answer.

Comprehensive Problems

87. Review the vitamin C controversy discussed in this chapter. How is it possible that a compound can be both good and bad for your health?

Thinking Beyond the Calculation

98. Xylene (ZIGH-leen) is an important organic molecule isolated from petroleum oil. It is often used as a thinner for oil-based paints.
   a. Elemental analysis of a sample of xylene shows that the mass percent of carbon is 90.51% and the mass percent of hydrogen is 9.49%. What is the empirical formula of xylene?

Learning Resources for Students

An extensive print and media package has been designed to assist students in working problems, visualizing molecular-level interactions, and building study strategies to fully comprehend concepts.

Technology for Students

■ **Your Guide to an A** with passkey is the portal to all of the premium student resources available from the Online Study Center (*college.hmco.com/pic/kelter*). From the Online Study Center, students will have access to *Visualizations* (animated molecular concepts and lab demonstration videos), *interactive tutorials, electronic flashcards, ACE practice tests,* and *over 50 hours of video lessons from Thinkwell.* These resources will help students prepare for class, study for quizzes and exams, and improve their grade. If students have bought a used textbook, they can purchase *Your Guide to an A* separately.

• *Visualizations* Animations and videos bring chemical concepts to life with animated molecular-level interactions and lab demonstrations. Each animation and video includes practice questions to test the student's knowledge of that concept.

• *Tutorials* These interactive tutorials guide students from preparation to comprehension using a variety of learning techniques, including preview and practice questions, concept overviews, animated demonstrations, and interactive activities.

• *Video Lessons from Thinkwell* Over 50 hours of video lessons are delivered via streaming video. Each 8- to 10-minute mini-lecture features a chemistry expert lecturing on key topics. These lessons combine video, audio, and whiteboard examples to help students understand and review concepts.

Also included in the Online Study Center are an *interactive periodic table, molecule library of chemical structures,* and *Careers in Chemistry page,* which has links to career information in industry, education, medicine, law, and other fields. A passkey is not required to access these resources.

■ **Eduspace®, Houghton Mifflin's Complete Online Learning Tool,** features all of the student resources included within the *Online Study Center* (described above), such as *tutorials, Visualizations, video lessons from Thinkwell, flashcards,* and *ACE practice tests,* as well as *text-specific end-of-chapter problems, ChemWork online homework assignments,* an online multimedia eBook, and SMARTHINKING—live, online tutoring. End-of-chapter problems include helpful links to equations, tables, and art from the textbook for student review, as well as links to the online multimedia eBook.

Also available are *ChemWork* assignments that help students begin to think and solve problems like chemists. As students work through unique, individual assignments, a series of gradual interactive hints guide them through the problem-solving process to help them arrive at a solution. *ChemWork* exercises go beyond the typical online homework system because they are designed to help students approach the problems in much the same way as if an instructor were sitting right next to them—directing them when they get stuck but not giving them the answer. These *ChemWork* problems also are automatically graded and recorded in the grade book.

The online multimedia eBook available within Eduspace integrates reading textbook content with interactive media. Students can visualize molecular concepts, work through interactive *tutorials,* watch *video lessons,* practice problem solving, and quiz themselves on key terms by clicking the embedded icons within the eBook.

- **Live, Online Tutoring available through SMARTHINKING®** provides personalized, text-specific tutoring during peak study hours when students need it most (terms and conditions subject to change; some limits apply). It allows students to use a powerful whiteboard with full scientific notation and graphics to interact with a live e-structor; submit a question to get a response, usually within 24 hours; view past online sessions, questions, or essays in an archive on their personal academic homepage; and view their tutoring schedule. E-structors help students with the process of problem solving rather than supply answers. SMARTHINKING® is available through Eduspace or, upon instructor request, with new copies of the student textbook.

Print Supplements: For Students

- The **Study Guide,** by Gretchen M. Adams (University of Illinois at Urbana-Champaign) and Frank J. Torre (Springfield College), expands on the problem-solving methods of the textbook with *First Thoughts, Solutions,* and *Further Insights* to help students further understand concepts that are particularly difficult. Each chapter of the guide includes 45–50 exercises for additional student practice. Tables and section descriptions also are included.

- The **Student Solutions Manual,** by Scott A. Darveau (University of Nebraska at Kearney), provides detailed solutions for half of the end-of-chapter exercises (designated by the blue question numbers) using the strategies emphasized in the text. This supplement has been thoroughly checked for precision and accuracy.

- The **Lab Manual,** by James Almy (Cornell University), offers a unique mix of both traditional and guided-inquiry experiments. This mix of experiments gives the instructor power in choosing the student's level of autonomy in the laboratory, and guidelines for use of these two types of experiments is discussed extensively in the "To the Instructor" section of the manual. Students will find each experiment to be clear, engaging, and thought-provoking. The front of the manual, with the sections "To the Student," "Safety," and "How to Use Lab Equipment," and the appendixes give students a solid base of knowledge (and instructors a solid base of comfort) to perform well in the laboratory.

Resources for Instructors

A complete suite of customizable teaching tools accompanies *Chemistry: The Practical Science.* Whether online or via CD, these integrated resources are designed to save you time and help make class preparation, presentation, assessment, and course management more efficient and effective.

Technology: For Instructors

- The **Media Integration Guide for Instructors** gives an overview of instructor and student media resources available with the text, provides the passkey to the *Online Teaching Center,* and includes the instructor CD's: *HM Testing™* (*powered by Diploma®*) and *HM ClassPresent™.* Throughout the guide, recommendations are given that suggest how, why, and when to use the media offered in this program.

- **HM Testing™ (powered by Diploma®)** combines a flexible test-editing program with a comprehensive grade-book function for easy administration and tracking. With *HM Testing,* instructors can administer tests via print, network server, or the web. Questions can be selected based on chapter, section, topic, format, and level of difficulty. Instructors also have the option of accessing the test bank content from *Eduspace*. With *HM Testing* you can

- Choose from over 2000 test items designed to measure the concepts and principles covered in the text.
- Ensure that each student gets a different version of the problem by selecting from the 777 algorithmic questions within the computerized test bank.
- Edit or author algorithmic questions.
- Choose problems designated as single-skill (easy), multi-skill (moderate), and challenging and multi-skill (difficult). Create questions, which then become part of the question database for future use.
- Customize tests to assess the specific content from the text.
- Create several forms of the same test where questions and answers are scrambled.

The *Complete Solutions Manual* files are included on this CD.

- **HM ClassPresent™ General Chemistry CD-ROM** features animations and video demonstrations arranged by chapter and topic. *HM ClassPresent* provides a library of high-quality, scaleable lab demonstration videos and animations covering core chemistry concepts. The resources within it can be browsed by thumbnail and description or searched by chapter, title, or keyword. Instructors can export the animations and videos to their own computers or use them for presentation directly from the CD. Full transcripts accompany all audio commentary to reinforce visual presentations and to accommodate different learning styles.

- **Online Teaching Center** (*college.hmco.com/pic/kelter*) includes everything instructors need to develop lectures: *Lecture Outline PowerPoint slides; virtually all of the text figures, tables, and photos* available in PPT slides and digital files; the *Instructor's Resource Manual* for both the main text and *Lab Manual* (PDF formats); *transparencies* (PDF format); animation and videos; and Classroom Response System (CRS) content.
  - *Lecture Outline PowerPoint slides* include lecture outlines, animations and video demonstrations, art from the textbook, and questions to gauge students' comprehension.
  - *Classroom Response System* (*CRS*) *content* transforms traditional lectures into student-centered learning environments that promote peer interaction and collaboration. The instructor has a formative assessment tool that provides real-time feedback when the histogram of student responses to the questions is displayed. CRS offers a dynamic way to facilitate interactive learning with students—perform immediate assessments, deliver quick quizzes, gauge comprehension, and take class attendance easily. These text-specific slides pose multiple-choice questions to students and challenge them to answer using wireless "clickers." Questions are conceptual and quantitative, and many also include applications. A variety of responses display anonymously in a bar graph, pie chart, or other graphic and can be exported to a grade book. (Additional hardware and software are required. Contact your sales representative for more information.)

- **Eduspace®, Houghton Mifflin's Complete Online Learning Tool,** is an instructor's "one-stop" resource for all course material. Through Eduspace, instructors have access to all of the media included within the Online Teaching and the Online Study Centers, plus additional homework problems and assignments. This additional content includes *algorithmic end-of-chapter problems* and *ChemWork assignments*. Text-specific end-of-chapter problems are automatically graded and include links to equations, tables, and art from the textbook, as well as optional hints that link to the *online multimedia eBook*. The majority of the end-of-chapter problems are algorithmically generated, ensuring that each student receives a different version. *ChemWork's* interactive assignments help students learn the process of problem solving with a series of interactive hints as they work through the assignments and are graded automatically. Multiple, randomizing versions of each assignment ensure that students do not get the same one. *ChemWork* is designed to help students think about problems in much the same way as if you, the instructor, were sitting right next to them—guiding them when they get stuck but not giving them the answer. SMARTHINKING®, live, online tutoring, is also included through Eduspace for students.

Eduspace includes all of Blackboard's powerful tools for teaching and learning, as well as customized functions that allow instructors to tailor these materials to their specific needs. Instructors can select, create, and post homework assignments and tests, communicate with students in a variety of ways, track student progress, and manage their portfolio of course work in the grade book.

- **Online Course Content for Blackboard® and WebCT** allows delivery of text-specific content online using your institution's local course management system. Through these course management systems, Houghton Mifflin offers access to all assets within Eduspace, such as *ChemWork, end-of-chapter problems, tutorials, video lessons,* and other resources.

Print Supplements: For Instructors

- The **Complete Solutions Manual,** by Scott A. Darveau (University of Nebraska at Kearney), includes every solution to the end-of-chapter problems using the strategies emphasized in the text. This supplement has been thoroughly checked for precision and accuracy.

Acknowledgments

We would like to thank the following friends and colleagues whose professional skills, understanding, and commitment have made this textbook possible.

Frank Torre and Gretchen Adams, dear friends both, thanks for your work on the study guide and for Frank's work on the PowerPoint slides. Frank, continue to work for peace and fly high. Gretchen, you throw like a guy.

Scott Darveau, how lucky we are to have you on our team. Thanks for putting together the solutions manual and offering so much valued counsel during the construction of this text.

Jeff Woodford and Jason Overby, many thanks for your excellent work on the test bank. Jeff, your work as a reviewer of the manuscript was marvelous. Mike Perona, we are grateful for your exceptional eye on the manuscript review as well.

Margaret Asirvatham, valued friend and colleague, thanks for your ability to peer into the future with your work on the clickers. Estelle Lebeau and Linda Bush, thank you for your many efforts in helping us to put our problems online into Eduspace. Laura Pence, teller of great stories, thank you for helping us to make our story come alive.

We also thank Laura McGinn, our marketing manager, for helping others to see what we have written; Andrea Cava, project editor, who was so good at keeping the process together over three continents; Connie Day, copyeditor, for her careful attention to detail; Cia Boynton, designer, for the attractive and flexible design; Jessyca Broekman, art development editor, to whom we owe much thanks for developing the lovely art program for the text; Naomi Kornhauser, for finding the photos that have added so much to the story; and Charles Hartford, vice president and publisher, for overseeing the project. Thanks also to Liz Hogan and Amy Galvin, assistant editors; Chip Cheek, editorial assistant; and Lynne Blaszak, senior media producer.

Special thanks to two who will be our friends forever: Richard Stratton and Katherine Greig, always with the right words to say and always there, no matter where our separate paths might take us.

Finally, thanks to Rebecca Berardy Schwartz, kindred spirit, confidante, soul-sister, and top-notch developmental editor. Thanks, Rebecca, for knowing so well that communicating science requires both the brain and the heart.

Reviewers

We sincerely appreciate our colleagues' help in reviewing the text and instructor and student resources.

Shawn B. Allin, *Spring Hill College*
Olujide T. Akinbo, *Butler University*
David Ball, *Cleveland State University*
Mufeed M. Basti, *North Carolina A&T State University*
Vladimir Benin, *University of Dayton*
Conrad Bergo, *East Stroudsburg University*
Fereshteh Billiot, *Texas A&M, Corpus Christi*
Richard E. Bleil, *Dakota State University*
Mary J. Bojans, *Pennsylvania State University*
Christine Bilicki, *Pasadena City College*
Sean Birke, *Jefferson College*
Iona Black, *Yale University*
Robert Blake, *Texas Tech University*
Jabe Breland, *St. Petersburg College*
James Carr, *University of Nebraska, Lincoln*
Annina Carter, *Adirondack Community College*
Tsun-Mei Chang, *University of Wisconsin–Parkside*
Paul J. Chirik, *Cornell University*
Kurt Christoffel, *Augustana College, Illinois*
Douglas S. Cody, *Nassau Community College*
Donald Cotter, *Mount Holyoke College*
Robert Cozzens, *George Mason University*
Janet DeGrazia, *University of Colorado*
Phillip Davis, *University of Tennessee, Martin*
Luther F. Elrod, *Piedmont College*
Dale D. Ensor, *Tennessee Tech University*
Cheryl Baldwin French, *University of Oklahoma*
Lois Hansen-Polcar, *Cuyahoa Community College*
Alton Hassell, *Baylor University*
HollyAnn Harris, *Creighton University*
Richard Hartmann, *Nazareth College*
Bert Holmes, *UNC, Asheville*
Martha Jackson-Carter, *Community College of Aurora*
Milton Johnston, *University of South Florida*
Don Jones, *Lincoln Land College*
Andy Jorgensen, *University of Toledo*
Phillip C. Keller, *University of Arizona*
Shahed Khan, *Duquesne University*
Bette A. Kreuz, *University of Michigan, Dearborn*
Shannon Lieb, *Butler University*
Art Landis, *Emporia State University*
Mark Masthay, *Murray State University*
Ursula Mazur, *Washington State University*
Craig McLauchlan, *Illinois State University*
Gary Mercer, *Boise State University*
Sally A. Meyer, *Colorado College*
Clyde Metz, *College of Charleston*
Steven Mylon, *Lafayette College*
Gary Mort, *Lane Community College*
Jim Niewahner, *Northern Kentucky University*
Stuart Nowinski, *Glendale Community College*
John M. Oakes, *Grossmont College*
G. S. Owens, *University of Utah*
Diane Payne, *Villa Julie College*
Yasmin Patell, *Kansas State*
Cynthia Peck, *Delta Community College*
Laura E. Pence, *University of Hartford*

Michael J. Perona, *CSU Stanislaus*
Giuseppe A. Petrucci, *University of Vermont*
John R. Pollard, *University of Arizona*
Parris Powers, *Volunteer Community College*
Mike Rennekamp, *Columbus State Community College*
Catherine Reck, *Indiana University*
Margaret Rempe, *Seattle University*
Scott W. Reeve, *Arkansas State University*
Dale D. Russell, *Boise State University*
David Rusak, *University of Scranton*
Ray Sadeghi, *University of Colorado*
Karl Sohlberg, *Drexel University*
Mary Sohn, *Florida Institute of Technology*
Jerry L. Sarquis, *Miami University*
Todd P. Silverstein, *Willamette University*
Les Sommerville, *Fort Lewis College*
Jacquelyn Thomas, *Southwestern College*
Lorena Tribe, *Pennsylvania State University, Berks Campus*
Rachel E. Ward, *East Carolina University*
Brian D. Williams, *Kings College*
Thomas Whelan, *University of Massachusetts, Amherst*
Kazushige Yokoyama, *SUNY, Geneseo*
Jenny Y. Yom, *Marshall University*
Timothy Vail, *Northern Arizona University*
John Vincent, *The University of Alabama*
Jeffrey Woodford, *Eastern Oregon University*
Kim Woodrum, *University of Kentucky*
James Worman, *Rochester Institute of Technology*
Timothy Zauche, *University of Wisconsin, Platteville*
Noel Zaugg, *Brigham Young University, Idaho*

Advisory Board Members

Iffat A. Ali, *Lake Land College*
Margaret R. Asirvatham, *University of Colorado at Boulder*
Mary J. Bojan, *The Pennsylvania State University*
Sean R. Birke, *Jefferson College*
Byron K. Christmas, *University of Houston, Downtown*
Patricia Dooley, *United States, Military Academy*
Daniel Domin, *Tennessee State University*
Nick Flynn, *Angelo State University*
Thomas J. Greenbowe, *Iowa State University*
Gregory R. Hale, *University of Texas, Arlington*
C. Alton Hassell, *Baylor University*
Milton D. Johnston, *University of South Florida*
Phillip C. Keller, *University of Arizona*
Bette A. Kreuz, *University of Michigan, Dearborn*
Laura E. Pence, *University of Hartford*
Alan M. Stolzenberg, *West Virginia University*
Marcy Hamby Towns, *Purdue University*
Edmund L. Tisko, *University of Nebraska–Omaha*
Edward A. Walters, *University of New Mexico*
Edward D. Walton, *California State Polytechnic University*
Rachel E. Ward, *East Carolina University*
Patrick Wegner, *California State University, Fullerton*
William H. Zoller, *University of Washington*

Developing effective problem-solving skills using an interrogative approach

The problem-solving approach encourages students to first think about the problem, use logic to arrive at a solution efficiently, and then think beyond the calculation to uncover related information about the concepts being explored. Worked-out examples throughout the text reflect this problem-solving method with a Question, followed by a series of First Thoughts, a worked-out Solution, Further Insights, and a Practice problem.

EXERCISE 5.3 **The First Law of Thermodynamics**

Calculate the change in the energy of a system if 51.8 J of work is done *by* the system with an associated heat loss of 12.3 J.

First Thoughts

We must pay particular attention to the sign conventions for heat and work in this problem. In this case, work is done by the system. Is this work positive or negative? A useful system to keep in mind is you! That is, when you do work—by running, dancing, or even moving your textbooks from one class to the next—you are using energy. After the process of moving your body or your books, you have less energy than you had before, so the work has a "−" sign. Similarly, the 51.8 J of work done by the system means that its energy change, w_{system}, is −51.8 J. The energy loss as heat *by the system* (such as that accompanying your run as your body tries to stay cool) also has a "−" sign, so $q_{system} = -12.3$ J.

Solution

From the standpoint of the system,

$$\Delta U = q + w$$
$$\Delta U = -12.3 \text{ J} + (-51.8 \text{ J}) = -64.1 \text{ J}$$

Further Insights

We want to reinforce the point that there is no such thing as heat or work within a system. In other words, *a system does not contain heat or work.* Rather, heat and work exist only as *types of energy transfer* between the system and the surroundings. Work is done by or on a system to move it through a distance. A system can transfer 64.1 J of energy as heat and work. It does not contain 64.1 J of heat and work.

PRACTICE 5.3

Calculate the change in the energy of a system if 84.7 J of work is done on the system, with an associated loss of energy as heat of 39.9 J.

See Problems 11–14, 19, 20, and 89.

HERE'S WHAT WE KNOW SO FAR

- There are three natural forces: the gravitational, electroweak, and strong nuclear forces.
- Potential energy is the energy stored within a system.
- Kinetic energy is the energy associated with motion.
- The law of conservation of energy states that energy can be neither created nor destroyed. Instead, it just moves between the system and the surroundings and can be transformed from one form to another.
- Work and heat are two ways in which energy can move between the system and the surroundings.
- The flow of energy as heat from the system to the surroundings involves an exothermic process. An endothermic process involves the flow of energy as heat from the surroundings to the system.
- Changes in the energy of a reaction can be studied by examining a reaction profile diagram.

Additional aids for student comprehension include Here's What We Know So Far in-chapter summaries, The Bottom Line bulleted reviews of key chapter topics, and Key Words.

The text models an interrogative style of learning through investigation by posing questions to the students to introduce various topics. These highlighted questions appear throughout the chapter and prompt students to think critically about topics.

Dilution

How do municipal water treatment plant workers prepare water so that it contains a fluoride ion concentration of about 1 part per million? They use a concentrated source of fluorine, hydrofluorosilicic acid, H_2SiF_6 ("HFSA"), which they then dilute in the drinking water. HFSA reacts with water in a fairly complex way that releases fluoride ion into the water. In Ireland, a company in the town of New Ross,

Engaging students through integrated applications

A space shuttle launch is an awe-inspiring demonstration of the ability of energy to transport humans and material away from Earth's surface with an eye toward planetary exploration. The energy to launch the craft and its crew comes from the explosive violence of chemical reactions. When these reactions are used in a carefully controlled way, they can lift the massive shuttle (which weighs in at a robust 2,000,000 kg), the booster rockets, and the fuel tank and propel the ship into orbit hundreds of miles above Earth in a very brief 10-minute ride.

Two chemical reactions, indicated in Figure 5.1, power the launch of the space shuttle. The combustion of hydrogen gas (the combination of hydrogen and oxygen to form water) takes place in the main engines. At the same time, the solid rocket boosters attached to the sides of the shuttle release a host of products resulting from the oxidation of aluminum by ammonium perchlorate, though we show only the primary equation here.

Main engin

Boosters:

As the ergy that cle is quie booster ro

Application

CHEMICAL ENCOUNTERS: Setting the Stage with the Space Shuttle

Interwoven throughout the chapter, chemistry concepts are explained through the use of real-world examples. **Application icons** throughout the text show at a glance where chemical concepts are applied.

4. Diagram, using circles for atoms, a crystal of KCl versus the same crystal of KCl dissolved in water.

Chemical Applications and Practices

5. Earth's oceans contain tons of dissolved sodium chloride. Yet, when a ship develops an oil leak, almost none of the oil dissolves in the ocean. Explain this phenomenon.

6. When an ion dissolves, it is surrounded by a hydration sphere. If water molecules surrounded the ion so that the hydrogen portion of the water was closer to the ion, would the ion most likely be a cation or an anion?

7. Pure water does not conduct an electric current. However, aqueous solutions of some compounds do form solutions that conduct electricity. Explain why the presence of some solutes converts nonconducting water into a conducting solution.

8. Glycerin can be produced as a by-product in soap making. The compound dissolves so easily in water that water from the air. This latter characteristic is wh is often found in many skin lotions. As glyceri the water, the skin can be kept moist. Glycerin's st shown below. What aspects of glycerin's structure most to its ease of dissolving in water?

$$H - \overset{\overset{\displaystyle OH}{|}}{\underset{\underset{\displaystyle H}{|}}{C}} - \overset{\overset{\displaystyle OH}{|}}{\underset{\underset{\displaystyle H}{|}}{C}} - \overset{\overset{\displaystyle OH}{|}}{\underset{\underset{\displaystyle H}{|}}{C}} -$$

Glycerin

9. A conductivity-testing apparatus, such as the one this chapter, possesses a light bulb whose brightness to how much current is flowing through it (and als the solution.) A small, but measurable, amount must be present before the bulb becomes visibly What effect would this characteristic of the appar

(a)   (b)

(c)   (d)

● Mg²⁺ ● Cl⁻ ● H₂O

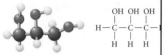

12. Which of the following would best represent water?

Applications are also found in **How Do We Know?** and **NanoWorld / MacroWorld** features, chapter openers, photos, and end-of-chapter exercises. Students will see how chemistry connects to their lives, their future careers, and their world.

How do we know?

The moons of Jupiter

The moons of the outer planets make most elegant chemical laboratories, because conditions on these worlds are so very different from those here at home. When we look at photos of Jupiter's moons, Europa and Ganymede (Figure 11.17), we see some vexing geological features. How do we know what caused these features? We can't visit the moons, at least not directly. However, our space probes can gather various types of electromagnetic radiation—including light, ultraviolet radiation, and X-rays—that give us data from which to draw conclusions.

The probes' data seem to show that deep within the surface of these moons, there are layers of ice, each in a different phase, mixed with rocks. The phase diagram of water that we showed as Figure 11.18 is inadequate to account for the low temperatures and massive pressures found within these moons. A more comprehensive phase diagram for water, emphasizing its solid phases, is given as Figure 11.20. The ice that is made in our kitchen freezer or found in an ice storm—what we might call "normal ice"— is technically called Ice Ih. Its structure is shown in Figure 11.21. There are 11 other forms of ice that have been made in the laboratory or simulated by computer.

The phase diagram shows that as the temperature and pressure inside the moons change, different types of ice are formed. Each ice has its own density. As layers form versions of ice of different densities, they form the geological features, such as cracking and grooves, that we see on the surface of these incredible satellites. Part of the task of scientists is to develop phase diagrams that tell us about the conditions at which each type of ice exists.

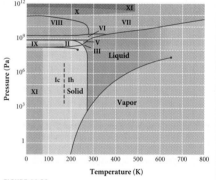

FIGURE 11.20

This is an expanded phase diagram for water, taking into account the phase changes among the various solid (ice) forms. These forms of ice are thought to occur in layers beneath the surface of some of the moons of the outer planets.

FIGURE 11.21

The arrangement of water molecules within a crystal of "normal" ice (Ice Ih).

Dynamic, contemporary art program

This **contemporary art and photo program** appeals to tech-savvy students who expect exciting and visually appealing graphics regardless of medium.

FIGURE 4.10
To visualize the idea of parts per million, per billion, and per trillion, consider that one drop of ink could be placed in these quantities of water. (a) Placing that drop of ink in a 12-gallon bucket results in 1 ppm. (b) Placing it in a tanker truck results in 1 ppb. (c) Placing it in a 12-million-gallon reservoir results in 1 ppt.

(a)   (b)   (c)

...tly different way. As an example, ...C_6Cl_6), a pesticide used on wheat ...ns that the maximum allowable ...$_6$ per billion grams of solution.

$$\frac{Cl_6}{\text{...ution}}$$

...ake the key assumption that *the ...o that of water*, then

$$\text{...ns} = \frac{1 \text{ g solution}}{1 \text{ mL solution}}$$

...on of hexachlorobenzene as the

$$= \frac{10^{-6} \text{ g } C_6Cl_6}{\text{L solution}} = \frac{1 \text{ } \mu\text{g } C_6Cl_6}{\text{L solution}}$$

...ions, we can express parts per

Water boils and creates steam.

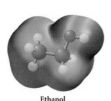
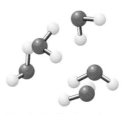

Five molecules of liquid water interact with each other. Note the positions of the hydrogen atoms. They are being shared with neighboring oxygen atoms.

Molecular-level illustrations of key concepts help students connect nanoscale activity to macroscale phenomena.

An electrostatic potential map of glucose and ethanol. The electrostatic potential is plotted on the surface of a computer-generated model of the molecules. Note how the electron density is distributed in each molecule, and compare these models to that of water (Figure 4.3).

Ethanol

D-glucose

In addition, **electrostatic potential maps** use vibrant color to show how electron density changes across a molecule.

Comprehensive
end-of-chapter materials

Focus Your Learning

The answers to the odd-numbered problems appear at the back of the book.

Section 4.1 Water—A Most Versatile Solvent

Skill Review

1. Explain how water molecules can dissolve both cations and anions.
2. Why doesn't pure water conduct an electric current?
3. Explain what is meant by the term *hydration sphere*?
4. Diagram, using circles for atoms, a crystal of KCl versus the same crystal of KCl dissolved in water.

Section 4.2 The Concentration of Solutions

Skill Review

11. Which of the following would best represent $MgCl_2$ dissolved in water?

   (a)   (b)

Comprehensive Problems

85. Individual atoms and molecules are so small that they have very low values of kinetic energy. However, given their mass and velocity, it is possible to calculate the value. What is the kinetic energy of an oxygen molecule (O_2) in air that you are breathing if its velocity is 460 m/s? Would you expect a nitrogen molecule (N_2) moving at the same speed to have more or less kinetic energy than the oxygen molecule? Explain.

86. Distinguish between the two terms in each of the following pairs:
    a. Heat and temperature
    b. System and surroundings
    c. Exothermic and endothermic
    d. q and ΔU

tions of muffins) are needed to provide 1 joule?

93. a. Suppose you are heating water (225 g) in a mug that you have placed in a microwave oven. As you wait to add the instant hot chocolate, please calculate, from the following data, the amount of energy as heat that the water has absorbed: The original water temperature was 15.0°C. When you remove the mug of hot water, you find that the temperature has risen to 98°C.
    b. What additional information would you need in order to determine the heat absorbed by the mug?

94. You have just removed a hot cheese pizza from the oven, and all of the ingredients are presumably at the same temperature. Without waiting for it to cool, you take a bite of the pizza. As you bite the pizza, the bread is hot on your tongue but does not burn. However, as you continue to bite, pizza sauce (mostly tomatoes and water) squeezes out and burns the roof of your mouth. Which has the higher specific heat,

---

96. A student's coffee cup calorimeter, including the water it contains, has been calibrated in a manner similar to that described in Problem 46. The heat capacity was found to be $55.5 \frac{J}{°C}$. If a 65.8-g sample of an unknown metal, at 100.0°C, was placed in the calorimeter initially at 25°C, and an equilibrium temperature of 29.1°C was reached, what is the specific heat of the metal?

97. The foods we eat provide fuel to keep us alive. Burning a 0.500-g sample of vegetable oil provides enough heat to raise the temperature of a calorimeter by 2.5 K. Assuming the heat capacity of the calorimeter to be $7.5 \frac{kJ}{K}$, determine the heat of combustion for 1 g of the oil.

98. A student performs the experiment shown graphically here. What is the specific heat of the block of metal used in the experiment? (Assume that the heat capacity of the empty calorimeter is $7.5 \frac{J}{°C}$.)

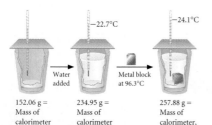

   −22.7°C   −24.1°C

         Water   Metal block
         added   at 96.3°C

152.06 g =   234.95 g =   257.88 g =
Mass of   Mass of   Mass of
calorimeter   calorimeter   calorimeter,
           and water   water, and
                      metal block

Thinking Beyond the Calculation

99. Phosphoric acid is used in many soft drinks to add tartness. This acid can be prepared through the following reaction:

$$P_4O_{10}(s) + 6H_2O(l) \rightarrow 4H_3PO_4(aq)$$

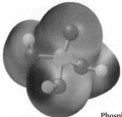

Phosphoric acid

a. If the value of ΔH for the reaction is -453 kJ, what is the value of ΔH for the reverse of the reaction?
b. What is the value of ΔH for this reaction if 10.0 g of phosphoric acid is produced?
c. Is this reaction endothermic or exothermic?
d. If 1.50 g of $P_4O_{10}(s)$ and 2.50 mL of water were mixed, how many grams of phosphoric acid would result?
e. What is the enthalpy change for the process outlined in part d?
f. If 10.0 g of P_4O_{10} were mixed with 1.00 kg of water at 25.0°C, what would be the final temperature of the water?

Online Study Center
college.hmco.com/pic/kelter

From the Online Study Center with passkey, students will have access to *Visualizations* (animated molecular concepts and lab demonstration videos), *interactive tutorials with pedagogy, electronic flashcards, ACE practice tests,* and *over 50 hours of video lessons from Thinkwell.* These resources will help students prepare for class, study for quizzes and exams, and improve their grade.

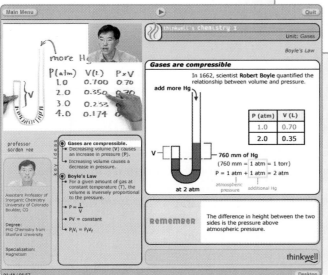

Video Lessons from Thinkwell are mini-lectures that combine video, audio, and whiteboard examples for student review. Each 8- to 10-minute segment features a chemistry expert lecturing on key concepts.

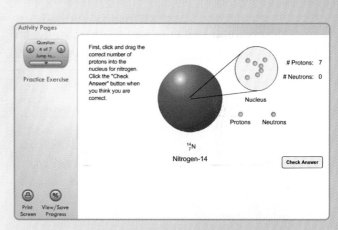

Interactive tutorials guide students from preparation to comprehension using a variety of learning techniques, including preview and practice questions, concept overviews, animated demonstrations, and interactive activities, allowing them to gauge their mastery of concepts from the text.

Visualizations include molecular-level animations and video lab demonstrations. Each animation and video includes practice questions to test the student's knowledge of that concept.

Online Teaching Center
college.hmco.com/pic/kelter

The Online Teaching Center includes everything instructors need to develop lectures:
- Lecture Outline PowerPoint slides
- Virtually all of the text figures, tables, and photos available in PPT slides and digital files (JPEG/GIF)
- The *Instructor's Resource Manual* for both the main text and *Lab Manual* (PDF formats)
- Transparencies (PDF format)
- Classroom Response System (CRS) content
- Animations and lab demonstration videos

Lecture Outline PowerPoint slides include lecture outlines, animations and video demonstrations, art from the textbook, and questions to gauge students' comprehension.

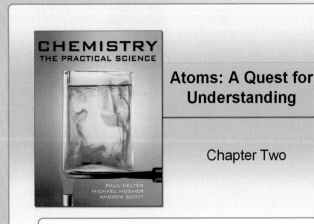

Chapter 1

- *Which of these elements that impacts our day-to-day lives occurs as a diatomic molecule?*
  1. Copper
  2. Gold
  3. Oxygen
  4. Silver
  5. Zinc

Classroom Response System (CRS) content transforms traditional lectures into student-centered learning environments that promote peer interaction and collaboration. The instructor has a formative assessment tool that provides real-time feedback by displaying a histogram of student responses to the questions. CRS offers a dynamic way to facilitate interactive learning with students—perform immediate assessments; deliver quick, text-specific quizzes; gauge comprehension; and take class attendance easily.

Atoms and Isotopes

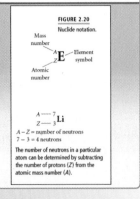

- The number of neutrons = A–Z
- Isotopes have the same atomic number but different mass numbers

$$^1_1H \quad ^2_1H \quad ^3_1H$$

FIGURE 2.20
Nuclide notation.

Mass number
Element symbol
Atomic number

$^A_Z E$

$A \longrightarrow 7$
$Z \longrightarrow 3$ Li

$A - Z$ = number of neutrons
$7 - 3 = 4$ neutrons

The number of neutrons in a particular atom can be determined by subtracting the number of protons (Z) from the atomic mass number (A).

Eduspace®

Eduspace®, Houghton Mifflin's complete online learning tool, is an instructor's "one-stop" resource for all course material. Through Eduspace, instructors have access to all of the media included within the Online Teaching and the Online Study Centers, plus additional homework problems and assignments.

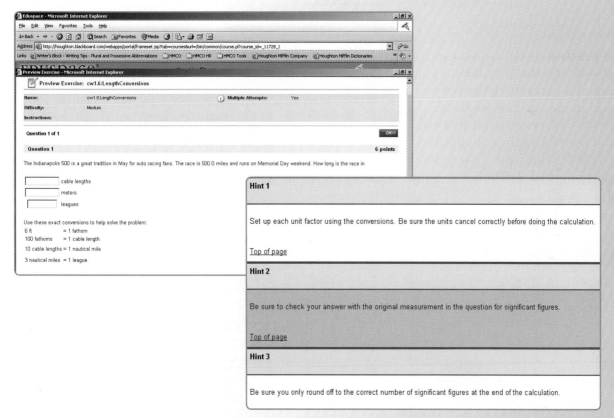

The online homework within *Eduspace* includes *algorithmic end-of-chapter problems* and *ChemWork assignments*. Text-specific end-of-chapter problems are automatically graded and include links to equations, tables, and art from the textbook, as well as optional hints that link to the *online multimedia eBook*. ChemWork's interactive assignments help students learn the process of problem solving with a series of interactive hints as they work through the assignments. Each assignment is also automatically graded.

Testing and presentation

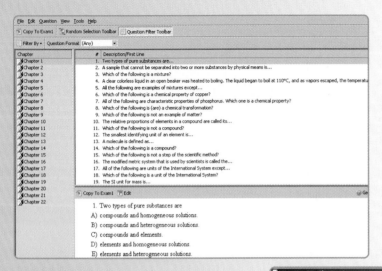

HM Testing™ (*powered by Diploma®*) combines a flexible test-editing program with a comprehensive gradebook function for easy administration and tracking via print, network server, or the web. Questions can be selected based on the chapter, section or topic, format, and level of difficulty. Instructors also have the option of accessing the test bank content from *Eduspace*.

With *HM Testing*, you can choose from over 2000 test items designed to measure the concepts and principles covered in the text. You can ensure that each student gets a different version of the problem by selecting from the 777 algorithmic questions within the computerized test bank.

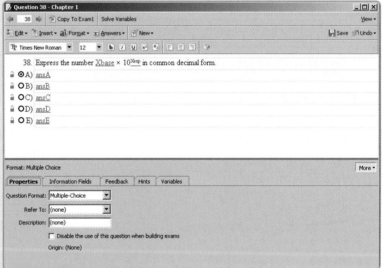

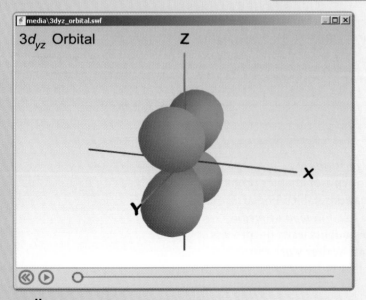

HM ClassPresent™ General Chemistry CD-ROM provides a library arranged by chapter and topic of high-quality, scaleable lab demonstration videos and animations covering core chemistry concepts. The resources within it can be browsed by thumbnail and description or searched by chapter, title, or keyword. Instructors can export the animations and videos to their own computers or use them for presentation directly from the CD.

14

Thermodynamics: A Look at Why Reactions Happen

Contents and Selected Applications

Sugary between-meal snacks are a good source of energy. Each contains sucrose, which is broken down in the body into glucose and fructose. Both of these molecules undergo complete oxidation and provide energy for the body.

After a hearty breakfast, we leave for work full of energy and ready to conquer the day. However, the midmorning hours can be difficult to get through because our energy level drops a couple of hours after we eat. This is especially true if we had a big bowl of sugar-coated, sugar-injected cereal for breakfast. To make matters worse, the mid-afternoon hours are no easier—they seem to be the longest of the day. Why does this happen and what can we do to give ourselves that "burst of energy" we need when we feel so tired? Enter the snack. Whether it takes the form of a chocolate bar, a donut, or a bottle of juice, it has the effect of raising our energy level. Just like breakfast, lunch, and dinner, the snack provides our bodies with a source of glucose. How does the consumption of glucose give us energy?

Antoine Lavoisier (the scientist we met in Chapter 3, whose measurements led to the formulation of the law of conservation of mass before he was guillotined in the French Revolution) noticed that living things consume foods and transform them into the energy that maintains life. Lavoisier's views on the process seem rudimentary given our modern understanding, but they were quite revolutionary in his day. The addition of glucose to living cells is an example of this food-to-energy transformation process. To the biochemist, this is part of the broader field of bioenergetics, the study of the energy changes that occur within a living cell.

In this chapter we will discuss some of the chemical reactions in the field of bioenergetics. Although we'll soon introduce terms such as *entropy, spontaneity, free energy,* and *equilibrium,* the underlying concept of probability demands our immediate attention. Chemists benefit from understanding these topics. They use probability in many ways: to locate electrons, to determine the macroscopic properties of compounds and mixtures, and to predict the outcome of chemical reactions. *We will use probabilities to discover why chemical processes occur*—including the chemical transformations of the body and their relationship to our ability to live.

14.1 Probability as a Predictor of Chemical Behavior

FIGURE 14.1

An interesting arrangement of the students in a classroom.

If you entered a classroom or movie theater and noticed all the males seated on one side and all the females on the other, as shown in Figure 14.1, would you think that some announcement, rule, or social convention had dictated that arrangement? Perhaps. But this seating pattern could also have emerged from purely random choices. In fact, there are numerous ways in which a room full of people could be sitting, and "separate seating" is just one of many possibilities.

Let's shift our focus to the room in which you are now sitting as you read this. As we know, the air in the room is a mixture of primarily oxygen and nitrogen gases. Oxygen and nitrogen molecules do not chemically interact with each other, so they can occupy essentially any unfurnished position in the room. Is it *possible* that these gases could be arranged such that all of the oxygen molecules were in one corner of the room and all of the nitrogen molecules in another, as shown in Figure 14.2? Possible? Yes. Likely? No. Is there something that these two seemingly unrelated situations—the room of people and the room of molecules—share?

The short answer is yes, the two situations have a lot in common. To understand how this could be so, let's introduce some common terminology to help in our discussion. We refer to the macrostate of a system (whether seated people or

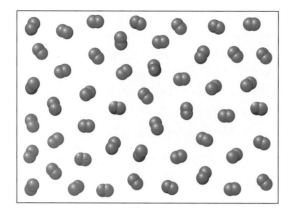

FIGURE 14.2

Is this arrangement of oxygen molecules within a room possible?

 = O_2

= N_2

A macrostate is a snapshot description of an overall situation.

A microstate is a snapshot description of a particular representation of individual particles. Each of these three pictures includes a different microstate for a single person in a movie theater.

molecular positions in a room) when we want to take a *snapshot* of the overall situation. The macrostate of the theater seating is that it is sorted by gender. The dispersed oxygen and nitrogen molecules in the room exert a certain pressure and have a certain composition; this is all part of the macrostate of the gases in the room.

If we wanted to describe the *individuals* in the theater, we might discuss which seat they are in, which way they are facing, and whether their arms or ankles are crossed. Each of these individual descriptions is referred to as a **microstate**. For instance, each arrangement of people in the theater indicates a different microstate. How does this apply to molecules? *The total of the microstates in a system defines, or describes, the macrostate of the system.* For individual molecules, the microstate can include their translational motion (changing from one location to another), their vibrational–rotational state (this involves the atomic movements around a chemical bond), and their electron configuration (ground state versus the excited state, even the oxidized state).

How might you describe the macrostate of the gases in your room? You could measure their temperature and pressure. You could also assess the number of molecules of each component in the room. Given the huge number of molecules of gas in the room, we would predict an even larger number of microstates for the gas. We mentioned the hypothetical condition of all the oxygen molecules being in one corner. To bring about that unlikely macrostate of air, the oxygen molecules (being restricted to the corner) would have to assume a limited number of the multitude of possible microstates in the room.

Why have you never encountered the macrostate that has all the oxygen molecules stuck in one corner of the room? One answer can be found in looking at

FIGURE 14.3

George Mallory and Andrew Irvine on Mt. Everest pack heavy cylinders of oxygen on their backs. This photo, taken in 1924 during their ascent to the summit, is the last known image of the pair.

Two individual macrostates.

the *probability* that such an event could occur. Out of all the possible macrostates, what are the chances that "all O_2 on one side, all N_2 on the other side" would occur? In short, there isn't a very good probability that this situation would happen. (Read on for a more detailed answer!)

Think back to the seating choices for a person entering a room. Which situation has more choices, the strict division by gender or "open seating"? Which situation would you consider to have the greater number of microstates that satisfy the conditions for a particular macrostate? Ludwig Boltzmann (1844–1906), an Austrian mathematician/physicist, dealt with this idea, along with its powerful implications, mathematically. We can get a sense of what he did by looking inside the tanks of oxygen that scuba divers and mountain climbers carry with them as they set off on their quests. Look closely at Figure 14.3. This photo, taken of mountain climbers George Leigh Mallory and Andrew Irvine before their fateful June 1924 attempt to scale the summit of Mt. Everest, shows the climbers each with two tanks of oxygen strapped to their backs. Let's assume that these tanks are connected by a valve and that one of the tanks is empty and the other full. What will happen to the distribution of the gas if the valve is opened? The final volume of the two tanks, which we'll call V_f, is double the initial volume of just one tank, V_i. We can also express this by saying that the ratio $\frac{V_f}{V_i} = 2$. How many ways can the individual molecules be distributed within the two tanks? (That is, how many "microstates" are there?) To make things a little simpler, let's assume that the tanks contain only two molecules of a gas. If we call the molecules A and B, we can have a total of four microstates, as shown in Figure 14.4. We will call the final number of microstates W_f (for the German word *Wahrscheinlichkeit*, "probability"), and $W_f = 4$ in this case. The initial number of microstates, W_i, is equal to 1, representing A and B both present in one tank, before the valve was opened allowing the gases to spread apart. This means that for two molecules in two tanks, the ratio $\frac{W_f}{W_i} = \frac{4}{1}$.

How is the number of microstates, $\frac{W_f}{W_i}$, related to the volume, $\frac{V_f}{V_i}$? For N molecules,

$$\frac{W_f}{W_i} = \left(\frac{V_f}{V_i}\right)^N$$

FIGURE 14.4

The possible arrangements of two molecules into two tanks.

Microstate	Tank 1	Tank 2
1	AB	
2		AB
3	A	B
4	B	A

That is the equation that Boltzmann derived. Using our numbers,

$$4 = 2^2$$

What if our tanks contained three molecules ($N = 3$) instead of two?

$$\frac{W_f}{W_i} = \left(\frac{V_f}{V_i}\right)^N \qquad \frac{W_f}{W_i} = 2^3 = 8$$

In this case, there would be eight possible microstates. *More molecules in the tanks make available more microstates—more ways in which the molecules can distribute themselves among the two tanks.* This means that the probability of all of the molecules being in only one tank—a single microstate among all other possibilities—becomes smaller. This is the key point: *As the number of molecules increases, the likelihood of their all being in one tank decreases sharply, and the probability of the gases tending toward an equal distribution increases.* Let's look further into this point and discuss its vital implications.

Let's put four oxygen molecules in the full tank. Here Boltzmann's equation indicates that there should be 16 ($2^N = 2^4 = 16$) different microstates of the oxygen molecules in the two-tank system. This is exactly what we predict by drawing each of the arrangements as in Figure 14.5. But if we look closely, we see that some of the microstates would give the same macrostate for the system. Figure 14.5 shows that only 5 unique *macro*states could arise from the 16 different *micro*states. Only 6 of these 16 microstates describe the equal distribution of the gases. The probability is therefore 6/16, or 37.5%, that the four molecules will arrange themselves into the two tanks equally. The probability of *exactly* equal distribution has diminished. However, there are many more microstates at or near equal distribution than microstates that are all on one side of either tank. Only 2 of the 16 microstates, or 12.5%, describe all of the molecules being on one side or the other.

As illustrated in Figure 14.6, greatly increasing the number of molecules in our experiment (from 8 to 32 to 128) also greatly increases the number of microstates that are available. As a result, the probability *of equal or nearly equal distribution of the molecules between the two tanks increases.* At the same time, the probability of *all* of the molecules being in one tank or the other is approaching zero. For even small real-world-sized samples of molecules (such as 0.01 mol or 0.1 mol), *equal or nearly equal distribution of the gases becomes the most likely outcome.* The bottom line is that probability—a mathematical construct—governs physical behavior, and in this case, probability says that the gases will spread from one tank to occupy both tanks evenly.

5 different macrostates

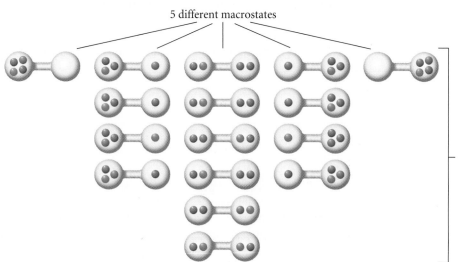

FIGURE 14.5

Microstates describing the possible arrangements of four molecules between two tanks.

16 different microstates

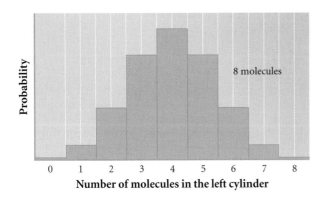

FIGURE 14.6

Probability of distribution of a gas between two cylinders. As the number of molecules increases in the system, the tanks' containing equal numbers of molecules becomes the more likely event. Note that the probability of equal distribution is a bell-shaped (Gaussian) curve.

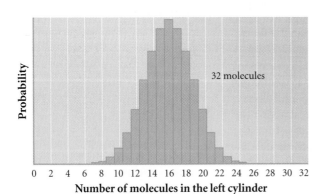

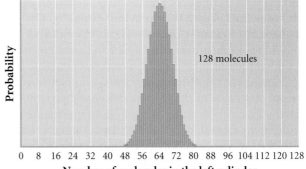

EXERCISE 14.1   **Probability**

A valve connects two glass jars. One of the jars contains six atoms of gaseous helium, and the other is empty. Determine the probability of the macrostate in which each jar will fill equally (that is, each jar will contain three atoms of helium) after the valve is opened. For the same system, what is the probability of finding four molecules in the left-hand jar and two in the right? What about the probability of finding all six molecules in the left-hand jar?

Solution

Because there are six molecules in this example, there are $2^6 = 64$ possible microstates. Drawing each of them out and grouping them into similar macrostates leads us to the conclusion that there are only 7 macrostates (see Figure 14.7). There are 20 microstates that indicate equal distribution, so the probability of equal distribution of the six molecules of gas is 20/64, or 31%. The probability of finding two molecules of gas in the right-hand jar and four in the jar on the left is 15/64, or 23%. The probability of finding all of the molecules in the left-hand jar is 1/64, or 1.6%.

FIGURE 14.7

Probability distribution for six molecules of gas in two tanks.

7 different macrostates

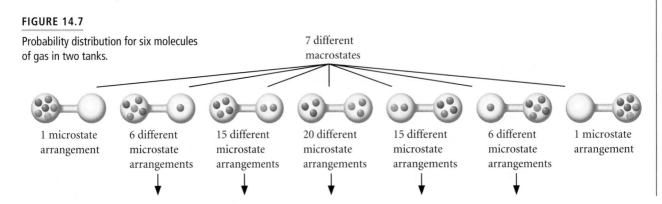

| 1 microstate arrangement | 6 different microstate arrangements | 15 different microstate arrangements | 20 different microstate arrangements | 15 different microstate arrangements | 6 different microstate arrangements | 1 microstate arrangement |

PRACTICE 14.1

Let's use the same valve and glass jar set-up, with one jar containing eight atoms of gaseous helium. Then the valve is opened. Determine the probability of the macrostate that shows three atoms of He in one jar and five atoms of He in the other jar.

See Problems 1–4, 7, and 8.

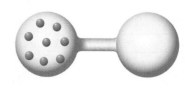

14.2 Why Do Chemical Reactions Happen? Entropy and the Second Law of Thermodynamics

Application

CHEMICAL ENCOUNTERS: Glycolysis

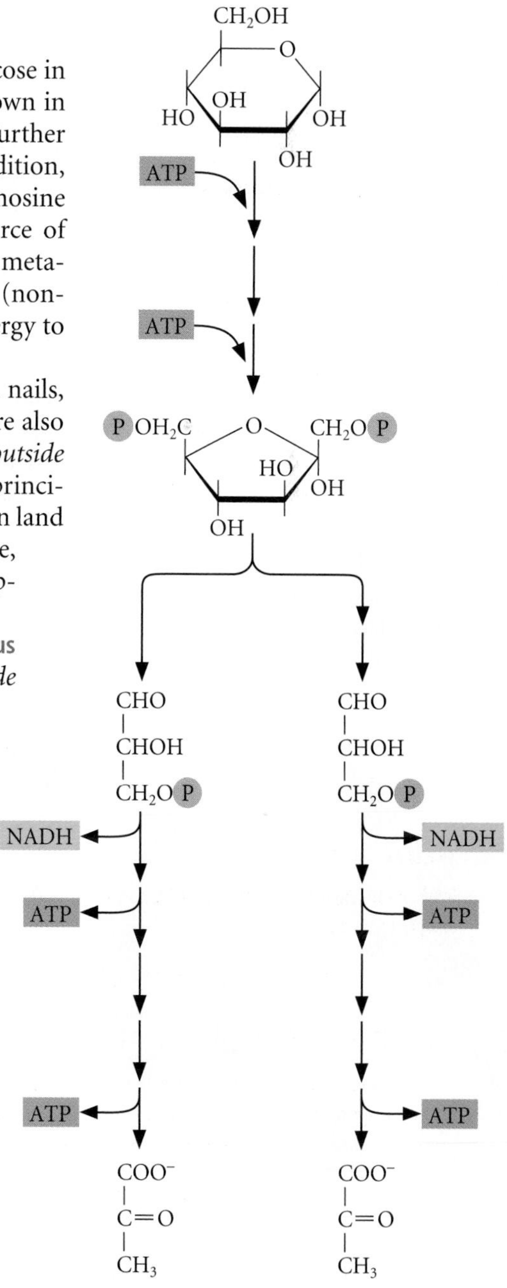

When sucrose enters the body, it is broken down into two simpler molecules, glucose and fructose. Glucose and fructose are structural isomers, both with the formula $C_6H_{12}O_6$.

$$C_{12}H_{22}O_{11}(s) + H_2O(l) \rightarrow C_6H_{12}O_6(aq) + C_6H_{12}O_6(aq)$$

Sucrose   Fructose   Glucose

Both molecules are used by the body to generate energy. For example, glucose in a cell undergoes **glycolysis**, the series of ten chemical transformations, shown in Figure 14.8, that produces two molecules of pyruvate. The pyruvate is further converted, releasing energy via a different set of transformations. In addition, during glycolysis two new energy storage molecules known as ATP (adenosine triphosphate, Figure 14.9) are produced. Glucose provides a major source of energy for living cells via the glycolysis pathway, which is the sole source of metabolic energy in some mammalian tissues and cell types. Many anaerobic (non-oxygen-consuming) microorganisms depend entirely on glycolysis for energy to carry out other biological reactions and survive.

Glycolysis is an example of a **spontaneous process**. The rusting of iron nails, the melting of ice in a glass, and the decay of wood buried in moist soil are also spontaneous processes. That is, these processes occur *without continuous outside intervention*. Say a brand new deck of cards falls off the kitchen table. The principles of probability say that there are many more ways in which the cards can land out of order than ways in which they can land sequentially. Furthermore, some of the cards will land face up and some face down. This disorder happens without our assistance—the process occurs spontaneously.

The reverse of a spontaneous process is known as a **nonspontaneous process**. Nonspontaneous processes *do not occur without continuous outside*

FIGURE 14.8

Glucose enters the glycolysis pathway on its way to complete oxidation. The reactions along the pathway produce two molecules of pyruvate and energy.

FIGURE 14.9

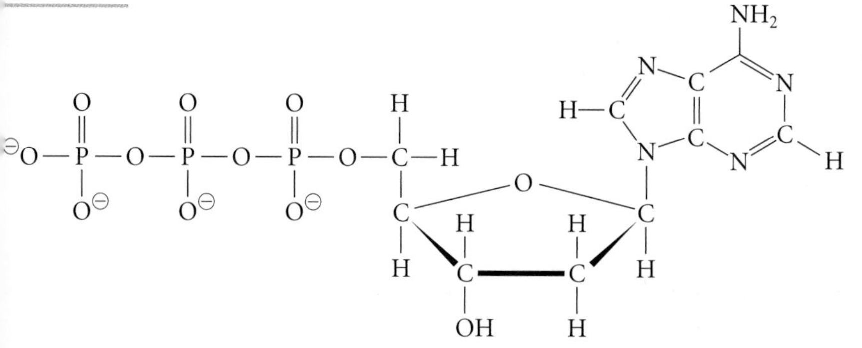

Adenosine triphosphate (ATP)

A disordered pile of playing cards.

 Application

intervention. A rusty nail does not revert to a polished iron nail without continuous help. Decayed wood buried in moist soil does not re-form freshly cut pieces of wood, and a deck of cards spread out on the ground does not leap into numerical and suit-based order. Just like these transformations, the reactions in chemistry can be considered either spontaneous or nonspontaneous.

What happens to a copper or bronze statue when it is exposed to the environment? As illustrated by the Newfoundland memorial erected to the memory of those lost in the worst plane crash in Canadian history (see Figure 14.10), a green patina forms on the surface. This patina is a complex mixture of colored compounds, such as antlerite ($Cu_3SO_4(OH)_4$, blue-green), brochantite ($Cu_4(SO_4)(OH)_6$, pale green), chalcanthite ($CuSO_4 \cdot 5H_2O$, blue-green), cuprite (Cu_2O, dark red), and tenorite (CuO, black). All of these compounds include either Cu^+ or Cu^{+2}, so they are oxidation products of the copper metal. Although the chemistry is much more complex, we can represent this patina by showing its formation as the simple oxidation of copper:

$$2Cu(s) + O_2(g) \rightarrow 2CuO(s)$$

A chemical reaction causes the green patina to form without our assistance, so this is a spontaneous process. The reverse process,

$$2CuO(s) \rightarrow 2Cu(s) + O_2(g)$$

is nonspontaneous; it does not occur without some outside assistance. *The reverse reaction of a spontaneous process is always nonspontaneous.*

The spontaneous oxidation of metals due to exposure to the environment is quite common. Table 14.1 lists some of the patinas that form on other metals.

Does the spontaneity of the oxidation of copper imply anything about the speed of the process? The short answer is no. It takes years for the green patina on a new copper roof to form completely. Under standard conditions, the conversion of diamond into graphite is also a spontaneous process, but luckily for people with diamond jewelry, the rate of this reaction is incredibly (almost immeasurably) slow. Rust forming on a nail and the decay of a buried log, even though they are spontaneous, are also slow processes. Biochemical reactions of glucose, on the other hand, are spontaneous and very rapid. The combustion of methane used to heat a pot of soup on the stovetop is even faster. **Thermodynamics**, the study of the changes in energy in a reaction (see also Chapter 5), determines *whether* a process is possible. In Chapter 15, we'll study the chemical kinetics of these processes to determine *how fast, and by what mechanism, they occur.*

FIGURE 14.10

A green patina on the bronze Silent Witness Memorial near Gander, Newfoundland, Canada.

TABLE 14.1	Patinas That Spontaneously Form on Metals		
Metal	**Element Symbol or Composition**	**Natural Color**	**Patina Color**
Aluminum	Al	Silvery white	Light gray
Brass	copper and zinc	Gold	Dark brown to black
Bronze	copper and tin	Yellow to olive brown	Dark brown to black
Copper	Cu	Light red brown	Green
Iron	Fe	Lustrous silvery white	Reddish brown
Silver	Ag	White to gray	Black

EXERCISE 14.2 | **Spontaneity in Common Processes**

Which of these processes are spontaneous?

a. Ice melting in a hot oven

b. Carbon dioxide and water reacting at STP to form methane and oxygen

c. A basketball player jumping to dunk a basketball

d. NaOH(*aq*) and HCl(*aq*) reacting when combined in a beaker

Solution

The processes described in parts (a) and (d) are spontaneous, because they happen without continuous outside intervention. The combination of sodium hydroxide and hydrochloric acid is often used in chemical analysis precisely because the reaction is not only spontaneous but also rapid. We will have much more to say about reaction speed in the next chapter, in which we discuss chemical kinetics. The process described in part (b) is nonspontaneous, which suggests that the reverse process, the combustion of methane, is spontaneous. The basketball player in part (c) must intervene (by adding energy to oppose the force of gravity) in order to dunk the basketball. This process is nonspontaneous.

PRACTICE 14.2

Indicate whether each of these processes is spontaneous or nonspontaneous.

a. Potassium and water reacting   c. A puddle evaporating from the sidewalk

b. Leaves falling from a tree   d. Photosynthesis

See Problems 15–16.

Entropy

The overall **catabolism** (the biological degradation of molecules to provide smaller molecules and energy to an organism) of glucose via glycolysis is a spontaneous process similar to the combustion of glucose. When glucose is burned in air, six molecules of oxygen gas and one molecule of glucose combine to produce six molecules of water vapor and six molecules of carbon dioxide gas.

$$C_6H_{12}O_6(s) + 6O_2(g) \rightarrow 6CO_2(g) + 6H_2O(g)$$

When this reaction occurs, the number of gaseous molecules increases, which corresponds to a dramatic increase in the number of microstates that describe the system. Because of this increase, the probability that the reaction will produce products is greater than the probability that carbon dioxide and water will spontaneously form glucose and oxygen. In short, *an increase in the number of microstates favors spontaneous reactions.* We can describe this principle in more practical terms by introducing entropy.

Glucose

Entropy (*S*) can be thought of as a measure of how the energy and matter of a system are distributed throughout the system. Investigations related to the concept of entropy began in the 1820s and 1830s with Nicolas Léonard Sadi Carnot (1796–1832) and Benoit Paul Emile Clapeyron (1799–1864). However, the concept wasn't mathematically developed until Rudolf Julius Emmanuel Clausius (1822–1888) worked on it in 1865. And although Clausius properly illustrated entropy, its relationship to the molecular level wasn't illuminated until Boltzmann did so several decades later.

Entropy isn't an easy concept to master, but we can gain important insight by considering the probabilities that have been the focus of our discussion. If the **multiplicity**—the number of microstates—increases, the number of ways in

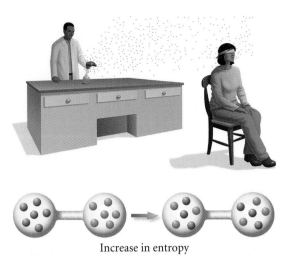

Increase in entropy

FIGURE 14.11

An experiment to explain entropy. Diffusion of gases is driven by entropy.

which energy and matter can be distributed also increases. Probability predicts that if the multiplicity of the system increases, there should be a corresponding increase in the number of ways in which energy and matter can be distributed in the system. This growth in the number of microstates increases the entropy of a system. *In other words, the more probable outcome of a spontaneous process is that an increase in entropy occurs.*

We can perform a simple experiment to help explain entropy. Say we have a friend place a bottle of perfume at one end of a room while we sit blindfolded in a chair on the opposite side of the room, as illustrated in Figure 14.11. Our friend opens the bottle. Still blindfolded, can we tell that the bottle has been opened? At first we would say it is still closed. Given a little time, though, we begin to notice the fragrance of the perfume and conclude that the bottle was opened. Why do we smell the perfume? The fragrance was released from the bottle on the opposite side of the room, so shouldn't it remain near the opened bottle? You know from experience that this isn't the case. What causes the perfume molecules to diffuse throughout the room and, eventually, into the noses of people at its most distant points? There is no pressure difference across the room, but still the perfume mixes spontaneously with the air. We can assume from the kinetic molecular theory that the attractive forces between the molecules of perfume and of those in the air are negligible, so there should be no significant change in the enthalpy of the process. Diffusion is neither exothermic nor endothermic for ideal gases. Instead, diffusion increases the distribution of the molecules throughout the room. Diffusion also increases the distribution of energy. The entropy of the system has increased.

We need to be extremely careful when we think of entropy. In processes represented by the perfume experiment, it appears that the level of disorder of the molecules has increased. Sometimes, we *incorrectly* think of entropy as a measure of the disorder of a system. But even though the increase in entropy often parallels the increase in disorder, entropy is not a measure of how disorganized a system has become. Disorder is a *macroscopic* description of a system, whereas entropy is related to the number of *microstates*.

The Second Law

 Application

Inside the cells of your body lie the enzymes (polymers of amino acids; see Chapter 12) that release energy from glucose. As shown in Figure 14.12, these large polymers start out as long flexible strands but, shortly after being made, fold into a small globular shape that contains pockets for binding glucose, ATP, ADP, water, and other compounds. The structure and type of amino acids around the binding pockets determine what type of reaction the enzyme will catalyze. Protein folding into the correct shape is a spontaneous process. **Does this make sense?** The flexible extended chain has many more motions than the folded enzyme; the number of ways to distribute energy in the system decreases as the enzyme folds. On the basis of this information alone, we might predict that protein folding is nonspontaneous. A closer look reveals our need for a deeper understanding of entropy and spontaneity.

As a rule, we say that a spontaneous process is accompanied by an increase in the entropy of the universe. This is the **second law of thermodynamics**. Mathematically, the change in the entropy of the universe is greater than zero for a spontaneous process:

$$\Delta S_{\text{universe}} > 0$$

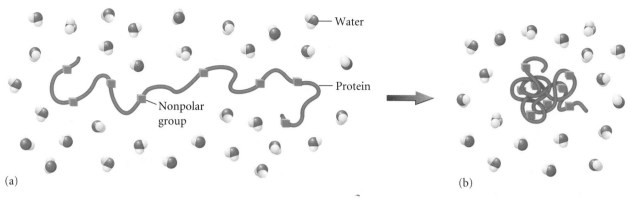

(a)

(b)

FIGURE 14.12

The folding of proteins is driven by entropy. The unfolded protein (a) disrupts the interactions of the water molecules. The nonpolar groups are tucked inside the protein, removing them from interaction with the solvent (b). The folding also increases the intermolecular forces of attraction between different regions of the protein and increases the number of interactions between solvent molecules.

However, recall the first law of thermodynamics (from Chapter 5), which says that the *energy* of the universe is constant ($\Delta E_{universe} = 0$). This contrasts with the second law, which implies that the *entropy* of the universe constantly increases. In other words, the number of possibilities for the distribution of the energy and matter of the universe constantly increases. This increase is related to the entropy changes in the system and surroundings (see Chapter 5 if you wish to review our definitions of the terms *universe, system,* and *surroundings*). Because the total entropy of the universe is the sum of the change in entropy for a particular system (ΔS_{system}) and the change in entropy of the surroundings ($\Delta S_{surroundings}$), we can describe the change in entropy of the universe as follows:

$$\Delta S_{universe} = \Delta S_{system} + \Delta S_{surroundings}$$

- If $\Delta S_{universe} > 0$, the process is spontaneous.
- If $\Delta S_{universe} < 0$, the process is nonspontaneous and is the reverse of the spontaneous process.
- If $\Delta S_{universe}$ is zero, we say that the process is neither spontaneous nor nonspontaneous but is at equilibrium, a condition of energetic stability that we will discuss shortly.

Because we take the sum of the change in entropy of the system and the change in entropy of the surroundings to obtain the change in entropy of the universe, ΔS_{system} could be a *negative* number and the overall process could still remain *spontaneous.* For example, if $\Delta S_{system} = -50$ J/K·mol and $\Delta S_{surroundings} = +80$ J/mol·K, then

$$\Delta S_{system} \quad + \quad \Delta S_{surroundings} \quad = \quad \Delta S_{universe}$$

$$-50 \text{ J/mol·K} + (+80 \text{ J/mol·K}) = +30 \text{ J/mol·K}$$

In this case, $\Delta S_{surroundings}$ increases more than ΔS_{system} decreases, so $\Delta S_{universe}$ increases and the process is spontaneous. Table 14.2 outlines the effects of $\Delta S_{universe}$ as a function of the change in entropy of the system and surroundings. Pick some

TABLE 14.2	$\Delta S_{universe}$ **Is the Sum of** ΔS_{system} **and** $\Delta S_{surroundings}$		
$\Delta S_{surroundings}$	ΔS_{system}	$\Delta S_{universe}$	**Spontaneity**
+	+	+	Spontaneous
+	−	?	Spontaneous if $\Delta S_{system} < \Delta S_{surroundings}$
−	+	?	Spontaneous if $\Delta S_{system} > \Delta S_{surroundings}$
−	−	−	Nonspontaneous

FIGURE 14.13

The unfolded protein reduces the inter-actions of the solvent molecules. By fold-ing, it allows those favorable interac-tions to take place.

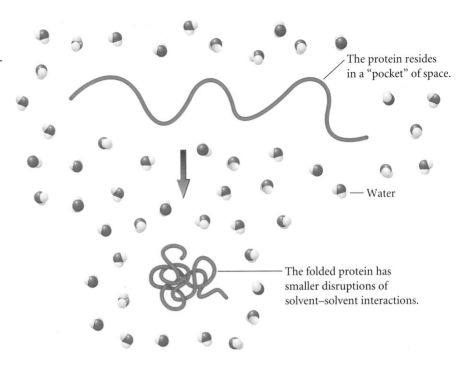

The protein resides in a "pocket" of space.

Water

The folded protein has smaller disruptions of solvent–solvent interactions.

sample values for ΔS_{system} and $\Delta S_{surroundings}$, as we did just above, to help clarify the outcomes in the table.

In the case of our folding protein, we must take into account the entropy of the system *and* that of the surroundings if we are to properly assess the change in entropy of the universe and determine whether the process is spontaneous. As an extended chain, the enzyme's nonpolar groups must interact with the aqueous cellular environment—the surroundings—as shown in Figure 14.13. The un-folded enzyme disrupts many of the interactions that occur among the solvent molecules (water). To reduce those disruptions within the surroundings, the folding enzyme tucks its *nonpolar* groups into the center of the globular struc-ture, effectively removing their interaction with the water inside the cell. The folding allows the *polar* groups in the enzyme to interact with the *polar* water molecules in the surroundings. The water molecules are also able to interact with each other with minimal disruption. The number of microstates for the protein decreases during the process of folding, but the number of microstates for the water and the water–protein interaction increases. The result is a $\Delta S_{surroundings}$ that is more positive than the negative ΔS_{system}. And the overall process, the fold-ing of a protein, is spontaneous ($\Delta S > 0$).

EXERCISE 14.3   **Reaction Spontaneity**

Determine whether the values shown below will produce a spontaneous process.

$$\Delta S_{system} = 140 \text{ J/mol·K}; \ \Delta S_{surroundings} = -155 \text{ J/mol·K}$$

Solution

In a spontaneous process the entropy of the universe increases, so we must add the values for the system and surroundings to answer the question.

$$\Delta S_{universe} = \Delta S_{system} + \Delta S_{surroundings}$$

$$= 140 \text{ J/mol·K} + (-155 \text{ J/mol·K})$$

$$= -15 \text{ J/mol·K}$$

Because our calculated value for the entropy of the universe is negative, the process is nonspontaneous.

PRACTICE 14.3

Determine whether the values for entropy in each of these cases will produce a spontaneous process.

   a. $\Delta S_{system} = -23$ J/mol·K; $\Delta S_{surroundings} = -55$ J/mol·K

   b. $\Delta S_{system} = 38$ J/mol·K; $\Delta S_{surroundings} = 59$ J/mol·K

   c. $\Delta S_{system} = -84$ J/mol·K; $\Delta S_{surroundings} = 132$ J/mol·K

See Problems 17, 18, 29, and 30.

14.3   Temperature and Spontaneous Processes

Living organisms have been found all over the Earth, from the mouths of near-boiling geysers to the depths of the Arctic Ocean. These living organisms, just like the species that live near the tropics, require energy to survive. Many of them use glucose as a source of energy. In fact, some of the psychrotrophs (bacteria that can survive exposure to low temperatures) and psychrophiles (bacteria that thrive in low temperatures) employ a concentrated solution of glucose as an "antifreeze" because such a solution lowers their freezing point. Research by microbiologists and biochemists into the life processes of the psychrophiles indicates that these organisms, like a lot of other living things on the planet, break down glucose to produce energy through glycolysis. Does the temperature at which these organisms live affect the spontaneity of the reactions involved in glycolysis? To answer this question, we need to consider the signs on the change in entropy of the system (ΔS_{system}) and of the surroundings ($\Delta S_{surroundings}$). A positive change in the entropy of the universe is required for the process to be spontaneous.

Application

CHEMICAL ENCOUNTERS: Psychrotrophs and Psychrophiles

In general, as compounds undergo changes in their physical states from solid to liquid to gas, the entropy of the *system* increases ($\Delta S_{system} = +$), as shown in Figure 14.16. Water molecules in an ice cube have a well-defined order in an ice cube. As the ice begins to melt, this well-defined order disappears and the water molecules increase their range of motions and, therefore, the number of microstates. The number of microstates that are possible in the liquid water suggests that the melting of ice corresponds to an *increase* in the entropy of the system. The same holds true when water is converted into steam. Conversely, the reverse of these processes (gas to liquid to solid) is typically accompanied by a *loss* of entropy ($\Delta S_{system} = -$).

Water molecules gain increased freedom of motion in changing phase from solid to liquid.

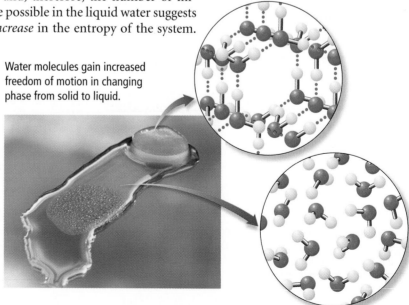

What is the effect of energy transfer on ΔS? When steam condenses to liquid water, energy as heat flows out of the system and into the surroundings, and the kinetic energy of the particles in the surroundings increases. The motions of the atoms in the surroundings increase, and the sign of $\Delta S_{surroundings}$ is positive. On the other hand, if energy as heat flows from the surroundings to the system (liquid to vapor), we'd expect the kinetic

NanoWorld / MacroWorld

Big effects of the very small: Industrial uses for the extremophiles

Imagine living at the bottom of the Arctic Ocean, thinking life was grand inside glacial ice, enjoying the weather near a thermal vent, or relaxing under the crush of 1 mile of bedrock. These conditions sound fairly extreme to us, but not to a class of bacteria known as the extremophiles. Some of these microorganisms thrive near the hot bubbling mud-pots of Yellowstone National Park, others in the sulfur-laden waters near a geothermal vent at the bottom of the Atlantic Ocean. Extremophiles, some examples of which are listed in Table 14.3, survive in conditions that we humans would find extreme.

Biochemists, microbiologists, and geologists from around the world study these creatures because of the extreme conditions in which they live and to learn more about the enzymes that continue to work under the equally extreme conditions inside them. For instance, millions of Americans are lactose-intolerant and have difficulty digesting the lactose in almost every dairy product, including milk and ice cream. Imagine if you could isolate beta-galactosidase (an enzyme that breaks down sugars like lactose into more easily digested compounds) from an extremophile that lived in icy environments. The extremophile's beta-galactosidase should be capable of working quite well in cold environments. By adding the isolated beta-galactosidase to milk and related products like ice cream, you could make lactose-free dairy products without having to heat them. Researchers at Pennsylvania State University have been able to show that this is possible by isolating a strain of bacteria, known as *Arthrobacter psychrolactophilus* that has a modified beta-galactosidase that works best when the temperature is 15°C and continues to work well when the temperature is as low as 0°C.

Thomas D. Brock isolated the first example of a true extremophile from hot springs, such as that shown in

TABLE 14.3	Classes of Extremophiles	
Class	**Extreme Environment**	**Locations Where They Live**
Acidophiles	Low pH	Sulfurous springs and acid mine drainage
Alkaliphiles	High pH	Alkaline lakes and basic soils
Anaerobes	Non-oxygen-containing environments	Fermenting juices
Barophiles	High pressure	Deep sea vents and deep within the Earth
Copiotrophs	High nutrient levels	Sugar solutions
Halophiles	High ion concentration	Saline lakes and salt deposits
Hyperthermophiles	Temperatures above 70°C	Hydrothermal vents, hot springs
Methanogens	Methane-rich	Deep-sea vents, oil deposits
Oligotrophs	Low nutrient levels	Desert, rocks
Psychrophiles	Low temperatures, typically below 10°C	Glaciers, Arctic Ocean, cold soils
Thermophiles	Temperatures above 50°C	Hydrothermal vents, hot springs

FIGURE 14.16

Entropy increases as a compound changes state from solid to liquid to gas. Note that the increased molecular motions allow more microstates to exist in the compound.

S_{solid} < S_{liquid} <<< S_{gas}

FIGURE 14.14

The Morning Glory Pool at Yellowstone National Park is named for the brightly colored thermophiles that flourish in this high-temperature environment.

FIGURE 14.15

Hydrothermal vent in the North Pacific west of Vancouver Island on the Juan de Fuca Ridge. Extremophiles such as *Pyrolobus fumarii* and *Methanopyrus* live on the sides of these chimneys. The "smoke" flowing from the vents is actually made up of minerals from the lava under the ocean floor.

Figure 14.14, in Yellowstone National Park in Wyoming. This bacterium, called *Thermus aquaticus,* grows most rapidly at temperatures near 70°C. Other thermophiles, or heat-loving bacteria, include *Sulfolobus acidocaldarius,* which lives in sulfur-laden hot springs at temperatures as high as 85°C, and *Pyrolobus fumarii,* which is isolated from deep-sea hydrothermal vents (Figure 14.15), grows only at temperatures above 90°C, and reproduces best at 105°C). These bacteria are of industrial interest because of their ability to grow at such high temperatures. For example, the enzyme Taq polymerase (isolated from *T. aquaticus*) is used in DNA fingerprinting because it can survive the severe temperature variations in the polymerase chain reaction used to make multiple copies of purified DNA (see Chapter 22).

The acid-tolerant extremophiles (acidophiles) are of interest because their enzymes are capable of operating in highly acidic environments. A potential application for the acidophile's enzymes is their addition to cattle feed, because they would work well in the acidic gut of an animal as an aid in digesting food. Their use would improve the usefulness of cheap food as a source of energy for the animals. The alkaliphiles (base-tolerant bacteria) thrive in basic soils such as those in the western United States and in Egypt. Proteases (enzymes that break down proteins) and lipases (enzymes that break down oils) isolated from these bacteria could find potential use in the detergent industry. Their addition to laundry detergents (which typically are basic) would improve the ability of the detergent to clean stains from clothing.

Investigators are currently searching, and finding, bacteria that live in environments we originally thought were sterile. After determining the types and properties of the enzymes that these bacteria possess, scientists are exploiting their industrial utility. The uses of these enzymes as catalysts to aid human life are endless. Will we find extremophiles that proliferate on Mars? . . . on Io, the volcanic innermost major moon of Jupiter? . . . on our own Moon? And, if so, what uses might we find for the enzymes they produce?

energy of the particles in the surroundings to decrease and the motions of the atoms (and, therefore, the entropy) in the surroundings to decrease also. In short, a flow of energy as heat *out of the system* and *into the surroundings* (an exothermic process) corresponds to a *positive sign for* $\Delta S_{\text{surroundings}}$. An endothermic process has an opposite effect on the surroundings; endothermic processes correspond to a negative sign for $\Delta S_{\text{surroundings}}$.

What is this exchange of energy to which we refer? If our process occurs under reversible conditions at a constant pressure, we can relate the energy of the process (q_{rev}) to the change in enthalpy of the process (ΔH). **Reversible conditions** occur when *the process is allowed to proceed in infinitesimally small steps.* At any point during the reaction, we could change the direction of the reaction with

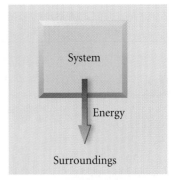

Exothermic processes involve the transfer of energy from the system to the surroundings.

merely slight modifications. *Often, reversible conditions exist during phase changes.* Quantitatively, we can summarize our statements by saying that the change in the entropy is equal to the change in enthalpy of the phase change (a reversible process) divided by the temperature:

$$\Delta S_{system} = \frac{q_{rev}}{T} = \frac{\Delta H_{system}}{T}$$

where the temperature (T) is reported in kelvins (K) and the enthalpy (ΔH_{system}) is reported in joules per mole. Because of some assumptions we've made to arrive at this equation, its use is limited to describing heat transfers when the temperature remains constant. For example, the equation works well for describing phase transitions but poorly for describing a reaction.

Because $q_{surroundings} = -q_{system}$, and $q_{system} = \Delta H_{system}$, the value of $\Delta S_{surroundings}$ can be obtained using a similar equation.

$$\Delta S_{surroundings} = \frac{-\Delta H_{system}}{T}$$

EXERCISE 14.4 | **Entropy Change at a Phase Change**

Instead of carrying water in their backpacks, hikers can melt ice to make drinking water. They also boil water for drinking and food preparation. What is the entropy change of the system for melting 1 mol of ice at 0.00°C and 1 atm? What is the entropy change for melting 125 g of ice? The enthalpy of fusion at this phase change, $\Delta_{fus}H$ is 6.01 kJ/mol.

$$H_2O(s) \rightarrow H_2O(l) \qquad \Delta_{fus}H = 6.01 \text{ kJ/mol at } 0.0°C$$

First Thoughts

The entropy change for the system or surroundings can be calculated if we know the temperature and the enthalpy of the system. Because the units of entropy are usually reported in J/mol·K, we should convert the units for the enthalpy and the temperature to match, so our calculation is simplified. The second part of the question asks us to examine the specific entropy change for a quantity of water that is not equal to 1 mol. We may do this part of the calculation by dimensional analysis.

Solution

The change in the entropy of this reversible process can be calculated using the formula we just discussed. This process involves an increase in the entropy of the system.

Melting ice into water.

$$\Delta S_{system} = \frac{\Delta H_{system}}{T} = \frac{6010 \text{ J/mol}}{273 \text{ K}} = 22.0 \text{ J/mol·K}$$

We've calculated the change in entropy ($\Delta S = 22.0$ J/mol·K) for the phase change, so we can use this value to determine the change in entropy for melting 125 g of water.

$$\Delta S_{system} = 125 \text{ g} \times \frac{1 \text{ mol}}{18.02 \text{ g}} \times \frac{22.0 \text{ J}}{\text{mol·K}} = \frac{153 \text{ J}}{K}$$

Further Insights

Reactions can occur with either an increase or a decrease of entropy. It is interesting to note that this change is based on the number of moles of the compounds in the reaction. If this relationship appears to be similar to what we observed in our discussion of enthalpy in Chapter 5, it should. Also, as we'll see later, entropy can be manipulated in ways that are very similar to those we used for enthalpy.

Moreover, because the temperature remains constant, we can calculate the value of $\Delta S_{surroundings}$. We find that the value is −22.0 J/mol·K. Therefore, the entropy change for the universe ($\Delta S_{universe}$) should be 0.0 J/mol·K ($\Delta S_{universe} = \Delta S_{system} + \Delta S_{surroundings}$). This process is neither spontaneous nor nonspontaneous. It is reversible.

PRACTICE 14.4

Calculate ΔS_{system} for each of these processes at 25°C. Assume that each is a reversible process.

$$I_2(g) \rightarrow I_2(s) \qquad\qquad \Delta_{sub}H = +62.4 \text{ kJ}$$

$$H_2O(l) \rightarrow H_2O(g) \qquad\qquad \Delta_{vap}H = +40.7 \text{ kJ}$$

See Problems 35 and 36. ∎

HERE'S WHAT WE KNOW SO FAR

- Spontaneous processes are associated with an increase in the entropy of the universe.
- The rate of a spontaneous reaction is not related to its spontaneity.
- The reverse of a spontaneous process is a nonspontaneous process.
- The change in entropy of the universe can be calculated as the sum of the change in entropy of the system and the change in entropy of the surroundings.
- The entropy of the system can be calculated for reversible processes by dividing the enthalpy for the process by the temperature of the process.

14.4 Calculating Entropy Changes in Chemical Reactions

Metabolism (the biochemical reactions of an organism) releases energy. In this process, the potential energy stored in food is used by an organism, and some of the food is converted via chemical reactions into molecules that are needed for the organism to survive. All of these reactions are spontaneous in the body and vital to the living processes that occur at the cellular level. For instance, the body breaks down sucrose, perhaps contained in a sugar-laden gumdrop, into glucose and fructose. The glucose then enters a series of reactions, the glycolytic pathway being the first (Figure 14.9), as the body converts it into carbon dioxide and water. Along the way it produces ATP (Figure 14.10), a molecule used to store potential energy. Plants, on the other hand, synthesize glucose by combining carbon dioxide and water. This reaction is energetically uphill for the plant, so it uses the high-energy ATP molecule to drive the reaction to completion. Why is the breakdown of glucose energetically downhill, whereas the formation of glucose is uphill? In other words, why does it take energy to make glucose, and why is energy released when glucose is broken down? We can answer this question by examining the entropy changes in the combustion of glucose. *Qualitatively,* is the sign of

Application

CHEMICAL
ENCOUNTERS:
More Glycolysis

The reaction of glucose with oxygen generates carbon dioxide and water. Compare the number of molecules of gaseous products made to the number of molecules of gaseous reactants.

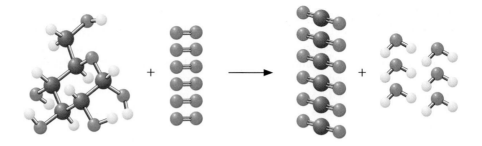

ΔS_{system} positive or negative? The reactants include 1 mol of glucose molecules and 6 mol of gaseous oxygen molecules.

$$C_6H_{12}O_6(s) + 6O_2(g) \rightarrow 6O_2(g) + 6H_2O(g)$$

The combustion proceeds as 7 mol of reactants are converted into 12 mol of products (6 mol of gaseous carbon dioxide and 6 mol of gaseous water). Prior to the reaction, there were a large number of possible microstates because of the large number (7 mol) of reactants. Because gases occupy a larger volume in a flask than do equivalent quantities of solids, the 6 mol of oxygen in our reaction occupy the majority of the locations within the flask as they rapidly travel within it. After the reaction, there are 12 mol of gas inside the flask. The number of microstates increased because of the larger number of gaseous products. The increase in the number of microstates is an increase in the entropy of the system (ΔS_{system} is positive), as shown in Figure 14.17. If we examine the reverse of this reaction (from the viewpoint of the glucose-producing plant), the entropy of the system is lowered because we are combining 12 mol of gaseous carbon dioxide and water to make 6 mol of gaseous oxygen and 1 mol of solid sugar.

What we've discussed is a method by which one can usually predict the sign of the entropy change accurately. As a rule, *the change in entropy of a reaction is positive if the number of gaseous molecules increases.* Although the number of moles of solid and liquid molecules contributes to the overall number of microstates, the large volume occupied by gaseous molecules contributes much more. By simply examining a reaction, we can predict the entropy change. The change is much harder to assess for reactions that do not involve gaseous molecules.

FIGURE 14.17

An increase in the number of gaseous molecules increases the entropy of the system.

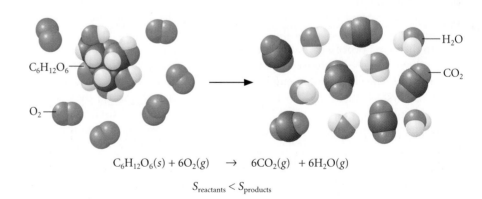

$$C_6H_{12}O_6(s) + 6O_2(g) \quad \rightarrow \quad 6CO_2(g) + 6H_2O(g)$$

$$S_{\text{reactants}} < S_{\text{products}}$$

EXERCISE 14.5 **Predict the Sign**

1. Some camp stoves use butane as fuel. The combustion of butane is exothermic, providing heat to cook food and boil water. Predict the sign of ΔS_{system} for the combustion of butane.

$$2CH_3CH_2CH_2CH_3(g) + 13O_2(g) \rightarrow 8CO_2(g) + 10H_2O(g)$$

2. The Haber process, the combination of hydrogen and nitrogen gases to form ammonia gas (NH_3) is one of the most widely used manufacturing processes because of worldwide demand for ammonia-based fertilizer. Predict the sign of ΔS_{system} for the production of ammonia.

$$3H_2(g) + N_2(g) \rightarrow 2NH_3(g)$$

3. Barium hydroxide ($Ba(OH)_2 \cdot 8H_2O$) reacts with ammonium chloride (NH_4Cl) to form several products, including ammonia, water, and barium chloride. Predict the sign of ΔS_{system} for this reaction.

$$Ba(OH)_2 \cdot 8H_2O(s) + 2NH_4Cl(s) \rightarrow BaCl_2(aq) + 2NH_3(g) + 10H_2O(l)$$

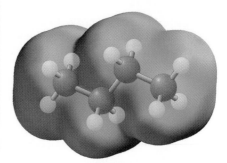

Butane

Solution

1. There are 18 mol of gaseous products and only 15 mol of gaseous reactants. Consequently, the number of microstates should increase for the reaction. This leads us to predict that the change in entropy should be a positive number for this reaction. Based on calculations that we'll discover later, $\Delta S_{system} = +789$ J/mol·K. This agrees with our prediction.

2. The Haber process takes 4 mol of gaseous reactants and forms 2 mol of gaseous products. The entropy change of the system is likely to be negative for this reaction. The actual ΔS_{system} value is –199 J/mol·K.

3. The reaction results in the formation of 2 mol of ammonia gas for each mole of barium hydroxide octahydrate that reacts with solid ammonium chloride. Consequently, we would predict that the change in system entropy would be positive. One factor to keep in mind is that the waters of hydration (that is, the eight H_2O molecules that are part of the barium hydroxide crystal) would be released as part of the process. These molecules would tend to raise the system entropy further as they join the liquid state. The actual ΔS_{system} value is 468 J/mol·K.

PRACTICE 14.5

Predict the sign of the change in entropy for each of these reactions.

$$H_2O(l) \rightarrow H_2O(g)$$

$$CH_3OH(l) + HCl(g) \rightarrow CH_3Cl(l) + H_2O(l)$$

See Problems 39–42, 45, and 47. ▌

Qualitatively, our prediction of the sign of ΔS_{system} can be based on the number of gaseous molecules in the reaction. Quantitatively, the value for the change in the entropy (ΔS_{system}) is nearly as easy to determine. However, a problem arises. In order to calculate a change in a state function, we subtract the final value from the initial value. How do we determine the initial value of entropy for a compound?

FIGURE 14.18

Based on the distance traveled by the mountain climbers, Mt. McKinley appears to be taller than Mt. Everest. However, with our reference point in place, it is clear that Mt. Everest is much taller.

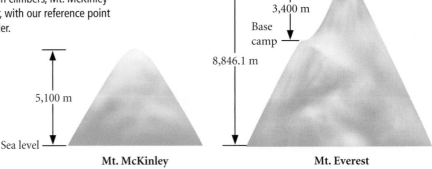

We can find the answer by returning to our Mt. Everest climbers from Section 14.1. Typically, such adventurers climb about 3,400 m (11,400 ft) from the base camp at the foot of the mountain to reach the summit. Using this information, can we accurately say that the mountain is the tallest in the world? Mt. McKinley in Alaska, with an ascent of 5,100 m (17,000 ft) appears to be taller. In order to accurately say that Mt. Everest is the tallest, we must consider that the base camp itself is 5,400 m above sea level. That is, we must establish a *reference point* from which to compare the heights, as we've done in Figure 14.18. In the same way, values of entropy are based on some reference point that is common to all compounds. The **third law of thermodynamics** establishes this point for entropy. The law states that the entropy of a pure perfect crystal at 0 K is zero. A "perfect" crystal, one in which all of the molecules are rigidly and uniformly aligned, has negligible kinetic energy at 0 K. In other words, if the excess kinetic energy of the crystal is zero, the crystal has zero entropy. We qualify the phrase *kinetic energy* with the word *excess* because there is still some atomic (electron) motion in a perfect crystal at 0 K.

We convert this perfect crystal into a collection of molecules at some higher temperature by adding kinetic energy. This increases the number of microstates, resulting in an increase in entropy, as illustrated in Figure 14.19. Under the standard conditions of 298 K and 1 atm, the compound has an associated standard molar entropy that we designate as $S°$. This value is the same as that for ΔS_{system} at this temperature and pressure. By measuring the change in entropy from 0 K to 298 K, researchers have determined the standard molar entropies of a wide variety of compounds (see Table 14.4).

Note that the magnitude of the standard molar entropies is larger for those molecules that are more complex: $S°_{H_2(g)} = 131$ J/mol·K and $S°_{H_2O(g)} = 189$ J/mol·K.

FIGURE 14.19

Adding kinetic energy to a perfect crystal at 0 K increases the number of microstates. The result: The entropy of a compound is always a positive number. (a) Crystal at 0 K. (b) Crystal at some higher temperature.

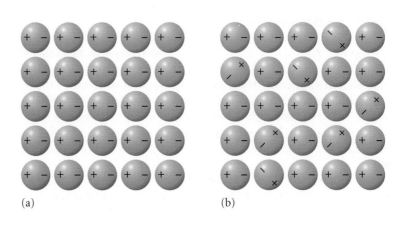

TABLE 14.4   Standard Molar Entropies and Free Energies for Selected Elements and Compounds at 25.0°C

Substance	$\Delta_fH°$ (kJ/mol)	$\Delta_fG°$ (kJ/mol)	$S°$ (J/mol·K)	Substance	$\Delta_fH°$ (kJ/mol)	$\Delta_fG°$ (kJ/mol)	$S°$ (J/mol·K)
$Br_2(l)$	0	0	152	$C_2H_5OH(l)$	−278	−175	161
$Br_2(g)$	+31	+3	245	$CH_3Cl(g)$	−84	−60	234
$HBr(g)$	−36	−53	199	$HCl(g)$	−92	−95	187
$CaF_2(s)$	−1220	−1167	69	$HCl(aq)$	−168	−131	55
$CaCl_2(s)$	−796	−748	105	$H_2(g)$	0	0	131
$CaCO_3(s)$	−1207	−1129	93	$Fe_2O_3(s)$	−826	−740	90
$C(graphite)$	0	0	6	$N_2(g)$	0	0	192
$C(diamond)$	+2	+3	2	$NO(g)$	90	87	211
$CO_2(g)$	−394	−394	214	$NO_2(g)$	33	51	240
$CO_2(aq)$	−414	−386	118	$NH_3(g)$	−46	−16	192
$CH_4(g)$	−75	−50	186	$H_2O(g)$	−242	−229	189
$C_2H_2(g)$	+227	+209	201	$H_2O(l)$	−286	−237	70
$C_2H_4(g)$	+52	+68	220	$NaOH(s)$	−426	−379	64
$C_2H_6(g)$	−85	−33	230	$H_2SO_4(aq)$	−909	−745	20
$CH_3OH(l)$	−239	−166	127	$ZnO(s)$	−348	−318	44

As more and more atoms are incorporated within a compound, the entropy of the compound increases. Similarly, note that the standard molar entropies are different for compounds in different states. For example, liquid water ($S° = 70$ J/mol·K) has a lower entropy than gaseous water ($S° = 189$ J/mol·K). This is understandable, because the molecules in the gaseous state have more freedom of movement and hence have a greater possible distribution of energies.

Computationally, we use these standard molar entropy values in much the same way that we used enthalpy values to calculate $\Delta H°$ for a reaction. The basic principles of Hess's law (see Chapter 5), which we used to calculate the change in enthalpy for a reaction, also work for determining the change in the entropy of a reaction. To summarize, the net standard state entropy gain (or loss) for a reaction is calculated by subtracting the total standard state entropy change for the reactants from the total standard state entropy change for the products:

$$\Delta S° = \sum nS°_{products} - \sum nS°_{reactants}$$

where n is the stoichiometric coefficient of each of the compounds in the reaction, and Σ indicates that the standard state entropy ($S°$) is summed. Just as in the determination of the change in enthalpy of a reaction, $\Delta S°$ for a reaction depends on the way the reaction is written.

EXERCISE 14.6   **Calculating $\Delta S°$**

In the oxidation of glucose at 25°C, the products are different from those we considered early in Section 14.4. In that discussion, glucose reacted at body temperature. Here, at 25°C, both oxygen and carbon dioxide are gases and water is a liquid. Use the table of thermodynamic values in the appendix to assess the change in entropy for this reaction under standard conditions.

$$C_6H_{12}O_6(s) + 6O_2(g) \rightarrow 6CO_2(g) + 6H_2O(l)$$

First Thoughts

If the water were written as a gas, we would predict a very large increase in the number of moles of gaseous products, leading to the prediction of a positive entropy change for the reaction. However, in this reaction as written, the number of moles of gas remains constant, and we are unable to assert that the entropy change would be positive from that standpoint alone. However, we might predict that the entropy of the system would increase slightly, because we are forming six molecules of a liquid where we had one molecule of solid reactants. We can use the summation equation to calculate the change in entropy for the reaction.

$$\Delta S° = \sum nS°_{products} - \sum nS°_{reactants}$$

Solution

From Table 14.4 we obtain $S°$ values for each of the compounds in the reaction. Using the equation shown above, we can calculate the value of $\Delta S°$:

$$6 \text{ mol } CO_2 \times 214 \text{ J/mol·K} = \quad 1284 \text{ J/K}$$

$$6 \text{ mol } H_2O \times 70 \text{ J/mol·K} = \quad 420 \text{ J/K}$$

$$\text{Total } S°_{products} = \quad 1704 \text{ J/K}$$

$$1 \text{ mol } C_6H_{12}O_6 \times 212 \text{ J/mol·K} = \quad 212 \text{ J/K}$$

$$6 \text{ mol } O_2 \times 205 \text{ J/mol·K} = \quad 1230 \text{ J/K}$$

$$\text{Total } S°_{reactants} = \quad 1442 \text{ J/K}$$

$$\text{Total } S°_{products} = \quad 1704 \text{ J/K}$$

$$-\text{Total } S°_{reactants} = -1442 \text{ J/K}$$

$$\Delta S° = \quad 262 \text{ J/K}$$

The reaction has an increase in entropy.

Further Insight

Does this answer make sense? Although the number of molecules of gas is the same for the reactants and the products, we can reasonably assert that the gain in entropy is due to the formation of six molecules of liquid from every molecule of solid. The effect is not as profound as for the formation of a gas ($\Delta S° = 262$ J/K versus $\Delta S° = 974$ J/K), but it does contribute, as in this case. Our answer makes sense.

PRACTICE 14.6

Predict the sign of $\Delta S°$ for each of these reactions. Then calculate the values of $\Delta S°$. You will need to use the table of thermodynamic values in the appendix. Do your calculations agree with your predictions?

$$CH_3OH(l) + HCl(g) \rightarrow CH_3Cl(g) + H_2O(g)$$
$$3O_2(g) \rightarrow 2O_3(g)$$

See Problems 46 and 48–52.

14.5 Free Energy

Application

CHEMICAL
ENCOUNTERS:
Pyruvate
and Lactate

In exercising muscles, the level of oxygen often is a limiting reagent. As the muscles consume glucose to provide the energy needed to contract and relax, the limited supply of oxygen forces a buildup of pyruvate (see Figure 14.20). This molecule can continue on the typical glycolysis pathway toward complete oxidation, but with limited oxygen this does not happen. Instead, the exercising muscle obtains energy by converting pyruvate into lactate (a reduction!) by the pathway shown in Figure 14.21. The reduced form of a biological molecule known as NAD^+ (nicotinamide adenine dinucleotide) is oxidized in the process. (Remember that we must have an oxidation and a reduction for a redox reaction to occur.)

FIGURE 14.20

Pyruvate is a product of the glycolysis pathway.

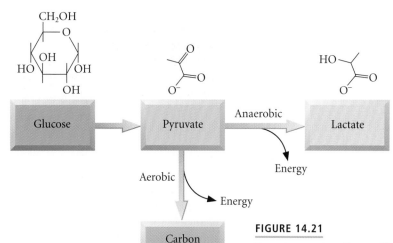

FIGURE 14.21

Pyruvate cannot continue oxidation (aerobic pathway) without oxygen. Instead, energy is derived by the conversion of pyruvate to lactate (anaerobic pathway).

Unfortunately, lactate is potentially a metabolic dead end in humans; further catabolism of lactate may not occur. Eventually, the lactate can be changed back to pyruvate by the reverse reaction and then catabolized in the presence of oxygen. While early research indicated that the body signals the presence of excess lactate (and a decrease in oxygen in the muscles) with a burning sensation, recent results seem to contradict this claim.

The reaction of pyruvate to make lactate is energetically favorable. Some energy is harvested from the pyruvate. However, *qualitatively*, it is difficult to predict this by just looking at the reaction. Determining the spontaneity of the reaction by simply looking at the states of the reaction is also difficult.

$$H^\oplus \ + \ NADH \ + \ \begin{matrix} COO^\ominus \\ | \\ C=O \\ | \\ CH_3 \end{matrix} \ \xrightarrow{\text{Lactate dehydrogenase}} \ \begin{matrix} COO^\ominus \\ | \\ HO-C-H \\ | \\ CH_3 \end{matrix} \ + \ NAD^\oplus$$

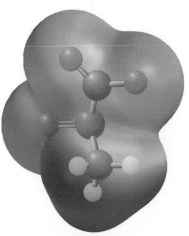

Pyruvate

After some calculations, we can determine the value of ΔS° (that is, ΔS_{system}), but we also have to determine the entropy of the surroundings ($\Delta S_{\text{surroundings}}$) in order to calculate the change in entropy of the *universe* (system + surroundings) and, therefore, the spontaneity of the reaction. A simpler and more useful way to determine reaction spontaneity was identified by Josiah Willard Gibbs (1839–1903), professor of mathematical physics at Yale from 1871 to 1903.

Gibbs showed that calculating a property he called the free energy (*G*) makes possible the straightforward determination of reaction spontaneity. The equation is indicative of two ideas that we have discussed.

■ *Idea 1:* An increase in the number of microstates available to the system favors an increase in the entropy of the universe.

■ *Idea 2:* An exothermic reaction increases the kinetic energy of the surroundings, therefore increasing the range of motions of its particles, leading to an increase in the entropy of the surroundings and favoring an increase in the entropy of the universe.

The Gibbs equation is

$$G = H - TS$$

where H is the enthalpy of the system, T is the temperature in kelvins, and S is the entropy of the system. We are interested in the *change* in the free energy of the system, so the Gibbs equation becomes

$$\Delta G = \Delta H_{\text{system}} - T\Delta S_{\text{system}}$$

at constant temperature and pressure.

TABLE 14.5	Effect of Enthalpy, Entropy, and Temperature on the Spontaneity of a Process		
ΔH	ΔS	Low Temperature	High Temperature
+	+	$\Delta G = +$; nonspontaneous	$\Delta G = -$; spontaneous
+	−	$\Delta G = +$; nonspontaneous	$\Delta G = +$; nonspontaneous
−	+	$\Delta G = -$; spontaneous	$\Delta G = -$; spontaneous
−	−	$\Delta G = -$; spontaneous	$\Delta G = +$; nonspontaneous

This equation doesn't seem very useful at first. However, the value of the change in the free energy (ΔG) of a process is related to $\Delta S_{universe}$ by the equation shown below. In other words, the free energy change of a process can be used to determine the spontaneity of that process. Because of the negative sign in the relationship, negative free energy changes ($\Delta G = -$) imply spontaneous processes, and positive free energy changes ($\Delta G = +$) indicate nonspontaneous processes Table 14.5 lists the outcomes of the change in free energy based on the relationship between ΔH and ΔS.

$$\Delta S_{universe} = \frac{-\Delta G}{T}$$

Therefore, the Gibbs equation can be used to calculate the change in free energy for a process, because we know how to calculate ΔH and ΔS using tabulated values (see Table 14.4). All we need, then, is the temperature of the process and the application of some assumptions. First, as a requirement of the Gibbs equation, we must assume that the pressure remains constant. We also have to assume that both ΔH and ΔS are temperature independent, which is not always a good assumption, especially for ΔS.

Let's reexamine the conversion of pyruvate to lactate under anaerobic conditions. Qualitatively, we cannot use the change in the number of moles of gas from reactants to products to help us assess whether the reaction will be spontaneous, because there are no gases in the reaction.

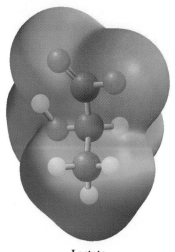

Lactate

$$H^{\oplus} \ + \ NADH \ + \ \begin{array}{c} COO^{\ominus} \\ | \\ C=O \\ | \\ CH_3 \end{array} \xrightarrow{\text{Lactate dehydrogenase}} \begin{array}{c} COO^{\ominus} \\ | \\ HO-C-H \\ | \\ CH_3 \end{array} \ + \ NAD^{\oplus}$$

However, because the values of ΔH and ΔS have been measured for this reaction, we can determine the change in free energy. In this system, $\Delta H = -78.7$ kJ/mol and $\Delta S = -88.75$ J/mol·K. On the basis of these data alone, we identify the reaction as exothermic with a decrease in system entropy. What is the value of ΔG for the reaction at 298 K?

$$\Delta G = \Delta H - T\Delta S$$
$$\Delta G = -78,700 \text{ J/mol} \ - (298 \text{ K} \times -88.75 \text{ J/mol·K})$$
$$\Delta G = -52,253 \text{ J/mol} \ = -52.3 \text{ kJ/mol}$$

Our calculations show that the free energy of this reaction decreases. One thing to keep in mind during such calculations is that in order to use the Gibbs equation, we must modify the values of ΔH and ΔS so that they have the same units. In our calculation, we converted them into units of J/mol and J/mol·K.

We previously mentioned that the change in free energy is negatively related to the change in the entropy of the universe. That is, a negative value for the change in free energy implies a spontaneous process. For a reaction, such as the conversion of pyruvate to lactate, in which the change in free energy is a negative value ($\Delta G = -$), the entropy of the universe has a positive value ($\Delta S_{universe} = +$). The reaction is spontaneous under standard conditions. We might not have predicted this solely on the basis of our examination of $\Delta S°$ for the reaction. Similarly, a process can be considered nonspontaneous if there is an increase in the free energy of the system ($\Delta G = +$). This means that if the reaction, as written, is nonspontaneous, the reverse reaction is spontaneous. For instance, the formation of lactate from pyruvate is spontaneous (a lowering of free energy), but the formation of pyruvate from lactate is nonspontaneous.

EXERCISE 14.7   Spontaneity and Biochemical Reactions

Yeast cells operate under anaerobic conditions to convert glucose to pyruvate, and pyruvate to ethanol and CO_2. Humans are unable to convert pyruvate to ethanol and must make lactate instead. What is the value of the change in the free energy (ΔG) for the conversion of glucose to ethanol at 25°C? (Assume that both the enthalpy and the entropy were also determined at 25°C.)

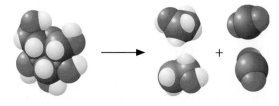

$$C_6H_{12}O_6(s) \rightarrow 2C_2H_6O(l) + 2CO_2(g) \qquad \Delta H = -70.0 \text{ kJ/mol}$$

Glucose   Ethanol $\Delta S = 534 \text{ J/mol·K}$

Solution

$$\Delta G = \Delta H - T\Delta S$$

$$\Delta G = -70,000 \text{ J/mol} - (298 \text{ K}) \times (534 \text{ J/mol·K})$$

$$\Delta G = -229,132 \text{ J/mol}$$

$$\Delta G = -229 \text{ kJ/mol}$$

Because the entropy is given in J/K·mol, the units of the enthalpy have been changed (from kilojoules to joules) so that the two values can be added easily. The reaction is spontaneous, with a rather large negative free energy change.

PRACTICE 14.7

Calculate ΔG at $-10°C$ and at 45°C for the ice-to-water phase transition. Which do you predict to be spontaneous? Do your calculations agree with your predictions? (Assume that the enthalpy and entropy are temperature independent.)

$$H_2O(s) \rightarrow H_2O(l) \qquad \Delta H = 6.01 \text{ kJ/mol}$$

$$\Delta S = 22.0 \text{ J/mol·K}$$

See Problem 56.

A Second Way to Calculate ΔG

Just like enthalpy and entropy, free energy is a state function. Remember from Chapter 5 that when we are determining the value of a state function, it doesn't matter how we calculate it because the end result is independent of the path. To illustrate this, we return to the trek up Mt. Everest. Climbers can take either the more popular south route up the Khumbu icefall or the north route along the ridge to the summit. No matter which way the climbers ascend, no matter how many steps there are in each of the two routes, and no matter how long their ascent takes the climbers, if they make it to the top they have climbed to a point 29,035 ft above sea level. As we saw before, altitude change is a state function. It doesn't matter how two climbers arrive at the summit of Mt. Everest; their change in altitude from the base camp to the top is the same.

Because free energy is a state function, we can obtain ΔG by using the same method we used to calculate ΔH. Adding a series of reactions, each with a known free energy, is often a good way to arrive at a particular calculation of the free energy, because many reactions cannot be performed directly in the lab. For example, the combustion of carbon, as occurs in our charcoal grills, can never give just carbon monoxide but, rather, always results in a mixture of oxides. For another example, say we were interested in the calculation of ΔG for the formation of ice from steam at $-18°C$ (255 K) and 1 atm, another reaction that is difficult to do in the lab. We could sum the equations (and the free energy terms) that describe the stepwise conversion from gas to liquid and from liquid to ice to arrive at ΔG for the process. Note that the free energy terms are specific to this temperature:

$$H_2O(g) \rightarrow H_2O(l) \qquad \Delta G = -13.6 \text{ kJ/mol}$$
$$\underline{H_2O(l) \rightarrow H_2O(s) \qquad \Delta G = -0.39 \text{ kJ/mol}}$$
$$H_2O(g) \rightarrow H_2O(s) \qquad \Delta G = -14.0 \text{ kJ/mol}$$

Application

We see that the process of converting water vapor to ice has a negative change in free energy at $-18°C$. What does this value of ΔG tell us, and does it agree with what we expect for this system? Under these conditions (1 atm, $-18°C$), the formation of ice from steam is spontaneous, whereas the converse process, sublimation of solid to the vapor, is not.

The summation procedure is not limited to phase changes. For example, glycogen (a polymer of glucose used as storage for quick energy release) is degraded to glucose-1-phosphate (Glu-1-P) when the body signals that energy is needed. In order for this derivative of glucose to be used in glycolysis, it must first be converted to glucose-6-phosphate (Glu-6-P) by a two-step process. The hydrolysis reaction of each of these phosphates has been extensively studied and the free energy change noted. What is the net free energy change for the direct conversion of glucose-1-phosphate to glucose-6-phosphate? On the basis of our previous discussion, we can calculate ΔG:

$$\text{Glu-1-P} + \cancel{H_2O} \rightarrow \cancel{\text{glucose}} + \cancel{\text{phosphate}} \qquad \Delta G = -21 \text{ kJ/mol}$$
$$\underline{\cancel{\text{glucose}} + \cancel{\text{phosphate}} \rightarrow \text{Glu-6-P} + \cancel{H_2O} \qquad \Delta G = +14 \text{ kJ/mol}}$$
$$\text{Glu-1-P} \qquad \rightarrow \qquad \text{Glu-6-P} \qquad \Delta G = -7 \text{ kJ/mol}$$

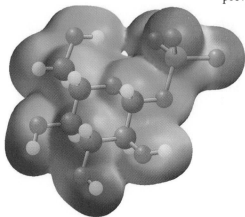

Glu-1-P

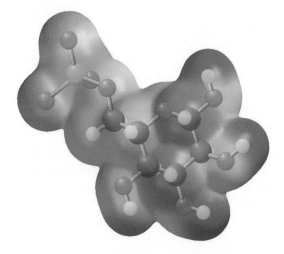

Glu-6-P

The net reaction is spontaneous. The reverse of this reaction, the conversion of glucose-6-phosphate into glucose-1-phosphate, is nonspontaneous with $\Delta G = +7$ kJ/mol. Does the result make sense? If the body needs energy, production of glucose-6-phosphate should be spontaneous.

As you can see, we can use the summation method for determining the spontaneity of a reaction in cases where the free energy of each in a series of reactions is known. In some cases, we can even measure the spontaneity of supposed reactions or processes that we do not wish to perform in the laboratory. The summation of a series of reactions makes possible the quick and easy calculation of the spontaneity of a reaction.

Free Energy of Formation

We can also calculate the spontaneity of a reaction using standard free energies of formation ($\Delta_f G°$). The standard molar free energy of formation ($\Delta_f G°$) is the change in the free energy of 1 mol of a substance in its standard state as it is made from its constituent elements in their standard states. The equation relating the standard free energy of formation for any compound is analogous to the equation written for the standard enthalpy of formation. For example,

$$H_2(g) + \tfrac{1}{2}O_2(g) \rightarrow H_2O(l)$$

The standard molar free energy of formation, $\Delta_f G°$, for all elements in their standard states is zero, just as it is for the standard molar enthalpy of formation, $\Delta_f H°$. Recall from our previous discussion on the third law of thermodynamics that the standard molar entropy of an element, $S°$, is *not* equal to zero.

The tabulation of $\Delta_f G°$ values is given in Table 14.4 and in the appendix. Access to this and similar tables enables us to determine quickly the free energy change for an unknown reaction. In much the same manner that we use $\Delta S°$ and $\Delta H°$, we can find the change in the standard free energy of a reaction. The sum of the free energies of formation for the reactants is subtracted from the sum of the free energies of formation for the products:

$$\Delta G° = \sum n \Delta_f G°_{products} - \sum n \Delta_f G°_{reactants}$$

where n is the stoichiometric coefficient of each of the compounds in the reaction.

EXERCISE 14.8   **I'm Hungry. What's for Dinner? Free Energy and Spontaneity**

In a fasting organism, there is no more glucose left to make energy. Glycogen supplies become depleted. The organism must find a way to make molecules that can be catabolized for energy. One such source of energy is found in the amino acid alanine. This molecule is converted to pyruvate for use in the production of energy (remember that pyruvate is an intermediate during the complete oxidation of glucose). Given the equation for the production of pyruvic acid, the acidic form of pyruvate, from alanine, as well as the values of the free energy of formation for both, determine the spontaneity of this reaction under standard conditions.

First Thoughts

The existence of $\Delta_f G°$ values for both the starting materials and the products means that we can use the summation equation to calculate the standard free energy change for the reaction.

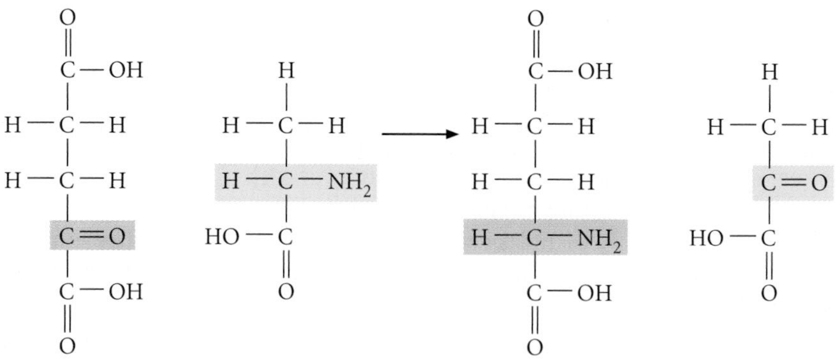

Ketoglutaric acid + **Alanine** ⟶ **Glutamic acid** + **Pyruvic acid**
−195.5 $\Delta_f G°$ (kJ/mol) −88.5 $\Delta_f G°$ (kJ/mol)   −174 $\Delta_f G°$ (kJ/mol)   −111 $\Delta_f G°$ (kJ/mol)

Solution

$$1 \text{ mol glutamic acid} \times -174 \text{ kJ/mol} = \quad -174 \text{ kJ}$$
$$1 \text{ mol pyruvic acid} \times -111 \text{ kJ/mol} = \quad \underline{-111 \text{ kJ}}$$
$$\text{Total } \Delta_f G°_{products} = \quad -285 \text{ kJ}$$

$$1 \text{ mol ketoglutaric acid} \times -195.5 \text{ kJ/mol} = \quad -195.5 \text{ kJ}$$
$$1 \text{ mol alanine} \times -88.5 \text{ kJ/mol} = \quad \underline{-88.5 \text{ kJ}}$$
$$\text{Total } \Delta_f G°_{reactants} = \quad -284 \text{ kJ}$$

$$\text{Total } \Delta_f G°_{products} = \quad -285 \text{ kJ}$$
$$-\text{Total } \Delta_f G°_{reactants} = \quad \underline{-(-284 \text{ kJ})}$$
$$\Delta G° = \quad -1 \text{ kJ}$$

Judging on the basis of our calculations, the change in free energy is negative and the reaction is spontaneous.

Further Insight

Pyruvate is so important to the production of energy that its formation is vital to the survival of an organism. Because of this, reactions that make pyruvate are typically spontaneous. One way to obtain pyruvate is from a source of alanine, as shown here. Where does the organism get alanine? Because alanine is an amino acid, we might predict that it comes from stores of excess alanine. However, there are few stores of this amino acid in the body, so it must come from another source. In particular, alanine can be obtained from the degradation of existing proteins (which contain alanine and other amino acids). Although there are other ways to make pyruvate, the only way to obtain pyruvate when an organism is starved is to consume proteins. *And the consumption of proteins means that muscle tissue is destroyed.* For this and other reasons, starvation diets are not the best way to lose weight.

PRACTICE 14.8

Use the table of thermodynamic values in the appendix to determine whether each of these oxidations is spontaneous. You may need to balance the equations.

$$C_6H_{12}O_6(s) + 6O_2(g) \rightarrow 6CO_2(g) + 6H_2O(g)$$

$$CH_3CH_2CH_3(g) + O_2(g) \rightarrow CO_2(g) + H_2O(g)$$

$$Mg(s) + N_2(g) \rightarrow Mg_3N_2(s)$$

See Problems 59–62.

HERE'S WHAT WE KNOW SO FAR

- Entropy and free energy are state functions.
- The change in entropy and free energy for a reaction can be determined by subtracting the sum of these quantities for the reactants from the sum for the products.
- Negative ΔG values are indicative of spontaneous processes.
- The Gibbs equation ($\Delta G = \Delta H - T\Delta S$) can be used to determine the spontaneity of a process.
- Like enthalpy changes, ΔS and ΔG for a multi-step process are simply the sum of the entropy or free energy changes for each individual process.

14.6 When $\Delta G = 0$; A Taste of Equilibrium

We've already mentioned that the complete oxidation of glucose in the body produces ATP. This molecule is a source of potential energy to force nonspontaneous reactions in the body to become spontaneous. For example, the preparation of glucose-6-phosphate from glucose and phosphate is nonspontaneous. Coupling the hydrolysis of ATP with the production of glucose-6-phosphate helps to make the overall process spontaneous. In this way, the ATP molecule is used to force a reaction to become spontaneous. Although the majority of the ATP in the body comes from the oxidation of glucose, ATP can be made in many other ways. One such way is through the reaction of two molecules of ADP (adenosine diphosphate), which can occur in vigorously active muscles. When the supply of glucose runs low and the level of ATP in the muscle drops, muscle cells gather energy by converting ADP to ATP and AMP. This enables the cells to continue their activity. Let's examine more closely the preparation of one molecule each of ATP and AMP (adenosine monophosphate) from two molecules of ADP. What is the first thing that you note about the reaction as written?

Application

CHEMICAL
ENCOUNTERS:
ATP Formation

$$2\text{ADP} \rightarrow \text{ATP} + \text{AMP} \qquad \Delta G \approx 0 \text{ kJ/mol}$$

CHO
H—OH
HO—H
H—OH
H—OH
CH$_2$OH

Glucose

$+ \text{ HPO}_4{}^{2-} \longrightarrow$

CHO
H—OH
HO—H
H—OH
H—OH
CH$_2$OPO$_3{}^{2-}$

Glucose-6-phosphate

$+ \text{ H}_2\text{O} \qquad \Delta G = 13.8 \text{ kJ/mol}$

$$\text{ATP} + \text{H}_2\text{O} \longrightarrow \text{ADP} + \text{HPO}_4{}^{2-} \qquad \Delta G = -30.5 \text{ kJ/mol}$$

CHO
H—OH
HO—H
H—OH
H—OH
CH$_2$OH

Glucose

$+ \text{ ATP} \longrightarrow$

CHO
H—OH
HO—H
H—OH
H—OH
CH$_2$OPO$_3{}^{2-}$

Glucose-6-phosphate

$+ \text{ ADP} \qquad \Delta G = -16.7 \text{ kJ/mol}$

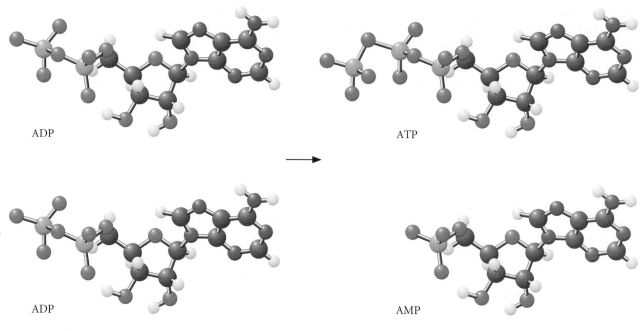

ADP

ATP

ADP

AMP

A phosphate group can be transferred from an ADP molecule to make ATP.

FIGURE 14.22

Trying to boil water at a camp on the Lhotse Face of Mt. Everest (23,500 ft).

Application

The change in the free energy of the reaction is zero. Is this reaction spontaneous? Is it nonspontaneous? We can look at the phase transition of water from solid to liquid to help sort all this out.

$$H_2O(s) \rightarrow H_2O(l)$$

At temperatures below the melting point of water, the reaction is spontaneous in the direction of $H_2O(s)$; that is, water freezes. At temperatures above the melting point of water, the reaction is spontaneous in the opposite direction; ice melts. At 0°C and 1 atm, the process is not spontaneous in either direction. At this temperature, the change in free energy for the process is zero ($\Delta G = 0$) and the reaction proceeds neither toward the products nor toward the reactants. We say that the reaction has reached **equilibrium**. We will focus on this important concept in Chapter 16, but for now, we need to know that a reaction at equilibrium hasn't stopped; it is just at a point where moving toward either the reactants or toward the products is not thermodynamically favored. The reaction continues to make both products and reactants at equal rates.

Remember that ΔG is *temperature-dependent* ($\Delta G = \Delta H - T\Delta S$), so the value of ΔG can be changed by adjusting the temperature. That is, we can melt ice or freeze water, depending on the temperature we pick. Active muscles do not change their temperature in order to drive the production of ATP from ADP, but this information can be used to calculate the temperature at which a process becomes spontaneous. Back to Mt. Everest. ... The base camp experiences temperatures ranging from a high of about −3°C in July to a low of about −16°C in January. High up on the slopes of the mountain, the temperature drops even lower, to around −36°C. For trekkers huddled in a tent, it may take a lot of effort to get a propane stove to light (especially if the temperature drops below the boiling point of propane; see Figure 14.22). How cold must it get before the propane gas liquefies? To answer this question, we need to consider the phase transition shown below.

$$CH_3CH_2CH_3(l) \rightarrow CH_3CH_2CH_3(g) \qquad \Delta H = 15.1 \text{ kJ/mol}$$

$$\Delta S = 65.4 \text{ J/mol·K}$$

When this reaction is at equilibrium, neither the forward nor the backward reaction will be spontaneous ($\Delta G = 0$). The temperature to which this corresponds is the boiling point. Because we know the equation that relates ΔG to the temperature, we can calculate the boiling point of this reaction.

$$\Delta G = \Delta H - T(\Delta S)$$
$$0 = 15{,}100 \text{ J/mol} - T(65.4 \text{ J/mol·K})$$
$$T(65.4 \text{ J/mol·K}) = 15{,}100 \text{ J/mol}$$
$$T = 231 \text{ K}$$
$$T = -42°\text{C}$$

Our calculations suggest that if the temperature falls to $-42°\text{C}$ ($-44°\text{F}$), the change in the free energy of the process will be zero. The reaction will be at equilibrium, and propane will be at its boiling point. If the temperature gets any lower than $-42°\text{C}$, the propane will be liquid, and the portable stove will become very difficult to light.

EXERCISE 14.9 **Temperature Dependence of ΔG**

In one of the final reactions to produce copper metal from its ore (chalcocite), copper(I) oxide reacts with carbon to produce gaseous carbon monoxide and copper metal. Above what temperature does the reaction become spontaneous?

$$Cu_2O(s) + C(s) \rightarrow 2Cu(s) + CO(g) \qquad \begin{aligned} \Delta H &= 59 \text{ kJ/mol} \\ \Delta S &= 165 \text{ J/mol·K} \end{aligned}$$

Solution

$$\Delta G = \Delta H - T(\Delta S)$$
$$0 = 59{,}000 \text{ J/mol} - T(165 \text{ J/mol·K})$$
$$T(171 \text{ J/mol·K}) = 59{,}000 \text{ J/mol}$$
$$T = 358 \text{ K}$$
$$T = 85°\text{C}$$

Above 85°C, this reaction becomes spontaneous ($\Delta G < 0$). So, at room temperature, the reaction doesn't proceed without outside assistance. In practice, this reaction is often run at very high temperatures to produce copper metal. The copper can be further purified by electrolytic deposition (see Chapter 19).

PRACTICE 14.9

What is the boiling point of methanol? ... of water?

$$CH_3OH(l) \rightarrow CH_3OH(g) \qquad\qquad H_2O(l) \rightarrow H_2O(g)$$
$$\Delta_{vap}H = 35.27 \text{ kJ/mol} \qquad\qquad \Delta_{vap}H = 40.66 \text{ kJ/mol}$$
$$\Delta_{vap}S = 104.6 \text{ J/mol·K} \qquad\qquad \Delta_{vap}S = 109.0 \text{ J/mol·K}$$

See Problems 67 and 68. ▌

Changes in Pressure Affect Spontaneity

As the temperature changes, the value of ΔG for a reaction changes. In fact, a nonspontaneous reaction can often be made spontaneous if the temperature is adjusted enough, such that $\Delta H - T\Delta S$ becomes negative (see Table 14.5). For a muscle cell in need of a quick energy fix, changing the temperature in order to make the conversion of ADP into ATP and AMP (adenosine monophosphate) spontaneous is not an option. Thankfully, temperature isn't the only variable that can change the spontaneity of a reaction. Pressure and concentration also play a major role in determining reaction spontaneity.

The entropy change of a reaction depends on its pressure. This occurs because there are fewer microstates in a compressed gas than there are if the pressure of the same sample is reduced by expanding the volume of the container. Mathematically, it has been shown that the pressure causes a change in the standard free energy of a reaction in accordance with the following equation:

$$\Delta G = \Delta G° + RT \ln Q_p$$

where ΔG is the change in the nonstandard state free energy

$\Delta G°$ is change in the standard state free energy

R is the universal gas constant, 8.3145 J/mol·K

T is the temperature in kelvins

Q_p is a term called the **pressure reaction quotient**

We'll discuss the pressure reaction quotient in much greater detail in Chapter 16. However, for purposes of our current discussion, you may consider the pressure reaction quotient, Q_p, to be *the ratio of the pressures of all of the gaseous products to the pressures of the gaseous reactants, raised to their respective stoichiometric coefficients.* For example, here is the equation for the Haber process for the formation of ammonia (part 2 of Exercise 14.5), along with the expression for its Q_p:

$$3H_2(g) + N_2(g) \rightarrow 2NH_3(g)$$

$$Q_p = \frac{P_{NH_3}^2}{P_{N_2} P_{H_2}^3}$$

For a reaction such as the fermentation of glucose, Q_p is equal to the pressure of carbon dioxide squared, because neither glucose nor ethanol is represented as a gas in the equation.

$$C_6H_{12}O_6(s) \rightarrow 2C_2H_6O(l) + 2CO_2(g)$$
Glucose   Ethanol

$$Q_p = \frac{P_{CO_2}^2}{1}$$

 Application

The brewmaster at a local brewpub knows about the effect of pressure on the fermentation of glucose. If the vat is left open to the atmosphere (1 atm), the yeast carries out the fermentation at 25°C. The reaction, as we saw earlier in this chapter, is spontaneous (−229 kJ/mol). If the brewmeister shuts the hatch on the vat and seals it, the formation of carbon dioxide begins to build up pressure as the glucose is catabolized. At some point, the pressure could reach 52.0 atm (assuming the vat is strong enough to hold that pressure). Is the reaction spontaneous at that pressure?

$$\Delta G = \Delta G° + RT \ln Q_p$$

$$\Delta G = -229,000 \text{ J/mol} + (8.3145 \text{ J/mol·K})(298 \text{ K}) \ln\left(\frac{(52.0)^2}{1}\right)$$

$$\Delta G = -229,000 \text{ J/mol} + 19,580 \text{ J/mol}$$

$$\Delta G = -209,420 \text{ J/mol}$$

$$\Delta G = -209 \text{ kJ/mol}$$

The reaction is still spontaneous, as you might expect for a reaction that produces energy for a living organism. However, the reaction has a lower free energy than it had at lower pressure.

Changes in Concentrations Affect Spontaneity

In a manner similar to that for gaseous reactions, the free energy of a reaction changes as the concentrations of the reactants and products change. **Does this make sense?** The equation relating the concentrations of reactants and products to the observed free energy change (ΔG) is

$$\Delta G = \Delta G° + RT\ln Q$$

Note that this equation is mathematically similar to the equation for determining the effect of changing pressure.

The greatest difference between this equation and the one presented in the previous section is the value of the **reaction quotient (Q)**. For reactions in *solution,* this reaction quotient is calculated by multiplying the initial molar concentrations of all of the products, raised to the power of their respective stoichiometric coefficients, divided by the initial molar concentrations of all of the reactants, raised to the power of their stoichiometric coefficients. Mathematically, for the reaction

$$rA + sB \rightarrow tC + uD$$

the reaction quotient is

$$Q = \frac{[C]_0^t[D]_0^u}{[A]_0^r[B]_0^s}$$

where $[\ ]_0 =$ the initial molar concentration of the substance.

What does this mean? Reactions with large concentrations of reactants have a Q value less than 1. This means that $RT\ln Q$ is negative and that the observed free energy (ΔG) is less than the standard free energy ($\Delta G°$). In other words, large concentrations of reactants and small concentrations of products increase the spontaneity of the forward reaction (this situation decreases the value of the observed ΔG). When the concentration of reactants is small and the concentration of products is large ($Q > 1.0$), the value of $RT\ln Q$ is greater than zero and the observed ΔG is more positive than $\Delta G°$. In this case, the reaction is less spontaneous. Again, we will examine a similar relationship in much greater detail in Chapter 16 and will explore more deeply what happens when $\Delta G = \Delta G°$, the equilibrium condition.

Coupled Reactions

Many reactions, such as the formation of glucose-6-phosphate from glucose, are nonspontaneous. Metabolic sequences have developed to account for this. As we've seen in this chapter, biological reactions are often coupled with other reactions to produce a spontaneous process. Organisms typically couple a reaction that has a very large negative ΔG with reactions that have positive free energy changes, as shown in Figure 14.23. The result is a spontaneous reaction.

In glycolysis, there are four coupled reactions. Two of these reactions use the negative free energy change of ATP $\rightarrow$ ADP ($\Delta G = -30.5$ kJ/mol) to place phosphate groups on a glucose molecule before it is broken down. Then, as the resulting carbohydrate is catabolized, the organism uses the stored energy of the carbohydrate to drive the reverse of this reaction (ADP $\rightarrow$ ATP; $\Delta G = +30.5$ kJ/mol). In doing so, the glycolytic pathway consumes two molecules of ATP but produces four molecules of ATP using the stored energy of the carbohydrate. The net result is the accumulation of two molecules of ATP for each glucose molecule.

In this chapter we have examined why chemical reactions proceed and have shown that it is directly related to an increase in the entropy of the universe. We

Nonspontaneous
reaction

Spontaneous
reaction

FIGURE 14.23

Biochemical reactions typically involve the coupling of a spontaneous reaction with a nonspontaneous reaction. Coupling the reactions makes the nonspontaneous reaction spontaneous.

 Application

Elevators are raised by a motor. To facilitate the motion of the elevator, a counterweight helps pull the elevator up. The motor and the counterweight couple their action to produce a working elevator.

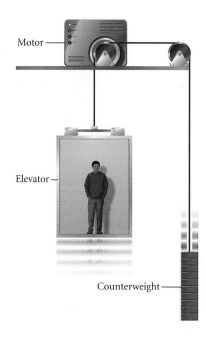

routinely consider the spontaneity of a reaction as a function of the values of ΔH, ΔS, and reaction conditions such as temperature, pressure, and concentration. We've noted that the free energy change (ΔG) depends on all of these things.

Although we now know *whether* a reaction will proceed, we haven't discussed *how fast* reactions proceed. We know that the production of energy from glucose is a spontaneous process, as is the rusting of a nail. But the rates of these two reactions are quite different, with important effects on us and our surroundings. In the next chapter, we'll discover that the degree of spontaneity implies nothing about the speed of a reaction.

The Bottom Line

- The multiplicity of a system can be used to determine the behavior of the system. The most probable macrostate is the one that has the most contributing microstates. (Section 14.1)

- Spontaneous processes occur without outside assistance. The reverse of the spontaneous process is nonspontaneous. (Section 14.2)

- Entropy is a measure of how energy and matter can be distributed in a chemical system. Entropy is *not* disorder. (Section 14.2)

- The second law of thermodynamics says that the entropy of the universe (as we defined the term *universe* in Chapter 5) continues to increase. Any process that is spontaneous must correspond to an increase in the entropy of the universe ($\Delta S_{universe} > 0$). (Section 14.2)

- The third law of thermodynamics says that the entropy of a pure perfect crystalline material is zero. This law enables us to calculate the entropy of any compound in any state. (Section 14.4)

- The free energy, ΔG, can be calculated via the Gibbs equation ($\Delta G = \Delta H - T\Delta S$) to determine the spontaneity of a process. (Section 14.5)

- When $\Delta G = 0$, the system is at equilibrium. The forward and reverse reactions still proceed, but their rates are equal. (Section 14.6)

- Coupled reactions are used by the body to make nonspontaneous processes become spontaneous. The use of ATP in this manner assists in the overall production of energy from glucose. (Section 14.6)

Key Words

bioenergetics The study of the energy changes that occur within a living cell. (*p. 580*)

catabolism The biological degradation of molecules to provide an organism with smaller molecules and energy. (*p. 587*)

entropy A measure of how the energy and matter of a system are distributed throughout the system. (*p. 587*)

equilibrium The state of a reaction when $\Delta G = 0$. The reaction hasn't stopped; rather, the rates of the forward and reverse reactions are equal. (*p. 608*)

free energy (G) The state function that is equal to the enthalpy minus the temperature multiplied by the entropy. Used to determine the spontaneity of a process. (*p. 601*)

Gibbs equation $\Delta G = \Delta H - T\Delta S$ (*p. 601*)

glycolysis A series of biochemical reactions that convert glucose into two molecules of pyruvate. The process results in the formation of two molecules of ATP. (*p. 585*)

macrostate The macroscopic state of a system that indicates the properties of the entire system. (*p. 580*)

metabolism The biochemical reactions of an organism. (*p. 595*)

microstate The state of the individual components within a system. (*p. 581*)

multiplicity The number of microstates within a system. (*p. 587*)

nonspontaneous process A process that occurs only with continuous outside intervention. (*p. 585*)

pressure reaction quotient (Qp) The ratio of the pressures of all of the gaseous products raised to their respective stoichiometric coefficients, divided by the pressures of all of the gaseous reactants raised to their stoichiometric coefficients. (*p. 610*)

reaction quotient (Q) The ratio of the initial molar concentrations of all of the products raised to the power of their respective stoichiometric coefficients, divided by the initial molar concentrations of all of the reactants raised to the power of their stoichiometric coefficients. (*p. 611*)

reversible conditions The conditions that occur when a process proceeds in a series of infinitesimally small steps. (*p. 593*)

second law of thermodynamics A spontaneous process is accompanied by an increase in the entropy of the universe; $\Delta S_{universe} > 0$. (*p. 588*)

spontaneous process A process that occurs without continuous outside intervention. (*p. 585*)

standard molar free energy of formation ($\Delta_fG°$) The free energy of a compound formed from its elements in their standard states. (*p. 605*)

thermodynamics The study of the changes in energy in a reaction. (*p. 586*)

third law of thermodynamics The entropy of a pure perfect crystal at 0 K is zero. (*p. 598*)

Focus Your Learning

The answers to the odd-numbered problems appear at the back of the book.

Section 14.1
Probability as a Predictor of Chemical Behavior

Skill Review

1. Suppose that four pennies fall from your pocket to the floor. How many microstates for the four pennies would exist? (Consider only heads up versus tails up in your explanation.)

2. What is the probability that all four coins from Problem 1 would land heads up?

3. What is the probability that the four coins from Problem 1 would land two heads up and two tails up?

4. What is the most probable outcome for the four coins in Problem 1?

5. Contrast the meanings of the terms *macrostate* and *microstate*.

6. Define the term *multiplicity*.

7. One hundred chemistry students are about to take an exam. There are two equal 200-seat classrooms for the students. Knowing that students must have vacant seats next to them during the exam, describe at least two macrostate arrangements you could predict for the two rooms.

8. In the situation defined in Problem 7, how could the positions of the students allow you to use microstates to explain your answer?

Chemical Applications and Practice

9. Even a sample of only 1,000 atoms is too small to weigh accurately, and yet we can calculate a probable distribution of their numbers between two equal containers. How many microstates are possible if 1,000 atoms of He become distributed between two containers of equal size? Explain why an equal distribution becomes more probable as the number of He atoms increases.

10. A certain lecture hall is 25 m long, 12 m wide, and 15 m tall. The oxygen molecules necessary to sustain life in the room are, of course, free to circulate throughout the room. Explain, using probability and microstates, why a student sitting in the back should not be concerned that all the freely moving oxygen molecules might concentrate at the front row of the classroom.

11. Some powdered creamer is added to a cup of hot coffee. Compare the initial macrostate to the final macrostate as the creamer dissolves. Has the number of microstates for the creamer and coffee increased from the initial state to the final state? Explain the evidence you would use to explain your answer.

12. A glass of tea is cooled by placing ice cubes in it. However, after a few minutes, the ice has melted. Compare the initial macrostate to the final macrostate. Has the number of microstates for the ice and tea increased from the initial state to the final state? Explain the evidence you would use to explain your answer.

13. Which of these would you classify as increasing the number of microstates?
    a. Water in a glass evaporates.
    b. A precipitate of AgCl forms from the addition of a drop of a 0.10 M solution of $AgNO_3$ into a glass of chlorinated tap water.
    c. An icicle forms from a downspout.

14. Which of these would you classify as increasing the number of microstates?
    a. A chunk of ice melts when placed in a glass of tap water at room temperature.
    b. A glass of tap water freezes when placed in a refrigerator freezer compartment.
    c. The combustion of gasoline produces carbon dioxide and water vapor.

Section 14.2 Why Do Chemical Reactions Happen? Entropy and the Second Law of Thermodynamics

Skill Review

15. Which of these, if any, need outside intervention to take place? Describe the necessary intervention.
    a. Combustion (combination with oxygen) of a piece of paper in the air
    b. Making a hard-boiled egg
    c. Increasing muscle mass
    d. Formation of calcium carbonate (bathtub ring) from evaporating hard water

16. Which of these, if any, need outside intervention to take place? Describe the necessary intervention.
    a. The melting of butter on a warm pancake
    b. Opening this book to this page
    c. Paddling a canoe upstream
    d. Cooking eggs for breakfast

17. What is the relationship between entropy and a nonspontaneous process?

18. What is the relationship between entropy and rate of change?

19. What is the relationship between entropy and number of microstates?

20. What is the relationship between a nonspontaneous process and the number of microstates?

21. Suppose you were studying in a residence hall. Down the hall someone is preparing popcorn. The irresistible aroma eventually reaches your room. To take your mind off this, explain how the second law of thermodynamics enables you to detect this tasty temptation from so far away.

22. A scientist on the planet Zoltan expresses the third law of thermodynamics by saying that the entropy of any compound under standard state conditions is zero. Would this change the ΔS values for the reaction of pyruvate to lactate mentioned in the chapter? Explain.

Chemical Application and Practice

23. While pumping gasoline into your car, you might spill some gasoline on your hands. However, the gasoline quickly evaporates with a cooling sensation on your skin. How can this process be spontaneous if it requires the input of the energy from your skin?

24. In a previous problem you were asked about the freezing of water in a refrigerator. Water poured in a tray will spontaneously freeze in a freezer. Explain why this process arranges the water molecules in a more orderly crystal form and yet is still spontaneous.

25. Solid carbon dioxide is called dry ice. At room temperature, this material spontaneously changes from an orderly solid to a gas, bypassing the liquid phase entirely. When undergoing this change, the molecules absorb heat from the nearby surroundings. This, in turn, slows down the molecules of the surroundings. What can be said about the change in entropy for the carbon dioxide molecules relative to nearby air molecules? What can be said about the change in the entropy of the universe for this process?

Dry ice.

26. The entropy of molecules can also depend on their relative atomic motions. The atoms in molecules can twist, rotate, and vibrate around a chemical bond. For which molecule would you be able to predict more microstates: a molecule of nitrogen or a molecule of ammonia (NH_3)? Explain the basis of your choice.

27. The following equation illustrates a gaseous reaction that is possible in the atmosphere. Which direction in the reaction shows the greater entropy for the system? Explain your choice.

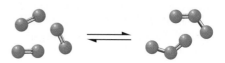

28. Another reaction common in the lower atmosphere is the formation of ozone from NO_2. Which direction in the reaction shows the greater entropy for the system? Explain your choice.

$$O_2(g) + NO_2(g) \rightleftharpoons O_3(g) + NO(g)$$

Section 14.3 Temperature and Spontaneous Processes

Skill Review

29. Classify each of these as representing either a positive change in entropy for the universe or a negative change in entropy for the universe, or indicate that you would need more information to determine this.
   a. $\Delta S_{sys} = +; \Delta S_{surr} = +$
   b. $\Delta S_{sys} = +; \Delta S_{surr} = -$
   c. $\Delta S_{sys} = -; \Delta S_{surr} = +$

30. Classify each of these as representing either a positive change in entropy for the universe or a negative change in entropy for the universe, or indicate that you would need more information to determine this.
   a. $\Delta S_{sys} = -; \Delta S_{surr} = -$
   b. $\Delta S_{sys} = +; \Delta S_{surr} = 0$
   c. $\Delta S_{sys} = -; \Delta S_{surr} = 0$

31. How does the multiplicity of a system change as the molecular motions increase in the system?

32. How does the molecular motion of the surroundings change as energy from the surroundings flows into a system?

33. How does the entropy of the surroundings change as energy flows out of a system?

34. Can we predict the change in entropy of the universe as energy flows into the system? Explain.

Chemical Applications and Practice

35. Mercury remains a liquid over a fairly wide temperature range, which is one reason why it has been used in thermometers. Classify each of these changes as a positive or a negative change in the entropy of a sample of mercury.
   a. Liquid mercury changes to a solid.
   b. Liquid mercury expands as it is heated.
   c. A small amount of mercury evaporates from the surface of a column of mercury in a sealed thermometer.

36. Chlorine gas (Cl_2) is a very toxic compound that can form as a result of the improper use of bleach and ammonia cleaning solutions. Classify each of these changes as a positive or a negative change in the entropy of a sample of this green gas.
   a. Chlorine gas condenses to a liquid.
   b. Chlorine gas is heated in a container.
   c. Chlorine gas deposits on a cold surface.

37. If you are enjoying an iced carbonated soft drink while studying, you may have noticed that the carbon dioxide used to carbonate the beverage bubbles slowly out of the beverage as it warms. Is this a positive or a negative entropy change for the CO_2? Explain.

38. In the bubbling of carbon dioxide mentioned in Problem 37, did the surroundings gain or lose heat? Is the sign for $\Delta S_{universe}$, at this temperature, positive or negative?

Section 14.4
Calculating Entropy Changes in Chemical Reactions

Skill Review

39. Propane stoves make use of the following combustion reaction:

$$\_\_ C_3H_8(g) + \_\_ O_2(g) \rightarrow \_\_ CO_2(g) + \_\_ H_2O(g)$$

Balance the equation, report the number of moles of gas molecules on each side of the equation, and predict the change in entropy of the system.

40. Methane can be combusted by the following reaction:

$$\_\_ CH_4(g) + \_\_ O_2(g) \rightarrow \_\_ CO_2(g) + \_\_ H_2O(g)$$

Balance the equation, report the number of moles of gas molecules on each side of the equation, and predict the change in entropy of the system.

41. Repeat the prediction for Problem 39, but assume that the reaction is performed under temperatures that cause the propane and water to be liquid, yet the oxygen and carbon dioxide remain as gases.

42. Repeat the prediction for Problem 40, but assume that the reaction is performed under temperatures that cause the methane and water to be liquid, yet the oxygen and carbon dioxide remain as gases.

43. Explain why the change in the number of moles of gases, from reactant to product, is typically more influential in determining the sign on entropy changes than the change in moles of liquids and solids.

44. The third law of thermodynamics specifies a particular condition for a perfect crystal. Why must the temperature be 0 K instead of 0°C?

45. Predict the sign on the entropy change for each of these reactions.
   a. $NH_3(g) + HCl(g) \rightarrow NH_4Cl(s)$
   b. $2HgO(s) \rightarrow 2Hg(l) + O_2(g)$
   c. $Cd(s) + \frac{1}{2}O_2(g) \rightarrow CdO(s)$

46. Using the values for $\Delta S°$ found in the appendix, determine the actual values for the standard change in entropy for the reactions in Problem 45.

47. Predict the sign on the entropy change for each of these reactions.
   a. $2SO_2(g) + O_2(g) \rightarrow 2SO_3(g)$
   b. $2NH_3(g) \rightarrow N_2(g) + 3H_2(g)$
   c. $CO(g) + 2H_2(g) \rightarrow CH_3OH(l)$

48. Using the values for $\Delta S°$ found in the appendix, determine the actual values for the standard change in entropy for the reactions in Problem 47.

Chemical Applications and Practices

49. Several states have implemented regulations for fuel alternatives in automobiles. One such gasoline alternative is ethanol (C_2H_5OH). Balance the following combustion reaction and determine the change in entropy for the reaction.

$$\_\_ C_2H_5OH(l) + \_\_ O_2(g) \rightarrow \_\_ CO_2(g) + \_\_ H_2O(g)$$

616 Chapter 14 | Thermodynamics: A Look at Why Reactions Happen

50. One important source of salt (NaCl) is the evaporation of ocean water. Calculate the change in the standard molar entropy as the dissolved ions precipitate the solid.

$$Na^+(aq) + Cl^-(aq) \rightarrow NaCl(s)$$

51. Graphite and diamond are both made only of carbon. However, pencils (incorporating the graphite form) sell for a few cents, whereas engagement rings (displaying diamonds) often sell for thousands of dollars. Using the appendix, determine the change in entropy for the conversion of diamond to graphite.

52. Using the appendix to note the standard $\Delta S°$ value for a metal, explain why the value for the metal alone is lower than the value for any of the listed compounds of that metal.

Section 14.5 Free Energy

Skill Review

53. Predict the relative magnitude of the temperature that would result in a spontaneous process in each of these combinations.
    a. $\Delta H = +$; $\Delta S = +$
    b. $\Delta H = +$; $\Delta S = -$

54. Predict the relative magnitude of the temperature that would result in a spontaneous process in each of these combinations.
    a. $\Delta H = -$; $\Delta S = +$
    b. $\Delta H = -$; $\Delta S = -$

55. Determine the value of ΔH in each of these.
    a. $\Delta G = -24.5$ kJ/mol; $\Delta S = 287$ J/mol·K; $T = 298$ K
    b. $\Delta G = 1.38$ kJ/mol; $\Delta S = 24$ J/mol·K; $T = 298$ K
    c. $\Delta G = 500.0$ kJ/mol; $\Delta S = -6439$ J/mol·K; $T = 325$ K
    d. $\Delta G = -24.5$ kJ/mol; $\Delta S = 187$ J/mol·K; $T = 39.9°C$

56. Determine the value of ΔG in each of these cases.
    a. $\Delta H = -20.5$ kJ/mol; $\Delta S = 259$ J/mol·K; $T = 298$ K
    b. $\Delta H = 350$ kJ/mol; $\Delta S = 73$ J/mol·K; $T = 157$ K
    c. $\Delta H = 299$ kJ/mol; $\Delta S = -639$ J/mol·K; $T = 325$ K
    d. $\Delta H = -4505$ kJ/mol; $\Delta S = 107$ J/mol·K; $T = 19.3°C$

57. Determine the value of ΔS in each of these cases.
    a. $\Delta G = -20.5$ kJ/mol; $\Delta H = 259$ kJ/mol; $T = 298$ K
    b. $\Delta G = 150$ kJ/mol; $\Delta H = -73$ kJ/mol; $T = 157$ K
    c. $\Delta G = 209$ kJ/mol; $\Delta H = -639$ kJ/mol; $T = 35.0$ K
    d. $\Delta G = -4505$ kJ/mol; $\Delta H = 107$ kJ/mol; $T = 135.8°C$

58. Determine the value of T in each of these cases.
    a. $\Delta G = -20.5$ kJ/mol; $\Delta H = 259$ kJ/mol;
       $\Delta S = 260$ J/mol·K
    b. $\Delta G = 150$ kJ/mol; $\Delta H = -73$ kJ/mol;
       $\Delta S = -290$ J/mol·K
    c. $\Delta G = 209$ kJ/mol; $\Delta H = 639$ kJ/mol; $\Delta S = 560$ J/mol·K
    d. $\Delta G = -4505$ kJ/mol; $\Delta H = 107$ kJ/mol;
       $\Delta S = 1160$ J/mol·K

59. Determine the spontaneity of each of these reactions at 298 K.
    a. $NH_3(g) + HCl(g) \rightarrow NH_4Cl(s)$
    b. $2HgO(s) \rightarrow 2Hg(l) + O_2(g)$
    c. $Cd(s) + \frac{1}{2}O_2(g) \rightarrow CdO(s)$

60. Determine the spontaneity of each of these reactions at 298 K.
    a. $2SO_2(g) + O_2(g) \rightarrow 2SO_3(g)$
    b. $2NH_3(g) \rightarrow N_2(g) + 3H_2(g)$
    c. $CO(g) + 2H_2(g) \rightarrow CH_3OH(l)$

Chemical Application and Practices

61. One of the authors of this text formerly drove an automobile that could best be described as blue and rust. Consider that the rust was formed, at least partially, by the reaction illustrated by this equation:

$$3O_2(g) + 4Fe(s) \rightarrow 2Fe_2O_3(s)$$

Assuming standard conditions, what would you calculate as the $\Delta G°$ for this reaction?

62. The impressive white cliffs of Dover in England have stood without significant change from their basic structure of calcium carbonate for eons. One possible reaction for the decomposition of calcium carbonate is

$$CaCO_3(s) \rightarrow CaO(s) + CO_2(g)$$

Use the $\Delta_f G°$ values of these compounds to determine the value of $\Delta G°$ for the reaction. Comment on how thermodynamics helps explain the relative stability of this beautiful landmark.

63. Sulfur dioxide and sulfur trioxide are important anhydrides for making sulfurous and sulfuric acid, respectively. When sulfur-containing coal is burned, sulfur gases pose environmental threats to air quality. Given the following two combustion reactions, determine the $\Delta G°$ value for the change from SO_2 to SO_3.

$S(s) + \frac{3}{2}O_2(g) \rightarrow SO_3(g)$ $\Delta G° = -371$ kJ/mol
$S(s) + O_2(g) \rightarrow SO_2(g)$ $\Delta G° = -300$ kJ/mol
$SO_2(g) + \frac{1}{2}O_2(g) \rightarrow SO_3(g)$ $\Delta G° = ?$

64. As we note earlier, graphite and diamond are both composed entirely of carbon atoms. Using the following reactions at 298 K, determine the value of $\Delta G°$ for the conversion of graphite into diamond.

$C_{diamond}(s) + O_2(g) \rightarrow CO_2(g)$ $\Delta G° = -397$ kJ/mol
$C_{graphite}(s) + O_2(g) \rightarrow CO_2(g)$ $\Delta G° = -394$ kJ/mol
$C_{graphite}(s) \rightarrow C_{diamond}(s)$ $\Delta G° = ??$

65. As we saw in earlier in this chapter, the production of glucose requires the input of energy. This is typically shown as green plants using sunlight to help combine carbon dioxide with water to form glucose through photosynthesis. However, in some deep areas of the ocean, sunlight does not reach bacteria that may grow around thermal vents. These organisms have been shown to produce energy through oxidation of a sulfur compound, H_2S. Determine $\Delta H°$, $\Delta S°$, and $\Delta G°$ for this biochemically important reaction. Assume sulfur is in the standard form—rhombic allotrope.

$$H_2S(aq) + O_2(g) \rightarrow 2H_2O(l) + 2S(s)$$

66. Smog produced over a city is formed from trace amounts of automobile exhaust in a reaction with atmospheric oxygen. One of the steps in the formation of ozone is the oxidation of oxygen gas by nitrogen dioxide (a by-product of the combustion of gasoline). Determine $\Delta H°$, $\Delta S°$, and $\Delta G°$ for this reaction.

$$NO_2(g) + O_2(g) \rightarrow NO(g) + O_3(g)$$

Section 14.6
When $\Delta G = 0$; A Taste of Equilibrium

Skill Review

67. Determine the temperature at which the indicated system reaches equilibrium.
    a. $\Delta H° = 46.4$ kJ/mol; $\Delta S° = 27.6$ J/mol·K
    b. $\Delta H° = 10.6$ kJ/mol; $\Delta S° = 77$ J/mol·K
    c. $\Delta H° = 124$ kJ/mol; $\Delta S° = 295.5$ J/mol·K

68. Determine the temperature at which the indicated system reaches equilibrium.
    a. $\Delta H° = 57.6$ kJ/mol; $\Delta S° = 17.4$ J/mol·K
    b. $\Delta H° = 94$ kJ/mol; $\Delta S° = 306$ J/mol·K
    c. $\Delta H° = 32.1$ kJ/mol; $\Delta S° = 552$ J/mol·K

69. At equilibrium, what is the pressure for the following process at 298 K?

    $$CaCO_3(s) \rightleftharpoons CaO(s) + CO_2(g) \quad \Delta G° = 131 \text{ kJ/mol}$$

70. What is the free energy change for the following reaction at 298 K, given that the pressures of NH_3 and N_2 are 1.0 atm each and the pressure of H_2 is 2.0 atm? (*Hint:* Use the appendix to determine the free energy change under standard conditions.)

    $$2NH_3(g) \rightleftharpoons N_2(g) + 3H_2(g)$$

Chemical Applications and Practices

71. At 1 atm of pressure the boiling point of pure water is 100.0°C. If 1000.0 g of water were brought to this point and then completely boiled away, what would you calculate as the entropy change for the water? (*Note:* The heat of vaporization for water is 40.7 kJ/mol.)

72. There is a historical approximation known as Trouton's rule. This approximation states that at the normal boiling point for nonpolar compounds, the standard molar entropy of vaporization is 87 J/mol·K. Using Trouton's rule, determine the approximate heat of vaporization of water. The actual molar entropy of vaporization for water is close to 110 J/mol·K. Explain why the Trouton value is so much different for polar substances such as water but is often found to be much closer to the actual value for nonpolar substances.

73. Under proper conditions, phase changes can be classified as reversible processes. The energy involved with melting or freezing of a sample is called the enthalpy of fusion. The enthalpy of fusion ($\Delta_{fus}H$) for the rare radioactive element actinium, $Z = 89$, is 10.50 kJ/mol. If the entropy of fusion is 9.6 J/mol·K, what would you calculate as the melting point for this silvery white metal?

74. One of the reasons why you are able to read this question is that the cellular functions necessary are supplied with energy from the molecule ATP (adenosine triphosphate), which couples with many biochemical reactions. The formation of ATP can be accomplished as follows:

    $$ADP(aq) + H_2PO_4^-(aq) \rightleftharpoons ATP(aq) + H_2O(l)$$

    $\Delta G°$ for the reaction is 31 kJ/mol. Using that information, what would you estimate for the reaction quotient, Q, at 25°C, for the reaction at equilibrium?

75. The gas commonly used in chemical laboratory burners is methane (CH_4). Shown here is the combustion reaction that takes place when you light your lab burner.

    $$CH_4(g) + 2O_2(g) \rightleftharpoons CO_2(g) + 2H_2O(g)$$

    a. Use $\Delta_f G°$ data to calculate the $\Delta G°$ value for the reaction.
    b. What would the value of ΔG be if the pressure of O_2 were reduced to 0.20 atm from 1.00 atm, at room conditions, with the remaining gases at standard conditions?
    c. Explain why, if ΔG has a negative value indicating a spontaneous change, we still have to bring a flame or spark to the system to get it to react in the lab.

76. Nitrogen gas and oxygen gas make up essentially 100% of our air. The following reaction has $\Delta G° = 174$ kJ. Fortunately, the two do not easily combine through this reaction under the Earth's atmospheric conditions.

    $$N_2(g) + O_2(g) \rightleftharpoons 2NO(g)$$

    a. What is the value of Q_p at 298 K for the reaction at equilibrium?
    b. What temperature would be needed for the reaction to be spontaneous if the pressures were returned to 1.0 atm? (Assume that enthalpy and entropy values do not change significantly over this range.)
    c. What would be the value of ΔG at 25°C if the pressure of both N_2 and O_2 were increased to 5.0 atm each, while the pressure of NO_2 was decreased to 0.50 atm?

Comprehensive Problems

77. Butane, burned in small portable lighters, combusts according to the following unbalanced equation:

    $$\_\_\_ C_4H_{10}(g) + \_\_\_ O_2(g) \rightarrow \_\_\_ CO_2(g) + \_\_\_ H_2O(g)$$

    First balance the equation, and then explain your answer to this question: "Does the combustion show an increase or a decrease in entropy for the system?"

78. Suppose a particularly noxious compound was entering a water supply at only one point. If it would stay at the entry point, it might easily be removed. However, this does not happen. Explain why environmental scientists must be aware of the second law of thermodynamics.

79. Because it was already known that a positive change in the entropy of the universe indicated a spontaneous reaction, why was it important to develop the Gibbs equation, which is also used to predict the spontaneity of a reaction? What advantage does the Gibbs equation offer?

80. In the ongoing research to find a cure or treatment for Alzheimer's disease, some investigators have focused on the appearance of plaque-like formations in brain cells. The solid masses form from protein fibers called beta-amyloids. Use Internet resources and journal sources to find out if the process is based on a positive or a negative value for the $\Delta S°$ of the plaque-forming reaction.

81. In calculations involving Gibbs energy and equilibrium, you must always be aware of the differences between ΔG and $\Delta G°$. When $\Delta G = 0$, at 25°C, what is true about Q?

82. A certain reaction is nonspontaneous at one temperature. If raising the temperature caused the reaction to become spontaneous, what could you conclude about the entropy change of the reaction? Explain your answer.

Thinking Beyond the Calculation

83. The oxidation of glucose was discussed in detail in this chapter. A similar compound, fructose, also undergoes oxidation in biological organisms to give (eventually) CO_2 and water:

$$\_\_\_ C_6H_{12}O_6(s) + \_\_\_ O_2(g) \rightarrow \_\_\_ CO_2(g) + \_\_\_ H_2O(l)$$

   a. Balance the equation and predict the numerical value of the change in entropy for this process.
   b. Use the appendix to calculate the values of $\Delta H°$, $\Delta S°$, and $\Delta G°$ for this reaction. Compare your calculated value for the entropy change to the predicted value. Assume that the thermodynamic values for fructose are equivalent to those for glucose.
   c. If the combustion reaction is done in the laboratory, the water is isolated as vapor. Recalculate the values of $\Delta H°$, $\Delta S°$, and $\Delta G°$ for the reaction where both products are gases.
   d. If 5.0 g of fructose is consumed, how many liters of $CO_2(g)$ would be produced? Where does this CO_2 go in a living organism? (Assume 25°C and 1 atm.)

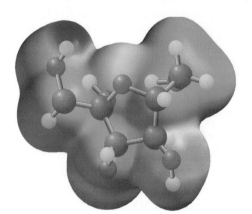

Fructose

   e. How much heat is liberated from the combustion of 5.0 g of fructose in the laboratory?
   f. In the first step of the catabolism of fructose, a phosphate is attached to the sugar unit:

$$C_6H_{12}O_6(aq) + ATP(aq) \rightarrow ADP(aq) + C_6H_{11}O_9P^{2-}(aq)$$
$$\Delta G = -16.7 \text{ kJ/mol}$$

   We also know that ATP can be made from ADP and inorganic phosphate in the body:

$$ATP(aq) + H_2O(l) \rightarrow ADP(aq) + HPO_4^{2-}(aq)$$
$$\Delta G = -30.5 \text{ kJ/mol}$$

   What is the free energy change for the reaction of fructose with phosphate?

$$C_6H_{12}O_6(aq) + HPO_4^{2-}(aq) \rightarrow C_6H_{11}O_9P^{2-}(aq) + H_2O(l)$$
$$\Delta G = ?$$

   g. Why would an organism have a need to utilize fructose in the same manner as glucose? What is a typical source of fructose?

15

Chemical Kinetics

Contents and Selected Applications

Aerial spraying. No, this plane isn't parked in that field. It's flying inches above it, spraying to control pests and weeds. Pesticides and herbicides enhance crop production, result in greener lawns, and eliminate nasty pests from our homes. But once they're added to the environment, how long do they stick around?

In 2004, American farmers continued a decades-long increase in food production, harvesting over 700 million metric tons of wheat, corn, rice, and other grains. According to the U.S. Department of Agriculture, corn production in Iowa alone more than quadrupled, from 40 bushels per acre to 180 bushels per acre, in the 75 years between 1930 and 2004. Although the introduction of the tractor and other automated farm machinery has played a large role in this increase in production, the use of insecticides and herbicides (compounds used to kill unwanted plants) has had a substantial impact. No longer do insects and weeds run rampant through cornfields and destroy crop yields. Atrazine, a herbicide, is one of the agents most commonly sprayed onto the soil from which corn crops grow in order to control weeds; approximately 15 million pounds are used annually in Nebraska alone.

When it is introduced into a farmer's field, atrazine works well to control broadleaf weeds, such as pigweed, cocklebur, velvetleaf, and certain grass weeds, without harming the corn plants. What happens to the atrazine that doesn't land on weeds? Some of it travels into the soil, where microbes and water can degrade it into by-products. This degradation process has been studied extensively by scientists. One particular reaction, the hydrolysis of atrazine, in which the chlorine atom on atrazine is replaced with a hydroxy (—OH) group, is of particular interest to researchers. The product, hydroxyatrazine, is rapidly metabolized by microbes living in the soil and groundwater and is viewed by the U.S. Environmental Protection Agency as not harmful to humans. The length of time it takes atrazine to metabolize is largely determined by this initial hydrolysis reaction.

Atrazine + H_2O ⟶ **Hydroxyatrazine** + HCl

Environmental chemists study the interaction of compounds and the environment, including the chemistry of the soil, water, and air. Their work proves that pesticides (a pesticide is any compound used to kill unwanted organisms) do not always rapidly disappear from the environment. For example, their analyses of lakes, rivers, and streams in states that use atrazine show that it persists in the environment for quite a long time. Depending on certain environmental and biological factors (including soil depth, temperature, and the presence of microorganisms, especially fungi), the

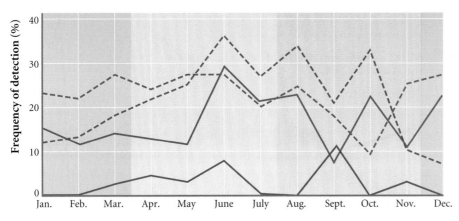

Little River—Agricultural basin
- - - - Herbicides
——— Pesticides

Lafayette Creek—Urban basin
- - - - Herbicides
——— Pesticides

The frequency of pesticide detections in a stream draining an agricultural basin was related to the agricultural cycle.

FIGURE 15.1

Atrazine and other herbicides persist in the environment long after they are first applied.

concentration of atrazine in *soil* can decline by half in less than a month, though about 60 days is typical. However, in natural *water* samples, atrazine typically degrades to one-half of its original concentration more slowly, in about 400 days. Because its degradation is relatively slow, atrazine is present in many water samples throughout the year, as shown in Figure 15.1. Laboratory studies, however, indicate that the hydrolysis of atrazine is spontaneous ($\Delta G < 0$ kJ/mol) and exothermic ($\Delta H = -35$ kJ/mol). **Does it make sense for a process to be so slow, compared to (for example) the combustion of propane in a propane torch, even if it is spontaneous?** As we noted in Chapter 14, the answer is a resounding yes. Values for free energy, enthalpy, and entropy are useful only in determining the thermodynamic properties of a reaction (that is, whether the reaction is spontaneous). The spontaneity of a reaction does not indicate anything about its rate. In order for us to determine how quickly the reaction occurs, we have to examine **chemical kinetics**—the study of the rates and mechanisms of chemical reactions, including the factors that influence these properties. To begin our study of chemical kinetics, we will briefly leave the farm fields and travel to the Olympic Games.

15.1 Reaction Rates

The Olympic Games rely heavily on the use of accurate timekeeping. In the bobsled and luge events, such as that shown in Figure 15.2, the accuracy of the timekeeping determines whether an athlete or team wins a gold or no medal at all. For example, at the 1998 Winter Olympic Games in Nagano, Japan, Silke Kraushaar of Germany placed first in the women's luge with a time of 50.617 s for her best run. The silver medal went to Barbara Niedernhuber, also from Germany, with a time of 50.625 s. The difference between these times is very small.

Let's examine the luge event more closely to help us introduce some new terms related to kinetics, the main topic of this chapter. The women's luge course at Nagano in 1998 was 1194 m long. Judging on the basis of her winning time, how fast did Silke Kraushaar travel? Speed is calculated by dividing the distance traveled by the change in time. Kraushaar traveled 1194 m in 50.617 s, so her **rate** of travel (speed) was 84.92 km/h (52.77 mi/h).

Application

$$\text{Speed} = \frac{\text{distance}}{\text{time}} = \frac{1194 \text{ m}}{50.617 \text{ s}} \times \frac{1 \text{ km}}{1000 \text{ m}} \times \frac{3600 \text{ s}}{\text{h}} = \frac{84.92 \text{ km}}{\text{h}}$$

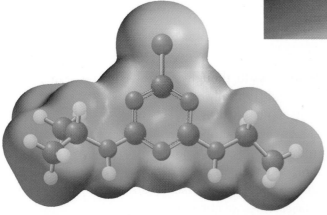

Atrazine

But *top* speeds for luge and bobsled events routinely hit 135 km/h (84 mi/h)! What we've calculated is the average rate of her travel.

Chemical reactions also have rates. Whereas the speed of a bobsledder can be listed in kilometers per hour (or miles per hour), the speed of a reaction is often described in units of concentration, often molarity, per second. For instance, under certain laboratory conditions, a 0.50 M solution of the herbicide atrazine can be completely hydrolyzed in 24 h. We can calculate the rate of the reaction by dividing the concentration that is consumed in the reaction by the time it took to complete the hydrolysis.

$$\text{Average rate} = \frac{0.50\ M}{24\ \text{h}} \times \frac{1\ \text{h}}{3600\ \text{s}} = 5.8 \times 10^{-6}\ M/\text{s}$$

We can say that the rate of this reaction for the 24 h period is $5.8 \times 10^{-6}\ M/\text{s}$.

Determining the average rate of a reaction is one of the tasks accomplished in chemical kinetics. However, when we study kinetics, we have to be careful to note the difference between the *extent* of a reaction and the *rate* of the reaction. The extent of a reaction (which we'll cover in Chapter 16) is a measure of the completeness of a reaction. The rate of a reaction describes how quickly it gets to that point. For example, the combustion of methane to make the flame on your cooking stove is an essentially complete reaction that is also relatively fast. The oxidation of iron on a suspension bridge is also complete, but it is quite slow. *Kinetics deals only with "how fast or slow and by what route." Kinetics tells us nothing about the extent of a reaction.*

Instantaneous Rate, Initial Rate, and Average Rate

At the 2001 Grand Nationals in Chicago, Whit Bazemore in his Matco Tools Pontiac Firebird "funny car" finished the quarter-mile drag strip in 4.750 s (Figure 15.3). Using this information (0.2500 mi in 4.750 s), we can calculate the average speed of the funny car as 0.05263 mi/s, or 189.5 mi/h. However, the speed of the funny car at the start was much less than this (0 mi/h), and the speed at the finish line was a lot faster (323.3 mi/h) than the average speed. The rate of a chemical reaction changes throughout, much like the rate of travel of a funny car at a drag race. However, chemical reactions differ because they typically start rapidly and then slow down with time. In other words, at the start of a reaction, the rate of chemical change is typically fast. As the reaction nears its end, the rate is typically slow. Over a given time period (Δt), though, it has an average rate that describes how long it took to reach that certain point in the reaction.

$$\text{Average rate} = \frac{\Delta \text{concentration}}{\Delta t}$$

In short, just as the speed of a dragster changes during a race, *the rate of the reaction changes as the reaction proceeds.*

What if we consider a change in time that is negligible ($\Delta t \approx 0$)? When this happens, we are examining the instantaneous rate of a reaction. This is what we determine at the finish line in the funny car race (323.3 mi/h). It is also what we measure as the lights turn green at the start of the race (0 mi/h). At these points, and at any other point we pick, we are measuring the instantaneous rate. In a chemical reaction, the rate at the start of a reaction, when the reactant concentrations are greatest, is important. The instantaneous rate of the reaction measured at the start is referred to as the initial rate of reaction. Instantaneous rates can be measured if we have a plot of the reaction such as that shown in Figure 15.4. If, on the plot of our reaction, we draw a line that is tangent to the curve (that is, a line that just touches the curve and is going in the same direction *at that point*), as is done in Figure 15.5, and we measure the slope of that line, we get the instantaneous rate of the reaction at that specific time. This is a useful way to measure instantaneous rates.

Environmental chemists often measure the rate of a reaction. For example, the environmental hydrolysis of alachlor (also known as Lasso™, a common herbicide) occurs more rapidly than the hydrolysis of atrazine. However, the rate is still slow enough that new ways to decrease the time that the herbicide spends in the environment before chemically degrading are being sought. One such way includes the reduction of alachlor to an acetanilide via electrochemical techniques such as those that we will discuss in Chapter 19.

FIGURE 15.3

"Funny cars," with their characteristic powerful engines and oversized rear wheels, get ready to race the quarter-mile. Bazemore powered his Matco Tools Pontiac Firebird to a national record time of 4.750 s at a track record speed of 323.27 mph to lead the 16-car field.

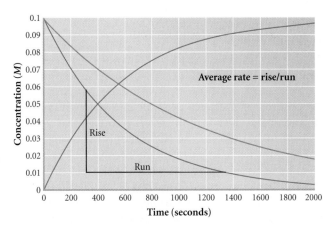

FIGURE 15.4

Calculating the average rate of a reaction from a sample plot of the reactant concentration versus time. Average rates and instantaneous rates differ in the length of time used to calculate them. The average rate of a reaction is calculated by dividing the rise by the run.

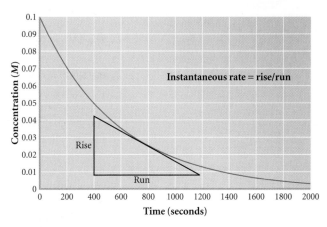

FIGURE 15.5

Calculating the instantaneous rate of a reaction from the same sample plot used to calculate the average rate in Figure 15.5. The slope of a tangent line can be used to find an instantaneous rate.

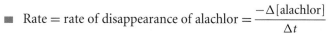

Alachlor (Lasso)   **Acetanilide product**

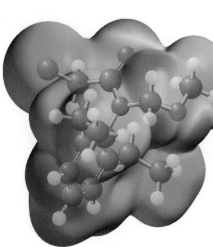

Alachlor

The rate of this reaction can be determined in the laboratory by measuring the change in the concentration of one of the compounds over a period of time. Mathematically, the rate of the reaction is equal to the rate of the disappearance of alachlor, the rate of appearance of the acetanilide, or the rate of the appearance of Cl^-, because they are all in a 1-to-1 mole ratio. The sign placed in the equation is used to indicate whether the compound being measured is disappearing (minus sign) or appearing (plus sign). Remember that the Δ symbol represents a change, measured by taking the final value minus the initial value. Even though the sign of the rate for the disappearance would appear to generate a negative value for the rate, it does not. In fact, *reaction rates are always positive.*

- Rate = rate of disappearance of alachlor = $\dfrac{-\Delta[\text{alachlor}]}{\Delta t}$

- Rate = rate of disappearance of H^+ = $\dfrac{-\Delta[H^+]}{\Delta t}$

- Rate = rate of appearance of product = $\dfrac{\Delta[\text{acetanilide}]}{\Delta t}$

- Rate = rate of appearance of Cl^- = $\dfrac{\Delta[Cl^-]}{\Delta t}$

The rate of the decomposition of hydrogen peroxide into water and oxygen can also be written using these rules. The rate of the reaction could be set equal to the rate of appearance of oxygen. In this case, the rate is simply the change in its

$$2H_2O_2(aq) \rightarrow 2H_2O(l) + O_2(g)$$

concentration divided by the change in time. *However, if we consider the rate of appearance of water as a measure of the rate of the reaction,* we must somehow note that two molecules of water are appearing for every molecule of $O_2(g)$ that is produced. This is done by dividing the rate by the mole ratio from the balanced equation. For instance, the rate of appearance of H_2O times $\dfrac{1 \text{ mol } O_2}{2 \text{ mol } H_2O}$ gives the rate of the reaction.

Our rate descriptions are

- Rate based on disappearance of $H_2O_2(g) = \dfrac{-\Delta[H_2O_2]}{\Delta t} \times \dfrac{1}{2}$

- Rate based on appearance of $O_2(g) = \dfrac{\Delta[O_2]}{\Delta t}$

- Rate based on appearance of $H_2O(l) = \dfrac{\Delta[H_2O]}{\Delta t} \times \dfrac{1}{2}$

EXERCISE 15.1   Rate of the Haber Process

Farmers apply ammonia to their cornfields during spring planting by injecting it directly into the soil. The ammonia they use is made by the Haber process; the chemical reaction for this process is indicated by the equation shown below. Describe the rate of the reaction in terms of the rate of appearance or disappearance of the components of the reaction.

$$N_2(g) + 3H_2(g) \rightarrow 2NH_3(g)$$

Solution

The rate of the reaction can be measured by measuring the changes in concentration of each of the species. Mathematically, the rate of the reaction of N_2 is equal to one-third the rate of disappearance of H_2, because 1 mol of N_2 disappears for every 3 mol of H_2 that react. The rate of the reaction of N_2 is also equal to one-half the rate of appearance of ammonia (NH_3), because 1 mol of N_2 disappears for every 2 mol of NH_3 that are produced. Note that the disappearance of H_2 is indicated with a minus sign and the appearance of NH_3 a plus sign.

$$\text{Rate} = -\dfrac{\Delta[N_2]}{\Delta t} = -\dfrac{1}{3}\dfrac{\Delta[H_2]}{\Delta t} = \dfrac{1}{2}\dfrac{\Delta[NH_3]}{\Delta t}$$

PRACTICE 15.1

What is the rate of the following reaction in terms of the rates of disappearance and appearance of the components of the reaction?

$$2HI(aq) \rightarrow H_2(g) + I_2(aq)$$

See Problems 5, 6, 9, 10, and 13.

We can examine this further by actually calculating the average rate of the reaction. Assume that an environmental chemist begins an experiment with a 0.400 M alachlor solution. After 10 days, the concentration of alachlor is determined to be 0.350 M, and the concentration of acetanilide and that of chloride are both 0.050 M. What is the average rate of the reaction? We know the final value (0.350 M alachlor at 10 days) and the initial value (0.400 M alachlor at 0 days). Although time can be used with almost any unit, we often report rates as M/s. So, we convert the time into seconds (10 days = 864,000 s) and fill in our equations, keeping in mind that the rate measures the change in concentration per unit change in time. In this example, however, we don't know the concentration of H^+ at either time, so we can't use it to determine the rate of the reaction. Note: It would be perfectly fine to report rates with units of M/day, M/hr, etc.

- Rate = disappearance of alachlor $= \dfrac{-(0.350\ M - 0.400\ M)}{(864{,}000\ \text{s} - 0\ \text{s})}$

$$= 5.79 \times 10^{-8}\ M/s$$

The slope of a line that is tangent to the plot of concentration versus time for a reaction gives the instantaneous rate of the reaction. Instantaneous rates can be measured at any specific time.

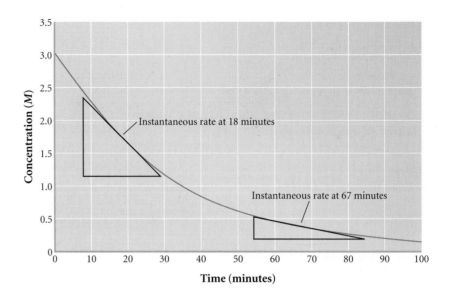

■ $\text{Rate} = \text{appearance of acetanilide} = \dfrac{(0.050\ M - 0.000\ M)}{(864,000\ s - 0\ s)} = 5.79 \times 10^{-8}\ M/s$

■ $\text{Rate} = \text{appearance of } Cl^- = \dfrac{(0.050\ M - 0.000\ M)}{(864,000\ s - 0\ s)} = 5.79 \times 10^{-8}\ M/s$

Note that no matter which calculation we complete, we should always obtain the same rate of reaction because of the 1-to-1-to-1 mole ratio of reactants and products.

Remember that average rates, instantaneous rates, and initial rates are calculated in the same manner. *The only difference is that the length of the time period is different.* Long changes in time determine the average rate over those long changes. Instantaneous rates are measured when the change in time (Δt) is very small (that is, $\Delta t \rightarrow 0$). Experimentally, average rates, instantaneous rates, and initial rates can be found by measuring the color, temperature, electrochemical voltage (Chapter 19), or some other physical property of the reactants or products that changes over time. Then by determining the slope of a line that is tangent to the curve drawn when the concentrations of reactants or products are plotted against time, the rate can be obtained. Initial rates are measured as instantaneous rates at the start of the reaction.

EXERCISE 15.2	The Rate of a Reaction

Methoxychlor is an important insecticide used to control parasites on livestock and a variety of pests on vegetables and fruits. Its breakdown by soil microbes may proceed through the following reaction. Calculate the average rate of this reaction in M/s of methoxychlor, assuming that the concentration of CH_3OH starts at $0.000\ M$ and after $60.0\ h$ climbs to $0.100\ M$.

First Thoughts

The equation that describes this reaction includes two starting materials and two types of product molecules. We could use any of these compounds to determine the average rate of the reaction, but the question asks us to work with the formation of methanol to determine the rate. By examining the balanced equation, we see that the rate of methanol formation is two times the rate of the reaction of methoxychlor. That is, 2 mol of methanol are formed for every mole of methoxychlor that is consumed.

Solution

The rate of the reaction can be determined on the basis of the rate of appearance of methanol (CH_3OH). Because methanol is forming at twice the rate of the reaction of methoxychlor, the rate of the reaction of methoxychlor is one-half the rate of appearance of methanol.

$$\text{Rate} = \frac{1}{2}\left(\frac{\Delta[CH_3OH]}{\Delta t}\right) = \frac{1}{2}\left(\frac{(0.100\ M - 0.00\ M)}{(216{,}000\ s - 0.00\ s)}\right)$$

$$= \frac{1}{2}\left(\frac{0.100\ M}{216{,}000\ s}\right) = 2.31 \times 10^{-7}\ M/s$$

Further Insights

The rate we have calculated in this problem is an average rate of reaction, which can be determined by examining the length of time that was used to measure the rate over this time period. To measure the initial rate or the instantaneous rate of the reaction, we would need to measure the concentrations of methanol (or another of the compounds in the equation) during a much shorter reaction time. Currently, rates based on time changes on the order of *femtoseconds (10^{-15})* can be determined with laser-based measurement techniques.

PRACTICE 15.2

Calculate the average rate of the Haber process (Exercise 15.1), assuming that at 12.5 s the concentration of $H_2(g)$ was 0.355 M and at 83.3 s the concentration was 0.258 M.

See Problems 7 and 8. ∎

15.2 ▸ An Introduction to Rate Laws

We pointed out in the introduction to this chapter that under certain conditions, atrazine can degrade to one-half of its original concentration in 60 days. This means that in a sample containing $5.0 \times 10^{-7}\ M$ atrazine, the concentration reduces to $2.5 \times 10^{-7}\ M$ after 60 days. We can calculate the rate of this reaction using the concepts we learned in Section 15.1. **Can we predict the concentration of atrazine after 120 days?** This question highlights a complicating factor in kinetics: *The rate of a reaction typically decreases as the reaction progresses, because fewer reactant molecules exist after the reaction begins.* The lower concentration of reactant reduces the likelihood that molecules will interact to make products. As a result, determining concentrations of reactants and products at a certain time during a reaction requires greater understanding of how the reaction rate changes with time. In the end, we cannot say that the concentration of atrazine should be 0 M after 120 days (see Figure 15.6). Similarly, we cannot say that the concentration is $3.75 \times 10^{-7}\ M$ after only 30 days.

The decomposition of hydrogen peroxide can be used to illustrate how the rate of a reaction can be related to the reaction conditions. Hydrogen peroxide, a common staple in the home medicine cabinet, is used to clean cuts and scrapes

 Application

FIGURE 15.6

The environmental decomposition of atrazine in groundwater. The half-life is the time it takes for a given concentration to be halved.

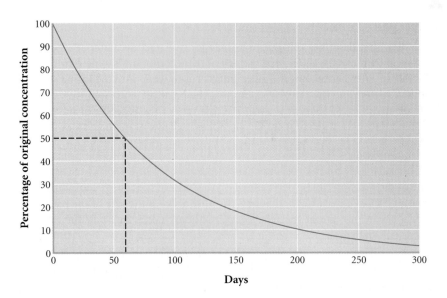

because of its ability to oxidize microbes. We observe by experiment that the rate of the reaction depends on the concentration of hydrogen peroxide. As the concentration decreases, the rate of the reaction decreases.

$$\text{Rate} \propto [H_2O_2]$$

When we examine the relationship more closely, the following mathematical equation, called a **rate law**, emerges. This rate law states that the rate of the reaction of hydrogen peroxide is equal to the product of a constant (which we call the **rate constant**) times the concentration of H_2O_2.

$$2H_2O_2(aq) \rightarrow 2H_2O(l) + O_2(g)$$

$$\text{Rate} = k[H_2O_2]$$

From the rate law, we determine that the reaction is **first order** in hydrogen peroxide. That is, *the rate depends on the concentration of H_2O_2 raised to the first power*. The reaction is first order *overall* because the rate equation for the reaction is dependent only on the concentration of H_2O_2 to the first power—that is, it is linearly related. It is important to remember that the value of the rate constant, the compounds included in the rate law, and the orders of the compounds in the equation *can be found only experimentally*.

The rate law, as we will see, can be used to determine the rate of a reaction at any reactant concentration. It will also tell you which species are the most important contributors to the rate of a reaction. The typical rate law has the following form:

$$\text{Rate} = k[A]^n[B]^m$$

where k is the rate constant, [A] and [B] are the concentrations of substances involved in the reaction, and n and m are the orders of the corresponding compounds. The values of n and m are measures of how dependent the rate is on the concentration of a particular reactant, and they *must be* experimentally determined. The reaction also can be described in terms of the overall order, which is calculated by adding n and m (and the exponents of any other reactants in the rate law). The order of a compound or the overall order of a reaction can certainly be negative or even a noninteger number. Again, it is important to remember that *the order of a compound in a reaction cannot be determined just by looking at the reaction*.

The reaction of nitrogen monoxide gas with hydrogen gas is

$$2NO(g) + 2H_2(g) \rightarrow 2H_2O(l) + N_2(g)$$

The experimentally determined rate law is

$$\text{Rate} = k[\text{NO}]^2[\text{H}_2]$$

The reaction is said to be second order in nitrogen monoxide, because the rate depends on [NO] to the second power. The rate is first order with respect to hydrogen gas, because the exponent is 1, which means there is a linear relationship between the rate and [H_2]. The reaction is third order (the sum of the individual orders, $2 + 1$) overall. A reaction can have fractional orders, though we will not deal with that here.

EXERCISE 15.3   The Rate Law

Environmental chemists are concerned with the damaging effects of compounds on the ozone layer. One such class of compounds is the nitrogen oxides, such as NO(g) and NO_2(g). Under certain conditions, the reaction of NO(g), an air pollutant released in automobile exhaust, with oxygen can produce N_2O_4(g). The rate law for this reaction was determined experimentally and is shown below. What is the reaction order of each of the compounds in the rate law? What is the overall order of the reaction?

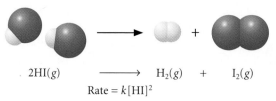

$$2\text{NO}(g) \quad + \quad \text{O}_2(g) \quad \longrightarrow \quad \text{N}_2\text{O}_4(g)$$
$$\text{Rate} = k[\text{NO}][\text{O}_2]$$

Solution

The experimentally determined rate law says that the reaction is first order in NO(g) and first order in O_2(g). Overall, then, the reaction is second order.

PRACTICE 15.3

The following reaction proceeds at 300°C. What is the reaction order of the compound in the following reaction with the given rate law? What is the order of the reaction?

$$2\text{HI}(g) \quad \longrightarrow \quad \text{H}_2(g) \quad + \quad \text{I}_2(g)$$
$$\text{Rate} = k[\text{HI}]^2$$

See Problems 19 and 20.

Collision Theory

In Exercise 15.3 and Practice 15.3, the rate law is expressed as the concentration of the reactants raised to a power. This is not uncommon, but as we've mentioned before, it isn't true for reactions in general. Why do the orders of the rate law and the stoichiometric factors of a reaction often differ? Reactions are typically more complex than they appear when written on paper. To understand how this can cause the rate law to differ from what we may expect, we need to consult collision theory. This theory *describes how the rate of a reaction is related to the number of properly oriented collisions of the molecules involved.* Collision theory is heavily based on the kinetic molecular theory we discussed in Chapter 11.

Kinetic molecular theory says that the thermal motion of particles (the kinetic energy) can be used to explain how a gas behaves. For instance, the pressure

Increasing the temperature of a reaction increases the kinetic energy of the components of the reaction. This means that the particles move faster and, as a result, have many more collisions than they do in the colder reaction. More collisions mean a faster reaction.

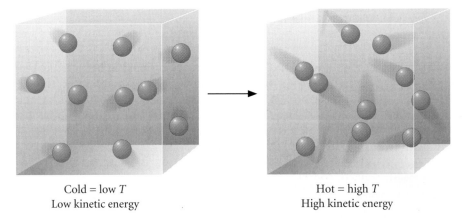

Cold = low T
Low kinetic energy

Hot = high T
High kinetic energy

of a gaseous system is related to the number of collisions of the molecules with the sides of their container in a given time. If we increase the number of molecules per unit volume, the number of collisions per second also increases, assuming the temperature is constant. The pressure of the system can be increased if we raise the temperature of the gas and leave the volume constant. This is because the molecules are moving faster (more kinetic energy) and engage in more collisions per second. In short, higher kinetic energy equals more collisions.

Collision theory, which is summarized in Table 15.1, requires that molecules collide in order to react. One of the more important statements in collision theory, as shown in Figure 15.7(a), says that the collisions must be energetic enough to make a product. The minimum energy required, the activation energy (E_a), is specific to a particular reaction. However, an energetic collision alone is not enough to cause a reaction to occur. The collision must also occur between properly oriented molecules; see Figure 15.7(b). Because the equation we write to describe a reaction doesn't address all of these issues, rate laws are difficult to derive by simply examining the overall equation. We'll revisit this statement in Section 15.6.

TABLE 15.1	Collision Theory

A reaction occurs when the following conditions have been met:
- Molecules collide.
- Molecules have enough kinetic energy.
- Molecules are oriented properly.

Implications:
- Larger concentrations have faster reaction rates.
- Reactions with higher temperatures have faster rates.
- Rates depend on the number of properly oriented collisions.
- Predicting the rate of a reaction is difficult.

FIGURE 15.7

Collision theory. (a) Collisions must be energetic enough to be considered successful. (b) Successful collisions only occur between properly oriented molecules.

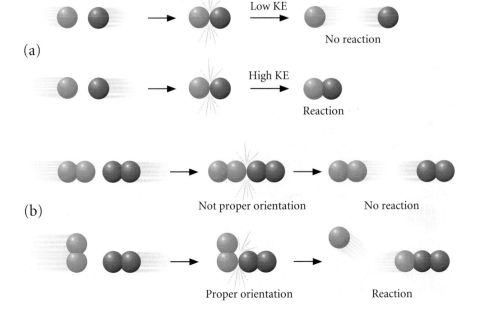

Low KE
No reaction

High KE
Reaction

(a)

Not proper orientation
No reaction

Proper orientation
Reaction

(b)

HERE'S WHAT WE KNOW SO FAR

■ The rate of a reaction is the change in concentration (M) per unit time. Rates are always positive numbers, often reported in M/s.

■ Average rates and instantaneous rates differ only in the time measurement. Instantaneous rates have $\Delta t \approx 0$.

■ The rate law (Rate = $k[A]^n[B]^m$) indicates the relationship between the rate and the concentrations of reactants.

■ The order of a reactant can be used to indicate quickly the relationship between the reactant concentration and the rate.

■ Collision theory explains why the rate of a reaction typically decreases as time passes.

15.3 ⟩ Changes in Time—The Integrated Rate Law

After the discovery in 1939 that DDT (1,1,1-trichloro-2,2-bis-(4′-chlorophenyl) ethane, or **d**ichloro**d**iphenyl**t**richloroethane) can be used to control mosquito-borne malaria, its use soared. Especially important was its use to protect soldiers who were fighting in the Pacific Rim countries in World War II. Since its discovery, DDT has been sprayed to eliminate insects from cotton crops, spiders from residences, and mosquitoes from towns all across the globe (Figure 15.8). Initial testing showed that the compound wasn't very toxic to mammals. However, because the metabolism of DDT is very slow, small amounts of DDT in the environment tended to accumulate in animals (including humans) until toxic levels were present. Evidence of this caused Sweden in 1970 and the United States in 1972 to ban the use of DDT as a pesticide, although it is still used in some other countries, such as Ethiopia and South Africa. Despite the 30-year ban on DDT use in the United States, the insecticide can still be found in the environment, mostly in waterways like that shown in Figure 15.9. The hazard of DDT accumulation in the food chain versus the benefit of saving human lives by preventing malaria in the populations of, for example, East African countries is still a topic of intense debate.

In organisms that are resistant to DDT, an enzyme known as dehydrochlorinase converts DDT into dichlorodiphenyldiethene (DDE). Unfortunately, DDE can accumulate within birds and weaken their eggshells by interfering with the

Application

CHEMICAL
ENCOUNTERS:
Decomposition
of DDT

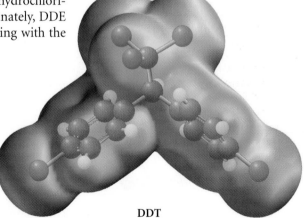

DDT

FIGURE 15.8

DDT and the mosquito. DDT is still one of the most cost-effective methods of controlling mosquito-borne malaria. Although many countries have banned its use because of DDT's persistence in the environment, many homes in central Africa are still sprayed inside and out.

FIGURE 15.9

Even though the use of DDT has been banned in the United States since the 1970s, DDT is still present in the environment. This plot of New York harbor shows that the sediments in the East River harbor still contain large quantities of DDT.

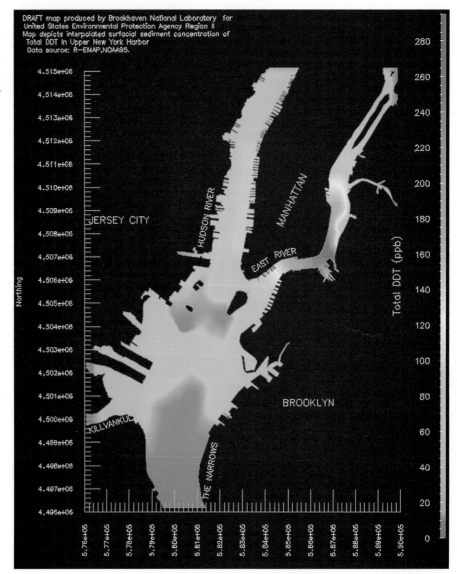

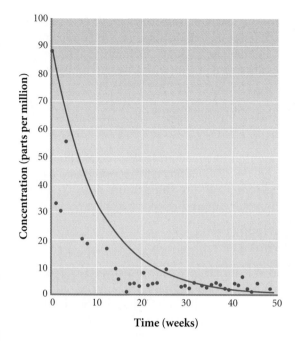

FIGURE 15.10

An experiment to illustrate the bioremediation (biological recycling) of DDT-contaminated ground by soil microbes and nutrients. The decomposition of DDT occurs rapidly at first and then slows. Note that the concentration of DDT is reported in parts per million (1 ppm of DDT = 1 µg of DDT per gram of soil). Although the curve appears to be placed incorrectly, it is not. Computer analysis of this set of data, and additional data not shown, produced this curve.

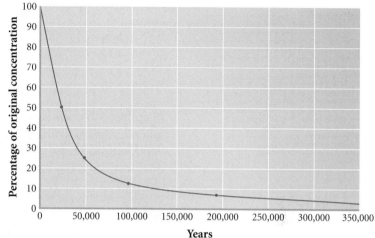

FIGURE 15.11

Plot of the radioactive decay of plutonium-239.

complex process of constructing the shells. This leads to shells that break under the normal pressures naturally associated with nesting. For this reason, several species of birds, such as the peregrine falcon, were nearly wiped out in the United States.

The rate of decomposition of DDT by soil microbes is plotted against time in Figure 15.10. Initially the rate is relatively high; then, as time passes, the rate begins to decline. Does this make sense according to what we know about collision theory? Yes. Reducing the number of reactant molecules reduces the number of collisions that would result in the formation of the product.

What if we're interested in determining what concentration of a chemical will exist after a certain amount of time has passed? For example, the Hanford Nuclear Reservation on the banks of the Columbia River just north of Richland, Washington, has produced 54 million gallons of radioactive plutonium waste over the past half-century. The waste is currently being stored in 177 underground tanks as a watery sludge. How long will it take for the radioactive waste stored at the Hanford Nuclear Reservation to decay to 1% of its current concentration? We could examine the plot shown in Figure 15.11 to figure this out, but we would need either to have a plot of the radioactive decay reaction or to know the rate law, the rate, and rate constant of the reaction. Can we determine the concentration at a specific time without knowing the rate or even having a plot of the reaction? Calculus comes to our rescue. With some manipulation of the rate law, we can make a more useful description of the rate of a reaction that will enable us to perform these calculations. These equations are referred to as the integrated rate laws.

   **Application**

Integrated First-Order Rate Law

We discussed the decomposition of hydrogen peroxide to make oxygen and water near the start of Section 15.2. Experimentally, it has been determined that the rate law for this process describes a first-order reaction. Unfortunately, this doesn't tell us the concentration of H_2O_2 at any point during the reaction, unless we know the rate of the reaction at that time and the rate constant (k). In order to calculate the concentration of H_2O_2 at any point during the reaction, we can mathematically convert the rate law into an **integrated first-order rate law**.

$$2H_2O_2(aq) \rightarrow 2H_2O(l) + O_2(g)$$

$$\text{Rate} = k[H_2O_2]$$

The integrated rate law gets its name from the mathematical process, known as integration, that we follow to *generate the relationship between concentration and time*. When we integrate the rate law from $t = 0$ to some future time, the integrated rate law for the decomposition of hydrogen peroxide becomes

$$\ln\left(\frac{[H_2O_2]_t}{[H_2O_2]_0}\right) = -kt$$

where $[H_2O_2]_0$ is the concentration of hydrogen peroxide initially, $[H_2O_2]_t$ is the concentration of hydrogen peroxide at a particular time t, and k is the rate constant. In practice, we need know only three of the four values in the equation (time, rate constant, initial concentration, and concentration at time t) in order to find the fourth.

This equation is general for all first-order reactions, which we will designate using the general form

$$A \rightarrow \text{Products}$$

where A is any single reactant. Note that the stoichiometric coefficient for A is 1. The natural logarithm (ln) of the quotient of the final reactant concentration, $[A]_t$, divided by the initial concentration $[A]_0$ is equal to the negative of the rate constant, k, times the time, t, shown in the left-hand side of the box below. We can use this equation to calculate the time required to reach a given concentration. Alternatively, we can rearrange the equation to that shown on the right-hand side of the box if we wish to calculate the concentration at a particular time:

$$\ln\left(\frac{[A]_t}{[A]_0}\right) = -kt \qquad [A]_t = [A]_0 e^{-kt}$$

We can transpose this into an equation in the form $y = mx + b$ by recognizing that

$$\ln\left(\frac{[A]_t}{[A]_0}\right) = \ln[A]_t - \ln[A]_0$$

Substituting for $\ln\left(\frac{[A]_t}{[A]_0}\right)$ yields

$$\ln[A]_t - \ln[A]_0 = -kt$$

which enables us to come up with the final $y = mx + b$ form:

$$\ln[A]_t = -kt + \ln[A]_0$$
$$y \;\;\; = \;\; mx + \;\;\; b$$

where the y axis $= \ln[A]_t$

     the x axis $= t$

     the slope $m = -k$

     the intercept $b = \ln[A]_0$

How do we use the first-order equation to find the concentration of hydrogen peroxide after 5.00 min if we have a solution in which the initial concentration,

$[H_2O_2]_0$, is equal to 0.100 M? The rate constant for this reaction was determined by experiment to be 3.10×10^{-3} s^{-1}. Using this equation, we can calculate the amount of peroxide still remaining after 5.00 min. We first *convert our time to match the units for the rate constant* (5.00 min $= 3.00 \times 10^2$ s) and then insert our known values into the integrated first-order rate law.

$$\ln[H_2O_2]_t - \ln[H_2O_2]_0 = -kt$$
$$\ln[H_2O_2]_t - \ln(0.100\ M) = -(3.10 \times 10^{-3}\ \text{s}^{-1})(3.00 \times 10^2\ \text{s})$$
$$\ln[H_2O_2]_t - \ln(0.100\ M) = -0.930$$
$$\ln[H_2O_2]_t + 2.3026 = -0.930$$
$$\ln[H_2O_2]_t = -3.2326$$
$$[H_2O_2]_t = e^{-3.2326} = 0.0395\ M$$

The concentration of hydrogen peroxide remaining after 5.00 min is 0.0395 M.

EXERCISE 15.4   **Working with the Integrated First-Order Rate Law**

Archaeologists near the Dead Sea in 1998 reported the discovery of a substance that they believe ancient peoples used as glue. A sample of *newly prepared* collagen exhibits 15.2 disintegrations per minute per gram (15.2 dis/min/g) of carbon. (A disintegration is the decomposition of a radioactive nucleus such as ^{14}C; see Chapter 21.) The ^{14}C decay rate for a sample of the *ancient* glue (made from collagen) was found to be 5.60 disintegrations per minute per gram (5.60 dis/min/g) of carbon. What is the age of the glue? The decomposition of ^{14}C is a first-order process with a rate constant of 1.209×10^{-4} year^{-1}.

First Thoughts

This problem shows that the integrated first-order rate law can be used with radioactive compounds to determine decay rates, concentrations, or times. In these cases, we consider the concentration of a reactant to be directly proportional to the number of disintegrations per minute per gram. In the laboratory, this method can be used to accurately determine the date of objects that are between 200 and 50,000 years old. Also note that we do not need to convert dis/min/g to dis/yr/g because the units cancel in the equation.

Solution

If we assume that fresh collagen has the same activity of ^{14}C that the ancient glue did when it was first made, we can calculate the length of time it would take a fresh sample of collagen to have the same activity of ^{14}C as the glue.

$$\ln\left(\frac{5.60\ \text{dis/min/g}}{15.2\ \text{dis/min/g}}\right) = -(1.209 \times 10^{-4}\ \text{year}^{-1})t$$
$$\ln(0.3684) = -(1.209 \times 10^{-4}\ \text{year}^{-1})t$$
$$-0.9985 = -(1.209 \times 10^{-4}\ \text{year}^{-1})t$$
$$t = 8259\ \text{year} = 8260\ \text{year}$$

The calculation reveals that it would take 8260 years for the activity in the fresh sample to decay to the level observed in the ancient piece of wood. This implies that the glue is 8260 years old.

Further Insight

Radiocarbon dating has been used extensively in determining the age of archaeological artifacts. The process relies on the assumption that the ratio of carbon-14 to carbon-12 in nature has always been constant. However, when an organism dies, the ratio begins to change as the radioactive carbon-14 decays. Controversy over the validity of this dating method has been addressed by compensating for small fluctuations in the original ratio. These fluctuations have been determined by dating objects with an age known by other methods. More information about radiocarbon dating can be found in Chapter 21.

PRACTICE 15.4

Hanford's nuclear waste contains large quantities of plutonium (mostly ^{239}Pu). Researchers have determined that approximately 875 kg of solid waste plutonium are buried there. How long will it take for the mass of plutonium-239 to drop to 10% of its original value? Assume the rate constant that describes the decay of ^{239}Pu is 2.874×10^{-5} year^{-1}. How long will it take for the mass of plutonium-239 to reach half of its original concentration?

See Problems 33 and 34.

Half-life

Application

CHEMICAL
ENCOUNTERS:
Persistent
Pesticides

The persistence of pesticides and herbicides in the environment is often reported as the amount of time that it takes for half of the original concentration to decompose. In general, any reaction can be reported in this manner by calculating the amount of time it takes for the reaction to proceed to *50% completion*. This value is known as the **half-life ($t_{1/2}$)** of the reaction (Figure 15.12). Perhaps you've heard this term used to express the rate of decay for a radioactive element, such as the radioactive waste stored at the Hanford Nuclear Reservation, or in accounts of the dating of ancient artifacts. The half-lives of pesticides and herbicides indicated in Table 15.2 are used to judge the safety of the compounds and to establish guidelines for the frequency of their application. How does the half-life fit in with our description of the integrated first-order rate law?

Consider the first-order hydrolysis of atrazine in groundwater. The rate constant for this reaction in water has been found to be 0.001733 day^{-1}. Note that we're using a rate constant with units of day^{-1} instead of s^{-1}. This will be important in the answer we generate from the integrated rate law equation.

$$\ln \left(\frac{[\text{atrazine}]_t}{[\text{atrazine}]_0} \right) = -kt$$

FIGURE 15.12

The half-life of a reaction is the amount of time required for the reaction to reach 50% of the original concentrations. In terms of radioactive decay or the decomposition of pesticides, the passage of one half-life reduces the concentration in half. Two half-lives reduce the concentration to one-quarter of the original.

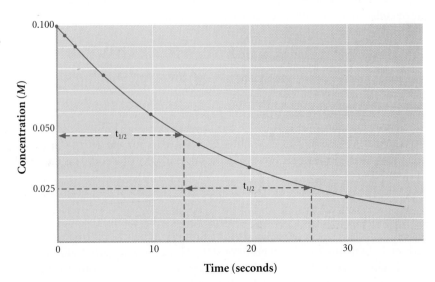

TABLE 15.2	Solubility and Half-life in Soil for Selected Pesticides

The sorption index is the ratio of pesticide concentration bound to soil particles divided by the concentration in the aqueous phase. Pesticides with low sorption indices are more likely to be leached into groundwater supplies, because a low proportion of each binds to the soil. The half-life is reported for the pesticide in sterile soil. 2,4-D, for example, is of greater environmental concern because of its sorption index value than is DDT.

Trade Name/ Brand Name	Water Solubility (ppm)	Sorption Index (higher = greater binding to the soil)	Soil Half-life (days)
2,4-D	890	20	10
Alachlor/Lasso	240	170	15
Atrazine/Aatrex	33	100	60
Dicamba/Banvel	400,000	2	14
Carbaryl/Sevin	110	300	10
Chlorsulfuron/Glean	7000	40	160
DDT	0.0055	24,000	3000
Diazinon	60	1000	40
Malathion/Cythion	145	1800	1
Metolachlor/Dual	530	200	90
Methoxychlor/Marlate	0.10	80,000	120
Pendimethalin/Prowl	<1	5000	90
Pronamide/Kerb	15	200	60
Terbacil/Sinbar	710	55	120
Terbufos/Counter	4.5	500	5
Trifluralin/Treflan	<1	8000	60

Source: Institute of Agriculture and Natural Resources, Univ. Nebraska Lincoln, *Factors That Affect Soil-Applied Herbicides*, 2005.

When the hydrolysis has consumed half of the original concentration of atrazine, $[\text{atrazine}]_t = \frac{1}{2}[\text{atrazine}]_0 = 0.5[\text{atrazine}]_0$. Substituting this into the equation above, we find that

$$\ln\left(\frac{0.5[\text{atrazine}]_0}{[\text{atrazine}]_0}\right) = -kt_{1/2}$$

The concentration of atrazine ($[\text{atrazine}]_0$) cancels. Simplifying the equation further yields

$$\ln 0.5 = -kt_{1/2}$$
$$-0.693 = -kt_{1/2}$$
$$t_{1/2} = \frac{0.693}{k}$$

Our derivation reveals that *the half-life ($t_{1/2}$) of a first-order reaction is, throughout the reaction, a constant that depends only on the rate constant and not on the concentration of the reactant.* This means that if we know the half-life for a particular first-order reaction, we can calculate the rate constant, and vice versa.

Substituting the rate constant for atrazine into this equation, we find that the half-life for the hydrolysis in water agrees with the experimental observation we noted at the start of this chapter. Half of the atrazine added to water in the environment disappears after 400 days.

$$t_{1/2} = \frac{0.693}{0.001733 \text{ day}^{-1}} = 4.00 \times 10^2 \text{ days}$$

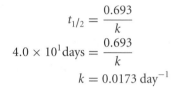

EXERCISE 15.5   How Long Will It Take?

Diazinon crystals are sprinkled around a home's foundation to kill and repel ants from the home. How long will it take for the diazinon to decompose, assuming first-order kinetics, to 25% of its original concentration in the soil? (From Table 15.2, the half-life of diazinon is 4.0×10^1 days.)

First Thoughts

The problem doesn't state the original concentration of the diazinon in the soil. However, we don't need to know the concentration to determine the answer, because we have the ratio of initial concentration to final concentration (that is, $[\text{diazinon}]_t = 0.25[\text{diazinon}]_0$).

Solution

Using the half-life, we first calculate the rate constant for the reaction:

$$t_{1/2} = \frac{0.693}{k}$$

$$4.0 \times 10^1 \text{days} = \frac{0.693}{k}$$

$$k = 0.0173 \text{ day}^{-1}$$

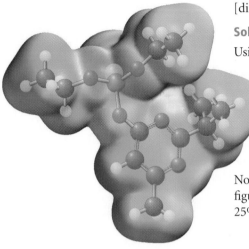

Diazinon

Note that the unit of the rate constant is reciprocal days and that we retain an extra figure in the value because we will use the data in the next part of the calculation. If 25% of the diazinon remains, then

$$\ln\left(\frac{0.25[\text{diazinon}]_0}{[\text{diazinon}]_0}\right) = -(0.0173 \text{ day}^{-1})t$$

$$\ln 0.25 = -0.0173 \text{ day}^{-1}t$$

$$-1.386 = -0.0173 \text{ day}^{-1}t$$

$$t = 8.0 \times 10^1 \text{ days}$$

Further Insight

There is an alternative method by which we can calculate the answer. One half-life reduces the original concentration by 50% (50% = 0.5 = ½). Two half-lives reduce the concentration to 25% (½ × ½ = ¼). Three reduce the concentration to 12.5% (½ × ½ × ½ = ⅛). Because we want to know the time required for the reaction to reduce the concentration of starting material to 25% of the initial concentration, we need two half-lives (4.0×10^1 days + 4.0×10^1 days = 8.0×10^1 days). Therefore, for a first-order process, the fraction remaining, $[A]_t/[A]_0$ equals 2^{-n}, where n = number of half-lives. For example, for n = 3 half-lives, $[A]_t/[A]_0$ = 2^{-3} or 0.125.

PRACTICE 15.5

What is the length of time you would have to wait for alachlor to decompose to 25% of its original value? . . . to 6.25%? . . . to 0.001%?

See Problems 27 and 28.

Other Rate Laws

Not all reactions follow first-order kinetics. Other orders do exist, even noninteger orders. Reactions that take place on metal surfaces typically follow zero-order kinetics. Hydrogenation of vegetable oils, the decomposition of ammonia on a tungsten wire, and the reaction of N_2O with oxygen in your car's catalytic converter are reactions on metal surfaces. They follow zero-order kinetics.

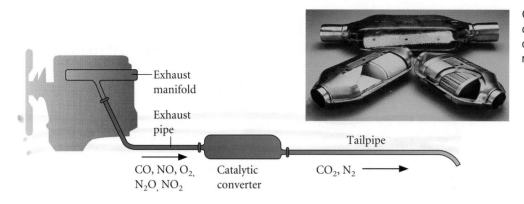

Catalytic converters catalyze the reaction of N_2O into N_2. The reaction is zero order.

In a **zero-order reaction**, the rate law does *not* depend on the concentration of any of the compounds in the reaction. The rate of the zero-order reaction is constant. No matter what the original concentration happens to be, the reaction always proceeds at the same rate.

$$\text{Rate of disappearance of A} = -\frac{\Delta[A]}{\Delta t}$$

$$\text{Rate} = k[A]^0 = k$$

The **integrated zero-order rate law**, determined by integrating the rate law over time, for a zero-order reaction is different from the integrated first-order rate law:

$$[A]_t = -kt + [A]_0$$

Substituting $0.5[A]_0$ for the concentration of A at time t, we can rearrange the equation to get the formula for the half-life of the zero-order reaction:

$$t_{1/2} = \frac{[A]_0}{2k}$$

The half-life of a zero-order reaction directly depends on the initial concentration of the reactant. Larger concentrations of the reactant will mean a larger half-life for the reaction. Note that the rate of a zero-order reaction is constant but that the half-life depends on the initial concentration of reactant. For example, consider a zero-order reaction where the rate constant $k = 2.5 \times 10^{-4}$ *M*/s. When $[A]_0 = 1.00$ *M*, the half-life of the reaction is 2000 s. If $[A]_0 = 0.25$ *M*, the half-life of the reaction is 500 s. The rate of the reaction (rate $= k$) is a constant, but the half-life changes as the concentration changes.

The **second-order rate law** can be more complicated, because there are two cases that fit the definition of a second-order reaction. In one of those cases, the reaction is second order in only one reactant:

$$\text{Rate} = k[A]^2$$

In the other case involving a second-order rate law, the reaction could be first order in two different species:

$$\text{Rate} = k[A][B]$$

In second-order reactions with only one reactant, the integrated rate law is determined using the method we have explored for the zero-order and first-order reactions. After integration and rearrangement, the **integrated second-order rate law** takes the form

$$\frac{1}{[A]_t} = kt + \frac{1}{[A]_0}$$

The half-life of this type of second-order reaction can be determined by assuming that the concentration of A at some time, t, is equal to one-half the initial concentration ($[A]_t = 0.5[A]_0$). Simplifying the equation gives

$$t_{1/2} = \frac{1}{k[A]_0}$$

The half-life for a second-order reaction (involving only one compound in the rate law) is inversely dependent on the initial concentration of the reactant. Smaller initial concentrations of the reactant will mean a longer half-life for the reaction.

If the second-order reaction contains two species in the rate law, the integrated rate law becomes much more complicated. In fact, the math gets so complicated that chemists typically *manipulate the experimental conditions to reduce the amount of calculation.* Consider the reaction of one of the components of smog with ozone:

$$NO(g) + O_3(g) \rightarrow NO_2(g) + O_2(g)$$

$$\text{Rate} = k[NO][O_3]$$

The reaction is first order in NO, first order in O_3, and second order overall.

To calculate the concentration of a reactant, determine the rate constant, or find the time required to reach a certain concentration with this type of rate law, we conduct the reaction with a relatively small concentration of one of the reactants and a very large concentration of the other. **What effect does this have on the rate law?** Because one of the concentrations is very large, any change in its concentration is negligible, and *we can assume that its concentration remains constant through the course of the reaction.* An analogy is having someone who is rich spend $1 in a day (decreasing to 50 cents after one half-life!) from a fortune of $1 billion. The change is hardly noticeable. The fortune is essentially constant. Someone who had only $10, however, would notice the effect of spending $1 immediately. Having the concentration of one component much larger than that of the other reduces the rate law to a much simpler form. For example, if we perform the reaction with 0.100 M NO and 0.001 M O_3, the concentrations of the species after the reaction is complete can be determined:

$$[O_3]_f = 0.001\ M - 0.001\ M = 0.000\ M$$
$$[NO]_f = 0.100\ M - 0.001\ M = 0.099\ M \approx 0.100\ M$$

The O_3 is consumed in the reaction, but the concentration of NO is only slightly affected. We can make the assumption that the concentration doesn't change. Because the final concentration of NO has essentially remained constant, it can be combined with the rate constant. And the rate equation for the reaction can be reduced to

$$\text{Rate} = k\,[NO][O_3] = k\,[NO]_0\,[O_3]$$

and, because $k' = k\,[NO]$,

$$\text{Rate} = k'\,[O_3]$$

where k' is the new rate constant. What is the order of our new rate law? Because of our choice of the initial concentrations, the kinetics for this reaction has taken on the form of a first-order rate law. Because of our modification, we say that this is a **pseudo-first-order rate** equation.

We can do this manipulation with any reaction. By increasing the concentration of a particular reactant to a very large value, any order of a rate law can be simplified to a pseudo-first order rate equation. This enables us to study reactions no matter what order they appear to be. We must remember, however, that any modification of the rate equation means that the new rate constant is not the same rate constant as in the original reaction.

HERE'S WHAT WE KNOW SO FAR

- ■ The integrated rate laws enable researchers to calculate one of four things about a reaction (rate, rate constant, initial concentration, or final concentration) if three of these are known.

- ■ The half-life of a reaction indicates the time required for the reaction to reach 50% completion.

- ■ Modifying a second-order reaction by using a large concentration of one of the reactants reduces the integrated rate law to a pseudo-first-order rate law.

15.4   Methods of Determining Rate Laws

Glyphosate herbicides are absorbed through the foliage of weeds, inhibiting a plant's ability to make new amino acids. Because these herbicides react relatively quickly with water ($t_{1/2} < 7$ days), the rate of their biological reaction in plants is important. Weed scientists study the rates of amino acid inhibition and environmental degradation in order to suggest modifications to improve glyphosate effectiveness (Figure 15.13). The greatest benefit of the glyphosate herbicides is attributable to their rapid degradation in the environment. The rapid degradation means this class of herbicide causes less harm to the environment than other herbicides. The rates of the degradation of these compounds have been measured by experiment, and the overall rate laws have been determined from those experiments.

We, too, can use the information from a chemical reaction to obtain the final rate law for a reaction. The first of two commonly used procedures that we will consider is the **method of initial rates**. In this approach, we measure and compare initial rates rather than comparing instantaneous rates later in the reaction. We use initial rates to determine the rate law because we can precisely measure and control the starting concentrations of the reactants and precisely identify the time for the reaction to reach a given point. In addition, limited side reactions (reactions that make products other than what we're interested in), rapid determination of the rate, and a well-defined time period make the comparison of multiple reactions experimentally straightforward.

We'll use as our example the reaction of nitrogen monoxide, NO(g), with oxygen to make nitrogen dioxide, NO$_2$(g), a component of smog. We can measure the initial rate of this reaction as we change the concentrations of both NO(g) and O$_2$(g). We conduct three separate reactions with different concentrations of reactants, measure the initial rate, and complete the table on the next page. Note that we have carefully chosen our starting concentrations to keep one reactant the same in two experiments while doubling the other reactant.

$$2NO(g) + O_2(g) \rightarrow 2NO_2(g)$$

We can determine the rate law for this reaction by assuming that the rate is based solely on the two reactants in the equation. We write

$$\text{Rate} = k[\text{NO}]^n[\text{O}_2]^m$$

where n and m are the orders of the two reactants. If we compare the rate of the third reaction to the rate of the second reaction, in which [NO] is constant and [O$_2$] changes, the equation simplifies dramatically. To do this, let's divide the rate law for the third experiment into the rate law for the second experiment.

$$\frac{\text{rate}_2}{\text{rate}_3} = \frac{k[\text{NO}]^n[\text{O}_2]^m}{k[\text{NO}]^n[\text{O}_2]^m}$$

Application

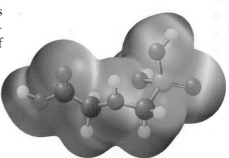

FIGURE 15.13

Roundup herbicide contains glyphosate. The general herbicide is sold for use on farms and in removing unwanted weeds around the yard.

Glyphosate

Automobile exhaust produces nitrogen compounds that react with oxygen.

Experiment	[NO] (M)	[O$_2$] (M)	Initial Rate (M/s)
1	0.0126	0.0125	1.41×10^{-2}
2	0.0252	0.0250	1.13×10^{-1}
3	0.0252	0.0125	5.64×10^{-2}

Next, we add the values from the table to the equation. Then we simplify the equation. Although the value of the rate constant, k, is not known, it should be the same in both reactions:

$$\frac{1.13 \times 10^{-1}\,M \cdot s^{-1}}{5.64 \times 10^{-2}\,M \cdot s^{-1}} = \frac{k(0.0252)^n(0.0250)^m}{k(0.0252)^n(0.0125)^m}$$

$$2 = \frac{(0.0250)^m}{(0.0125)^m}$$

$$2 = 2^m$$

$$m = 1$$

Why did we divide the second equation by the third? When one of the reactant concentrations is held constant ([NO], in this case) and the other concentration ([O$_2$]) is doubled, the effect on the rate is *due only to the change in [O$_2$]*. This effect is related to a power of 2 and reveals the order of the second reactant ($m = 1$). To continue, we divide the third rate law by the first because [O$_2$] is constant while [NO] changes, so *the effect on the rate is due only to the change in [NO]*. We substitute concentrations and solve:

$$\frac{5.64 \times 10^{-2}\,M \cdot s^{-1}}{1.41 \times 10^{-2}\,M \cdot s^{-1}} = \frac{k(0.0252)^n(0.0125)^1}{k(0.0126)^n(0.0125)^1}$$

$$4 = \frac{(0.0252)^n}{(0.0126)^n}$$

$$4 = 2^n$$

$$n = 2$$

We are nearly ready to write the rate law for the reaction because we know the order of the reactants. We are missing only the rate constant. We can solve for k by choosing one of the experiments we've completed and substituting the concentrations into the rate law. Solving for the rate constant, we obtain

$$\text{Rate} = k[NO]^2[O_2]$$

$$1.41 \times 10^{-2} = k(0.0126)^2(0.0125)$$

$$k = 7.11 \times 10^3\ M^{-2} \cdot s^{-1}$$

The method of initial rates requires that we can obtain and compare the initial rates of reactions. We need at least three reactions to solve for two unknown orders. And in every case, we've used *experimentally determined data* to calculate the rate law for the reaction.

Note that the units for the rate constant are different depending on the order of the rate law. Specifically, the units are $M^{-(\text{order}-1)} \cdot s^{-1}$.

EXERCISE 15.6 | **Initial Rates**

The reaction of Cl_2 with NO occurs at a very rapid pace. Use the data in the table below to determine the rate law for the reaction. Then calculate the rate constant.

$$2NO(g) + Cl_2(g) \rightarrow 2NOCl(g)$$

Experiment	[NO] (M)	[Cl_2] (M)	Initial Rate (M/min)
1	0.10 M	0.10 M	0.18
2	0.10 M	0.20 M	0.36
3	0.20 M	0.20 M	1.45

Solution

The rate law for the reaction can be determined by using the method of initial rates. The overall rate law, based on the reaction, is

$$\text{Rate} = k[NO]^m[Cl_2]^n$$

The order of the reaction with respect to NO is

$$\frac{\text{Rate 3}}{\text{Rate 2}} = \frac{1.45 \ M \cdot min^{-1}}{0.36 \ M \cdot min^{-1}} = \frac{k(0.20)^m(0.20)^n}{k(0.10)^m(0.20)^n}$$

$$\frac{1.45}{0.36} = \frac{(0.20)^m}{(0.10)^m}$$

$$4 = 2^m$$

$$m = 2$$

The order of the reaction with respect to Cl_2 is

$$\frac{\text{Rate 2}}{\text{Rate 1}} = \frac{0.36 \ M \cdot min^{-1}}{0.18 \ M \cdot min^{-1}} = \frac{k(0.10)^m(0.20)^n}{k(0.10)^m(0.10)^n}$$

$$\frac{0.36}{0.18} = \frac{(0.20)^n}{(0.10)^n}$$

$$2 = 2^n$$

$$n = 1$$

The overall rate law and the value for the rate constant can then be calculated. Note that the rate is still expressed in concentration per unit time. Also note that while the orders in this rate law equal the coefficients in the equation for this example, this is not always true. We will deal with this in Section 15.6.

$$\text{Rate} = k[NO]^2[Cl_2]^1$$

$$k = \frac{0.18}{(0.10)^2(0.10)} = 1.8 \times 10^2 \ M^{-2} \cdot min^{-1}$$

PRACTICE 15.6

Use the initial rates for the reaction of carbon monoxide (CO) with hemoglobin (Hb) to determine the rate law and the rate constant. What is the overall order of the reaction?

Experiment	[Hb] (M)	[CO] (M)	Initial Rate (M/s)
1	$2.21 \times 10^{-6} \ M$	$1.00 \times 10^{-6} \ M$	0.619×10^{-6}
2	$4.42 \times 10^{-6} \ M$	$1.00 \times 10^{-6} \ M$	1.24×10^{-6}
3	$4.42 \times 10^{-6} \ M$	$3.00 \times 10^{-6} \ M$	3.71×10^{-6}

See Problems 57–60, 66, and 67. ■

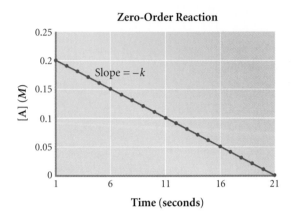

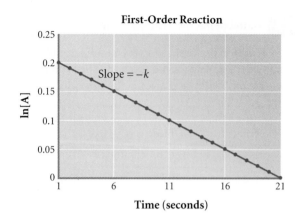

FIGURE 15.14

A linear relationship exists for the data if time is plotted versus [A] for zero-order reactions, versus ln[A] for first-order reactions, and versus 1/[A] for second-order reactions. Note that the slope of the line is equal to the negative of the rate constant for zero-order and first-order plots. The slope of the second-order plot is equal to the rate constant.

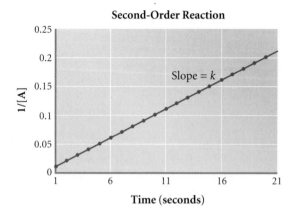

The second method for determining the rate law of a reaction has us examine only one reaction instead of a series of reactions. In this **method of graphical analysis** (also known as the method of integrated rate laws), we plot how the concentration of a reactant changes with time. Although this method does require us to measure the rate of the reaction as it proceeds over a long time period, little mathematical manipulation of the data is needed to determine the rate law. Various versions of the plot can be quickly constructed in order to establish a linear relationship between time and a measure of concentration that confirms one of our common rate laws. Figure 15.14 displays plots of zero-order, first-order, and second-order reactions. Each is a linear relationship that is derived from the integrated rate law. If our data are linear when plotted in one of these ways, it suggests that the data fit that model. Computer-based data acquisition can also help us to do statistical analyses to determine the model that best fits the data.

Here are the possible outcomes that we will consider:

- The zero-order reaction produces a linear plot when the concentration of reactant is plotted against time. The slope of the line is equal to $-k$.

- The first-order reaction produces a linear plot when the natural logarithm (ln) of the concentration of reactant is plotted against time. The slope in this case is also equal to the negative of the rate constant, $-k$.

- The second-order reaction produces a linear relationship when the reciprocal concentration is plotted against time. The slope, which is equal to the rate constant, is positive in this case.

If the concentration of a reactant is followed as a function of time, this is the best method to use in determining the rate law. By graphing the data in three different ways, we can determine the overall order of the reaction (zero order, first order, or second order).

EXERCISE 15.7 **Determining the Reaction Order**

The decomposition of atrazine in the presence of titanium dioxide has been studied and the rate of the reaction measured. Plot the data shown in the table, and determine whether the reaction follows zero-order, first-order, or second-order kinetics.

Time (h)	[Atrazine] (M)
0	4.65×10^{-5}
3	2.98×10^{-5}
8	1.49×10^{-5}
15	6.98×10^{-6}
22	3.67×10^{-6}

First Thoughts

We must plot the data for each of the three models we have discussed: zero order, first order, and second order. If might be useful to add two columns to your table for ln[atrazine] and 1/[atrazine], respectively.

Solution

Using a graphical analysis software package (or three sheets of graph paper), we plot the data on three different graphs. In the first, the concentration is plotted versus time, the second relates the ln[atrazine] versus time, and the third illustrates 1/[atrazine] versus time. Examination of the results leads us to the conclusion that the middle plot—the one that relates first-order kinetics—is the appropriate graph. We choose this one because the data points seem to lie closest to the line of best fit, without being systematically curved. The reaction must be first order overall and first order in atrazine (the reactant).

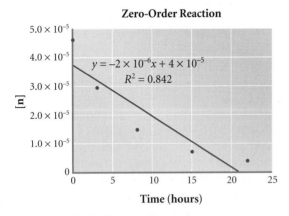

Zero-Order Reaction

$y = -2 \times 10^{-6}x + 4 \times 10^{-5}$
$R^2 = 0.842$

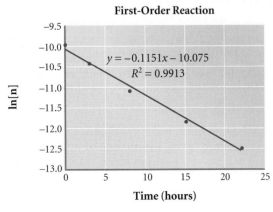

First-Order Reaction

$y = -0.1151x - 10.075$
$R^2 = 0.9913$

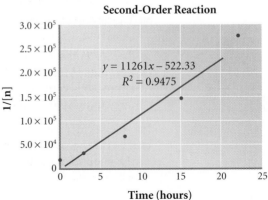

Second-Order Reaction

$y = 11261x - 522.33$
$R^2 = 0.9475$

Further Insights

There are a number of mathematical tools we can use to compute the best fit of the data to one of our reaction orders. One of these tools is the correlation coefficient, r, which tells how well any two measures are mathematically related to each other. A perfect directly linear relationship would yield a correlation coefficient, r, of 1. As infants grow, their height and weight give correlation coefficients tending toward 1. A perfect inverse relationship gives r values of -1. As we increase in age past about 45 years old, we inevitably run more slowly. Age and running speed in older runners are inversely related and give an r value that is closer to -1. If there is no relationship between variables, such as between human hair color and the number of strawberries people eat in July, we get an r value of 0. If a first-order model were to fit our data, it would have the highest correlation coefficient of the three possible models that we have introduced.

PRACTICE 15.7

Plot the data for the following reaction as was done in Exercise 15.7. Determine the overall order of this reaction. You may wish to use a graphing program to determine which graph gives the straightest line.

$$2NO_2(g) \rightarrow 2NO(g) + O_2(g)$$

Time (s)	[NO$_2$] (M)
0	0.0100
50	0.0079
100	0.0065
150	0.0055
200	0.0048
300	0.0038
400	0.0031

See Problems 53, 54, 61, 62, 65, and 68.

15.5 Looking Back at Rate Laws

A summary of the data that we have discussed thus far is appropriate. In short, here's what we know so far:

■ Reaction rates determine the speed at which a reaction progresses but do not reveal anything about the extent to which they produce a product.

■ We can measure the average rate if we know the initial and final concentrations over a particular time period.

■ The instantaneous rate is the rate at a given point in the reaction. It can be determined by measuring the concentrations at points when the time difference approaches zero, or it can be measured by determining the slope of a line tangent to a plot of the rate versus time.

■ The initial rate is the instantaneous rate as the reaction starts.

■ The rate law is experimentally determined using the method of initial rates or the method of graphical analysis.

TABLE 15.3 | **Rate Laws**

The value of the rate is reported in the units of concentration per unit time. The value of the rate constant is different for each of the three orders (zero order $= M/s$; first order $= 1/s$; and second order $= 1/M \cdot s$).

Order	Rate Law	Integrated Rate Law	Half-life	Linear Plot
Zero	Rate $= k$	$[A]_t = -kt + [A]_0$	$t_{1/2} = \dfrac{[A]_0}{2k}$	$[A]$ versus t slope $= -k$
First	Rate $= k[A]$	$\ln\left(\dfrac{[A]_t}{[A]_0}\right) = -kt$	$t_{1/2} = \dfrac{0.693}{k}$	$\ln[A]$ versus t slope $= -k$
Second	Rate $= k[A]^2$	$\dfrac{1}{[A]_t} = kt + \dfrac{1}{[A]_0}$	$t_{1/2} = \dfrac{1}{k[A]_0}$	$\dfrac{1}{[A]}$ versus t slope $= +k$

- The half-life of a reaction is the time required for the concentration of a reaction to reach 50% of the initial value.
- Complex reaction orders can often be reduced to pseudo-first-order reactions by keeping the concentration of one of the reactants relatively large.

Specific information for the three rate orders that we have discussed is included in Table 15.3. There are many more overall orders for reactions than those listed here.

15.6 Reaction Mechanisms

At this point, we need to do some detective work. In Exercise 15.2 we determined the rate of metabolism of methoxychlor, an organochlorine insecticide, using actual values for the concentrations. However, upon deeper investigation, chemists have found that the reaction proceeds in two sequential steps. In the first step, the methoxychlor undergoes reaction with water and cytochrome P450 (an enzyme in the liver) to make mono-hydroxymethoxychlor. In a second step, the mono-hydroxymethoxychlor reacts with another molecule of water and cytochrome P450 and is converted into the product bis-hydroxymethoxychlor.

Application

CHEMICAL
ENCOUNTERS:
Metabolism of
Methoxychlor

Step 1

H$_2$O + Methoxychlor $\xrightarrow{\text{Cytochrome P450}}$ (mono-hydroxymethoxychlor) + CH$_3$OH

Step 2

H$_2$O + (mono-hydroxymethoxychlor) $\xrightarrow{\text{Cytochrome P450}}$ *bis*-Hydroxymethoxychlor + CH$_3$OH

Why is it useful to know the individual steps that make up the overall reaction? Chemists often are interested in more detailed descriptions of chemical reactions, including how the reactions occur at the molecular level. We know from our previous discussions that chemical equations contain a wealth of information about a reaction. We can determine the spontaneity of the process, the enthalpy of the process, and the stoichiometry of the reactants by examining the chemical equation. However, the overall chemical equation doesn't show how the reactants collide to become products. To address this concern, investigators study a single reaction to determine exactly how each molecule moves during the course of the process. *The knowledge of exactly how a reaction proceeds is useful in predicting new reactions, determining the rates of those reactions, discovering new applications of chemistry, and learning how substances interact with humans and our environment.* Their study is part of the field of mechanistic chemistry.

A mechanism for a reaction is the set of steps that compounds take as they proceed from reactant to product. The mechanism of a reaction accounts for the *experimentally determined rate of the reaction* and is consistent with *the overall stoichiometry of the reaction.* In some cases, a mechanism is only one step. In others, there are a multitude of steps. However, we can't tell this by looking at the overall chemical equation.

Each of the single steps in a chemical reaction is called an elementary step. For example, as shown in Figure 15.15, the overall process of turning off the lights in a room is made up of two elementary steps: (1) walking to the light switch and (2) flipping the light switch. One of these steps, walking to the light switch, is slower. The other, flipping the switch, is so fast that its contribution to the time required to complete the overall process is negligible. Any calculations of the time required to turn off the lights, then, can be reduced to the time it takes to walk to the light switch. In other words, the time it takes to turn off the lights in the room is nearly equal to the length of time it takes to walk to the light switch. This slow step is known as the rate-determining step.

Within each elementary step, reactants come together and undergo successful collisions to make products. The number of molecules that collide in this process defines the molecularity of the step (Figure 15.16). A unimolecular reaction involves one molecule as the only reactant. When two molecules collide, the reaction is said to be a bimolecular reaction. Reactions that involve the collision of three molecules simultaneously (which are called termolecular reactions, or trimolecular reactions) are also known, but they are rare because they require that three molecules collide at the same time and in the proper orientation. In such cases, the decrease in the entropy associated with three molecules coming together at one time is often prohibitive (see Chapter 14). In general, an elementary step has only a single bond breakage or formation.

FIGURE 15.15

The elementary steps completed in turning off the lights.

Step 1: Walk to light
Slow

Step 2: Turn off light
Fast

FIGURE 15.16

Molecularity of reactions. The number of molecules that must collide at one time to produce the reaction determines the molecularity.

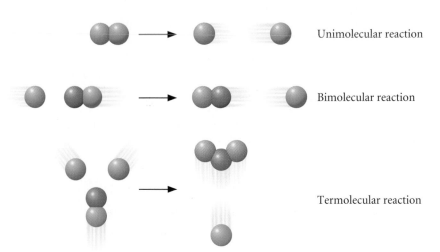

Unimolecular reaction

Bimolecular reaction

Termolecular reaction

If we know the elementary steps in a reaction, we can obtain a wealth of information about the rate of the reaction. Most important, *rate laws can be written directly from elementary steps*. Specifically, the rate orders for the reactants in an elementary step are given by the stoichiometric coefficients of the reactants in that step. Moreover, the rates of the elementary steps in a mechanism need not be the same—indeed, in most cases they are not. A mechanism with two elementary steps typically has a fast step and a slow step. The slow step in a mechanism is the one that will determine the rate of the overall reaction.

The reaction of NO_2 and F_2 gas is a useful case study:

$$2NO_2(g) + F_2(g) \rightarrow 2NO_2F(g)$$

After careful experimentation, a mechanism involving two elementary steps has been suggested for the reaction. This first step was determined to be slow; the second was determined to be relatively fast:

$$NO_2(g) + F_2(g) \rightarrow NO_2F(g) + F(g) \quad \text{(slow)}$$
$$\underline{F(g) + NO_2(g) \rightarrow NO_2F(g) \qquad\qquad \text{(fast)}}$$
$$2NO_2(g) + F_2(g) \rightarrow 2NO_2F(g)$$

Note that the sum of the elementary steps gives the balanced equation. From these steps, we can determine the rate law for the overall reaction in a way that is similar to our discussion of the length of time required to turn off the lights. The slow elementary step will determine the rate of the reaction, so we can use this rate-determining step to write the rate law. Judging on the basis of the stoichiometric coefficients of the reactants in the slow step, the overall reaction is first order in NO_2, first order in F_2, and second order overall.

$$\text{Rate} = k[NO_2][F_2]$$

Not all mechanisms are so easy to work with. For instance, the reaction of NO with O_2 to make NO_2 is much more complicated than our first glance suggests. From our previous discussion in Section 15.4, we know the overall equation for the reaction:

$$2NO(g) + O_2(g) \rightarrow 2NO_2(g)$$

We saw that the experimentally determined rate equation for the reaction is

$$\text{Rate} = k[NO]^2[O_2]$$

This implies that the reaction is a termolecular process, which is unlikely because it would require three molecules to collide simultaneously. The mechanism of this reaction is known, and it has the elementary steps shown below.

$$2NO(g) \underset{k_{-1}}{\overset{k_1}{\rightleftharpoons}} N_2O_2(g) \quad \text{(fast)}$$
$$N_2O_2(g) + O_2(g) \overset{k_2}{\longrightarrow} 2NO_2(g) \quad \text{(slow)}$$

What is the meaning of the double arrows in the fast equation? These arrows indicate that the reaction can proceed in both the forward direction and the reverse direction at the same time. Moreover, each of these directions has a rate constant associated with it (k_1 and k_{-1}). The slow step in our mechanism is the reaction of $N_2O_2(g)$ with oxygen, and we could write the rate equation on the basis of this information. Note that we've specified the rate constants for both reactions:

$$\text{Rate} = k_1[NO]^2 \qquad \text{for the fast step } (k_1 \gg k_2)$$
$$\text{Rate} = k_2[N_2O_2][O_2] \qquad \text{for the slow step } (k_2 \ll k_1)$$

It follows that the rate law for the overall reaction should be

$$\text{Rate} = k_2[N_2O_2][O_2] \qquad \text{for the overall reaction}$$

However, this doesn't agree with the experimentally determined rate law that we noted above:

$$\text{Rate} = k[\text{NO}]^2[\text{O}_2]$$

This difference arises because $\text{N}_2\text{O}_2(g)$ is an intermediate in the reaction. ~~An intermediate is a compound that is formed and consumed during the course of a reaction.~~ If we examine the overall reaction, we don't see the intermediate N_2O_2 as one of the reactants. Measuring the concentration of this species, then, could be difficult. We need to rewrite the rate equation so that the rate reflects only the compounds in the overall reaction. To deal with this, *we will assume that the fast reaction reaches equilibrium,* an assumption that greatly simplifies our determination of the overall rate law for the reaction. What does this assumption mean? Within a reaction that is at equilibrium, the rate of the forward reaction is equal to the rate of the reverse reaction.

$$2\text{NO}(g) \underset{k_{-1}}{\overset{k_1}{\rightleftharpoons}} \text{N}_2\text{O}_2(g) \qquad \text{(fast)}$$

$$k_1[\text{NO}]^2 = k_{-1}[\text{N}_2\text{O}_2]$$

Then we can rearrange our equation to solve for $[\text{N}_2\text{O}_2]$:

$$[\text{N}_2\text{O}_2] = \frac{k_1[\text{NO}]^2}{k_{-1}} = k'[\text{NO}]^2$$

where the new rate constant k' is equal to $\dfrac{k_1}{k_{-1}}$.*

We can now substitute for the concentration of the intermediate, $[\text{N}_2\text{O}_2]$, in our original rate equation and simplify:

$$\text{Rate} = k_2[\text{N}_2\text{O}_2][\text{O}_2]$$

$$[\text{N}_2\text{O}_2] = k'[\text{NO}]^2$$

$$\text{Rate} = k_2 k'[\text{NO}]^2[\text{O}_2] = k''[\text{NO}]^2[\text{O}_2]$$

where the new rate constant k'' is equal to $k_2 k'$.

This agrees with our experimentally determined rate equation. The mathematics used to convert our rate law containing the intermediate into the experimentally observed rate law are based on the assumption that the fast reaction has reached equilibrium. This assumption requires that the rate constant for the reverse of the fast reaction be much larger than the rate constant for the slow step.

EXERCISE 15.8 **Rate Laws**

Write the overall reaction, identify any intermediates, and write the rate law for the following proposed mechanism for the decomposition of $\text{IBr}(g)$ to $\text{I}_2(g)$ and $\text{Br}_2(g)$.

$$\text{IBr}(g) \rightarrow \text{I}(g) + \text{Br}(g) \qquad \text{(slow)}$$

$$\text{IBr}(g) + \text{Br}(g) \rightarrow \text{I}(g) + \text{Br}_2(g) \qquad \text{(fast)}$$

$$\text{I}(g) + \text{I}(g) \rightarrow \text{I}_2(g) \qquad \text{(fast)}$$

---

* *Note:* Alternatively, we could rearrange this equation to place the rate constants on one side and the concentrations of compounds on the other side:

$$\frac{k_1}{k_{-1}} = \frac{[\text{N}_2\text{O}_2]}{[\text{NO}]^2}$$

This gives rise to something that looks remarkably similar to Q, the reaction quotient from Chapter 14. We'll explore this in much greater detail in Chapter 16.

Solution

The overall reaction is the sum of the elementary steps in the mechanism.

$$2IBr(g) \rightarrow I_2(g) + Br_2(g)$$

The intermediates are produced and consumed in the reaction. They are $I(g)$ and $Br(g)$. Because the first step in the mechanism is the slow step, it is rate determining. Therefore, the rate law for the reaction can be written directly from this step:

$$rate = k\,[IBr]$$

It is first order in $IBr(g)$ and first order overall.

PRACTICE 15.8

Write the overall reaction, identify any intermediates, and write the rate law for the following proposed mechanism for the production of nitrogen dioxide (NO_2).

$$NO(g) + O_2(g) \rightleftharpoons NO_3(g) \quad \text{(fast)}$$

$$NO_3(g) + NO(g) \rightarrow 2NO_2(g) \quad \text{(slow)}$$

See Problems 85 and 86.

Transition State Theory

The destruction of ozone by atomic oxygen is one of the ways in which stratospheric ozone can be depleted:

$$O_3(g) + O(g) \rightarrow 2O_2(g)$$

By examining this reaction in the laboratory, we can determine the change in enthalpy ($\Delta H = -392$ kJ/mol) and measure the rate of the reaction. However, it is often helpful to examine a reaction by consulting a plot of the energies for the reactants, products, and any intermediates. If we make a graph of the energies as the reactants proceed along a **reaction coordinate** (the pathway describing the changes in each molecule in the reaction, even though they are happening at different times) to become product, we obtain a **reaction profile** like that shown in Figure 15.17. On the basis of our earlier discussion of collision theory, we know that the reactants must have enough energy to overcome a barrier known as the activation energy (E_a)—assuming that the reactants collide in the proper orientation. For the reaction of atomic oxygen and ozone, the barrier is rather small ($E_{a(forward)} = 19$ kJ/mol) compared to the reverse reaction. The reaction profile illustrates this.

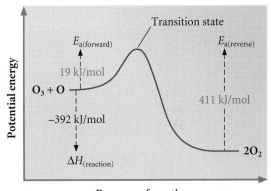

FIGURE 15.17

Reaction profile.

The reaction profile is used to explore **transition state theory** and how it applies to a reaction. This theory describes how the bonds in the reacting molecules reorganize to represent the bonds in the products. At some point on the reaction coordinate the collision occurs, and the atoms in the reactants occupy a **transition state**. The collection of atoms at the transition state, called the **activated complex**, is very energetic at this point in the reaction—more so than the reactants, products, or intermediates. The activated complex is not a separate isolable compound. Rather, *it is a snapshot of the reaction at the point in time when the molecules have collided.* From the activated complex, the reaction could proceed to products, or the complex could dissociate back into the reactants.

The reaction profile shows the activation energy for the forward reaction, the activation energy for the backward reaction, and the overall change in the energy of the reaction (ΔE) in a graphical way. This change in energy (ΔE) is equal to ΔH

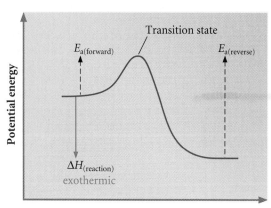

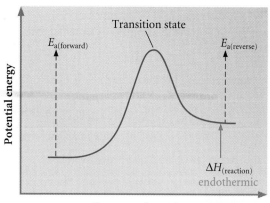

FIGURE 15.18

Exothermic reaction profile. The reactants are more energetic than the products in the endothermic reaction. $E_{a(reverse)}$ is larger than $E_{a(forward)}$.

FIGURE 15.19

Endothermic reaction profile. The products are more energetic than the reactants in the endothermic reaction. $E_{a(forward)}$ is larger than $E_{a(reverse)}$.

for the reaction at constant pressure and volume. Even for cases where ΔE and ΔH are not equal (unequal volumes or pressures), the difference is usually very small. By looking at the reaction profile, we can tell whether a reaction is exothermic (Figure 15.18) or endothermic (Figure 15.19).

$$\Delta H_{reaction} \cong \Delta E = E_{a(forward)} - E_{a(reverse)}$$

To what is the activation energy related? In 1888, Svante Arrhenius (1859–1927), a Swedish chemist, studied how temperature affected the rate of a reaction. What came out of this work is a relationship between the activation energy and the rate of a reaction. His mathematical equation is

$$k = Ae^{-E_a/RT}$$

where k is the rate constant, A is the **frequency factor** that relates how many successfully oriented collisions occur in a particular reaction, E_a is the activation energy, T is the temperature in kelvins, and R is the universal gas constant (8.314 J/mol·K). This equation says that the rate constant of a reaction is related to the size of E_a. As E_a gets larger, the rate constant gets smaller and the rate of the reaction decreases.

This equation can be used to determine the rate of a reaction on the basis of the temperature of the reaction and the amount of energy the reactants require to make the activated complex. To use it, however, we must know the activation energy (E_a) *and* the frequency factor (A) for the reaction. Fortunately, by performing the reaction at two different temperatures, we can utilize this equation to calculate the activation energy without knowing the frequency factor. Alternatively, if we know the activation energy and the rate of reaction at a particular temperature, we can determine the rate of reaction at any other temperature. The equation that relates this calculation can be derived by taking the natural logarithm of the Arrhenius equation above, at two temperatures:

$$\ln\left(\frac{k_2}{k_1}\right) = \frac{E_a}{R}\left(\frac{1}{T_1} - \frac{1}{T_2}\right)$$

where k_1 and k_2 are the rate constants for the reaction obtained at two different temperatures, T_1 and T_2.

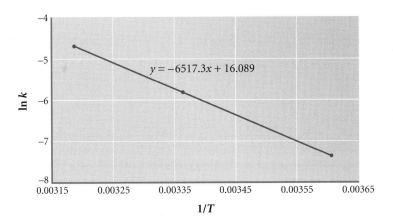

FIGURE 15.20

A plot of ln k versus $1/T$ gives a straight line whose slope is $-E_a/R$. Each data point on this plot corresponds to the measurement of the temperature and rate constant in separate reactions. The slope of the line of best fit (-6517.3) is equal to $-E_a/R$. Therefore, $E_a = 54.2$ kJ/mol for this reaction. If the axes went to zero, the intercept (16.089) corresponding to ln A would be found. The frequency factor is 9,710,000.

This equation provides a quick method to determine the energy of activation for a reaction, but the resulting answer can contain significant error, because its value is based on only two reactions. Alternatively, we can determine the value of E_a graphically by using a series of rate constants calculated at different temperatures. To see how this is done, let's examine the original equation produced by Arrhenius:

$$k = Ae^{-E_a/RT}$$

If we take the natural log of both sides of the equation, we get

$$\ln k = \ln A - \frac{E_a}{RT}$$

Rearranging this equation as shown enables us to determine the activation energy by plotting the rate constant of a reaction at several temperatures.

$$\ln k = -\frac{E_a}{R}\left(\frac{1}{T}\right) + \ln A$$
$$y \quad = \quad mx \quad + \quad b$$

If we construct an "Arrhenius plot" of ln k versus $1/T$ for a series of reactions, we obtain a straight line whose slope is equal to $-E_a/R$ and whose intercept is ln A, as shown in Figure 15.20. This method not only enables us to determine the energy of activation quite accurately but also provides a convenient way to determine the frequency factor A.

EXERCISE 15.9   **Energy Barrier**

The reaction of NO, a component in smog, with ozone has been extensively studied. Data for the temperature dependence are tabulated below. What is the activation energy for this reaction?

$$NO(g) + O_3(g) \rightarrow NO_2(g) + O_2(g)$$

Temperature (K)	k (1/M·s)
195	1.08×10^9
298	12.0×10^9

Solution

The activation energy can be calculated by substituting the values from the table into the equation:

$$\ln\left(\frac{k_2}{k_1}\right) = \frac{E_a}{R}\left(\frac{1}{T_1} - \frac{1}{T_2}\right)$$

$$\ln\left(\frac{12.0 \times 10^9}{1.08 \times 10^9}\right) = \frac{E_a}{8.314 \text{ J·mol}^{-1}\text{·K}^{-1}}\left(\frac{1}{195 \text{ K}} - \frac{1}{298 \text{ K}}\right)$$

$$2.408 = \frac{E_a}{8.314 \text{ J·mol}^{-1}\text{·K}^{-1}}\left(1.773 \times 10^{-3} \text{ K}^{-1}\right)$$

$$20.02 \text{ J·mol}^{-1} = E_a\left(1.773 \times 10^{-3} \text{ K}\right)$$

$$E_a = 11292 \text{ J·mol}^{-1} = 11.3 \text{ kJ·mol}^{-1}$$

PRACTICE 15.9

More data on the reaction of NO and O_3 are shown in the table below. Calculate E_a for each pair of reactions. Are the values the same? Explain.

Temperature (K)	k (1/M·s)
230	2.95×10^9
260	5.42×10^9
369	35.5×10^9

See Problems 83, 84, 87, 88, and 101.

15.7 Applications of Catalysts

Environmental chemists have comprehensively explored the rate of decomposition of atrazine in aqueous solutions. Because the rate in water is so slow ($t_{1/2} = 400$ days), they've spent time considering how the decomposition could be accelerated to clean up the environment more quickly. The exercise in the previous section showed that the rate of a reaction increases with an increase in temperature. That's one way to speed up a reaction. However, raising the temperature of groundwater, rivers, and lakes is not a feasible way to increase the rate of decomposition of herbicides and pesticides. Researchers at the University of Wisconsin have found a better way to enhance the rate of the decomposition. They have discovered that filtering atrazine-contaminated water through a container full of titanium(IV) oxide in the presence of ultraviolet light greatly increases the rate of decomposition (to $t_{1/2} = 15$ min). What does the titanium(IV) oxide do?

The titanium(IV) oxide is used as a **catalyst** in the decomposition of atrazine. A catalyst is a compound that, when added to a reaction mixture, changes the mechanism of the reaction to a new pathway with a lower activation energy. Rather than lowering the activation energy of the existing mechanism, it creates a new set of elementary steps whose rate-determining step has a lower energy of activation than the reaction would have without the catalyst. Because E_a is lower, the new mechanism is faster, so we often say that a catalyst increases the rate of the reaction. Another useful aspect of catalysts is that they can be recovered from the reaction; catalysts are not consumed in a reaction. Because of this, they don't appear in the net chemical equation. However, because they are involved in the reaction, they do appear in the mechanism. To show that a particular reaction involves a catalyst, we typically place it over or under the arrow in the overall equation. There are two types of catalysts, homogeneous catalysts and heterogeneous catalysts. The type of catalyst, as well as the reaction profile that results, depends on how the catalyst is mixed with the reaction.

A homogeneous catalyst is part of a reaction that is *catalyzed in a homogeneous mixture* (that is, the catalyst is intimately mixed with the reactants). For example, the destruction of ozone by chlorine radicals (a homogeneous catalyst) is illustrated by the net reaction of ozone with oxygen atoms:

$$O_3 + O \xrightarrow{\text{Cl}} 2O_2$$

The mechanism of this reaction consists of two elementary steps:

Step 1: The ozone molecule reacts with elemental chlorine (the catalyst) to make a molecule of ClO and a molecule of oxygen.

Step 2: The ClO reacts with an oxygen atom (the other reactant in the net equation) to make another molecule of oxygen and regenerate elemental chlorine.

Application

CHEMICAL ENCOUNTERS:
Destruction of Ozone

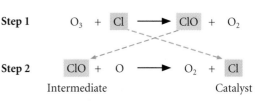

The chlorine atom appears first as a reactant and later as a product; chlorine begins and escapes the reaction without being changed and therefore is not consumed. This is exactly what catalysts do. Is ClO a catalyst too? No. It is formed in the course of the reaction and then consumed before products are made. The ClO never escapes the reaction. As we saw earlier, this is exactly what happens to an intermediate.

The presence of chlorine atoms causes a tremendous increase in the rate of the decomposition of ozone. How does a catalyst cause a reaction's rate to increase? Consider the reaction profile, shown in Figure 15.21, for the first-order decomposition of hydrogen peroxide by a homogeneous catalyst. In the noncatalyzed reaction, the reaction follows a unimolecular mechanism with a clearly defined high-energy barrier (the activation energy) separating the reactants from the products. If a catalyst such as iodide is added to this reaction, the mechanism of the reaction changes. The iodide is the catalyst, and it is shown over the reaction arrow to identify it as such. **What is the role of OI⁻ in the reaction?** The reaction makes an intermediate, which is more stable than the activated complex. The solid line in the reaction profile in Figure 15.21 illustrates the new reaction.

What is the outcome of adding a catalyst? Remember that our catalyst has produced a new mechanism for the reaction. If we plot the reaction profile for this new mechanism, we can see that the activation energy is lower. This means that more molecules will have the

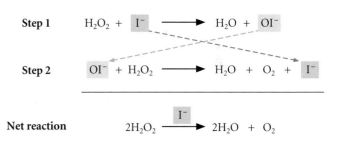

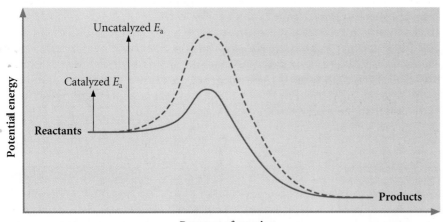

FIGURE 15.21

Decomposition of H_2O_2 with and without a homogeneous catalyst. The dotted line represents the reaction profile without the catalyst; the solid line indicates the effect of a homogeneous catalyst.

FIGURE 15.22

Heterogeneous catalysis of NO.

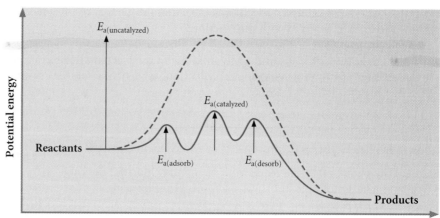

All of the different-colored heterogeneous catalysts in this collection work in a similar manner. The reactants must adsorb to the surface of the catalyst before the reaction can be catalyzed. After reaction, the products desorb from the catalyst. The reaction shown here illustrates the catalytic hydrogenation of ethylene to make ethane.

requisite energy to become activated complexes in the mechanism. Although the overall reaction enthalpy (ΔH) hasn't changed, the activation energy has been reduced dramatically. A reduction in the activation energy causes the rate of the reaction to increase.

In systems with a **heterogeneous catalyst**, the catalyst and the reactants are in *different* physical states. The catalyst is typically a metal in solid form, whereas the reactants are typically in gaseous, aqueous, or liquid form. The TiO_2 decomposition of atrazine is an example of this type of catalysis. The catalytic converter (usually made up of platinum, palladium, and/or rhodium metal) in your automobile is another. One of the reactions in the catalytic converter cuts down on smog-forming NO by reducing it to N_2. The general unbalanced reaction is

$$NO(g) \rightarrow N_2(g)$$

The heterogeneous catalyst works in a three-step process. In the first step shown in Figure 15.22, the reactant molecules **adsorb** to the catalyst—that is, they sticks to the catalyst's surface. Note that the word *adsorb* is different than the word **absorb**, which means being taken up or mixed into a substance. A small activation energy barrier must be crossed to achieve the surface binding of the reactant. Often, there is only a very small barrier for binding of a reactant to the surface of a catalyst. Then the reactants migrate around on the surface until they collide to make the product. A larger, yet still low, activation energy barrier exists for this step. In the final step, the products are **desorbed**, or released from the surface of the catalyst (the reverse of being adsorbed). The resulting reaction profile diagram has a characteristic shape.

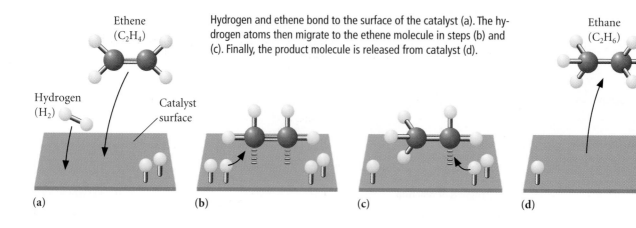

Hydrogen and ethene bond to the surface of the catalyst (a). The hydrogen atoms then migrate to the ethene molecule in steps (b) and (c). Finally, the product molecule is released from catalyst (d).

(a)   (b)   (c)   (d)

NanoWorld / MacroWorld

Big effects of the very small: Enzymes—nature's catalysts

The modern confectionery industry operates a booming business, helping to satisfy that sweet tooth in most of us. Fanciful desserts require sucrose as a sweetener. Fortunately, the American farmer can meet the large demand for sweeteners. For instance, sugar beet production in Colorado, Montana, Nebraska, and Wyoming yields 4.5 to 6 million tons of sucrose per year. Sugar cane production, primarily in Hawaii, Louisiana, and Florida, adds another 6 million tons to the total. But even more sugar is needed. One of the ways to meet the public's demand for sweeteners involves corn starch and a biological molecule known as D-glucose isomerase, shown in Figure 15.23. The product of these molecules is sweeter than sucrose alone. It is known as high-fructose corn syrup, and its use has surpassed that of sucrose in the confectionery industry.

Like other enzymes, D-glucose isomerase acts as a catalyst that speeds up a reaction. The enzymes work by binding selectively to a particular molecule, forcing it into just the right shape, and then assisting in the

FIGURE 15.23

High-fructose corn syrup is made from corn starch using an enzyme. D-Glucose isomerase catalyzes the reaction that converts glucose into fructose. The reaction proceeds much more rapidly with the enzyme than without it. The enzyme is shown here as a series of ribbons that represent the atoms that make up the strands of protein polymers. The strands loop and wind their way together to make a pocket that can catalyze the reaction of glucose to make fructose.

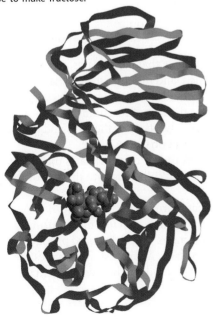

reaction that makes the product. They increase the value of A (the frequency factor from the Arrhenius equation) and decrease the energy of activation (E_a) at the same time. This activity arises because the backbone of the amino acid polymer weaves the enzyme into a structure similar to a catcher's mitt. Along the inside of the catcher's mitt (the active site of the enzyme) lie portions of the enzyme that are polar and portions that are nonpolar. The arrangements of the polar and nonpolar groups provide a template that exactly matches that of the molecule they bind (the reactant or substrate). When the substrate binds, the enzyme bends it into a conformation similar to that of the product of the reaction. Then, when the conformation is just right, the reaction takes place. After releasing the product, the enzyme returns to its original shape, ready to accept another substrate (Figure 15.24). The net result is an increase in the reaction rate without an increase in temperature, which is particularly useful in the food industry.

For example, lactase (an enzyme that converts lactose into glucose and galactose) is used in the dairy industry to make digestible milk products. Because many of these products spoil at temperatures warmer than those found in a refrigerator, the use of enzymes to speed the reaction without a temperature increase is quite helpful. After the lactase has been added to milk, lactose-intolerant people can drink all of the milk they want. And they owe their settled stomach to one of nature's catalysts.

FIGURE 15.24

Diagram of an enzyme-catalyzed reaction. The substrate binds to the active site on an enzyme, where the reaction is catalyzed.

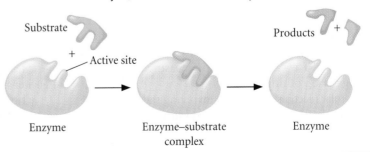

Substrate

Products

+ Active site

Enzyme

Enzyme–substrate complex

Enzyme

The principles of chemical kinetics are important not only to chemists but to anyone concerned with the rate of a process. The rate of decay at the landfill, the rate of ozone depletion, and the persistence of pesticides and herbicides in the environment can easily be determined by examining the rate laws associated with these processes. Our work in the lab can provide the rate laws for these reactions. And, after determining the thermodynamics of a reaction (Chapter 14), we can determine not only whether a reaction will take place but also how long it will take to complete.

The Bottom Line

- Reaction rates determine the speed at which a reaction progresses but do not reveal anything about the extent to which they produce a product. (Section 15.1)

- The average rate can be measured if you know the initial and final concentrations over a particular time period. (Section 15.1)

- The instantaneous rate is the rate at a given point in the reaction. It can be determined by measuring the concentrations at points when the time difference approaches zero, or it can be measured by determining the slope of a line tangent to a plot of the rate versus time. (Section 15.1)

- The initial rate of a reaction is the instantaneous rate as the reaction starts. (Section 15.1)

- The half-life of a reaction is the time required for the concentration of a reaction to reach 50% of the initial value. (Section 15.3)

- Complex reaction orders can often be reduced to pseudo-first-order reactions by keeping the concentration of one of the reactants large. (Section 15.3)

- The rate law is experimentally determined using the method of initial rates or the method of graphical analysis. (Section 15.4)

- Transition state theory, which is based on collision theory, describes the energy of a reaction during the course of a reaction. A plot of the reaction coordinate versus the energy can give meaningful information, such as the activation energy, the presence of any intermediates, the effect of a catalyst, and the enthalpy for the forward and reverse process. (Section 15.6)

- Catalysts speed up a reaction without being consumed in the reaction. (Section 15.7)

Key Words

absorb To be associated, through intermolecular forces of attraction, by being taken up or mixing into a substance. (*p. 656*)

activated complex The unstable collection of atoms that can break up either to form the products or to re-form the reactants. (*p. 651*)

activation energy (E_a) The minimum energy of collision that reactants must have in order to successfully create the activated complex. (*p. 630*)

adsorb To be associated, through intermolecular forces of attraction, with a surface. (*p. 656*)

average rate The rate of a reaction measured over a long period of time. (*p. 622*)

bimolecular reaction A reaction involving the collision of two molecules in the rate-determining step. (*p. 648*)

catalyst A substance that participates in a reaction, is not consumed, and modifies the mechanism of the reaction to provide a lower activation energy. Catalysts increase the rate of reaction. (*p. 654*)

chemical kinetics The study of the rates and mechanisms of chemical reactions. (*p. 621*)

collision theory A theory that correlates the number of properly oriented collisions with the rate of the reaction. (*p. 629*)

desorbed Released from a surface. (*p. 656*)

elementary step A single step in a mechanism that indicates how reactants proceed toward products. (*p. 648*)

environmental chemist A scientist who studies the interactions of compounds in the environment. (*p. 620*)

first order A reaction is first order in a particular species when the rate of the reaction depends on the concentration of that species raised to the first power. (*p. 628*)

frequency factor A term in the Arrhenius equation that indicates the rate of collision and the probability that colliding reactants are oriented for a successful reaction. (*p. 652*)

half-life ($t_{1/2}$) The time required for a reaction to reach 50% completion. (*p. 636*)

herbicide Any compound used to kill unwanted plants. (*p. 620*)

heterogeneous catalyst A specific catalyst that exists in a different physical state than the reaction. (*p. 656*)

homogeneous catalyst A specific catalyst that exists in the same physical state as the compounds in the reaction. (*p. 655*)

initial rate The instantaneous rate of reaction when $t = 0$. (*p. 623*)

insecticide Any compound used to kill unwanted insects. (*p. 620*)

instantaneous rate The rate of reaction measured at a specific instant in time. The instantaneous rate is typically measured by calculating the slope of a line that is tangent to the curve drawn by plotting [reactant] versus time. (*p. 623*)

integrated first-order rate law An expression derived from a first-order rate law that illustrates how the concentrations of reactants vary as a function of time. (*p. 634*)

integrated rate law A form of the rate law that illustrates how the concentrations of reactants vary as a function of time. (*p. 633*)

integrated second-order rate law An expression derived from a second-order rate law that illustrates how the concentrations of reactants vary as a function of time. (*p. 639*)

integrated zero-order rate law An expression derived from a zero-order rate law that illustrates how the concentrations of reactants vary as a function of time. (*p. 639*)

intermediate A compound that is produced in a reaction and then consumed in the reaction. Intermediates are not indicated in the overall reaction equation. (*p. 650*)

mechanism The series of steps taken by the components of a reaction as they progress from reactants to products. (*p. 648*)

method of graphical analysis A method of determining the rate law for a reaction where the rate of a reaction is plotted versus time. Also known as the method of integrated rate laws. (*p. 644*)

method of initial rates A method of determining the rate law for a reaction where the initial rates of different trials of a reaction are compared. (*p. 641*)

molecularity A description of the number of molecules that must collide in the rate-determining step of a reaction. (*p. 648*)

pesticide Any compound used to kill unwanted organisms (whether they be animals, insects, or plants). (*p. 620*)

pseudo-first-order rate A modification of the second-order rate that enables one to use first-order kinetics. (*p. 640*)

rate The "speed" of a reaction, recorded in M/s. (*p. 621*)

rate constant A constant that is characteristic of a reaction at a given temperature, relating to the rate of disappearance of reactants. (*p. 628*)

rate-determining step The slowest elementary step in a reaction sequence. (*p. 648*)

rate law An equation that indicates the molecularity of a reaction as a function of the rate of the reaction. (*p. 628*)

reaction coordinate A measure that describes the progress of the reaction. (*p. 651*)

reaction profile A plot of the progress of a reaction versus the energy of the components. (*p. 651*)

second-order rate law The rate of a reaction is directly related either to the square of the concentration of a single reactant or to the product of the concentrations of two reactants. (*p. 639*)

termolecular (trimolecular) reaction A reaction in which three molecules collide in the rate-determining step of the reaction. (*p. 648*)

transition state The point along the reaction coordinate where the reactants have collided to form the activated complex. (*p. 651*)

transition state theory The theory that describes how the energy of activation is related to the rate of reaction. (*p. 651*)

unimolecular reaction A reaction in which one molecule alone is involved in the rate-determining step of the reaction. (*p. 648*)

zero-order reaction A reaction in which the rate is not related to the concentrations of any species in the reaction. (*p. 639*)

Focus Your Learning

The answers to the odd-numbered problems appear at the back of the book.

Section 15.1 Reaction Rates

Skill Review

1. Use the analogy of a runner in a 10-km road race to define each of these pertinent reaction kinetics terms:
   a. Extent of reaction
   b. Average rate
   c. Instantaneous rate
   d. Initial rate

2. Use the analogy of firing a bullet from a gun to define each of these kinetics terms:
   a. Extent of reaction
   b. Average rate
   c. Instantaneous rate
   d. Initial rate

3. For the following reaction in a 4.00-L container, it was found that 1.00×10^{-4} mol of C_4H_8 reacted over a time period from 10:58 A.M. to 11:15 A.M.

$$C_4H_8(g) \rightarrow 2C_2H_4(g)$$

   What is the average rate, in M/s, for this reaction? Is it possible to have an instantaneous rate faster than the average rate? Explain.

4. The reaction described in Problem 3 was performed a second time. Into a 1.5-L flask was placed 3.25 mol of $C_4H_8(g)$. After 56 min, 1.00 mol of $C_2H_4(g)$ was obtained. What is the average rate, in M/s, for this reaction?

5. Using the same reaction as in Problem 3 ($C_4H_8 \rightarrow 2C_2H_4$), compare the rate of appearance of C_2H_4 to the rate of disappearance of C_4H_8. Write out this relationship using the style presented in the chapter that depicts the rate, as it would be expressed based on either of the components.

6. The following reaction shows PH_3 decomposing into two products.

$$4PH_3(g) + 3O_2(g) \rightarrow 4P(g) + 6H_2O(g)$$

   Write the rate expression that depicts the rate of disappearance of the reactant when compared to the appearance of each product.

7. Determine the rate of reaction, in M/s, for each of these systems over the time period indicated. Assume that the reaction is

$$A \rightarrow B$$

   a. $[A]_0 = 0.350\ M$; $[A]_t = 0.300\ M$; $t_0 = 0$ s; $t = 100$ s
   b. $[A]_0 = 1.522\ M$; $[A]_t = 0.350\ M$; $t_0 = 0$ min; $t = 15$ min
   c. $[A]_0 = 0.050\ M$; $[A]_t = 0.010\ M$; $t_0 = 0$ days; $t = 399$ days
   d. $[A]_0 = 0.280\ M$; $[A]_t = 0.140\ M$; $t_0 = 35$ min; $t = 2.5$ h

8. Determine the rate of reaction, in M/s, for each of these systems over the time period indicated. Assume that the reaction is

$$A \rightarrow 2B$$

   a. $[A]_0 = 0.350\ M$; $[A]_t = 0.280\ M$; $t_0 = 0$ s; $t = 100$ s
   b. $[A]_0 = 2.50\ M$; $[A]_t = 0.250\ M$; $t_0 = 0$ s; $t = 15$ min
   c. $[A]_0 = 1.750\ M$; $[A]_t = 0.010\ M$; $t_0 = 0$ days; $t = 250$ days
   d. $[A]_0 = 0.125\ M$; $[A]_t = 0.105\ M$; $t_0 = 15$ s; $t = 2.5$ min

9. In the general reaction shown below, the rate of disappearance of A is $4.5 \times 10^{-2}\ M/s$.

$$2A + 3B \rightarrow C + 2D$$

   a. What is the rate of disappearance of B?
   b. What is the rate of appearance of C?
   c. What is the rate of appearance of D?

10. In the general reaction shown below, the rate of disappearance of A is $1.85 \times 10^{-4}\ M/s$.

$$A + 2B \rightarrow 2C + 3D$$

   a. What is the rate of disappearance of B?
   b. What is the rate of appearance of C?
   c. What is the rate of appearance of D?

11. Either on a piece of graph paper or using a computer, plot the data given in the accompanying table, which are from a drag race. Then determine:
   a. The initial speed
   b. The instantaneous speed at $t = 8$ s
   c. The instantaneous speed at $t = 25$ s
   d. The average speed of the dragster
   e. In your own words, how does this compare to the typical plot of a reaction?

Distance (mi)	Time (s)
0	0
0.055	5
0.193	10
0.611	20
1.120	30

12. Plot the accompanying data on a piece of graph paper or using a computer. Then determine the following:
   a. The initial rate, in M/min, of the reaction
   b. The instantaneous rate, in M/min, at $t = 15$ min
   c. The instantaneous rate, in M/min, at $t = 45$ min
   d. The average rate, in M/min, of the reaction

[Pesticide]	Time (min)
$0.10000\ M$	0
$0.055294\ M$	15
$0.030575\ M$	30
$0.016906\ M$	45
$0.009348\ M$	60

Chemical Applications and Practice

13. The common disinfectant hydrogen peroxide (H_2O_2) can decompose according to the following balanced equation:

$$2H_2O_2(aq) \rightarrow 2H_2O(l) + O_2(g)$$

   a. How much faster is the appearance of H_2O than the appearance of O_2?
   b. Write the expression that defines the rate of the reaction based on the rate of disappearance of H_2O_2 and the rates of appearance of H_2O and O_2.

14. Reducing the level of nitrogen monoxide compounds emitted in automobile exhaust is a priority of environmentally concerned citizens. One response to this has been the development of catalytic converters. The NO in the exhaust passes over a rhodium-containing converter and is changed to the components already present in clean air.

$$2NO(g) \rightarrow N_2(g) + O_2(g)$$

If the rate of appearance of N_2 were 1.5×10^{-6} mol/s, what would you calculate as the rate of disappearance of NO?

15. The relationship between ozone and humans has a rather unique feature. Whether ozone benefits humans depends largely on proximity. Ozone is considered beneficial when it occurs in the upper atmosphere, but it can cause serious respiratory problems if it is in the atmosphere layer closest to us. Ozone can be formed by the following reaction:

$$O_2(g) + O(g) \rightarrow O_3(g)$$

This graphical representation shows the decomposition of oxygen over time. Redraw the graph and sketch a line that would depict the appearance of ozone over the same time period.

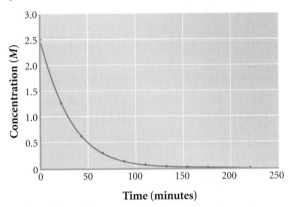

Time (minutes)

16. As we have seen, the reaction that is used to produce the agriculturally critical fertilizer ammonia combines nitrogen and hydrogen gas in the following manner:

$$3H_2(g) + N_2(g) \rightarrow 2NH_3(g)$$

a. Using the following graph of the disappearance of N_2 as a guide, sketch two additional lines that factor in the ratios of the different species for the disappearance of H_2 and appearance of NH_3, respectively.

b. If the disappearance of N_2 in a particular reaction were 1.2×10^{-3} mol/min, what would be the rate of appearance of NH_3?

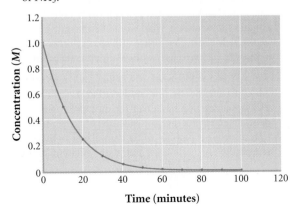

Time (minutes)

15.2 An Introduction to Rate Laws

Skill Review

17. Judging on the basis of collision theory, indicate whether each of these modifications would increase the rate of a reaction. Explain your answers.
a. increasing the temperature
b. decreasing the temperature
c. increasing the initial concentration of reactant
d. diluting the reaction with more solvent

18. Judging on the basis of collision theory, indicate whether each of these modifications would have an effect on the rate of a reaction. Explain your answers.
a. increasing the volume of the reaction
b. decreasing the number of reactant molecules
c. adding some product molecules to the reaction
d. removing the product molecules as they form

19. The following equation represents the rate law for the decomposition of an important pesticide (symbolized here as Pest).
a. What is the order of the reaction?
b. What is the meaning of k?
c. What effect would doubling the concentration of pesticide have on the rate of the reaction?
d. What effect would doubling the concentration of the pesticide have on the value of k?

$$\text{Rate} = k \, [\text{Pest}]^2 [\text{H}^+]$$

20. Report the overall order of each of these reactions:
a. Rate = $k[NO][O_3]$ c. Rate = $k[H_2][Cl_2]^{1/2}$
b. Rate = $k[NO][H_2][H_2O]^{-1}$

21. Calculate the rate of the following reaction, if the rate constant is 3.95×10^{-4} s^{-1} and $[A] = 0.509$ M. The reaction is first order in A and zero order in B.

$$A + B \rightarrow 2C + D$$

22. Calculate the rate constant for a reaction if, when $[A] = 0.672$ M, the rate of the reaction is 2.99×10^{-3} M/s. The reaction is second order in A.

$$A \rightarrow B$$

Chemical Applications and Practices

23. The hypochlorite ion (ClO^-) is present in commercial bleach. One aqueous reaction in which this ion participates is

$$3ClO^- \rightarrow ClO_3^- + 2Cl^-$$

Without any further information, give two reasons why we could not claim that the rate law is Rate = $k[ClO^-]$.

24. If the rate law for the hypochlorite reaction from the equation in Problem 23 ($3ClO^- \rightarrow ClO_3^- + 2Cl^-$), is Rate = $k[ClO^-]^2$, what would you report as the order of the reaction? If the concentration of hypochlorite were tripled, what effect would this have on the rate of the reaction (assuming no change in temperature)? The order of the reaction does not match the stoichiometry of the equation. What does this indicate?

Section 15.3
Changes in Time—The Integrated Rate Law

Skill Review

25. Determine the rate constant for each of these first-order reactions:
    a. decomposition of peroxyacetyl nitrate; $t_{1/2} = 1920$ s
    b. decomposition of sulfuryl chloride; $t_{1/2} = 525$ min
    c. radioactive decay of ^{40}K; $t_{1/2} = 1.25 \times 10^9$ years
    d. radioactive decay of ^{14}C; $t_{1/2} = 5730$ years

26. Determine the half-life for each of these first-order reactions:
    a. radioactive decay of ^{131}I; $k = 0.08619$ day^{-1}
    b. radioactive decay of ^{24}Na; $k = 0.0473$ h^{-1}
    c. decomposition of DDT; $k = 2.31 \times 10^{-4}$ day^{-1}
    d. metabolism of malathion; $k = 0.693$ day^{-1}

27. In the following first-order reaction, the half-life was determined to be 43 min.
    a. How long would it take for the concentration of A to drop to 50% of the original amount?
    b. To 25% of the original amount?
    c. To 10% of the original amount?

$$A \rightarrow B$$

28. The radioactive decay of ^{14}C is a first-order reaction.
    a. If a sample originally contains 1.59×10^{-5} M ^{14}C, how long will it take before the concentration is 0.795×10^{-5} M? The half-life of ^{14}C is 5730 years.
    b. How long will it take before the concentration is 1.00×10^{-6} M?

29. For each case below, calculate the concentration of A at the time indicated. The reaction is first order with a half-life of 3.95×10^2 s.
    a. $[A]_0 = 0.100$ M; $\Delta t = 50.0$ s
    b. $[A]_0 = 0.100$ M; $\Delta t = 100.0$ s
    c. $[A]_0 = 0.200$ M; $\Delta t = 50.0$ s
    d. $[A]_0 = 0.200$ M; $\Delta t = 20.0$ s

30. For each case below, calculate the time required to reach the concentration shown. The reaction is first order with a half-life of 1.25×10^{-3} s.
    a. $[A]_0 = 0.100$ M; $[A] = 0.010$ M
    b. $[A]_0 = 0.350$ M; $[A] = 0.095$ M
    c. $[A]_0 = 0.200$ M; $[A] = 0.010$ M
    d. $[A]_0 = 0.250$ M; $[A] = 0.100$ M

31. What was the initial concentration of A if $[A] = 0.0388$ M after 2.75 days? Assume that the half-life of the first-order reaction is 1.18 days.

$$A \rightarrow B$$

32. Determine the rate constant (in s^{-1}) for the first-order decomposition of the pesticide 2,4-D, if the initial concentration was 2.73×10^{-3} M and the concentration after 60.0 days was 8.44×10^{-4} M.

33. In the following cases of first-order reactions, something is wrong with the data. Determine which value is incorrect and indicate why.
    a. $[A]_0 = 0.100$ M; $[A]_t = 0.900$ M; $t_0 = 0$ s; $t = 10$ s
    b. $[A]_0 = 0.090$ M; $[A]_t = 0.010$ M; $t_0 = 10$ s; $t = 0$ s

34. In the following cases of first-order reactions, something is wrong with the data. Determine which value is incorrect and indicate why.
    a. $[A]_0 = 0.100$ M; $[A] = 0.050$ M; $t_0 = 0$ s; $t = 10$ s; $t_{1/2} = 24$ min
    b. $[A]_0 = 0.900$ M; $[A] = 0.450$ M; $t_0 = 0$ s; $t = 10$ s; $k = 0.085$ s^{-1}

35. What is the half-life of the decomposition of ammonia on a metal surface, a zero-order reaction, if $[NH_3] = 0.0333$ M initially and $[NH_3] = 0.0150$ M at $t = 450.0$ s?

36. Determine the concentration of ammonia from Problem 35 when $t = 800.0$ s.

37. What is the value of the rate constant for a zero-order reaction with $t_{1/2} = 3.55$ h? Assume the original concentration $[A]_0 = 0.100$ M.

38. What is the value of the rate constant for a second-order reaction with $t_{1/2} = 300.0$ days? Assume the original concentration $[A]_0 = 1.50$ M.

39. What is the half-life of a second-order reaction if the concentration of A drops to 10% of its original value of 2.00×10^{-3} M in 520 min?

$$2A \rightarrow B$$

40. What is the concentration of A after 3.5 h in the second-order reaction illustrated in Problem 39, if $[A]_0 = 0.100$ M and $k = 1.2 \times 10^{-4}$ M$^{-1} \cdot$s^{-1}?

41. Determine the concentration of the reactant in each of these cases. Assume that the reaction is second order with $k = 0.0312$ M$^{-1} \cdot$min^{-1}.
    a. $[A]_0 = 0.100$ M; $t = 10.0$ s
    b. $[A]_0 = 0.500$ M; $t = 10.0$ s
    c. $[A]_0 = 0.339$ M; $t = 200.0$ s
    d. $[A]_0 = 0.0050$ M; $t = 24$ days

42. Determine the concentration of the reactant in each of these cases. Assume that the reaction is second order with $k = 0.410$ M$^{-1} \cdot$h^{-1}.
    a. $[A]_0 = 0.100$ M; $t = 10.0$ h
    b. $[A]_0 = 0.500$ M; $t = 10.0$ h
    c. $[A]_0 = 0.222$ M; $t = 1.75$ h
    d. $[A]_0 = 0.0010$ M; $t = 14$ days

43. A graphical plot of concentration of a reactant versus time during a reaction will reveal, for reactions above zero order, a changing rate. Use collision theory to explain why the rate slows over time.

44. When you examine the three integrated rate expressions mentioned in the chapter, you can easily note that all three contain the symbol k. What would be the units for k in each of the zero-order, first-order, and second-order rate expressions? (If necessary, use any time unit merely as "time.")

45. Suppose two students are discussing their recent chemistry lab experiment. The first student, Pablo, remarks that his first-order reaction has a half-life of 25 min. The other student, Peter, replies that coincidentally, his second-order reaction also has a half-life of 25 min. Then both go back to repeat their experiments, but with different amounts of

starting materials. Neglecting experimental error, explain any differences, or lack of, that they might find this time.

46. a. What advantage does changing a reaction to pseudo-first-order kinetics give to an experimenter?

b. Describe how to alter a kinetics experiment in order to study it in the pseudo-first-order kinetic model.

c. Explain why the concentration of one component in the pseudo-first-order model can be made to be part of the specific rate constant of a reaction.

Chemical Applications and Practices

47. An agricultural chemist is attempting to detect the decomposition of a new herbicide. The chemist notes that after application, the compound decays from 100.0% potency to 75.0% potency over a time period of 1 week (168 h). Assume that the original concentration $[A]_0 = 1.00 \times 10^{-3} M$.

a. What would be the specific rate constant if the reaction were first order with respect to the herbicide?

b. What would be the specific rate constant if the reaction were second order with respect to the herbicide?

c. What would be the specific rate constant if the reaction were zero order with respect to the herbicide?

48. Use the values obtained in Problem 47 to determine the half-life of the herbicide, assuming:

a. first-order kinetics

b. second-order kinetics

c. zero-order kinetics

49. Assume that the fermentation of glucose by yeast, to produce ethanol, is a first-order process. Under certain conditions the value of the specific rate constant is $0.00205\ h^{-1}$. If the initial concentration of glucose were $0.980\ M$, what would be the concentration after 244 h of fermentation?

50. The precipitation of metal ions with sulfide is often used as an identifying technique for the metal ions. The production of hydrogen sulfide to be used in the precipitation, however, can be dangerous. Consequently, H_2S can be generated by placing thioacetamide (CH_3CSNH_2) in an aqueous acid solution. If the first-order decay constant for thioacetamide under those conditions were $0.46\ min^{-1}$, what would you calculate as the time required for $0.100\ M$ thioacetamide to reach a concentration of $0.0100\ M$?

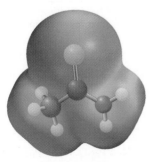

Thioacetamide
CH_3CSNH_2

51. All nuclear decay processes (alpha, beta, and gamma decay) follow first-order kinetics. The isotope americium-241 is used in many smoke detectors. It has a half-life of approximately 241 years. How long would it take the americium in a smoke detector to decay (into neptunium) from its initial radiation level to 66.6% of its original value?

52. Explain why nuclear decay processes can be considered always to follow first-order kinetics?

15.4 Methods of Determining Rate Laws

Skill Review

53. Plot the following data and determine whether they follow zero-order, first-order, or second-order kinetics.

Time (s)	Concentration (M)
0	0.500
5	0.274
10	0.189
20	0.116
30	0.084

54. Plot the data in Problem 12 and determine whether they follow zero-order, first-order, or second-order kinetics.

55. Explain the change in the rate of the reaction in each case below.

$$\text{Rate} = k[A][B]$$

a. We double $[A]$.

b. We double $[B]$.

c. We double $[A]$ and $[B]$.

56. Explain the change in the rate of the reaction in each case below.

$$\text{Rate} = k[A]^2[B]$$

a. We double $[A]$.

b. We double $[B]$.

c. We triple $[A]$.

57. Use the method of initial rates to determine the order of each component, along with the general rate law and the value of the rate constant, in the following hypothetical reaction. What is the overall order of the reaction?

$$A + B \rightarrow 2C$$

Experiment	[A] (M)	[B] (M)	Initial Rate (M/s)
1	0.10	0.10	0.222
2	0.10	0.20	0.444
3	0.20	0.20	0.444

58. Use the method of initial rates to determine the order of each component, along with the general rate law and the value of the rate constant, in the following hypothetical reaction. What is the overall order of the reaction?

$$A + B \rightarrow 2C$$

Experiment	[A] (M)	[B] (M)	Initial Rate (M/s)
1	0.10	0.10	0.286
2	0.10	0.20	0.143
3	0.20	0.20	0.286

59. Use the method of initial rates to determine the order of each component, along with the general rate law and the value of the rate constant, in the following hypothetical reaction. What is the overall order of the reaction?

$$A + 2B \rightarrow 2C$$

Experiment	[A] (M)	[B] (M)	Initial Rate (M/s)
1	0.10	0.10	0.105
2	0.10	0.20	0.420
3	0.20	0.20	0.840

60. Use the method of initial rates to determine the order of each component, along with the general rate law and the value of the rate constant in the following hypothetical reaction. What is the overall order of the reaction?

$$2A + 2B \rightarrow 2C$$

Experiment	[A] (M)	[B] (M)	Initial Rate (M/s)
1	0.050	0.10	0.074
2	0.10	0.20	0.888
3	0.050	0.20	0.222

61. Use the method of graphical analysis to determine the order for the hypothetical reaction $A \rightarrow C + D$. What is the rate constant (with appropriate units) for this reaction?

[A] (M)	Time (min)
0.432	0
0.385	1
0.291	3
0.197	5
0.103	7

62. Use the method of graphical analysis to determine the order for the hypothetical reaction $A \rightarrow B$. What is the rate constant (with appropriate units) for this reaction?

[A] (M)	Time (s)
0.100	0
0.050	62
0.025	124
0.013	186
0.0065	248

63. The following two diagrams represent two different containers. Within each container, two different compounds are placed.

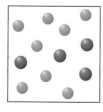 

a. If the reaction about to take place is first order with respect to the large dark atoms and zero order with respect to the small light atoms, which graphical plot would yield a straight line for each component?

b. How would the overall reaction rate compare between the first and second containers?

c. What units would you assign to the rate constant for the reaction between the two components? (You may use seconds for the time unit.)

64. The following diagram represents a container with two gas components in their initial conditions. The reaction is zero order with respect to the large atoms and first order with respect to the small atoms. Prepare a similar diagram, but show what would be needed to produce a reaction that would be three times faster than the first (assuming no change in temperature or any other reaction conditions).

Chemical Applications and Practices

65. Municipal water supplies are often treated with chlorine compounds in order to take advantage of the oxidizing ability of chlorine to react with potential pollutants. In some industrial settings, other oxidizing substances are used. One example of such an application is use of the powerful oxidizing potential of iron(VI) compounds. Given the information below, what order would you report for the reaction of the iron(VI) compound? What would you report as the value for k?

[Fe^{6+}] (M)	Time (min)
0.100	0.00
0.0682	1.00
0.0517	2.00
0.0300	5.00
0.00920	10.00

66. The gas phase hydrogenation of ethene is shown in the following reaction:

$$C_2H_2(g) + 2H_2(g) \rightarrow C_2H_6(g)$$

a. If the following data were collected, using the method of initial rates, for four experiments at a fixed temperature, what would you determine as the rate law for the reaction?

Experiment	$P_{C_2H_2}$ (atm)	P_{H_2} (atm)	Initial Rate (atm/s)
1	0.10	0.10	11
2	0.20	0.10	22
3	0.10	0.20	22
4	0.20	0.05	11

b. What would you calculate as the rate constant for the reaction?

c. If the experiment were run once again, at the same temperature, with initial pressures of 0.020 atm for ethene and 0.020 atm for hydrogen, what would you determine as the rate?

67. Suppose the following represents the kinetic study of the oxidation of a new plastic stabilizer being proposed for use in automobile upholstery.

$$\text{Stabilizer}(aq) + H^+(aq) + O_2(g) \rightarrow \text{oxidation product}$$

Experiment	Stabilizer (aq) (M)	H$^+$(aq) (M)	O$_2$(g) (M)	Rate (M/s)
1	0.400	0.300	0.560	7.14×10^{-4}
2	0.100	0.500	0.200	4.55×10^{-5}
3	0.100	0.100	0.200	4.55×10^{-5}
4	0.400	0.300	0.750	1.28×10^{-3}
5	0.100	0.300	0.560	3.57×10^{-4}

a. What is the rate law for the reaction?

b. What is the rate constant for the reaction at this temperature?

c. What would you calculate as the rate of the reaction, at the same temperature, if the respective initial concentrations were 0.111, 0.200, and 1.00 for the stabilizer, hydrogen ion, and oxygen, respectively?

d. If the rate of the same reaction, at the same conditions, were determined to be 2.55×10^{-4} M/s when the initial concentration of stabilizer was 0.300 M with a hydrogen ion concentration of 0.100, what would the initial oxygen pressure have to be?

68. Brewed coffee left on a warming device will gradually change flavor as a consequence of several complex reactions that occur as the flavor oils decompose. Suppose a flavor chemist for Dr. Beans Coffee Company collected the following data on one such oil as it decomposed over time.

Concentration (M)	Time (min)
0.00128	0
0.00120	10.0
0.00113	20.0
0.00107	30.0
0.000781	100.0
0.000561	200.0

a. Using graphical techniques, determine the order of the decay process.

b. What is the rate constant for the decay?

c. Starting with the initial concentration, how long would it take for half the ingredient to decompose (half-life)?

69. The naturally occurring isotope of hydrogen known as tritium has two neutrons and one proton. The reaction between tritium and deuterium may provide the basis for controlled fusion reactions. The half-life of the radioactive tritium isotope is approximately 12 years. How much radioactive tritium, starting with a sample producing a beta decay count rate of 545 cpm (counts per minute), would remain after 3 years?

70. Sodium hypochlorite (NaOCl) is the active ingredient in many aqueous commercial bleaching products. If the NaOCl added to a particular sewage treatment process had a half-life of 15 days, what percentage of the original concentration would remain after 1 year? (Assume first-order kinetics.)

15.5 Looking Back at Rate Laws

Skill Review

71. What mathematical effect would there be on the three graphs for first, second, and third order, respectively, if before plotting the terms on each y axis you first subtracted the initial concentration, ln of the initial concentration, and 1/(initial concentration), respectively, from each reading?

72. A researcher mistakenly plots the data from a first-order reaction using log [A] instead of ln [A]. What effect would this have on the resulting graph?

73. What sign do you expect for the slope of the line in a plot of [A] versus t for a zero-order reaction?

74. What sign do you expect for the slope of the line in a plot of ln[A] versus t for a first-order reaction?

75. Which indicates a faster reaction for a first-order process: $k = 1.66 \times 10^{-2}\,s^{-1}$ or $k = 8.95 \times 10^{-2}\,s^{-1}$?

76. Which indicates a faster reaction for a first-order process: $t_{1/2} = 24$ days or $t_{1/2} = 15$ days?

Chemical Applications and Practices

77. One method of producing yellow lead chromate pigment is via a reaction of sodium chromate. Chromium(III) ions can be made to undergo a three-electron oxidation to the chromate ion (CrO_4^{2-}) with the addition of cerium(IV) ions. The rate law was found to be

$$\text{Rate} = k[Cr^{3+}]^2\,[Ce^{4+}]\,[CrO_4^{2-}]^x$$

Suppose the concentration of each component in the rate law were doubled. If this caused the rate to quadruple, what would you calculate as the value of x?

78. An approximation that chemists may sometimes casually use is that increasing the temperature of a system by 10 degrees Celsius may double the rate. Suppose you wanted to increase a reaction rate by using only concentration changes. How much would a concentration have to change to cause a reaction to become ten times faster? (Assume the reaction is first order.)

15.6 Reaction Mechanisms

Skill Review

79. Explain the relationship among a reaction mechanism, elementary steps, and the rate-determining step.

80. Explain how it is possible for the proposed mechanism of a reaction to be acceptable, yet perhaps not represent the actual occurrence of events in the mechanism of that reaction.

81. You are seated at your kitchen table. Describe each of the steps involved in answering the telephone in your home (be very detailed). Which of these steps is the rate-determining step for this process?

82. What is the rate-determining step in the process you use to go to your first-period chemistry class from your bedroom?

83. What is the activation energy for a hypothetical reaction ($A \rightarrow B$) if $k = 1.74 \times 10^{-2}$ s^{-1} at 300 K and $k = 4.22 \times 10^{-2}$ s^{-1} at 400 K?

84. Calculate the rate constant of a first-order reaction at 35°C, given that $k = 8.5 \times 10^{-4}$ s^{-1} at 25°C and $E_a = 144$ kJ.

Chemical Applications and Practices

85. The aqueous reaction between hydrogen peroxide and iodide in an acid solution is represented here:

$$H_2O_2 + 3I^- + 2H^+ \rightarrow 2H_2O + I_3^-$$

$$Rate = k[H_2O_2][I^-][H^+]$$

One of the following mechanisms can be accepted for the above rate law, and one cannot. Select the acceptable mechanism and show proof for your selection as well as giving the basis for rejection of the other.

Mechanism A

$H^+ + I^- \rightleftharpoons HI$ (fast)

$H_2O_2 + HI \rightarrow H_2O + HOI$ (slow)

$HOI + H^+ + I^- \rightarrow H_2O + I_2$ (fast)

$I^- + I_2 \rightarrow I_3^-$ (fast)

Mechanism B

$H_2O_2 + I^- \rightarrow H_2O + OI^-$ (slow)

$H^+ + I^- \rightleftharpoons HI$ (fast)

$H^+ + OI^- + HI \rightarrow H_2O + I_2$ (fast)

$I_2 + I^- \rightarrow I_3^-$ (fast)

86. When one reactant produces two products, the reaction is said to be a disproportionation reaction. The following shows the disproportionation of the hypochlorite ion used to make commercial bleaching products:

$$3ClO^-(aq) \rightarrow 2Cl^-(aq) + ClO_3^-(aq)$$

On the basis of the following proposed mechanism, what would you write as the rate law for this interesting reaction?

$$ClO^- + ClO^- \rightarrow ClO_2^- + Cl^- \quad (slow)$$

$$ClO^- + ClO_2^- \rightarrow ClO_3^- + Cl^- \quad (fast)$$

87. The solvent acetone has many industrial uses and is also a common ingredient in nail polish remover. It does decompose to a weak acid, carbonic acid. At 10.0°C, the rate constant for that decomposition is approximately 6.4×10^{-5} L/mol·s. At 78°C, the rate constant for the reaction has a value of 2.03×10^{-1} L/mol·s.
    a. What is the activation energy for this reaction?
    b. What is the rate constant for this reaction at 37°C?

88. At 78°C, what would you calculate as the value of the Arrhenius frequency factor, A, for the decomposition of acetone (Problem 87)?

15.7 Applications of Catalysts

Skill Review

89. Provide clear and concise definitions for each term:
    a. Reaction intermediate
    b. Activated complex
    c. Homogeneous catalyst
    d. Heterogeneous catalyst

90. a. Explain how a catalyst increases the rate of a chemical reaction.
    b. Explain why a catalyst does not appear as part of the stoichiometry in a balanced equation.

91. Consider the following elementary steps for the decomposition of N_2O.

$$N_2O \rightarrow N_2 + O$$

$$N_2O + O \rightarrow N_2 + O_2$$

    a. What is the overall reaction?
    b. Indicate any intermediates or catalysts involved in the reaction.
    c. Experimental evidence reveals that the rate law for this reaction is Rate $= k[N_2O]$. Which of the steps is the rate-limiting step in the mechanism?

92. The following mechanism has been proposed for the reaction of $ICl(g)$ and $H_2(g)$.

$$H_2 + ICl \rightarrow HI + HCl$$

$$HI + ICl \rightarrow I_2 + HCl$$

    a. What is the overall reaction?
    b. Indicate any intermediates or catalysts involved in the reaction.
    c. The first step in the mechanism is slow compared to the second. What is the rate law for the reaction?

93. A schematic mechanism for the reaction of lactose and lactase (an enzyme) to produce glucose and galactose is shown below.

$$lactose + lactase \rightarrow (lactase–lactose)$$

$$(lactase–lactose) \rightarrow (lactase–glucose–galactose)$$

$$(lactase–glucose–galactose) \rightarrow lactase + glucose + galactose$$

    a. What is the overall reaction?
    b. Indicate any intermediates or catalysts involved in the reaction.
    c. The first step in the mechanism is slow compared to the rest. What is the rate law for the reaction?

94. Each of the following represents an elementary step in a different mechanism. Classify each as unimolecular, bimolecular, or termolecular.
    a. $^{40}K \rightarrow {}^{40}Ar$
    b. $N_2 + Fe \rightarrow FeN_2$
    c. $2NO \rightarrow N_2O_2$
    d. $2NO + Cl_2 \rightarrow 2NOCl$

Chemical Applications and Practices

95. The industrial production of ammonia makes use of catalysts. One generalized mechanism may be presented as follows:

$$N_2(g) + Fe(s) \rightarrow FeN_2(s)$$

$$3H_2(g) + 3Fe(s) \rightarrow 3FeH_2(s)$$

$$FeN_2(s) + 3FeH_2(s) \rightarrow 4Fe(s) + 2NH_3(g)$$

    a. What is the overall stoichiometry of the reaction?
    b. What intermediates, if any, are present?
    c. What catalyst is present?
    d. Is the catalyst homogeneous or heterogeneous?

96. Diagram a reaction profile that illustrates the exothermic reaction whose mechanism is shown here. Next use a dotted line to show the same profile with any changes that would reflect the role of a heterogenous catalyst.

$$A(aq) + B(aq) \rightarrow C(aq) \quad \text{(slow)}$$
$$C(aq) \rightarrow D(g) \quad \text{(fast)}$$

Comprehensive Problems

97. In the reaction shown below, the initial concentration of H_2O_2 is 0.250 M, and 8 s later the concentration is 0.223 M. What is the initial rate of this reaction expressed in M/s and M/h?

$$2H_2O_2(aq) \rightarrow 2H_2O(l) + O_2(g)$$

98. What is the half-life for the first-order decomposition of dimethyl ether at 500°C if the rate constant for the reaction is 2.567×10^{-2} min^{-1}?

$$(CH_3)_2O \rightarrow CH_4 + H_2 + CO$$

99. A first-order reaction, $A \rightarrow B$, has a rate of 0.0875 M/s when $[A] = 0.250\ M$.
    a. What is the rate constant?
    b. What is the half-life for this reaction?

100. If the order of a reaction component were -1, what would be the effect of tripling the concentration of that component?

101. If the ΔH° value for a reaction were $+125$ kJ and the activation energy for the reverse of the reaction were $+75$ kJ, what would you calculate as the value for the activation energy for the forward reaction?

102. Consider the following reaction mechanism.

$$C_2H_6O(aq) + HCl(aq) \rightleftharpoons C_2H_7O^+(aq) + Cl^-(aq) \quad \text{(fast)}$$
$$C_2H_7O^+(aq) + Cl^-(aq) \rightarrow C_2H_5Cl(aq) + H_2O(l) \quad \text{(slow)}$$

a. Write the overall reaction that is indicated by the mechanism.
b. What would you predict as the rate law for the reaction?

103. Consider the following reaction mechanism.

$$C_2H_4(aq) + HCl(aq) \rightarrow C_2H_5^+(aq) + Cl^-(aq) \quad \text{(slow)}$$
$$C_2H_5^+(aq) + Cl^-(aq) \rightarrow C_2H_5Cl(aq) \quad \text{(fast)}$$

a. Write the overall reaction that is indicated by the mechanism.
b. What would you predict as the rate law for the reaction?

Thinking Beyond the Calculation

104. Draw a hypothetical reaction profile for the Haber process involving 1 mol of nitrogen and 3 mol of hydrogen in a 1.0 L flask.

$$N_2(g) + 3H_2(g) \rightarrow 2NH_3(g)$$

a. Use information you have learned in previous chapters to determine whether the reaction is exothermic or endothermic.
b. Is this reaction spontaneous at room temperature? At what temperature is the reaction at equilibrium?
c. On the reaction profile you drew, indicate what you'd expect to see if the reaction were homogeneously catalyzed.
d. Draw what you'd expect to see if the reaction were heterogeneously catalyzed.
e. If the catalyzed reaction were accomplished at 300°C using the quantities outlined in the start of this question, what would be the yield, in grams, of ammonia ($NH_3(g)$)? Assume the reaction produces only a 45% yield.
f. If 10.0 kg of nitrogen and 30.0 kg of hydrogen were combined in the catalyzed reaction, what would be the theoretical yield, in kilograms, of ammonia?

16

Chemical Equilibrium

Just as this balance settles at a fixed position of lowest energy, chemical reactions "strive" toward a position of lowest free energy—that is, chemical equilibrium.

Contents and Selected Applications

"I'm running late." We seem to hear that expression so often in our hyper-charged, have-to-do-it-now world. Running late might mean being stuck in traffic or on mass transit. There is not much you can do in a sea of cars and trucks. But sometimes you actually do run to get where you are going. As you struggle to make up time, you breathe more heavily than normal, desperately sucking air into your lungs. Your body's efforts to get more oxygen to the muscles are greatly enhanced by a protein in muscle cells called myoglobin.

When you are resting, the myoglobin becomes loaded up with oxygen molecules. These oxygen molecules can be quickly released when your muscle cells undergo activity. How does the myoglobin acquire and release oxygen when we need it?

Strenuous activities such as running require a sharp change in the amount of oxygen your muscles require. The interaction of myoglobin and oxygen in the muscles accommodates this need.

Myoglobin (Mb), shown in Figure 16.1, is a protein with a molecular weight of about 16,900 g/mol. A key part of the protein is the heme group, shown in Figure 16.2. The heme contains an Fe^{2+} ion that can form a bond with one molecule of oxygen, creating a myoglobin–oxygen complex as follows:

$$Mb + O_2 \rightarrow MbO_2$$

When your cells need the oxygen, it is released from the complex by reversing the direction of the reaction:

$$MbO_2 \rightarrow Mb + O_2$$

The free myoglobin is then available to bind more oxygen, which it can later release as needed, and continue in this *reversible* cycle of bind–release–bind–release. Let's examine this reaction more closely to help us understand the concepts of reversible reactions and the essential details of reactions such as this, which are known as chemical equilibria.

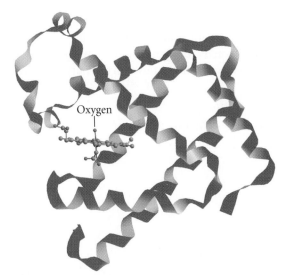

FIGURE 16.1

Myoglobin (Mb) is a protein with a molecular weight of about 16,900 g/mol. A key part of the protein is the heme group, highlighted on the left, which can bind to an oxygen molecule.

FIGURE 16.2

This drawing of a heme group highlights the Fe^{2+} ion, which can bind to one molecule of oxygen as shown.

16.1 The Concept of Chemical Equilibrium

Why does myoglobin's reversible cycle of binding and releasing oxygen take place? We know from our understanding of thermodynamics (Chapter 14) that spontaneous reactions lower the free energy, G, of the chemicals involved. When we consider myoglobin and oxygen in living systems, we find that the two competing reactions exist. In one, myoglobin combines with oxygen. In the other, the MbO_2 complex releases oxygen. The end result is that the molecules in each reaction will never be completely converted into products, because these products are always being converted back into reactants. *In a closed system*, these reversible reactions will settle into a state in which the forward and reverse reactions occur at equal rates, where *no net change in the concentrations occurs*, even though both reactions continue. We describe this state as the position of chemical equilibrium, or just **equilibrium** (the plural is *equilibria*). What thermodynamic parameter determines when an equilibrium exists? *The concentrations will no longer change when the free energy of the system is at a minimum for the process.* At that point, the *change* in free energy of the system, ΔG, is 0 kJ/mol.

We symbolize a system that can settle into equilibrium by using double arrows, to represent the fact that both the forward and reverse reactions occur. For example, the myoglobin and oxygen reaction equilibrium is written

$$Mb + O_2 \rightleftharpoons MbO_2$$

As discussed in Chapter 15, we express the *molar* concentration of a substance by placing its chemical symbol in brackets, [ ], such as [Mb] or [MbO_2].

Let's examine what happens to the concentrations of the reactants and products as the minimum free energy is approached (see Figure 16.3.) To make things as straightforward as possible, we will consider the reaction occurring in a beaker, rather than in the human body where all kinds of complications (such as "running late") affect the chemistry.

Let's assume that we place oxygen in our beaker so that its concentration is $3.0 \times 10^{-4} M$. We would say $[O_2]_0 = 3.0 \times 10^{-4} M$, where the subscript 0 means the concentration at "time = 0," which is another way of saying the initial concentration. In fact, the amount of myoglobin normally present in muscle cells varies a great deal among, and within, biological species. In humans, a mid-range value is $[Mb]_0 = 2.0 \times 10^{-4} M$. We will assume for this discussion that we have a closed system (not the human body) and that there is no MbO_2 complex initially, so $[MbO_2]_0 = 0\ M$. As the reaction proceeds, oxygen binds to myoglobin. The forward reaction proceeds with a rate constant of k_1, known in this particular reaction as the **binding rate constant**.

$$Mb + O_2 \xrightarrow{k_1} MbO_2$$

FIGURE 16.3

Like a ball finding its lowest energy point in a valley, reactions find their lowest free energy position. This is the equilibrium position (*B*).

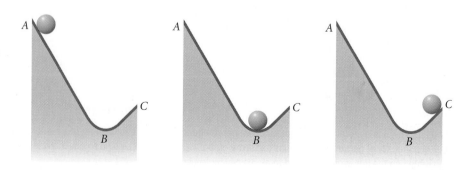

The concentration of oxygen *decreases,* as does that of free myoglobin, as shown in Figure 16.4. The concentration of the MbO_2 complex *increases* from zero as the reaction proceeds. As soon as the MbO_2 complex forms, however, it begins to dissociate back into Mb and O_2 with a rate constant of k_{-1}, known in this particular reaction as the **release rate constant**.

$$MbO_2 \xrightarrow{k_{-1}} Mb + O_2$$

Both reactions proceed until the free energy of the system is at a minimum, which occurs when *the rates of the forward and reverse reactions are equal.* That statement embodies the two key ways to define chemical equilibrium:

Definitions of Equilibrium

1. The free energy *change* of both forward and reverse reactions is zero ($\Delta G = 0$), and the free energy of the system is at its minimum.
2. The rates of the forward and reverse reactions are equal.

$$\text{rate}_f = \text{rate}_r$$
$$k_1[Mb][O_2] = k_{-1}[MbO_2]$$

This is shown in Figure 16.5. The forward and reverse reactions that bind and release oxygen are still occurring. In fact, they are occurring at the same rate. Therefore, *equilibrium is a dynamic process.* And there is no overall change in the concentration of Mb, O_2, or MbO_2 at equilibrium.

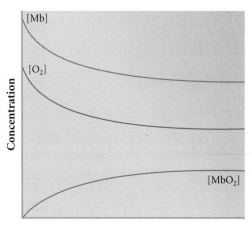

FIGURE 16.4

When myoglobin and oxygen are mixed, the concentration of oxygen decreases, as does that of free myoglobin, as shown. The concentration of the MbO_2 complex increases from 0 *M*. As soon as the MbO_2 complex forms, however, it begins to dissociate back into Mb and O_2.

FIGURE 16.5

Equilibrium is a dynamic process. The forward and reverse reactions are occurring at equal rates. The result is no net change in concentration of Mb (the blue shapes), O_2 (the red dots), or MbO_2 at equilibrium.

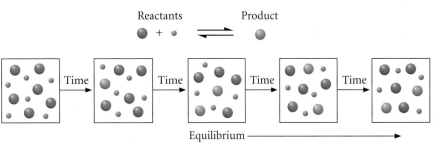

The initial concentrations of reactants and products change over time until equilibrium is reached. At this point, the forward and reverse reactions continue to produce their respective products, but the overall concentrations of each component in the reaction remain constant.

EXERCISE 16.1 **Equilibrium Concentrations**

Hydrogen and iodine gases can be combined to form hydrogen iodide,

$$H_2(g) + I_2(g) \rightleftharpoons 2HI(g)$$

Given the following initial and final concentrations, calculate the equilibrium concentration of HI.

$[I_2]_0 = 0.037\ M$ $[H_2]_0 = 0.121\ M$ $[HI]_0 = 0.099\ M$

$[I_2] = 0.022\ M$ $[H_2] = 0.106\ M$ $[HI] = ???\ M$

First Thoughts

The mole ratios of reactants to product are 1-to-1-to-2, so 1 mol each of H_2 and I_2 react to produce 2 mol of HI in a constant volume. Because the volume remains constant, we can think of the reaction stoichiometry this way: 1 M H_2 and 1 M I_2 react to produce 2 M HI.

Solution

The concentrations of I_2 and H_2 both decrease by 0.015 M.

$$0.015\ M\ H_2\ (\text{or } I_2) \times \frac{2M\ HI}{1M\ H_2\ (\text{or } I_2)} = 0.030\ M\ HI\ \text{produced}$$

$$[HI] = [HI]_0 + 0.030 = 0.13\ M$$

Further Insights

Much of the discussion in this chapter and in those that follow will consider how we can *predict* equilibrium concentrations when we know only about the system and the initial conditions. We will spend considerable time later in this chapter discussing how the ability to predict what will happen in a system is important in the chemical industry. For example, in the development of a manufacturing process, understanding how changes in conditions affect the equilibrium process enables the manufacturer to produce the largest possible yield of product, as well as save the company (and ultimately the consumer) money.

PRACTICE 16.1

Calculate the equilibrium concentration of HI if $[I_2]_0 = 0.050\ M$, $[H_2]_0 = 0.044\ M$, $[HI]_0 = 0.206\ M$, and $[I_2] = 0.041\ M$.

See Problem 21. ▮

It has been shown by experiment that the equilibrium concentrations of myoglobin, oxygen, and the MbO_2 complex are related by the ratio of the product to reactant concentrations known as the **mass-action expression** or, often, the **equilibrium expression**, of the reaction.

$$K = \frac{[MbO_2]}{[Mb][O_2]}$$

The value K is called the **equilibrium constant** for the reaction at a given temperature. We can get the equivalent result by separating the rate constants from the concentrations in the rate expressions as follows. At equilibrium, the rate of the forward and reverse reaction are equal.

$$k_1[Mb][O_2] = k_{-1}[MbO_2]$$

Rearranging the equation to put the rate constants on one side gives

$$\frac{k_1}{k_{-1}} = \frac{[MbO_2]}{[Mb][O_2]}$$

Therefore, the equilibrium constant, K, is the ratio of the forward rate constant to the reverse rate constant.

$$K = \frac{k_1}{k_{-1}}$$

The value for k_1 in the myoglobin–oxygen reaction at 20°C is $1.9 \times 10^7 \ M^{-1} \cdot s^{-1}$, and k_{-1} is $22 \ M^{-1} \cdot s^{-1}$, so we can calculate the value of K:

$$K = \frac{k_1}{k_{-1}} = \frac{1.9 \times 10^7}{22} = 8.6 \times 10^5$$

We typically would express a calculation such as this by including the units. However, the equilibrium constant does not have units. This is true because the actual thermodynamic definition of an equilibrium constant is based on the ratio of a substance's concentration to a standard state concentration. Even though the reasoning is subtle, the bottom line is that the equilibrium constant is typically given without units. In the reaction of myoglobin and oxygen, K is simply 8.6×10^5.

These last two results—that there exists a mass-action expression to find the equilibrium concentrations of Mb, O_2, and MbO_2, and that there exists an equilibrium constant for this expression at a particular temperature—can be extended to any reversible reaction. For example, in a general equilibrium (reactants A and B yielding products C and D) represented with stoichiometric coefficients m, n, p, and q,

$$mA + nB \rightleftharpoons pC + qD$$

The mass-action expression is

$$K = \frac{[C]^p [D]^q}{[A]^m [B]^n}$$

Exercise 16.2 explains why each equilibrium concentration is raised to the power of its coefficient in the mass-action expression.

EXERCISE 16.2   The Mass-Action Expression

The production of ammonia for use in fertilizers, via the Haber process, can be depicted as

$$H_2(g) + H_2(g) + H_2(g) + N_2(g) \rightleftharpoons NH_3(g) + NH_3(g)$$

Write the mass-action expression for the formation of ammonia.

First Thoughts

We did something unusual by breaking the equation down to list each individual molecule without the coefficients, a rather cumbersome way of displaying an equation. Our goal in doing this is to demonstrate how the product of the coefficients in the mass-action is displayed in exponential form.

Solution

If we base the mass-action expression on the reaction *exactly as it is written*, we get the following mass-action expression:

$$K = \frac{[NH_3][NH_3]}{[H_2][H_2][H_2][N_2]} = \frac{[NH_3]^2}{[H_2]^3 [N_2]}$$

Further Insights

The exponential form on the right-hand side is what we would have obtained had we written the Haber process in the usual way:

$$3H_2(g) + N_2(g) \rightleftharpoons 2NH_3(g)$$

This shows *why* the mass-action expression includes the equilibrium concentration of each substance raised to the power of its coefficient. If the coefficient is 1, as with N_2, it is not shown as an exponent, because raising anything to the power of 1 does not change its value.

PRACTICE 16.2

One of the ways to produce hydrogen gas industrially involves the reaction of methane with high-temperature steam. The reaction can be written as

$$CH_4(g) + H_2O(g) \rightleftharpoons CO(g) + H_2(g) + H_2(g) + H_2(g)$$

Write the mass-action expression for this reaction.

See Problems 5 and 6. ■

EXERCISE 16.3   Practice with Mass-Action Expressions

Write the mass-action expression for each of these reactions:

a. $PCl_5(g) \rightleftharpoons PCl_3(g) + Cl_2(g)$
b. $S_8(g) \rightleftharpoons 8S(g)$
c. $Cl_2O_7(g) + 8H_2(g) \rightleftharpoons 2HCl(g) + 7H_2O(g)$

Solution

In each case, the mass-action expression for the general reaction

$$mA + nB \rightleftharpoons pC + qD$$

is of the form in which the equilibrium concentration of each reactant or product is raised to the power of its coefficient.

$$K = \frac{[C]^p[D]^q}{[A]^m[B]^n}$$

a. $K = \dfrac{[Cl_2][PCl_3]}{[PCl_5]}$ (Products ↑; Reactant ↓)

b. $K = \dfrac{[S]^8}{[S_8]}$ (Coefficient of S ↑)

c. $K = \dfrac{[H_2O]^7[HCl]^2}{[Cl_2O_7][H_2]^8}$ (Coefficient of H_2O ↑; Coefficient of HCl ↑; Coefficient of H_2 ↓)

Note: Mathematically $[C]^p[D]^q = [D]^q[C]^p$, so the order in which we write these terms doesn't matter, as long as we keep each exponent with its term. For instance, the exponent p must remain with $[C]$.

PRACTICE 16.3

Write the equilibrium expression for each of these reactions:

a. $NO(g) + O_3(g) \rightleftharpoons NO_2(g) + O_2(g)$
b. $HCl(aq) + NH_3(aq) \rightleftharpoons NH_4Cl(aq)$
c. $C_2H_2(g) + 2H_2(g) \rightleftharpoons C_2H_6(g)$

See Problems 9 and 10. ■

Concentration-based mass-action expressions are generally suitable representations for the equilibria that occur in chemical reactions. However, in some aqueous solutions, especially where the solute concentrations are high, chemists often make a correction using activities instead of molarities, to get the most meaningful results. For example, if we prepare a solution that contains 3.0 mol of hydrochloric acid (HCl) in a liter of water, we say that the HCl concentration is 3.0 molar. We expect this strong acid to dissociate into H^+ and Cl^- ions, and we therefore assert that in the solution, the concentration of each ion, H^+ and Cl^-, is 3.0 M. However, this is not completely true. Some of the hydrogen cations do interact with the chloride anions in solution, and the ions interact with the water solvent through ion–dipole interactions, as we discussed in Chapter 10. This means that the *effective* concentration is likely to be somewhat different from the intended concentration, especially in relatively concentrated solutions. This effective concentration of the solute is called its activity. We will generally not consider the impact of activity in our discussions, but it is important for you to know that such an idea exists and can be dealt with quantitatively.

HERE'S WHAT WE KNOW SO FAR

- Most reactions do not go to completion. Rather, they reach a point of minimum free energy. We call this the point the position of chemical equilibrium.
- At chemical equilibrium, the rates of the forward and reverse reactions are equal.
- Chemical equilibrium is a dynamic, not static, condition.
- A reaction at chemical equilibrium can be described by a mass-action expression for which there is an equilibrium constant, K, that depends on temperature.

16.2 Why Is Chemical Equilibrium a Useful Concept?

The reaction of myoglobin with oxygen is just one of countless examples of equilibrium processes in living systems. In fact, the chemistry of blood is filled with equilibria. The chemistry of the environment also involves equilibrium chemistry. As we will explore in Section 16.6, we can control the position of equilibrium—that is, we can make it possible for reactions to proceed almost all the way toward products or to reach a point at which mostly reactants exist. For example, we can select the conditions so that the greatest possible amount of ammonia is formed from hydrogen and nitrogen in the Haber process. We can also maximize the amount of sulfur trioxide that is formed from the reaction of sulfur dioxide with oxygen as part of the industrial-scale preparation of sulfuric acid. We can attempt to reduce the concentrations of acid in lakes and streams. We can learn about the impact of chlorofluorocarbons (CFCs) on stratospheric ozone levels. We can prepare pharmaceuticals to work in the most effective ways. We can analyze for the presence of an extraordinary variety of substances, from silver to steroids. We can do these things because we understand the fundamental ideas of equilibrium. Our ability to use equilibrium concepts to control the extent of chemical processes has the following vital implications:

Application

CHEMICAL ENCOUNTERS: Important Processes That Involve Equilibria

1. Economic implications via the trillions of dollars of manufactured products prepared and sold by the chemical industry.
2. Environmental implications for the quality of air, water, and land in the closed system that is Earth.
3. Personal implications for our health.

Achievement of chemical equilibrium occurs in living systems, chemical manufacturing, and the environment. Equilibrium figures in widely disparate processes related to the chemistry of blood, ammonia manufacture, steroid analysis, and lakes and waterways.

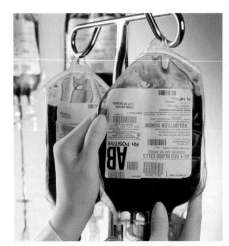

TABLE 16.1	Chemical Equilibrium Processes	
Category	**Process**	**Important Reaction**
Industrial	Contact process	$2SO_2(g) + O_2(g) \rightleftharpoons 2SO_3(g)$
Industrial	Haber process	$3H_2(g) + N_2(g) \rightleftharpoons 2NH_3(g)$
Biological	Myoglobin uptake of oxygen	$Mb(aq) + O_2(aq) \rightleftharpoons MbO_2(aq)$
Analytical	Chromatographic analysis	$A_{\text{mobile phase}} \rightleftharpoons A_{\text{stationary phase}}$
Analytical	Metal analysis with EDTA	$Ca^{2+} + EDTA^{4-} \rightleftharpoons CaEDTA^{2-}$
Environmental	Leaching of lead into water	$PbCO_3(s) + 2H^+(aq) \rightleftharpoons Pb^{2+}(aq) + CO_2(g) + H_2O(l)$

Table 16.1 lists some significant processes that involve chemical equilibria. Among them is chromatography, the subject of the accompanying boxed feature on equilibrium and chromatographic analysis.

16.3 The Meaning of the Equilibrium Constant

Application

CHEMICAL ENCOUNTERS: The Manufacture of Sulfuric Acid

More sulfuric acid (H_2SO_4) is produced in the United States than any other chemical; 37.5 billion kg were produced in 2004. Sulfuric acid has a wide range of uses, the most important being the production of agricultural fertilizers. Its industrial and agricultural importance makes examining the manufacture of sulfuric acid an excellent way to illustrate the meaning of the equilibrium constant.

Most of the sulfuric acid produced in the United States is made via the **Contact process**, which began to be used on an industrial scale in 1880. The process is a set of steps performed on readily available materials.

Step 1: The process begins with the sulfur provided by minerals such as iron pyrite (FeS_2) or hydrogen sulfide gas (H_2S). The sulfur combines with oxygen from the air.

$$S(s) + O_2(g) \rightleftharpoons SO_2(g)$$

Step 2: In this step, sulfur trioxide (SO_3) is generated by the oxidation of SO_2 produced in step 1.

$$2SO_2(g) + O_2(g) \rightleftharpoons 2SO_3(g)$$

Sulfur dioxide gas is passed over a catalyst bed containing 6–10% vanadium(V) oxide (V_2O_5) at 600°C and then at 400°C. *Temperature has a major effect on the equilibrium of this reaction, as we will see.*

Step 3: Sulfur trioxide (SO_3) is then combined with concentrated sulfuric acid and water to give *more* sulfuric acid in a net process that can be written as

$$SO_3(g) + H_2O(l) \rightleftharpoons H_2SO_4(aq)$$

Let's revisit step 2 of the contact process, the reaction of SO_2 and oxygen to make SO_3. The equilibrium constant, K, for this reaction at 27°C is 4.0×10^{24}. What does this value tell us about the relative amounts of reactants and products when the reaction reaches equilibrium? When the value for K is very large, the equilibrium lies essentially all the way to the products side. (When we say, "reactants and products side," we are always referring to these in terms of the forward reaction, written from left to right.) The reaction goes almost, but not fully, to completion. We can use a line chart, as shown to the right, to visualize the meaning of the equilibrium constant for this reaction by comparing the equilibrium position (E) to the starting position (S). We start with only reactants (R) and have no products (P). In practice, the contact process is not carried out at 27°C because it takes too long for this reaction to reach equilibrium at that temperature. In the chemical industry, time is money. To speed up the process, the temperature is raised, which lowers the equilibrium constant for this reaction. Unfortunately, for this and many other equilibria, *the extent of the reaction indicated by the equilibrium constant and the kinetics of the reaction (how fast it gets there), can force us into a compromise between reaction speed and reaction yield.* We will discuss the interplay of these variables and their effect on selecting reaction conditions in Section 16.6.

Every reaction has its own set of temperature-dependent values of K (which is also known as K_c when only concentrations are used to determine its value), the equilibrium constant. Our chapter-opening reaction of myoglobin with oxygen has $K = 8.6 \times 10^5$ at 20°C, which is fairly large. The opposite, a small equilibrium constant, is also possible. For example, an equation can be written that illustrates the formation of silver and chloride ions in a saturated solution of silver chloride (AgCl) from solid AgCl. Recall from Chapter 11 that a saturated solution is one in which no more solute will dissolve. The *small* equilibrium constant of 1.7×10^{-10} indicates that the *product* concentrations are quite small, $[Ag^+] = [Cl^-] = 1.3 \times 10^{-5} M$. This implies that very little silver chloride dissolves at 25°C before equilibrium (the saturated solution) is reached.

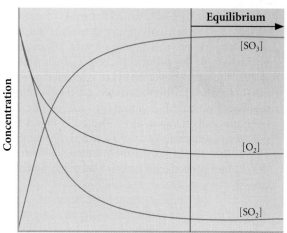

As the reaction proceeds, the concentration of product increases and the concentrations of reactants decrease. At some point, the concentrations of each component reach and maintain a constant value. This is the point when equilibrium is reached.

$$AgCl(s) \rightleftharpoons Ag^+(aq) + Cl^-(aq) \qquad K = 1.7 \times 10^{-10}$$

When the value for K is very small, the equilibrium lies nearly all the way to the reactants side. We can show this using our line chart. In this case, the equilibrium position is quite close to the silver chloride reactant, and we would say that silver chloride isn't very soluble in water.

How do we know?

Equilibrium and chromatographic analysis

If you were to take a vote among chemists as to the single most important technique for finding out what you have, and how much of it there is in a sample, the winner might well be **chromatography**, which was the subject of the boxed feature in Chapter 12. This technique has been used in many chemical analyses. For instance, the analysis of steroids and other banned substances in the urine of baseball players, football players, and Olympic athletes is done by separating out the chemicals via chromatography. As another example, the compounds that make up gasoline can be separated out and identified chromatographically. The technique has even been used to identify the gases on the planet Venus.

In a chromatograph, the components of a sample can be separated on the basis of how they distribute themselves between two chemical or physical phases. Figure 16.6 shows the essential parts of a gas chromatograph. The sample to be analyzed is injected into the instrument and pushed by an inert gas (in **gas chromatography**) or by a liquid (in liquid chromatography) into a long tube known as a column. The gas or liquid that pushes the sample moves, so it is called the **mobile phase**. The sample and the mobile phase pass through the column packed with a **stationary phase**, so called because it stays in place on the column.

On the ride through the column, all of the components of the sample (called the analytes) interact physically or chemically with the stationary phase. Here is where our study of equilibria comes in. The interaction of each analyte, "A," with the mobile and stationary phases can be described by the reversible reaction

$$A_{\text{mobile phase}} \rightleftharpoons A_{\text{stationary phase}}$$

The equilibrium constant (called a **distribution constant**, K_D) has the mass-action expression

$$K_D = \frac{[A_{\text{stationary phase}}]}{[A_{\text{mobile phase}}]}$$

If an analyte interacts considerably with the stationary phase, the concentration of the analyte in the stationary phase will be greater than its concentration in the mobile phase. Therefore, the value of K_D will be a number greater than 1. In such cases, the analytes will slow down and take more time to travel through the column. If the analytes do not interact well with the stationary phase, the value of K_D will be small, and the analytes will move quickly through the column. For a given set of conditions in the chromatograph, each analyte will have

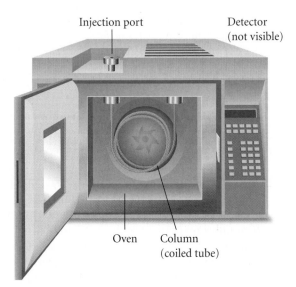

FIGURE 16.6

The essential parts of a gas chromatograph. There is an inlet connected to a column into which the sample is fed. The sample is then pushed through the column by a carrier gas such as helium (in gas chromatography) or by a liquid, often an aqueous solution (in liquid chromatography). This phase moves, so it is called the mobile phase. It passes through the column containing a stationary phase, so called because it stays in place on the column.

its own distribution constant (K_D) and will exit the column at a different time.

Figure 16.7 shows chromatograms of the compounds in refinery gas processed by a petroleum company, as well as the important compounds in a sample of caffeine and some "street drugs." The components in a sample from an athlete or a refinery can be identified by using chromatography. However, the method has even more uses. For instance, chromatography is often one of the first steps in many very sophisticated analyses. Once the analytes are separated in a chromatography instrument, they can immediately be fed into other instruments, such as a mass spectrometer or infrared spectrometer, to confirm their identity. In some cases, the information from the other instruments is used to determine the identity of an unknown component in a mixture. (Figure 16.8 shows two of the more important multistep analyses, which are commonly referred to as hyphenated techniques.) For this reason, chemical equilibrium, the basis of chromatography, is often the most important process in a multistep instrumental analysis.

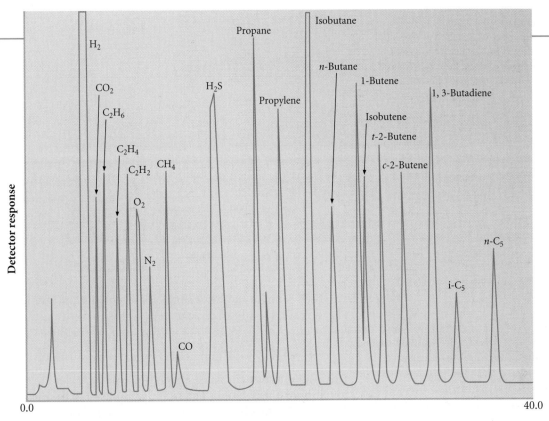

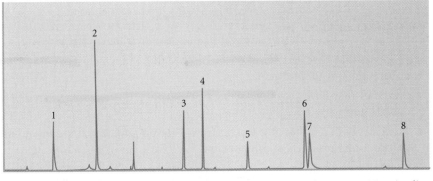

FIGURE 16.7

Chromatograms of compounds in refinery gas (top) and common drugs (left) show the importance of chromatography as a separation technique.

1 Methamphetamine   3 Amobarbital   5 Procaine   7 Nortriptyline
2 Nicotine   4 Caffeine   6 Cocaine   8 Heroin

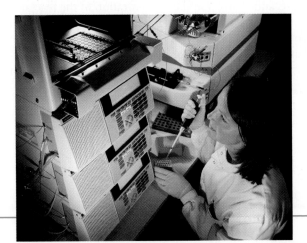

FIGURE 16.8

Multistep analyses are commonly referred to as hyphenated techniques. They include techniques such as GC-MS (gas chromatography–mass spectrometry) and LC-NMR (liquid chromatography–nuclear magnetic resonance) (see photo). These techniques are used to separate, identify, and quantitate the solutes within a solution.

The value of the equilibrium constant for the ionization of sulfurous acid (H_2SO_3) indicates that a significant amount of un-ionized reactant remains at equilibrium. Note, as well, that when equilibrium is finally reached, the concentrations of each component in the reaction become constant.

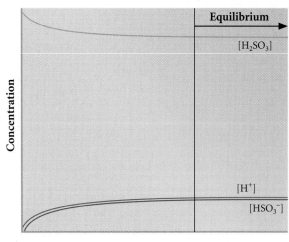

Let's examine another example of an equilibrium constant. The ionization of sulfurous acid (H_2SO_3) to form hydrogen ions and bisulfite ions (HSO_3^-) has a value for K of 0.0120 at 25°C.

$$H_2SO_3(aq) \rightleftharpoons H^+(aq) + HSO_3^-(aq) \qquad K = 0.0120$$

This is an intermediate value; that is, K is relatively close to 1. At equilibrium, there remain significant amounts of both reactants and products. When the value for K is close to 1, the equilibrium lies somewhere between the reactants and products sides. Again, our line chart helps us see the equilibrium position.

HERE'S WHAT WE KNOW SO FAR

- Processes that have very large values of K are those in which mostly products are present at equilibrium.
- Processes that have very small values of K have mostly reactants present at equilibrium.
- Processes with K values not too far from 1 have significant amounts of both reactants and products at equilibrium.

The meaning of the equilibrium constant is shown graphically in Figure 16.9. As we continue to build our understanding of equilibria, we will learn that the equilibrium position for a reaction is related to the equilibrium constant as well as to the temperature, the pressure, and changes in the concentration of the reactants and products. As we explore these relationships, our goal is not only to interpret the meaning of K but also to understand how we can manipulate our reaction conditions to produce what we want (products or reactants) under the best possible conditions. In industrial-scale manufacturing, such as the production of sulfuric acid, these "best possible conditions" can include chemical, environmental, *and* economic factors.

FIGURE 16.9

The relative equilibrium points of typical reactions based on their equilibrium constants. High values of K favor product formation. Small values of K favor the reactants side. Intermediate values favor a middle-of-the-road position.

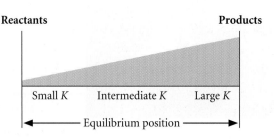

EXERCISE 16.4   Interpreting K

One of the most important chemicals in the toolbox of analytical chemists has the chemical name ethylenediaminetetraacetic acid, or, more simply, EDTA. A chemist would like to determine the concentration of several metal ions, including Co^{2+}, Zn^{2+}, Ni^{2+}, and Ca^{2+}, in a solution by titrating them (recall titrations from Section 4.3) with the ionic form of EDTA known as $EDTA^{4-}$ (shown below). The values of K for the reaction of the metal ion with $EDTA^{4-}$ are listed next to each cation. Judging solely on the basis of these values, and assuming the equilibrium is established very quickly, would EDTA be a reasonable choice to react almost completely with each of these metal ions?

Application

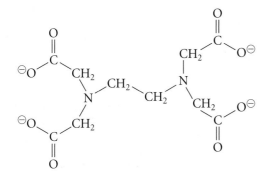

Ethylenediaminetetraacetate

(sample reaction) $Ca^{2+}(aq) + EDTA^{4-}(aq) \rightleftharpoons CaEDTA^{2-}(aq)$

Element	Cation	K
cobalt	Co^{2+}	2×10^{16}
zinc	Zn^{2+}	3×10^{16}
nickel	Ni^{2+}	4×10^{18}
calcium	Ca^{2+}	5×10^{10}

First Thoughts

What does a large value of the equilibrium constant mean? Recall our discussion in the text, where we noted that if K is very large, the equilibrium lies essentially all the way to the products side. This means that looking only at the value for K (and ignoring how quickly or slowly the reactions might occur) suggests that the reactions will be essentially complete.

Solution

Because each of the equilibrium constants are considerably larger than 1, $EDTA^{4-}$ will react essentially completely with these metals.

Further Insights

EDTA is a remarkable analytical reagent because of its ability to react with nearly every metal ion. Examples of its uses include determining water "hardness" by titrating to find the concentrations of calcium and magnesium in water, and determining the composition of metal alloys and metals in pharmaceuticals.

PRACTICE 16.4

Which of these reactions provide(s) mostly products? . . . mostly reactants?

a. $NH_4^+(aq) + H_2O(l) \rightleftharpoons NH_3(aq) + H_3O^+(aq)$ $K = 5.6 \times 10^{-10}$

b. $HF(aq) + H_2O(l) \rightleftharpoons H_3O^+(aq) + F^-(aq)$ $K = 7.2 \times 10^{-4}$

c. $HOCl(aq) + H_2O(l) \rightleftharpoons H_3O^+(aq) + OCl^-(aq)$ $K = 3.5 \times 10^{-8}$

d. $HClO_4(aq) + H_2O(l) \rightleftharpoons H_3O^+(aq) + ClO_4^-(aq)$ $K = 1.0 \times 10^7$

See Problems 25 and 26.

Homogeneous and Heterogeneous Equilibria

Let's look again at the reaction of the calcium and EDTA ions in the previous exercise. Compare that to the dissolution of silver chloride, as well as the Haber process for the combination of H_2 and N_2 to produce ammonia (NH_3), the focus of Exercise 16.2.

$$Ca^{2+}(aq) + EDTA^{4-}(aq) \rightleftharpoons CaEDTA^{2-}(aq)$$

$$3H_2(g) + N_2(g) \rightleftharpoons 2NH_3(g)$$

$$AgCl(s) \rightleftharpoons Ag^+(aq) + Cl^-(aq)$$

Note the phases of each substance. In the EDTA titration of calcium ion, the reactants and products are all in the aqueous phase. When all of the phases are the same in a reaction, we say that the reaction establishes a homogeneous equilibrium. The formation of ammonia is another example of homogeneous equilibrium because all of the substances are gases. On the other hand, the dissolution of silver chloride in water begins with a solid and forms ions in the aqueous phase. When there are different phases present in the reaction, we have a heterogeneous equilibrium.

The mass-action expressions for homogeneous and heterogeneous equilibria differ in one vital aspect, which we can examine by focusing on the formation of a saturated solution of silver chloride. The density of solid AgCl is 5.56 g/cm³. We can think of density as a measure of the concentration, because it is the amount of substance per unit volume. Density is independent of the quantity of substance; therefore, the *concentration of pure AgCl is the same whether we have 10 g or 100 tons*. Constants, such as the concentration of any pure solid or liquid, are said to be part of the equilibrium constant and are not included in the mass-action expression. This is a general result that is valid for pure solids and pure liquids and is approximately correct for solvents such as water, but only when the solutes are very dilute. This means that for the dissolution of silver chloride, our original mass-action expression,

$$K = \frac{[Ag^+][Cl^-]}{[AgCl]}$$

can be simplified by recognizing that AgCl is a solid:

$$K = [Ag^+][Cl^-]$$

We can apply this same reasoning to derive the mass-action expression for one step in the large-scale cleanup of sulfur dioxide emitted from industrial smokestacks. In this process, SO_2 is converted to solid $CaSO_4$.

$$2CaO(s) + 2SO_2(g) + O_2(g) \rightleftharpoons 2CaSO_4(s)$$

$$K = \frac{1}{[SO_2]^2[O_2]}$$

16.4 Working with Equilibrium Constants

In this section, we begin to learn how we can work with reactions, mass-action expressions, and equilibrium constants. This is the next step in learning how to control experimental conditions *by using equilibria to achieve desired chemical outcomes*. As with our previous section, we begin by looking at the reaction of sulfur dioxide and oxygen.

The mass-action expressions for the known reactions are

$$K_1 = \frac{[CH_3COO^-][H_3O^+]}{[CH_3COOH]} \qquad K_2 = \frac{1}{[H_3O^+][OH^-]}$$

If we multiply the two known mass-action expressions, we get

$$\frac{[CH_3COO^-][H_3O^+]}{[CH_3COOH]} \times \frac{1}{[H_3O^+][OH^-]} = \frac{[CH_3COO^-][H_3O^+]}{[CH_3COOH][H_3O^+][OH^-]} =$$

$$K_1 K_2 = \frac{[CH_3COO^-]}{[CH_3COOH][OH^-]}$$

This is the mass-action expression for the titration reaction! For this process, then,

$$K_{\text{titration}} = K_1 K_2 = (1.8 \times 10^{-5})(1.0 \times 10^{14}) = 1.8 \times 10^9$$

In short, when the overall reaction is the *sum* of other reactions, the overall equilibrium constant is the *product* of the equilibrium constants for these other reactions. In the case of the titration of acetic acid with sodium hydroxide, $K_{\text{titration}}$ is sufficiently large (and the reaction is quite fast). Therefore, the titration of acetic acid with sodium hydroxide should (and does!) work well.

Calculating Equilibrium Concentrations from K and Other Concentrations

We know from our previous discussion that it is possible to calculate the equilibrium constant by substituting equilibrium concentrations of reactants and products into the mass-action expression. We have one equation, the mass-action expression, and one unknown, K. In your day-to-day work as a chemist, biologist, medical technologist, or soil scientist, the more likely scenario is that the value of K is already known and you will need to calculate the equilibrium concentration of one or more of the reactants or products.

Let's use the Contact process to show how this is done for one unknown concentration when the other equilibrium concentrations and K are known. At 27°C, $K = 4.0 \times 10^{24}$ for the reaction

$$2SO_2(g) + O_2(g) \rightleftharpoons 2SO_3(g)$$

If the equilibrium concentrations of SO_2 and O_2 are 6.4×10^{-12} M and 1.2×10^{-3} M, respectively, what is the equilibrium concentration of SO_3? We have one equation with one unknown, so we can solve for $[SO_3]$.

$$K = \frac{[SO_3]^2}{[SO_2]^2[O_2]}$$

$$4.0 \times 10^{24} = \frac{[SO_3]^2}{[6.4 \times 10^{-12}]^2[1.2 \times 10^{-3}]}$$

$$[SO_3]^2 = 4.0 \times 10^{24} \, (6.4 \times 10^{-12})^2 \, (1.2 \times 10^{-3})$$

$$[SO_3] = \sqrt{0.197} = 0.443 \approx 0.44 \ M$$

Does our answer make sense? We ought to check our math, and we can do so by substituting the values back into the mass-action expression to verify the value of the equilibrium constant.

$$\frac{[SO_3]^2}{[SO_2]^2[O_2]} = \frac{[0.443]^2}{[6.4 \times 10^{-12}]^2[1.2 \times 10^{-3}]} = 4.0 \times 10^{24}$$

We can make such substitutions because the reaction is *at equilibrium*. When this is not the case, a different way of thinking, the subject of Section 16.5, will prove useful.

Using Partial Pressures

Most of the equilibrium constants that chemists employ are derived using concentrations measured in molarity because much of the chemistry we do is in solution. However, when working with gases, we can use partial pressures in units of atmospheres. **What is the relationship between the pressure of a gas and its concentration?** We can use the ideal gas equation, which holds well for gases in low concentration (see Chapter 10).

$$PV = nRT$$

$$\text{Concentration} = \frac{\text{moles}}{\text{volume}} = \frac{n}{V} = \frac{P}{RT}$$

The mass-action expression for the reaction of oxygen with sulfur dioxide can be written using molarity, as usual, or by substituting the equivalent variables from the ideal gas law $\left(\frac{P}{RT}\right)$ in place of the concentration.

$$2SO_2(g) + O_2(g) \rightleftharpoons 2SO_3(g)$$

$$K = \frac{[SO_3]^2}{[SO_2]^2[O_2]} = \frac{\frac{P_{SO_3}^2}{(RT)^2}}{\frac{P_{SO_2}^2}{(RT)^2} \times \frac{P_{O_2}}{RT}}$$

We can combine all of the RT terms and put them on the side with the pressure-based mass-action expression.

$$K = \frac{P_{SO_3}^2}{P_{SO_2}^2 \, P_{O_2}} \, (RT)^1$$

where K = the mass-action expression solved using only molar concentrations
P = the pressure in atmospheres
T = the temperature in kelvins
R = the universal gas constant

If we set K_p equal to the pressure-based mass-action expression and rearrange the equation, we get

$$K_p = \frac{P_{SO_3}^2}{P_{SO_2}^2 \, P_{O_2}}$$

$$K = K_p \, (RT)^1$$

We have introduced a new equilibrium constant, K_p, which is based on the mass-action expression for the partial pressures of substances in the reaction. K_p is often calculated with partial pressures, P, in units of atmospheres. However, remember that the actual definition of K involves the use of activities. Therefore, in the end, K_p has no units. As a matter of nomenclature, we use K_p when dealing with partial pressures and K (or, in some literature, K_c) when dealing with concentrations. *Note in this equation that the value of the exponent of RT indicates the difference in the number of moles of gas between reactants and products.* In general, then, we can write the relationship between K and K_p in two ways:

$$K_p = K(RT)^{\Delta n} \qquad \text{or} \qquad K = K_p(RT)^{-\Delta n}$$

where Δn = the change in the number of moles of gas (products minus reactants)
R = 0.08206 L·atm·mol^{-1}·K^{-1}
T = temperature in kelvins

In the reaction of sulfur dioxide with oxygen, there is one fewer mole of gaseous products ($2SO_3$) than of reactants ($2SO_2$ and O_2), so the change in the number of moles of gas from reactant to product, Δn, is equal to -1. We can relate K to K_p in two ways, depending on which equilibrium constant we are given.

$$K_p = K(RT)^{-1} \quad \text{or} \quad K = K_p(RT)^1$$

At 673 K and 1 atm total system pressure, the value of K_p for the oxidation of SO_2 to SO_3 is 1.58×10^5, measured using the equilibrium partial pressure of each gas. We can calculate K using this information.

$$K = K_p(RT)^{-\Delta n}$$

$$K = (1.58 \times 10^5)(0.08206 \text{ L·atm·mol}^{-1}\text{·K}^{-1} \times 673 \text{ K})^{-(-1)} = 8.73 \times 10^6$$

EXERCISE 16.6 **Converting K to K_p**

Calculate K_p for the production of ammonia via the Haber process.

$$3H_2(g) + N_2(g) \rightleftharpoons 2NH_3(g) \qquad K = 0.060 \text{ (at 500°C)}$$

Solution

We lose 2 mol of gas going from reactants to products, so $\Delta n = -2$.

$$K_p = K(RT)^{\Delta n}$$

$$K_p = 0.060 \ (0.08206 \text{ L·atm·mol}^{-1}\text{·K}^{-1} \times 773 \text{ K})^{-2}$$

$$K_p = 0.060 \ (62.43)^{-2}$$

$$K_p = 1.5 \times 10^{-5}$$

PRACTICE 16.6

Calculate the value of K_p at 25°C for the reaction of chlorine and carbon monoxide.

$$CO(g) + Cl_2(g) \rightleftharpoons COCl_2(g) \qquad K = 3.7 \times 10^9 \text{ (at 25°C)}$$

See Problems 41 and 42.

16.5 Solving Equilibrium Problems— A Different Way of Thinking

The world is not at equilibrium. Its shifts are seen and felt in the massive upheavals of earthquakes, volcanoes, and hurricanes and in the smallest electronic interactions of atoms. Life itself is a process in which reversible reactions within us keep shifting their equilibrium positions, always chasing a moving target, in ways that make our survival possible. If one aspect of being human is our ability to understand our world, then one expression of this understanding is *the ability to manipulate our starting reaction conditions to control the position of equilibrium.* We cannot stop earthquakes, but we can reliably make ammonia, sulfuric acid, and a whole host of other chemicals. We can examine the complex interactions of carbon with the environment. We can understand the interaction of myoglobin and oxygen. We can pick the best conditions for chemical analyses. All these things are based on knowing how the conditions change from the starting point to equilibrium. How can we do this? We must first develop a different way of thinking.

This way of thinking is based on two questions: **"Given the chemical and physical conditions, how do I judge what is likely to happen?"** and **How can I use my** understanding to change these conditions to obtain the outcome I want?" Here are some judgments we must make when we combine substances:

1 What chemical reactions will occur?

2 Which among these are important? Which are unimportant?

3 Given the initial concentrations of substances, in which direction (toward the formation of more reactants or toward the formation of more products) is the reaction likely to proceed?

4 How can we solve for the amounts of substances of interest that are present at equilibrium?

5 How can we manipulate the conditions to maximize the concentration of the desired components and minimize that of the others?

A Case Study

We discussed the analysis of acetic acid (CH_3COOH) previously. Here, we will look at the equilibrium established when an acetic acid solution is prepared with an initial concentration of 0.500 M. Remember the overarching question: **"Given the chemical and physical conditions, how do I judge what is likely to happen?"** Specifically, what are the concentrations of all the substances in my flask at equilibrium? Let's approach this by answering the other questions, in order.

1 What chemical reactions will occur?

One reaction is the ionization of the acid as shown in reaction A, and this will supply CH_3COO^- and H^+. Another reaction that always occurs in aqueous solution is the ionization of water itself, also supplying H^+, as shown in reaction B.

A: $CH_3COOH(aq) \rightleftharpoons CH_3COO^-(aq) + H^+(aq)$ $K = 1.8 \times 10^{-5}$

B: $H_2O(l) \rightleftharpoons H^+(aq) + OH^-(aq)$ $K = 1.0 \times 10^{-14}$

2 Which among these are important? Which are unimportant?

The "important chemistry" is that which affects the outcome of the overall process. The unimportant chemistry (in this context) is that which has no significant bearing on the outcome. The extent of the reactions and their relative importance to us are indicated by their equilibrium constants. Even though neither reaction proceeds very far, the ionization of acetic acid is far more significant than the ionization of water (we will test this assertion later.) We can make this claim because the value of K for equation A is about 10^8 times larger than the value of K for equation B. The mass-action expression for the ionization of acetic acid (equation A) is

$$K = \frac{[CH_3COO^-][H^+]}{[CH_3COOH]} = 1.8 \times 10^{-5}$$

In many systems, it is entirely possible that more than one reaction is important to our calculations. However, in this chapter, we will typically deal with one important reaction in each process that we discuss.

3 Given the initial concentrations of substances, in which direction is the reaction likely to proceed?

We can predict the direction of change in a reaction by using the **reaction quotient** (Q), which we introduced in Section 14.6. This is the numerical outcome of the mass-action expression using *initial concentrations*, which are designated [ ]$_0$.

$$Q = \frac{[CH_3COO^-]_0[H^+]_0}{[CH_3COOH]_0}$$

Q is then compared to the equilibrium constant, K, in order to determine the direction in which the reaction will proceed. Keep in mind that Q deals with *initial conditions* and K deals with *equilibrium conditions*. Calculation of the reaction quotient indicates which way the reaction will proceed in order to establish equilibrium.

- If Q is equal to K, the system is *at equilibrium*.

- If Q is greater than K, there is too much product present. The system will *shift to the left* to reach equilibrium. Mathematically, the numerator is much larger, and the denominator much smaller, than the equilibrium values.

- If Q is less than K, there is too much reactant present. The system will *shift to the right* to reach equilibrium.

In our current example, the reaction must go toward formation of products ("to the right") because we initially have no products ($Q = 0$), and this will be the case in many equilibrium problems you will encounter.

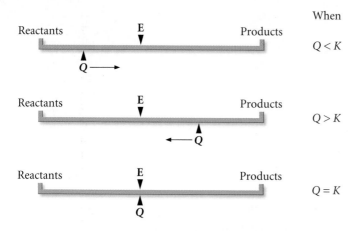

If we were to change the initial concentration of our substances, such that $[H^+]_0 = 0.0100$ M, $[CH_3COO^-]_0 = 0.200$ M and $[CH_3COOH]_0 = 0.150$ M, we could calculate Q for these initial concentrations.

$$Q = \frac{[CH_3COO^-]_0[H^+]_0}{[CH_3COOH]_0} = \frac{(0.200\ M)(0.0100\ M)}{(0.150\ M)} = 0.0133$$

What does this value tell us? Q is much greater than K (1.8×10^{-5}), so the reaction will shift toward the formation of reactants ("to the left"). Mathematically, this makes sense, because reducing the product concentration and increasing the reactant concentration will reduce the quotient of the mass-action expression. What does this indicate about the chemistry? If chemical change is an inevitable part of our world, it is especially useful to be able to control that chemical change in order to have a desirable impact on manufacturing, human biology, and the environment.

EXERCISE 16.7	Predicting the Direction of Equilibrium

Predict the direction in which the reaction of myoglobin and oxygen will proceed to reach equilibrium for each set of conditions.

$$Mb + O_2 \rightleftharpoons MbO_2 \qquad K = 8.6 \times 10^5$$

a. $Q = 1500$

b. $Q = 8.3 \times 10^6$

c. $[Mb]_0 = 2.04 \times 10^{-4}\ M$; $[O_2]_0 = 3.00 \times 10^{-6}\ M$; $[MbO_2]_0 = 2.50 \times 10^{-4}\ M$

d. $[Mb]_0 = 5.00 \times 10^{-5}\ M$; $[O_2]_0 = 9.21 \times 10^{-7}\ M$; $[MbO_2]_0 = 1.00 \times 10^{-4}\ M$

e. $[Mb]_0 = 1.0 \times 10^{-4}\ M$; $[O_2]_0 = 2.25 \times 10^{-6}\ M$; $[MbO_2]_0 = 1.94 \times 10^{-4}\ M$

First Thoughts

Keep in mind the significance of the reaction quotient, Q. It helps us see in which direction the reaction will go to reach equilibrium. When the value for K is small, it is true that the equilibrium position will favor the reactants. However, if you started off with *no* products at all, even such a reaction will move (slightly) to the right to form a little product. We can show this graphically:

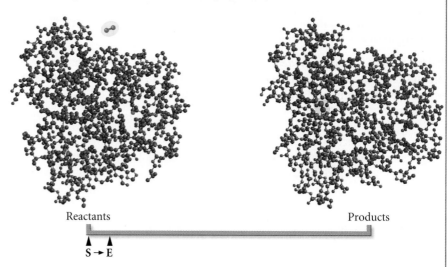

Reactants   Products

S → E

Solution

a. $Q < K$, so the reaction will form more products and shift to the right.

b. $Q > K$, so the reaction will form more reactants and shift to the left.

c. $Q = \dfrac{[MbO_2]_0}{[Mb]_0[O_2]_0} = \dfrac{[2.50 \times 10^{-4}]}{[2.04 \times 10^{-4}][3.00 \times 10^{-6}]} = 4.08 \times 10^5$

   $Q < K$, so the reaction will form more products and shift to the right.

d. $Q = \dfrac{[1.00 \times 10^{-4}]}{[5.00 \times 10^{-5}][9.21 \times 10^{-7}]} = 2.17 \times 10^6$

   $Q > K$, so the reaction will form more reactants and shift to the left.

e. $Q = \dfrac{[1.94 \times 10^{-4}]}{[1.0 \times 10^{-4}][2.25 \times 10^{-6}]} = 8.6 \times 10^5$

   $Q = K$, so the reaction is at equilibrium.

Further Insights

Food for thought: How might these shifts in the direction of the reaction toward equilibrium allow the muscles in the body to obtain needed oxygen during vigorous exercise?

PRACTICE 16.7

Under certain specific conditions, the formation of ozone from NO_2 has an equilibrium constant $K = 120$. Predict the direction of the following reaction, given the conditions in each case below.

$$NO_2(g) + O_2(g) \rightleftharpoons NO(g) + O_3(g) \qquad K = 120$$

a. $Q = 1.5 \times 10^5$

b. $[O_3] = 1.0\ M;\ [O_2] = 1.0\ M;\ [NO] = 0.50\ M;\ [NO_2] = 0.25\ M$

c. $[O_3] = 0.0010\ M;\ [O_2] = 2.55\ M;\ [NO] = 1.78 \times 10^{-6}\ M;\ [NO_2] = 5.4 \times 10^{-3}\ M$

d. $[O_3] = 0.033\ M;\ [O_2] = 0.019\ M;\ [NO] = 9.3\ M;\ [NO_2] = 0.044\ M$

See Problems 45–48. ■

4 How can we solve for the amounts of substances of interest that are present at equilibrium?

The present case study concerns a small value of K. After this, we will look at large and then intermediate values of K.

Small Value of K

We have a system that contains $0.500\ M\ CH_3COOH$, which ionizes with the relatively small K of 1.8×10^{-5}. What will be the equilibrium concentrations of acetate ions (CH_3COO^-) and hydrogen ions (H^+)?

$$CH_3COOH(aq) \rightleftharpoons CH_3COO^-(aq) + H^+(aq) \qquad K = 1.8 \times 10^{-5}$$

The lack of products initially present, along with the small equilibrium constant, suggests that the reaction will proceed to the right, but not very far. Our view of where we start and where we end looks something like this on our equilibrium line chart:

Tracking the changes that take place as we go from the start to equilibrium requires a bit of bookkeeping. Bookkeepers keep track of a company's finances using tables that show changes in financial data in an organized, clear way. We will do the same thing for our equilibrium data by setting up a table that contains the following rows:

Initial row: The "initial" row includes the initial concentration of each species.

$$CH_3COOH(aq) \rightleftharpoons CH_3COO^-(aq) + H^+(aq)$$

▶ initial	$0.500\ M$	$0\ M$	$0\ M$

Change row: The "change" row describes the change in concentration of each species that occurs in order to reach equilibrium. This must take into account the stoichiometric ratios among reactants and products in the reaction (all 1-to-1 in this example) and the magnitude of the equilibrium constant, which in this case is small enough to indicate that the reaction will not go very far before equilibrium is reached. Because we don't yet know the amount of acetic acid that will ionize, we call it "x." The concentration of acetic acid will *decrease* by "x" M, and the acetate and hydrogen ion concentrations will *increase* by "x" M. Again, the stoichiometry of the equation is included in this line of the table.

$$CH_3COOH(aq) \rightleftharpoons CH_3COO^-(aq) + H^+(aq)$$

initial	$0.500\ M$	$0\ M$	$0\ M$
▶ change	$-x$	$+x$	$+x$

Equilibrium row: When the free energy *change* of the reaction equals zero, such that the free energy itself is at a minimum, the reaction will be at equilibrium. The value for each substance in the "equilibrium" row equals the initial amount plus the change (so that $0.500 + \text{"}-x\text{"} = 0.500 - x$). This is sufficient for us to proceed with the problem, especially via programmable calculators, which can solve the necessary equations with a few keystrokes.

$$CH_3COOH(aq) \rightleftharpoons CH_3COO^-(aq) + H^+(aq)$$

initial	0.500 M	0 M	0 M
change	$-x$	$+x$	$+x$
▶ equilibrium	$0.500 - x$	$+x$	$+x$

Assumptions row: Whether or not we have a programmable calculator, we can get a deeper understanding of the equilibria in solution by making key assumptions. We can simplify the problem solving by assuming that because the value for K is small, the value of "x" will also be small—that is, there is negligible ionization compared to our initial acetic acid concentration. We'll assume that it will be so small as to be unimportant *compared to the initial concentration of 0.500 M.* Making that assumption enables us to say that $0.500 - x \approx 0.500$. However, because "x" is *not* unimportant compared to 0 M (any quantity is infinitely large compared to zero!), we cannot neglect "x" in the other columns of the table. The "assumptions" row shows the final equilibrium amounts with any assumptions we make.

$$CH_3COOH(aq) \rightleftharpoons CH_3COO^-(aq) + H^+(aq)$$

initial	0.500 M	0 M	0 M
change	$-x$	$+x$	$+x$
equilibrium	$0.500 - x$	$+x$	$+x$
▶ assumptions	0.500	x	x

The table that we have worked with is an expanded version of what is often called an ICE table, which stands for Initial, Change, Equilibrium table. Our expanded version includes the Assumptions row, so we will call this an ICEA table. We will often use ICEA tables in our equilibrium problem solving because they give us an organized way to assess the changes in concentration that occur in our reactions.

We can now substitute the equilibrium concentrations generated in the assumptions row of our table into the mass-action expression and solve for "x."

$$K = \frac{[CH_3COO^-][H^+]}{[CH_3COOH]}$$

$$1.8 \times 10^{-5} = \frac{(x)(x)}{0.500}$$

$$1.8 \times 10^{-5} = \frac{x^2}{0.500}$$

$$9.0 \times 10^{-6} = x^2$$

$$3.0 \times 10^{-3} = x$$

Now, if we return the value of "x" to our ICEA table and solve for the assumptions row, we obtain the equilibrium concentrations of all species in the reaction, assuming our assumption is justified.

$$x = [CH_3COO^-] = [H^+] = 3.0 \times 10^{-3} \, M$$

The actual equilibrium concentration of acetic acid is $0.500 - 3.0 \times 10^{-3} = 0.497 \, M$, or $0.50 \, M$ to two significant figures. **Do our results make sense? That is, are they reasonable?** We can determine that our results are mathematically correct by substituting the concentration values back into the equilibrium expression to show that this results in K.

$$\frac{(3.0 \times 10^{-3})^2}{0.50} = 1.8 \times 10^{-5}$$

Was our assumption justified? In other words, was "x" negligible compared to the original acetic acid concentration? We say that our assumption is valid if the change as a result of the assumption is less than 5% of the original concentration.

$$\frac{x}{\text{original concentration}} \times 100\% \leq 5\%$$

Although we will use this "5% rule" in our work, professional chemists sometimes require a smaller tolerance, and sometimes a larger, depending on the process with which they are working. With our data,

$$\frac{3.0 \times 10^{-3}}{0.500} \times 100\% = 0.6\%$$

and using the 5% rule, we find that our assumption of negligible ionization (0.6%, in this case) was valid.

Let's revisit our equilibrium line chart and see what 0.6% ionization means in terms of the extent of the reaction.

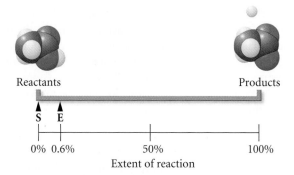

This confirms our initial thinking that with the very small value for K, the reaction would not proceed—acetic acid would not ionize—appreciably.

To be sure our calculations are valid, we should also test our other assumption, that the ionization of water is unimportant. This is a more complex issue that we will consider in Chapter 17.

$$H_2O \rightleftharpoons H^+ + OH^- \qquad K = 1.0 \times 10^{-14}$$

EXERCISE 16.8   **Concentration of Lead Ion in Saturated Lead Bromide**

Determine the concentration of lead ion in a saturated solution that would result from the dissolution of solid lead(II) bromide, $PbBr_2(s)$.

$$PbBr_2(s) \rightleftharpoons Pb^{2+}(aq) + 2Br^-(aq) \qquad K = 4.6 \times 10^{-6} \text{ at } 25°C$$

First Thoughts

What is the important chemistry that occurs in solution? The only important chemistry of interest is the dissolution of the lead bromide, which is a largely insoluble salt, judging by the small value of K. In which direction will the reaction proceed? Even though the equilibrium constant is quite small, the reaction will proceed (minimally) to the products side because there were no products present initially.

Reactants   Products

$S \rightarrow E$

Our equilibrium line chart is similar to that for the dissociation of acetic acid. What are the equilibrium concentrations of substances? We can use the same style of table as we did with the acetic acid dissociation. Our only modification arises because lead bromide is a pure solid, so it is not part of the equilibrium expression. We show this in the ICEA table below.

$$PbBr_2(s) \rightleftharpoons Pb^{2+}(aq) + 2Br^-(aq)$$

	$PbBr_2(s)$	$Pb^{2+}(aq)$	$2Br^-(aq)$
initial	—	$0\ M$	$0\ M$
change	—	$+x$	$+2x$
equilibrium	—	x	$2x$

The concentration of the solid reactant is constant. In this table, "x" represents the amount of $PbBr_2(s)$ that dissolves. This value is therefore equal to the solubility of the salt. Because the initial amount of each product was $0\ M$, the amount gained, "x" and "$2x$," is not negligible compared to $0\ M$; therefore, we made no assumptions. Note that we use "$2x$" to represent the change in $[Br^-]$ because bromide has a stoichiometric factor of 2 in the equation. This stoichiometric factor will also come in to play when we write the mass-action expression.

Solution

How can we solve for the amounts of substances of interest that are present at equilibrium? We can substitute our concentrations into the mass-action expression for the equation:

$$K = [Pb^{2+}][Br^-]^2$$

$$4.6 \times 10^{-6} = (x)(2x)^2$$

$$4.6 \times 10^{-6} = 4x^3$$

$$[Pb^{2+}] = x = 1.048 \times 10^{-2}\ M \approx 1.0 \times 10^{-2}\ M$$

$$[Br^-] = 2x = 2.096 \times 10^{-2}\ M \approx 2.1 \times 10^{-2}\ M$$

We check our answer by solving for K.

$$K = (1.048 \times 10^{-2}) \times (2.096 \times 10^{-2})^2 = 4.6 \times 10^{-6}$$

This agrees well with the actual value of K.

Further Insights

Do our results make sense? The concentrations for the ions that we calculated are quite low, and that makes sense, given the very low value for K.

PRACTICE 16.8

What is the concentration of lead ion in a saturated solution of $PbCl_2$?

$$PbCl_2(s) \rightleftharpoons Pb^{2+}(aq) + 2Cl^-(aq) \qquad K = 1.6 \times 10^{-5} \text{ at } 25°C$$

See Problems 49, 50, 55, 56, and 60.

In Exercise 16.8, only one important equilibrium needed to be considered. As our understanding of equilibrium deepens, we will find that more than one reaction may well be important. For example, although it wasn't illustrated, the chemical interaction of Pb^{2+} and Br^- with water were considered. In both of these cases, the interaction is minimal, so the dissolution of $PbBr_2$ was the only equilibrium of importance. However, if instead of $PbBr_2$ we had attempted to calculate the concentration of lead ion from the dissolution of PbS, the reaction of S^{2-} with water would have been very important, as illustrated by the equilibria below. In this case, both equations would need to be considered.

$$PbS(s) \rightleftharpoons Pb^{2+}(aq) + S^{2-}(aq) \qquad K = 7 \times 10^{-29}$$

$$S^{2-}(aq) + H_2O(l) \rightleftharpoons HS^- + OH^- \qquad K = 0.083$$

Including the formation of HS^- in our calculations would modify the solubility of lead(II) sulfide. We will learn how to deal quantitatively with multiple equilibria in Chapter 18.

Large Value of K

The reaction of sulfur dioxide and oxygen to form sulfur trioxide at 400°C serves as an excellent model with which to examine systems that have large equilibrium constants, in which the reaction is essentially complete.

$$2SO_2(g) + O_2(g) \rightleftharpoons 2SO_3(g) \qquad K = 8.7 \times 10^6$$

If the initial concentrations of SO_2 and O_2 are 1.0×10^{-3} *M* and 2.0×10^{-3} *M*, respectively, what is the equilibrium concentration of SO_3? Given the large equilibrium constant, we can assume that the reaction goes to completion, except for a small amount, "2x," that remains unreacted. Remember that the "2x" indicates the stoichiometry of the reaction. An equilibrium line chart can help us visualize the extent of reaction.

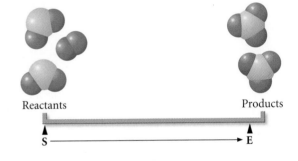

Reactants   Products

This is, in effect, a limiting reactant problem in which SO_2 is the limiting reactant. On the basis of the reaction stoichiometry and the large value of K, we can develop an ICEA table. We complete the first row of the table by writing the initial concentration of each species in the reaction.

	$2SO_2(g)$	$+$	$O_2(g)$	$\rightleftharpoons$	$2SO_3(g)$
initial	1.0×10^{-3} *M*		2.0×10^{-3} *M*		0 *M*

The "change" row in our ICEA table will be a little different than before. We have said that the equilibrium constant is large, and this means the reaction will go essentially to completion. However, *we must hold a tiny amount of each reactant back because the reaction will not go all the way to products.* Let's indicate the small amount that remains behind as "2x" for SO_2 and "x" for O_2. That is the "+2x" and "+x" that we place in the respective concentrations in the change row. *Other than those small amounts that remain, all of the SO_2 that can react will do so.* That means, based on the reaction stoichiometry, that 1.0×10^{-3} *M* SO_2 and 0.5×10^{-3} *M* O_2 will react (less the "2x" and "x" amounts of reactants that remain) to form $1.0 \times 10^{-3}\,M\,SO_3$ (less the "$2x$" that is unreacted). The total $[SO_2]$ that will react, then, is *all of it* except for the $2x$ that remains. This is where we get the change of $-1.0 \times 10^{-3} + 2x$. In other words, all of it forms products except for the small amount, "$2x$," that does not react and remains. Because of the 2-to-1 mole ratio of SO_2 to O_2, $0.5 \times 10^{-3}\,M\,O_2$ will react with $1.0 \times 10^{-3}\,M\,SO_2$. And if $2x$ mol of SO_2 remains unreacted, x mol of O_2 will be unreacted. This is why the change in concentration of O_2 is $-0.5 \times 10^{-3} + x$.

	$2SO_2(g)$	$+$	$O_2(g)$	$\rightleftharpoons$	$2SO_3(g)$
initial	$1.0 \times 10^{-3}\,M$		$2.0 \times 10^{-3}\,M$		$0\,M$
change	$-1.0 \times 10^{-3} + 2x$		$-0.5 \times 10^{-3} + x$		$1.0 \times 10^{-3} - 2x$

The equilibrium row is, again, the result of adding together the initial and change entries in each column.

	$2SO_2(g)$	$+$	$O_2(g)$	$\rightleftharpoons$	$2SO_3(g)$
initial	$1.0 \times 10^{-3}\,M$		$2.0 \times 10^{-3}\,M$		$0\,M$
change	$-1.0 \times 10^{-3} + 2x$		$-0.5 \times 10^{-3} + x$		$1.0 \times 10^{-3} - 2x$
equilibrium	$2x$		$1.5 \times 10^{-3} + x$		$1.0 \times 10^{-3} - 2x$

In the last row of the table, the "assumptions" row, we make the assumption that "x" is small. If this is true, then $1.5 \times 10^{-3} + x \approx 1.5 \times 10^{-3}$. And, if *that* is true, then $1.0 \times 10^{-3} - 2x \approx 1.0 \times 10^{-3}$ must be true as well.

	$2SO_2(g)$	$+$	$O_2(g)$	$\rightleftharpoons$	$2SO_3(g)$
initial	$1.0 \times 10^{-3}\,M$		$2.0 \times 10^{-3}\,M$		$0\,M$
change	$-1.0 \times 10^{-3} + 2x$		$-0.5 \times 10^{-3} + x$		$1.0 \times 10^{-3} - 2x$
equilibrium	$2x$		$1.5 \times 10^{-3} + x$		$1.0 \times 10^{-3} - 2x$
assumptions	$2x$		1.5×10^{-3}		1.0×10^{-3}

We then write the mass-action expression, plug our assumptions row values into the equation, and solve for "x":

$$K = \frac{[SO_3]^2}{[SO_2]^2[O_2]} = \frac{(1.0 \times 10^{-3})^2}{(2x)^2(1.5 \times 10^{-3})} = 8.7 \times 10^6$$

$$4x^2 = 7.66 \times 10^{-11}$$

$$x = 4.38 \times 10^{-6}\,M$$

$$2x = [SO_2] = 8.75 \times 10^{-6} \approx 8.8 \times 10^{-6}\,M$$

Does this answer make sense? Substituting back into the mass-action expression shows that our equation is mathematically valid.

$$\frac{(1.0 \times 10^{-3})^2}{(8.75 \times 10^{-6})^2(1.5 \times 10^{-3})} = 8.7 \times 10^6\,M$$

Is our assumption valid? That is, is the value of "x" negligible compared to $1.5 \times 10^{-3}\,M$?

$$\frac{x}{\text{original concentration}} \times 100\% = \frac{4.38 \times 10^{-6}\,M}{1.5 \times 10^{-3}\,M} \times 100\% = 0.29\%$$

This easily passes the 5% test, so our assumption that "x" is negligible compared to the initial concentrations of O_2 and SO_3 is valid.

EXERCISE 16.9   **The Myoglobin–Oxygen System**

Solve for the equilibrium concentrations of myoglobin, oxygen, and the MbO_2 complex, given the following initial concentrations. Assume that the myoglobin-oxygen reaction is the most important reaction in this system. In other words, you may neglect the ionization of water because its equilibrium constant is relatively very small.

$$[Mb]_0 = 2.0 \times 10^{-4}\, M; \quad [O_2]_0 = 1.9 \times 10^{-5}\, M; \quad [MbO_2]_0 = 0\, M$$

$$Mb + O_2 \rightleftharpoons MbO_2 \quad K = 8.6 \times 10^5$$

First Thoughts

The value of the equilibrium constant, K, is large, so the reaction will be nearly complete at equilibrium. We have a 1-to-1 mole ratio of myoglobin to oxygen, but we don't have enough oxygen ($[O_2]_0 = 1.9 \times 10^{-5}\, M$) to react with all of the myoglobin ($[Mb]_0 = 2.0 \times 10^{-4}\, M$). Therefore, *this is a limiting reactant problem, with oxygen as the limiting reactant—there is excess myoglobin.*

Solution

We set up the ICEA table, write the mass-action expression, and solve for "x." Our assumption, that "x" is small compared to 1.9×10^{-5}, will need to be checked.

	Mb	+	O_2	$\rightleftharpoons$	MbO_2
initial	$2.0 \times 10^{-4}\, M$		$1.9 \times 10^{-5}\, M$		$0\, M$
change	$-1.9 \times 10^{-5} + x$		$-1.9 \times 10^{-5} + x$		$1.9 \times 10^{-5} - x$
equilibrium	$1.81 \times 10^{-4} + x$		x		$1.9 \times 10^{-5} - x$
assumptions	1.81×10^{-4}		x		1.9×10^{-5}

$$K = \frac{[MbO_2]}{[Mb][O_2]} = \frac{(1.9 \times 10^{-5})}{(1.81 \times 10^{-4})(x)} = 8.6 \times 10^5$$

$$x = [O_2] = 1.22 \times 10^{-7}\, M \approx 1.2 \times 10^{-7}\, M$$

$$[Mb] = 1.81 \times 10^{-4} + x \approx 1.8 \times 10^{-4}\, M$$

$$[MbO_2] = 1.9 \times 10^{-5} - x \approx 1.9 \times 10^{-5}\, M$$

The value of "x" is well under 5% of our initial concentrations, so our assumption that "x" is negligible is valid. Checking our math yields

$$\frac{(1.9 \times 10^{-5})}{(1.81 \times 10^{-4})(1.22 \times 10^{-7})} = 8.6 \times 10^5 = K$$

Further Insights

A famous advertising campaign used to talk about pork as "the other white meat," the conventional white meat being chicken. Beef is redder than chicken or pork because of its myoglobin content in the muscles, which averages (give or take quite a bit) about 8 mg of myoglobin per gram of meat. Pork averages only about 2 mg of myoglobin per gram of meat, and chicken has about 1 to 3 mg of myoglobin per gram of meat. Dogs average about 7 mg/g, rats about 2 mg/g, and whales, who require relatively immense myoglobin concentrations to hold needed oxygen for their extended stays underwater, have levels between about 20 and 70 mg/g, depending on the species.

PRACTICE 16.9

Determine the equilibrium concentration of each compound in the following reaction at 25°C, given the data indicated.

$$[C_2H_4O_2]_0 = 0 \ M; \quad [C_2H_3O_2^-]_0 = 0.100 \ M; \quad [H^+]_0 = 0.0500 \ M$$

$$C_2H_3O_2^-(aq) + H^+(aq) \rightleftharpoons C_2H_4O_2(aq) \qquad K = 5.6 \times 10^4 \ (\text{at } 25°C)$$

See Problems 54, 59, 63, 65, 66, and 67. ∎

Intermediate Value of K

Sulfurous acid dissociates in water to produce ions. The equilibrium constant is not very small, nor is it very large:

$$H_2SO_3(aq) \rightleftharpoons H^+(aq) + HSO_3^-(aq) \qquad K = 0.0120 \ (\text{at } 25°C)$$

Other chemistry also occurs in an aqueous solution of sulfurous acid, including the ionization of water and the ionization of the HSO_3^- ion:

$$H_2O(l) \rightleftharpoons H^+(aq) + OH^-(aq) \qquad K = 1.0 \times 10^{-14} \ (\text{at } 25°C)$$

$$HSO_3^-(aq) \rightleftharpoons H^+(aq) + SO_3^{2-}(aq) \qquad K = 1.0 \times 10^{-7} \ (\text{at } 25°C)$$

The equilibrium constants of these reactions are quite small compared to the initial ionization of sulfurous acid, so we will focus only on the first equation. Let's calculate the equilibrium concentrations of all species. That is, if $[H_2SO_3]_0 = 1.50 \ M$ and $[H^+]_0 = [HSO_3^-]_0 = 0 \ M$, what is the equilibrium concentration of each species in solution?

Although the value of K is intermediate (close to 1), we will *assume* that we can *neglect dissociation of H_2SO_3* (that is, we assume that the dissociation reaction does occur but that the change in concentration, "x," is negligible compared to the concentrations of our initial substances).

	$H_2SO_3(aq)$	$\rightleftharpoons$	$H^+(aq)$	$+$	$HSO_3^-(aq)$
initial	1.50 M		0 M		0 M
change	$-x$		$+x$		$+x$
equilibrium	$1.50 - x$		x		x
assumptions	1.50		x		x

$$K = \frac{[H^+][HSO_3^-]}{[H_2SO_3]}$$

$$0.0120 = \frac{x^2}{1.50}$$

$$x = 0.134 \ M = [H^+] = [HSO_3^-]$$

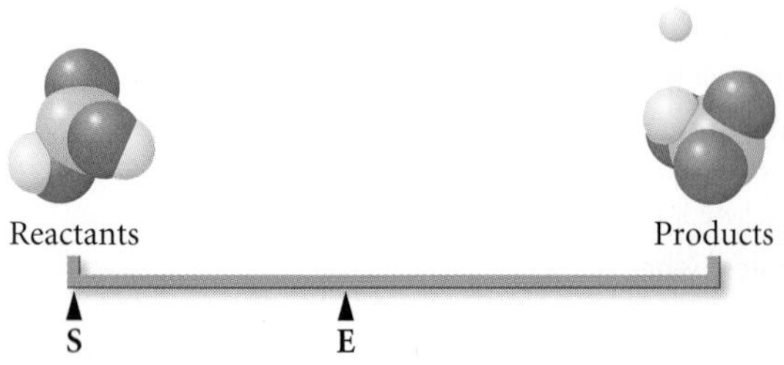

Before going on, we must test our assumption that "x" is negligible compared to 1.50 M, because our assumptions row in the ICEA table indicates that $1.50 - x = 1.50$. We do this by dividing "x" by 1.50 and multiplying by 100%. Unfortunately, "x" *(0.134)* is *9% of 1.50! Our assumption is not valid.* This suggests that our

Reactants

Products

S   E

equilibrium line chart might look something like that on page 698 (recall this same chart from Section 16.3), which shows more than a little forward reaction.

To arrive at the correct answer for this problem, we must solve the problem explicitly—that is, without making the assumption that the dissociation of H_2SO_3 is unimportant compared to its original concentration of 1.50 M. In order to solve the problem, we must substitute the *equilibrium* row of our ICEA table into the mass-action expression:

$$0.0120 = \frac{x^2}{1.50 - x}$$

Unfortunately, the presence of both an "x" and an "x^2" in the same equation complicates the math somewhat. One useful way to solve for "x" in these situations is to arrange the values so that we have a **quadratic equation** of the general form $ax^2 + bx + c$. For our example, we multiply both sides of the equation by $(1.50 - x)$:

$$0.0120 \times (1.50 - x) = x^2$$

$$0.0180 - 0.0120x = x^2$$

Then we collect all of our terms onto one side of the equals sign by adding $0.0120x$ and subtracting 0.0180 from both sides of the equation. The result has set our equation equal to zero:

$$x^2 + 0.0120x - 0.0180 = 0$$

$$ax^2 + \quad bx \quad + \quad c \quad = 0$$

Comparing this to the general form for a quadratic equation, we obtain the values for the constants a, b, and c:

$$a = 1; \quad b = +0.0120; \quad c = -0.0180$$

Some programmable calculators will solve for the values of "x" in the equation by entering the constants a, b, and c. The other, perfectly satisfactory option is to employ the **quadratic formula**, the equation used to solve for "x":

$$x = \frac{-b \pm \sqrt{b^2 - 4ac}}{2a}$$

Inserting our values for a, b, and c into this equation and solving, we obtain two values for x:

$$x = \frac{-b \pm \sqrt{b^2 - 4ac}}{2a}$$

$$x = \frac{-0.0120 \pm \sqrt{(0.0120)^2 - 4(1)(-0.0180)}}{2(1)}$$

$$x = \frac{-0.0120 \pm \sqrt{0.000144 + 0.072}}{2(1)}$$

$$x = \frac{-0.0120 \pm 0.2686}{2(1)}$$

$$x = 0.128, -0.140$$

The existence of two values for "x" would appear to be a problem. However, it is not. One of these values gives equilibrium concentrations that are physically impossible to obtain. Let's determine the concentrations in both cases and see why only one works:

If "x" = −0.140, then

$$[H_2SO_3] = 1.50 + 0.140 = 1.64\ M; \quad [H^+] = [HSO_3^-] = -0.140\ M$$

If "x" = 0.128, then

$$[H_2SO_3] = 1.50 - 0.128 = 1.37\ M; \quad [H^+] = [HSO_3^-] = 0.128\ M$$

When "x" = −0.140, we obtain negative values for both $[H^+]$ and $[HSO_3^-]$. This is impossible, so "x" must be 0.128. The correct answer to this problem must be $[H_2SO_3] = 1.37\ M$ and $[H^+] = [HSO_3^-] = 0.128\ M$. Using these values, we need to check our answer:

$$K = \frac{(0.128)^2}{1.37} = 0.0120$$

The invalid answer from the quadratic equation will generate a negative value for a concentration. We must never assume, however, that a negative value of "x" will always produce the invalid answer. In the end, the key to doing equilibrium problems is to *make assumptions when you can* to simplify the math. However, you must *test the assumptions that you make*. When the assumptions fail, we use the equilibrium row in the ICEA table to solve for "x" explicitly.

In Summary

We have seen that our ability to interpret the meaning of equilibrium constants and to make assumptions that simplify our problem solving are the ideas at the core of this different way of thinking about chemistry. We raised five questions at the beginning of this section:

1 What chemical reactions will occur?

2 Which among these are important? Which are unimportant?

3 Given the initial concentration of substances, in which direction (toward the formation of more reactants or toward the formation of more products) is the reaction likely to proceed?

4 How can we solve for the amounts of substances of interest that are present at equilibrium?

5 How can we create the conditions to maximize the concentration of the desired components and minimize that of the others?

We have now answered the first four of these questions. We are now ready for question 5, which concerns the human control of chemical processes—one big payoff of our study of equilibrium.

FIGURE 16.10

Henry Louis Le Châtelier (1850–1936), a French chemist, was a mining engineer before working as a professor. In addition to inspiring his work on thermodynamics, his interest in high temperatures, dating from his studies of mineralogy, led to the development of the oxyacetylene torch for cutting and welding steel.

16.6 Le Châtelier's Principle

We have discussed understanding chemical equilibrium as "a different way of thinking." **Le Châtelier's principle**, described by Henry Louis Le Châtelier (1850–1936; Figure 16.10) in 1884, extends this to *changes* in a system at equilibrium. Its implications are profound. This useful principle can be summarized as follows: *If a stress is applied to a system at equilibrium, it will change in such a way as to partially undo the applied stress and restore the equilibrium.* Although the system moves back *toward* its original set of equilibrium conditions, it never quite makes it, so there is a net change (often substantial) in equilibrium concentrations as a result of changes in the system. For people, the equivalent saying might be "Push me and I'll push back." This is shown graphically in Figure 16.11.

This principle has several implications for a system at equilibrium:

- If the *concentration* of a component is changed, the system will respond in such a way that the concentration returns toward (but doesn't make it to) its original equilibrium value.

- If the *pressure* of a system is changed, it will respond in such a way as to return the pressure toward (but not to) the original equilibrium value.

- If the *temperature* of a system is changed, it will respond by exchanging heat such that the temperature returns toward the original equilibrium value.

Let's look at the effect on equilibrium of each of these changes—concentration, pressure, and temperature—in more detail.

Changes in Concentration

If the concentration of a component is changed, the system will respond in such a way that the concentration returns toward its original equilibrium value. We began this chapter by discussing the interaction of oxygen and myoglobin to form a complex that stores and transports oxygen within muscle cells. How is the control of oxygen levels in the muscle cells indicative of this statement of Le Châtelier's principle? Let's look at it mathematically, using two separate sets of conditions. We saw one set of equilibrium conditions in Exercise 16.9. Recall the data for the reaction:

$$Mb + O_2 \rightleftharpoons MbO_2 \qquad K = 8.6 \times 10^5$$

$$[Mb] = 1.8 \times 10^{-4}\,M; \quad [O_2] = 1.2 \times 10^{-7}\,M; \quad [MbO_2] = 1.9 \times 10^{-5}\,M$$

Let's change the conditions so that the oxygen level in the blood increases to $1.0 \times 10^{-5}\,M$. How will the system respond to this change? We can use our reaction quotient, Q, to determine which way the reaction will go to reestablish equilibrium.

$$Q = \frac{[MbO_2]_0}{[Mb]_0[O_2]_0} = \frac{(1.9 \times 10^{-5})}{(1.8 \times 10^{-4})(1.0 \times 10^{-5})} = 1.1 \times 10^4$$

Because $Q < K$, the reaction will shift to the right (see Section 16.5) to produce more product and reduce the concentration of the reactants. Let's solve for the concentrations of myoglobin, oxygen, and the MbO_2 complex at this new equilibrium position. The ICEA table can be set up as follows:

	Mb	+	O_2	$\rightleftharpoons$	MbO_2
initial	$1.8 \times 10^{-4}\,M$		$1.0 \times 10^{-5}\,M$		$1.9 \times 10^{-5}\,M$
change	$-x$		$-x$		$+x$
equilibrium	$1.8 \times 10^{-4} - x$		$1.0 \times 10^{-5} - x$		$1.9 \times 10^{-5} + x$

When we solve, we find that "x" $= 9.8 \times 10^{-6}\,M$, and

$$[Mb]_{new} = 1.7 \times 10^{-4}\,M; \quad [O_2]_{new} = 2.0 \times 10^{-7}\,M; \quad [MbO_2]_{new} = 2.9 \times 10^{-5}\,M$$

compared to the starting position,

$$[Mb]_0 = 1.8 \times 10^{-4}\,M; \quad [O_2]_0 = 1.0 \times 10^{-5}\,M; \quad [MbO_2]_0 = 1.9 \times 10^{-5}\,M$$

The reactant concentrations (myoglobin and oxygen) have decreased, and the concentration of the product (the myoglobin–oxygen complex) has increased. We added more reactant and the system shifted to the right to make more

FIGURE 16.11

Le Châtelier's principle is somewhat analogous to this situation. The wrestler in red pushes the defender out of position (applying a stress). The defender pushes back, trying to restore his original position, but not fully succeeding.

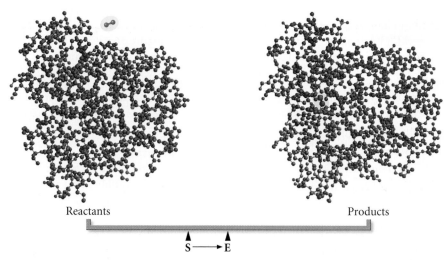

Reactants   Products

S ———→ E

product. In the end, the system moved to restore the equilibrium. In our human analogy, the system was pushed and it pushed back. A snapshot of the changes on our equilibrium line chart is shown above.

During exercise, the body uses large amounts of oxygen. Some of that oxygen is supplied by the equilibrium position shifting to the left, in response to the fall in free oxygen levels that occurs because so much oxygen is being consumed. This releases more oxygen and free myoglobin, enabling athletes to run freely, for example. When the need for oxygen is less, the free myoglobin combines with oxygen (the reaction shifts to the right) and forms more of the MbO_2 complex. The complex can act as a storage location for oxygen, making it ready for release when it is needed.

Concentration changes make possible the industrial-scale manufacturing of chemicals. As the chemicals are produced in a reaction, they are removed, forcing the reaction to produce products continually in an "attempt" to restore the original equilibrium position. This is an important part of the contact process, in which the SO_3 that is produced from the reaction of SO_2 and O_2 is continually removed, forcing continued production of SO_3.

Changes in Pressure

If the pressure of a system is changed (at constant temperature and volume), it will respond in such a way as to return the pressure toward the original equilibrium value.

To illustrate the importance of this statement of Le Châtelier's principle, let's look at a reaction in which changes in pressure are meaningful—one that involves gases. Recall the reaction for the manufacture of ammonia from hydrogen and nitrogen via the Haber process:

$$3H_2(g) + N_2(g) \rightleftharpoons 2NH_3(g)$$

If the pressure of the system is substantially increased from 1 atm to 300 atm, how will it respond? The system will shift in a direction that will lower the pressure toward the original equilibrium value. Recall from our discussion of gases (Chapter 10) that the pressure of a gas is approximately proportional to the number of moles of a real gas. Fewer moles means lower pressure, so the reaction used in the Haber process will shift to the right when the pressure is increased. Typically, we observe changes in volume as the reaction seeks to accommodate pressure changes. As the volume is decreased, the pressure increases, and as the volume is increased, the pressure decreases.

An increase in pressure favors the side with fewer moles of gas.

A decrease in pressure favors the side with more moles of gas.

TABLE 16.2	Mole Percent of Ammonia Present at Various Pressures and Temperatures					
	Pressure (atm)					
	1	10	50	100	300	1000
Temperature (°C)						
200	15.3	50.7	74.4	81.5	89.9	98.3
400	0.4	3.9	15.3	25.1	47.0	79.8
600	—	0.5	2.3	4.5	13.8	31.4

Source: Hocking, M. B., *Handbook of Chemical Technology and Pollution Control;* Academic Press: New York, 1998, p. 313.

How does this help in the manufacture of ammonia? Table 16.2 shows the mole percent of ammonia present at equilibrium at various pressures for the Haber process.

At every temperature, higher pressure means a shift toward ammonia. In practice, the industrial manufacture of ammonia is done between 100 and 300 atm.

Changes in Temperature

The reaction for the manufacture of ammonia is exothermic:

$$3H_2(g) + N_2(g) \rightleftharpoons 2NH_3(g) \qquad \Delta H° = -92.0 \text{ kJ}$$

How will the system respond if the temperature is raised from 200°C to 500°C at constant pressure? The change in enthalpy for the formation of ammonia is negative. Therefore, the reaction gives off heat. **What shift is necessary to attempt to restore the original temperature of the system?** The reaction will proceed in the direction that *absorbs* heat ("attempting" to lower the temperature) rather than proceeding in the direction that releases more heat, which would raise the system temperature. In the formation of ammonia, equilibrium would be restored with a shift to the left resulting in the formation of more reactants.

Exothermic reactions shift toward the left (the reactants side) when heated. (Note that this can be seen in Tables 16.2 and 16.3.)

Endothermic reactions shift toward the right (the products side) when heated.

There is another implication to the shift that occurs when a system at equilibrium is heated or cooled. The temperature itself is changing the concentrations of the components in the equation. The system is responding and we aren't adding or removing a component. This can happen only if *the equilibrium constant itself changes with temperature*. As we noted in Exercise 16.10, equilibrium constants are temperature dependent. Table 16.3 shows the change in K_p at various temperatures for the exothermic contact process addition of oxygen to SO_2 to form SO_3. Although the data in the table show that the value of K decreases as the temperature increases, there are many cases where K increases with increasing temperature. The direction of the change is dependent on the enthalpy of the process.

TABLE 16.3	Dependence of the Equilibrium Constant (K_p) on Temperature
$2SO_2(g) + O_2(g) \rightleftharpoons 2SO_3(g) \quad \Delta H = -198 \text{ kJ}$	
Temperature (°C)	K_p
400	1.6×10^5
500	2.3×10^3
600	91
700	6.9
800	0.84
900	0.15
1000	0.034
1100	0.0096

Source: Based on data from Hocking, M. B., *Handbook of Chemical Technology and Pollution Control;* Academic Press: New York, 1998, p. 260.

The position of equilibrium and, hence, the value of the equilibrium constant change when the temperature of the reaction is changed. The value of the equilibrium constant of an exothermic reaction decreases with an increase in temperature; the value of the equilibrium constant of an endothermic reaction increases with an increase in temperature.

For an exothermic reaction

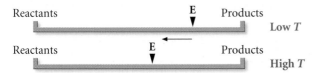

For an endothermic reaction

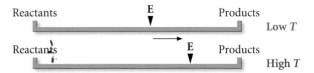

The Importance of Catalysts

Application

CHEMICAL
ENCOUNTERS:
Catalysts in
Industry

Economics plays an important part in the chemical industry. A production process that reaches equilibrium more rapidly will allow more product to be manufactured. More product means the opportunity for increased sales. Catalysts—substances that substantially increase the rate of a reaction without being consumed—are therefore vital to the chemical process industries.

A catalyst does not affect the equilibrium position, but it allows the process to achieve equilibrium more rapidly than it would without a catalyst.

Fritz Haber used magnetite (Fe_3O_4) for the preparation of ammonia. Iron-related catalysts are still used for ammonia production (via the Haber process), although other metals can also be used, including osmium and mixtures of ruthenium and barium.

The nitrogen gas used in the synthesis of ammonia is obtained by distilling liquid air. The hydrogen gas for the Haber process is derived from the iron(II) oxide– and chronium(III) oxide–catalyzed reaction of carbon monoxide (derived from coal tar) with water. The equation illustrating the formation of hydrogen by this method is

$$CO(g) + H_2O(g) \underset{}{\overset{FeO + Cr_2O_3}{\rightleftharpoons}} CO_2(g) + H_2(g) \qquad (500°C)$$

The nickel-catalyzed reaction of methane (from natural gas) and water vapor also produces hydrogen:

$$CH_4(g) + H_2O(g) \underset{}{\overset{Ni, 400 \text{ psi}}{\rightleftharpoons}} CO(g) + 3H_2 \qquad (800°C)$$

This means that when the price of coal or natural gas rises, the cost of fertilizer can rise as well. This is another example of the relationship between industrial chemical processes and international economics.

The Contact process uses vanadium(V) oxide on pumice as the catalyst for the conversion of SO_2 to SO_3. Although the catalyst can last for up to 20 years, replacing it each year helps ensure efficiency in the reaction. Platinum is a better catalyst but costs much more. Platinum catalysts can also become less effective in the presence of impurities such as arsenic.

A look at metal catalysts through a scanning electron microscope reveals a porous crystal surface.

EXERCISE 16.10 Le Châtelier's Principle

The reaction for the combination of hydrogen gas and oxygen gas to give water vapor is

$$2H_2(g) + O_2(g) \rightleftharpoons 2H_2O(g) \qquad \Delta H° = -484 \text{ kJ}$$

Predict the effect of each of these changes to the system on the direction of equilibrium.

a. H_2O is removed as it is being generated.

b. H_2 is added.

c. The pressure on the system is decreased.

d. The system is cooled.

Solution

a. Moves to the right (removal of product forces Q to be less than K, and the system compensates by making more product).

b. Moves to the right (same as above, except Q is less than K because $[H_2]_0$ is larger than at the previous equilibrium).

c. Moves to the left because decreasing the pressure favors the side with more moles of gas.

d. Moves to the right because an exothermic reaction gives off heat. Cooling the system increases the temperature gradient between the system and the surroundings, therefore allowing a continued flow of heat to the surroundings.

PRACTICE 16.10

Predict the effect of each of these changes to the following system on the direction at equilibrium.

$$2C_2H_6O(aq) + 2CO_2(g) \rightleftharpoons C_6H_{12}O_6(aq) \qquad \Delta H = 70.0 \text{ kJ/mol}$$

Ethanol　　　　　　　　　　　　Glucose

a. Heat is added.
b. Some ethanol (C_2H_6O) is removed from the reaction.
c. A catalyst is added.
d. More glucose is added to the flask.

See Problems 69, 70, and 74. ▮

Le Châtelier's principle is one of the most important ideas in all of chemistry. Through its application, we understand and control reactions that have the most far-reaching importance, from the essential reactions in the human body to the production of billions of kilograms of material goods used in everything from fertilizers to plastics. Table 16.4 summarizes the impact of changing the concentration, pressure, or temperature, as well as the impact of the addition of a catalyst, on the direction of chemical equilibria.

TABLE 16.4	Impact of External Changes on the Equilibrium Direction	
Change	**System Response**	**Change in K**
Concentration	Shifts toward restoring initial concentration	None
Pressure (of the system)		
Increase	Shifts toward side with fewer moles of gas	None
Decrease	Shifts toward side with more moles of gas	None
Temperature		
Exothermic reaction	Raising temperature shifts toward reactant	Decreases
	Lowering temperature shifts toward product	Increases
Endothermic reaction	Raising temperature shifts toward product	Increases
	Lowering temperature shifts toward reactant	Decreases
Catalyst	No change in direction; reaches equilibrium more rapidly	None

16.7 Free Energy and the Equilibrium Constant

We introduced the relationship between free energy and the reaction quotient, Q, in Section 14.6 of our thermodynamics chapter. We listed the quantitative relationship as

$$\Delta G = \Delta G° + RT \ln Q$$

where ΔG = the free energy of the reaction

$\Delta G°$ = the free energy at standard conditions

R = the universal gas constant, $8.3145 \text{ J·mol}^{-1}\text{·K}^{-1}$

T = the temperature in kelvins

Q = the reaction quotient illustrating the current concentrations in the reaction

Our thermodynamic definition says that at equilibrium, $\Delta G = 0$. Therefore, at equilibrium, the reaction quotient, Q, becomes the thermodynamic equilibrium constant, K_{eq}.

$$0 = \Delta G° + RT \ln(K_{eq})$$

Solving for $\Delta G°$, we obtain

$$\Delta G° = -RT \ln(K_{eq})$$

This equation is very useful. It enables us to calculate the equilibrium constant for a process if we know the standard free energy change for that process.

One word of caution is needed. The equilibrium constant in this equation requires that we use its thermodynamic definition. This means that all concentrations in the mass-action expression must be expressed in activities and that all gases must be expressed in fugacities (f). A fugacity is similar to an activity in that it measures the effective pressure of a gas. To simplify this, we'll assume that the activity values are close to the values of concentration expressed in molarity and that the fugacity values are close to the values of pressure expressed in atmospheres. Let's write the equilibrium constant expression for the environmental leaching of lead into acidic waters in order to illustrate this definition.

$$PbCO_3(s) + 2H^+(aq) \rightleftharpoons Pb^{2+}(aq) + CO_2(g) + H_2O(l)$$

$$K_{eq} = \frac{a_{Pb^{2+}} f_{CO_2} a_{H_2O}}{a_{PbCO_3} a_{H^+}^2} \approx \frac{[Pb^{2+}] P_{CO_2}}{[H^+]^2}$$

where: $a_{Pb^{2+}} \approx [Pb^{2+}]$ and $a_{H^+}^2 \approx [H^+]^2$

$f_{CO_2} \approx P_{CO_2}$ (the partial pressure of CO_2) in atmospheres

$a_{PbCO_3} \approx 1.0$ and $a_{H_2O} \approx 1.0$

In this equation, $PbCO_3$ is a solid and H_2O is a liquid. As with K and K_p, we consider their activity to be 1.0 and their concentration to be part of the equilibrium constant. As before, we simply remove them from the equation.

EXERCISE 16.11   **Free Energy and the Equilibrium Constant**

Using the standard free energy values given below, calculate the equilibrium constant at STP for the formation of $SO_3(g)$.

$$2SO_2(g) + O_2(g) \rightleftharpoons 2SO_3(g)$$

| $\Delta G°$ (kJ/mol) | -300 | 0 | -371 |

Solution

$$\Delta_{rxn}G° = \Delta G°_{products} - \Delta G°_{reactants} = 2(-371 \text{ kJ/mol}) - 2(-300 \text{ kJ/mol})$$

$$\Delta_{reaction}G° = -142 \text{ kJ/mol}$$

In order to cancel units properly, we must convert $\Delta_{reaction}G°$ to J/mol.

$$\Delta_{reaction}G° = -142{,}000 \text{ J/mol}$$

$$\Delta G° = -RT \ln(K_{eq})$$

$$-142{,}000 \text{ J/mol} = -8.3145 \text{ J·mol}^{-1}\text{·K}^{-1} (298 \text{ K})\ln(K_{eq})$$

$$\ln(K_{eq}) = \frac{-142{,}000 \text{ J·mol}^{-1}}{-8.3145 \text{ J·mol}^{-1}\text{·K}^{-1}(298 \text{ K})} = 57.31$$

We can take the inverse natural log of both sides.

$$K_{eq} = e^{57.31} = 7.76 \times 10^{24}$$

When we compare this value to the value we mentioned for the reaction at 400°C ($K = 8.7 \times 10^6$), we notice that it is different. Why is it different? The equilibrium constant is highly temperature dependent. We've calculated it at 25°C, and so it should be different from K at 400°C.

PRACTICE 16.11

Use the thermodynamic data in the appendix to calculate the equilibrium constant for the ionization of sulfurous acid.

$$H_2SO_3(aq) \rightleftharpoons H^+(aq) + HSO_3^-(aq) \qquad K = 0.0120 \ (25°C)$$

How does the calculated value for K_{eq} compare to the value of K reported here? Explain any differences.

See Problems 77–82.

We will apply the concepts we learned in this chapter (including the nature of equilibrium, our new way of thinking about problem solving, and Le Châtelier's principle) to look at aqueous equilibria. Our immediate focus will be on a most important set of reactions—acid–base equilibria.

The Bottom Line

- Reactions can proceed reversibly toward the products or back toward the reactants. (Section 16.1)

- The point in a reaction at which there is no net change in the concentration of reactants or products is known as chemical equilibrium—or, often, simply as equilibrium. (Section 16.1)

- The free energy, G, of a reaction is at a minimum at equilibrium. (Section 16.1)

- The free energy change, ΔG, is equal to 0 at equilibrium. (Section 16.1)

- The rates of the forward and reverse reactions are equal at equilibrium. (Section 16.1)

- The mass-action expression relates the equilibrium concentrations of reactants and products in a reaction. (Section 16.1)

- The equilibrium constant is temperature dependent. (Sections 16.1, 16.6)

- The size of the equilibrium constant gives us information about the extent of a reaction. (Section 16.3)

- Modifying the coefficients of a reaction modifies the value of its equilibrium constant. (Section 16.4)

- The equilibrium constant can be converted for use with partial pressures or molarities. (Section 16.4)

- The equilibrium constant for the sum of chemical reactions is the mathematical product of the individual K values. (Section 16.4)

- We can use the equilibrium constant and mass-action expression to calculate the equilibrium concentration of substances in a reaction. (Section 16.5)

- Solving problems relating to reaction equilibria involves asking and answering a series of systematic questions. (Section 16.5)

- We can use the reaction quotient, Q, to assess which way a reaction will proceed to reach equilibrium. (Section 16.5)

- Le Châtelier's principle concerns the impact of changing the pressure, temperature, and concentration conditions of a reaction at equilibrium. (Section 16.6)

- A catalyst does not affect the equilibrium position. It changes the reaction mechanism in such a way as to speed up the reaction. (Section 16.6)

- The free energy change of a reaction can be determined from the equilibrium constant for that reaction and vice versa. (Section 16.7)

Key Words

activity The effective concentration of a solute in solution. (*p. 675*)

binding rate constant The rate constant that indicates the association of two molecules. (*p. 670*)

chromatography A chemical technique involving the partition of a solute between a stationary phase and a mobile phase. The technique can be used to separate or purify mixtures of solutes. (*p. 678*)

contact process An industrial method used to produce sulfuric acid from elemental sulfur. (*p. 676*)

distribution constant The equilibrium constant that describes the partitioning of a solute between two immiscible phases. (*p. 678*)

equilibrium A system of reversible reactions in which the forward and reverse reactions occur at equal rates, such that *no net change in the concentrations occurs,* even though both reactions continue. (*p. 670*)

equilibrium constant (*K*) The value of the equilibrium expression when it is solved using the equilibrium concentrations of reactants and products. (*p. 672*)

equilibrium expression The ratio of product to reactant concentrations raised to the power of their stoichiometric coefficients. This expression relates the equilibrium concentrations to the equilibrium constant. It is also known as the mass-action expression. (*p. 672*)

gas chromatography A specific chromatography technique in which the mobile phase is a gas and the stationary phase is a solid. (*p. 678*)

heme group A compound that, when bound to hemoglobin and iron cations, is responsible for binding oxygen. (*p. 669*)

heterogeneous equilibrium An equilibrium that results from reactants and products in different phases or physical states. (*p. 682*)

homogeneous equilibrium An equilibrium that results from reactants and products in the same phase, or physical state. (*p. 682*)

Le Châtelier's principle If a system at equilibrium is changed, it responds by returning toward its original equilibrium position. (*p. 700*)

mass-action expression The ratio of product to reactant concentrations raised to the power of their stoichiometric coefficients. This expression relates the equilibrium concentrations to the equilibrium constant. It is also known as the equilibrium expression. (*p. 672*)

mobile phase In chromatography, the phase that moves. (*p. 678*)

myoglobin (Mb) A biochemical compound responsible for storing and releasing oxygen in a living organism. (*p. 669*)

quadratic equation A mathematical equation written in the form $ax^2 + bx + c = 0$. (*p. 699*)

quadratic formula The method used to solve for *x* from the quadratic equation,

$$x = \frac{-b \pm \sqrt{b^2 - 4ac}}{2a} \quad (p.\ 699)$$

reaction quotient (*Q*) The ratio of product concentrations to reactant concentrations raised to the power of their stoichiometric coefficients for a reaction that is not at equilibrium. (*p. 688*)

release rate constant The rate constant of the reaction in which oxygen is released from the myoglobin-oxygen reaction. (*p. 671*)

stationary phase In chromatography, the phase that does not move. (*p. 678*)

Focus Your Learning

The answers to the odd-numbered problems appear at the back of the book.

Section 16.1 The Concept of Chemical Equilibrium

Skill Review

1. The word *dynamic* refers to changes. Explain how the descriptive term *dynamic equilibrium* can be applied to a chemical system where the concentrations of reactants and products do not change.

2. Match each of these conditions of a chemical system to the appropriate description of the Gibbs free energy: +, −, or 0.
   a. System reacting toward products
   b. System at equilibrium
   c. System reacting toward reactants

3. When describing a reacting system, a scientist may say that the reaction "does not go to completion." Use free energy and equilibrium to explain the meaning of that phrase.

4. Assume the expression "rate$_1$" represents the rate of a reaction, and "rate$_2$" represents the expression for the rate of the reverse of that reaction. Which of these statements is *not* true of a reaction at equilibrium, and why?
   a. rate$_1$/rate$_2$ = 1   c. rate$_1$/rate$_2$ = K^2
   b. rate$_2$/rate$_1$ = −1   d. rate$_2$ = rate$_1$ × K

5. Write the equilibrium expression for each of these reactions:
   a. $HCl(g) + C_2H_4(g) \rightleftharpoons C_2H_5Cl(g)$
   b. $CH_4(g) + 2O_2(g) \rightleftharpoons CO_2(g) + 2H_2O(g)$
   c. $2H_2(g) + O_2(g) \rightleftharpoons 2H_2O(l)$

6. Write the equilibrium expression for each of these reactions:
   a. $CaCO_3(s) \rightleftharpoons CaO(s) + CO_2(g)$
   b. $SO_3(aq) + H_2O(l) \rightleftharpoons H_2SO_4(aq)$
   c. $4NH_3(g) + 7O_2(g) \rightleftharpoons 4NO_2(g) + 6H_2O(g)$

Chemical Applications and Practices

7. Phosphoric acid (H_3PO_4) is used in soft drinks and in producing fertilizers. As shown in the following reaction, phosphoric acid can be produced by the action of sulfuric acid on rocks that contain calcium phosphate.

   $Ca_3(PO_4)_2(s) + 3H_2SO_4(aq) \rightleftharpoons 3CaSO_4(aq) + 2H_3PO_4(aq)$

   Describe the system at equilibrium, using each of these three concepts:
   a. Reaction rates
   b. Concentration conditions
   c. Gibbs free energy

8. Batteries in cars, watches, and the like all depend on a drive from reactants to products that produces electricity. When the production of electricity stops, we typically say that the battery is "dead." A chemical way to express this is to say that the battery has attained equilibrium. Explain why this chemical statement also describes why the battery no longer produces electricity.

9. Hydrogen chloride gas (used in the production of hydrochloric acid) can be produced directly by the combination of hydrogen and chlorine gas as follows:

   $$H_2(g) + Cl_2(g) \rightleftharpoons 2HCl(g)$$

   At equilibrium, $k_1[H_2][Cl_2] = k_{-1}[HCl]^2$. Write the mass-action expression (that is, the equilibrium expression) for the reaction.

10. Chlorofluorocarbons, including Freon-12, have been used in air conditioning units. However, their use is being phased out in most countries as a consequence of their breakdown into chlorine atoms that attack our planet's protective ozone layer. Atmospheric scientists studied the following reaction to understand the breakdown process:

    $$CCl_2F_2(g) \text{ (Freon-12)} \rightleftharpoons CClF_2(g) + Cl(g)$$

    At equilibrium, $k_1[CCl_2F_2] = k_2[CClF_2][Cl]$. Write the mass-action expression, i.e. equilibrium expression for the reaction.

Section 16.2
Why Is Chemical Equilibrium a Useful Concept?

Skill Review

11. In your own words, explain the economic outcome to the petroleum industry if equilibria could not be controlled.

12. What types of interactions might exist in a chromatographic system to make a solute interact strongly with the mobile phase instead of the stationary phase?

Chemical Applications and Practices

13. The following chromatogram was developed when ink from a black felt-tip pen was drawn on a plate containing a stationary phase. The plate was then dipped in solvent, and the solvent moved up the plate by capillary action. After development of the plate, it was obvious that the original black ink

had separated into the different dyes used to make the ink black.
a. Which color dye in the ink has the largest value of K_D?
b. Which color dye interacts least with the stationary filter paper?

14. The following is a chromatogram from a gas chromatography analysis of the vapor above a sample of gasoline. Each peak corresponds to a component in the gasoline vapor mixture. It is important to blend gasoline components for better performance at certain altitudes. From the chromatogram, which component has the lower value for K_D? Which has the most interaction with the stationary phase?

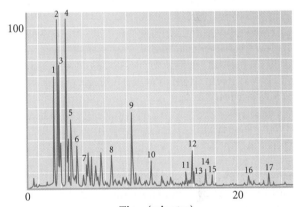

Time (minutes)

1 Butane	10 Octane
2 2-Methylbutane	11 Ethylbenzene
3 Pentane	12 Xylene
4 2-Methylbutane	13 Xylene
5 Hexane	14 Xylene
6 Methylcyclopentane	15 Nonane
7 Benzene	16 1-Ethyl-2-methylbenzene
8 Methylcyclopentane	17 1, 2, 4-Trimethylbenzene
9 Toluene	

Section 16.3 The Meaning of the Equilibrium Constant

Skill Review

15. For each of the following systems, an equilibrium expression is given. If any errors are present in the expressions, correct them and rewrite the equilibrium expression.
    a. $2PbO(s) + O_2(g) \rightleftharpoons 2PbO_2(s)$ $K = [PbO_2]/[PbO]^2[O_2]$
    b. $H_2O(l) + SO_3(g) \rightleftharpoons H_2SO_4(aq)$ $K = 1/[SO_3]$

16. For each of the following systems, an equilibrium expression is given. If any errors are present in the expressions, correct them and rewrite the equilibrium expression.

a. $H_2CO_3(aq) \rightleftharpoons H_2O(l) + CO_2(g)$ $K = 1/[CO_2]$

b. $H_2O(l) + NH_3(g) \rightleftharpoons NH_4^+(aq) + OH^-(aq)$
$K = [NH_4^+][OH^-]/[NH_3][H_2O]$

17. Using the equilibrium line chart for the reaction of carbon monoxide and water:

$$CO(g) + H_2O(g) \rightleftharpoons CO_2(g) + H_2(g) \quad K = ????$$

$CO(g) + H_2O(g)$ $CO_2(g) + H_2(g)$

Reactants   Products

E

a. Estimate the value of K.

b. Based on this information, what can you say about the relative concentrations of carbon monoxide and carbon dioxide when the reaction has reached equilibrium?

18. Based on the equilibrium line charts for the following hypothetic reactions, which reaction would produce fewer moles of product? Explain why this is possible. (Assume that each reaction has the same initial conditions.)

$A(aq) + B(aq)$ $C(aq)$

Reactants   Products

E

$X(aq) + Y(aq)$ $2C(aq)$

Reactants   Products

E

Chemical Applications and Practices

19. Some camp stoves and portable burners operate via the combustion of propane (C_3H_8). Balance the following combustion equation, and write the equilibrium expression for the reaction.

$$C_3H_8(g) + O_2(g) \rightleftharpoons CO_2(g) + H_2O(g)$$

20. Ethanol (C_2H_5OH) is widely used as a fuel additive in gasoline.

a. Balance the following combustion equation, and write the equilibrium expression for this important reaction.

$$C_2H_5OH(g) + O_2(g) \rightleftharpoons CO_2(g) + H_2O(g)$$

b. Would you expect the value for K for this reaction, at combustion temperatures, to be large or small? Explain.

21. Hydrogen peroxide, in a dilute solution, is a very commonly used disinfectant. The following balanced equation shows the decomposition reaction for gas-phase hydrogen peroxide.

$$2H_2O_2(g) \rightleftharpoons 2H_2O(g) + O_2(g)$$

Given the following initial and final concentrations, determine the equilibrium concentration of O_2.

$[H_2O_2]_0 = 0.100;$ $[H_2O]_0 = 0.050;$ $[O_2]_0 = 0.025$

$[H_2O_2] = 0.050;$ $[H_2O] = 0.100;$ $[O_2] = ?$

22. The Haber process, at 450°C, has an equilibrium constant $K = 0.30$. What is the equilibrium concentration of hydrogen in a system containing the following equilibrium concentrations of nitrogen and ammonia?

$[N_2] = 0.100;$ $[NH_3] = 0.100;$ $[H_2] = ?$

23. Molybdenum, element 42, has many uses, perhaps most notably in the production of a strong type of steel. The reaction shown here is involved in one of the steps in recovering molybdenum from its natural ore.

$$2MoS_2(s) + 5O_2(g) \rightleftharpoons 2MoO_3(s) + 4SO(g)$$

Write the proper mass-action expression for the equilibrium constant for this reaction.

24. The following reaction shows the dissociation of magnesium hydroxide into ions. This compound can be found in several commercial antacids.

$$Mg(OH)_2(s) \rightleftharpoons Mg^{2+}(aq) + 2OH^-(aq)$$

Write the proper mass-action expression for the equilibrium constant for this reaction.

25. At 450°C, the Haber process has a K value of approximately 0.30. At 25°C, the reaction between NO from airplane exhaust and ozone has a K value of approximately 3.0×10^{34}. The ionization reaction of acetic acid in vinegar, at 25°C, is approximately 1.8×10^{-5}. Complete the following table and compare the three systems.

System	K	Reactant Favored	Product Favored	Mixture
Ammonia synthesis	0.30			
Ozone depletion	3.0×10^{34}			
Acid ionization	1.8×10^{-5}			

26. Aqueous solutions of hydrofluoric acid (HF) have the unique property of being able to dissolve glass. The ionization of HF in water has an equilibrium value, at 25°C, of approximately 3.5×10^{-4}. The decomposition of gaseous dinitrogen tetroxide ($N_2O_4(g)$), rocket fuel used on the lunar landers of the Apollo missions, has a K value of 0.133. The reaction of chlorine gas (Cl_2) and carbon monoxide (CO) to form phosgene ($COCl_2$), a deadly nerve gas, has a K value of 3.7×10^9 at 25°C. Complete the following table and compare the three systems.

System	K	Reactant Favored	Product Favored	Mixture
Ionization of HF	3.5×10^{-4}			
Decomposition	0.133			
Phosgene reaction	3.7×10^9			

27. Water hardness is a property of water that depends on the concentration of calcium and magnesium ions. One method used to determine these concentrations is titration with a known solution of EDTA. The goal in the titration is to produce a reaction between the dissolved metal ions and EDTA that converts essentially all the dissolved ions into compounds involving EDTA.

a. Explain why this is a desirable outcome in the analysis of water hardness.

b. Explain why K values on the order 10^{10} for the reactions between calcium and EDTA give us more confidence in the analysis than we would have if the K values were on the order of 10.

28. In aqueous solutions, acids dissociate to produce hydronium ions and a negative ion. If the reverse reaction is favored, the acid is considered weak. Judging on the basis of the following two acid dissociation reactions, which acid is the weaker acid?

Acetic acid (found in vinegar) $K = 1.8 \times 10^{-5}$

Benzoic acid (found in berries) $K = 6.5 \times 10^{-5}$

Section 16.4 Working with Equilibrium Constants

Skill Review

29. Water is a product in many chemical reactions. It can be directly made from its elements:

$$2H_2(g) + O_2(g) \rightleftharpoons 2H_2O(g)$$

a. Write the equilibrium expression for the reaction.

b. If the equilibrium concentrations for the compounds, at a specific temperature, were as follows, what would be the numerical value for K?

$$[H_2] = 0.134; \quad [O_2] = 0.673; \quad [H_2O] = 1.00$$

c. What is the value for K for the reverse reaction?

d. What is the value of K for the reaction of only 1 mol of hydrogen and 0.5 mol of oxygen to make 1 mol of water (that is, if we halve the coefficients in this reaction)?

30. If a solid bar of zinc is placed in a solution containing 1 M silver ions (Ag^+), a spontaneous reaction takes place producing zinc ions and silver metal with an equilibrium constant value of approximately 8×10^{52}.

a. What would you calculate as the equilibrium constant for the reverse reaction?

b. What would you calculate as the equilibrium constant if the stoichiometric coefficients were doubled?

Chemical Applications and Practices

31. When scientists seek information about air pollution in large cities, one of the reactions they study is

$$2NO(g) + O_2(g) \rightleftharpoons 2NO_2(g)$$

If K for the reaction, at 25°C, is approximately 1.7×10^{12} and the specific rate constant for the reverse reaction is approximately 6.6×10^{-12}, what would you calculate as the value of the rate constant for the forward reaction? (Units have been omitted for this problem.)

32. Ethyl acetate, a common laboratory solvent, can be prepared by the following reaction of acetic acid and ethanol:

$$C_2H_4O_2 \; + \; C_2H_6O \; \rightleftharpoons \; C_4H_8O_2 + H_2O$$

$\qquad$ Aetic acid $\qquad$ Ethanol $\qquad\quad$ Ethyl acetate

If K for the reaction, at 25°C, is 2.2 and the specific rate constant for the forward reaction is 4.22×10^{10}, what is the value

of the rate constant for the reverse reaction? (Units have been omitted for this problem.)

33. Producing industrially useful amounts of acetylene (C_2H_2) is important for more than acetylene torches. Acetylene is also used as a starting compound for many important polymers, such as vinyl chloride (used in PVC materials) and acrylonitrile.

a. Using the equation $CH_4(g) \rightleftharpoons \frac{1}{2}C_2H_2(g) + \frac{3}{2}H_2(g)$, write the appropriate mass-action equilibrium expression.

b. Rewrite the equation showing the stoichiometric ratios for the production of 1 mol of $C_2H_2(g)$. Write the appropriate mass-action equilibrium expression for this equation.

c. If the mathematical value for the equilibrium constant for the reaction in part a were known, how would it be mathematically converted to the equilibrium constant for the reaction in part b?

34. One of the reactions used to produce formaldehyde (CH_2O) is

$$CH_3OH(g) + \frac{1}{2}O_2(g) \rightleftharpoons CH_2O(g) + H_2O(g)$$

a. Write the mass-action equilibrium constant for the reaction.

b. Rewrite the reaction, keeping the same stoichiometric ratio, but showing the reaction utilizing 1 mol of oxygen. Write the mass-action equilibrium expression for this reaction.

c. How are the two equilibrium expressions mathematically related?

35. The reaction that allows many biochemical reactions to take place involves the breakdown of ATP (adenosine triphosphate) into ADP (adenosine diphosphate), as discussed in Chapter 14. The equilibrium constant of this reaction, at 37°C, is approximately 1.4×10^5. One of the early steps in the breakdown of glucose from food is the attachment of a phosphate group. The equilibrium constant for this process is approximately 4.7×10^{-3}. In living cells these two reactions are combined. What would be the equilibrium constant for the resulting combined reaction?

36. The production of tin is important because it has many practical uses, from plating iron objects to helping deliver fluoride in toothpaste as SnF_2. Combine the first two of the following reactions, and use the appropriate equilibrium constants, to obtain the equilibrium constant for the third reaction.

$$SnO_2(s) + 2CO(g) \rightleftharpoons Sn(s) + 2CO_2(g) \qquad K_1 = 14$$
$$CO(g) + H_2O(g) \rightleftharpoons CO_2(g) + H_2(g) \qquad K_2 = 1.3$$
$$SnO_2(s) + 2H_2(g) \rightleftharpoons Sn(s) + 2H_2O(g) \qquad K_3 = ?$$

37. Many compounds have more than one important use. Such is the case with the weak acid phenol (C_6H_5OH). It can be used, in dilute form, as an antiseptic and as a component in making some plastics. In water, phenol dissociates slightly as shown here:

$$C_6H_5OH(aq) \rightleftharpoons H^+(aq) + C_6H_5O^-(aq)$$

The equilibrium constant for this reaction is 1.3×10^{-10}. To analyze a solution containing phenol, you may carefully add measured amounts of aqueous NaOH. Recall that in water, the following reaction also takes place:

$$H^+ + OH^- \rightleftharpoons H_2O \qquad K = 1.0 \times 10^{14}$$

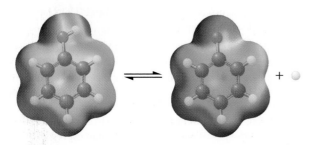

Adding these two equations produces a third that represents the reaction between sodium hydroxide and phenol. Using equilibrium constants, evaluate the feasibility of the analysis—that is, whether the reaction will proceed toward products enough for the analysis to be performed.

38. Procaine ($C_{13}H_{20}N_2O_2$) can be used to produce the anesthetic novocaine ($C_{13}H_{21}N_2O_2Cl$). Procaine is a weak base that undergoes the following reaction in aqueous solutions:

$$C_{13}H_{20}N_2O_2 + H_2O \rightleftharpoons OH^- + C_{13}H_{20}N_2O_2H^+$$

$$K = 7.1 \times 10^{-6}$$

If a solution of procaine were to be analyzed by adding carefully measured amounts of hydrochloric acid (HCl), explain how you could use the following reaction to assist in the evaluation of the viability of the analysis.

$$H^+ + OH^- \rightleftharpoons H_2O \qquad K = 1.0 \times 10^{14}$$

39. Using information from Problems 37 and 38, determine the equilibrium constant value for the reaction between phenol and procaine. Would it be a reasonable analytical strategy to employ phenol as a reactant to determine the concentration of procaine in solution?

40. Using the information from Problems 37 and 38, determine the equilibrium constant value for the reaction between HCl and NaOH. Would it be a reasonable analytical strategy to employ HCl as a reactant to determine the concentration of a NaOH solution?

41. At temperatures near 400°C, the K_p value for the synthesis of ammonia is 2.5×10^{-4}. At 400°C, what would be the approximate value of K for the following reaction?

$$3H_2(g) + N_2(g) \rightleftharpoons 2NH_3(g)$$

42. The reaction of nitrogen monoxide and chlorine gas has a large value for the equilibrium constant, K, at 298 K. However, it is often easier to measure the partial pressures of each component of a gaseous system than it is to measure their concentration. What is the value of K_p at this temperature?

$$2NO(g) + Cl_2(g) \rightleftharpoons 2NOCl(g) \quad K = 6.3 \times 10^4 \text{ (at 298 K)}$$

**Section 16.5 Solving Equilibrium Problems—
A Different Way of Thinking**

Skill Review

43. Consider the acetic acid system described earlier in the text:

$$CH_3COOH(aq) \rightleftharpoons CH_3COO^-(aq) + H^+(aq) \quad K = 1.8 \times 10^{-5}$$

What is the equilibrium hydrogen ion concentration, [H^+], given each of these initial concentrations?
a. $[CH_3COOH]_0 = 0.500\ M$; $[CH_3COO^-]_0 = 0.0\ M$
b. $[CH_3COOH]_0 = 0.100\ M$; $[CH_3COO^-]_0 = 0.100\ M$
c. $[CH_3COOH]_0 = 0.010\ M$; $[CH_3COO^-]_0 = 0.0\ M$

44. Consider the chemical system:

$$2NOCl(g) \rightleftharpoons 2NO(g) + Cl_2(g) \qquad K = 1.6 \times 10^{-5}$$

What is the equilibrium concentration of nitrogen monoxide, [NO], given each of these initial concentrations?
a. $[NOCl]_0 = 0.500\ M$; $[Cl_2]_0 = 0.0\ M$
b. $[NOCl]_0 = 1.500\ M$; $[Cl_2]_0 = 2.00\ M$
c. $[NOCl]_0 = 2.25\ M$; $[Cl_2]_0 = 1.20\ M$

45. At some temperature, the reaction $H_2 + I_2 \rightleftharpoons 2HI$ has $K = 617$. Predict in which direction, forward or reverse, the reaction would proceed when:
a. $[H_2]_0 = 0.240\ M$; $[I_2]_0 = 0.080\ M$; $[HI]_0 = 0.20\ M$
b. $[H_2]_0 = 0.030\ M$; $[I_2]_0 = 0.100\ M$; $[HI]_0 = 1.50\ M$

46. At some temperature, the reaction $H_2 + I_2 \rightleftharpoons 2HI$ has $K = 617$. Predict in which direction, forward or reverse, the reaction would proceed when:
a. $[H_2]_0 = 0.990\ M$; $[I_2]_0 = 0.280\ M$; $[HI]_0 = 0.500\ M$
b. $[H_2]_0 = 0.250\ M$; $[I_2]_0 = 1.000\ M$; $[HI]_0 = 0.500\ M$

47. Using the value of $K = 8.6 \times 10^{-5}$ for the myoglobin and oxygen reaction described in the text, $Mb + O_2 \rightleftharpoons MbO_2$, indicate which of the systems described in the following table are at equilibrium. If an example is not at equilibrium, predict the direction of change (forward or reverse) that would take place to attain the equilibrium condition.

	[Mb] (M)	[O_2] (M)	[MbO_2] (M)
a.	3.5×10^{-4}	2.5×10^{-4}	0
b.	1.0×10^{-4}	1.0×10^{-4}	8.6×10^{-13}
c.	2.0×10^{-4}	1.5×10^{-4}	2.6×10^{-11}
d.	0	2.5×10^{-4}	1.0×10^{-10}

48. The decomposition of 2 moles of carbon dioxide into carbon monoxide and oxygen gas can occur under certain conditions. If, at a particular temperature, $K = 4.5 \times 10^{-5}$, predict the direction of change (forward or reverse) that would take place to attain the equilibrium condition. (*Hint:* Start by writing the balanced equation.)

	[CO_2] (M)	[CO] (M)	[O_2] (M)
a.	0.44	1.0×10^{-5}	1.0×10^{-5}
b.	1.0×10^{-4}	0.22	1.5×10^{-8}
c.	6.3×10^{-8}	3.9×10^{-2}	4.7×10^{-12}

49. Barium sulfate ($BaSO_4$) is a slightly soluble compound that has some medical applications when used to diagnose gastrointestinal problems. Because barium can be toxic, it is important to keep the concentration of barium ions at a minimum. Given the following reaction and equilibrium value, determine the maximum equilibrium concentration of $Ba^{2+}(aq)$ when in the presence of solid $BaSO_4$.

$$BaSO_4(s) \rightleftharpoons Ba^{2+}(aq) + SO_4^{2-}(aq) \qquad K = 1.1 \times 10^{-10}$$

50. Many municipal water supplies are treated with fluoride ions (F^-) in an attempt to strengthen dental enamel. If the water contains significant amounts of calcium ions, a precipitation reaction can take place. When solid calcium fluoride is present in water, the following equilibrium is established:

$$CaF_2(s) \rightleftharpoons Ca^{2+}(aq) + 2F^-(aq) \qquad K = 4.0 \times 10^{-11}$$

What would be the equilibrium concentration of fluoride ion present in this equilibrium?

51. One of the least soluble compounds known is antimony sulfide (Sb_2S_3). If the concentration of antimony ion in a solution in which Sb_2S_3 was present were 2.2×10^{-19}, and no other solute was present, what would you calculate as the equilibrium constant for the following reaction?

$$Sb_2S_3(s) \rightleftharpoons 2Sb^{3+}(aq) + 3S^{2-}(aq)$$

52. The equilibrium constant for a reaction is very temperature dependent. Assume 0.060 is the equilibrium constant for the Haber process at a given temperature.

$$N_2(g) + 3H_2(g) \rightleftharpoons 2NH_3(g)$$

What is the equilibrium concentration of H_2 if the equilibrium concentrations of N_2 and NH_3 are found both to be 0.0010 M?

53. Using the same value of K for the ammonia synthesis reaction in Problem 52, solve for:
   a. The equilibrium concentration of NH_3 when $[N_2] = 0.0010$ M and $[H_2] = 0.010$ M
   b. The equilibrium concentration of H_2 when $[NH_3] = 0.020$ M and $[N_2] = 0.015$ M

54. Calculate the $[NO_2]$ given the equilibrium concentrations based on the reaction

$$2NO(g) + O_2(g) \rightleftharpoons 2NO_2(g) \qquad K = 1.71 \times 10^{12}$$

   a. $[NO] = 0.00020$ M; $[O_2] = 0.000050$ M; $[NO_2] = ?$
   b. $[NO] = 0.00010$ M; $[O_2] = 0.000010$ M; $[NO_2] = ?$

Chemical Applications and Practices

55. Codeine ($C_{18}H_{21}NO_3$), an analgesic drug obtained by prescription, produces the following reaction when added to water.

$$C_{18}H_{21}NO_3(aq) + H_2O(l) \rightleftharpoons OH^-(aq) + C_{18}H_{21}NO_3H^+(aq)$$
$$K = 1.6 \times 10^{-6}$$

   a. What reactions are taking place in the solution?
   b. Which among these are important? Which are unimportant?
   c. If a solution had the following concentrations, in which direction would it proceed?
   $[C_{18}H_{21}NO_3]_0 = 0.10$ M; $[OH^-]_0 = 0$ M; $[C_{18}H_{21}NO_3H^+]_0 = 0$ M
   d. Once equilibrium was achieved, what would be the concentrations of the species mentioned in part c?

56. Acetylsalicylic acid ($C_9H_8O_4$, also known as aspirin) dissociates in water with an equilibrium constant, at 25°C, of 3.0×10^{-4}.

$$C_9H_8O_4(aq) \rightleftharpoons H^+(aq) + C_9H_7O_4^-(aq)$$

   a. If the initial concentration of $C_9H_8O_4$ were 0.10 M, what would you calculate as the amount of $C_9H_8O_4$ remaining at equilibrium?
   b. What percentage of $C_9H_8O_4$ reacted?
   c. Draw an equilibrium line chart that illustrates this system.

57. One method to obtain silver metal from impure lead samples is named after the work of Samuel Parkes (1761–1825). A silver-containing lead sample is melted, and zinc is added to the molten sample. The molten zinc makes a coating on the surface. The molten silver is approximately 300 times more soluble in the molten zinc than in the impure molten lead. (The zinc–silver mixture is later removed, and pure silver is obtained by distilling away the zinc.) An equilibrium constant can be written for the concentration of silver in the lead mixture versus the amount in the zinc: $K_D = [Ag_{(Zn)}]/[Ag_{(Pb)}]$. If the $[Ag_{(Zn)}]$ was 0.0010 M and the $[Ag_{(Pb)}]$ was 0.000011 M, would it be wise to wait to see whether more Ag could be extracted? Or has the extraction for this system reached a maximum? Explain your answer.

58. The solubility of a solute in one solvent compared to another can be used to our advantage. The ratio of the dissolved amounts of solute to solvent, called a partition coefficient, may be used in a similar way as the distribution constant described earlier. The K_D value for a compound between a water layer and an ether layer is 0.024. (*Note:* This represents the amount dissolved in ether divided by the amount dissolved in water.) Suppose that the compound was ether-extracted from a plant and is now 0.015 M in ether. What will be the molarity of the compound that will form, in water, when water is placed in contact with the ether?

59. At relatively high temperatures, the following reaction can be used to produce methyl alcohol:

$$CO(g) + 2H_2(g) \rightleftharpoons CH_3OH(l) \qquad K = 13.5$$

   a. If the concentration of CO, at equilibrium, were found to be 0.010 M, what would be the equilibrium concentration of hydrogen gas?
   b. Draw an equilibrium line chart that illustrates this system.

60. Pyruvic acid is produced as an intermediate during the metabolism of carbohydrates in cells; see Chapter 14. In water it undergoes the following reaction:

$$CH_3COCOOH(aq) \rightleftharpoons H^+(aq) + CH_3COCOO^-(aq)$$
$$K = 6.6 \times 10^{-3}$$

   a. If the equilibrium concentration of $CH_3COCOOH$ were found to be 0.0010 M, what would be the equilibrium concentration of CH_3COCOO^-?
   b. Draw an equilibrium line chart that illustrates this system.

61. At high temperatures, methane (CH_4) can be reacted with steam to produce carbon monoxide and hydrogen gas, as shown in the following reaction:

$$CH_4(g) + H_2O(g) \rightleftharpoons CO(g) + 3H_2(g)$$

If the equilibrium constant is 0.25, at a specific temperature and the equilibrium concentrations of $[CH_4] = 0.11$ M, $[H_2O] = 0.28$ M, and $[CO] = 0.75$ M, what would you calculate as the $[H_2]$?

62. The aroma of rotten eggs can be partially attributable to the foul-smelling sulfur compound H_2S. Hydrogen sulfide decomposes according to the following reaction:

$$2H_2S(g) \rightleftharpoons 2H_2(g) + 2S(s)$$

The equilibrium constant for the process at a specific temperature is 0.020. If the initial concentration of H_2S were 0.0010 M, what would you determine to be the equilibrium concentrations of H_2S and H_2?

63. We discussed hydrogenation, the addition of hydrogen atoms to a carbon–carbon double or triple bond, in Chapter 12. One source of ethylene (C_2H_4) is the hydrogenation of acetylene (C_2H_2). The equilibrium constant for the reaction varies greatly with temperature. If the equilibrium constant for the following reaction is 4.2×10^{15}, what would be the equilibrium concentration of hydrogen gas in a system when the equilibrium concentrations of C_2H_2 and C_2H_4 were, respectively, 1.2×10^{-5} M and 0.025 M?

$$C_2H_2(g) + H_2(g) \rightleftharpoons C_2H_4(g)$$

64. Butanoic acid ($CH_3CH_2CH_2COOH$) has the aroma of spoiled butter. A better-smelling compound, an ester, can be made when butanoic acid is treated with methanol and an acid catalyst.

$$CH_3CH_2CH_2COOH + CH_3OH \rightleftharpoons$$
$$CH_3CH_2CH_2COOCH_3 + H_2O$$

Under certain conditions, the equilibrium constant for the reaction is 1.5×10^{-2}. What would be the equilibrium concentration of the product ester if the initial concentrations of each reactant were 0.500 M? Note that water is not the solvent and must be included in K.

65. The element vanadium is unusually resistant to corrosion. Alloyed with iron (approximately 5% vanadium) it produces a useful type of steel. One reaction used to obtain vanadium has a K value of 14 at 298 K.

$$VO^+(aq) + 2H^+(aq) \rightleftharpoons V^{3+}(aq) + H_2O(l)$$

Starting with $[VO^+]_0 = 0.15$ M and $[H^+] = 0.100$ M, what would you calculate as the equilibrium concentrations of $VO^+(aq)$, $H^+(aq)$, and $V^{3+}(aq)$?

66. Using the reaction in Problem 65, decide in which direction the reaction would proceed when the following concentrations were known. (Prove your answers.)
    a. $[VO^{2+}] = 0.10$ M; $[H^+] = 0.25$ M; $[V^{3+}] = 0.85$ M
    b. $[VO^{2+}] = .0025$ M; $[H^+] = 0.10$ M; $[V^{3+}] = 0.025$ M

67. Using the K value of 8.6×10^{-5} presented in the text for the myoglobin and oxygen reaction $Mb + O_2 \rightleftharpoons MbO_2$, what would you calculate as the $[Mb]$, $[O_2]$, and $[MbO_2]$ when the initial concentrations were as follows: $[Mb] = 0.00100$ M; $[O_2] = 0$ M, and $[MbO_2] = 0.000020$ M?

68. As was mentioned in Problem 32, ethyl acetate can be prepared by the reaction of acetic acid and ethanol.

$$C_2H_4O_2 + C_2H_6O \rightleftharpoons C_4H_8O_2 + H_2O \qquad K = 2.2 \text{ (at } 25°C)$$

What would you calculate as the equilibrium concentration of each component of the mixture if the initial concentrations of each component in the mixture were 0.100 M? (Assume that water is not the solvent.)

Section 16.6 Le Châtelier's Principle

Skill Review

69. Using Le Châtelier's principle, decide whether each of these changes would cause the equilibrium of the system presented to shift to the left, would cause it to shift to the right, or would have no effect on the equilibrium.

$$CH_4(g) + 2O_2(g) \rightleftharpoons CO_2(g) + 2H_2O(g)$$

(This is the exothermic reaction of burning methane in a lab burner.)

a. Removing CO_2 from the system
b. Adding heat to the system
c. Decreasing the volume of the container
d. Adding $H_2O(g)$ to the system
e. Adding inert He to the system

70. Calcium oxide (CaO) is also known as lime. It is one of the leading chemicals produced worldwide, thanks to its many uses in plant and animal foods, insecticides, paper making, and plaster products. It is produced, at high temperatures, from calcium carbonate.

$$CaCO_3(s) \rightleftharpoons CaO(s) + CO_2(g) \text{ (endothermic reaction)}$$

If the system were in a closed container, what effect (shift to the left, shift to the right, or no effect) would each of these changes have on the favored direction of the reaction?
a. Removing CO_2
b. Adding CaO
c. Raising the temperature
d. Enlarging the size of the container
e. Adding a suitable catalyst

Chemical Applications and Practices

71. The following equilibrium constant values are found for dissolving two solids in water to produce aqueous solutions of the ions shown. Note that the stoichiometry for the process is the same in both systems.

$$AgCl(s) \rightleftharpoons Ag^+(aq) + Cl^-(aq) \qquad K = 1.7 \times 10^{-10}$$
$$CuCl(s) \rightleftharpoons Cu^+(aq) + Cl^-(aq) \qquad K = 1.9 \times 10^{-7}$$

a. In which system would you find the greater number of moles of dissolved ions?
b. Would adding more solid to the other system increase the number of dissolved ions so that it might equal the total found in the choice for part a? Explain your reasoning.

72. The production of ethylene is important in the manufacture of polyethylene products. The following reaction shows how ethylene can be made from ethane by removing hydrogen from ethane.

$$CH_3CH_3(g) \rightleftharpoons CH_2CH_2(g) + H_2(g)$$

a. At 298 K, the equilibrium constant is 0.96. If a 1-liter container initially contained 0.10 M CH_3CH_3, what would be the equilibrium concentration of all three species?
b. After equilibrium is reached, an additional 0.010 mol of H_2 is injected into the container without changing its volume. What would be the concentration of all three species when equilibrium was once again restored?

73. A dilute solution of $Na_2Co(H_2O)_6Cl_4$ has a faint pink color and can be used as "invisible ink." When some of the loosely held water is driven off, with gentle heating, Na_2CoCl_4 forms, with a visible change to blue. If you stored your "invisible ink" solution in a refrigerator, would it appear pink or blue? Explain the basis of your answer.

74. The recognizable aromas of many fruits are due to a group of compounds known as esters, as we learned in Chapter 12. For example, the following reaction shows the production of pentyl acetate. (Assume that water is not the solvent.)

$$CH_3CH_2CH_2CH_2CH_2OH \;+\; CH_3COOH \;\rightleftharpoons$$

Pentanol   **Ethanoic acid**
(acetic acid)

$$CH_3CH_2CH_2CH_2CH_2OOCCH_3 \;+\; H_2O$$

Pentyl ethanoate
(pentyl acetate)

Which of these methods would increase the amount of product formed, and why?
a. Add water so that the pentyl ethanoate would dissolve better.
b. Add magnesium sulfate so it would react with any water formed.

75. One way to produce rubbing alcohol ($CH_3CHOHCH_3$) is from propene:

$$CH_3-CH=CH_2 + H_2O \underset{\text{Catalyst}}{\rightleftharpoons} CH_3-\overset{\displaystyle OH}{\overset{\displaystyle |}{C}H}-CH_3$$

Explain what the role of the catalyst is, in relation to the equilibrium, in this reaction.

76. Tungsten's unusually high melting point (over 3000°C) and its efficiency at producing light from electrical energy led to its use in light bulb filaments. It can be obtained via the following reaction:

$$WO_3(s) + 3H_2(g) \rightleftharpoons W(s) + 3H_2O(g)$$

Like most reactions in which a metal is obtained from another compound, this reaction is endothermic. Explain why pressure changes are not considered significant factors when tungsten is obtained in this manner.

Section 16.7 Free Energy and the Equilibrium Constant

Skill Review

77. Determine the equilibrium constant, K_{eq}, associated with reactions that have these free energy changes at 25°C.
a. $\Delta G° = -1.05$ J/mol
b. $\Delta G° = 0.230$ J/mol
c. $\Delta G° = 2.55$ kJ/mol
d. $\Delta G° = -9.80$ kJ/mol

78. Determine the free energy change, $\Delta G°$, for each of these equilibrium constants at 25°C.
a. $K_{eq} = 1.8 \times 10^{-5}$
b. $K_{eq} = 6.67 \times 10^{-1}$
c. $K_{eq} = 2.30 \times 10^{-2}$
d. $K_{eq} = 125$

79. What is the free energy change, $\Delta G°$, in kilojoules per mole, for the formation of methanol from carbon monoxide and hydrogen gas at 25°C?

$$CO(g) + 2H_2(g) \rightleftharpoons CH_3OH(l) \qquad K_{eq} = 13.5$$

80. Use the tables of $\Delta G°$ in the Appendix to determine the value of the equilibrium constant, K_{eq}, for the following reaction at 25°C.

$$CaCO_3(s) \rightleftharpoons CaO(s) + CO_2(g)$$

Chemical Applications and Practices

81. Hydrogen sulfide (H_2S), which is responsible for the odor of rotten eggs, decomposes by the reaction illustrated in Problem 62. Given the value of the equilibrium constant in Problem 62, calculate the free energy change, in kilojoules per mole, for the decomposition reaction at 25°C.

82. The ionization of HF in water (see Problem 26) has an equilibrium constant $K_{eq} = 3.5 \times 10^{-4}$ at 25°C. Calculate the free energy change, in kilojoules per mole, for the decomposition reaction.

Comprehensive Problems

83. Acids react by donating hydrogen ions. The strength of the acid reaction is determined by the ability the acid has to donate the H^+ to water. Symbolically, the reaction in water can be represented as follows:

$$HA \rightleftharpoons H^+ + A^-$$

The following is a list of some common weak acids followed by their water reaction equilibrium values. All are compared at the same temperature. Which acid in the list is the weakest? Which is the strongest?

Acetic acid, $HC_2H_3O_2$ (found in vinegar) $K = 1.8 \times 10^{-5}$

Formic acid, $HCHO_2$ (found in ants) $K = 1.8 \times 10^{-4}$

Benzoic acid, $HC_7H_5O_2$ (found in some berries)
$$K = 6.3 \times 10^{-5}$$

84. Scientists have investigated hydrazine (N_2H_4) and nitrogen monoxide (NO) in their study of rocket fuels. Use the following reaction to write the chemical equilibrium expression for this hydrazine reaction.

$$N_2H_4(g) + 2NO(g) \rightleftharpoons 2N_2(g) + 2H_2O(g)$$

85. Suppose there are two synthetic routes by which a pharmaceutical company can make the same prescription drug. Method A uses expensive starting materials but has a large value for K. Method B uses inexpensive starting materials but has a small value for K. You have been asked to discuss briefly, in a planning meeting, the various considerations involved in deciding between these two methods. What would you say about the arguments for making a profit with either method?

86. Is it possible for K_p to equal K? Explain your answer.

87. Using only whole-number coefficients, write a balanced chemical equation that represents the conversion of oxygen molecules into ozone. If the equilibrium constant for that reaction were 7×10^{-58}, what would you calculate as the equilibrium constant for the reaction that produces 1 mol of ozone?

88. The electrochemical reaction powering a nickel–cadmium rechargeable battery has an equilibrium constant value, at 298 K, of approximately 1.5×10^{11}, as written below. What is the value for the reverse reaction of this process? The reaction takes place in an alkaline solution.

$$Cd(s) + NiO_2(s) \rightleftharpoons Ni(OH)_2(s) + Cd(OH)_2(s)$$

89. An owner of a coffee shop, who happens to be a former chemistry student, notices that there are some similarities between customers (that is, people in the shop and those not entering the shop) and the reactants and products at equilibrium in a chemical system. What type of customer movement would represent equilibrium for the shop? What type of equilibrium would the profit-minded owner prefer, one with a large value of K or a small value of K? Explain. If Q were less than K, would it be a good business day or a poor business day? Explain.

$$K = \frac{[\text{customers}]}{[\text{people on the street}]}$$

90. As we have noted previously, the presence of fluoride in some municipal water systems can bring about the precipitation of CaF_2 if the concentration of Ca^{2+} is very high.

$$CaF_2(s) \rightleftharpoons Ca^{2+}(aq) + 2F^-(aq) \qquad K = 4.0 \times 10^{-11}$$

a. How many moles per liter of CaF_2 would dissolve in pure water?

b. If the concentration of Ca^{2+} in a water sample were 0.0050 M, as might be present in hard water samples, how many moles per liter of CaF_2 would dissolve?

91. The following reaction has historical importance as it was once used to produce a useful fuel called "water gas." The process involved using steam to convert coal into carbon monoxide and hydrogen gas.

$$C(s) + H_2O(g) \rightleftharpoons CO(g) + H_2(g) \qquad K_p = 21 \ (\text{at } 1000°C)$$

If the initial partial pressure of $H_2O(g)$ were 52 atm, what would you calculate as the equilibrium partial pressures of $H_2O(g)$; $CO(g)$ and $H_2(g)$?

92. Carbonic acid, present in carbonated beverages, can participate in two reactions that both involve removing a H^+ from the molecule.

$$H_2CO_3\,(aq) \rightleftharpoons H^+\,(aq) + HCO_3^-(aq) \qquad K = 4.3 \times 10^{-7}$$
$$HCO_3^-(aq) \rightleftharpoons H^+(aq) + CO_3^{2-}(aq) \qquad K = 5.6 \times 10^{-11}$$

Starting with an initial concentration of H_2CO_3 of 0.10 M, what would you calculate as the equilibrium concentrations of $[H_2CO_3], [HCO_3^-]$, $[H^+]$, and $[CO_3^{2-}]$? Be sure to justify any assumptions you made to solve the problem.

93. Examine the hypothetical reaction illustrated below. A snapshot of each reaction was taken at specific times during the course of the reaction. Which frame represents the first frame in which equilibrium has been reached? Explain your answer.

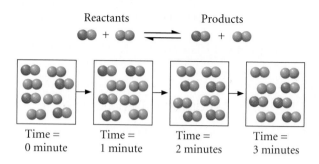

Reactants   Products

| Time = 0 minute | Time = 1 minute | Time = 2 minutes | Time = 3 minutes |

Thinking Beyond the Calculation

94. The industrial preparation of methanol, a potential gasoline substitute, is accomplished by the hydrogenation of carbon monoxide. The reaction is

$$CO(g) + 2H_2(g) \rightleftharpoons CH_3OH(g)$$

a. Calculate the thermodynamic parameters for this reaction using the Appendix. Is this reaction spontaneous at 25°C?

b. Using your calculated value of $\Delta G°$, determine the equilibrium constant for the reaction. Does this reaction favor products or reactants?

c. What is the value of K for the reverse reaction?

d. If the rate of the forward reaction was determined to be 3.56×10^{-12} M/s, what is the rate of the reverse reaction at equilibrium?

e. If a researcher began the synthesis of methanol by adding 1.5 mol of CO and 3.5 mol of H_2 to a 5.0-L flask, what would be the equilibrium concentration of methanol?

f. What effect, if any, would the addition of more CO have on the equilibrium concentration of methanol?

g. With added catalyst and removal of the methanol as it is formed in the reaction, the reaction can quickly produce 100% yield. If 1.0 L of $H_2(g)$ at 25°C cost $0.10 and 1.0 L of $CO(g)$ at 25°C cost $0.30, what would it cost to produce 1.0 L of $CH_3OH(l)$ at 25°C? Assume the expense associated with the experimental procedure is negligible. (*Hint:* Note that the problem asks for the cost to produce liquid methanol from gaseous reactants.)

17

Acids and Bases

Contents and Selected Applications

Acids and bases are an integral part of our everyday life. For instance, the acidity of the local swimming pool is monitored daily. Adjustments to the pH can be made by adding chemicals.

"Home is where the heart is." Home is also where the phosphoric acid is and where other important acids are, including nitric, sulfuric, acetic, and even acetylsalicylic and ascorbic acids. Most homes also have products containing bases, among which we count ammonia and sodium hydroxide as the two most important. Given the continuing increase in population, the resulting need for more food, the frantic pace of new home construction (see Figure 17.1), and the increase in sales of consumer products, we can understand why many acids and bases are among the top 20 chemicals produced in the United States, as shown in Table 17.1.

Application

CHEMICAL
ENCOUNTERS:
Common Uses of
Acids and Bases

Why are acids and bases worth knowing about? As we will see in this chapter, they are a part of every household, the people in it, and the house itself. Acid–base reactions in our blood keep us alive. Amino acids combine to form proteins that are enzymes, hormones, and structural materials in our bodies. DNA and RNA are formed from nucleotides that are made by the chemical combination of phosphoric acid, a sugar, and a base. Our food is mostly acidic. Many of us take daily supplements of vitamin C (ascorbic acid) for its health benefits. We clean our homes with products that include both acids, such as acetic acid (CH_3COOH) and sulfuric acid (H_2SO_4) and bases, such as ammonia (NH_3) and

TABLE 17.1	Acids and Bases in Top Chemicals Produced in U.S. Industry in 2004	
Substance	**Key Commercial Uses**	**Billions of kg Produced**
Sulfuric acid	Fertilizer	37.5
Calcium oxide	Cement, paper	18.4*
Phosphoric acid	Fertilizers, animal feed	11.5
Ammonia	Fertilizers, plastics	10.8
Sodium carbonate	Glass, cleansers	10.3*
Sodium hydroxide	Industrial synthesis	9.5
Nitric acid	Fertilizers, explosives	6.7

*2002 data.
Source: Chemical & Engineering News, July 11, 2005, pp. 69–75.

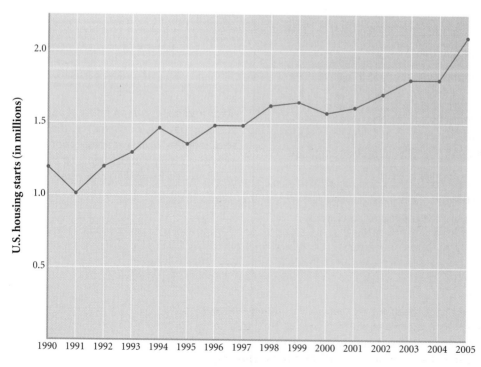

FIGURE 17.1

Housing starts in the United States for the 16-year period ending in 2005. Acids and bases are a part of home construction, household furnishings, and appliances. This trend in new home construction indicates a robust demand for the industrial production of acids and bases.

TABLE 17.2	Common Acids and Bases and Examples of Their Uses
Acid or Base	**Example of Use**
Acetylsalicylic acid	Aspirin
Ammonia	Household cleaners, fertilizer, manufacture of fertilizers
Lauric acid, $CH_3(CH_2)_{10}COOH$	Key ingredient in toothpaste manufacture
Nitric acid	Key ingredient in acid precipitation
Nicotine (a base)	Tobacco products
Sodium hydroxide	Manufacture of soap, many industrial compounds

Sodium hydroxide — NaOH   Magnesium hydroxide — $Mg(OH)_2$

Acetic acid — CH_3OOH Acetylsalicylic acid — $C_9H_8O_4$ Ascorbic acid — $C_6H_8O_6$

Acids and bases are worth knowing about because they are ubiquitous in the world both around us and within our bodies. Those household products containing bases are listed in blue; those containing acids are listed in red.

sodium hypochlorite (NaOCl). The walls of our house or apartment are likely to be made of gypsum, another name for calcium sulfate ($CaSO_4$), formed from the reaction of phosphate rock and sulfuric acid. Municipal water supplies are monitored, and (when required) chemically treated, to maintain safe acid concentrations.

Acids, such as aluminum sulfate ($Al_2(SO_4)_3$) and bases, such as sodium hydroxide (NaOH) and sodium carbonate (Na_2CO_3), are used in the manufacture of the paper on which you are now reading these ideas. Other acids and bases are used in the manufacture of plastics and polymer-based clothing, such as polyester and rayon. Computer chips are etched with hydrofluoric acid. Fertilizer for the garden is often made with ammonia-based compounds. Gold is isolated from its ores with a base known as sodium cyanide (NaCN). Toothpaste contains a base known as tetra-sodium pyrophosphate ($Na_4P_2O_7$). The list goes on and on and on. Whether the context we discuss is biological, medical, agricultural, environmental, or industrial, acids and bases are a part of it (see Table 17.2). How much of a part? As we will learn in Chapter 18, acids and bases are used to answer that as well.

17.1 What Are Acids and Bases?

There are several models we can use to define an acid. One of these is the Arrhenius model, named after the Swedish chemist Svante Arrhenius (1859–1927), in which an **acid** is any species that produces *hydrogen* ions in solution and a **base** is any species that produces *hydroxide* ions in solution. For example, nitric acid can be classified as an Arrhenius acid because it produces hydrogen ions in aqueous solution.

$$HNO_3(aq) \rightleftharpoons H^+(aq) + NO_3^-(aq)$$

Similarly, sodium hydroxide is an Arrhenius base because it produces hydroxide ions in aqueous solution.

$$NaOH(aq) \rightarrow Na^+(aq) + OH^-(aq)$$

In truth, hydrogen ions (H^+) do not exist free in solution. Rather, they *always* interact with the solvent, often water. Just as metal cations such as Na^+ are surrounded by water molecules through ion–dipole interactions, hydrogen cations (which are just protons because they have no neutrons or electrons) similarly

FIGURE 17.2

Data show that hydrogen ions interact with several water molecules. One possible structure involves a shell of 21 water molecules surrounding a H_3O^+ ion. (*Source:* Mark Johnson, Yale University.)

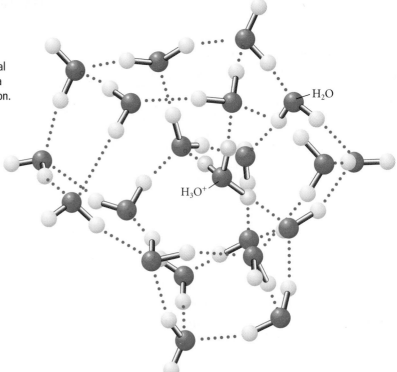

FIGURE 17.3

Johannes Nicolaus Brønsted (1879–1947) was a Danish physical chemist. In addition to studying quantum mechanics and developing an acid–base theory, he became interested in politics during the German occupation of Denmark in World War II. He was elected to the Danish parliament in 1947 but became ill and died before he could take office.

interact with water molecules that surround them. In fact, protons interact so strongly that they become directly incorporated into the fabric of one or more water molecules, and are easily passed among them. Experimental data show that each proton is immediately surrounded by at least four water molecules and is most likely surrounded by many more. Recent research by several groups in the U.S. suggests that, when H^+ is surrounded by twenty-one (21) water molecules, a most wonderful structure, shown in Figure 17.2, is formed! However, in room temperature aqueous solution, no single well-defined structure exists, because hydrogen bonds are being continually broken and formed. For simplicity, chemists typically refer to the hydrogen ion as either H^+ or H_3O^+ (the hydronium ion), understanding all the while that H^+ actually exists surrounded by several water molecules.

A more useful way of describing acids and bases is the Brønsted–Lowry model (named after the Danish scientist Johannes Nicolaus Brønsted (1879–1947, Figure 17.3) and the English chemist Thomas Lowry (1874–1936), who proposed the definition in 1923). In his model, a **Brønsted–Lowry acid** is defined as any species that *donates* a hydrogen ion (proton) to another species. This definition of an acid is applicable to *all solvents* in which protons can be exchanged, and, being more far-reaching than the Arrhenius model, it is the definition we will use. A **Brønsted–Lowry base** is any species that can *accept* a hydrogen ion (proton) from an acid. As an example of a Brønsted–Lowry acid and base, consider what happens when hydrogen chloride gas is dissolved in water.

$$HCl(g) \ + \ H_2O(l) \rightleftharpoons Cl^-(aq) \ + \ H_3O^+(aq)$$

Hydrochloric acid   Hydronium ion

Figure 17.4 shows the Lewis structures of the reactants and products. In the Brønsted–Lowry model, HCl is the acid and water is the base. The chloride ion (Cl^-) is called the **conjugate base** of HCl because it is the base that results after the HCl donates a proton to water. Similarly, H_3O^+ is the **conjugate acid** of water because it is the acid that results after the water accepts the proton from HCl. The word *conjugate* comes from the Latin word *conjugare*, which means "join together."

HCl and Cl^- are a conjugate acid–base pair.

H_3O^+ and H_2O are a conjugate acid–base pair.

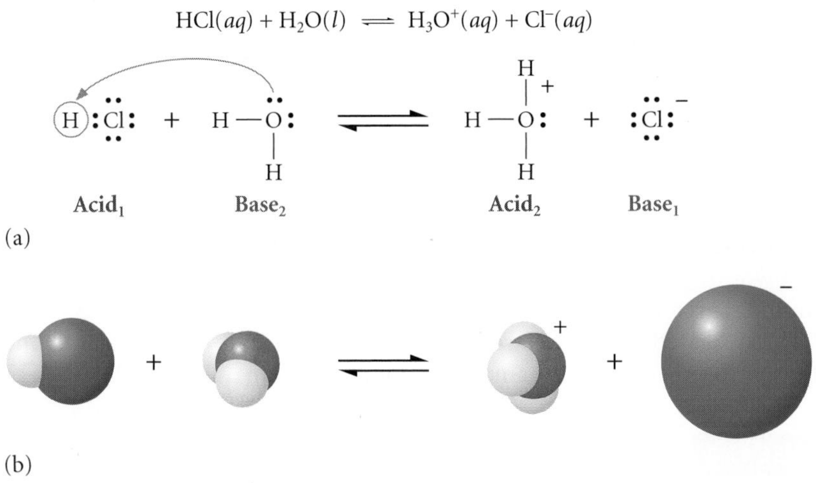

$$HCl(aq) + H_2O(l) \rightleftharpoons H_3O^+(aq) + Cl^-(aq)$$

Acid₁   Base₂   Acid₂   Base₁

(a)

(b)

Note that a conjugate base is paired with an acid (Cl⁻ and HCl) and a conjugate acid is paired with a base (H₃O⁺ and H₂O).

$$\underset{\text{[Acid]}}{HCl(g)} + \underset{\text{[Base]}}{H_2O(l)} \rightleftharpoons \underset{\text{[Conjugate base]}}{Cl^-(aq)} + \underset{\text{[Conjugate acid]}}{H_3O^+(aq)}$$

EXERCISE 17.1   Acids, Bases, and Their Conjugates

Complete the equation for the reaction of formic acid (HCOOH) and water. Identify the conjugate acid–base pairs.

$$HCOOH(aq) + H_2O(l) \rightleftharpoons$$

First Thoughts

Formic acid can donate a hydrogen ion to water. Is water an acid or a base in this process? The products will be the formate and hydronium ions. When deciding on the conjugate pairs, think about what each reactant forms when it either donates or accepts a hydrogen ion. We will denote the conjugate pairs as "1" and "2."

Solution

$$\underset{\text{[Acid}_1\text{]}}{HCOOH(aq)} + \underset{\text{[Base}_2\text{]}}{H_2O(l)} \rightleftharpoons \underset{\text{[Conjugate base}_1\text{]}}{HCOO^-(aq)} + \underset{\text{[Conjugate acid}_2\text{]}}{H_3O^+(aq)}$$

Further Insights

Conjugate acid–base pairs can exist in nonaqueous solvents (that is, the solvent is something other than water). For example, phenol (C₆H₆OH) acts as an acid when it reacts with the basic solvent ethylenediamine (H₂NCH₂CH₂NH₂) in the following way:

$$\underset{\text{[Acid}_1\text{]}}{C_6H_6OH} + \underset{\text{[Base}_2\text{]}}{H_2NCH_2CH_2NH_2} \rightleftharpoons \underset{\text{[Conjugate base}_1\text{]}}{C_6H_6O^-} + \underset{\text{[Conjugate acid}_2\text{]}}{H_2NCH_2CH_2NH_3^+}$$

PRACTICE 17.1

Complete the equation for the reaction of ethylenediamine with water. Identify the conjugate acid–base pairs.

$$H_2NCH_2CH_2NH_2(aq) + H_2O(l) \rightleftharpoons$$

See Problem 7. ■

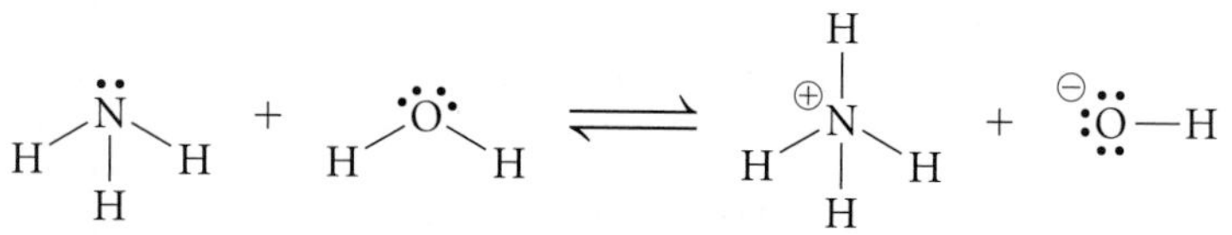

FIGURE 17.5

Ammonia is an Arrhenius base because it generates OH⁻ in water. It is also considered a Brønsted–Lowry base because it accepts a proton from water.

We previously mentioned that ammonia (NH_3) is an important chemical, and the 2004 worldwide production figure of 10.8 billion kg would seem to confirm this. Ammonia is a Brønsted–Lowry base because it accepts a hydrogen ion from water. The unshared pair of electrons on the nitrogen can form a covalent bond with the hydrogen, forming the ammonium ion, as shown in Figure 17.5.

EXERCISE 17.2   Ammonia as a Base

Identify the conjugate acid–base pairs in the reaction of ammonia with water. How does water behave differently in this reaction than when it reacts with HCl?

First Thoughts

This contrasts with Exercise 17.1 because ammonia (NH_3) is a base. Water takes on a very different role than in the previous exercise, that of an acid. Yet the concept of the conjugates is still the same—both ammonia and water will have conjugate pairs.

Solution

$$\underset{[\text{Base}_1]}{NH_3(aq)} + \underset{[\text{Acid}_2]}{H_2O(l)} \;\rightleftharpoons\; \underset{[\text{Conjugate acid}_1]}{NH_4^+(aq)} + \underset{[\text{Conjugate base}_2]}{OH^-(aq)}$$

Further Insights

We devote many words in this text to the important properties of water. Here we see another one. As the "universal solvent," water can be an acid or, as in Exercise 17.1, a base, depending on the solute. Any substance that can be an acid or a base is called amphiprotic. We will explore this property later in the chapter.

PRACTICE 17.2

Identify the conjugate pairs in the reaction of lauric acid ($CH_3(CH_2)_{10}COOH$) with water.

See Problems 3–6, 11, and 12. ∎

G. N. Lewis (remember him from Chapter 8 for his work representing substances via Lewis structures) proposed a *third* model of acids and bases in which a Lewis base donates a previously nonbonded pair of electrons (a lone pair) to form a coordinate covalent bond. Electrons are not transferred entirely but, rather, are shared to make a bond. Reduction and oxidation are not taking place when a Lewis base donates a pair of electrons. All Brønsted–Lowry acids are also Lewis acids, and all Brønsted–Lowry bases are also Lewis bases. However, many metal ions, such as Al^{3+}, are Lewis acids, because they can accept electrons, although they do not donate protons. For example, when Al^{3+} is in aqueous solution, it combines with water:

$$Al^{3+}(aq) + 6H_2O(l) \rightleftharpoons Al(H_2O)_6^{3+}(aq)$$

It then can act as a Brønsted–Lowry acid:

$$Al(H_2O)_6^{3+}(aq) + H_2O(l) \rightleftharpoons Al(H_2O)_5OH^{2+}(aq) + H_3O^+(aq)$$

In another example, we could identify borane (BH_3) in the reaction below as a Lewis acid and ammonia as a Lewis base. This reaction and the specific bonding patterns were discussed in detail in Chapter 8.

$$BH_3(g) + NH_3(g) \rightleftharpoons H_3B—NH_3(s)$$
Lewis acid   Lewis base

We mentioned in the opening of the chapter that aluminum sulfate is added to wood pulp as it is formed into paper. The compound is used as a "sizing agent," a substance that prevents ink from spreading. Unfortunately, this acid slowly breaks down the cellulose in paper, causing it to turn light brown with age. That is why many newspapers and paperback books look old even after only weeks or months.

We will have more to say about Lewis acids in the next chapter. In our present discussion, because we are dealing primarily with water as a solvent, and because Lewis acids become Brønsted–Lowry acids in water, the Brønsted–Lowry model will be the most useful to us.

How do we know an acid when we see one? Even though nearly all common foods (including milk!) are acidic, we often associate acids specifically with citrus juices. Orange juice and grapefruit juice can taste sour. This is a characteristic property of acids. Bases, on the other hand, are slippery and often taste bitter.

We learned in Chapter 12 that hydrochloric acid reacts with zinc to produce hydrogen gas:

$$Zn(s) + 2HCl(aq) \rightarrow Zn^{2+}(aq) + 2Cl^-(aq) + H_2(g)$$

This is typical of another characteristic of acids: that they react with many metals to form solutions and often release hydrogen gas. In this sense, acids corrode metals. Bases often react with metal ions to produce insoluble hydroxides, such as $Fe(OH)_3$. A vital property that acids and bases share is that they modify the structure of some types of organic molecules, often found in plants, to cause color changes. In the next chapter, we will discuss how we use these color changes to help us analyze the amount of substances present in a sample. All of these things—sour or bitter, slimy, reactions with metals, color changes, and more—are properties that signal that a material is acidic or is basic (see Table 17.3).

Aluminum is a Lewis acid because it combines with water. Although aluminum sulfate is useful as a sizing agent in books and newspapers to prevent ink from spreading, the aluminum ion acting as an acid breaks down cellulose in paper, causing the pages to become yellow and brittle after only months.

TABLE 17.3	**Properties of Acids and Bases**
Acids	**Bases**
Taste sour	Taste bitter
Donate protons during an acid–base reaction	Accept protons during an acid–base reaction
React with some metals to produce hydrogen gas and metal ions	Form insoluble hydroxides with many metal ions

17.2   Acid Strength

We now know what acids and bases are, and we have seen some typical acid–base reactions. We have shown that acids and bases are present throughout our world and within ourselves. However, just as people come in all shapes and sizes, acids and bases come in different *strengths*. These differences have a profound impact on their chemical behavior and their uses.

We can begin to understand acid (and, by extension, base) strength by recalling that nearly all of our foods are acidic. Let's turn that statement around and see whether it still makes sense. If nearly all foods are acidic, are nearly all acids suitable as foods? That is, we know that citrus fruits contain citric acid ($C_6H_8O_7$) and that ingesting it in reasonable amounts is safe. Oranges and grapefruits also contain ascorbic acid ($H_2C_6H_6O_6$), which is also called vitamin C. Aspirin ($C_8H_8O_4$) is known chemically as acetylsalicylic acid. We eat these things. Some are necessary for good health (vitamin C); some can relieve headaches and may

Ascorbic acid

Acid and base *strength* is an inherent property of a substance and is unaffected by dilution. Sulfuric acid, found in car batteries, is inherently strong, whereas citric acid, found in oranges, is inherently weak.

 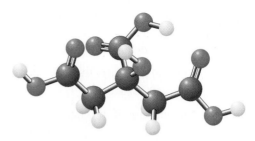

Sulfuric acid   **Citric acid**

even help prevent heart attacks (aspirin). Yet ingesting sulfuric acid (H_2SO_4) at the concentration found in a car battery would be lethal. This is also true of the hydrochloric acid that is used as a 30% solution in water to clean stains on concrete.

Application

CHEMICAL ENCOUNTERS: Acids in Foods

There are two issues here. The first is that sulfuric acid and hydrochloric acid are *strong* acids (a term defined below). Many acids found in foods are *weak* acids. The other point is that in batteries and concrete cleaners, the acids are relatively *concentrated,* whereas in an orange or other food, the acids are fairly *dilute.* Diluting the hydrochloric acid by a factor of 1000 with water would render it ineffective for cleaning concrete, even though *it would remain a strong acid.* Some acids are inherently strong and some are weak. Solute concentration, whether 10 *M* or 1×10^{-6} *M*—that is, whether relatively concentrated or dilute—doesn't change the inherent strength of the acids or bases.

Strong and Weak Acids

In aqueous solution, a **strong acid** is one that at 1 molar concentration *dissociates (or, in some cases, ionizes) essentially completely.* "Dissociates" means separates or, in this case, loses a hydrogen cation—a proton. Molecules in which the hydrogen atom is covalently bonded actually do ionize when they go into solution. *Whether the process is called dissociation or ionization, the result is the same: the production of H^+ in the solution.* A **weak acid** *only partially ionizes (or dissociates)* at 1 molar concentration in aqueous solution. We can reinforce these ideas by comparing a strong acid, nitric acid (HNO_3), to a weak acid, acetic acid (CH_3COOH). The ionization equations for 1 molar aqueous solutions of these two acids can be written as follows:

$$HNO_3(aq) + H_2O(l) \rightleftharpoons NO_3^-(aq) + H_3O^+(aq)$$

$$CH_3COOH(aq) + H_2O(l) \rightleftharpoons CH_3COO^-(aq) + H_3O^+(aq)$$

The ionization of nitric acid proceeds essentially all the way to products, so it is a strong acid. The reverse reaction will not occur to any extent because nitric acid donates a proton to water (forward direction) much more effectively than the hydronium ion (H_3O^+) donates a proton to nitrate ion (reverse direction). Acetic acid *only slightly dissociates* (typically less than 1%, depending on its initial concentration), so it is a weak acid. This occurs because H_3O^+ can donate a proton to the acetate ion (CH_3COO^-), the conjugate base of acetic acid, regenerating the initial reactants (see Figure 17.6).

The equilibrium constant for the dissociation of an acid is called the **acid dissociation constant** (K_a) and has the same relationship to the extent of an acid–base reaction as any other equilibrium constant to that of its own reaction. This is a key point:

The principles of equilibrium are consistent no matter what system we are working with.

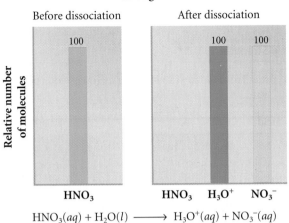

1.0 *M*
Strong acid

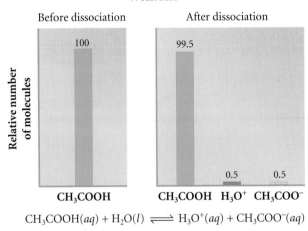

1.0 *M*
Weak acid

$HNO_3(aq) + H_2O(l) \longrightarrow H_3O^+(aq) + NO_3^-(aq)$

$CH_3COOH(aq) + H_2O(l) \rightleftharpoons H_3O^+(aq) + CH_3COO^-(aq)$

FIGURE 17.6

There is a competition between acetic acid (CH_3COOH) and hydronium ion (H_3O^+) to get rid of a hydrogen ion. The hydronium ion is a stronger acid, so the acetic acid does not dissociate to a great extent. The single-headed arrow in the ionization of nitric acid indicates that the reaction goes essentially to completion.

The equilibrium constant may be called K_a for acids, K_b for bases, or K_{sp} for solids; and there are others. *But their fundamental meaning as equilibrium constants, and how we use them in our problem solving, are the same.*

Table 17.4 lists several weak acids and their K_a values.

The mass-action expressions for the reactions shown for nitric and acetic acids with water can be written in the following "shorthand" form (neglecting the presence of water because it is the solvent, and neglecting activity effects).

$$K_a = \frac{[NO_3^-][H^+]}{[HNO_3]}$$

$$K_a = \frac{[CH_3COO^-][H^+]}{[CH_3COOH]}$$

Nitric and other strong acids have K_a values much greater than 1, often regarded as infinity in aqueous solution. Weak acids, such as acetic acid ($K_a = 1.8 \times 10^{-5}$), have K_a values less than 1. We can use the equilibrium line chart that we introduced in Chapter 16 to see the extent of the reaction for HNO_3, the strong acid, compared to CH_3COOH, the weak acid.

There are differences in acid strength among strong acids. For example, $HClO_4$ is inherently stronger than HCl. However, this difference not observable in water, in which HCl, or any other strong acid, appears to be just as

TABLE 17.4	K_a of Selected Weak Acids	
Formula	**Name**	**K_a**
HSO_4^-	Hydrogen sulfate ion	1.2×10^{-2}
$HClO_2$	Chlorous acid	1.2×10^{-2}
HF	Hydrofluoric acid	7.2×10^{-4}
HNO_2	Nitrous acid	7.0×10^{-4}
$HC_3H_5O_3$	Lactic acid	1.3×10^{-4}
$HC_2H_3O_2$ (CH_3COOH)	Acetic acid	1.8×10^{-5}
$[Al(H_2O)_6]^{3+}$	Hydrated aluminum ion	1.4×10^{-5}
HOCl	Hypochlorous acid	3.5×10^{-8}
HCN	Hydrocyanic acid	6.2×10^{-10}
NH_4^+	Ammonium ion	5.6×10^{-10}
HOC_6H_5	Phenol	1.6×10^{-10}

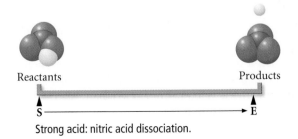

Strong acid: nitric acid dissociation.

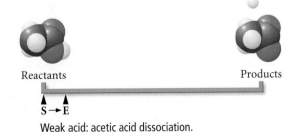

Weak acid: acetic acid dissociation.

strong as $HClO_4$, because their strength makes their reaction with water essentially complete. It is possible to use nonaqueous solvents to show differences in strength even among strong acids.

EXERCISE 17.3 | **Relative Acid Strength**

Arrange the following acids in order from weakest to strongest. How is your placement of them related to their K_a values?

Acid	K_a
$HClO_2$	1.2×10^{-2}
CH_3COOH	1.8×10^{-5}
H_2SO_4	>1
HCN	6.2×10^{-10}

First Thoughts

Recall that a strong acid is one that dissociates (or ionizes) completely at 1 molar concentration, whereas a weak one does not. This is measured by the value of K_a.

Solution

The larger the value of K_a, the stronger the acid. Based on our values of K_a, the order of acids from weakest to strongest is $HCN < CH_3COOH < HClO_2 < H_2SO_4$.

Further Insights

The significance of the *magnitude* of the equilibrium constant is the same for acids (K_a) and bases (called "K_b") in a given solvent. For example, an acid with $K_a = 1 \times 10^{-5}$ has the same meaning for *the extent of reaction in water* as does a base with an equilibrium constant, K_b, of 1×10^{-5}, even though the specific reactions are different. This shows that understanding the concept of equilibrium goes well beyond a particular situation—a consistent theme in this discussion.

PRACTICE 17.3

The Appendix of this textbook has a list of many acids. On the basis of the K_a values, pick three acids that are weaker than hydrofluoric acid (HF) and three that are stronger than hypochlorous acid (HOCl).

See Problems 15 and 16.

Given the relative acid strengths of nitric acid and acetic acid, what might we conclude about the strengths of their conjugate bases, nitrate ions and acetate ions? Nitric acid is strong, so its ionization equilibrium to produce H^+ will lie all the way to the right. In other words, the nitrate ion is such a weak base that it stays as is and essentially doesn't go back to form nitric acid at all. Another way of expressing this is to say that in the tug of war for protons between water (which acts as a base on the reactant side) and nitrate (which acts as a base on the product side), the water wins because water is a much stronger base than the nitrate ion. This battle, and its outcome, are shown in Figure 17.7.

Let's consider acetic acid, which we call a weak acid because its acid ionization reaction doesn't go very far to the right in water. This means that most of the acetic acid stays as acetic acid when it is added to water. When water (on the reactant side) and acetate ion (on the product side) enter into the tug of war for protons, the acetate ion wins because it is a much stronger base than water. These reactions are shown in Figure 17.8. The bottom line is that *strong acids* have *very weak conjugate bases* and *weak acids* have *somewhat stronger conjugate bases*.

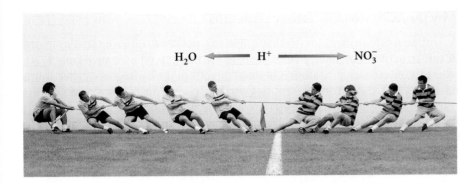

FIGURE 17.7

There is a "tug of war" for hydrogen ions between water and the nitrate ion. The water wins because water is a much stronger base than the nitrate ion.

$$H_2O \longleftarrow H^+ \longrightarrow NO_3^-$$

$CH_3COOH + H_2O \Longleftarrow CH_3COO^- + H_3O^+ \Longrightarrow CH_3COOH + H_2O$

FIGURE 17.8

In the reaction of acetate (CH_3COO^-) and water, the acetate wins because it is a stronger base than water.

EXERCISE 17.4   **Strength of the Conjugates**

For each of the following acids in water—hydrofluoric acid (HF, $K_a = 7.2 \times 10^{-4}$), acetic acid (CH_3COOH, $K_a = 1.8 \times 10^{-5}$), and hypochlorous acid (HOCl, $K_a = 3.5 \times 10^{-8}$):

a. Write the mass-action expression for dissociation of each acid.

b. Place the conjugate bases of these acids in order from strongest to weakest.

c. State which of the conjugate bases are stronger than water and which are weaker than water.

Solution

a. $K_a = \dfrac{[F^-][H^+]}{[HF]}$

   $K_a = \dfrac{[CH_3COO^-][H^+]}{[CH_3COOH]}$

   $K_a = \dfrac{[OCl^-][H^+]}{[HOCl]}$

b. Based on the K_a values, the acid strengths are ordered as follows:

$$HF > CH_3COOH > HOCl$$

The relative strengths of the conjugate bases are therefore in reverse order:

$$OCl^- > CH_3COO^- > F^-$$

c. All of these bases are stronger than water.

PRACTICE 17.4

Using Table 17.4, pick two acids with conjugate bases that are weaker than the acetate ion (CH_3COO^-).

See Problem 18. ▮

Why Do Acids Have Different Strengths?

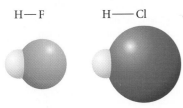

FIGURE 17.9

Compare the relative sizes of the atoms in HCl and HF.

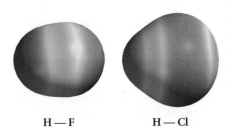

Electrostatic potential maps for HF and HCl indicate the location of electron density in the molecules. Note the color of the map near the hydrogen end of each molecule. The more intense blue color indicates less electron density around the hydrogen. How does this compare to the relative acidities for HF and HCl?

As with so many answers to chemical questions, the key to differing acid strengths lies in structure. For binary acids such as HCl or HF (shown in Figure 17.9), where the electronegative atom is bonded directly to the hydrogen, smaller atoms have the valence electrons present in a smaller space. This *higher electron density* results in stronger bonds between the electronegative atom and hydrogen, which makes these acids weaker (less likely to donate the proton). That is why HF is weaker than HCl. However, if the sizes of the atoms bonded to hydrogen are about the same, *the acidity increases with increasing electronegativity of the atom bonded to hydrogen,* because the polarity of the bond also increases. This is why HF is a stronger acid than H_2O, which, though it is not binary, has two H—O bonds.

Consider a "generic" oxygen-containing compound with a central atom, A, as shown in Figure 17.10. If A has a high electronegativity, then it will have a tendency to form a covalent bond with oxygen, which is also highly electronegative, while weakening the bond between the oxygen and hydrogen. The hydrogen can then be easily removed, which means the compound is acidic. *The more electronegative the central atom (A), the more acidic the compound* (see Figure 17.11). Chlorine is more electronegative than sulfur, which, in turn, is more electronegative than phosphorus. This means that perchloric acid ($HClO_4$) is inherently stronger than sulfuric acid (H_2SO_4), which is stronger than phosphoric acid (H_3PO_4). We do not see the difference between perchloric and sulfuric acids in aqueous solution, but phosphoric acid is noticeably weaker in water than either of these other compounds.

For the same central atom (sulfur, for example), the higher the oxidation state, the higher the attraction for electrons and the stronger the covalent bond between the sulfur and oxygen atom. This tends to weaken the O—H bond in these compounds, as described above. This is why H_2SO_4 (with sulfur in the +6 oxidation state) is a stronger acid than H_2SO_3 (where sulfur is in the +4 oxidation state). For the same reason, HNO_3 is stronger than HNO_2, and the strength of so-called chlorine "oxoacids" is $HClO_4 > HClO_3 > HClO_2 > HClO$.

This model explains why a compound such as NaOH is basic. Let's look again at Figure 17.10, where "A" is Na. Sodium has a relatively low electronegativity and therefore will not form a strong covalent bond with the oxygen atom. The bond

FIGURE 17.10

In this "generic" oxygen-containing compound the central atom, A, is bonded to an oxygen atom, which is itself bonded to a hydrogen atom. If A is highly electronegative, it will weaken the bond between oxygen and hydrogen.

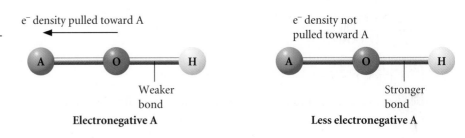

FIGURE 17.11

Chlorine is more electronegative than sulfur, which, in turn, is more electronegative than phosphorus. The result is that $HClO_4$ is inherently stronger than sulfuric acid (H_2SO_4), which is stronger than H_3PO_4. The listed structures are examples of resonance structures of each molecule.

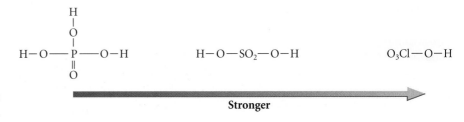

EXERCISE 17.8   **[H⁺] and pH: One Implication**

In Exercise 17.6, we discussed the sensitivity of aquatic species to the hydrogen ion concentration. Let's extend this discussion. Mussels can survive in waterways with a pH of 6.8. They cannot survive at pH 5.2. What is the ratio of the hydrogen ion concentrations in the two solutions? That is, how many times greater is one than the other?

First Thoughts

The pH scale is logarithmic. That is, each pH unit represents a difference in $[H^+]$ of a factor of 10. The pH values of 6.8 and 5.2 therefore have very different hydrogen ion concentrations. *In order to find the ratio of the concentrations, we must convert the pH of each solution into its hydrogen ion concentration. We cannot compare the pH values, themselves, as a measure of the hydrogen ion concentration ratio.* Which one has the higher hydrogen ion concentration, $[H^+]$? *The lower the pH, the higher the $[H^+]$,* so the pH 5.2 solution has a greater $[H^+]$ than the pH 6.8 solution.

Solution

$[H^+] = 10^{-pH}$, so for the waterway that has a pH = 6.80,

$$[H^+] = 10^{-6.80} = 1.6 \times 10^{-7} \, M$$

For the waterway that has a pH = 5.20,

$$[H^+] = 10^{-5.20} = 6.3 \times 10^{-6} \, M$$

The ratio of the hydrogen ion concentrations is the quotient of the two values:

$$\frac{6.3 \times 10^{-6} \, M}{1.6 \times 10^{-7} \, M} = 39$$

Further Insights

The waterway at pH 5.20 has an acid concentration that is about 40 times greater than that of the pH 6.80 waterway. This shows that seemingly small changes in pH can translate into large changes in hydrogen ion concentration. This is of particular importance in discussions involving the chemistry of life, where small changes in the pH of blood, for example, can be hazardous or fatal.

PRACTICE 17.8

If the hydrogen ion concentration of a body of water is 500 times that of another waterway, and the pH of the less acidic water is 8.84, what is the pH of the more acidic water?

See Problems 29 and 30.

Water and the pH Scale

Pure water can undergo **autoprotolysis**, proton transfer within only the solvent itself. Such a proton transfer would indicate that one of the water molecules is acting as a base and the other is acting as an acid.

$$H_2O(l) + H_2O(l) \rightleftharpoons H_3O^+(aq) + OH^-(aq) \qquad K_w = 1.00 \times 10^{-14} \text{ at } 24°C$$

The ability of a compound to act both as an acid and as a base (not necessarily in the same reaction) isn't unique to water. Those compounds capable of such a feat are called **amphiprotic**. They include, among many others, water, ammonia (NH_3), and, as we shall discover in Section 17.7, the amino acids that make up the proteins in the human body. In the autoprotolysis of water, the reaction is often simplified as

$$H_2O(l) \rightleftharpoons H^+(aq) + OH^-(aq) \qquad K_w = 1.00 \times 10^{-14} \text{ at } 24°C$$

It is understood that the H^+ and OH^- really aren't naked ions; they are solvated by the aqueous solution. However, we can write the equation this way to simplify our equation. In any case, this equation has the mass-action expression

$$K_w = [H^+][OH^-] = 1.00 \times 10^{-14}$$

Taking the log of both sides gives

$$pK_w = pH + pOH = 14.00$$

In pure water, the only source of $[H^+]$ and $[OH^-]$ is water itself, so the concentrations of H^+ and OH^- (formed in a 1:1 ratio) will be equal. **What are the concentrations of H^+ and OH^- in pure water?** If we call each "x," then

$$[H^+][OH^-] = x^2 = 1.00 \times 10^{-14}$$

$$x = [H^+] = [OH^-] = 1.00 \times 10^{-7}\ M$$

This means that in pure water at 24°C, $[H^+] = [OH^-] = 1.00 \times 10^{-7}\ M$, and the solution will have pH $= 7.0$. We define this as **neutral pH** when the solvent is water and the system is at 24°C. This pH value also equals pOH because both $[H^+]$ and $[OH^-]$ are equal to $1.0 \times 10^{-7}\ M$ under these conditions. The K_w value is temperature dependent, as shown in Table 17.5.

Unless otherwise stated, we will assume a temperature of 24°C for the remainder of our discussion, so that $K_w = 1.00 \times 10^{-14}$. In aqueous solution, we can always determine pH, $[H^+]$, pOH, or $[OH^-]$ in a solution if any one of these factors is known.

TABLE 17.5	K_w at Several Temperatures	
Temperature	K_w	pK_w
0°C	1.14×10^{-15}	14.94
10°C	2.92×10^{-15}	14.54
20°C	7.81×10^{-15}	14.11
24°C	1.00×10^{-14}	14.00
25°C	1.01×10^{-14}	14.00
30°C	1.47×10^{-14}	13.83
50°C	5.47×10^{-14}	13.26
60°C	9.71×10^{-14}	13.01

EXERCISE 17.9 Water in a Pristine Lake

Pure water has a pH $= 7.0$. But "pristine" rainwater (unaffected by pollutants from sources such as nitrogen oxides from automobile tailpipe emissions or sulfur oxides from industrial smokestack emissions) generally has a pH of between 5.5 and 6.0. This results from the dissolving and equilibration of carbon dioxide from the atmosphere and the subsequent release of a hydrogen ion to the water.

$$CO_2(g) + H_2O(l) \rightleftharpoons H_2CO_3(aq) \rightleftharpoons H^+(aq) + HCO_3^-(aq)$$

Many waterways in the United States have pH values significantly lower than this range as a consequence of acid precipitation, in which the stronger acids HNO_3 and H_2SO_4 combine with the water. We discussed the implications of this in Exercises 17.6 and 17.8. If the pH of the water in a pristine lake is 5.90, determine the value of $[H^+]$, $[OH^-]$, and pOH in this water.

Solution

There are several ways to do this problem. We'll show just one.

$$pOH = 14.00 - pH = 14.00 - 5.90 = 8.10$$
$$[H^+] = 10^{-pH} = 10^{-5.9} = 1.3 \times 10^{-6}\ M$$
$$[OH^-] = 10^{-pOH} = 10^{-8.10} = 7.9 \times 10^{-9}\ M$$

We can check the result by noting that $[H^+][OH^-] = K_w$ and

$$(1.3 \times 10^{-6})(7.9 \times 10^{-9}) = 1.0 \times 10^{-14}.$$

PRACTICE 17.9

What are the pH, $[H^+]$, and $[OH^-]$ values for a solution with pOH $= 12.35$?

See Problems 27 and 28. ∎

The sum of the pH and pOH values is 14.00. This is the basis of the common pH scale, shown in Figure 17.13. Note that the hydrogen ion and hydroxide ion concentrations are inversely related. Aqueous solutions with a pH less than 7.0 are said to be **acidic**, and those with a pH greater than 7.0 are **basic**. Also, as the solutions become more acidic or basic, their pH moves farther away from 7.0, as shown in the figure. The pH values of some common substances are also listed in Table 17.6 and illustrated graphically in Figure 17.14.

FIGURE 17.13

The sum of the pH and pOH values is 14.00 in water at 24°C. This is the basis of the common pH scale, shown here. Note the inverse relationship between the concentration of hydrogen and that of the hydroxide ion.

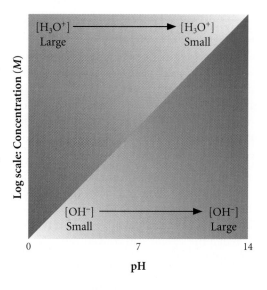

TABLE 17.6   pH of Some Common Substances

Substance	Contains This Acid or Base	pH
Battery acid	Sulfuric acid	1.3
Stomach acid	Hydrochloric acid	1.5–3.0
Vinegar	Acetic acid	2.5
Wines	Tartaric acid	2.8–3.8
Apples	Malic acid	2.9–3.3
Food preservative	Benzoic acid	3.1
Cheese	Lactic acid	4.8–6.4
Blood	Carbonate ion and others	7.3–7.5
Baking soda	Bicarbonate ion	8.3
Detergents	Carbonate, phosphate ions	10–11
Milk of magnesia	Magnesium hydroxide	10.5
Drain cleaner	Sodium hydroxide	13+

Very basic

Household lye — 14.0
Bleach — 13.0
— 12.0
Ammonia — 11.0
— 10.0
— 9.0
Egg whites — 8.0 — Seawater
— Swimming pool water
Distilled water — 7.0
— 6.0
Pure rain — Egg yolks
— 5.0
Beer — 4.0 — Orange juice
Pickle processing —
— 3.0
— Vinegar
Lemon juice — 2.0
— Battery acid
— 1.0
— 0.0

Very acidic

FIGURE 17.14

pH of some common substances.

HERE'S WHAT WE KNOW SO FAR

- We now understand what is meant when we read or hear about acids and bases.
- We know the difference between strong and weak acids and the difference between concentrated and dilute acids.
- We have a frame of reference—the pH scale—with which we can categorize solutions of acids and bases.
- We now know where many common substances fit within this frame of reference.

At its heart, chemistry is about the *interactions* of substances. The applications of chemistry concern the *changes* that result from these interactions. To understand the nature of change in acid–base chemistry, we first need to consider how to determine the changes that occur when an aqueous acidic or basic solution is prepared. This will be the focus of the remainder of this chapter. In the next chapter, we will consider how changing a prepared acidic or basic solution affects its chemical behavior.

17.4 Determining the pH of Acidic Solutions

We have learned that strong acids essentially completely dissociate in aqueous solution ($K_a \gg 1$) and that weak acids as a rule dissociate only partially ($K_a < 1$). We also noted that the concentration of [H$^+$] (and therefore the pH) in solution will be determined by both the strength and the initial concentration of the acid.

pH of Strong Acid Solutions

A monoprotic acid is an acid (such as HCl) that contains only one acidic hydrogen ion, or proton. H_2SO_4, by contrast, contains two acidic protons and is called a diprotic acid. In a strong monoprotic acid, the hydrogen ion concentration in aqueous solution roughly equals the initial concentration of the acid (neglecting activity effects). This is approximately true at any concentration greater than about 10^{-6} M. When the strong acid concentration is less than this, the autoprotolysis of water supplies relatively few hydrogen ions that exist in solution, and the pH becomes more difficult to calculate, as we will discuss later in this section. Even with an HCl solution of concentration 10^{-8} M or less, the pH is still held just below 7.0 because of the supply of H$^+$ from the autoprotolysis of water.

| EXERCISE 17.10 | Calculating the pH of a Strong Acid Solution |

Your stomach contains hydrochloric acid. If we were going to prepare a solution that had a hydrogen ion concentration within the range of that in the stomach, we might work with a 3×10^{-2} M aqueous solution of HCl. What is the pH of this solution?

First Thoughts

This strong acid would essentially completely dissociate to give [H$^+$] = 3×10^{-2} M and [Cl$^-$] = 3×10^{-2} M.

Solution

We can calculate the pH of this solution as follows:

$$\text{pH} = -\log[\text{H}^+] = -\log(3 \times 10^{-2}\,M) = 1.5$$

Further Insights

Does the answer make sense? We have a moderately concentrated strong acid, so we would expect the pH to be in the range of, perhaps, 1 to 3. We can narrow our expected answer down further by noting that [H$^+$] is between 10^{-1} and 10^{-2} M, which means that the pH will be between 1 and 2. Our answer to this problem does make sense.

| PRACTICE 17.10 |

What is the pH of a 0.0010 M HNO$_3$ solution? . . . of a 0.0000250 M HClO$_4$ solution?

See Problem 37. ∎

Le Châtelier's Principle and the Supply of Hydroxide Ion in Acidic Solutions

Consider a strong acid at pH 3.0. On the basis of our previous discussion, we know that the pOH is 11.0, and $[OH^-] = 1 \times 10^{-11}$ M. Where does that small amount of hydroxide ion come from? The only source is the autoprotolysis of water:

$$H_2O(l) \rightleftharpoons H^+(aq) + OH^-(aq) \qquad K_w = 1.00 \times 10^{-14}$$

If the liquid were *pure* water, $[OH^-]$ would equal 1×10^{-7} M. However, the addition of H^+ from the strong acid imposed a stress on the aqueous system, to which it responded by lessening the extent of dissociation of water. To put it another way, when the acid was added, *the reaction shifted to the left to compensate*. This is an example of Le Châtelier's principle, which we discussed in Section 16.6, and is known as the **common-ion effect**. We added an ion *common* to one of the products (H^+), and the result was that the reaction did not proceed to the right as much as it would have without the acid. We will look at many of the practical outcomes of Le Châtelier's principle and the common-ion effect in the next chapter. The key in this introduction to acids and bases is that the addition to an aqueous solution of any substance that produces H^+ will reduce the supply of H^+ and OH^- from the autoprotolysis of water. Therefore, in all but the dilute acid solutions, the autoprotolysis of water as a source of H^+ is generally *negligible*.

For example, let's consider the pH of a 1.0×10^{-8} M solution of HCl, a strong acid. We might predict that the HCl produces 1.0×10^{-8} M H^+ in solution. We would be correct in our prediction.

$$HCl(aq) \rightarrow H^+(aq) \quad + \quad Cl^-(aq)$$
$$1.0 \times 10^{-8} \, M \rightarrow 1.0 \times 10^{-8} \, M \quad 1.0 \times 10^{-8} \, M$$

Determining the pH of this solution gives

$$pH = -\log[H^+]$$
$$pH = -\log(1.0 \times 10^{-8})$$
$$pH = 8.00$$

Does our answer make sense? *No it doesn't*. Adding HCl to water, even a very small amount, shouldn't cause the pH to increase! What have we forgotten to consider? The concentration of hydrogen ions in the solution is made up of all sources of $[H^+]$.

$$[H^+]_{total} = [H^+]_{HCl} + [H^+]_{water}$$

This means we should add all of the sources of hydrogen ion together and then determine the pH of the solution. What is the $[H^+]$ due to water? Recall our autoprotolysis equation:

$$H_2O(l) \rightleftharpoons H^+(aq) + OH^-(aq) \qquad K_w = 1.00 \times 10^{-14}$$

On the basis of this, we might be inclined to say that $[H^+]_{water} = [OH^-]_{water} = 1.0 \times 10^{-7}$ M. However, we must keep in mind the effect of Le Châtelier's principle, in which having hydrogen ions supplied by the HCl suppresses the ionization of H_2O. Therefore, $[H^+]_{water}$ will be less than 1.0×10^{-7} M. Although we won't go into the details here, it is possible to determine that in this solution, $[H^+]_{water} = 9.5 \times 10^{-8}$ M.

$$[H^+]_{total} = [H^+]_{HCl} + [H^+]_{water}$$
$$[H^+]_{total} = 1.0 \times 10^{-8} \, M + 9.5 \times 10^{-8} \, M$$
$$[H^+]_{total} = 1.05 \times 10^{-7} \, M$$
$$pH = 6.98$$

This is more reasonable than our initial answer of pH = 8 (after all, an acid solution should be acidic, not basic!), and it also shows the importance of Le Châtelier's principle as well as the autoprotolysis of water.

pH of Weak Acid Solutions

As we noted in Section 14.5, lactic acid ($HC_3H_5O_3$) is produced in our muscle cells when we work too strenuously to maintain aerobic respiration (respiration in the presence of sufficient oxygen). Recent evidence shows that contrary to long-time assumptions, lactic acid is a normal product of metabolism and not the barrier to athletic performance that was previously assumed. Lactic acid can be prepared commercially and is used in products ranging from biodegradable polymers to a spray to help extend the shelf life of beef strips. Its wide range of biological applications makes lactic acid a useful prototype for our discussion about the pH of weak acids.

Let's determine the pH of a 0.10 M solution of lactic acid. We considered the steps in accomplishing this task in Chapter 16. This is an equilibrium problem, and we may solve it using the same principles that we use to solve any other equilibrium problem.

Steps in Solving for the pH of a Weak Acid in Aqueous Solution

Step 1: Determine the equilibria, and the resulting species, that are in the solution.

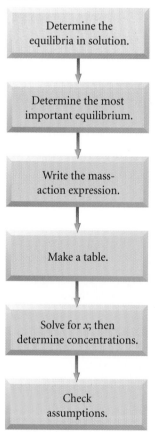

There are two important equilibria occurring simultaneously in this solution: the ionization of lactic acid ($HC_3H_5O_3$, written here for simplicity as HL) and the autoprotolysis of water.

$$HL(aq) \rightleftharpoons H^+(aq) + L^-(aq) \qquad K_a = 1.38 \times 10^{-4}$$

$$H_2O(l) \rightleftharpoons H^+(aq) + OH^-(aq) \qquad K_w = 1.00 \times 10^{-14}$$

Step 2: Determine the equilibria that are the most important contributors to $[H^+]$ in the solution.

As we discussed previously, an acid that is much stronger than water will significantly depress the ionization of water in accordance with Le Châtelier's principle. Let's assume that this holds true for a relatively concentrated solution of the weak acid so that *we can safely neglect the autoprotolysis of water as a contributor of H^+*. We will test this assumption later.

Step 3: Write the equilibrium expression for the important contributors to $[H^+]$ (which usually means just the weak acid).

$$K_a = \frac{[L^-][H^+]}{[HL]}$$

Step 4: Set up a table of the initial and equilibrium concentrations of each pertinent species.

Weak acids are called weak because the extent of their ionization is normally quite small. As a first approximation, we may *assume* that "x" is far less than 0.100 M, or, equivalently, that $[HL] \approx [HL]_0$. We do this because it greatly simplifies our problem solving, but we will also test this assumption later. *The assumption will generally work if K_a is less than about $10^{-2} \times [HL]_0$*. In the present problem, $10^{-2} \times 0.10 = 1 \times 10^{-3}$. Our K_a of 1.38×10^{-4} is less than that, so our assumption is probably valid.

	HL	$\rightleftharpoons$	H^+	$+$	L^-
initial	0.10 M		0 M		0 M
change	$-x$		$+x$		$+x$
equilibrium	$0.10 - x$		$+x$		$+x$
assumptions	0.10		$+x$		$+x$

Step 5: Solve for the estimated concentration of each species.

$$1.38 \times 10^{-4} = \frac{x^2}{0.10}$$

$$x = [H^+] = [C_3H_5O_3^-] = 3.7 \times 10^{-3} \, M$$

$$[HC_3H_5O_3] = 0.10 - 3.7 \times 10^{-3} = 0.096 \, M$$

Step 6: Check our assumption that the extent of ionization of lactic acid is negligibly small.

This is done using the "5% rule," which we introduced in Section 16.5. Also as discussed in that section, you can ignore the 5% simplification if you want to program your calculator to solve the quadratic equation in all cases. We present the 5% rule there, and here, because it shows that it is possible to use our understanding of chemistry to arrive at a solution strategy that is straightforward whether or not a programmable calculator is available.

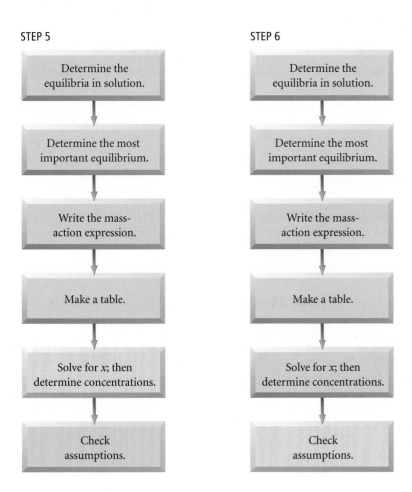

STEP 5

Determine the
equilibria in solution.

Determine the most
important equilibrium.

Write the mass-
action expression.

Make a table.

Solve for x; then
determine concentrations.

Check
assumptions.

STEP 6

Determine the
equilibria in solution.

Determine the most
important equilibrium.

Write the mass-
action expression.

Make a table.

Solve for x; then
determine concentrations.

Check
assumptions.

STEP 7

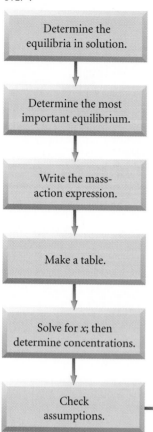

If less than 5% of the original amount of the weak acid ionizes, this is considered "negligible." If more than 5% ionizes, then we must take this into account in our problem solving during Step 4. We will show how this is done below. What percentage of the lactic acid has ionized?

$$\% \text{ dissociated} = \frac{[C_3H_5O_3^-]}{HC_3H_5O_3} \times 100\% = \frac{3.7 \times 10^{-3}}{0.10} \times 100\% = 3.7\%$$

We can consider the ionization to be negligible because less than 5% of the original acid reacted to form products.

Step 7: Solve for the pH of the solution.

$$pH = -\log[H^+] = -\log(3.7 \times 10^{-3}\, M) = 2.43$$

Remember that the number of significant figures after the decimal point in the pH is equal to the number of significant figures in the pre-exponential term. Because the pre-exponential term is 3.7, we use two figures after the decimal point (".43"). The pH = 2.43.

EXERCISE 17.11 **pH of a Weak Acid**

We have mentioned aqueous hydrofluoric acid (HF) several times in this chapter, and we have found it to be a weak acid, $K_a = 7.2 \times 10^{-4}$. It is employed in the chemical industry to produce alkylated (see Section 12.3) compounds in gasoline and fluorocarbons used, for example, in refrigerants. Calculate the pH in a $1.0 \times 10^{-3}\, M$ HF solution.

First Thoughts

Our understanding of equilibrium tells us that even though the specific exercise is different from the one we just went over together, the questions that we ask about the chemical system remain the same, and therefore our approach is consistent. We understand our chemical system (and, in doing so, get a reasonable answer for the pH) by asking the right questions.

Solution

Step 1: Equilibria in solution.

The two important equilibria in the solution are the ionization of HF and the autoprotolysis of water.

$$HF(aq) \rightleftharpoons H^+(aq) + F^-(aq) \qquad K_a = 7.2 \times 10^{-4}$$
$$H_2O(l) \rightleftharpoons H^+(aq) + OH^-(aq) \qquad K_w = 1.00 \times 10^{-14}$$

Step 2: Determine the equilibria that are the most important contributors to $[H^+]$ in the solution.

We will assume that the HF ionization is the only important contributor to $[H^+]$ in solution because its K_a value is far greater than the K_w value of water.

Step 3: Write the equilibrium expression for the important contributors to $[H^+]$.

$$K_a = \frac{[F^-][H^+]}{[HF]}$$

Step 4: Table of concentrations.

	HF	$\rightleftharpoons$	H^+	$+$	F^-
initial	$1.0 \times 10^{-3}\ M$		$0\ M$		$0\ M$
change	$-x$		$+x$		$+x$
equilibrium	$1.0 \times 10^{-3} - x$		$+x$		$+x$
assumptions	1.0×10^{-3}		$+x$		$+x$

Although we assume that the ionization of HF is negligibly small (that is, "x" is essentially irrelevant compared to $1.0 \times 10^{-3}\ M$), the assumption is hazardous because K_a, 7.2×10^{-4}, is not less than about $10^{-2} \times [HF]_0$ ($= 1.0 \times 10^{-5}\ M$). Rather, *it is nearly equal to* $[HF]_0$! Let's determine the implications of making the assumption.

Step 5: Solve.

$$7.2 \times 10^{-4} = \frac{x^2}{1.0 \times 10^{-3}}$$

$$x = [H^+] = [F^-] = 8.5 \times 10^{-4}\ M$$

Step 6: Check our assumption of negligible ionization.

$$\% \text{ dissociated} = \frac{[F^-]}{[HF]} \times 100\% = \frac{8.5 \times 10^{-4}}{1.0 \times 10^{-3}} \times 100\% = 85\%$$

Wow! This is certainly not negligible compared to 5%, so we may *not* claim that the ionization of HF is negligibly small. We must solve the following equation, which uses the "equilibrium" row of the ICEA table, rather than the "assumptions" row.

$$7.2 \times 10^{-4} = \frac{x^2}{1.0 \times 10^{-3} - x}$$

We can set up the quadratic equation by multiplying K_a, 7.2×10^{-4}, by $[HF]$, $1.0 \times 10^{-3} - x$, to give

$$x^2 = 7.2 \times 10^{-7} - 7.2 \times 10^{-4}x$$

Setting the equation $= 0$ so we may solve for x yields

$$x^2 + (7.2 \times 10^{-4}x) - 7.2 \times 10^{-7} = 0$$

As we discussed in Section 16.5, we can solve the quadratic equation by substituting values for a, b, and c in the quadratic formula:

$$x = \frac{-b \pm \sqrt{b^2 - 4ac}}{2a}$$

In the present exercise,

$$a = 1 \qquad b = 7.2 \times 10^{-4} \qquad c = -7.2 \times 10^{-7}$$

Substituting into the quadratic formula yields

$$x = \frac{-7.2 \times 10^{-4} \pm \sqrt{(7.2 \times 10^{-4})^2 - 4(1)(-7.2 \times 10^{-7})}}{2(1)}$$

$$x = \frac{-7.2 \times 10^{-4} \pm 1.843 \times 10^{-3}}{2}$$

$$x = [H^+] = [F^-] = 5.62 \times 10^{-4}\ M \approx 5.6 \times 10^{-4}\ M$$

$$[HF] = 1.0 \times 10^{-3} - x = 1.0 \times 10^{-3} - (5.62 \times 10^{-4})$$

$$= 4.38 \times 10^{-4} \approx 4.4 \times 10^{-4}\ M$$

Step 7: Solve for the pH of the solution.

$$pH = -\log[H^+] = -\log(5.62 \times 10^{-4}) = 3.25$$

We can check our math by substituting back into the mass-action expression.

$$K_a = \frac{(5.62 \times 10^{-4})^2}{4.38 \times 10^{-4}} = 7.2 \times 10^{-4}$$

Our answer is confirmed.

Further Insights

We often assume, on the basis of the low value of K_w, that the autoprotolysis of water is unimportant, and we assumed that in Step 2 above. *Did this make sense?* What is the hydrogen ion concentration due to the autoprotolysis of water? It is equal to the hydroxide ion concentration due to water. That is,

$$[H^+]_{water} = [OH^-]_{water}$$

Also, water is the *only* source of hydroxide ion in this weak acid solution. Therefore,

$$[OH^-]_{total} = \frac{K_w}{[H^+]_{total}} = \frac{1.00 \times 10^{-14}}{5.62 \times 10^{-4}} = 1.8 \times 10^{-11}\ M = [OH^-]_{water} = [H^+]_{water}$$

This is so much smaller than 5.62×10^{-4} M that it can be safely neglected. Our decision to neglect the autoprotolysis of water as a source of H^+ ions made sense.

PRACTICE 17.11

What is the pH of a 0.250 M acetic acid solution ($K_a = 1.8 \times 10^{-5}$)?

See Problems 39–50. ∎

---

pH of a Mixture of Monoprotic Acids

If you ingest some vinegar, 3% acetic acid, does it significantly change the pH of your HCl-containing stomach? This question falls within the general topic of the pH of *a mixture of acids that differ greatly in strength*. Consider a solution that is 0.50 M HCl and 0.90 M acetic acid (CH_3COOH), $K_a = 1.8 \times 10^{-5}$. To solve for the pH of the mixture, we employ our usual approach. The relevant equilibria in the solution are

$$HCl(aq) \rightleftharpoons H^+(aq) + Cl^-(aq) \qquad\qquad K_a > 1$$
$$CH_3COOH(aq) \rightleftharpoons H^+(aq) + CH_3COO^-(aq) \qquad K_a = 1.8 \times 10^{-5}$$
$$H_2O(l) \rightleftharpoons H^+(aq) + OH^-(aq) \qquad\qquad K_w = 1.00 \times 10^{-14}$$

This says that there are three sources of hydrogen ion: HCl, CH_3COOH, and H_2O. We can write this in equation form:

$$[H^+]_{total} = [H^+]_{HCl} + [H^+]_{CH_3COOH} + [H^+]_{H_2O}$$

The hydrochloric acid is a substantially stronger acid than either the acetic acid or the water and is present in a concentration that is large enough so that we may make the *assumption* that neither the acetic acid nor the water ionizes significantly. In fact, the presence of hydrogen ion (the common ion!) from HCl further suppresses the acetic acid and water ionization in accordance with Le Châtelier's principle.

$$[H^+]_{total} = [H^+]_{HCl} \approx 0.50\ M$$

We will test this assumption later.

What is the hydrogen ion contribution due to the acetic acid? We know that $[H^+]_{total} = 0.50\ M$. We also know that the $[H^+]$ contributed by the acetic acid will be essentially equal to the $[CH_3COO^-]$. The concentration of acetic acid at equilibrium will be essentially equal to its initial concentration.

$$[CH_3COOH] = 0.90 \, M$$

$$[H^+]_{acetic \, acid} = [CH_3COO^-] = \text{``}x\text{''}$$

We can use the mass-action expression for acetic acid ionization to solve for $[H^+]_{acetic \, acid}$.

$$K_a = \frac{[CH_3COO^-][H^+]}{[CH_3COOH]}$$

$$1.8 \times 10^{-5} = \frac{x(0.50)}{0.90}$$

$$x = [CH_3COO^-] = [H^+]_{acetic \, acid} = 3.2 \times 10^{-5} \, M$$

This shows that acetic acid is not a significant contributor to the hydrogen ion concentration of the solution, and although we did not quantify it here, the water is even less important. Further, if we had had an aqueous solution of only 0.90 M CH_3COOH (without the HCl), the equilibrium concentration of the acetate ion, $[CH_3COO^-]$, would have been

$$K_a = \frac{[CH_3COO^-][H^+]}{[CH_3COOH]}$$

$$1.8 \times 10^{-5} = \frac{x^2}{0.90}$$

$$x = [H^+] = [CH_3COO^-] = 4.0 \times 10^{-3} \, M$$

This is nearly 100 times *higher* than the equilibrium acetate ion concentration of $3.2 \times 10^{-5} \, M$ in the HCl solution. This confirms what we said previously, that "the presence of hydrogen ion (the common ion!) from HCl further suppresses the acetic acid and water ionization in accordance with Le Châtelier's principle."

The main message to keep in mind from this discussion is that when you calculate the pH of a mixture of acids, you must look for the dominant equilibrium. This will determine the pH of the solution.

Application

17.5 ▷ Determining the pH of Basic Solutions

We have noted in this chapter the impact of acids and bases on ourselves and our world. A useful, though perhaps unfortunate, example concerns tobacco, which, according to the World Health Organization, prematurely kills well over 4 million people worldwide each year. Tobacco companies have used scientists' understanding of acid–base chemistry to increase by a factor of 100 the amount of nicotine that leaves solid burned tobacco particles and enters the gas phase to be absorbed by the lungs. The two important compounds involved in this chemistry are the nicotine itself ($C_{10}H_{14}N_2$) and ammonia, both of which are bases (see Figure 17.15). We will look at how ammonia can be used to increase the amount of gaseous nicotine that enters the lungs of smokers. As a first step in our analysis, we need to see how and why ammonia acts as a base.

Ammonia (NH_3) has many applications, including those shown in Table 17.1. It is the fourth-ranked industrial chemical, with 10.8 billion kg produced in 2004. Ammonia is quite soluble in water, acting as a weak base. Using the Arrhenius model of base behavior, it supplies hydroxide ions to the solution.

FIGURE 17.15

Ammonia and nicotine are both bases.

Ammonia

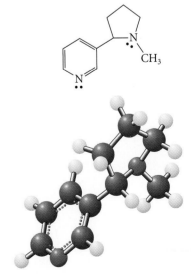

Nicotine

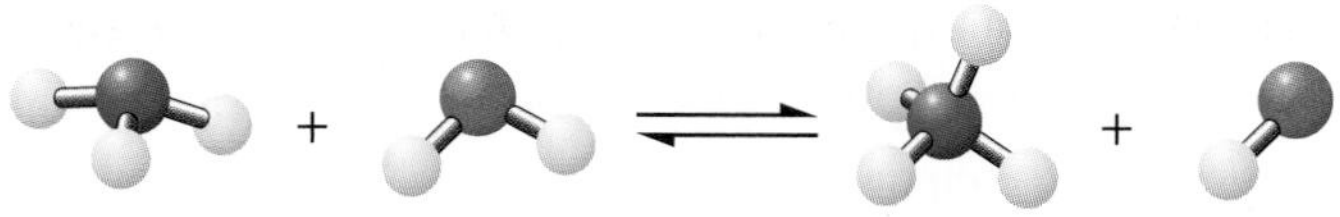

$$NH_3(aq) \quad + \quad H_2O(l) \quad \rightleftharpoons \quad NH_4^+(aq) \quad + \quad OH^-(aq) \qquad K_b = 1.8 \times 10^{-5}$$

Ammonia is typical of many bases in that it has an unshared pair of electrons on the nitrogen atom that can accept a proton from, in this case, the water molecule, as shown in the illustration.

Ammonia is considered a weak base because the K_b value is much less than 1. On the other hand, Group IA hydroxides, such as NaOH and KOH, *completely* dissociate in water ($K_b \gg 1$) to supply hydroxide ion and are considered strong bases.

$$NaOH(s) \rightarrow Na^+(aq) + OH^-(aq)$$

The solubility of Group IIA hydroxides increases from the essentially insoluble $Be(OH)_2$ to the more soluble (0.01 M) $Ca(OH)_2$ to the still more soluble (up to 0.1 M) $Ba(OH)_2$. Soluble Group IIA hydroxides, such as $Ca(OH)_2$, are strong bases like their Group IA counterparts, but they supply *two* moles of hydroxide for every mole of base that dissolves.

$$Ca(OH)_2(s) \rightleftharpoons Ca^{2+}(aq) + 2OH^-(aq)$$

Drawing on your understanding of equilibrium (that is, what are the right questions to ask in order to understand what happens in the solution?) and your sense of the pH scale, try the following two exercises dealing with the pH of a strong base solution and of the weakly basic ammonia solution. Even though we are now looking at bases rather than acids, the *equilibrium processes and the thinking involved are largely the same.*

EXERCISE 17.12 **pH of a Strong Base**

Calculate the pH of a 0.60 M aqueous solution of KOH.

First Thoughts

As a strong base, KOH completely dissociates. This is consistent with the behavior of Group IA and soluble Group IIA hydroxides.

$$KOH(s) \rightarrow K^+(aq) + OH^-(aq) \qquad K \gg 1$$

The other acid–base reaction that occurs in solution is the autoprotolysis of water, although it is unimportant as a source of OH^- because the K value is so small compared to that of the strong base.

$$H_2O(l) \rightleftharpoons H^+(aq) + OH^-(aq) \qquad K_w = 1.0 \times 10^{-14}$$

Solution

Potassium hydroxide is a strong base and will completely dissociate in aqueous solution.

$$KOH(s) \rightarrow K^+(aq) + OH^-(aq)$$

$$[OH^-] = 0.60 \ M$$

$$pOH = 0.22; \ pH = 13.78$$

Further Insights

Does the answer make sense? We expect the pH to be quite high, analogous to the very low pH of a strong acid, so our answer makes sense. In addition, the pH is considerably higher than with the same concentration of ammonia, a weak base. This is shown in the next exercise.

PRACTICE 17.12

Calculate the pH of a 1.06 M solution of NaOH. (*Hint:* It is possible to have aqueous solutions with a pH below 0 or above 14, although the actual pH is somewhat difficult to measure.)

See Problems 38 and 54. ∎

EXERCISE 17.13   pH of a Weak Base

Determine the pH of a 0.600 M solution of ammonia.

First Thoughts

We may proceed as with any equilibrium problem, by listing the equilibria that occur in solution.

$$NH_3(aq) + H_2O(l) \rightleftharpoons NH_4^+ + OH^-(aq) \qquad K_b = 1.8 \times 10^{-5}$$
$$H_2O(l) \rightleftharpoons H^+(aq) + OH^-(aq) \qquad K_w = 1.0 \times 10^{-14}$$

The autoprotolysis of water is insignificant compared to the hydrolysis of ammonia. In fact, the OH^- produced by the ammonia reaction will further depress the autoprotolysis of water (via Le Châtelier's principle), so the OH^- and H^+ due to water will be less than in neutral solution, as discussed previously. The only relevant equilibrium expression is

$$K_b = \frac{[NH_4^+][OH^-]}{[NH_3]}$$

Solution

We set up the table of concentration changes in the usual fashion.

	NH$_3$	$\rightleftharpoons$	NH$_4^+$	+	OH$^-$
initial	0.600 M		0 M		0 M
change	$-x$		$+x$		$+x$
equilibrium	$0.600 - x$		$+x$		$+x$
assumptions	0.600		$+x$		$+x$

$$1.8 \times 10^{-5} = \frac{x^2}{0.600}$$
$$x = [NH_4^+] = [OH^-] = 3.3 \times 10^{-3}\ M$$
$$pOH = 2.48;\ pH = 11.52$$

Further Insights

Were we justified in neglecting "x"? The percent dissociation was

$$\frac{3.3 \times 10^{-6}}{0.600} \times 100\% = 0.5\%$$

Our assumption was valid. Were we justified in neglecting the autoprotolysis of water as a source of hydroxide ions? The only source of hydrogen ions in this solution is the autoprotolysis of water. If pH = 11.52, then $[H^+]_{water} = 3.0 \times 10^{-12}\ M$. This also equals $[OH^-]_{water}$, and this is insignificant compared to $3.3 \times 10^{-3}\ M$, the total $[OH^-]$. Does our answer make sense? To the extent that our pH reflects a moderately basic solution, our answer does make sense.

"Crack" cocaine

PRACTICE 17.13

Calculate the pH of a 0.500 M solution of dimethylamine, $(CH_3)_2NH$, $K_b = 5.9 \times 10^{-4}$.

See Problems 51–53, 55, and 56.

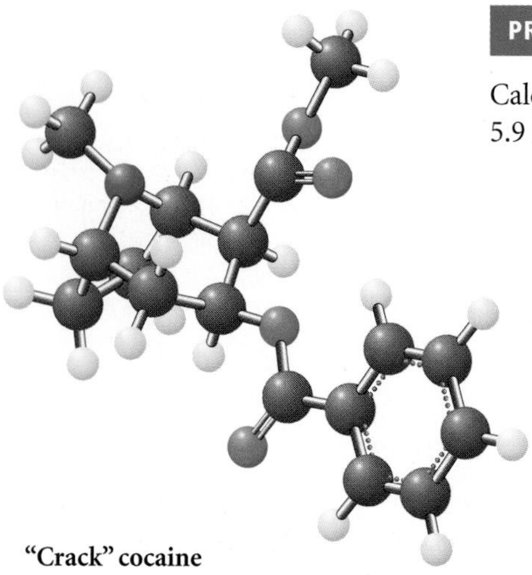

One class of alkaloids, *ephedrines*, are used as dietary supplements to help in weight loss, to enhance body building, and to increase the user's energy level. In doses of more than 8 mg per serving, the compounds are considered dangerous for routine use. Another of the alkaloids, cocaine, has a severe psychological impact. It can be made basic to create the free-base form called "crack."

Issues and Controversies

Nicotine and pH Control in Cigarettes

Nicotine can exist in three forms, depending on the pH of its environment (see Figure 17.16). Below pH 3, it is in the diprotonated form. Between about pH 3 and pH 8, most of it is in the monoprotonated form.

If the pH is above 8, most of the nicotine exists in the volatile "free-base" form, which readily evaporates at the temperature of burning tobacco. This free-base is effectively absorbed by the lung tissue. Ammonia is added to tobacco leaves to raise the pH, making available more free-base nicotine for inhalation. The Food and Drug Administration has also determined that pH levels have been manipulated in smokeless tobacco products. The products for new users are at a relatively low pH, so there is not that much free-base nicotine available. Smokeless tobacco for "experienced" users has a higher pH, which leads to a higher level of nicotine absorption.

Nicotine is an **alkaloid**, one of many nitrogen-containing bases found in vegetables and other plants. Table 17.7 lists the structures and uses of some alkaloids. You might recognize the names of some of the compounds in the table. They often have a substantial impact on the central nervous system and brain.

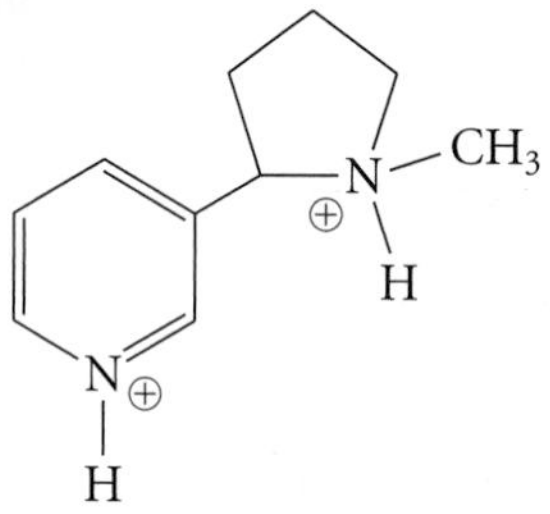

$pk_{a_1} = 3.12$

(a)

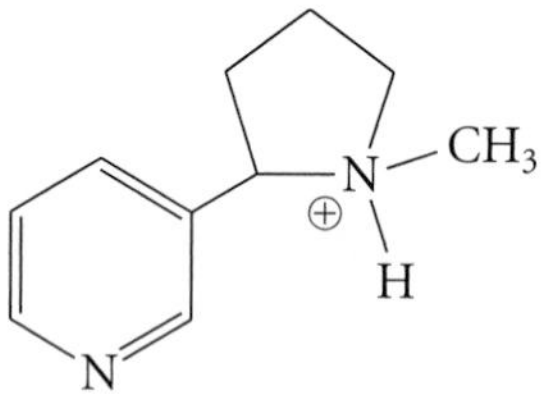

$pk_{a_2} = 8.02$

(b)

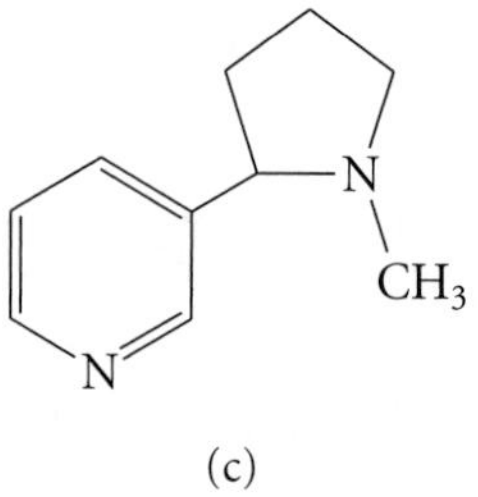

FIGURE 17.16

The three forms of nicotine. (a) The form that predominates below pH 3.12. (b) The form that predominates between pH 3.12 and 8.02. (c) The form that predominates above pH 8.02. This "free-base" form is readily vaporized and absorbed into the lungs when the cigarette burns.

(c)

17.6 Polyprotic Acids

Our theme is *impact*—the impact of acids and bases on the chemical industry, on our environment, and on ourselves. Phosphoric acid (H_3PO_4) fits well with that theme. It is different from other acids we have mentioned thus far, because it is a **polyprotic acid**. Like all polyprotic acids, phosphoric acid contains *more than one acidic hydrogen*. The structure of this **triprotic acid** (three acidic hydrogen atoms) acid is shown in Figure 17.17, with its three acidic hydrogen atoms highlighted. The acid is produced from "phosphate rock," which is largely composed of fluoroapatite ($Ca_5(PO_4)_3F$) and other compounds containing iron, calcium, silicon, aluminum, and fluorine.

Application

CHEMICAL ENCOUNTERS:
Production and Uses
of Phosphoric and
Sulfuric Acids

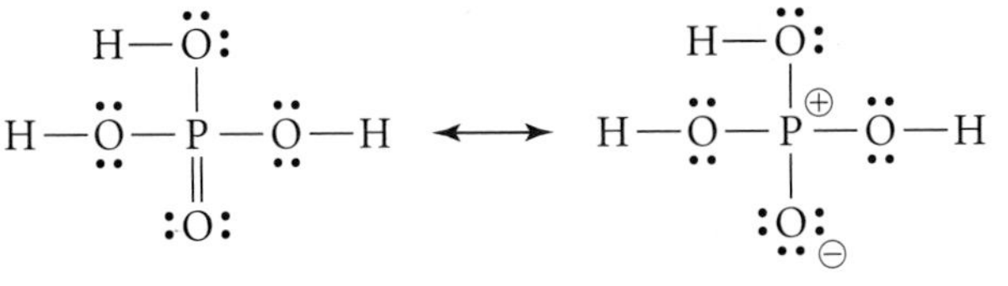

FIGURE 17.17

Phosphoric acid (H_3PO_4) is triprotic acid because it contains three acidic hydrogen atoms.

TABLE 17.7	Structures and Uses of Selected Alkaloids		
Structure	**Common Use**	**Structure**	**Common Use**
Morphine 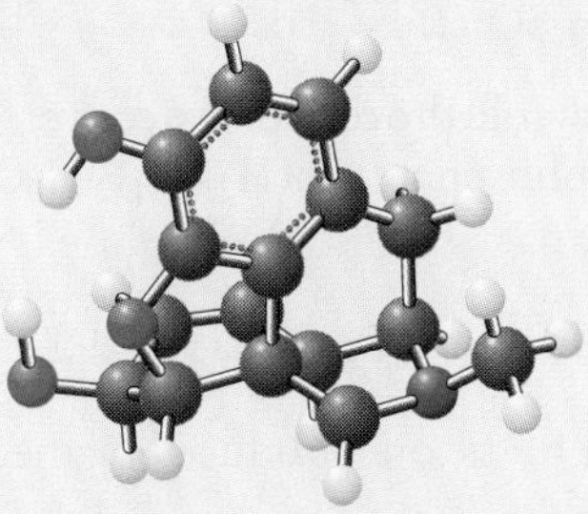	Addictive pain reliever	Methadone 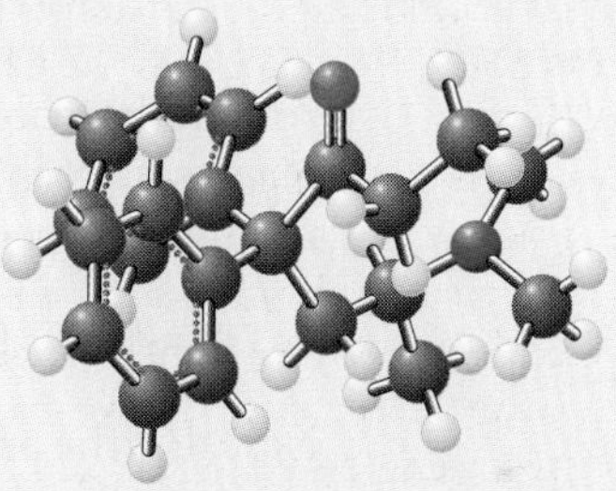	Therapy for heroin addiction
Procaine 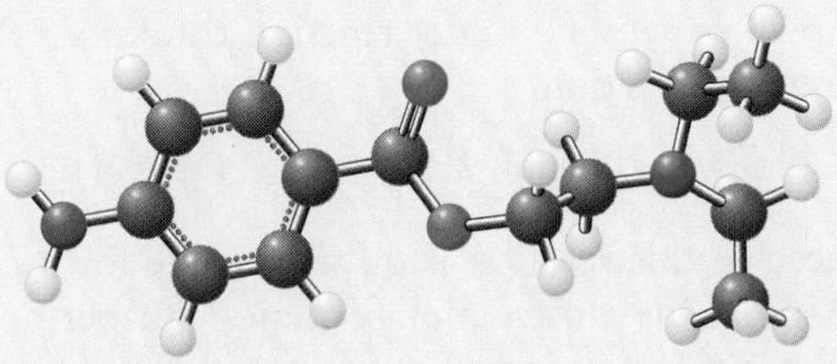	Local anesthetic	Valium 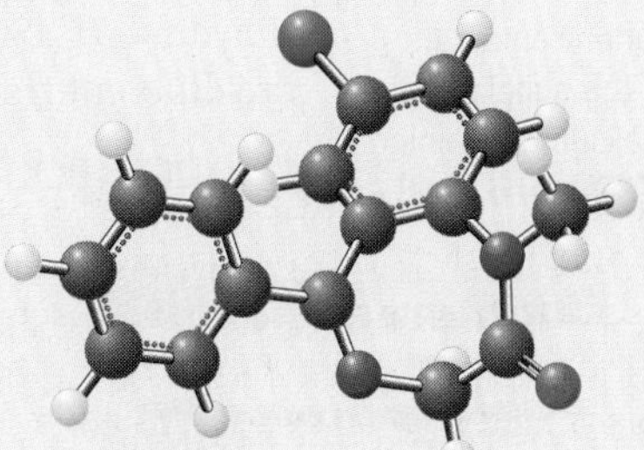	Tranquilizer
Fentanyl 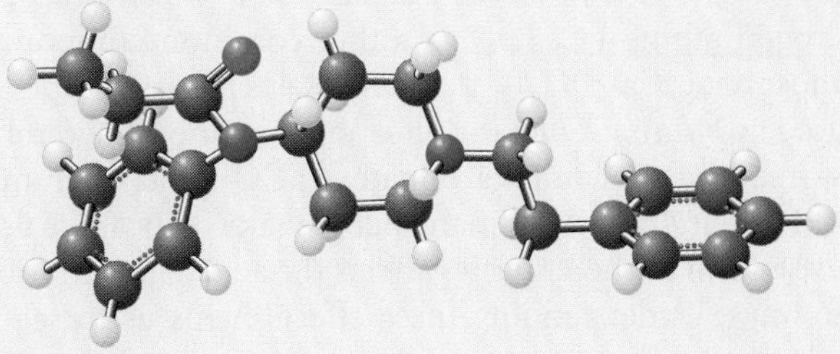	Anesthetic in most surgical procedures		

TABLE 17.8	Uses of Phosphoric Acid in Manufacturing

Fertilizer
Dentifrices
Soaps
Detergents
Fire control agents
Soft drinks
Incandescent light filaments
Corrosion inhibitors in metals
Organic chemicals such as
    ethylene and propylene

In 2003, over 33.3 million tons of marketable phosphate rock was mined in the United States, mostly from Florida and North Carolina, according to the U.S. Geological Survey. In fact, the U.S. production is about 24% of the world's phosphate rock production. Significant amounts of phosphates are also produced in China and in the Morocco and Western Sahara regions of Africa. This ore is converted into phosphoric acid for use in our society. Table 17.8 indicates the wide variety of uses of phosphoric acid. Phosphoric acid can be used to convert fluoroapatite into a soluble fertilizer, as shown in the following reaction:

$$2Ca_5(PO_4)_3F + 14H_3PO_4 \rightleftharpoons 10Ca(H_2PO_4)_2 + 2HF$$

In the human body, phosphate ion is important in maintaining the pH of blood in a fairly narrow range of 7.3 to 7.5. We will explore how it does so in the next chapter.

Phosphoric acid is one of two inorganic polyprotic acids that have a worldwide impact on our ability to convert what nature has given us into products that sustain and improve our quality of life. Sulfuric acid is the other.

Sulfuric acid is a diprotic acid that is prepared by the Contact process, as we discussed in Section 16.3. Sulfur is burned in oxygen to form sulfur dioxide, which is then converted into sulfur trioxide via a catalyst such as vanadium:

$$S(s) + O_2(g) \rightleftharpoons SO_2(g)$$

$$2SO_2(g) + O_2(g) \rightleftharpoons 2SO_3(g)$$

The sulfur trioxide is then combined with water to give sulfuric acid:

$$SO_3(g) + H_2O(l) \rightleftharpoons H_2SO_4(l)$$

Among the many uses for sulfuric acid is a century-old process for the conversion of phosphate rock to the fertilizer monocalcium phosphate, $Ca(H_2PO_4)_2 \cdot H_2O$. The reaction can be summarized as follows:

$$2Ca_5(PO_4)_3F + 7H_2SO_4 + 3H_2O \rightleftharpoons 3Ca(H_2PO_4)_2 \cdot H_2O + 7CaSO_4 + 2HF$$

Note that the product of this reaction is similar to the one produced by the treatment of phosphate rock with phosphoric acid.

Among the other uses of sulfuric acid is in the manufacture of phosphoric acid itself from fluoroapatite, with the resulting production of calcium sulfate dihydrate ($CaSO_4 \cdot 2H_2O$, also known as **gypsum**) under reaction conditions that are different from those in the previous reaction.

$$2Ca_5(PO_4)_3F + 10H_2SO_4 + 20H_2O \rightleftharpoons 10CaSO_4 \cdot 2H_2O + 6H_3PO_4 + 2HF$$

FIGURE 17.18

Calcium supplements often contain the tribasic phosphate ion. This supplement contains a mixture of calcium-containing minerals including $Ca_3(PO_4)_2$ and $CaCO_3$.

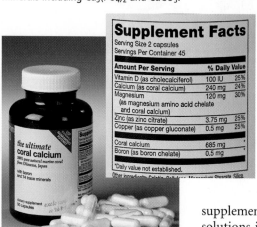

The gypsum produced in this reaction is quite valuable for use as Sheetrock and wallboard in the construction of homes. Furthermore, HF is a useful product in the glass industry.

In the reactions we have just shown, the phosphates and sulfates are present in a variety of forms: as polyprotic acids (H_3PO_4 and H_2SO_4); as a **monobasic salt** (it can accept one acidic hydrogen atom—$Ca(H_2PO_4)_2 \cdot H_2O$); and as a **dibasic salt** (it can accept two acidic hydrogen atoms—$CaSO_4$). Another common compound is calcium phosphate, $Ca_3(PO_4)_2$, a **tribasic salt** (it can accept three acidic hydrogen atoms). Calcium phosphate is one of several calcium salts, including calcium carbonate, $CaCO_3$, and calcium citrate, $Ca_3(C_6H_5O_7)_2 \cdot 4H_2O$, that many people take daily as a calcium supplement (Figure 17.18). Each of these species affects the acid concentration of solutions in predictable ways. Understanding these effects helps us to see how these acids are employed in manufacturing the products that we use.

Formula	Name	K_{a_1}	K_{a_2}	K_{a_3}
H_3PO_4	Phosphoric acid	7.4×10^{-3}	6.2×10^{-8}	4.8×10^{-13}
H_3AsO_4	Arsenic acid	5.0×10^{-3}	8.0×10^{-8}	6.0×10^{-10}
H_2CO_3	Carbonic acid	4.3×10^{-7}	5.6×10^{-11}	
H_2SO_4	Sulfuric acid	>1	1.2×10^{-2}	
H_2SO_3	Sulfurous acid	1.5×10^{-2}	1.0×10^{-7}	
H_2S	Hydrosulfuric acid	1.0×10^{-7}	1.0×10^{-15}	
$H_2C_2O_4$	Oxalic acid	6.5×10^{-2}	6.1×10^{-5}	
$H_2C_6H_6O_6$	Ascorbic acid	7.9×10^{-5}	1.6×10^{-12}	

TABLE 17.9 K_a Values for Selected Polyprotic Acids

The pH of Polyprotic Acids

Phosphoric acid is so common that it represents an important and useful model for our introduction to the pH of polyprotic acids. We begin by calculating the pH of 4.0 M aqueous phosphoric acid (neglecting activity effects).

As with any equilibrium problem, the first step is to establish the equilibria of the species in solution that contribute hydrogen ions. Phosphoric acid can donate three hydrogen ions per molecule, the second being more difficult to donate than the first because of the negative charge on the resultant dihydrogen phosphate anion ($H_2PO_4^-$). The third will be tougher still as a consequence of the greater charge on the monohydrogen phosphate anion (HPO_4^{2-}). This is reflected in the values for K_a of each step in the process, in which K_{a_1} is the equilibrium constant for the first acidic ionization, K_{a_2} refers to the second ionization, and K_{a_3} describes the third. Table 17.9 lists K_a values for several polyprotic acids. K_{a_1} values are not only larger than those of K_{a_2}, but they are often *considerably* so, and this is frequently true for acids. Water is also a source of hydrogen ions.

$$H_3PO_4 \rightleftharpoons H_2PO_4^- + H^+ \qquad K_{a_1} = 7.5 \times 10^{-3}$$
$$H_2PO_4^- \rightleftharpoons HPO_4^{2-} + H^+ \qquad K_{a_2} = 6.2 \times 10^{-8}$$
$$HPO_4^{2-} \rightleftharpoons PO_4^{3-} + H^+ \qquad K_{a_3} = 4.8 \times 10^{-13}$$
$$H_2O \rightleftharpoons OH^- + H^+ \qquad K_w = 1.0 \times 10^{-14}$$

The total concentration of hydrogen ion will equal the sum of the contributions from all the reactions.

$$[H^+]_{total} = [H^+]_{H_3PO_4} + [H^+]_{H_2PO_4^-} + [H^+]_{HPO_4^{2-}} + [H^+]_{H_2O}$$

Which reactions are *important* contributors of hydrogen ions to the solution? The K_{a_1} value is considerably larger than the others, so we may assume that it is the only important equilibrium. That is,

$$[H^+]_{total} \cong [H^+]_{H_3PO_4}$$

We will eventually want to prove that the other reactions are *not* important contributors if we make this assumption.

We may now solve the problem, determining the pH of a 4.0 M solution of H_3PO_4, as we have other equilibrium problems. We'll remember to test any assumptions we make along the way.

$$K_{a_1} = \frac{[H_2PO_4^-][H^+]}{[H_3PO_4]}$$

	H_3PO_4	$\rightleftharpoons$	H^+	+	$H_2PO_4^-$
initial	$4.0\ M$		$0\ M$		$0\ M$
change	$-x$		$+x$		$+x$
equilibrium	$4.0 - x$		$+x$		$+x$
assumptions	4.0		$+x$		$+x$

$$7.4 \times 10^{-3} = \frac{x^2}{4.0}$$

$$x = [H_2PO_4^-] = [H^+] = 0.17\ M$$

$$pH = 0.76$$

$$[H_3PO_4] = [H_3PO_4]_0 - [H_2PO_4^-] = 4.0 - 0.17 = 3.83\ M \approx 3.8\ M$$

We have made the assumption that "x" is negligible relative to 4.0 M. In this case,

$$\frac{0.17}{4.0} \times 100\% = 4.3\%$$

Our assumption is valid.

We must now test our assumptions that the other equilibria were not important contributors of hydrogen ion to the solution. We may begin with water, knowing that

$$[H^+]_{water} = [OH^-]_{total} = \frac{K_w}{[H^+_{total}]} = \frac{1.0 \times 10^{-14}}{0.17} = 5.9 \times 10^{-14}\ M$$

Our assumption that water was a negligible source of hydrogen ion was fine (with thanks to Le Châtelier!). What about $[H^+]_{HPO_4^{2-}}$, which results from the loss of a hydrogen ion by $H_2PO_4^-$?

$$H_2PO_4^- \rightleftharpoons HPO_4^{2-} + H^+ \qquad K_{a_2} = 6.2 \times 10^{-8}$$

We showed above that $[H_2PO_4^-]$ is equal to 0.17 M. What is $[H^+]$ in this equation? It is roughly equal to the hydrogen ion concentration resulting from the first dissociation, that of H_3PO_4, $[H^+]_{total} \approx [H^+]_{H_3PO_4}$, and that is also equal to 0.17 M. We can substitute these values into the equilibrium expression to determine $[H^+]_{H_2PO_4^-}$ (which equals $[HPO_4^{2-}]$):

$$K_{a_2} = 6.2 \times 10^{-8} = \frac{[HPO_4^{2-}][H^+]}{[H_2PO_4^-]} = \frac{[HPO_4^{2-}](0.17)}{(0.17)}$$

Therefore,

$$[HPO_4^{2-}] = K_{a_2} = 6.2 \times 10^{-8}\ M$$

Also, $[H^+]_{HPO_4^{2-}}$ will equal $[HPO_4^{2-}]$, because they are both produced in the same reaction.

$$[H^+]_{HPO_4^{2-}} = 6.2 \times 10^{-8}\ M$$

This confirms the notion that only the first equilibrium, the dissociation of H_3PO_4, is an important contributor to $[H^+]_{total}$.

We can take this one step further and calculate the hydrogen ion concentration due to the dissociation of the dibasic anion HPO_4^{2-}:

$$HPO_4^{3-} \rightleftharpoons PO_4^{3-} + H^+ \qquad K_{a_3} = 4.8 \times 10^{-13}$$

In this case, $[H^+]_{total}$ is still $0.17\ M$ and $[HPO_4^{2-}] = 6.2 \times 10^{-8}\ M$. Substituting into the equilibrium expression for K_{a_3} yields

$$K_{a_3} = 4.8 \times 10^{-13} = \frac{[PO_4^{3-}][H^+]}{[HPO_4^{-2}]} = \frac{[PO_4^{3-}](0.17)}{6.2 \times 10^{-8}}$$

$$x = [PO_4^{3-}] = [H^+]_{PO_4^{3-}} = 1.8 \times 10^{-19}\ M$$

In summary, we have accounted for all of the phosphate species and all of the hydrogen ion.

$$[phosphate\ species] = [H_3PO_4] + [H_2PO_4^-] + [HPO_4^-] + [PO_4^{3-}]$$

$$4.0\ M \quad = \quad 3.83\ M \ + \ 0.17\ M \ + 6.2 \times 10^{-8}\ M + 1.8 \times 10^{-19}\ M$$

$$[H^+]_{total} = [H^+]_{H_3PO_4} + [H^+]_{H_2PO_4^-} + [H^+]_{HPO_4^{2-}} + [H^+]_{H_2O}$$

$$0.17\ M \quad \approx \quad 0.17\ M \ + 6.2 \times 10^{-8}\ M + 1.8 \times 10^{-19}\ M + 5.9 \times 10^{-14}\ M$$

We note that when the concentration of phosphoric acid is much greater than the value of K_{a_1}, only the dissociation of phosphoric acid itself contributes significantly to the hydrogen ion concentration. The concentration of each phosphate species changes in solution as the pH changes, with less of the acidic forms (H_3PO_4 and $H_2PO_4^-$) and more of the basic forms (HPO_4^{2-} and PO_4^{3-}) present at higher pH levels.

EXERCISE 17.14   **Concentration of Species in a Polyprotic Acid Solution**

Oxalic acid ($H_2C_2O_4$), which is found in beet leaves, rhubarb, and spinach, is used in the bookbinding industry, as well as in dye and ink manufacturing. In the analytical laboratory it can be used as a primary standard against which to determine the molarity of sodium hydroxide. Using the information in Table 17.9, determine the pH and $[H_2C_2O_4]$ of a $1.40\ M$ solution of oxalic acid.

$$H_2C_2O_4(aq) \rightleftharpoons HC_2O_4^-(aq) + H^+(aq) \qquad K_{a_1} = 6.5 \times 10^{-2}$$

$$HC_2O_4^-(aq) \rightleftharpoons H^+(aq) + C_2O_4^{2-}(aq) \qquad K_{a_2} = 6.5 \times 10^{-5}$$

Oxalic acid
$C_2H_2O_4$

First Thoughts

The major species in solution are $H_2C_2O_4$ and H_2O. There are a number of equilibria that will occur in the solution. Judging on the basis of the values of K_{a_1}, K_{a_2}, and K_w, by far the most significant equilibrium will be the dissociation of $H_2C_2O_4$.

$$H_2C_2O_4(aq) \rightleftharpoons HC_2O_4^-(aq) + H^+(aq)$$

	$H_2C_2O_4$	$HC_2O_4^-$	H^+
initial	1.40	0	0
change	$-x$	x	x
final	$1.40 - x$	x	x
assumptions	1.40	x	x

As always, we will test our "negligible ionization" assumption ($1.40 \sim x \approx 1.40$). However, because K_a is *not* less than $10^{-2} \times [H_2C_2O_4]_0$, our assumption may well not be valid.

Solution

$$K_{a_1} = \frac{[HC_2O_4^-][H^+]}{[H_2C_2O_4]} = 6.5 \times 10^{-2} = \frac{x^2}{1.40}$$

$$x = [H^+] = [HC_2O_4^-] = 0.302\ M$$

Testing the 5% rule, we find that

$$\frac{0.302}{1.40} \times 100\% = 21.5\%!$$

This confirms our prediction based on K_a and $[H_2C_2O_4]_0$. Therefore, $[H_2C_2O_4] \neq [H_2C_2O_4]_0$ but rather equals "$1.40 - x$."

$$6.5 \times 10^{-2} = \frac{x^2}{1.40 - x}$$

We can solve using the quadratic formula, as we did in Section 16.5. Clearing the fraction and setting equal to zero, we get

$$x^2 + 0.065(x) - 0.091 = 0$$

where $a = 1$, $b = 0.065$, and $c = -0.091$. Solving yields

$$x = \frac{-0.065 \pm \sqrt{(0.065)^2 - 4(1)(-0.091)}}{2(1)}$$

$$x = 0.271 \, M$$

$$[H^+] = [HC_2O_4^-] = 0.271 \, M$$

$$[H_2C_2O_4] = 1.40 - 0.271 \approx 1.13 \, M$$

$$pH = -\log(0.271) = 0.57$$

Checking our math, we find that

$$K_{a_1} = \frac{(0.271)^2}{1.13} = 0.0650$$

Further Insights

Does our answer make sense? Although we classify oxalic acid as "weak" because its K_{a_1} value is less than 1 (and its K_{a_2} value is even smaller,) it is still stronger than many common weak acids such as acetic and citric acids. It is therefore reasonable that this relatively concentrated solution should have a low pH.

PRACTICE 17.14

Determine the pH of an aqueous 0.200 M H_3PO_4 solution.

See Problems 59, 60, 63, and 64. ■

We have seen that we can get a sense of what the pH of a solution will be by *assessing the competing equilibria that occur in solution*. Using this understanding, the pH of seemingly complex systems can be solved in a structured and meaningful fashion. We can extend this understanding to salts that contain an anion and cation that have acid–base behavior.

17.7 Assessing the Acid–Base Behavior of Salts in Aqueous Solution

Salts, such as NaCl, NH_4NO_3, and $NaNO_2$, are ionic compounds. When they dissociate in water they may exhibit acid–base behavior. The key questions you need to ask when assessing whether a salt will be acidic, basic, or neutral in aqueous solution are **What are the acid–base properties of the cation and anion parts of the salt?** and **Which is more influential, the acid strength of the cation or the base**

Application

strength of the anion? Whichever is stronger will determine whether the salt solution is acidic or basic.

Sodium nitrite ($NaNO_2$) is an important example because it is a food additive that helps retard spoilage in meat and also is used in many industrial applications, including the production of nitrogen-containing dyes as well as anticorrosion agents. Its use in the food industry has been restricted by the Food and Drug Administration to 200 parts per million in meat and poultry that is ready for sale, because sodium nitrite was implicated in the 1970s as a possible precursor for some cancer-causing compounds. The salt essentially completely dissociates in aqueous solution to give Na^+ and NO_2^- ions. These are the main species in solution in addition to H_2O. **What are the acid–base properties of each of these species?** Remember the conjugate acid–base relationships:

- Strong acids and bases have weak conjugates. *Na^+ and other alkali and alkaline earth metal ions exhibit no important acid–base properties.*
- The nitrite ion (NO_2^-) is the conjugate base of the weak acid HNO_2 ($K_a = 4.6 \times 10^{-4}$). Remember that *weak* is a relative term. HNO_2 is weak compared to HNO_3, which has $K_a \gg 1$, but is far stronger than HCN ($K_a = 6.2 \times 10^{-10}$). *The NO_2^- ion will act as a weak base.*
- Water has relatively little acid–base effect.

Therefore, an aqueous solution of $NaNO_2$ should be slightly basic. We can now determine how basic by applying our understanding of equilibrium.

The Relationship of K_a to K_b

Consider an aqueous 0.500 M $NaNO_2$ solution. The process in which the nitrite ion (or any base) reacts with water to produce the conjugate acid and hydroxide ion is called **base hydrolysis**. The important equilibrium is

$$NO_2^-(aq) + H_2O(l) \rightleftharpoons HNO_2(aq) + OH^-(aq) \qquad K_b = ?$$

Note that this equation describes the equilibration of a base with water. What is the value for K_b? When we look in Appendix 5, we do not find an entry for NO_2^-. However, we do find a value for the K_a of nitrous acid:

$$HNO_2(aq) \rightleftharpoons H^+(aq) + NO_2^-(aq) \qquad K_a = 7.0 \times 10^{-4}$$

Is it possible to relate the two equilibria to get a value for K_b of the nitrite ion hydrolysis? The short answer is yes. If we take the expression for K_b and multiply by $\dfrac{[H^+]}{[H^+]}$, we get

$$K_b = \frac{[HNO_2][OH^-]}{[NO_2^-]} \times \frac{[H^+]}{[H^+]} = \frac{[HNO_2][OH^-][H^+]}{[NO_2^-][H^+]}$$

Because $K_w = [H^+][OH^-]$, we can substitute K_w into the equation, which gives

$$K_a = \frac{[HNO_2]K_w}{[NO_2^-][H^+]}$$

If you write the mass-action expression for K_a for the ionization of nitrous acid, you might note that $\dfrac{[HNO_2]}{[NO_2^-][H^+]}$ is equal to $1/K_a$. This means that the K_b expression may be rewritten as

$$K_b = \frac{K_w}{K_a}$$

or, as more often cited,

$$K_w = K_a \times K_b$$

This means that we can determine the K_a or K_b value for the conjugate of any weak acid or base, given its equilibrium constant. For the nitrite ion,

$$K_b = \frac{K_w}{K_a} = \frac{1.0 \times 10^{-14}}{7.0 \times 10^{-4}} = 1.4 \times 10^{-11}$$

We may now determine the pH of this weak base as we would any other weak base in solution. We will do this as Exercise 17.15.

EXERCISE 17.15   **pH of a Salt with a Cation with No Acidic Properties**

Determine the pH of a 0.500 M $NaNO_2$ solution.

First Thoughts

As we discussed previously, the Na^+ cation has no acid–base properties, and the hydrolysis of the NO_2^- ion will produce OH^- ions, leading to a basic solution.

$$NO_2^-(aq) + H_2O(l) \rightleftharpoons HNO_2(aq) + OH^-(aq)$$

$$K_b = \frac{[HNO_2][OH^-]}{[NO_2^-]} = 1.4 \times 10^{-11}$$

We may now proceed as with any other weak-base problem.

$$NO_2^-(aq) + H_2O(l) \rightleftharpoons HNO_2(aq) + OH^-(aq)$$

initial	0.500	−0	0
change	−x	−x	x
final	0.500 − x	−x	x
with assumption	0.500	−x	x

In this exercise, "x" = $[HNO_2]$ = $[OH^-]$.

Solution

$$1.4 \times 10^{-11} = \frac{x^2}{0.500}$$

$$x = [OH^-] = [HNO_2] = 2.6 \times 10^{-6}\,M$$

This passes the 5% test (K_b is so small!).

$$pOH = -\log(2.6 \times 10^{-6}) = 5.59$$

$$pH = 14 - 5.59 = 8.41$$

Further Insights

Does the answer make sense? We have a weak base, and the pH is indicative of this. Therefore, our calculation is reasonable.

PRACTICE 17.15

Determine the pH of a 0.250 M sodium acetate (CH_3COONa) solution.

See Problems 75–82.

What happens when *both* the cation and the anion have acid–base properties? That is, what if the cation can react to supply hydrogen ion to the solution and the anion can supply hydroxide ion? In a broad sense, we can determine whether the solution will be acidic or basic from the *relative strengths of the acidic and basic parts of the salt.* For example, we can view ammonium cyanide (NH_4CN) as undergoing two important equilibrium reactions:

$$NH_4^+(aq) \rightleftharpoons NH_3(aq) + H^+(aq) \qquad K_a = \frac{K_w}{K_{b(NH_3)}} = 5.6 \times 10^{-10}$$

$$CN^-(aq) + H_2O(l) \rightleftharpoons HCN(aq) + OH^- \qquad K_b = \frac{K_w}{K_{a(HCN)}} = 1.6 \times 10^{-5}$$

Based on the equilibrium constants for the reactions, the CN^- ion is a much stronger base than the NH_4^+ ion is an acid, and we would therefore expect the solution to be basic. However, unlike the previous example using $NaNO_2$, in which only the nitrite ion had any acid–base behavior, here *both* the cation and the anion could contribute to the pH of the solution, and we must take both equilibria into account. In the sense that we have one substance that acts as an acid and one that acts as a base, this is similar to an amphiprotic substance. The derivation for the pH of a substance that has both acid and base properties, such as this type of salt or an amphiprotic substance such as Na_2HPO_4, is fairly complex. The resulting formula, however, is simple and useful:

$$[H^+] = (K_{a(NH_4^+)} \times K_{a(HCN)})^{1/2}$$
$$pH = \tfrac{1}{2}(pK_{a(NH_4^+)} + pK_{a(HCN)})$$

If the concentration of the substance is greater than 0.100 M (true with amphiprotic substances as well), the pH of the aqueous salt solution is approximately concentration independent. Let's use these equations to calculate the pH of a 0.800 M NH_4CN solution.

$$[H^+] = (K_{a(NH_4^+)} \times K_{a(HCN)})^{1/2} = (5.6 \times 10^{-10} \times 6.2 \times 10^{-10})^{1/2}$$
$$= 5.9 \times 10^{-10}\ M \qquad pH = 9.23$$

Amino acids are biologically vital compounds that have the ability to act as an acid and as a base within the same molecule. That is, one part of the molecule is acidic and a different part of the molecule is basic. Amino acids can polymerize into large units to form proteins such as hemoglobin (which transports oxygen), pepsinogen (which digests other proteins), and human growth hormone (which promotes normal growth). Amino acids are water soluble because they carry both positive and negative charge in aqueous solution. An example of how this can happen, involving the amino acid alanine, is shown in Figure 17.19. When dissolved in water, the carboxylic acid group loses a hydrogen ion, and the amine group gains a hydrogen ion. Why does this happen? The $-NH_3$ is a stronger base than the $-COO^-$, so the hydrogen ion will move from the COOH to the amine group. Ions that are doubly ionized in this way are called zwitterions. They can act in the same way as any other amphiprotic substance, donating a hydrogen ion to water or accepting one from water.

FIGURE 17.19

Amino acids are soluble in water because they often exist as zwitterions—doubly charged amino acids. As shown here with alanine, this can occur because the $-NH_2$ is a stronger base than the $-COO^-$, so the hydrogen ion will move from the COOH to the amine group.

Neutral form   Zwitterion

Application

CHEMICAL ENCOUNTERS:
Acid–Base Properties
of Amino Acids

Some amino acids.

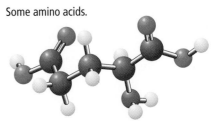

Glutamic acid

Glycine

Valine

EXERCISE 17.16   **pH of Zwitterions**

Given the following reactions and equilibrium constants, calculate the pH of a solution of 0.200 M alanine.

$$CH_3(NH_3^+)COO^-(aq) \rightleftharpoons CH_3(NH_2)COO^-(aq) + H^+(aq) \qquad K_{a_2} = 1.4 \times 10^{-10}$$

$$CH_3(NH_3^+)COO^-(aq) + H_2O(l) \rightleftharpoons CH_3(NH_3^+)COOH(aq) + OH^-(aq)$$
$$K_{b_2} = 2.2 \times 10^{-12}$$

First Thoughts

The donation of hydrogen ion by alanine is favored over its acceptance of a hydrogen ion. We therefore would expect the solution to be somewhat, though not strongly, acidic.

Solution

We must find K_{a_1} for the second equation, just as in the ammonium cyanide case described previously.

$$K_{a_1} = \frac{K_w}{K_{b_2}} = \frac{1.0 \times 10^{-14}}{2.2 \times 10^{-12}} = 4.5 \times 10^{-3}$$

$$[H^+] = (K_{a_2} \times K_{a_1})^{1/2} = (1.4 \times 10^{-10} \times 4.5 \times 10^{-3})^{1/2} = 7.9 \times 10^{-7} \, M$$

$$pH = 6.10$$

Further Insights

At this pH, alanine exists primarily as the zwitterion and is therefore electrically neutral. This is called the **isoelectric pH**. Each amino acid has a different isoelectric point, depending on its own acid–base properties. Chemists and biologists make use of the different isoelectric points (Figure 17.20) to separate amino acids in an electric field by changing the pH, because each amino acid will respond to the electric field differently depending on its isoelectric point.

Does our answer make sense? We asserted that the solution should be somewhat acidic because the acid-producing equilibrium is favored over the base-producing equilibrium. Food for thought: What would you expect to be the pH if the value of K_a for the hydrogen ion–producing reaction in a particular salt *is the same as* the value of K_b for the base-producing equilibrium of the salt? Can you think of any examples of this?

FIGURE 17.20

Isoelectric focusing can be used to purify and identify a mixture of compounds. For example, a sample of proteins from a particular cultivar of barley can be separated into the individual "bands" shown here. The proteins have been stained purple with a dye.

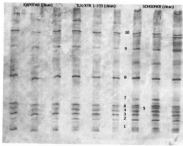

Photograph by Maria Sulman

PRACTICE 17.16

What is the pH of a 0.150 M alanine solution?

See Problems 83 and 84.

The principles that we have introduced for the evaluation of the pH of a salt can be extended from the two cases we have dealt with to a third case, in which the anion has no basic properties but the cation does have acidic properties. The thinking—that is, the questions that we raise—is the same. These questions about the nature of the equilibria in solution represent the unifying problem-solving theme in this chapter as well as the previous one dealing with chemical equilibrium.

Table 17.10 qualitatively summarizes the effect of the cation and of the anion on the pH of a salt.

Cation	Anion	Aqueous Solution	Example
TABLE 17.10	**Effect of Cation and Anion of the Acidity of a Salt**		
Acidic	Neutral	Acidic	NH_4NO_3
Neutral	Basic	Basic	Na_2CO_3
Neutral	Neutral	Neutral	NaCl
Acidic	Basic	Depends on the relative strength of each	

17.8 Anhydrides in Aqueous Solution

We started this chapter saying, "Home is where the heart is." The "home" that we talked about was not only our individual residence but ourselves and our world. In a sense, our final application, the set of reactions that cause acid deposition from the atmosphere, is a proper place to conclude the discussion, because the Earth is our communal home. To understand acid deposition, of which acid rain is one form, we need to understand the reactions of acidic and basic anhydrides (also known as acid and basic oxides) with water.

Basic anhydrides are binary compounds formed between metals with very low electronegativity and oxygen (see Section 17.2 for review of why these reactions would form bases). Strong bases are formed when Group IA and Group IIA anhydrides (*an* = "without" + *hydro* = "water") react with water. Metal hydroxides are often prepared this way instead of by reaction of the metal with water, which can sometimes be violent, as with the reaction of cesium with water to produce cesium hydroxide and hydrogen gas. Examples of anhydride and water reactions are

$$Li_2O(s) + H_2O(l) \rightleftharpoons 2LiOH(aq)$$

$$CaO(s) + H_2O(l) \rightleftharpoons Ca(OH)_2(aq)$$

Acid anhydrides are binary compounds formed between nonmetals and oxygen. Examples are SO_2, SO_3, NO_2, P_4O_{10}, and CO_2. These compounds react with water to form acids, their acid strength being related to the electronegativity of the nonmetal combined with oxygen. One example is the reaction of sulfur dioxide generated in industrial smokestacks with water:

$$SO_2(g) + H_2O(l) \rightleftharpoons H_2SO_3(aq)$$

The sulfurous acid generated in this reaction is not strong. However, dust in the air can catalyze the reaction between SO_2 and oxygen:

$$2SO_2(g) + O_2(g) \rightleftharpoons 2SO_3(g)$$

In a reaction analogous to the Contact process, the sulfur trioxide reacts with water vapor in the air to form sulfuric acid:

$$SO_3(g) + H_2O(l) \rightleftharpoons H_2SO_4(aq)$$

The acid that is formed can fall to Earth on a variety of surfaces, including snow, rain, and fog, and deposit on trees, lakes, and the like, and that is why we call the process acid deposition.

Nitrogen and oxygen released from the tailpipes of motorized vehicles during operation can react to form nitric oxide, which then slowly reacts with atmospheric oxygen to form nitrogen dioxide:

$$N_2(g) + O_2(g) \rightleftharpoons 2NO(g)$$

$$2NO(g) + O_2(g) \rightleftharpoons 2NO_2(g)$$

Application

CHEMICAL ENCOUNTERS:
Acid Deposition and
Acid-Neutralizing
Capacity

Acid deposition can severely damage the environment.

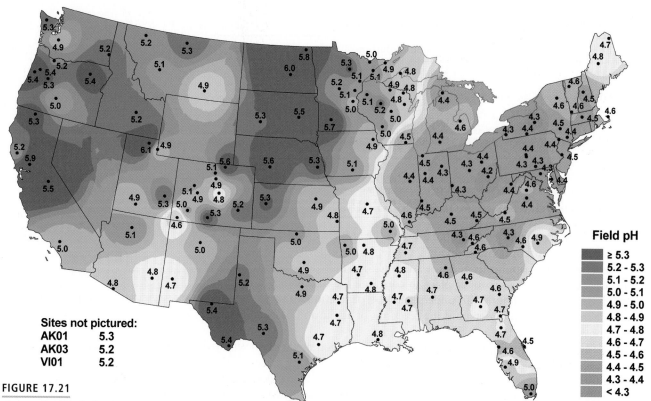

Sites not pictured:
AK01   5.3
AK03   5.2
VI01   5.2

FIGURE 17.21

The pH of materials that deposit on the United States varies across the country, 1999. The low pHs centered over Ohio are probably due to industrial processes.

Field pH

	≥ 5.3
	5.2 - 5.3
	5.1 - 5.2
	5.0 - 5.1
	4.9 - 5.0
	4.8 - 4.9
	4.7 - 4.8
	4.6 - 4.7
	4.5 - 4.6
	4.4 - 4.5
	4.3 - 4.4
	< 4.3

The nitrogen dioxide that is produced then reacts with water vapor to produce nitrous and nitric acids:

$$2NO_2(g) + H_2O(l) \rightleftharpoons HNO_2(aq) + HNO_3(aq)$$

The nitric acid adds to the problem of acid deposition. As can be seen in Figure 17.21, a lot of deposition that occurs throughout the United States has an unusually low pH. However, some places (for example, in the western United States) seem to be less affected by acid deposition than other places. Why?

The atmosphere acts as a large mixing chamber, and we've considered only the acidic inputs so far. Ammonia gas from agriculture and animal-feeding operations can react with water vapor to form aqueous ammonia, increasing the pH of the precipitation:

$$NH_3(g) + H_2O(l) \rightleftharpoons NH_4^+ + OH^-(aq)$$

There are more natural sources of ammonia gas in the western United States than sources of sulfur dioxide and nitrogen dioxide, so the pH of precipitation in this region is higher. The ability of some lakes to mitigate the effects of acid deposition has to do with acid-neutralizing capacity. This represents the theme of our next chapter: how and why acid–base and other types of reactions in aqueous solution are used in chemical analysis. This discussion will include acid–base neutralization, buffers, and titrations. Home is where the heart is. But we have shown that the home, and the people within it, are, chemically speaking, where the acids and bases also reside. Our global home, *Spaceship Earth,* is ever changing. It and we who occupy it owe much of this change to the acids and bases we have discussed here. In the next chapter, we will learn how.

The Bottom Line

- Acids and bases can be defined using three different models. (Section 17.1)

- Acids and bases come in different strengths. (Section 17.2)

- Both the strength and the initial concentration of the acid affect the acidity in solution at equilibrium. (Section 17.2)

- Acids and bases have conjugates pairs whose behavior is related to that of the acid or base from which they are derived. (Section 17.1)

- We use pH as our common measure of acidity. (Section 17.3)

- We can interconvert among H^+, OH^-, pH, and pOH for a given acidic or basic solution. (Section 17.3)

- We can calculate the pH of strong and weak acids and bases in aqueous solutions. (Sections 17.4 and 17.5)

- We can solve for the pH of a polyprotic acid or base, including salts. (Sections 17.6 and 17.7)

- K_a and K_b are related via K_w. (Section 17.7)

- The reaction of an acid anhydride with water results in an acid, and the reaction of a basic anhydride with water results in a base. (Section 17.8)

Key Words

acid According to the Arrhenius model, a species that produces hydrogen ions in solution. Compare the definitions of *Brønsted–Lowry acid* and *Lewis acid*. (*p. 719*)

acid deposition The precipitation of acidic compounds from the atmosphere. This includes wet deposition as rain and dry deposition of particles. (*p. 757*)

acid dissociation constant (K_a) The equilibrium constant for the dissociation of an acid. (*p. 724*)

acid-neutralizing capacity The capacity of a solution, such as lake water, to neutralize acidity. (*p. 758*)

acidic Having a pH less than 7.0 in aqueous solution at 24°C. (*p. 735*)

acid anhydrides Binary compounds formed between nonmetals and oxygen that react with water to form acids. (*p. 757*)

alkaloid Nitrogen-containing bases found in vegetables and other plants. (*p. 746*)

amphiprotic Having the ability to act as either an acid or a base in different circumstances. (*p. 733*)

autoprotolysis Proton transfer between molecules of the same chemical species, as in the autoprotolysis of water. (*p. 733*)

base According to the Arrhenius model, a species that produces hydroxide ions in solution. Compare the definitions of *Brønsted-Lowry base* and *Lewis base*. (*p. 719*)

base hydrolysis The process in which a base reacts with water to produce its conjugate acid and hydroxide ion. (*p. 753*)

basic Having a pH greater than 7.0 in aqueous solution at 24°C. (*p. 735*)

basic anhydrides Binary compounds that are formed between metals with very low electronegativity and oxygen and that react vigorously with water. (*p. 757*)

Brønsted–Lowry acid Any species that donates a hydrogen ion (proton) to another species. (*p. 720*)

Brønsted–Lowry base Any species that accepts a hydrogen ion (proton) from another species. (*p. 720*)

common-ion effect The addition of an ion common to one of the species in the solution, causing the equilibrium to shift away from production of that species. (*p. 737*)

conjugate acid The acid that results after accepting a proton. (*p. 720*)

conjugate base The base that results after donating a proton. (*p. 720*)

dibasic salt A salt that can accept two hydrogen ions. (*p. 748*)

diprotic acid An acid that contains two acidic protons. (*p. 736*)

gypsum Calcium sulfate dihydrate, $CaSO_4 \cdot 2H_2O$. (*p. 748*)

isoelectric pH pH value at which an amino acid is in the zwitterion form and so is electrically neutral overall. (*p. 756*)

Lewis acid Accepts a previously nonbonded pair of electrons (a lone pair) to form a coordinate covalent bond. (*p. 722*)

Lewis base Donates a previously nonbonded pair of electrons (a lone pair) to form a coordinate covalent bond. (*p. 722*)

monobasic salt A salt that can accept one hydrogen ion. (*p. 748*)

monoprotic acid An acid that contains one acidic proton. (*p. 736*)

neutral pH A pH of 7.0 in aqueous solution at 24°C. (*p. 734*)

pH A numerical value related to hydrogen ion concentration by the relationship $pH = -\log[H^+]$ or $pH = -\log[H_3O^+]$. (*p. 730*)

polyprotic acid An acid that can release more than 1 mol of hydrogen ions per mole of acid. (*p. 747*)

strong acid An acid that fully dissociates in water, releasing all of its acidic protons. (*p. 724*)

superacids Amazingly strong acids that can be used to add hydrogen ions to organic molecules that are otherwise impervious to such reaction. (*p. 729*)

tribasic salt A salt that can accept three acidic hydrogen atoms. (*p. 748*)

triprotic acid An acid that contains three acidic protons. (*p. 747*)

weak acid An acid that only partially dissociates in water. (*p. 724*)

zwitterion A molecular ion carrying both an acid group, which generates a negative ion, and a basic group, which generates a positive ion. (*p. 755*)

Focus Your Learning

The answers to the odd-numbered problems appear at the back of the book.

Section 17.1 What Are Acids and Bases?

Skill Review

1. Explain how ammonia (NH_3) qualifies as a base in both the Brønsted–Lowry and Arrhenius acid–base models.

2. Explain how HCl and NaOH are classified in both the Brønsted–Lowry and Arrhenius acid–base models.

3. List the conjugate base of each of these acids.
   a. HNO_3 b. HBr   c. H_2O d. $HClO_4$

4. List the conjugate base of each of these acids.
   a. HCl   b. NH_4^+ c. CH_3OH d. H_2SO_4

5. List the conjugate acid of each of these bases.
   a. NaOH   b. NH_3 c. H_2O d. NaF

6. List the conjugate acid of each of these bases.
   a. KBr   b. CH_3OH c. KNO_2 d. KSH

7. Acids react with active metals to produce hydrogen gas. Complete, balance, and name each of the products for these reactions.
   a. $Al(s) + HCl(aq) \rightarrow$ _____ + _____
   b. $Ca(s) + HNO_3(aq) \rightarrow$ _____ + _____
   c. $Na(s) + HCl(aq) \rightarrow$ _____ + _____
   d. $K(s) + HNO_3(aq) \rightarrow$ _____ + _____

8. Many bases react with metals to form insoluble hydroxides. Write the formula for each of these hydroxides.
   a. aluminum hydroxide   b. copper(II) hydroxide
   c. barium hydroxide   d. strontium hydroxide
   e. iron(III) hydroxide   f. calcium hydroxide

9. Being strong usually refers to the ability to carry out a task or produce an effect. (For example, a spice may have a strong flavor, and a weightlifter may display a lot of strength.) How is this term used when applied to acids? When an acid is said to be strong, what effect is being described?

10. What is the definition of a Lewis acid? Why are many metal ions capable of behaving as Lewis acids? Write out the reaction that depicts an aluminum cation behaving as a Lewis acid in an aqueous solution.

11. Balance and identify each of the species in the following reactions as either acid, base, conjugate acid, or conjugate base.
    a. $HCl + H_2O \rightarrow Cl^- + H_3O^+$
    b. $NaOH + CH_3COOH \rightarrow CH_3COONa + H_2O$
    c. $H_2SO_4 + Mg(OH)_2 \rightarrow MgSO_4 + H_2O$

12. Balance and identify each of the species in the following reactions as either acid, base, conjugate acid, or conjugate base.
    a. $HCOOH + NH_3 \rightarrow NH_4^+ + HCOO^-$
    b. $KOH + CH_3OH \rightarrow CH_3OK + H_2O$
    c. $H_3PO_4 + Ca(OH)_2 \rightarrow Ca_3(PO_4)_2 + H_2O$

Chemical Applications and Practices

13. One common antacid used in relief of upset stomachs is $Mg(OH)_2$. It helps to neutralize excess hydrochloric acid. Balance the following representative equation, and identify the conjugate acid–base pairs.

$$Mg(OH)_2 + HCl \rightarrow MgCl_2 + H_2O$$

14. Prizes in cereal boxes used to include little submarines that, when filled with baking soda ($NaHCO_3$) and placed in a cup of water containing a little vinegar (CH_3COOH), would rise and fall as though by magic. Balance the reaction of baking soda and vinegar, and identify the conjugate base and acid pairs.

$$CH_3COOH + NaHCO_3 \rightarrow CH_3COONa + H_2CO_3$$

Section 17.2 Acid Strength

Skill Review

15. Describe the characteristics of a strong acid with regard to each of the following:
    a. The numerical value of its K_a.
    b. The ability of its conjugate base to regain a H^+.
    c. The approximate percent dissociation of a 0.1 M solution.

16. Describe the characteristics of a weak acid with regard to each of the following:
    a. The numerical value of its K_a.
    b. The ability of its conjugate base to regain a H^+.
    c. The approximate percent dissociation of a 0.1 M solution.

17. Judging on the basis of electron density and electronegativity, which acid, HBr or HI, would you expect to be stronger? Explain your choice.

18. Which conjugate base, $Br^-(aq)$ or $I^-(aq)$, would you expect to be stronger? Explain your choice.

19. Using molecular structure and electronegativity, explain which acid, $HClO_4$ or $HBrO_4$, would be the weaker.

20. Which acid, phosphoric (H_3PO_4) or phosphorous (H_3PO_3), would you expect to be stronger? Explain your choice.

Chemical Applications and Practices

21. Formic acid, found in ants, and acetic acid, found in vinegar, have the K_a values 1.8×10^{-4} and 1.8×10^{-5}, respectively.
    a. Which acid has the stronger conjugate base?
    b. Which acid, if both were in 0.10 M solutions, would have the higher percent dissociation?

| Formic acid | Acetic acid |

22. The K_a value for an acid provides information about one type of reaction of the acid, its ability to provide H^+. However, a weak acid may have other very important reactions. For example, hydrofluoric acid, $K_a = 7.2 \times 10^{-4}$, has the ability to etch glass. Phenol, $K_a = 1.6 \times 10^{-10}$, can be used as a disinfectant.
    a. Which of these two is the weaker acid?
    b. Which has the stronger conjugate base?
    c. If both were 0.10 M, which would produce the greater concentration of H^+?

23. Propanoic acid is a weak acid that can be used to prepare a type of mold retardant. What is the value for K_a of the acid if, in a solution, the following equilibrium concentrations were found: [acid] = 0.10 M, [conjugate base] and [H^+] = 0.0011 M?

24. At 25°C the K_b for ammonia (NH_3) is 1.8×10^{-5}. What is the hydroxide concentration when [NH_3] = 0.103 M and [NH_4^+] = 0.00205 M?

Section 17.3 The pH Scale

Skill Review

25. Calculate the pH of each of these solutions.
    a. [H^+] = 4.55×10^{-3} M
    b. [H^+] = 3.27×10^{-6} M
    c. [H^+] = 8.11×10^{-9} M

26. Calculate the [H^+] for each of these solutions.
    a. pH = 1.50   b. pH = 10.25
    c. pH = 5.38   d. pH = 7.00

27. Calculate the values missing from the following table.

	[H^+] (M)	pH	[OH^-] (M)	pOH
a.		4.42		
b.	0.0056			
c.			0.000078	
d.				10.10

28. Calculate the values missing from the following table.

	[H^+] (M)	pH	[OH^-] (M)	pOH
a.		12.50		
b.	0.000035			
c.			0.00388	
d.				3.75

29. If the pH value in an aqueous sample were doubled, what effect would be detected in the hydronium ion concentration?

30. What would be the effect on the hydroxide ion concentration if the pH were doubled?

Chemical Applications and Practices

31. Paper is produced from the processed fibers of trees. Part of the process of sulfate pulping uses sodium hydroxide. What would be the pH of a solution in a wood-pulping mill if it contained 10.0 g of OH^- ions for every 10.0 L of solution?

32. One method to increase oil production in areas drilled through limestone deposits is to use hydrochloric acid to increase drainage channels through the stone. If such a solution had a pH of 2.59, what would you calculate as the grams of HCl dissolved per liter of solution?

33. Two samples of rainwater are being analyzed for an environmental impact study. What is the hydronium concentration in each sample? What is the pH of each sample?
    a. 500.0 mL containing 1.55×10^{-5} mol of H^+
    b. 250.0 mL containing 7.25×10^{-6} mol of H^+

34. The pH of human blood must be maintained within a very narrow range to ensure proper health. The following blood samples were analyzed to determine their pH values. What would you calculate as the hydronium concentration in each?
    a. pH = 7.42   b. pH = 7.38   c. pH = 7.51

35. Assuming a negligible change in volume, how many moles of either OH^- or H^+ would have to be added to change the pH of 1.00 L of a solution from 4.35 to 5.85?

36. Formic acid has a pK_a value of 3.74. Benzoic acid has a pK_a value of 4.20. Compare the electrostatic potential maps of formic acid and benzoic acid. Which is the stronger acid? Which of the two acids would have the weaker conjugate base?

| Formic acid | Benzoic acid |

Section 17.4 Determining the pH of Acidic Solutions

Skill Review

37. Determine the pH of each of these solutions of strong acids.
    a. 0.45 M HCl   b. 0.045 M HCl
    c. 0.000487 M HNO_3 d. 0.00026 M HBr

38. Determine the pH of each of these solutions of strong bases.
    a. 0.550 M NaOH   b. 0.00089 M KOH
    c. 0.00388 M KOH   d. 0.015 M KOH

39. Determine the pH of each of these solutions. (Use the table in the text to find the values for the appropriate K_a.)
    a. 0.45 M HOCl   b. 0.0250 M CH_3COOH
    c. 0.18 M HF

40. Determine the pH of each of these solutions. (Use the table in the text to find the values for the appropriate K_a.)
    a. 0.299 M HOCl   b. 0.18 M CH_3COOH
    c. 0.45 M lactic acid ($HC_3H_5O_3$)   d. 0.050 M HCN

41. Determine the value of pK_a for:
    a. $K_a = 3.75 \times 10^{-5}$ b. $K_a = 1.84 \times 10^{-2}$
    c. $K_a = 4.59 \times 10^{-8}$

42. Determine the value of K_a for:
    a. $pK_a = 3.50$ b. $pK_a = 4.74$ c. $pK_a = 6.17$

43. If the pH of a 0.015 M solution of codeine, a drug used in some pain relievers, is 10.19, what is the value of K_b for codeine ($C_{18}H_{21}NO_3$)?

44. What would be the resulting pH when a solution was made that was 0.0100 M in HCl and 0.100 M in HCN (hydrocyanic acid, a deadly poison, which has a K_a value of 6.2×10^{-10})?

Chemical Applications and Practices

45. Among the growth requirements for bacteria is the proper range of aqueous hydrogen ion concentration. Suppose a microbiologist was preparing growth media to study a specific bacterium. Examine both of the following situations and determine in which case the $H^+(aq)$ would be greater than 1.0×10^{-6} M?
    a. A 0.500-L solution containing 1.00 g of benzoic acid ($K_a = 6.5 \times 10^{-5}$; molar mass = 122 g)
    b. 100.0 mL of 0.0001 M sulfuric acid

46. Benzoic acid is often used to prepare a preservative known as sodium benzoate. If the K_a value of benzoic acid is 6.5×10^{-5}, what is the hydrogen ion concentration when the acid concentration is 0.0040 M and the conjugate base concentration is 0.0024 M?

47. The following reaction depicts an industrial process to manufacture gaseous hydrogen fluoride.
    $$CaF_2(s) + H_2SO_4(aq) \rightarrow CaSO_4(aq) + 2HF(g)$$
    a. How many grams of HF can be made from 1.00 kg of fluorospar (CaF_2)?
    b. HF can then be used to prepare fluorocarbon compounds. What would be the H^+, F^-, and OH^- concentrations in a solution that was 0.25 M in HF? (K_a of HF = 7.2×10^{-4})

48. An aspirin tablet may contain 325 mg of acetylsalicylic acid ($pK_a = 3.522$, 180.16 g/mol). What would be the approximate pH when two tablets were dissolved in 275 mL of water?

49. A vitamin C tablet may contain 500.0 mg of ascorbic acid ($C_6H_8O_6$). What would be the pH of a solution made from dissolving one such tablet in 355 mL of solution? (K_{a_1} of ascorbic acid = 8.0×10^{-5}) Does the 5% rule assumption apply in this example? Show your proof.

50. Benzoic acid ($K_a = 6.5 \times 10^{-5}$) and propionic acid ($K_a = 1.3 \times 10^{-5}$) can both be used to produce food preservatives. A 0.10 M solution of one of the acids has $[H^+] = 0.00255$ M. Which acid was used?

Section 17.5 Determining the pH of Basic Solutions

Skill Review

51. Determine the pH of each of these solutions.
    a. 0.100 M aniline ($K_b = 3.8 \times 10^{-8}$)
    b. 0.0100 M NaOH
    c. 0.250 M ammonia

52. Determine the pH of each of these solutions.
    a. 0.0333 M methylamine ($K_b = 5.9 \times 10^{-4}$)
    b. 0.0150 M $Ca(OH)_2$
    c. 0.016 M ammonia

Chemical Applications and Practices

53. Pyridine is a weak base that can be used to make a product used in some mouthwash preparations. The K_b value of pyridine is approximately 1.4×10^{-9}. What would be the hydroxide ion concentration, the pOH, and the pH of a solution that was 0.0010 M pyridine?

54. The base $Ca(OH)_2$ is known as slaked lime. It is widely used in the paper industry and in steel making. When properly heated, it gives off a bright light. In the 1800s, this light was used to illuminate some theaters. Actors began appearing in the "limelight."
    a. Write out the equation representing the dissociation of lime in water.
    b. $Ca(OH)_2$ is not very soluble in water. If 0.025 mol could dissolve per liter, what would you calculate as the pH of the solution?

55. The typical "fish aroma" is due to the production of amine compounds. What would be the K_b value of ethylamine ($CH_3CH_2NH_2$) if a 500.0 mL solution that contained 1.90 g of ethylamine had a pH of 11.87?

56. Metacaine is used to anesthetize groups of fish when scientific studies on them are conducted. The active ingredient of metacaine is a base known as ethyl 3-aminobenzoate. What would be the K_b value of ethyl 3-aminobenzoate ($C_9H_{11}NO_2$) if a 750.0 mL solution containing 1.00 g had a pH of 9.30?

Section 17.6 Polyprotic Acids

Skill Review

57. Write out the three hydrogen dissociation steps for phosphorous acid (H_3PO_3). What is the oxidation number of phosphorus in H_3PO_3?

58. Write out the two hydrogen dissociation steps for carbonic acid (H_2CO_3). What is the oxidation number of carbon in H_2CO_3?

59. The respective K_a values for the three dissociation steps of phosphoric acid are $7.4 \times 10^{-3}, 6.2 \times 10^{-8}$, and 4.8×10^{-13}. What would be the pH and HPO_4^{2-} concentration of a 1.0 M solution of H_3PO_4?

60. What are the pH and the HSO_4^- concentration of a 0.750 M solution of H_2SO_4?

Chemical Applications and Practices

61. Sulfurous acid (H_2SO_3) is a by-product of burning sulfur-containing coal. SO_2 is produced during the process and, when combined with water in the air, can produce H_2SO_3. Write the balanced equations that show the two-stage ionization of sulfurous acid. Identify the conjugate base produced in each stage.

62. Carbonic acid can be found in carbonated drinks. It forms when CO_2 reacts with water.
    a. Write the balanced equation that shows the formation of carbonic acid from dissolved carbon dioxide.
    b. Write out the equilibrium expressions for both ionization steps for this diprotic acid.
    c. Use Le Châtelier's principle to explain why increasing the pressure of CO_2 produces a lower pH in the solution.

63. Nicotine is dibasic because of the presence of two nitrogen atoms, each of which may accept hydrogen ions. The respective K_b values, at 25°C, are approximately 7.0×10^{-7} and 1.1×10^{-10}. What would be the pH of a solution that was 0.045 M in nicotine?

64. Tartaric acid ($H_2C_4H_4O_6$) is a diprotic acid used in some baking preparations. For the successive hydrogen ionizations, $K_{a_1} = 9.2 \times 10^{-4}$ and $K_{a_2} = 4.3 \times 10^{-5}$. What would be the pH of a solution that was 0.10 M in tartaric acid?

Section 17.7 Assessing the Acid–Base Behavior of Salts in Aqueous Solution

Skill Review

65. Arrange the following 0.10 M solutions in order of decreasing pH: NH_4Cl, $NaCl$, $NaC_2H_3O_2$.

66. Which of these ions could produce a basic aqueous solution? $S^{2-}, Cl^-, NO_3^-, NO_2^-, CO_3^{2-}, OCl^-$.

67. Two acids, HX and HY, have pK_a values of 4.55 and 5.44, respectively. Which salt, NaX or NaY, will produce the more basic aqueous solution when prepared as 0.10 M?

68. Two sodium salts, symbolized as NaW and NaY, are completely dissolved to produce 0.20 M solutions. The respective pH values of the two solutions are 8.55 and 9.55. Which acid, HW or HY, is stronger? Prove your choice.

69. What is isoelectric pH? Why is it useful information to know about amino acids?

70. If the isoelectric pH for an amino acid were above 7, what would that indicate about the relative values of its K_a and K_b?

71. The K_a value for the dissolved cation $Zn(H_2O)_6^{2+}$ is approximately 2.4×10^{-10}. What is the pH of a solution that is 0.10 M $ZnCl_2$? (Hint: What happens when $ZnCl_2$ dissolves?)

72. Will each of these salts be acidic, basic, or neutral?
    a. KI   b. NH_4F c. $(NH_4)_3PO_4$

73. Determine the value of K_a if:
    a. $K_b = 4.26 \times 10^{-5}$
    b. $K_b = 8.36 \times 10^{-9}$
    c. $pK_a = 2.85$

74. Determine the value of K_b if:
    a. $K_a = 6.90 \times 10^{-3}$
    b. $K_a = 1.77 \times 10^{-12}$
    c. $pK_a = 4.74$

75. Determine the pH of a solution that is 0.050 M in HCOONa.

76. Determine the pH of a solution that is 0.136 M in KNO_2.

Chemical Applications and Practices

77. The salt ammonium chloride is used in some chemical "cold packs" to absorb heat and cool muscle wounds. Ammonium chloride can be produced from an acid–base reaction.
    a. Write out the reaction using an acid and a base that would produce ammonium chloride.
    b. Would the resulting solution of ammonium chloride be acidic, basic, or neutral? Explain.
    c. Determine the pH of a solution of ammonium chloride that is 0.136 M.

78. The salt sodium hypochlorite (NaOCl) can be used in some bleaching actions needed for disinfecting aqueous systems.
    a. Write out the balanced equation that represents the complete dissociation of the salt in water.
    b. Would this be likely to produce an acidic, basic, or neutral solution?
    c. Determine the pH of a solution that is 0.250 M NaOCl.

79. Sodium carbonate, sometimes called soda ash, is used industrially in the manufacture of glass, paper, and soaps. What would be the pH of a 0.15 M solution of sodium carbonate?

80. Sodium bicarbonate, also known as baking soda or sodium hydrogen carbonate, is produced industrially by the addition of carbon dioxide to soda ash. Sodium bicarbonate has widespread uses in antacids, paper manufacturing, and some fire extinguishers, as well as to remove some harmful gases during coal combustion. What would be the pH of a 0.15 M solution of sodium bicarbonate?

81. Sodium benzoate, a salt of benzoic acid sometimes used as a food preservative, dissolves in water to produce the benzoate ion, $C_6H_5CO_2^-$. The K_a value for benzoic acid is approximately 6.5×10^{-5}.
    a. Write out the reaction of the benzoate ion in water and calculate the K_b value for the reaction.
    b. What would be the pH of a 0.010 M solution of sodium benzoate?

82. Novocain is often used as a local anesthetic. The compound is actually a salt of the base procaine. Procaine has a K_b value of 7.13×10^{-6}.
    a. What would be the K_a of Novocain?
    b. What would be the pH of a 0.010 M solution of Novocain?

83. Lysine is considered an essential amino acid. Essential amino acids are those that are not synthesized by humans and must, therefore, be part of a healthful diet. Lysine can be found in

beans. The formula of lysine is given below. Rewrite the formula showing lysine as a zwitterion.

$$H_2N-CH_2-CH_2-CH_2-CH_2-\overset{\overset{\displaystyle H}{|}}{\underset{\underset{\displaystyle COOH}{|}}{C}}-NH_2$$

84. Glycine has the simplest structure of the amino acids.

$$H-\overset{\overset{\displaystyle NH_2}{|}}{\underset{\underset{\displaystyle H}{|}}{C}}-COOH$$

a. Write out the reactions that show glycine acting as an acid and acting as a base.
b. What would be the pH of a 0.10 M solution of glycine? (The approximate K_{a_2} and K_{b_2} values, at 25°C, needed are 2.0×10^{-10} and 2.2×10^{-12}.)

17.8 Anhydrides in Aqueous Solution

Skill Review

85. Give the structure of the anhydride of sulfuric acid.

86. Indicate the structure of the substance that would be the anhydride of $Ba(OH)_2$.

Comprehensive Problems

87. The hydrogen ion donated by Brønsted–Lowry acids is typically represented in aqueous solutions as $H_3O^+(aq)$.
a. Explain the origin of the positive charge on this ion.
b. What other forms could the hydrogen ion take in water?
c. Would the shape of H_3O^+ be more likely to be flat or pyramidal? Explain.

88. Acetic acid, found in vinegar, has a small equilibrium constant. Hydrochloric acid is known as a strong acid. Which of these two representations depicts acetic acid? (*Note:* In the boxes, HX represents a general acid structure where X^- represents the conjugate base.)

(a)	(b)
HX HX HX X^- HX HX HX H^+ HX HX HX HX	H^+ X^- H^+ X^- H^+ X^- X^- H^+ H^+ H^+ X^- H^+ X^- H^+ X^- H^+ X^- H^+

89. Is it possible for a concentrated solution of a weak acid to have the same level of hydronium ion concentration as a dilute solution of a strong acid such as HCl?

90. Water, which has hydrogen bonded to oxygen, can form both H^+ ions and OH^- ions. KOH, which also has hydrogen bonded to oxygen, produces only OH^- ions in solution. Using structure and electronegativity, explain why this situation occurs.

91. When comparing the strengths of strong acids, one must use a solvent other than water. One such solvent is acetic acid. Explain why acetic acid would make a better solvent than water for comparing acid strength among strong acids.

92. At 25°C the K_w value for water is 1.0×10^{-14}. Using that value and the autoprotolysis of water, determine what percent of water molecules actually dissociate under these conditions.

93. Explain why the second ionization constant of a diprotic acid is typically much smaller than the first.

94. Only very pure phosphoric acid is used in food products. An older term for soft drinks is *phosphates*. This name was applied because pure phosphoric acid was used to produce a tart taste in some beverages and to help dissolve the other ingredients.
a. What is the pH of a solution that is known to be 5.44 M in H_3PO_4?
b. What would be the approximate concentration of $PO_4^{3-}(aq)$ in that solution?

95. a. Using the Internet reference http://www.fda.gov/medwatch/safety/1997/ephedr.htm explain why caffeine should not be mixed with stimulants that contain ephedrine alkaloids.
b. Use other searches to obtain the formula of an ephedrine alkaloid.
c. Is caffeine an alkaloid? What is meant by the term *alkaloid*?

96. Lactic acid is produced in muscle tissue during vigorous exercise. It is also found in spoiled milk. The K_a value of lactic acid ($CH_3CHOHCOOH$), at 25°C, is 1.3×10^{-4}. What is the $H^+(aq)$ concentration in a sample of cellular fluid that is 0.0000033 M in lactic acid and 0.0027 M in lactate ion?

Thinking Beyond the Calculation

97. A salt of sorbic acid ($HC_6H_7O_2$) has been used as mold inhibitor. The salt most commonly used in this practice is potassium sorbate ($KC_6H_7O_2$).

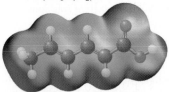

a. Will a solution of potassium sorbate produce a neutral, acidic, or basic solution?
b. Write a balanced chemical reaction that describes the processes that take place when potassium sorbate is dissolved in water.
c. The K_b value of the sorbate ion is 5.88×10^{-10}. What is the pH of a 0.0100 M solution of potassium sorbate?
d. If a researcher wanted to make 500.0 mL of a solution of potassium sorbate with a pH of 9.44, how many grams of this compound would need to be added to the water?
e. A solution is prepared that contains both 0.01000 M NH_3 and 0.01000 M potassium sorbate. What is the pH of the solution? What effect, if any, does the ammonia have on the pH of the solution (compare the answers to parts c and e).

18

Applications of Aqueous Equilibria

Contents and Selected Applications

Chemical Encounters: Industrial and Environmental Applications of Titrations

A chemical technician often performs titrations to analyze solutions for specific analytes.

Application

CHEMICAL
ENCOUNTERS:
Industrial and
Environmental
Applications of
Titrations

Water, so essential to life, makes up 70% of the Earth's surface and a nearly equal proportion of our own body mass. Water in living organisms is useful as a medium in which to dissolve the compounds necessary for life, and it also acts as a barrier to keep some compounds out of our bodies. As fundamental as it is to life, there are some everyday processes in which the presence of water can be harmful. Small amounts of water in your gas tank can reduce the efficiency of your car's engine; water in your motor oil increases the rate of decomposition of the lubricating properties (which can lead to the breakdown of the interior of your engine); and water in the coolant used in the manufacture of metal parts can damage the tooling machines, resulting in imperfections in the parts.

One job of people working as chemical technicians is to perform tests many times each day to determine the quality of the coolant, oil, or gasoline that their company uses or sells. Indeed, one of the many measures of quality oil is that it contains only a negligible amount of water. Technicians use the analytical method of titration, which we first discussed in Section 4.3, to measure the concentration of water in oil and to measure the quantity of a whole host of compounds and ions in water samples. A titration, shown in the photograph at the beginning of this chapter, is the controlled addition of just enough solution of *known concentration*, called a titrant, to react with essentially all of an analyte (the substance of interest) so that we can determine its concentration. Titrating oil to determine the amount of water present is only one of the multitudes of applications of titrations. These applications fall into several different categories, including those that

Water, essential for life, is not as desirable in some consumer products such as motor oil, where it adversely affects the oil's lubricating properties.

■ cause a reduction or oxidation to occur in an analyte
■ result in the formation of a precipitate
■ form a complex ion
■ involve an acid and a base reacting

Food and pharmaceutical manufacturers use titrations for quality control—making sure that the product contains what it is supposed to, and in the proper amounts. Environmental chemists use titrations for analyzing trace (very small) amounts of hazardous metals and other potentially harmful substances. Table 18.1 lists some analyses that are commonly accomplished using titrations. At the core of most titrations are many of the principles of aqueous equilibrium that we discussed in Chapters 16 and 17, and we will put those concepts to good use here. A good starting point is buffer solutions because they are commonplace both in industrial titration analyses and, more broadly, in biochemical systems (including us!).

TABLE 18.1	Selected Titration-Based Analyses
What the Titration Determines	**Primary Reagent**
Acidity	Sodium hydroxide
Alkalinity	Hydrochloric acid
Vitamin C	Iodine
Chloride ion	Silver nitrate
Water hardness	EDTA
Dissolved oxygen	Sodium thiosulfate
Salinity	Mercuric nitrate
Water	Iodine, sulfur dioxide, primary amines

18.1 ▸ Buffers and the Common-Ion Effect

The degree of "hardness" of water, a measure of the concentration of calcium (sometimes including magnesium and iron) in household water supplies, is determined by titration. When heated, the calcium ions in hard water form rock-hard carbonates and sulfates. The resulting solids, known as **boiler scale**, build up on the inside of pipes. In addition, ice cubes made with "hard" water melt to give an ugly-looking precipitate, as shown in Figure 18.1. Furthermore, very hard water has a bitter taste that many homeowners find unappealing.

The concentration of calcium ions in water can be determined by titration with ethylenediaminetetraacetic acid (EDTA), which we first discussed in Chapter 16 and will consider in greater detail later in this chapter as well as in Chapter 20. The equation describing the titration is

$$Ca^{2+}(aq) + EDTA^{4-}(aq) \rightleftharpoons CaEDTA^{2-}(aq) \qquad K = 5.0 \times 10^{10}$$

Application

Ca^{2+}

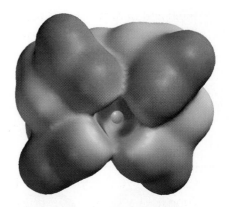
FIGURE 18.1
Hard water can deposit a white precipitate in your icy glass of water.

$Ca^{2+}(aq)$ $EDTA^{4-}(aq)$ $CaEDTA^{2-}(aq)$

In order to ensure that the EDTA exists as the tetraanion, the entire system must remain basic during the titration. An added buffer maintains the alkaline solution. As you will remember from our previous discussions, a **buffer** is a chemical system that is able to resist changes in pH. A buffer is the combination of a *weak acid and its conjugate base or of a weak base and its conjugate acid.* Buffers do *not* exist if a strong acid or strong base is paired with its conjugate. However, *buffers can accommodate the addition of strong acid and base, and can also withstand dilution, without large changes in the solution pH.*

One standard hard-water analysis protocol requires the addition of a buffer made from ammonia (a weak base) and ammonium chloride (a source of ammonia's conjugate acid). The required pH of the buffer for this analysis is 10. According to the protocol, this can be achieved when the initial concentrations are $[NH_3]_0 = 8.44\ M$ and $[NH_4^+]_0 = 1.27\ M$. How do these initial concentrations result in a solution with a pH close to 10?

To answer this question, we proceed as we do with any equilibrium process, by first examining the possible reactions that can take place in the aqueous solution. In doing so, we recognize that ammonium chloride (NH_4Cl) will dissociate

EDTA^{4-} complexes with a sodium ion. The complex involves each of the carboxylate oxygens (COO$^-$) and the two nitrogen atoms in the EDTA molecule. The resulting structure creates a pocket surrounding the sodium ion.

in water to give the ammonium ion (NH_4^+) with chloride (Cl^-) as a spectator ion. *The key reactants in the buffer are NH_4^+, NH_3, and H_2O.* Their specific reactions are given below.

Reaction 1: Ammonia, a weak base, reacts with water.

$$NH_3(aq) + H_2O(l) \rightleftharpoons NH_4^+(aq) + OH^-(aq) \qquad K_b = 1.8 \times 10^{-5}$$

Reaction 2: Ammonium ion, the conjugate acid of ammonia, reacts with water.

$$NH_4^+(aq) + H_2O(l) \rightleftharpoons NH_3(aq) + H_3O^+(aq) \qquad K_a = 5.6 \times 10^{-10}$$

(Recall from Section 17.7 that $K_a = K_w/K_b$ for NH_3.)

Reaction 3: Water undergoes autoprotolysis.

$$2H_2O(l) \rightleftharpoons H_3O^+(aq) + OH^-(aq) \qquad K_w = 1.0 \times 10^{-14}$$

The last reaction has a relatively small equilibrium constant, so its contribution to the pH of the solution is unimportant. Judging by their respective equilibrium constants, the base, ammonia, is stronger than its conjugate acid, ammonium ion, so we expect reaction 1 to be dominant. The reaction produces hydroxide ion, so we expect the solution to be basic.

The Impact of Le Châtelier's Principle on the Equilibria in the Buffer

Reaction 1 is producing NH_4^+. However, in the buffer used to determine the hardness of water, we already have a relatively high initial concentration of ammonium ion ($[NH_4^+]_0 = 1.27\ M$). How will this affect the extent of reaction 1? Le Châtelier's principle (Sections 16.6 and 17.4) suggests that the presence of the ammonium ion (a "common ion," in this case) will shift the equilibrium of reaction 1 to the reactants side, as shown in Figure 18.2. Reaction 1 will be *drastically suppressed* because of the common-ion effect, an outcome of Le Châtelier's principle.

What about reaction 2? It is producing ammonia (NH_3). However, the initial concentration is quite high, $[NH_3]_0 = 8.44\ M$. As with reaction 1, the presence of a large concentration of ammonia will shift the reaction to the left, the reactants side (Figure 18.3). Reaction 2 will also be *drastically suppressed* because of the common-ion effect, an outcome of Le Châtelier's principle.

FIGURE 18.2

Addition of NH_4^+ shifts the equilibrium of reaction 1 to the left.

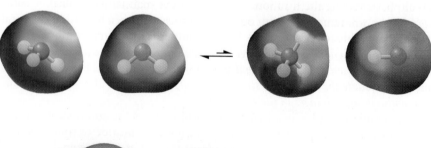

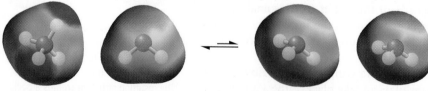

FIGURE 18.3

Addition of NH_3 shifts the equilibrium of reaction 2 to the left.

The impact of reactions 1 and 2 being suppressed (claims that we will prove after we solve for the pH of the buffer solution) is that we may assume that *the equilibrium concentrations of NH_3 and NH_4^+ are approximately equal to their initial concentrations.*

$$[NH_3] \approx [NH_3]_0 = 8.44 \ M \qquad \text{and} \qquad [NH_4^+] \approx [NH_4^+]_0 = 1.27 \ M$$

Because of this assumption, we can solve for the pH of this buffer solution using the mass-action expression derived from reaction 1, the hydrolysis of ammonia.

$$K_b = \frac{[NH_4^+][OH^-]}{[NH_3]} \qquad 1.8 \times 10^{-5} = \frac{(1.27)[OH^-]}{(8.44)}$$

$$[OH^-] = 1.2 \times 10^{-4} \ M$$

$$[H^+] = \frac{K_w}{[OH^-]} = \frac{1.0 \times 10^{-14}}{1.2 \times 10^{-4}} = 8.3 \times 10^{-11} \ M$$

$$pH = 10.08$$

Alternatively, we could have used the mass-action expression derived from reaction 2 to solve for the pH of the solution, as we will discover in Exercise 18.1.

What about our claim that reaction 1 was suppressed by the presence of the ammonium common ion? To show the impact of the common ion, let's calculate $[OH^-]$ in an 8.44 M NH_3 solution that has *no* NH_4^+—in other words, not a buffer, just a weak base—using the principles we learned in Chapters 16 and 17.

$$NH_3(aq) + H_2O(l) \rightleftharpoons NH_4^+(aq) + OH^-(aq) \qquad K_b = 1.8 \times 10^{-5}$$

$$K_b = \frac{[NH_4^+][OH^-]}{[NH_3]} \qquad 1.8 \times 10^{-5} = \frac{[NH_4^+][OH^-]}{(8.44)}$$

$$1.8 \times 10^{-5} = \frac{x^2}{8.44}$$

$$x = [NH_4^+] = [OH^-] = 0.012 \ M$$

Our calculations reveal that the total hydroxide and ammonium ion concentrations, which are equal in this solution of weak base, are $[OH^-] = [NH_4^+] = 0.012 \ M$. Moreover, when we compare the hydroxide ion concentration of the buffer, in which $[OH^-] = 1.2 \times 10^{-4} \ M$, to the value we just calculated for the weak base alone, we note that it is 100-fold less. *The presence of the ammonium ion in the buffer has suppressed reaction 1, the hydrolysis of ammonia, by 99%!* If we were to do a similar calculation with the ammonium ion, we would find that the buffer suppresses the acid dissociation of NH_4^+ by over 99.99%. Le Châtelier's principle has again proved its worth as a formidable part of the chemist's toolbox.

Our goal was to show how a mixture of these concentrations of ammonia and ammonium ion results in a buffer solution with a pH of about 10. Exercise 18.1 shows the implications of using a slightly different approach to achieve the same goal.

EXERCISE 18.1 | **Alternative Route to the pH of the Buffer**

Instead of calculating the pH of the system using reaction 1, calculate the pH of the buffer using reaction 2, the acid dissociation of the ammonium ion. What does your result tell you about solving for the pH of a buffer?

First Thoughts

We still assert that the extent of reaction in a buffer system is negligible; the starting position is the same as the equilibrium position, as shown by the equilibrium line chart.

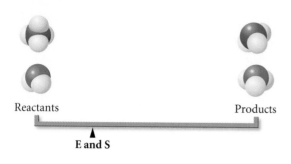

Reactants

Products

E and S

The implication is that the starting and equilibrium concentrations are essentially equal, so, as before,

$$[NH_3] \approx [NH_3]_0 = 8.44 \ M$$

and

$$[NH_4^+] \approx [NH_4^+]_0 = 1.27 \ M$$

Additionally, we are directed to solve the problem using reaction 2, so we will use its mass-action expression to solve for $[H^+]$ and pH.

Solution

$$NH_4^+(aq) + H_2O(l) \rightleftharpoons NH_3(aq) + H_3O^+(aq) \qquad K_a = 5.6 \times 10^{-10}$$

$$K_a = \frac{[NH_3][H_3O^+]}{[NH_4^+]} \qquad 5.6 \times 10^{-10} = \frac{(8.44)[H_3O^+]}{(1.27)}$$

$$[H^+] = 8.4 \times 10^{-11} \ M$$

$$pH = 10.08$$

Further Insights

Our answer is the same whether we use the mass-action expression for the hydrolysis of the base (ammonia) or the dissociation of its conjugate (ammonium ion). This is a useful outcome that is a result of the common-ion effect of suppressing both the acid reaction and the base reaction in the buffer. When working with buffers, we may use either the acid dissociation or the conjugate base hydrolysis mass-action expression, but we often work with the expression describing the reaction of *the stronger conjugate* (the ammonia hydrolysis, in this case).

PRACTICE 18.1

Determine the pH of a buffer made from 1.50 M NH_3 and 3.50 M NH_4^+.

See Problems 5 and 6.

EXERCISE 18.2   Practice Calculating the Initial pH of a Buffer

We have shown that an ammonia–ammonium ion buffer can have a pH of about 10. Are all buffers basic? To help answer the question, calculate the pH of a buffer that contains 0.200 M each of acetic acid (CH_3COOH) and its conjugate base, the acetate ion (CH_3COO^-). It is interesting, but nonetheless coincidental, that the K_a value for acetic acid is about the same as the K_b value for ammonia.

First Thoughts

We said in the last exercise that we normally use the reaction and mass-action expression for the stronger conjugate when calculating the pH of the buffer. The relevant conjugate reactions (using the shorthand form for the acid dissociation) and equilibrium constants are

$$CH_3COOH(aq) \rightleftharpoons H^+(aq) + CH_3COO^-(aq) \qquad K_a = 1.8 \times 10^{-5}$$

$$CH_3COO^-(aq) + H_2O(l) \rightleftharpoons CH_3COOH(aq) + OH^-(aq) \qquad K_b = 5.6 \times 10^{-10}$$

We will use the mass-action expression for the stronger conjugate, acetic acid. As with other buffer systems, we recognize that both reactions are suppressed as we have explained using Le Châtelier's principle, so *the equilibrium concentrations are about equal to the initial concentrations of the respective components.*

Solution

The mass-action expression for the reaction of acetic acid is

$$K_a = \frac{[CH_3COO^-][H^+]}{[CH_3COOH]}$$

Solving for $[H^+]$ and then pH, we find that

$$[H^+] = \frac{K_a[CH_3COOH]}{[CH_3COO^-]} = \frac{(1.8 \times 10^{-5})(0.200)}{(0.200)} = 1.8 \times 10^{-5} \, M$$

$$pH = 4.74$$

Further Insights

The ammonia–ammonium buffer has a basic pH, because the base, NH_3, is the stronger of the conjugate pairs. The acetic acid–acetate buffer system is acidic, because acetic acid is the stronger conjugate. This means that you can predict whether a buffer is likely to be acidic or basic judging by the strength of each of the conjugates. The acetic acid–acetate buffer cannot have a pH of 10.

PRACTICE 18.2

Would you predict that a buffer prepared from the mixture of 0.300 M formic acid (HCOOH) and 0.400 M sodium formate (HCOONa) would be acidic or basic? Why? Prove your assertion by calculating the pH of this buffer. K_a of formic acid $= 1.8 \times 10^{-4}$.

See Problems 21 and 22. ■

We have seen from this discussion that it is possible to determine the approximate pH of a buffer. Extending that idea a step further, it is also possible to pick a buffer that will be in the pH range we want by looking at whether the acid or the base conjugate is the stronger. There is often much more to the selection of a buffer than just pH, because we must consider factors such as whether the buffer will interact with the substances we are studying and whether the buffer's presence in the reaction system has any unintended health consequences. Once these factors are taken into account, we need to know how to prepare the buffers in order to use them.

HERE'S WHAT WE KNOW SO FAR

■ A buffer is a chemical system that is able to resist changes in pH.
■ A buffer consists of the combination of a weak acid and its conjugate base, or of a weak base and its conjugate acid.
■ A buffer contains a high enough concentration of each conjugate that acid–base equilibria are effectively suppressed, an outcome of Le Châtelier's principle.
■ A buffer will be acidic or basic, depending on which of the conjugates is the stronger.
■ It is possible to calculate the pH of the buffer system by applying the principles of equilibrium and acid–base chemistry that we learned in the last two chapters.

FIGURE 18.4

Phosphoric acid is often found in soft drinks.

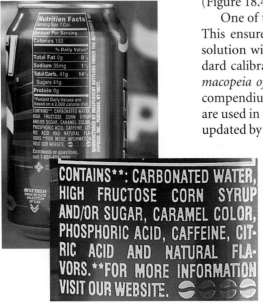

Buffer Preparation

The chemical technician working in the food industry often uses a pH meter to determine the acidity of the food that is being prepared. Sodas, for instance, often have phosphoric acid added to them to provide a tart taste, and pH control is vital (Figure 18.4).

One of the most common uses of a buffer solution is to calibrate pH meters. This ensures that the reading on the meter accurately represents the pH of a solution with which we are working. Recipes exist for the preparation of standard calibration buffer solutions. One source for these recipes is the *The Pharmacopeia of the United States of America/The National Formulary*, a 2400-page compendium of "standards and specifications for materials and substances that are used in the practice of the healing arts." Organized in 1884 and produced and updated by medical and pharmaceutical experts ever since, the resulting *Pharmacopeia* ("USP" for short) contains standard analysis procedures for a great many substances.

The USP recipe to prepare calibration buffers in the range of 2.2 to 4.0 recommends using a solution of potassium hydrogen phthalate, or "KHP" ($KHC_6H_4(COO)_2$), which dissociates when added to water to form K^+ and HP^- ($HC_6H_4(COO)_2$). The conjugate acid of this weak base, phthalic acid ("H_2P") is generated by addition of hydrochloric acid (a source of H^+) to the HP^-.

$$HP^-(aq) + H^+(aq) \rightleftharpoons H_2P(aq) \qquad K \approx 900$$

The equilibrium position (minimum free energy) of the reaction of the weak base with the strong acid is so far toward the formation of products that we can say the reaction is essentially complete. That is, although we will normally write the reaction to show that it settles at some equilibrium point,

$$HP^-(aq) + H^+(aq) \rightleftharpoons H_2P(aq)$$

we may also write it to show that the reaction is essentially complete,

$$HP^-(aq) + H^+(aq) \rightarrow H_2P(aq)$$

Suppose we wish to prepare a buffer with pH = 3.0, and assume that we want the total concentration of phthalate species to be 0.0500 *M*. That is,

$$[H_2P] + [HP^-] = 0.0500 \ M$$

Once the proper ratio of conjugate acid to base is present, the buffer will be at pH = 3.00. **How do we find the proper ratio? How do we then find the final concentrations of H$_2$P and HP$^-$?**

As has been true throughout these three chapters on equilibrium (Chapters 16–18), the answer lies in writing down the relevant equilibrium reaction and its mass-action expression. For the phthalate buffer system, the important reaction is the dissociation of phthalic acid (H$_2$P) in water:

$$H_2P(aq) + H_2O(l) \rightleftharpoons HP^-(aq) + H_3O^+(aq) \qquad K_{a_1} = 1.12 \times 10^{-3}$$

We can write it using our shorthand form:

$$H_2P(aq) \rightleftharpoons HP^-(aq) + H^+(aq) \qquad K_{a_1} = 1.12 \times 10^{-3}$$

The mass-action expression for the reaction is

$$K_{a_1} = \frac{[HP^-][H^+]}{[H_2P]}$$

Dividing both sides by [H$^+$] gives us an expression for the ratio of base to acid:

$$\frac{K_{a_1}}{[H^+]} = \frac{[HP^-]}{[H_2P]}$$

Solving, with the use of the pH = 3.00 ([H$^+$] = 1.0 $\times$ 10^{-3} M),

$$\frac{(1.12 \times 10^{-3})}{(1.00 \times 10^{-3})} = \frac{(1.12)}{(1.00)} = \frac{[HP^-]}{[H_2P]}$$

we find that the ratio of the base, HP$^-$, to its conjugate acid, H$_2$P, is 1.12 to 1. We'll call this Equation 1.

$$[HP^-] = 1.12\,[H_2P] \qquad \text{(Equation 1)}$$

We said initially that we had set the sum of concentrations of the two species to be a total of 0.0500 M. We'll call this Equation 2.

$$[H_2P] + [HP^-] = 0.0500\ M \qquad \text{(Equation 2)}$$

This gives us two equations (Equations 1 and 2) and two unknowns ([H$_2$P] and [HP$^-$]). We can solve Equation 2 by substituting 1.12[H$_2$P] in place of [HP$^-$], as allowed by Equation 1:

$$[H_2P] + 1.12[H_2P] = 0.0500\ M$$
$$2.12[H_2P] = 0.0500\ M$$
$$\mathbf{[H_2P] = 0.0236\ \textit{M}}$$

$$[HP^-] = 0.0500\ M - 0.0236\ M$$
$$\mathbf{[HP^-] = 0.0264\ \textit{M}}$$

Therefore, in order to obtain a buffer at pH = 3.00, we'll have to make up a solution that is 0.0236 M in H$_2$P and 0.0264 M in KHP. We can check that these quantities are reasonable by substituting back into the mass-action expression and solving for [H$^+$].

$$[H^+] = \frac{K_{a_1}[H_2P]}{[HP^-]} = \frac{(1.12 \times 10^{-3})(0.0236)}{(0.0264)}$$

$$[H^+] = 1.00 \times 10^{-3}\,M$$

This concentration of H$^+$ would produce a solution with a pH = 3.00.

EXERCISE 18.3 Practice with Buffer Preparation

How many grams of sodium formate (HCOONa), molar mass = 68.01 g/mol, must be dissolved in a 0.300 *M* solution of formic acid (HCOOH), to make 400.0 mL of a buffer solution with a pH = 4.60? Assume that the volume of the solution remains constant when you add the sodium acetate.

First Thoughts

We are asked to find the mass of sodium formate needed to combine with formic acid to prepare the buffer. Let's develop a stepwise approach to the problem.

Step 1: As in prior examples involving buffers, we need to establish the ratio of the concentrations of the acid and the conjugate base, $\frac{[\text{HCOO}^-]}{[\text{HCOOH}]}$, needed to produce a buffer with a pH = 4.60. To solve for the ratio of concentrations of acid and conjugate base needed, we must first write the important processes that occur in the solution. Two equilibria are important in this buffer system:

$$\text{HCOOH}(aq) + \text{H}_2\text{O}(l) \rightleftharpoons \text{H}_3\text{O}^+(aq) + \text{HCOO}^-(aq) \qquad K_a = 1.8 \times 10^{-4}$$
$$\text{HCOO}^-(aq) + \text{H}_2\text{O}(l) \rightleftharpoons \text{HCOOH}(aq) + \text{OH}^-(aq) \qquad K_b = 5.6 \times 10^{-11}$$

As we discussed in Exercise 18.1, we may use either reaction to solve for the acid-to-conjugate-base ratio.

Step 2: Knowing that the concentration of formic acid is 0.300 *M*, we can then find the concentration of the conjugate base. Remember that the sodium salt will completely dissociate in solution, leaving the formate anion (HCOO^-) as the conjugate base and Na^+ as the spectator ion.

Step 3: We may then convert from the concentration of formate (HCOO^-) to the number of moles of HCOO^- in 400.0 mL of solution.

Step 4: Finally, we may convert from moles of formate (as the sodium formate salt) to grams of sodium formate.

A flowchart of the process looks like this:

$$\frac{[\text{HCOO}^-]}{[\text{HCOOH}]} \xrightarrow{\text{mass-action expression}} [\text{HCOO}^-] \xrightarrow{\text{volume solution}} \text{mol HCOO}^- \xrightarrow{\text{molar mass HCOONa}} \text{g HCOONa}$$

Step 1 Step 2 Step 3 Step 4

Solution

Step 1:

$$K_a = \frac{[\text{HCOO}^-][\text{H}^+]}{[\text{HCOOH}]}$$

The pH of the solution is 4.60, so $[\text{H}^+] = 2.51 \times 10^{-5}$ *M*. We are retaining an extra figure because this is an intermediate calculation.

$$1.8 \times 10^{-4} = \frac{[\text{HCOO}^-](2.51 \times 10^{-5})}{[\text{HCOOH}]}$$

$$\frac{[\text{HCOO}^-]}{[\text{HCOOH}]} = \frac{1.8 \times 10^{-4}}{2.51 \times 10^{-5}} = \frac{7.17}{1.00}$$

The concentration of formate ion is about 7.2 times as great as the concentration of formic acid.

Step 2:

$$[\text{HCOO}^-] = 7.17 \times [\text{HCOOH}]$$
$$[\text{HCOO}^-] = 7.17 \times 0.300\ M$$
$$[\text{HCOO}^-] = 2.15\ M$$

Alternatively, we could have combined steps 1 and 2 to find [HCOO$^-$] directly by substituting 0.300 M into the mass-action expression, as follows:

$$1.8 \times 10^{-4} = \frac{[HCOO^-](2.51 \times 10^{-5})}{0.300}$$

$$[HCOO^-] = 2.15\ M$$

Step 3: $\dfrac{2.15\ \text{mol HCOO}^-}{\text{L solution}} \times 0.4000\ \text{L solution} =$

$$0.860\ \text{mol HCOO}^- = 0.860\ \text{mol HCOONa}$$

Step 4: $0.860\ \text{mol HCOONa} \times \dfrac{68.01\ \text{g HCOONa}}{1\ \text{mol HCOONa}} = 58\ \text{g HCOONa}$

Further Insights

Does it make sense that the buffer system should be acidic? Formic acid (HCOOH) is stronger than its conjugate, so the acid dissociation reaction will dominate, resulting in an acidic buffer solution. This is a reasonable conjugate pair to use to prepare an acidic buffer solution. Our answer makes sense.

PRACTICE 18.3

How many grams of sodium formate (HCOONa) must be dissolved in a 0.150 M solution of formic acid (HCOOH) to make 500.0 mL of a buffer solution with pH = 3.95? Assume that the volume of the solution remains constant when you add the sodium formate.

See Problems 17, 18, 25, and 26. ■

EXERCISE 18.4   **More Practice with Buffer Preparation**

How many milliliters of 0.200 M HCl must be added to 50.0 mL of a 0.200 M solution of NH$_3$ in order to prepare a buffer that has a pH of 8.60?

$$NH_3 + H_2O(l) \rightleftharpoons NH_4^+ + OH^- \qquad K_b = 1.8 \times 10^{-5}$$

First Thoughts

We have a solution of NH$_3$. We need to add enough strong acid, in the form of HCl, to convert NH$_3$ to NH$_4^+$ until the ratio of the weak base to its conjugate acid, $\dfrac{[NH_3]}{[NH_4^+]}$, will be the same as that in a pH 8.60 buffer.

As we think through a problem-solving strategy, let's write down what we know about the system.

■ The K_b value for the hydrolysis of NH$_3$ is 1.8×10^{-5}.
■ We know the mass-action expression for the formation of NH$_4^+$ from NH$_3$.
■ We also know that there is 0.0100 mol of NH$_3$ initially present in the solution:

$$0.0500\ \text{L NH}_3 \times \frac{0.200\ \text{mol NH}_3}{\text{L NH}_3\ \text{solution}} = 0.0100\ \text{mol NH}_3$$

Step 1: What is the ratio of the weak base to the conjugate acid, $\dfrac{[NH_3]}{[NH_4^+]}$, in the pH = 8.60 buffer ([H$^+$] = 2.5 × 10^{-9} M)? This ratio will be the first equation we need to solve in order to find the amounts of NH$_3$ and NH$_4^+$. The base hydrolysis equation contains [OH$^-$] rather than [H$^+$]. We can solve for [OH$^-$] from [H$^+$] and K_w. We are keeping an extra figure in for the intermediate calculation.

$$[OH^-] = \frac{K_w}{[H^+]} = \frac{1.00 \times 10^{-14}}{2.51 \times 10^{-9}} = 3.98 \times 10^{-6}$$

We can then set up our mass-action expression to solve for $\dfrac{[NH_3]}{[NH_4^+]}$.

$$NH_3(aq) + H_2O(l) \rightleftharpoons NH_4^+(aq) + OH^-(aq) \qquad K_b = 1.8 \times 10^{-5}$$

$$K_b = \frac{[NH_4^+][OH^-]}{[NH_3]}$$

$$\frac{K_b}{[OH^-]} = \frac{[NH_4^+]}{[NH_3]}$$

Inverting both sides of the equation, we get

$$\frac{[OH^-]}{K_b} = \frac{[NH_3]}{[NH_4^+]}$$

Step 2: The sum of the moles of NH_3 and NH_4^+ in the final solution must equal the initial 0.100 mol of NH_3 used to prepare the original solution because we are *changing* the NH_3 to NH_4^+, *not getting rid of any* from the reaction flask. This is the second equation we need to solve to find the amounts of NH_3 and NH_4^+.

$$mol\ NH_4^+ + mol\ NH_3 = 0.0100\ mol$$

Step 3: Finally, we can find how much 0.200 *M* HCl will be needed to react with our original 0.100 mol of NH_3 to generate the proper number of moles of NH_4^+.

Solution

Step 1: Finding the ratio of $\dfrac{[NH_3]}{[NH_4^+]}$ in the solution.

$$\frac{[OH^-]}{K_b} = \frac{[NH_3]}{[NH_4^+]}$$

Substituting for $[OH^-]$ and K_b yields

$$\frac{3.98 \times 10^{-6}}{1.8 \times 10^{-5}} = \frac{0.221}{1.00} = \frac{[NH_3]}{[NH_4^+]}$$

Because the volume of the buffer solution is the same for NH_3 and NH_4^+, we can work with moles rather than molarity (the liters cancel out on top and bottom).

$$mol\ NH_3 = 0.221 \times (mol\ NH_4^+)$$

Step 2: Finding moles of NH_4^+ and NH_3 so that the sum equals 0.0100 mol.

$$mol\ NH_4^+ + mol\ NH_3 = 0.0100\ mol$$

$$mol\ NH_4^+ + [0.221 \times (mol\ NH_4^+)] = 0.0100\ mol$$

$$1.221 \times (mol\ NH_4^+) = 0.0100\ mol$$

$$mol\ NH_4^+ = 0.00819\ mol$$

$$mol\ NH_3 = 0.00181\ mol$$

As a check of your work, you will find that substituting these values back into the mass-action expression will give you K_b.

Step 3: Finding how many milliliters of 0.200 *M* HCl we need to add to produce 0.00819 mol of NH_4^+ from NH_3.

$$0.00819\ mol\ HCl \times \frac{1\ L\ HCl\ solution}{0.200\ mol\ HCl} \times \frac{1000\ mL\ HCl\ solution}{1\ L\ HCl\ solution} = 41\ mL\ HCl\ solution$$

Further Insights

Although we used the base hydrolysis of ammonia to get the initial conjugate acid–base ratio, we could have used the acid ionization of ammonium just as well, because we are dealing with a buffer solution. If we had done this, the solution in step 1 would have looked like this:

$$NH_4^+(aq) + H_2O(l) \rightleftharpoons NH_3(aq) + H_3O^+(aq)$$

$$K_a = \frac{[K_w]}{[K_b]} = \frac{(1.0 \times 10^{-14})}{(1.8 \times 10^{-5})} = 5.56 \times 10^{-10}$$

(We retain an extra figure in K_a, which we would drop at the end of the calculation.)

$$K_a = \frac{[NH_3][H_3O^+]}{[NH_4^+]}$$

$$\frac{[K_a]}{[H_3O^+]} = \frac{[NH_3]}{[NH_4^+]}$$

$$\frac{[NH_3]}{[NH_4^+]} = \frac{(5.56 \times 10^{-10})}{(2.51 \times 10^{-9})} = \frac{0.221}{1.00}$$

$$mol\ NH_3 = 0.221\ (mol\ NH_4^+)$$

This agrees with the answer we got in step 1.

PRACTICE 18.4

How many milliliters of 0.10 M HCl must be added to 25.0 mL of a 0.2000 M solution of NH_3 to prepare a buffer that has a pH of 8.80?

See Problems 11, 12, 27, and 28.

In practice, even fairly dilute buffers with fairly low conjugate concentrations (not far above their equilibrium constants) will have pH values similar to those with equal ratios of higher conjugate concentrations. If the buffer is too dilute, other factors cause the pH to move toward neutrality.

The Henderson–Hasselbalch Equation: We Proceed, But with Caution

We have seen how the mass-action expression is used to find the approximate ratio of base to acid in a buffer. In 1902, seven years before Peter Sørenson coined the term *pH*, a Massachusetts physician named Lawrence Joseph Henderson, who was studying buffers in blood, published work relating $[H^+]$ to the acid and base concentrations in a buffer. For an acid, HA, and its conjugate base, A⁻, Henderson noted that $[H^+] = \dfrac{K_a[HA]}{[A^-]}$, as we showed in Exercise 18.2 for the acetic acid–acetate ion buffer system. Written a slightly different way for visual clarity, this is

$$[H^+] = K_a\frac{[HA]}{[A^-]} = K_a\frac{[weak\ acid]}{[conjugate\ base]}$$

Note the relationship between the acid and the base. The acid is a weak acid, and the base is the conjugate base of that weak acid. In 1916 K.A. Hasselbalch (pronounced "hassle-back"), a physiologist at the University of Copenhagen, used

Sørenson's "new" pH term, taking the negative log of both sides of Henderson's equation to give

$$pH = -\log(K_a) - \log\left\{ \frac{[\text{weak acid}]}{[\text{conjugate base}]} \right\}$$

This can be slightly modified by using pK_a (the same as $-\log(K_a)$) and changing the sign before the log term, which inverts the concentrations within the log term. This gives the final form of what is commonly known as the **Henderson–Hasselbalch equation**:

$$pH = pK_a + \log\left\{ \frac{[\text{conjugate base}]}{[\text{weak acid}]} \right\}$$

The equation is not necessary; we can solve any buffer problem without it, including the ammonia–ammonium ion system and the KHP buffer system we discussed earlier in this section. However, scientists in the medical and biological professions use the equation because it can be a timesaver for calculating the pH.

We added the phrase "we proceed, but with caution" to the title of this subsection because, in spite of how common the use of the Henderson–Hasselbalch equation is, there are two reasons why you must be cautious with its use. First, a system *must* contain both an acid and its conjugate base in order for the equation to be valid. If you don't have a buffer system, using this equation will lead you to incorrect results. Second, and more troublesome for many students, *is the tendency to invert the ratio of acid to base within the log term.* Proceed with caution!

EXERCISE 18.5   **The Henderson–Hasselbalch Equation**

Use the Henderson–Hasselbalch equation to find the ratio of conjugate base to weak acid in an acetic acid–acetate buffer solution with a pH of 5.0. $K_a = 1.8 \times 10^{-5}$.

Solution

$$pH = pK_a + \log\left\{ \frac{[\text{base}]}{[\text{acid}]} \right\}$$

$$5.0 = 4.74 + \log\left\{ \frac{[CH_3COO^-]}{[CH_3COOH]} \right\}$$

$$0.26 = \log\frac{[CH_3COO^-]}{[CH_3COOH]}$$

$$10^{0.26} = \frac{[CH_3COO^-]}{[CH_3COOH]} = 1.8$$

This means there is 1.8 times as much acetate ion as acetic acid in a solution with a pH just above the pK_a.

PRACTICE 18.5

Determine the pH of an acetic acid–acetate buffer containing 0.500 *M* acetic acid and 0.250 *M* sodium acetate. $K_a = 1.8 \times 10^{-5}$.

See Problems 19–22. ∎

The conclusion to Exercise 18.5 is important, because it says that *in order for the pH of the buffer to be higher than the pK_a, there must be more conjugate base than weak acid.* The opposite statement is also true (as illustrated in Practice 18.5); that is, pH values lower than the pK_a value require more conjugate acid than base. Take a quick look back at Exercises 18.1 through 18.3 to see that this is so. In Exercise 18.2, the concentrations of the weak acid and conjugate base are equal. When this is so, the pH is equal to the pK_a, and the buffer that results has the greatest possible capacity to neutralize strong acids and bases.

Buffer Capacity

The job of the chemical technician may include monitoring the emissions from a smoke stack. Recent laws enacted to protect the environment have made this a priority. To reduce the emissions, businesses often make use of a scrubber attached to the smoke stack. Scrubbing is used to remove sulfur dioxide from the smoke emitted by combustion of sulfur-rich coal. Chemically, the process can be accomplished by flue-gas desulfurization, in which a limestone slurry is combined with sulfur dioxide in a multistep process:

Application
CHEMICAL
ENCOUNTERS:
Scrubbing Sulfur
Dioxide Emissions

$$CaCO_3(s) + SO_2(g) \rightleftharpoons CaSO_3(s) + CO_2(g)$$

The calcium sulfite that is formed is further oxidized and hydrated to give gypsum ($CaSO_4 \cdot 2H_2O$), which is used to make wallboards for home construction, as discussed in Chapter 17.

$$CaSO_3(s) + \tfrac{1}{2}O_2(g) + 2H_2O(l) \rightleftharpoons CaSO_4 \cdot 2H_2O$$

To make this conversion of sulfur dioxide to calcium sulfate dihydrate more efficient, a mixture of formic acid (HCOOH) and sodium formate (HCOONa) is added to the scrubber. The low pH of this buffer (Exercise 18.3) enhances the reaction efficiency by converting some of the sulfite in solution to bisulfite, (HSO_3^-). Doing so allows the more soluble calcium bisulfite ($CaHSO_3$) to form, as well as minimizing calcium sulfite buildup on the processing machinery. **How can the formic acid–formate ion buffer system keep the system pH within a small range?** The buffer capacity of a system is a measure of the number of moles of strong acid or strong base that can be added while keeping the pH relatively constant. IUPAC defines "relatively constant" as between +/− 1 pH unit. Others have different parameters. Because this discussion serves as an introduction to acid–base titrations, we will define "relatively constant" as that point at which all of the conjugate acid (or base) is reacted.

Suppose we wish to determine the buffer capacity of 100.0 mL of a solution containing 0.200 *M* HCOOH and 0.400 *M* HCOONa. We first address this problem by noting all of the relevant equilibria in aqueous solution.

$$2H_2O(l) \rightleftharpoons H_3O^+(aq) + OH^-(aq) \qquad K = 1.0 \times 10^{-14}$$

$$HCOOH\ (aq) \rightleftharpoons HCOO^-(aq) + H^+(aq) \qquad K_a = 1.8 \times 10^{-4}$$

Again, the autoprotolysis of water is insignificant, based on the relative size of the equilibrium constant. Considering only the formic acid–formate equilibrium, the pH of this system is 4.05, shown by our calculation:

$$[H^+] = \frac{K_a[HCOOH]}{[HCOO^-]} = \frac{1.8 \times 10^{-4}(0.200)}{(0.400)}$$

$$[H^+] = 9.0 \times 10^{-5}\ M \qquad pH = 4.05$$

Let's look at the impact on the pH of adding strong acid and then strong base.

Change 1: Addition of a strong acid*

What happens to the pH of our buffer if we add 10.0 mL of a 1.00 M HCl solution to 100.0 mL of buffer (total solution volume = 110.0 mL)? We can set the stage by calculating the moles of each component initially in solution.

$$\text{mol HCOOH}_{\text{initial}} = 0.1000 \text{ L HCOOH} \times \frac{0.200 \text{ mol HCOOH}}{\text{L HCOOH solution}}$$

$$= 0.0200 \text{ mol HCOOH}$$

$$\text{mol HCOO}^-_{\text{initial}} = 0.1000 \text{ L HCOO}^- \times \frac{0.400 \text{ mol HCOO}^-}{\text{L HCOO}^- \text{ solution}}$$

$$= 0.0400 \text{ mol HCOO}^-$$

We continue by finding out how many moles of HCl were added.

$$\text{mol HCl}_{\text{added}} = 0.0100 \text{ L} \times \frac{1.00 \text{ mol}}{\text{L}} = 0.0100 \text{ mol HCl}$$

The addition of the strong acid supplies H^+ to the solution, and this H^+ essentially completely reacts with $HCOO^-$ to form HCOOH. ($K = 5.6 \times 10^3$).

How much HCOOH will be formed? We can organize our thinking using a table. At the top of our table we will write the equation that indicates the reaction of the added HCl (a source of H^+) with the conjugate base of formic acid ($HCOO^-$). We note that this is a *limiting-reactant* calculation in which the HCl is limiting and the $HCOO^-$ is in excess.

$$\text{HCOO}^-(aq) + \text{H}^+(aq) \rightleftharpoons \text{HCOOH}(aq) \qquad K = 5.6 \times 10^3$$

moles initial	0.0400		0.0200
moles added		0.0100	
change	−0.0100	−0.0100	+0.0100
moles at equilibrium	0.0300	≈0	0.0300

After addition of the HCl, which threw the system out of equilibrium, it returns again to its new equilibrium position, shown by

$$\text{HCOOH}(aq) \rightleftharpoons \text{HCOO}^-(aq) + \text{H}^+(aq)$$

We still have lots of conjugate acid and base—a buffer system, for which we can find the pH:

$$[\text{H}^+] = \frac{K_a[\text{HCOOH}]}{[\text{HCOO}^-]} = \frac{1.8 \times 10^{-4}(0.300)}{(0.300)} = 1.8 \times 10^{-4} \, M \qquad \text{pH} = pK_a = 3.74$$

The buffer has responded to the addition of HCl by having only a slightly lowered pH, from 4.05 to 3.74.

---

*The value for the equilibrium constant for the reaction of the strong acid with the formate anion ($HCOO^-$) to form HCOOH can be calculated by combining the following two equations, as we did in Section 16.4.

$\text{HCOO}^-(aq) + \text{H}_2\text{O}(aq) \rightleftharpoons \text{HCOOH}(aq) + \text{OH}^-(aq)$	$K_b = K_w/K_a = 5.6 \times 10^{-11}$
$\text{H}^+(aq) + \text{OH}^-(aq) \rightleftharpoons \text{H}_2\text{O}(aq)$	$K = 1/K_w = 1.0 \times 10^{-14}$
$\text{HCOO}^-(aq) + \text{H}^+(aq) \rightleftharpoons \text{HCOOH}(aq)$	$K = (K_b \times 1/K_w) = 1/K_a = 5.6 \times 10^3$

We use this method several times in this chapter to determine the equilibrium constant for the addition of strong acids or bases to weak bases or acids in a titration.

Change 2: Addition of a strong base

What happens to the pH of our *original* solution if we add 15.0 mL of a 1.00 M NaOH solution (total volume = 115.0 mL)? We already know how much formic acid (0.0200 mol) and formate ion (0.0400 mol) we started with. How many moles of NaOH were added?

$$\text{mol NaOH}_{\text{added}} = 0.0150 \text{ L NaOH solution} \times \frac{1.00 \text{ mol NaOH}}{\text{L NaOH solution}}$$

$$= 0.0150 \text{ mol NaOH}$$

The addition of the strong base supplies OH^- to the solution, and this OH^- essentially completely reacts with HCOOH to form $HCOO^-$ ($K = 1.8 \times 10^{10}$). Therefore, we will set up a table based on the reaction of OH^- with HCOOH.

$$\text{HCOOH}(aq) + \text{OH}^-(aq) \rightleftharpoons \text{HCOO}^-(aq) \quad K = 1.8 \times 10^{10}$$

	HCOOH	OH⁻	HCOO⁻
moles initial	0.0200		0.0400
moles added		0.0150	
change	−0.0150	−0.0150	+0.0150
moles at equilibrium	0.0050	≈ 0	0.0550

We still have both acid and conjugate base in the buffer, although the acid concentration is a little low. We can solve for the pH.

$$[H^+] = \frac{K_a[\text{HCOOH}]}{[\text{HCOO}^-]} = \frac{1.8 \times 10^{-4}(0.0050)}{(0.0550)} = 1.64 \times 10^{-5} \, M \quad \text{pH} = 4.79$$

The pH of the buffer has gone up, but the solution still has the capacity to keep the pH close to the original value of 4.05.

Change 3: Exceeding the buffer capacity

At what point will the buffer no longer have the capacity to keep the pH reasonably close to the original value? In other words, when will the pH rise or fall sharply? How much will the pH change before stabilizing? The addition of 50.0 mL 1.00 M HCl solution to the *original* buffer solution will stress the system. Let's see how much, again using our table.

$$\text{HCOO}^-(aq) + \text{H}^+(aq) \rightleftharpoons \text{HCOOH}(aq) \quad K = 5.6 \times 10^3$$

	HCOO⁻	H⁺	HCOOH
moles initial	0.0400		0.0200
moles added		0.0500	
change	−0.0400	−0.0400	+0.0400
moles at equilibrium	≈ 0	0.0100	0.0600

How did we calculate the moles at equilibrium in this case? *This is still a limiting-reactant problem,* with the $HCOO^-$ instead of the H^+ limiting the amount of product formed. We have 0.0500 mol of H^+, but only 0.0400 mol of $HCOO^-$ with which to react! This means that 0.0400 mol will react to form the HCOOH product, and there will be 0.0100 mol of H^+ in excess.

What is the final pH of the resulting solution? At equilibrium, we have a solution that contains 0.0600 mol of HCOOH and 0.0100 mol of H^+. *The formic acid is so much weaker than the hydrochloric acid (judging on the basis of their K_a values) that its presence will not affect the final hydrogen ion concentration.* Only the H^+

from the HCl is important. Therefore, the pH is based solely on the $[H^+]$ due to the ionization of the strong acid. The total volume of 150.0 mL (0.1500 L) is the sum of the initial 100.0 mL of solution and the 50.0 mL HCl solution added to it.

$$[H^+] = \frac{(0.0100 \text{ mol})}{(0.1500 \text{ L})} = 0.0667 \ M \qquad pH = 1.18$$

This reveals that the buffer's ability to resist a change in pH has been exceeded; the pH has changed dramatically. In the original solution, the formate ion ($HCOO^-$) could react with up to 0.0400 mol of the strong acid without having any excess H^+ to greatly lower the pH. *This is its buffer capacity toward strong acid.* Similarly, the formic acid could react with up to 0.0200 mol of strong base without having any excess strong base to greatly raise the pH. *This is its buffer capacity toward strong base.* As we saw with the addition of too much HCl, when the buffer capacity is exceeded, the pH changes quite sharply. For a monoprotic acid or base, the buffer capacity is greatest when $[HA] = [A^-]$. When this occurs, the buffer can neutralize equal amounts of both strong base and strong acid.

EXERCISE 18.6 | **Buffer Capacity**

Let's look at the buffer capacity of an ammonia–ammonium buffer system like the one we used for our calcium–EDTA analysis at the beginning of this chapter. We will start with 200.0 mL of a solution containing 0.500 M NH_3 and 0.200 M NH_4^+. What will be the initial pH of the buffer? Will we exceed the buffer capacity by adding 75.0 mL of 2.00 M NaOH? What will be the pH after that addition?

Solution

We have a total of 0.100 mol of NH_3 and 0.0400 mol NH_4^+. The solution has more conjugate base than acid, so the pH should be higher than the pK_a for ammonium, 9.26. We use the expression for K_a of NH_4^+ so that we can solve directly for $[H^+]$:

$$NH_4^+(aq) \rightleftharpoons NH_3(aq) + H^+(aq) \qquad K = 5.6 \times 10^{-10}$$

$$[H^+] = \frac{K_a[NH_4^+]}{[NH_3]} = \frac{5.6 \times 10^{-10}(0.200)}{(0.500)}$$

$$[H^+] = 2.2 \times 10^{-10} \ M \qquad pH = 9.65$$

We now take the system out of equilibrium by adding 75.0 mL of 2.00 M NaOH (0.150 mol of OH^- added). The OH^- will react with the weakly acidic ammonium ion to give more ammonia. Given the amount of OH^- added, what is the limiting reactant?

$$NH_4^+(aq) + OH^-(aq) \rightleftharpoons NH_3(aq) + H_2O(l) \qquad K = 5.6 \times 10^4$$

moles initial	0.0400		0.100
moles added		0.150	
change	−0.0400	−0.0400	+0.0400
moles at equilibrium	≈0	0.110	0.140

NH_4^+ is the limiting reactant, and we will have 0.110 mol of OH^- and 0.140 mol of NH_3 in excess. The $[OH^-]$ will determine the final pH because it is a much stronger base than NH_3. The total solution volume consists of the 200.0 mL with which we started and the 75.0 mL of strong base that we added, for a total of 275.0 mL.

$$[OH^-] = \frac{(0.0110 \text{ mol } OH^-)}{(0.2750 \text{ L } OH^- \text{ solution})} = 0.0400 \ M$$

$$pOH = 1.40 \qquad pH = 12.60$$

The excess of OH^-, and the resulting sharp increase in the pH, indicate that we have exceeded the buffer capacity.

PRACTICE 18.6

What is the pH of the ammonia–ammonium ion buffer in this exercise after the addition of 30.0 mL of 0.100 M HCl? . . . after the addition of 50.0 mL of 1.50 M HCl?

See Problems 29 and 30.

EXERCISE 18.7 | **Keeping the pH Within Specified Limits**

Our goal in buffer preparation is often to keep the pH within specific limits upon the addition of a strong acid or base. How many milliliters of 0.100 M HCl may be added to 100.0 mL of a buffer containing 0.150 M each of formic acid (HCOOH) and formate ion (HCOO$^-$) so that the pH will not change by more than 0.20?

First Thoughts

Our goal is to find out how many moles of HCl we can add to the system. We can then convert to milliliters of HCl via molarity. We can add only as many moles of HCl as will change the pH by only 0.20 unit. We can find this by determining the initial pH and the final pH and then calculating how the amounts of formic acid and formate ion change.

Solution

The initial amounts of formic acid and formate ion are equal:

$$\text{mol HCOOH} = \text{mol HCOO}^- = 0.1000 \text{ L} \times \frac{(0.150 \text{ mol})}{(1.00 \text{ L})} = 0.0150 \text{ mol of each}$$

$$[H^+] = \frac{K_a[\text{HCOOH}]}{[\text{HCOO}^-]} = \frac{1.8 \times 10^{-4}(0.0150)}{(0.0150)}$$

$$[H^+] = K_a = 1.8 \times 10^{-4} \text{ } M$$

$$\text{pH} = \text{p}K_a = 3.74$$

When we add HCl solution, the pH is not to drop below 3.54 (0.20 from the original pH). The concentration of H^+ at this pH is $[H^+] = 10^{-3.54} = 2.88 \times 10^{-4}$ M. We can solve for the ratio of acid to base:

$$\frac{[H^+]}{K_a} = \frac{2.88 \times 10^{-4}}{1.8 \times 10^{-4}} = \frac{[\text{HCOOH}]}{[\text{HCOO}^-]} = \frac{1.60}{1}$$

Therefore, retaining an extra figure in this immediate calculation,

$$[\text{HCOOH}] = 1.60[\text{HCOO}^-]$$

Because the volumes are equal,

$$\text{mol HCOOH} = 1.60(\text{mol HCOO}^-)$$

The total amount of formic acid and formate ion equals 0.0300 mol (it was originally 0.01500 mol each). We can substitute for HCOOH and solve.

$$1.60(\text{HCOO}^-) + \text{HCOO}^- = 0.0300 \text{ mol}$$

$$2.60(\text{HCOO}^-) = 0.0300 \text{ mol}$$

$$\text{mol HCOO}^- = \frac{0.0300 \text{ mol}}{2.60} = 0.0115 \text{ mol}$$

$$\text{mol HCOOH} = 1.60(0.0115 \text{ mol HCOO}^-) = 0.0184 \text{ mol}$$

Because our original amounts of HCOOH and HCOO⁻ were 0.01500 mol each, we can have an addition of 0.0035 mol of HCl and still have the pH stay within 0.20 of the original pH. We can now determine the maximum HCl solution volume.

$$\text{mL HCl} = 0.0035 \text{ mol HCl} \times \frac{1.000 \text{ L}}{0.1000 \text{ mol}} = 0.035 \text{ L} = 35 \text{ mL}$$

Further Insights

We see the importance of working in moles with buffer calculations. Keep in mind that this is possible only because the volumes of the conjugates cancel. This will be the case only when we are dealing with buffers.

PRACTICE 18.7

Solve the same problem using the Henderson–Hasselbalch equation instead of the mass-action expression for the buffer.

See Problems 29 and 30.

In Summary: What are the criteria for a suitable buffer?

A buffer should not react with the system it is buffering.

- The pK_a of a buffer should be as close as possible to the pH you want to maintain.
- The buffering capacity of a buffer must be sufficient to accommodate the addition of a strong acid or a strong base.

Food for Thought:
Are Strong Acids and Bases Buffers?

A buffer, as we noted before, is a mixture of a weak acid and its conjugate base or of a weak base and its conjugate acid. Is it possible that a solution containing only a strong acid (such as HCl) or a strong base (such as NaOH) could be a buffer? For example, 1 L of 0.10 M HCl has a pH of 1.0. The solution pH remains close to 1.0 even when some NaOH is added. Similarly, the pH of 0.10 M NaOH remains close to 13.0 even when some strong acid is added. In that sense, they meet the criterion of keeping the pH of the solution fairly constant upon addition of strong acid or base. However, buffers should also keep their pH constant when diluted, and this is where strong acids and bases fail as buffers. Dilution of a strong acid or a strong base solution causes the pH to change by roughly 1 unit with every 10-fold dilution. On the other hand, buffers made from conjugate acid–base pairs show very little change in pH with dilution. This is critical in biochemical processes, which require a fairly constant pH whatever the solution concentration.

The importance of buffers in medicine is illustrated by a class of drugs called antacids. These drugs are compounds that neutralize gastric acid and exert a buffering effect in the stomach for temporary relief of acid indigestion. Similarly, magnesium carbonate is added to certain brands of aspirin specifically to alter stomach pH. The magnesium carbonate, by neutralizing the "gastric juice," increases stomach pH. The net result is that the aspirin exists predominantly in its ionized form, as shown in Figure 18.5, and reduces the risk of aspirin-induced stomach bleeding or ulcers. Although this is desirable in some cases, it can reduce the amount of drug absorption. Unfortunately, antacids alone may also raise the pH of the stomach above the pK_a of other drugs, resulting in their ionization and in reduced absorption through the stomach. This reduced absorption means that the drug treatment is not effective. Consequently, many drugs bear the warning

NanoWorld / MacroWorld

Big effects of the very small: Buffers in biochemical studies and medicine

Enzymes, which catalyze nearly all the chemical reactions that occur in living organisms, are often highly sensitive to the hydrogen ion concentration of the environment in which they are found. Slight increases or decreases in pH can have a dramatic effect on an enzyme's ability to carry out its unique function. Consequently, living organisms typically have buffering systems in place to maintain a relatively constant pH. Technological advances in biochemistry and molecular biology have enabled chemists to prepare, purify, and study just about any enzyme they desire outside of its normal cellular environment, as long as they can maintain the pH at around 7. For example, members of the class of enzymes called cytochrome P450 are chemically active only between pH 6.5 and pH 8.5, with optimum activities usually occurring between pH 6.8 and pH 7.5. These enzymes are present in the human liver, where they help the body rid itself of foreign chemicals, including most pharmaceuticals.

In 1966, Norman Good and coworkers reported on the design of a dozen new buffers for use in biological research. These so-called **Good (or Good's) buffers** are now widely used, because they are fairly chemically stable in the presence of enzymes or visible light and do not interact with biological compounds. Moreover, they are easy to prepare. Several of the Good buffers (those shown with asterisks in Table 18.2) and boric acid are among the buffers most commonly used in the study of enzyme behavior. Their abbreviated names, structures, and pK_a values are listed in Table 18.2. An additional set of highly effective biological buffers were synthesized in the late 1990s and are now commercially available. Not too surprisingly, they are called "better buffers."

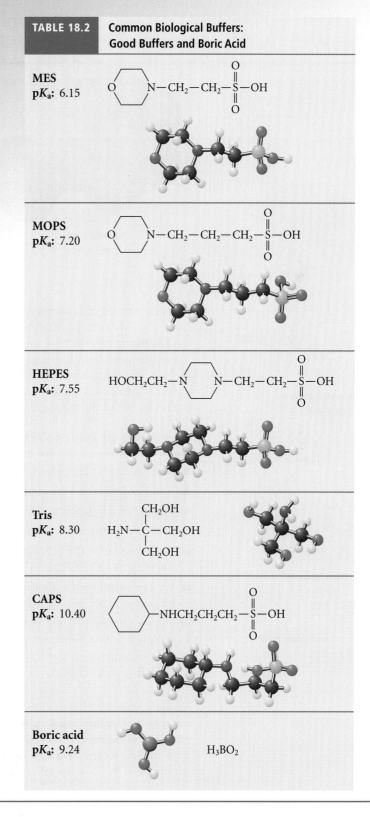

TABLE 18.2	Common Biological Buffers: Good Buffers and Boric Acid
MES pK_a: 6.15	
MOPS pK_a: 7.20	
HEPES pK_a: 7.55	$HOCH_2CH_2-N \quad N-CH_2-CH_2-\overset{O}{\underset{O}{S}}-OH$
Tris pK_a: 8.30	$H_2N-\overset{CH_2OH}{\underset{CH_2OH}{C}}-CH_2OH$
CAPS pK_a: 10.40	$\langle\;\rangle-NHCH_2CH_2CH_2-\overset{O}{\underset{O}{S}}-OH$
Boric acid pK_a: 9.24	H_3BO_2

FIGURE 18.5

The neutral and ionic forms of aspirin.

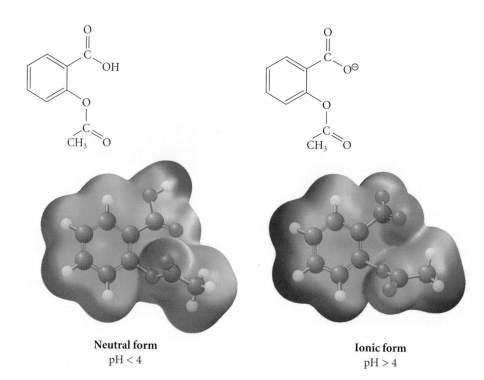

Neutral form
pH < 4

Ionic form
pH > 4

Protonated form
pH < 8.3

Neutral form
pH > 8.3

FIGURE 18.6

The ionic and neutral forms of tetracycline.

"Do not take antacids containing (hydroxides of) aluminum, calcium, or magnesium (e.g., Mylanta, Maalox) while taking this medication."

The buffering effects of antacids and other buffered medicines can give rise to a number of undesirable drug interactions with prescription medications. Tetracycline, for example, is an antibiotic drug that is absorbed primarily through the stomach lining in its protonated form, shown in Figure 18.6, thanks to the normally low pH of the stomach.

HERE'S WHAT WE KNOW SO FAR

- Many reactions are pH-sensitive and require buffers to control pH.
- A buffer resists change in pH upon addition of a strong acid or a strong base.
- The pH of a buffer is not changed when the solution is diluted.
- Buffers are typically composed of weak conjugate acid–base pairs.
- We can solve for the pH of buffers in a straightforward way by recognizing the importance of Le Châtelier's principle and the common-ion effect.
- We can calculate the approximate ratio of conjugate acid to base in order to prepare a buffer of a known pH.
- Solving for the pH of a buffer upon addition of strong acid or base is really solving a limiting-reactant problem.
- It is possible to exceed the buffer capacity, in which case the pH will move sharply higher (with excess base) or sharply lower (with excess acid).

We have seen that buffers are used to maintain the pH of all kinds of systems, ranging from municipal scrubbers to your body. Our overarching application of aqueous equilibria in this chapter is analysis of calcium in hard water via titration with EDTA. We are one step closer to completing our task. We next focus on titrations.

18.2 Acid–Base Titrations

We discussed the wide range of titrations, of which acid–base titration is one important type, in the opening section of this chapter. A small sample of the commercial, environmental and biological uses of acid–base titrations includes analysis of the acidity of food and drink, determination of the pH of water supplies, measurement of the solubility of pharmaceuticals, determination of amino acids in blood, and determination of the acidity or basicity (called the "total acid" or "total base" number) of motor oils.

In the lab, we typically set up an acid–base titration by monitoring the pH as shown in Figure 18.7. This normally includes a buret to accurately measure the volume of titrant delivered, a beaker or flask, and a calibrated pH meter. Industrial laboratories often use automated titrators to increase efficiency. The typical acid–base titrations fall into one of these main categories:

- strong-acid–strong-base titrations
- strong-acid–weak-base titrations
- weak-acid–strong-base titrations

A fourth type, weak-acid–weak-base titrations, is typically not used because the equilibrium constant for the overall reaction is not nearly as large as with the other systems, and the indication of the end of the titration is too gradual to tell us when the titration is complete.

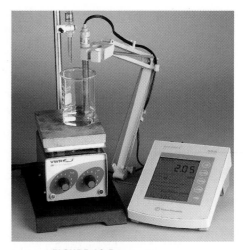

FIGURE 18.7

A typical set-up for an acid–base titration monitored by a pH meter includes a buret to accurately measure the volume of titrant delivered, a beaker, and the calibrated pH meter. An automatic titrator is used when there are many titrations to be done.

Strong-Acid–Strong-Base Titrations

The determination of HCl molarity based on titration with NaOH is a common process throughout all levels of chemistry and from the academic to the industrial laboratory setting. Let's examine *the changes* that take place during a strong-acid–strong-base titration by assuming that we wish to titrate 50.00 mL of 0.1000 M HCl by adding known amounts of 0.2000 M NaOH. The results of the titration are graphically shown in Figures 18.8a–f, which illustrates the relationship between pH and volume of OH^- added.

Part 1: Initial pH

We can calculate the pH of the initial 0.1000 M solution of HCl as we would that of any other strong acid:

$$pH = -\log[H^+] = -\log(0.1000) = 1.0$$

We enter this on the graph to the right (Figure 18.8a).

Part 2: Addition of 5.00 mL of NaOH solution

What will be the reaction of the strong acid with the strong base? We can write the reaction in molecular form:

$$HCl(aq) + NaOH(aq) \rightleftharpoons H_2O(l) + NaCl(aq)$$

However, the net ionic form gives a better sense of what is going on in the solution:

$$H^+(aq) + OH^-(aq) \rightleftharpoons H_2O(l) \qquad K = 1.0 \times 10^{14}$$

The equilibrium constant is very high and the reaction is fast, both good features to have when doing a titration. What, and how much, will be left over after addition of the NaOH titrant to the HCl solution? *This is a limiting-reactant problem*, and we can use the same type of table that we used when discussing

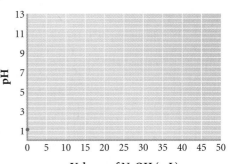

FIGURE 18.8a

Each plot follows the pH changes as we add 0.2000 M NaOH solution to 50.00 mL of 0.1000 M HCl solution. The initial pH is shown here, followed in turn by the pH after addition of the listed volumes.

buffers to help us sort it all out. For example, the initial concentration of our strong acid is

$$[H^+] = 0.1000\ M = \frac{(0.1000\ \text{mol})}{(1.000\ \text{L})} = \frac{(0.1000\ \text{mmol})}{(1.000\ \text{mL})}$$

How much H^+ is in the solution? Using the concentration in moles per liter and the volume in liters, we find that

$$\frac{(0.1000\ \text{mol})}{(1.000\ \text{L})} \times 0.05000\ \text{L} = 0.005000\ \text{mol}\ H^+$$

We can calculate the amount of strong base, OH^-, added to the solution in the same way.

$$\frac{(0.2000\ \text{mol})}{(1.000\ \text{L})} \times 0.00500\ \text{L} = 0.001000\ \text{mol}\ OH^-$$

Putting our values in tabular format shows that we still have plenty of strong acid in the solution. Note that because water is the solvent, it will not enter into the mass-action expression, and we can ignore it in our calculations.

$$H^+(aq) + OH^-(aq) \rightleftharpoons H_2O(l) \qquad K = 1.0 \times 10^{14}$$

moles initial	0.005000	
moles added		0.001000
change	−0.001000	−0.001000
moles at equilibrium	0.004000	≈ 0

We can calculate the pH, keeping in mind the total solution volume of 55.00 mL (50.00 mL of HCl solution + 5.00 mL of added NaOH solution).

$$[H^+] = \frac{(0.004000\ \text{mol})}{(0.05500\ \text{L})} = 0.0727\ M$$

$$pH = 1.14$$

The addition of the strong acid has raised the pH, but not much, because we still have plenty of excess acid. We have entered the data onto our graph in Figure 18.8b.

FIGURE 18.8b

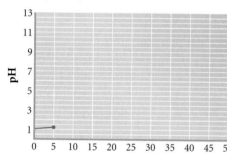

Volume of NaOH (mL)

Part 3: Addition of a total of 12.50 mL of NaOH solution

Half of the H^+ is neutralized at this point.

$$H^+(aq) + OH^-(aq) \rightleftharpoons H_2O(l) \qquad K = 1.0 \times 10^{14}$$

moles initial	0.005000	
moles added		0.002500
change	−0.002500	−0.002500
moles at equilibrium	0.002500	≈ 0

The total volume is 62.50 mL (50.00 mL of HCl solution + 12.50 mL of NaOH solution), which results in a pH of 1.4, as shown here and in Figure 18.8c.

$$[H^+] = \frac{(0.0025000\ \text{mol})}{(0.06250\ \text{L})} = 0.0400\ M$$

$$pH = 1.40$$

FIGURE 18.8c

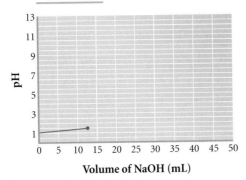

FIGURE 18.8c

Part 4: Addition of a total of 24.00 mL of NaOH solution

By the time we add 24.00 mL of 0.2000 M NaOH to the acid, we have neutralized nearly all of the hydrogen ion, as shown in the following data table.

$$H^+(aq) + OH^-(aq) \rightleftharpoons H_2O(l) \quad K = 1.0 \times 10^{14}$$

moles initial	0.005000	
moles added		0.004800
change	−0.004800	−0.004800
moles at equilibrium	0.000200	≈ 0

The total volume is 74.00 mL (50.00 mL of HCl solution + 24.00 mL of NaOH solution), which results in a pH of 2.57, as shown.

$$[H^+] = \frac{(0.000200 \text{ mol})}{(0.07400 \text{ L})} = 2.70 \times 10^{-3} \ M$$

$$pH = 2.57$$

Adding a bit more, so that the volume of base added is 24.95 mL, results in a pH of 3.87, shown in Figure 18.8d. As we get very close to neutralizing the acid, the pH starts to rise sharply.

FIGURE 18.8d

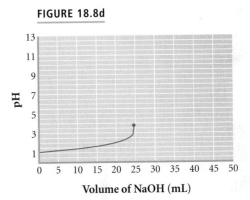

Part 5: Addition of a total of 25.00 mL of NaOH solution

At this point, all of the strong acid has been neutralized by the strong base. This is called the **equivalence point** of the titration, the exact point at which the reactant has been neutralized by the titrant.

$$H^+(aq) + OH^-(aq) \rightleftharpoons H_2O(l) \quad K = 1.0 \times 10^{14}$$

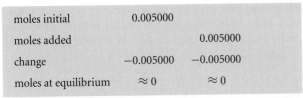

moles initial	0.005000	
moles added		0.005000
change	−0.005000	−0.005000
moles at equilibrium	≈ 0	≈ 0

We say that there are "≈ 0" hydrogen and hydroxide ions in the solution. *This really says that the amount is insignificant when compared to the original amounts of acid and base that were mixed.* How much is "≈ 0" in this neutral solution?

We have 75.00 mL of (ideally) pure water at equilibrium. The only reaction that is important in our solution at this point is the autoprotolysis of water. Finally, the equilibrium constant for this reaction has become very important.

FIGURE 18.8e

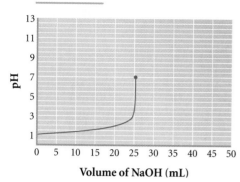

Volume of NaOH (mL)

Using the equation for this reaction, and the corresponding mass-action expression, we can solve for the concentration of H^+ in the solution.

$$H_2O(l) \rightleftharpoons H^+(aq) + OH^-(aq) \qquad K_w = 1.0 \times 10^{-14}$$

$$[H^+] = [OH^-] = 1.0 \times 10^{-7} M$$

$$pH = 7.00$$

The answer to our question here is $[H^+] = 1.0 \times 10^{-7} M$, which is insignificant compared to the initial concentration of strong acid and base. However, *in the absence of other sources of H^+, this is very significant*. The solution now has a neutral pH, as shown in Figure 18.8e. Note the sharp rise to the equivalence point, which makes it easy to identify.

Part 6: Addition of a total of 40.00 mL of NaOH solution

At this point, the additional strong base is just being added to water (neglecting the spectator ions Na^+ and Cl^-), so we would expect the pH to rise sharply. We are adding 15.00 mL of 0.2000 M NaOH, or 0.00300 mol, past the equivalence point, and our pH is calculated as shown for the total solution volume of 90.00 mL (50.00 mL of HCl solution + 40.00 mL of NaOH added).

$$[OH^-] = \frac{(0.003000 \text{ mol})}{(0.09000 \text{ L})} = 0.03333 M$$

$$pOH = 1.48$$

$$pH = 12.52$$

FIGURE 18.8f

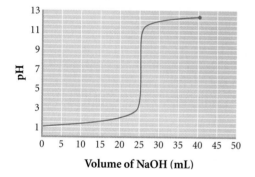

Volume of NaOH (mL)

The solution has become quite basic. The complete strong-acid–strong-base **titration curve** is shown in Figure 18.8f.

Summarizing, we have shown that a strong base will only slightly increase the pH of a strong acid until very close to the equivalence point, where it will rise sharply to pH = 7. After the equivalence point, the pH will continue its sharp increase to a point that depends on the concentration of the strong-base titrant.

A word of caution: *The pH at the equivalence point will equal 7 only in monoprotic strong-acid–strong-base titrations.* We will show why this is so immediately after Exercise 18.8.

EXERCISE 18.8 **Titrating Sodium Hydroxide with Hydrochloric Acid**

Calculate and draw a graph showing the relationship between the pH and the volume of HCl for the titration of 25.00 mL of 0.2500 M NaOH with the following total volumes of 0.1250 M HCl: a. 0 mL; b. 20.00 mL; c. 49.80 mL; d. 50.00 mL; e. 60.00 mL.

Solution

The net ionic reaction is the same as in the addition of NaOH to HCl, except that the reactant (now OH^-) and the titrant (now H^+) have switched roles.

$$OH^-(aq) + H^+(aq) \rightleftharpoons H_2O(l) \qquad K = 1.0 \times 10^{14}$$

a. 0 mL of acid added: The pH of this strong base can be found from the hydroxide ion concentration, which is equal to the initial concentration of the NaOH solution.

$$[OH^-] = 0.2500 M \qquad pOH = 0.60 \qquad pH = 13.40$$

b. 20.00 mL of acid added: We can use the same table setup that we used previously to calculate the moles of each after reaction. There are initially

$$\frac{(0.2500 \text{ mol})}{(1 \text{ L})} \times 0.02500 \text{ L} = 0.006250 \text{ mol } OH^-$$

in the solution. We add

$$\frac{(0.1250 \text{ mol})}{(1.000 \text{ L})} \times 0.02000 \text{ L} = 0.002500 \text{ mol of } H^+$$

in a total solution volume of 45.00 mL (25.00 mL of base + 20.00 mL of acid) = 0.04500 L.

$$OH^-(aq) + H^+(aq) \rightleftharpoons H_2O(l) \qquad K = 1.0 \times 10^{14}$$

	OH^-	H^+
moles initial	0.006250	
moles added		0.002500
change	−0.002500	−0.002500
moles at equilibrium	0.003750	≈ 0

$$[OH^-] = \frac{(0.003750 \text{ mol})}{(0.04500 \text{ L})} = 0.08333 \ M$$

$$pOH = 1.08$$

$$pH = 12.92$$

c. 49.8 mL of acid added: Using the same type of calculations, we find that

$$OH^-(aq) + H^+(aq) \rightleftharpoons H_2O(l) \qquad K = 1.0 \times 10^{14}$$

	OH^-	H^+
moles initial	0.006250	
moles added		0.006225
change	−0.006225	−0.006225
moles at equilibrium	0.000025	≈ 0

$$[OH^-] = \frac{(0.0000250 \text{ mol})}{(0.07480 \text{ L})} = 3.34 \times 10^{-4} \ M$$

$$pOH = 3.48$$

$$pH = 10.52$$

d. 50.00 mL of acid added:

$$OH^-(aq) + H^+(aq) \rightleftharpoons H_2O(l) \qquad K = 1.0 \times 10^{14}$$

	OH^-	H^+
moles initial	0.006250	
moles added		0.006250
change	−0.006250	−0.006250
moles at equilibrium	≈ 0	≈ 0

The solution is at the equivalence point, and pH = 7.0 for a strong-base–strong-acid titration.

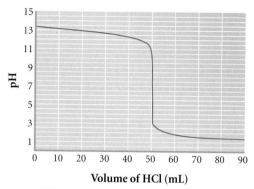

FIGURE 18.9

The titration curve for the addition of 0.125 M HCl to 25.00 mL of 0.250 M NaOH.

e. 60.00 mL of acid added: We have added 10.00 mL of excess acid, which is a total of 0.00125 mol. The total solution volume is 85.00 mL (25.00 mL of base + 60.00 mL of added acid) = 0.08500 L. We can calculate the pH from this information.

$$[H^+] = \frac{(0.001250 \text{ mol})}{(0.08500 \text{ L})} = 0.01471 \ M$$

$$pH = 1.83$$

The titration curve shown in Figure 18.9 has a shape similar to what we expected. It is fairly flat until close to the equivalence point, where it drops quite sharply and over a large pH range, so it is easily detectable.

PRACTICE 18.8

Calculate and draw a graph of the relationship between the pH and the volume of NaOH solution for the titration of 25.00 mL of 0.2500 M HCl with the following total volumes of 0.2500 M NaOH:

a. 0 mL   d. 25.00 mL
b. 10.00 mL   e. 30.00 mL
c. 20.00 mL   f. 40.00 mL

See Problems 33, 34, and 37. ▮

Acid–Base Titrations in Which One Component Is Weak and One Is Strong

Although the general problem-solving strategy is the same when we titrate a weak acid with a strong base (or a weak base with a strong acid) as when we perform a strong-acid–strong-base titration, there is a critical difference, the K_a (or K_b) of the analyte, that affects both the pH and the pH change at the equivalence point. *Our ability to do a titration analysis depends on having a large, sharp break in the equivalence point.* We can best see this by comparing the data from our HCl–NaOH titration with those from the titration of 50.00 mL of a 0.1000 M acetic acid solution (CH$_3$COOH, $K_a = 1.8 \times 10^{-5}$) with a 0.2000 M sodium hydroxide solution. The amounts and concentrations are the same. Only the acid has been changed from strong to weak.

FIGURE 18.10a

Each plot follows the pH changes as we add 0.2000 M NaOH solution to 50.00 mL of 0.1000 M acetic acid solution. The pH values at each volume are superimposed on those from Figure 18.9 to show the difference in the nature of the titration curve between the strong acid and the weak acid.

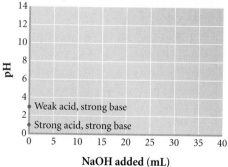

NaOH added (mL)

Part 1: Initial pH

We can determine pH in this weak acid as we would in any other weak acid, using principles we learned in Chapter 17.

$$CH_3COOH(aq) \rightleftharpoons CH_3COO^-(aq) + H^+(aq) \qquad K_a = 1.8 \times 10^{-5}$$

$$K_a = \frac{[H^+][CH_3COO^-]}{[CH_3COOH]} \qquad 1.8 \times 10^{-5} = \frac{x^2}{(0.1000)}$$

$$x = [CH_3COO^-] = [H^+] = 1.3 \times 10^{-3} \ M$$

$$pH = 2.87$$

We already see a difference in the titration curve (Figure 18.10a) because this weak acid pH is nearly 2 units higher than the initial pH of the strong acid, HCl, of the same concentration.

Part 2: Addition of 5.00 mL of NaOH solution

We will use the same thinking—and ask the same questions—to assess the chemistry here as in the strong-acid–strong-base titration. We begin with

$$0.005000 \text{ mol of acetic acid} \left(50.00 \text{ mL} \times \frac{0.1000 \text{ mol}}{L}\right),$$

to which we add 0.001000 mol of OH^- $\left(5.000 \text{ mL} \times \frac{0.2000 \text{ mol}}{L}\right)$.

Question 1: *What will be the reaction of the acetic acid with the NaOH solution?* The net ionic form of the reaction is useful because spectator ions are not part of the acid–base chemistry.

$$CH_3COOH(aq) + OH^-(aq) \rightleftharpoons CH_3COO^-(aq) + H_2O(l) \qquad K = 1.8 \times 10^9$$

The equilibrium constant is the same whether we describe a reaction by giving its molecular or net ionic form. For this reaction, K is quite high and the reaction is fast.

Question 2: *What, and how much, will be left over after addition of the titrant?* We can use a table to clarify the amounts involved when the system reaches its new equilibrium position.

$$CH_3COOH(aq) + OH^-(aq) \rightleftharpoons CH_3COO^-(aq) + H_2O(l)$$

moles initial	0.005000		0
moles added		0.001000	
change	−0.001000	−0.001000	+0.001000
moles at equilibrium	0.004000	≈ 0	0.001000

Because we have both a weak acid and its conjugate base, *we have produced a buffer*, and we can solve for the pH as with any buffer system. Note that we have substituted moles into the equation instead of molarities because the total volume of the solution will cancel out.

$$[H^+] = \frac{K_a[CH_3COOH]}{[CH_3COO^-]} = \frac{(1.8 \times 10^{-5})(0.004000)}{(0.001000)} = 7.2 \times 10^{-5} \text{ M}$$

$$pH = 4.14$$

We have entered the data point onto our graph in Figure 18.10b. How is the curve shaping up compared to that of the strong-acid–strong-base titration? Because the solution is a buffer at this point, this part of the titration is called the **buffer region**. We expect the pH to be relatively constant within the buffer region.

FIGURE 18.10b

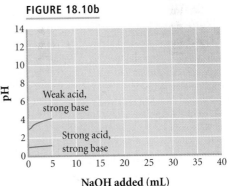

Part 3: Addition of 12.50 mL of NaOH solution

Proceeding as we did in part b, we can generate the following table and solve for pH. Again, in our calculation of the hydrogen ion concentration, we needn't worry about the volumes of acid and base because they will cancel out during our calculation.

$$CH_3COOH(aq) + OH^-(aq) \rightleftharpoons CH_3COO^-(aq) + H_2O(l)$$

moles initial	0.005000		0
moles added		0.002500	
change	−0.002500	−0.002500	+0.002500
moles at equilibrium	0.002500	≈ 0	0.002500

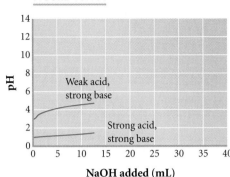

FIGURE 18.10c

FIGURE 18.10c

$$[H^+] = \frac{K_a[CH_3COOH]}{[CH_3COO^-]} = \frac{(1.8 \times 10^{-5})(0.002500)}{(0.002500)} = 1.8 \times 10^{-5}\,M$$

$$pH = 4.74$$

We are still in the buffer region, having neutralized precisely one-half of the acetic acid and forming an equal amount of acetate ion, the conjugate base. This is called the **titration midpoint**, at which the pH equals the pK_a of acetic acid. It is also possible to work backward, finding the pK_a of an acid from pH at the titration midpoint. As before, we have entered the data point onto our graph (see Figure 18.10c). How is the curve shaping up compared to that of the strong-acid–strong-base titration?

Part 4: Addition of a total of 24.00 mL of NaOH solution

Continuing, we generate the following table, which shows that we are still—though barely—in the buffer region. The pH is beginning to rise on the way to the equivalence point.

$$CH_3COOH(aq) + OH^-(aq) \rightleftharpoons CH_3COO^-(aq) + H_2O(l)$$

moles initial	0.005000		≈ 0
moles added		0.004800	
change	−0.004800	−0.004800	+0.004800
moles at equilibrium	0.000200	≈ 0	0.004800

FIGURE 18.10d

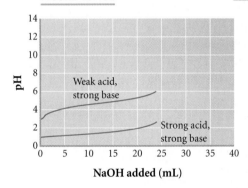

$$[H^+] = \frac{K_a[CH_3COOH]}{[CH_3COO^-]} = \frac{(1.8 \times 10^{-5})(0.000200)}{(0.004800)} = 7.5 \times 10^{-7}\,M$$

$$pH = 6.12$$

Continue to keep an eye on the data comparison (Figure 18.10d) between this titration and the strong-acid–strong-base titration.

Part 5: Addition of a total of 25.00 mL of NaOH solution

The completed table shows that we are at the equivalence point. We converted all of the acetic acid to acetate ion.

$$CH_3COOH(aq) + OH^-(aq) \rightleftharpoons CH_3COO^-(aq) + H_2O(l)$$

moles initial	0.005000		≈ 0
moles added		0.005000	
change	−0.005000	−0.005000	+0.005000
moles at equilibrium	≈ 0	≈ 0	0.005000

How do we calculate the pH of this solution? To answer that, we need to go back to our most important questions: "What is in solution?" and "What equation describes their behavior?"

The answer to the first question is "0.005000 mol of acetate ion in a total of 75.00 mL of solution." Using the chemist's shorthand,

$$[CH_3COO^-] = \frac{(0.005000 \text{ mol})}{(0.07500 \text{ L})} = 0.06667 \, M$$

We have neutralized all of the weak acid, and we now have a solution of its conjugate base. This acetate ion will hydrolyze, if only barely, to acetic acid.

$$CH_3COO^-(aq) + H_2O(l) \rightleftharpoons CH_3COOH(aq) + OH^-(aq)$$

We can calculate the equilibrium constant for the hydrolysis of this conjugate base of acetic acid, K_b, from K_w and the acetic acid K_a.

$$K_b = \frac{K_w}{K_a} = \frac{1.0 \times 10^{-14}}{1.8 \times 10^{-5}} = 5.6 \times 10^{-10}$$

We can now solve for the pH of the weak base.

$$K_b = \frac{[OH^-][CH_3COOH]}{[CH_3COO^-]}$$

$$5.6 \times 10^{-10} = \frac{[x^2]}{[0.06667]} \qquad x = [CH_3COOH] = [OH^-] = 6.1 \times 10^{-6} \, M$$

$$pOH = 5.21$$

$$pH = 8.79$$

The pH of the weak base is, in fact, basic, as we would predict. Compare this to the pH $= 7$ equivalence point of the strong-acid–strong-base titration. There, only water was present at the equivalence point. In this titration, however, we have an equivalence point solution of a weak base. The pH for this titration did rise sharply near the equivalence point, making it easy to determine, as shown in Figure 18.10e.

FIGURE 18.10e

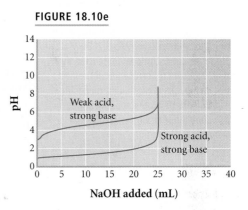

Part 6: Addition of a total of 40.00 mL of NaOH solution

We now add a 0.2000 M solution of a strong base to a very weak base. The weak base will not be an important contributor to the total hydroxide ion concentration because it is so weak. The hydroxide ion concentration will be strictly determined by the excess moles of OH^- and the total solution volume in which it is contained.

$$\text{excess mol } OH^- = 0.01500 \text{ L} \times \frac{(0.2000 \text{ mol})}{(1.000 \text{ L})} = 0.003000 \text{ mol}$$

$$[OH^-] = \frac{(0.003000 \text{ mol})}{(0.09000 \text{ L})} = 0.03333 \, M$$

$$pOH = 1.48$$

$$pH = 12.52$$

The pH has increased sharply. Compare this data point with that from the equivalent volume of strong base added to the strong acid in the previous titration, shown in Figure 18.10f. They are the same! In both cases, after the equivalence point, we added the same volume of the same concentration of strong base.

FIGURE 18.10f

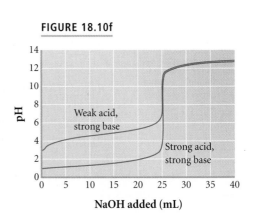

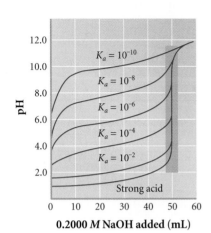

FIGURE 18.11

This plot shows the relationship between K_a value for 50.00 mL of a 0.2000 M acid and the change in pH at the equivalence point when titrated with a 0.2000 M NaOH solution. Notice two items in the plot. First, the concentration of the acid, not its relative strength, determines the equivalence point. Second, the larger the K_a value, the sharper the pH break at the equivalence point.

Summarizing the Key Ideas of the Weak-Acid–Strong-Base Titration Discussion

There are four key areas that define the titration curve and the information it yields.

Initial pH: This will be closer to neutral for weaker acids, further away for stronger acids.

Buffer region: This is where we have generated enough conjugate base, while still having the weak acid available to produce a buffer. This part of the titration curve will have a gently sloping pH until quite near the equivalence point. An important point in the buffer region is the titration midpoint (pH = pK_a). There is an inflection point at the titration midpoint that we do not see with strong-acid–strong-base titrations (compare Figures 18.9 and 18.11 in this regard).

Equivalence point: The starting weak acid has been exactly neutralized, and the solution is a weak base. The stronger the acid (the larger the K_a value), the sharper will be the break at the equivalence point. Figure 18.11 shows that when the K_a value of the weak acid is too small, the pH break at the equivalence point is too small to be of practical use.

Post-equivalence point: Excess strong base sharply raises the pH of the system.

EXERCISE 18.9 | **Titrating a Weak Base with a Strong Acid**

To further compare systems, calculate the pH values and draw the curve for the titration of 50.00 mL of 0.1000 M ammonia with 0.2000 M of hydrochloric acid using the same volumes of titrant as in our previous titrations:

a. 0 mL
b. 5.00 mL
c. 12.50 mL
d. 24.00 mL
e. 25.00 mL
f. 40.00 mL

Solution

a. Initial pH. The important reaction is the hydrolysis of ammonia.

$$NH_3(aq) + H_2O(l) \rightleftharpoons NH_4^+(aq) + OH^-(aq) \qquad K_b = 1.8 \times 10^{-5}$$

$$K_b = \frac{[NH_4^+][OH^-]}{[NH_3]}$$

$$1.8 \times 10^{-5} = \frac{x^2}{0.1000}$$

$$x = [OH^-] = 1.34 \times 10^{-3}\,M$$

$$pOH = 2.87$$

$$pH = 11.13$$

b. *Addition of 5.00 mL of HCl solution.* The system is thrown out of equilibrium by the addition of the HCl solution, much as the acetic acid system had to compensate for the addition of NaOH. We will generate a buffer, shown in the table.

$$NH_3(aq) + H^+(aq) \rightleftharpoons NH_4^+(aq) \qquad K_b = 1.8 \times 10^9$$

moles initial	0.005000		≈ 0
moles added		0.001000	
change	-0.001000	-0.001000	$+0.001000$
moles at equilibrium	0.004000	≈ 0	0.001000

When the system returns to equilibrium,

$$NH_3(aq) \rightleftharpoons NH_4^+(aq) + OH^-(aq) \qquad K_b = 1.8 \times 10^{-5}$$

$$[OH^-] = \frac{K_b[NH_3]}{[NH_4^+]} = \frac{(1.8 \times 10^{-5})(0.004000)}{(0.001000)} = 7.2 \times 10^{-5} \ M$$

$$pOH = 4.14$$

$$pH = 9.86$$

c. *Addition of 12.50 mL of HCl solution.* We can generate the following table and solve for pH.

$$NH_3(aq) + H^+(aq) \rightleftharpoons NH_4^+(aq) \qquad K_b = 1.8 \times 10^9$$

moles initial	0.005000		≈ 0
moles added		0.002500	
change	-0.002500	-0.002500	$+0.002500$
moles at equilibrium	0.002500	≈ 0	0.002500

When the system returns to equilibrium,

$$NH_3(aq) \rightleftharpoons NH_4^+(aq) + OH^-(aq) \qquad K_b = 1.8 \times 10^{-5}$$

$$[OH^-] = \frac{K_b[NH_3]}{[NH_4^+]} = \frac{(1.8 \times 10^{-5})(0.002500)}{(0.002500)} = 1.8 \times 10^{-5} \ M$$

$$pOH = pK_b = 4.74$$

$$pH = 9.26$$

d. *Addition of a total of 24.00 mL of HCl solution.* We are nearing the equivalence point. How do the various titration curves, shown in Figure 18.12 on page 798, compare?

$$NH_3(aq) + H^+(aq) \rightleftharpoons NH_4^+(aq) \qquad K = 1.8 \times 10^9$$

moles initial	0.005000		≈ 0
moles added		0.004800	
change	-0.004800	-0.004800	$+0.004800$
moles at equilibrium	0.000200	≈ 0	0.004800

When the system returns to equilibrium,

$$NH_3(aq) \rightleftharpoons NH_4^+(aq) + OH^-(aq) \qquad K = 1.8 \times 10^{-5}$$

$$[OH^-] = \frac{K_b[NH_3]}{[NH_4^+]} = \frac{(1.8 \times 10^{-5})(0.000200)}{(0.004800)} = 7.5 \times 10^{-7} \ M$$

$$pOH = 6.12$$

$$pH = 7.87$$

e. *Addition of a total of 25.00 mL of HCl solution.* We are at the equivalence point, at which we have added exactly the same number of moles of HCl as there were moles of ammonia at the start of the titration. We now have a solution that is weakly acidic as a consequence of the conversion of ammonia to the ammonium ion.

$$NH_3(aq) + H^+(aq) \rightleftharpoons NH_4^+(aq) \qquad K = 1.8 \times 10^9$$

moles initial	0.005000		≈ 0
moles added		0.005000	
change	−0.005000	−0.005000	+0.005000
moles at equilibrium	≈ 0	≈ 0	0.005000

$$[NH_4^+] = \frac{(0.005000 \text{ mol})}{(0.07500 \text{ L})} = 0.06667 \ M$$

$$K_a = \frac{K_w}{K_b} = \frac{1.0 \times 10^{-14}}{1.8 \times 10^{-5}} = 5.6 \times 10^{-10}$$

We can now solve for the pH of the weak acid.

$$K_a = \frac{[H^+][NH_3]}{[NH_4^+]}$$

$$5.6 \times 10^{-10} = \frac{x^2}{0.06667}$$

$$x = [NH_3] = [H^+] = 6.1 \times 10^{-6} \ M$$

$$pH = 5.21$$

f. *Addition of a total of 40.00 mL of HCl solution.*

$$\text{mol excess } H^+ = 0.01500 \text{ L} \times \frac{(0.2000 \text{ mol})}{(1.000 \text{ L})} = 0.003000 \text{ mol}$$

$$[H^+] = \frac{(0.003000 \text{ mol})}{(0.09000 \text{ L})} = 0.03333 \ M$$

$$pH = 1.48$$

PRACTICE 18.9

Calculate the pH values and draw the curve for the titration of 25.00 mL of 0.2500 M acetic acid with 0.2500 M sodium hydroxide using the same volumes of titrant as in our previous titrations: a. 0 mL; b. 5.00 mL; c. 12.50 mL; d. 24.00 mL; e. 25.00 mL; f. 40.00 mL. K_a (acetic acid) $= 1.8 \times 10^{-5}$

See Problems 35, 36, and 38.

FIGURE 18.12

This plot shows a comparison of the pH for strong-acid–strong-base, weak-acid–strong-base, and weak-base–strong-acid titrations using equal concentrations of acid and base.

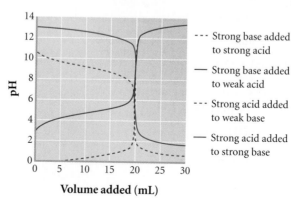

- - - Strong base added to strong acid

—— Strong base added to weak acid

- - - Strong acid added to weak base

—— Strong acid added to strong base

Volume added (mL)

We have seen that a successful monoprotic acid–base titration has an analyte (what you are titrating) that, when titrated with a strong acid or strong base, has a large K. The reaction is typically fast and reproducible. Polyprotic acid and base titrations are common, and the analysis of their titration curves presents interesting challenges, although we will not deal with these here.

Indicators

The pH meter, discussed in Chapter 19, can provide very accurate readings of the pH. Making successful measurements using a pH meter, however, relies on its having been properly maintained, calibrated, and operated. For speed and simplicity in a titration, the chemical technician often relies on a chemical pH reporter. This class of compounds, known as acid–base indicators or pH indicators, visually indicates the change in pH as we approach, reach, and pass the equivalence point. Indicators themselves are conjugate acid–base pairs of organic molecules that change color as they change between their acid and base forms. Perhaps the best-known example is phenolphthalein, which changes from colorless to rose-pink as the pH changes from 8.5 to 9.5. Figure 18.13 shows that phenolphthalein actually has several structural changes (and therefore color changes) from very low to very high pH.

Why is phenolphthalein such a popular acid–base indicator? Its color change occurs in the pH region where many acids titrated with strong bases reach their

FIGURE 18.13

The structure of phenolphthalein changes as we increase the pH from very low to very high.

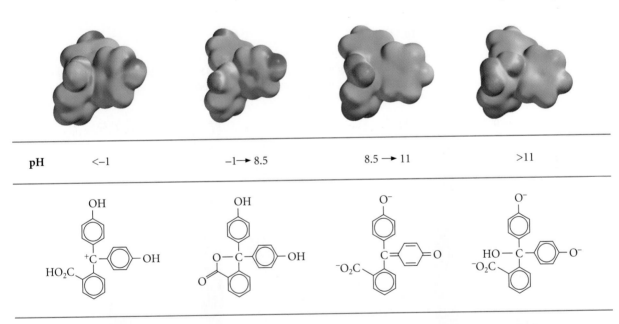

| pH | <−1 | −1 → 8.5 | 8.5 → 11 | >11 |

Orange-red
(formed in 65–98% H_2SO_4)

Colorless

Pink

Colorless
(formed above pH 11)

equivalence point. For example, acetic acid has an equivalence point, at which it is essentially all changed to acetate ion, at about pH 9, and the pH goes from about 6 to 11 within a small volume of titrant on either side of the equivalence point. The titration of a strong acid with base (or vice versa) changes very rapidly between the region of pH 6 to 11. An indicator that itself changes color anywhere in this area would, generally speaking, be a suitable reporter of the equivalence point.

In a given titration, how do we know which acid–base indicator to choose? We want to choose an indicator with a pK_a as close as possible to the pH at the equivalence point. A distinct color change is also useful. For example, the pK_a of phenolphthalein is about 9.5. This is well within the region of the pH at the equivalence point of titration of acetic acid by sodium hydroxide (pH ≈ 9, depending on acetic acid concentration). As a rule of thumb, *the color changes of pH indicators are visible to +/−1 pH unit on either side of the indicator pK_a.* This means that phenolphthalein will be completely colorless below a pH of 8.5 and will then be rose-pink from pH 8.5 to about pH 11. It will turn colorless again above pH 11. A selection of common pH indicators, their color changes, and their pH ranges is given in Figure 18.14.

During the chemical technician's analysis, only a few drops of an indicator solution are added to the analyte solution. Why so little? Because the indicator also undergoes an acid–base reaction. This means that in addition to adding the required volume to neutralize the analyte, we add just a bit more to cause the color change in the indicator. For example, if we titrate a solution of acetic acid

FIGURE 18.14

A selection of common pH indicators, their color changes, and their pH ranges. Our key criterion in selecting the proper indicator is that its pK_a should be as close as possible to the equivalence point of the titration in which it is used. Note that most indicators exhibit a color change over less than 2 pH units.

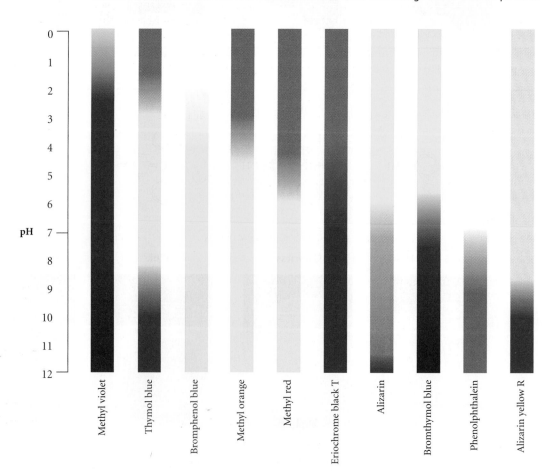

containing phenolphthalein indicator, we might need 35.27 mL of a sodium hydroxide solution to react with the acetic acid itself. Changing the indicator's structure (and therefore its color) might require *an additional 0.02 mL* of the strong base. The equivalence point is at 35.27 mL, but *the point at which you see the change in indicator color that tells you the titration is finished*, which is called the **titration endpoint**, is at 35.29 mL. Therefore, we would use 35.29 mL as our number for calculating the concentration of analyte. This could lead to very large errors if we had a lot of extra indicator in the solution. These errors are reduced if the endpoint is as close as possible to the equivalence point.

EXERCISE 18.10   **Picking an Indicator**

What would be a reasonable indicator for the titration of 0.10 *M* ammonia with 0.10 *M* HCl?

Solution

The key question is "What is the pH of the solution at the equivalence point?" When essentially all of the ammonia is converted to ammonium ion, the pH will be around 5.2, as we saw in Exercise 18.9, part e. As shown in Figure 18.14, several indicators change color around pH = 5.2, and methyl red appears to be a good choice.

PRACTICE 18.10

What would be a reasonable indicator for the titration of 0.10 *M* NaOH with 0.10 *M* HCl?

See Problems 39–42.

Some natural and commercially prepared indicators are made up of several colorful organic molecules, and they change color throughout the pH range. Notable among the natural indicators are the **anthocyanins**, which are responsible for most of the different colors found in vegetables and flowers. There are over 150 naturally occurring anthocyanins in foods such as the red cabbage that we cook and serve with dinner. The juice from the red cabbage can therefore be used as an indicator. Figure 18.15 shows the wide range of colors that can be obtained by adjusting the pH of red cabbage juice. Commercially prepared solutions of mixtures of indicators can mimic these color changes, but far more intensely, so far less is required. For instance, the commercially prepared "universal indicator" is a mixture of thymol blue, methyl red, bromthymol blue, and phenolphthalein. Because each indicator gains or loses protons at a different pH, the universal indicator has color changes over a wide pH range, as shown in Figure 18.16.

Application

CHEMICAL ENCOUNTERS:
Anthocyanins and
Universal Indicators

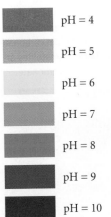

pH = 4

pH = 5

pH = 6

pH = 7

pH = 8

pH = 9

pH = 10

FIGURE 18.16

A typical universal indicator is a mixture of several common indicators.

FIGURE 18.15

The spectrum of colors in each sample of red cabbage juice is caused by the changes in structure of the anthocyanins as the pH moves from 1 to 13.

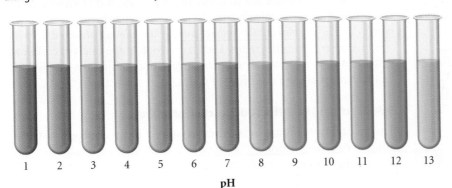

1 2 3 4 5 6 7 8 9 10 11 12 13

pH

HERE'S WHAT WE KNOW SO FAR

- Strong-acid–strong-base titrations show a relatively level pH until near the equivalence point, where the pH rises dramatically.

- Titration curves in which one component is weak and the other is strong contain four regions, including the initial pH, the buffer region, the equivalence point region and the post–equivalence point region.

- The buffer region contains a point at which one-half of the analyte has been converted to its conjugate. This is called the titration midpoint, and the pH at this point is equal to the pK of the analyte.

- The larger the pK of the analyte, the sharper will be the change in pH at the equivalence point.

- We can use an indicator to "see" the equivalence point of a titration.

- We add only a few drops of an indicator to the titration solution so that the equivalence point and titration endpoint can be as close together as possible.

 Application

18.3 Solubility Equilibria

The Pacific Ocean is an incredibly complex heterogeneous system. The bottom layers of this and other massive waterways are covered with a variety of soils and sediments, including **calcareous oozes**, calcium-containing detritus from dead single-celled, calcium-based sea life. One of the important compounds within the oozes is calcium carbonate ($CaCO_3$), some of which is in contact with ocean water, dissociating to form calcium and carbonate ions. The equation relating this dissociation is written so that the solid is a reactant and the dissolved ions are products:

$$CaCO_3(s) \rightleftharpoons Ca^{2+}(aq) + CO_3^{2-}(aq)$$

The mass-action expression that can be used to determine the solubility of $CaCO_3$ is called the **solubility product** when the equation is written as shown above. The solubility product is equal to the product of the concentrations of the ions (remember that the $CaCO_3$ is a solid and is not written as part of the mass-action expression).

$$K_{sp} = [Ca^{2+}][CO_3^{2-}]$$

FIGURE 18.17

Many processes, including the formation of bicarbonate ion and the reaction of hydrogen and hydroxide ions, affect the solubility of calcium carbonate in the ocean. These stromatolites are formations of calcium carbonate.

This equilibrium constant is called the **solubility product constant** (K_{sp}) and has the same conceptual meaning as any other equilibrium constant along with its mass-action expression. Because the values of K_{sp} tend to be very small, the concentrations of ions are quite low and that activities are not important here. Table 18.3 lists representative K_{sp} values for some of the sparingly soluble salts.

The difficulty with describing solubility using a single mass-action expression is that there are so many other processes that enter into the chemistry that our typically simple mass-action expression often just won't do. *The simple calculations we can perform do not always agree with what we observe in real systems.* Let's take a look at the calcium carbonate system in a somewhat nonmathematical approach as we discover the factors that affect the solubility of solids.

Side Reactions That Affect Our Reaction of Interest

The solubility of many ions, when dissolved in an aqueous system, is affected by side reactions. The solubility of calcium carbonate in a large ocean-based system is no exception (Figure 18.17).

TABLE 18.3   Selected K_{sp} Values at 25°C

Ionic Solid	K_{sp} (at 25°C)	Ionic Solid	K_{sp} (at 25°C)	Ionic Solid	K_{sp} (at 25°C)
Fluorides		$Hg_2CrO_4{}^*$	2×10^{-9}	$Co(OH)_2$	2.5×10^{-16}
BaF_2	2.4×10^{-5}	$BaCrO_4$	8.5×10^{-11}	$Ni(OH)_2$	1.6×10^{-16}
MgF_2	6.4×10^{-9}	Ag_2CrO_4	9.0×10^{-12}	$Zn(OH)_2$	4.5×10^{-17}
PbF_2	4×10^{-8}	$PbCrO_4$	2×10^{-16}	$Cu(OH)_2$	1.6×10^{-19}
SrF_2	7.9×10^{-10}			$Hg(OH)_2$	3×10^{-26}
CaF_2	4.0×10^{-11}	**Carbonates**		$Sn(OH)_2$	3×10^{-27}
		$NiCO_3$	1.4×10^{-7}	$Cr(OH)_3$	6.7×10^{-31}
Chlorides		$CaCO_3$	8.7×10^{-9}	$Al(OH)_3$	2×10^{-32}
$PbCl_2$	1.6×10^{-5}	$BaCO_3$	1.6×10^{-9}	$Fe(OH)_3$	4×10^{-38}
$AgCl$	1.6×10^{-10}	$SrCO_3$	7×10^{-10}	$Co(OH)_3$	2.5×10^{-43}
$Hg_2Cl_2{}^*$	1.1×10^{-18}	$CuCO_3$	2.5×10^{-10}		
		$ZnCO_3$	2×10^{-10}	**Sulfides**	
Bromides		$MnCO_3$	8.8×10^{-11}	MnS	2.3×10^{-13}
$PbBr_2$	4.6×10^{-6}	$FeCO_3$	2.1×10^{-11}	FeS	3.7×10^{-19}
$AgBr$	5.0×10^{-13}	Ag_2CO_3	8.1×10^{-12}	NiS	3×10^{-21}
$Hg_2Br_2{}^*$	1.3×10^{-22}	$CdCO_3$	5.2×10^{-12}	CoS	5×10^{-22}
		$PbCO_3$	1.5×10^{-15}	ZnS	2.5×10^{-22}
Iodides		$MgCO_3$	1×10^{-15}	SnS	1×10^{-26}
PbI_2	1.4×10^{-8}	$Hg_2CO_3{}^*$	9.0×10^{-15}	CdS	1.0×10^{-28}
AgI	1.5×10^{-16}			PbS	7×10^{-29}
$Hg_2I_2{}^*$	4.5×10^{-29}	**Hydroxides**		CuS	8.5×10^{-45}
		$Ba(OH)_2$	5.0×10^{-3}	Ag_2S	1.6×10^{-49}
Sulfates		$Sr(OH)_2$	3.2×10^{-4}	HgS	1.6×10^{-54}
$CaSO_4$	6.1×10^{-5}	$Ca(OH)_2$	1.3×10^{-6}		
Ag_2SO_4	1.2×10^{-5}	$AgOH$	2.0×10^{-8}	**Phosphates**	
$SrSO_4$	3.2×10^{-7}	$Mg(OH)_2$	8.9×10^{-12}	Ag_3PO_4	1.8×10^{-18}
$PbSO_4$	1.3×10^{-8}	$Mn(OH)_2$	2×10^{-13}	$Sr_3(PO_4)_2$	1×10^{-31}
$BaSO_4$	1.5×10^{-9}	$Cd(OH)_2$	2.5×10^{-14}	$Ca_3(PO_4)_2$	1.3×10^{-32}
		$Pb(OH)_2$	1.2×10^{-15}	$Ba_3(PO_4)_2$	6×10^{-39}
Chromates		$Fe(OH)_2$	1.8×10^{-15}	$Pb_3(PO_4)_2$	1×10^{-54}
$SrCrO_4$	3.6×10^{-5}				

*Contains $Hg_2{}^{2+}$ ions. $K = [Hg_2{}^{2+}][X^-]^2$ for Hg_2X_2 salts, for example.

1. *Hydrolysis of carbonate ion.* The carbonate ion formed from the dissolution of calcium carbonate is a base that reacts with water to form bicarbonate ion and hydroxide ion.

$$CO_3{}^{2-}(aq) + H_2O(l) \overset{K_{b_1}}{\rightleftharpoons} HCO_3{}^-(aq) + OH^-(aq)$$

Because the carbonate ion is involved in this reaction, some of it is removed from the calcium carbonate solubility equilibrium. The net result, in accordance with Le Châtelier's principle, is that more of the calcium carbonate dissolves than we would predict.

2. *The interplay between the atmosphere and the ocean water.* Dissolved CO_2 from the air mixes with ocean water to form carbonic acid and, ultimately, hydrogen ion and bicarbonate ion.

$$CO_2(aq) + H_2O(l) \overset{K}{\rightleftharpoons} H_2CO_3(aq) \overset{K_{a_1}}{\rightleftharpoons} H^+(aq) + HCO_3{}^-(aq)$$

FIGURE 18.18

Even a system that seems as simple as the solubility of lead(II) iodide isn't. Most of the Pb^{2+} ions precipitate upon the addition of a small amount of iodide. However, a significant concentrate of Pb^{2+} remains.

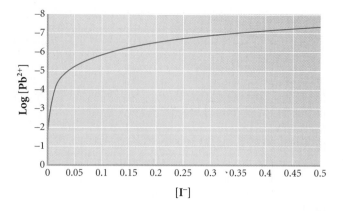

This interaction generates the bicarbonate ion, which influences the equilibrium shown at the bottom of page 803. The net result is to reduce the effect of the interaction of carbonate ions with water. The exact change depends on the amount of carbon dioxide dissolved in seawater.

3. *The formation of water from the reaction of hydrogen and hydroxide ions.* These are produced from the processes described in reactions 1 and 2.

$$H^+(aq) + OH^-(aq) \xrightleftharpoons{1/K_w} H_2O(l)$$

The effect of this reaction is an increase in the concentration of the bicarbonate ion generated from the carbon dioxide equilibrium.

As you can see, these three equilibria interact with others in the ocean as part of a remarkably complex system in which temperatures and concentrations change, making the calculation of calcium carbonate solubility at a given temperature most challenging.

Shifting our focus from the oceans to a more controlled setting, we find that side reactions can still confound apparently simple systems. Consider the solubility of lead(II) iodide (PbI_2) in distilled water. The amount of precipitated lead(II) iodide is related to the initial concentration of iodide as shown in Figure 18.18. *Not accounting for these changes can lead to massive errors in calculating the solubility of lead iodide.*

Molecular-Level Processes

We can take a simple view of the solubility of a salt such as calcium sulfate by considering only the dissociation reaction:

$$CaSO_4(s) \xrightleftharpoons{K_{sp}} Ca^{2+}(aq) + SO_4^{2-}(aq)$$

Our mass-action expression is

$$K_{sp} = [Ca^{2+}][SO_4^{2-}]$$

However, Meites, Pode, and Thomas wrote as early as 1966 that even in the absence of side reactions, the concentrations we would calculate would be wrong by about 60%, largely because of the tendency of the calcium and sulfate ions to stay together as individual **ion pairs**. When the small amount of calcium sulfate dissolves, most of it does not form individual ions. Rather, the ions associate intimately with each other. This is especially important in salts of highly charged (± 2 or ± 3) cations and anions. *The bottom line is that even in the absence of side reactions, such as the addition of H^+ to SO_4^{2-} to make HSO_4^- in acidic solution, there are several factors that affect solubility at the molecular level, making many such calculations challenging.* These factors include

1. *Formation of ion pairs,* as mentioned in the previous paragraph
2. *Ion activities,* a measure of the effective concentration of ions in solution
3. *Thermodynamic measures,* including enthalpy and entropy changes in the solution process

Some simple univalent (both cation and anion singly charged) systems do give reasonable answers when we do solubility calculations. In these cases, and others as well, the total number of moles of solute that dissolve per liter of solution is often called the **molar solubility**. For example, we can calculate the molar solubility of silver bromide (AgBr) by using its solubility product constant and mass-action expression.

$$AgBr(s) \rightleftharpoons Ag^+(aq) + Br^-(aq) \qquad K_{sp} = 5.0 \times 10^{-13}$$
$$K_{sp} = [Ag^+][Br^-]$$

We can set up our table, as we've done before. Although the solid AgBr will not enter into the mass-action expression, we'll include it in the K_{sp} ICE tables for the reasons mentioned below. In any case, the number of moles of silver bromide that will dissolve into solution and the number of moles of silver and bromide ions produced will all be equal, because there is a 1-to-1-to-1 mole ratio in the reaction. We can designate the molar solubility of AgBr as s, in which case the equilibrium concentrations, $[Ag^+]$ and $[Br^-]$, will also be s.

$$AgBr(s) \rightleftharpoons Ag^+(aq) + Br^-(aq)$$

initial	—		
change	$-s$	$+s$	$+s$
equilibrium	—	s	s

$$K_{sp} = [Ag^+][Br^-]$$
$$5.0 \times 10^{-13} = s^2$$
$$s = 7.1 \times 10^{-7}\ M = [Ag^+] = [Br^-]$$
$$s = \text{molar solubility of AgBr} = 7.1 \times 10^{-7}\ M$$

Qualitatively, what would we expect to happen to the solubility if we added a little sodium bromide, in which the added bromide is a common ion? According to Le Châtelier's principle, addition of an ion common to the product would push the dissociation reaction back to the left, further decreasing the solubility. Caution: If we add too much bromide ion, the solubility of silver bromide could actually *increase,* as a consequence of the formation of soluble species such as $AgBr_2^-$.

EXERCISE 18.11 **How Much Dissolves?**

One method of analyzing groundwater for nitrate requires that the chloride ions in the water sample be removed first. This is typically done by adding a solution of silver ions (Ag^+) in order to precipitate the sparingly soluble silver chloride salt (AgCl). What silver ion concentration is present when silver chloride is added to water?

$$AgCl(s) \rightleftharpoons Ag^+(aq) + Cl^-(aq) \qquad K_{sp} = 1.6 \times 10^{-10}$$

Solution

Setting up the table, we get

$$AgCl(s) \rightleftharpoons Ag^+(aq) + Cl^-(aq)$$

initial	—	0	0
change	$-s$	$+s$	$+s$
equilibrium	—	s	s

Then, as usual, we can find our equilibrium concentrations by solving the mass-action expression:

$$K_{sp} = [Ag^+][Cl^-]$$

$$1.6 \times 10^{-10} = (s)(s) = s^2$$

$$s = 1.3 \times 10^{-5}\ M$$

PRACTICE 18.11

Calculate the molar solubility of barium fluoride (BaF_2), $K_{sp} = 2.4 \times 10^{-5}$.

See Problems 49 and 50.

EXERCISE 18.12 **Calculating K_{sp}**

The concentration of calcium ions in a saturated solution of calcium fluoride was found to be $2.15 \times 10^{-4}\ M$. What is the apparent value for the solubility product constant, K_{sp}?

First Thoughts

This problem is asking the same question as the previous exercise, but in the reverse direction. The problem gives us the molar solubility of calcium ions, so we'll examine the equilibrium expression to determine how to calculate K_{sp}.

Solution

The equilibrium under consideration is

$$CaF_2(s) \rightleftharpoons Ca^{2+}(aq) + 2F^-(aq)$$

The mole ratio of Ca^{2+} to F^- is 1-to-2, so if the equilibrium concentration of Ca^{2+} is 2.15×10^{-4}, that of F^- must be twice as large, or $[F^-] = 4.30 \times 10^{-4}$. We can substitute these values into the mass-action expression.

$$K_{sp} = [Ca^{2+}][F^-]^2$$

$$K_{sp} = (2.15 \times 10^{-4})(4.30 \times 10^{-4})^2 = 3.98 \times 10^{-11}$$

Further Insight

The question asked us to calculate the apparent K_{sp} value. This was done because there may be some side reactions, activity considerations, or other factors that affect the molar solubility of the calcium fluoride salt. In particular, we have neglected the fact the fluoride ion (F^-) is a Brønsted base, which will affect the solubility of the calcium fluoride. (Can you propose how?) In this case, we've calculated a value for K_{sp} that is similar to the actual value, $K_{sp} = 4.00 \times 10^{-11}$.

PRACTICE 18.12

Calculate the apparent value of K_{sp} for lead bromide ($PbBr_2$) if the concentration of bromide in a saturated solution is $2.1 \times 10^{-2}\ M$.

See Problems 53 and 54.

Solubility, Precipitation, and Gravimetric Analysis

 Application

Chemical technicians can determine the concentration of substances in solution by causing them to form insoluble salt precipitates and weighing these precipitates or their related solids in a technique called gravimetric analysis. The quantitation of a sample on the basis of its mass is among the most powerful tools at the disposal of chemical technicians because good balances are both highly accurate and precise, and weighing a sample is fast and inexpensive. For example, the amount of chloride in a sample is routinely determined by combining the chloride ion with silver ion, forming the solid silver chloride as described in the Exercise 18.11.

$$Cl^-(aq) + Ag^+(aq) \rightleftharpoons AgCl(s)$$

Other substances can be routinely determined by gravimetric analysis. Aluminum ion concentrations can be found via the formation of aluminum hydroxide ($Al(OH)_3$). Igniting (driving off water at high temperature) the aluminum hydroxide forms aluminum oxide (Al_2O_3), which can then be weighed. Aluminum can also be determined by reaction with 8-hydroxyquinoline (C_9H_7ON) to form $Al(C_9H_6ON)_3$ without subsequent ignition.

$$Al^{3+}(aq) + 3C_9H_7ON(aq) \rightleftharpoons Al(C_9H_6ON)_3(s) + 3H^+(aq)$$

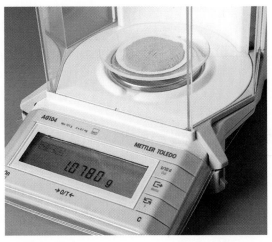

The concentration of aluminum in solution, like many metals, can be determined by gravimetric analysis. Here, aluminum is reacted to form the 8-hydroxyquinoline salt, which is made pure by recrystallization and weighed.

The solid forms good crystals that can be weighed after drying.

Sulfur can be determined by reaction of the sulfate (SO_4^{2-}) with barium ion to form barium sulfate:

$$SO_4^{2-}(aq) + Ba^{2+}(aq) \rightleftharpoons BaSO_4(s)$$

Calcium concentrations can be measured by reaction to form calcium oxalate (CaC_2O_4).

$$Ca^{2+}(aq) + C_2O_4^{2-}(aq) \rightleftharpoons CaC_2O_4(s)$$

In each of these analyses there are complicating factors, such as the presence of other elements that can react with the precipitating agents, as well as the complex nature of the precipitation process, so the procedures are a bit more involved than the simple reactions suggest. In fact, acid–base and other equilibria are nearly always a vital part of chemistry. Despite all of these concerns, a host of elements can be determined via precipitation. Understanding solubility equilibria and how we can affect them makes the analyses all the more meaningful.

Precipitation is also used in **metal recovery**, in which dissolved metals are reclaimed from processing wastes. Many metals in industrial effluents (runoff from manufacturing) are worth recovering because they are environmental hazards or they waste finite metal resources. Recycling these metals saves money and the environment. Such metals, which include copper, mercury, lead, and zinc, are typically recovered as their sulfide salts, although some metals can be precipitated as their corresponding carbonate salt.

 Application

To Precipitate or Not to Precipitate

Often, the formation of a precipitate is not as obvious as simply mixing two solutions containing ions that form a sparingly soluble salt. Let's say our chemical technician is interested in mixing two solutions, one containing silver ions and one containing chloride ions, so that the final concentrations are $[Ag^+] = 1.0 \times 10^{-4} M$ and $[Cl^-] = 1.0 \times 10^{-4} M$. Will mixing these solutions cause the formation of the insoluble AgCl? To answer this question, we can perform a calculation using our mass-action expression. However, because the concentrations do not reflect equilibrium conditions, we will be calculating the reaction quotient (recall this from Section 16.5) related to the solubility product. We'll call this Q_{sp}.

$$AgCl(s) \rightleftharpoons Cl^-(aq) + Ag^+(aq) \qquad K_{sp} = 1.6 \times 10^{-10}$$

$$Q_{sp} = [Ag^+]_0 [Cl^-]_0$$

$$Q_{sp} = (1.0 \times 10^{-4} M)(1.0 \times 10^{-4} M) = 1.0 \times 10^{-8}$$

The K_{sp} value for AgCl is 1.6×10^{-10}. This value is based on the equilibrium conditions of the sparingly soluble salt. The reaction quotient we calculated is 60 times greater than the equilibrium constant for the precipitation, so the AgCl precipitate forms. If the reaction quotient were smaller than the equilibrium value, no precipitate would form. To reiterate:

- If $Q_{sp} > K_{sp}$, a precipitate forms and continues to form until $Q_{sp} = K_{sp}$.
- If $Q_{sp} < K_{sp}$, no precipitate forms.

EXERCISE 18.13   Will It Make a Solid?

A chemical technician wishes to precipitate the lead ions in 100 mL of a water sample. If the water sample contains 3.10×10^{-10} M Pb^{2+}, and 100 mL of a solution containing 7.0×10^{-4} M Cl^- is added, will a precipitate form? K_{sp} for $PbCl_2 = 1.6 \times 10^{-5}$.

Solution

The solubility equilibrium is

$$PbCl_2(s) \rightleftharpoons Pb^{2+}(aq) + 2Cl^-(aq)$$

The mass-action expression is

$$K_{sp} = [Pb^{2+}] [Cl^-]^2$$

When the two solutions are mixed, the total volume is doubled, to 200 mL. Therefore the final concentrations of the respective ions after the two solutions are mixed become

$$[Pb^{2+}] = 1.55 \times 10^{-10} M$$

$$[Cl^-] = 3.5 \times 10^{-4} M$$

and Q_{sp} is

$$Q_{sp} = (1.55 \times 10^{-10}) (3.5 \times 10^{-4})^2 = 1.90 \times 10^{-17}$$

No, the chloride solution will not precipitate the lead in the sample.

PRACTICE 18.13

Will a precipitate form when equal volumes of the lead solution in the exercise above and 3.5×10^{-4} M sulfide ion are mixed? K_{sp} for PbS $= 7.0 \times 10^{-29}$.

See Problems 55 and 56. ▮

Acids, Bases, and Solubility

Application

The chemical technician who works at the water treatment center is often responsible for treating waste water before it is returned to the environment. One such treatment is **sedimentation**, in which aluminum sulfate, $Al_2(SO_4)_3$ and calcium hydroxide, $Ca(OH)_2$, are added to help clarify and purify the wastewater (Figure 18.19). The aluminum and hydroxide ions in the solution form a gelatinous precipitate.

$$Al^{3+}(aq) + 3OH^-(aq) \rightleftharpoons Al(OH)_3(s) \qquad K_{sp} = 2 \times 10^{-32}$$

The solid settles, carrying with it some dissolved organic material, microorganisms and other undesirable substances in a process called **coagulation**. Iron(III) hydroxide can also be used in this way.

On the other hand, increasing the acidity of waterways can increase the concentration of undesirable metals. For example, lead can be found naturally as the insoluble sulfide, PbS. When acidic waters contact the natural lead sulfide, hydrogen ions compete via Le Châtelier's principle to form hydrogen sulfide, H_2S. This

allows the lead ion to enter the waterway as Pb^{2+}. The equilibrium constant for the process is not especially high ($K \approx 10^{-7}$), but the leaching of metals, including lead, mercury, cadmium and aluminum into waterways, even at low concentrations, is of concern.

18.4 Complex-Ion Equilibria

We noted before that adding a common ion to a solution of a sparingly soluble salt affects its solubility. We said that if too much of the common ion were added, the sparingly soluble salt could dissolve instead of precipitate. This interesting phenomenon arises because of the formation of a chemical complex, which typically consists of one or more metal cations bonded to one or more Lewis bases known as ligands (recall that such bases donate electrons). Examples of ligands include Cl^-, F^-, OH^-, CN^-, NH_3, and H_2O. The complexes can be anions, as with $AgCl_4^{-3}$, or cations, such as $Co(NH_3)_6^{3+}$. Each of these ionic complexes has one or more ions of opposite charge to balance the total charge in the solution.

Introducing the Formation Constant

Our first example of a chemical complex begins with the zinc cation, which exists in aqueous solution bonded to four water molecules, written as $Zn(H_2O)_4^{2+}$. In an ammonia–ammonium ion buffer, an ammonia molecule replaces a water molecule.

$$Zn(H_2O)_4^{2+}(aq) + NH_3(aq) \rightleftharpoons ZnNH_3(H_2O)_3^{2+}(aq) + H_2O(l)$$

We will next simplify the expression by assuming the presence of water, as we often do in acid–base reactions, and simplify the expression.

$$Zn^{2+}(aq) + NH_3(aq) \rightleftharpoons Zn(NH_3)^{2+}(aq) \qquad K_{f_1} = 190$$

The equilibrium constant for the formation of the zinc–ammonia complex is called its formation constant (K_f) or stability constant, and conceptually, *it means the same thing as any other equilibrium constant*. Le Châtelier's principle teaches us that as we add more ammonia, more NH_3 ligands will form coordinate covalent bonds with the central atom, each step having its own formation constant.

$$Zn(NH_3)^{2+}(aq) + NH_3(aq) \rightleftharpoons Zn(NH_3)_2^{2+}(aq) \qquad K_{f_2} = 220$$

$$Zn(NH_3)_2^{2+}(aq) + NH_3(aq) \rightleftharpoons Zn(NH_3)_3^{2+}(aq) \qquad K_{f_3} = 250$$

$$Zn(NH_3)_3^{2+}(aq) + NH_3(aq) \rightleftharpoons Zn(NH_3)_4^{2+}(aq) \qquad K_{f_4} = 110$$

FIGURE 18.20

Here are the changes that occur in the equilibrium concentrations of the various zinc–ammonia complex ions as we increase the concentration of ammonia. The x-axis displays log [NH$_3$], so that each factor of 10 by which we change [NH$_3$] occupies equal space in the plot.

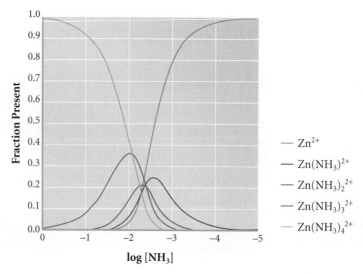

— Zn^{2+}
— Zn(NH$_3$)$^{2+}$
— Zn(NH$_3$)$_2^{2+}$
— Zn(NH$_3$)$_3^{2+}$
— Zn(NH$_3$)$_4^{2+}$

Figure 18.20 shows the distribution of the various zinc–ammonia complexes as the ammonia concentration is increased. Because the formation constants of the steps are so similar, several different zinc–ammonia species are typically present in solution, as shown in the figure. Going from Zn^{2+} to Zn(NH$_3$)$_4^{2+}$ does not give a clear, sharp endpoint, and in general, metal-ion concentrations cannot be analyzed by titration that involves a process with multiple formation constants. **Is it possible to have a titrant that will completely combine with a single reaction in a 1-to-1 mole ratio with the metal ion, in order to determine its concentration?** This is where EDTA, introduced as a titrant in Section 18.1, comes in.

Application

CHEMICAL ENCOUNTERS: Commercial Uses of Aminopolycarboxylic Acid Chelating Agents

FIGURE 18.21

EDTA is a most important chelating agent. Solutions of EDTA are typically prepared as the disodium salt (Na$_2$EDTA), with EDTA^{2-} shown here as a Lewis dot structure (top) and in a free-energy-minimized configuration (bottom), including the two sodium ions.

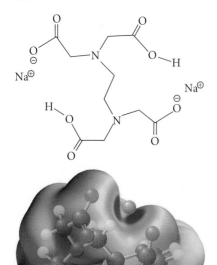

Extending the Discussion to EDTA

EDTA is a very useful compound for titrations. It is typically used in its most basic form, shown in Figure 18.21. It has *six* pairs of electrons, one pair on each of the two nitrogen atoms and one pair on each of four oxygen atoms, which form between four and six coordinate covalent bonds to a single metal ion such as Ca^{2+}. Substances that form multiple bonds in this way are called **chelates** (the Greek word *chele* means "claw") or chelating agents because they grab the metal ion like a set of claws. These substances are further characterized by the number of coordinate covalent bonds they make to the metal ion. Ammonia (NH$_3$) is a **monodentate ligand** (one-toothed ligand). EDTA can be a **tetradentate ligand** (four-toothed ligand) or a **hexadentate ligand** (six-toothed ligand). In Chapter 16, we saw the very high equilibrium constants (formation constants) for the reactions of EDTA with metals, shown in Table 18.4. Note in the table how the higher charge on the Fe^{3+} results in a dramatically higher formation constant with EDTA compared to that of Fe^{2+}. We now see that the great stability of such metal–chelate complexes is a result of the **polydentate** nature of the ligand. Several industrially important polydentate chelating agents are listed in Table 18.5. These compounds are so useful that well over 150 million kg are used annually in a host of different products and applications, some of which are listed in Table 18.6.

Complex formation with EDTA and its chemical relatives can be used to determine the concentration of many metals, such as zinc, aluminum, nickel, cobalt, iron, and, in the study of the hardness of water, calcium, and magnesium. We can write the reaction of the calcium ion with EDTA in ionic equation form:

$$Ca^{2+}(aq) + EDTA^{4-}(aq) \rightleftharpoons CaEDTA^{2-}(aq)$$

or we can give it more visual clarity by giving Lewis structures as well as space-filling models, as shown in Section 18.1. Because the equilibrium

TABLE 18.4	Formation Constants of Some Metal–EDTA Complexes	
Element	Cation	K_f
silver	Ag^+	2.1×10^7
calcium	Ca^{2+}	5.0×10^{10}
cobalt	Co^{2+}	2.0×10^{16}
zinc	Zn^{2+}	3.0×10^{16}
iron(II)	Fe^{2+}	2.1×10^{14}
nickel	Ni^{2+}	3.6×10^{18}
bismuth	Bi^{3+}	8.0×10^{27}
iron(III)	Fe^{3+}	1.7×10^{24}
vanadium	V^{3+}	8.0×10^{25}

TABLE 18.5 Industrially Important Aminopolycarboxylic Acid Chelating Agents

Name and Abbreviation

Ethylenediaminetetraacetic acid, EDTA

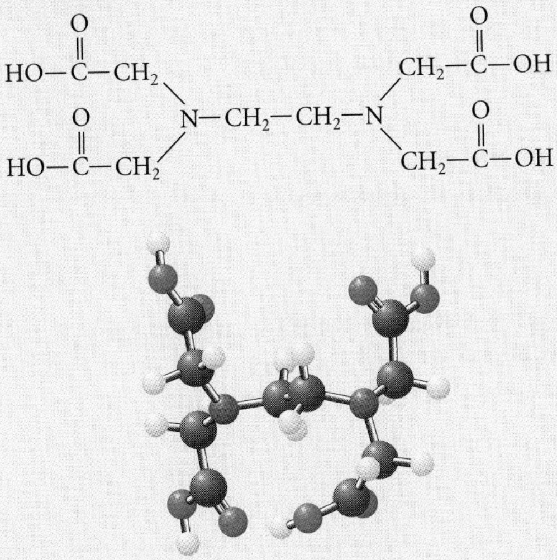

Name and Abbreviation

Diethylenetriaminepentaacetic acid, DTPA

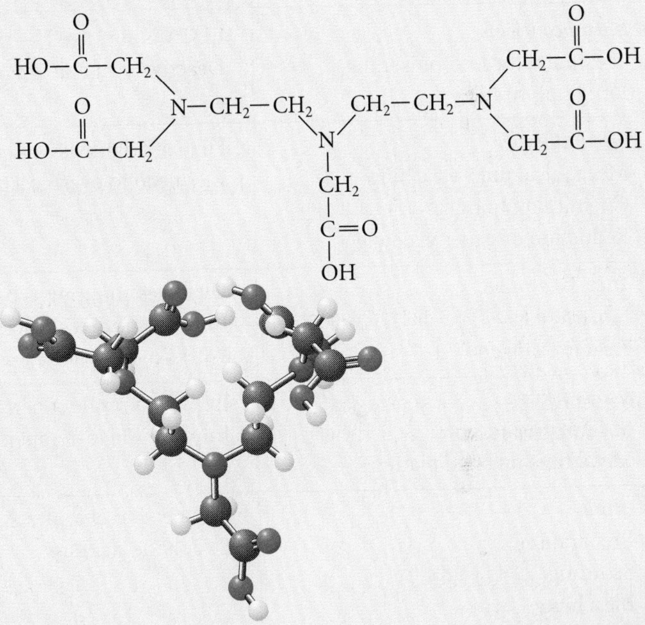

N-(hydroxyethyl)-ethylenediaminetriacetic acid, HEDTA

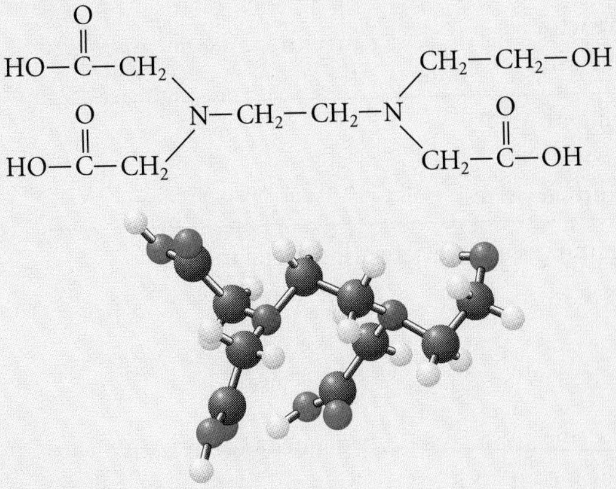

Nitrilotriacetic acid, NTA

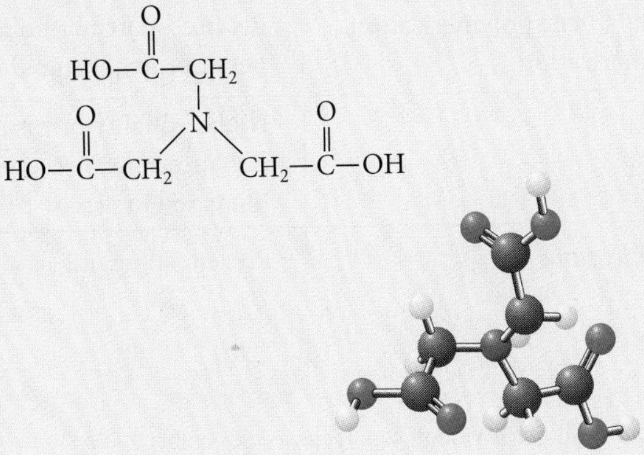

TABLE 18.6	Products and Applications of Chelating Agents	
Application	**Benefits of Using Chelating Agents**
Foods and Beverages Canned seafood products Dressings, sauces, spreads Canned beans Beverages	Protects the natural flavor, color, texture, and nutritive value of your food products Improves shelf life and consumer appeal
Cleaning Products Heavy-duty laundry detergents Hard-surface cleaners	Better foaming, detergency, and rinsing in hard water Helps remove metal oxides and salts from fabrics Enhances shelf life by inhibiting rancidity, clouding, and discoloration Improved consumer appeal and product value Improved germicidal action
Personal Care Products Creams, lotions Bar and liquid soaps Shampoos Hair preparations	Better lathering in shampoos and soaps, particularly in the presence of hard water Improves shelf life and consumer appeal Prevents softening, brown spotting, and cracking in bar soaps Improves stability of fragrances, fats, oils, and other water-soluble ingredients
Pharmaceuticals Treatment for lead poisoning Drug stabilization	EDTA is approved by the FDA for use in treatment of heavy-metal poisoning Deactivates metal ions that interfere with drug performance
Pulp and Paper Mechanical pulp bleaching Chemical pulping Reduction of paper yellowing	Higher brightness and/or lower bleaching costs Less need to overbleach to ensure specified brightness level
Water Treatment Boilers Heat exchangers	Dissolves common types of scale during normal operation Improves process efficiency and reduces downtime Works over a wide range of temperatures, pH levels, and pressures
Metalworking Surface preparation Metal finishing and plating	Improved product performance in hard water Improved high-temperature performance
Textiles Preparation Scouring Bleaching	Less need to overbleach to ensure specified brightness level Dye shade stability
Agriculture Chelated micronutrients	Excellent water solubility makes metal chelants more readily utilized by plants than the inorganic forms of metals
Polymerization Styrene–butadiene polymerization PVC polymerization	Stable polymerization rates Reduced polymer buildup in reactors Better polymer stability and shelf life
Photography Developers Bleaches	Higher-quality prints and negatives Enhanced silver recovery Increased longevity of prints and negatives
Oilfield Applications Drilling Production Recovery	Prevents plugging, sealing, precipitation by deactivating metal ions

Source: Dow Chemical, http://www.dow.com (accessed September 2005).

constant is so high, the reaction is essentially complete. This is important when designing a titration. It is also vital in another of EDTA's important uses: combining with metals in food products so that they are unavailable to participate in spoilage processes. To put it in a more formal way, the metal ions are **sequestered** (tied up) by EDTA.

The hard-water analysis at pH 10 allows EDTA to react with both calcium and magnesium ions in the water, which is a measure of "total hardness." At pH values above 12, magnesium ions precipitate as the hydroxide, and the analysis allows determination of the calcium ion concentration alone. Here again, as is our theme in this discussion, pH control is vital. Let's look more closely at the relationship of pH to the reaction. **Why should the titration of calcium with EDTA be more complete at basic than at acidic pH values?**

The Importance of the Conditional Formation Constant

Equilibrium represents a competition—a wrestling match between substances to acquire and release ions and molecules in their quest for energetic stability, as measured by the minimum system free energy. In an aqueous solution of calcium and EDTA, the primary competitor is hydrogen ion. The acidic H_4EDTA can lose four protons in stepwise fashion to form $EDTA^{4-}$.

$$H_4EDTA \rightleftharpoons H_3EDTA^- + H^+ \qquad K_{a_1} = 1.0 \times 10^{-2}$$

$$H_3EDTA^- \rightleftharpoons H_2EDTA^{2-} + H^+ \qquad K_{a_2} = 2.2 \times 10^{-3}$$

$$H_2EDTA^{2-} \rightleftharpoons HEDTA^{3-} + H^+ \qquad K_{a_3} = 6.9 \times 10^{-7}$$

$$HEDTA^{3-} \rightleftharpoons EDTA^{4-} + H^+ \qquad K_{a_4} = 5.5 \times 10^{-11}$$

The higher the pH, the greater the fraction of $EDTA^{-4}$ in the aqueous solution as hydrogen ions are sequentially removed from the molecule. Figure 18.22 shows that as the pH goes down (the solution is made more acidic), the fraction of EDTA present as $EDTA^{4-}$ (highlighted in the figure) diminishes drastically. The tendency to form protonated EDTA reduces the stability of the calcium–EDTA complex with reactions such as this:

$$CaEDTA^{2-} + H^+ \rightleftharpoons Ca^{2+} + HEDTA^{3-}$$

We show this reduction in stability via the **conditional formation constant (K′)**, which takes into account the fractions of the free (uncomplexed) metal ion and the $EDTA^{4-}$.

$$K' = K_f \, \alpha_{Ca^{2+}} \, \alpha_{EDTA^{4-}}$$

where $\alpha_{Ca^{2+}}$ = fraction of free Ca^{2+} (1, in this case)
$\alpha_{EDTA^{4-}}$ = fraction of EDTA present as $EDTA^{4-}$

For example, with our buffer system at pH = 10.0, the formation constant, K_f, for the titration reaction is 5×10^{10} and $\alpha_{Ca^{2+}} = 1$. It is possible to calculate $\alpha_{EDTA^{4-}}$, but we will simply estimate it from Figure 18.22 as being roughly 0.10.

$$K' = K_f \alpha_{Ca^{2+}} \alpha_{EDTA^{4-}} = 5 \times 10^{10} \, (1)(0.10) = 5 \times 10^9$$

The conditional formation constant is still sufficiently high for the titration to be essentially complete. If, however, we calculate the conditional formation constant at pH = 3.0, at which point very little of the EDTA is present as $EDTA^{4-}$ and $\alpha_{EDTA^{4-}} = 2 \times 10^{-11}$, we get

$$K' = K_f \alpha_{Ca^{2+}} \, \alpha_{EDTA^{4-}} = 5 \times 10^{10} \, (1)(2 \times 10^{-11}) = 1$$

The conditional formation constant is far too low for the titration to be feasible.

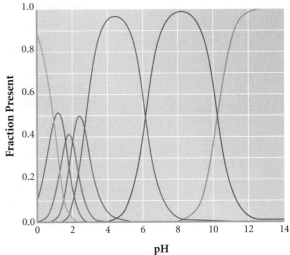

FIGURE 18.22

As the pH is lowered, the fraction of $EDTA^{4-}$ sharply decreases, reducing the conditional stability constant of any metal–EDTA titration. This is one of several factors that is important to consider when selecting the best pH for this type of analysis.

— $EDTA^{4-}$
— $HEDTA^{3-}$
— H_2EDTA^{2-}
— H_3EDTA^-
— H_4EDTA
— H_5EDTA^+
— H_6EDTA^{2+}

Fraction Present

pH

EXERCISE 18.14 **Conditional Formation Constant**

With some metals, the competition between EDTA and ammonia to bond to the metal ion can become important when we are judging the feasibility of a titration. If we were titrating zinc instead of calcium in our pH = 10 ammonia buffer, we would find that the zinc would form complex ions ranging from $Zn(NH_3)^{2+}$ to $Zn(NH_3)_4^{2+}$. This would make the fraction of free Zn^{2+}, $\alpha_{Zn^{2+}}$, less than 1, lowering the conditional formation constant.

$$Zn^{2+}(aq) + EDTA^{4-}(aq) \rightleftharpoons ZnEDTA^{2-}(aq) \qquad K_f = 3 \times 10^{16}$$

Calculate the conditional formation constant for the titration of zinc with EDTA in the pH = 10 buffer in which $\alpha_{Zn^{2+}} = 8 \times 10^{-6}$, and $\alpha_{EDTA^{4-}} = 0.10$. Is this titration still feasible in spite of the low fraction of uncomplexed zinc?

First Thoughts

We can solve for the conditional formation constant, K_f, just as we did with the calcium–EDTA system. Here, however, the fraction of free metal ion is very low.

Solution

$$K' = K_f \alpha_{Zn^{2+}} \alpha_{EDTA^{4-}} = 3 \times 10^{16} (8 \times 10^{-6})(0.10) = 2.4 \times 10^{10}$$

This value for K' is still quite large, and the titration works well.

Further Insights

Keep in mind that in spite of the various α and K terms we are working with, a key question with which we are concerned is "How much of each reactant is available to react?" In the case of the zinc ion, the answer is "Not much at all." With the EDTA, there is a much higher fraction available. To reinforce the point we have brought up before, it is the beauty of EDTA that even when the fraction of available reactant is low, the titration is still practical.

PRACTICE 18.14

Calculate the conditional formation constant, K_f, for the system in Exercise 18.14 at pH = 3.0.

See Problems 63 and 64. ∎

In the titration of metals with EDTA, we have seen equilibrium principles all come together in one of the most important types of aqueous analyses at the disposal of the chemical technician. Recall Table 18.1 at the beginning of the chapter, in which we listed the calcium–EDTA titration-based hard-water analysis among several ones that are commonly done. Equilibrium principles make these processes ideal for use in many everyday venues. That EDTA titrations are so very common in industrial and academic settings is testimony to the universal utility of equilibrium theory and practice.

EXERCISE 18.15 **Data for a Calcium–EDTA Analysis**

Here are some data obtained from the titration of calcium ion in water with EDTA. How many milligrams of calcium are there per liter of water?

The EDTA solution was prepared by combining the disodium salt Na_2H_2EDTA with water. Its molarity is 0.01944 M. About 5 mL of an ammonia–ammonium ion buffer are combined with a 50.00 mL aliquot of the water. The resulting solution is titrated with EDTA, and it requires 31.88 mL to reach the Eriochrome Black T indicator endpoint, shown by a color change from wine red to blue.

Solution

We begin by finding the mass of calcium in the 50.00 mL aliquot.

Grams of Ca in the 50.00 mL aliquot

$$= 0.03188 \text{ L EDTA solution} \times \frac{0.01944 \text{ mol EDTA}}{1 \text{ L EDTA sol'n}} \times \frac{1 \text{ mol Ca}}{1 \text{ mol EDTA}} \times \frac{40.08 \text{ g Ca}}{1 \text{ mol Ca}}$$

$$= 0.02484 \text{ g Ca in the 50.00 mL aliquot}$$

To convert to the 1 L sample, we use dimensional analysis to scale up to the 1 L volume:

$$0.02484 \text{ g} \times \frac{1000 \text{ mL}}{50 \text{ mL}} = 0.497 \approx 0.500 \text{ g/L calcium}$$

This is equal to 500 mg/L, which is the same as 500 parts per million, or 500 ppm (recall the discussion about ppm in Section 4.2), of calcium in the solution. This corresponds to fairly hard water.

PRACTICE 18.15

How many milliliters of the EDTA solution described in this exercise would be needed to titrate a 50.00 mL sample of water containing 123.8 ppm Ca?

See Problems 65 and 66.

The Bottom Line

- A titration is a technique used to find out how much of a substance is in a solution. (Section 18.2)

- There are several types of titrations, including reduction–oxidation, precipitation, complex-formation, and acid–base titration. (Section 18.2)

- Many reactions are pH-sensitive and require buffers to control pH. (Section 18.1)

- A buffer resists change in pH upon addition of a strong acid or strong base or upon dilution. (Section 18.1)

- Buffers are typically composed of weak conjugate acid–base pairs. (Section 18.1)

- We can solve for the pH of buffers in a straight-forward way by recognizing the importance of Le Châtelier's principle and the common-ion effect. (Section 18.1)

- We can calculate the approximate ratio of conjugate acid to base in order to prepare a buffer of a known pH. Activity effects are important, and our acid-to-base ratio will probably need to be slightly adjusted to be at the desired pH. (Section 18.1)

- Solving for the pH of a buffer upon addition of strong acid or base is really solving a limiting-reactant problem. (Section 18.1)

- It is possible to exceed the buffer capacity, in which case the pH will go sharply higher (with excess base) or lower (with excess acid). (Section 18.1)

- Strong-acid–strong-base titrations show a relatively level pH until near the equivalence point, where the pH dramatically changes. (Section 18.2)

- Titration curves in which one component is weak and the other is strong contain four regions: the initial pH, the buffer region, the equivalence-point region and the post–equivalence point region. (Section 18.2)

- The buffer region contains a point at which one-half of the analyte has been converted to its conjugate. This is called the titration midpoint, and the pH is equal to the pK_a of the analyte. (Section 18.2)

- The larger the pK of the analyte, the sharper will be the change in pH at the equivalence point. (Section 18.2)

- The higher the concentration of the weak acid (or base) and the strong base (or acid), the sharper the endpoint. (Section 18.2)

- An indicator is used to visually detect the equivalence point of a titration. (Section 18.2)

- Only a few drops of an indicator are added to the titration solution so that the equivalence point and endpoint can be as close together as possible. (Section 18.2)

■ Solubility equilibria can often be complex, involving several side reactions and molecular-level processes that make calculations challenging. (Section 18.3)

■ The effects of ion-pairing, activity, and other thermodynamic considerations add to the challenge of properly calculating the concentration of dissolved salts in aqueous solution. (Section 18.3)

■ Gravimetric analysis is based on weighing the precipitate that includes the substance of interest. (Section 18.3)

■ The pH of an aqueous solution can significantly affect the solubility of the substances in that solution. (Section 18.3)

■ A chemical complex typically consists of one or more metal cations bonded to one or more Lewis bases. (Section 18.4)

■ The formation constant is a measure of the extent of reaction between a Lewis base and metal ion in aqueous solution. (Section 18.4)

■ EDTA is the primary example of a highly effective chelating agent. (Section 18.4)

■ The reaction of chelating agents and metal ions has a very high formation constant. (Section 18.4)

■ The analysis of calcium in hard water by EDTA titration is an important application of complex-ion equilibrium. (Section 18.4)

Key Words

acid–base indicator A compound that changes color on the basis of the pH of the solution in which it is dissolved. The color change is often a result of structural changes due to protonation or deprotonation of acidic groups within the compound. (*p. 799*)

analyte A solute whose concentration is to be measured by a laboratory test. (*p. 766*)

anthocyanins A naturally occurring class of compounds responsible for many of the colors of plants. These compounds often act as acid–base indicators. (*p. 801*)

boiler scale A buildup of calcium and magnesium salts within pipes and water heaters. Typically composed of calcium carbonate and magnesium carbonate. (*p. 767*)

buffer A solution containing a weak acid and its conjugate base or a weak base and its conjugate acid. Buffers resist changes in pH upon the addition of acid or base or by dilution. (*p. 767*)

buffer capacity The degree to which a buffer can "absorb" added acid or base without changing pH. (*p. 779*)

buffer region The region of a titration indicated by the presence of a weak acid or base and its conjugate. The pH changes little within this region. (*p. 793*)

calcareous oozes The calcium-containing detritus from dead single-celled, calcium-based sea life. (*p. 802*)

chelates Substances capable of associating through coordinate covalent bonds to a metal ion. Also known as chelating agents. (*p. 810*)

coagulation The precipitation of a solid along with some dissolved organic material, microorganisms and other undesirable substances (*p. 808*)

conditional formation constant (K') The formation constant that accounts for the free metal ion and its associated ligand. (*p. 813*)

equivalence point The exact point at which the reactant in a titration has been neutralized by the titrant. (*p. 789*)

flue-gas desulfurization A process used to remove sulfur dioxide (and other sulfur oxides) from combustion smoke. (*p. 779*)

formation constant (K_f) The equilibrium constant describing the formation of a stable complex. Typically, K_f values are large. Also known as the stability constant. (*p. 809*)

Good (Good's) buffers Buffers typically used in biochemical research because they are chemically stable in the presence of enzymes or visible light and are easy to prepare. (*p. 785*)

gravimetric analysis A laboratory technique in which the concentration of substances in solution is determined by forming insoluble salt precipitates and weighing them or their related solids. (*p. 806*)

Henderson–Hasselbalch equation A shorthand equation used to determine the pH of a buffer solution. $pH = pK_a + \log(\text{base/acid})$. (*p. 778*)

hexadentate ligand A ligand that makes six coordinate covalent bonds to a metal ion. (*p. 810*)

ion pair Ions in solution that associate as a unit. (*p. 804*)

ligand A compound that associates with a metal ion through coordinate covalent bonds. (*p. 809*)

metal recovery Recycling of metals from waste streams by complexation with chelating agents. (*p. 807*)

molar solubility The total number of moles of solute that dissolve per liter of solution. (*p. 805*)

monodentate ligand A ligand that makes one coordinate covalent bond to a metal ion. (*p. 810*)

pH indicator A compound that changes color on the basis of the acidity or basicity of the solution in which it is dissolved. Also known as an acid–base indicator. (*p. 799*)

polydentate Capable of forming several coordinate covalent bonds from a single ligand to a metal. (*p. 810*)

quality control The practice in industry of ensuring that the product contains what it is supposed to, and in the proper amounts. (*p. 766*)

scrubbing The process of removing harmful impurities from smokestack gases. (*p. 779*)

sedimentation The process of removing dissolved organic matter, heavy metals, and other impurities from water. (*p. 808*)

sequester To tie up an ion or compound by chelation and make it unavailable for use. (*p. 813*)

solubility product The mass-action expression for the solubility reaction of a sparingly soluble salt. (*p. 802*)

solubility product constant (K_{sp}) The constant that is part of the solubility product mass-action expression. Typically, K_{sp} values are much less than 1. (*p. 802*)

stability constant *See* formation constant. (*p. 809*)

tetradentate ligand A ligand that makes four coordinate covalent bonds to a metal ion. (*p. 810*)

titrant The solution being added to a solution of an analyte during a titration. (*p. 766*)

titration The process used to determine the exact concentration of an analyte. (*p. 766*)

titration curve A plot of the pH of the solution versus the volume (or concentration) of titrant. (*p. 790*)

titration endpoint The volume and pH at which the indicator has changed color during a titration. The endpoint is not always the same as the equivalence point. (*p. 801*)

titration midpoint The pH of the titration where the concentration of weak acid or base is equal to the concentration of its conjugate. At this point, the pH is equal to the pK_a of the analyte. (*p. 794*)

Focus Your Learning

The answers to the odd-numbered problems appear at the back of the book.

Section 18.1 Buffers and the Common-Ion Effect

Skill Review

1. Write the equations that would describe the equilibria present in each of these solutions:
   a. $0.10\ M\ NH_3$
   b. $0.250\ M\ Fe(OH)_3$
   c. $0.125\ M\ HCOONa$

2. Write the equations that would describe the equilibria present in each of these solutions:
   a. $0.30\ M\ PbS$
   b. $0.150\ M\ NH_4Cl$
   c. $0.050\ M\ CH_3COOH$

3. Decide which, if any, of these pairs could be used to prepare a buffer solution.
   a. HF and NaF
   b. CH_3COOH and NH_3
   c. NH_4Cl and HF
   d. H_2SO_4 and $NaHSO_4$
   e. NH_4NO_3 and NH_3

4. Decide which, if any, of these pairs could be used to prepare a buffer solution.
   a. KBr and HBr
   b. NaOH and CH_3COOH
   c. HCOOH and HNO_3
   d. $NaNO_3$ and HNO_3
   e. CH_3COONa and HCl

5. Without using the Henderson–Hasselbalch equation, calculate the pH of a buffer made from each of these pairs. Assume that the concentrations given are those in the final mixture.
   a. $1.00\ M\ NH_3$ and $1.00\ M\ NH_4Cl$
   b. $4.50\ M\ NH_4Cl$ and $0.50\ M\ NH_3$
   c. $2.50\ M\ CH_3COOH$ and $0.75\ M\ CH_3COONa$

6. Without using the Henderson–Hasselbalch equation, calculate the pH of a buffer made from each of these pairs. Assume the concentrations given are those in the final mixture.
   a. $2.33\ M\ NH_3$ and $1.00\ M\ NH_4Cl$
   b. $2.50\ M\ HCOOH$ and $1.50\ M\ HCOONa$
   c. $0.100\ M\ CH_3COOH$ and $0.75\ M\ CH_3COONa$

7. Suppose an ammonia–ammonium buffer has pH of 10.1. Indicate the effect, if any, of each of these changes:
   a. Adding NH_3
   b. Adding NH_4^+
   c. Adding Cl^-

8. Suppose an acetic acid–acetate buffer has pH of 4.74. Indicate the effect, if any, of each of these changes:
   a. Adding NH_3
   b. Adding Na^+
   c. Adding HCl

9. Suppose you were to prepare a buffer solution using acetic acid and sodium acetate. What would be the molar ratio of acid to its conjugate when the pH was adjusted to each of these values?
   a. pH = 3.74
   b. pH = 4.74
   c. pH = 5.74

10. Suppose you were to prepare a buffer solution using ammonia and ammonium chloride. What would be the molar ratio of acid to its conjugate when the pH was adjusted to each of these values?
    a. pH = 10.10
    b. pH = 9.26
    c. pH = 8.40

11. How many milliliters of $0.20\ M$ HCl would we have to add to 100.0 mL of $0.2500\ M$ ammonia in order to prepare a buffer that has each of these pH values?
    a. pH = 9.26
    b. pH = 10.5
    c. pH = 8.5

12. How many milliliters of $0.150\ M$ NaOH would we have to add to 100.0 mL of $0.100\ M$ acetic acid in order to prepare a buffer that has each of these pH values?
    a. pH = 4.26
    b. pH = 3.75
    c. pH = 5.25

13. Indicate the approximate pH of a buffer made from equal concentrations of each of these pairs. You may need to use the appendix to determine K_a values.
    a. NH_3 / NH_4^+ b. CH_3COOH / CH_3COO^-
    c. $HCOOH$ / $HCOO^-$

14. Indicate the approximate pH of a buffer made from equal concentrations of each of these pairs. You may need to use the appendix to determine K_a values.
    a. $C_6H_5COOH/C_6H_5COO^-$ b. $CH_3NH_2/CH_3NH_3^+$
    c. H_3BO_3 / $H_2BO_3^-$

15. List and explain the factors that determine the pH of a buffered system.

16. List and explain the factors that determine the buffer capacity of a buffered system.

17. A buffer is prepared using chloroacetic acid ($ClCH_2COOH$, $K_a = 1.4 \times 10^{-3}$) and potassium chloroacetate ($ClCH_2COOK$).
    a. Write out the key equilibrium expressions.
    b. Calculate the pH of a solution made by diluting 1.5 g of potassium chloroacetate with 100.0 mL of 0.10 M chloroacetic acid.

18. A buffer is prepared using pyridine (C_5H_5N, $K_b = 1.7 \times 10^{-9}$) and pyridinium chloride (C_5H_5NHCl)
    a. Write out the key equilibrium expressions.
    b. Calculate the pH of a solution made by dissolving 2.50 g of pyridine and 1.25 g of pyridinium chloride into a solution with a final volume of 100.0 mL.

19. The K_b value of methylamine (CH_3NH_2) is 4.3×10^{-4}. The conjugate acid of this weak organic base is the methylammonium ion ($CH_3NH_3^+$, $K_a = 2.3 \times 10^{-11}$). Calculate the pH of a solution that is made from a solution containing 0.10 mol of methylamine and 0.20 mol of methylammonium ion, first using the K_a approach and then using the K_b approach.

20. The K_a value of benzoic acid (C_6H_5COOH) is 6.46×10^{-5}. The conjugate base of this weak organic acid is the benzoate anion ($C_6H_5COO^-$). Calculate the pH of a solution containing 0.025 mol of benzoic acid and 0.250 mol of benzoate anion, first using the K_a approach and then using the K_b approach.

21. Determine the pH of an ammonia–ammonium buffer ($K_b = 1.8 \times 10^{-5}$) with each of these concentrations:
    a. $[NH_3] = 0.10\ M$; $[NH_4^+] = 0.10\ M$
    b. $[NH_3] = 0.20\ M$; $[NH_4^+] = 0.050\ M$
    c. $[NH_3] = 1.50\ M$; $[NH_4^+] = 0.10\ M$
    d. $[NH_3] = 0.050\ M$; $[NH_4^+] = 0.750\ M$

22. Determine the pH of a phenol (C_6H_5OH) / phenoxide ($C_6H_5O^-$) buffer ($K_a = 1.28 \times 10^{-10}$) with these concentrations:
    a. $[C_6H_5OH] = 0.20\ M$; $[C_6H_5O^-] = 0.050\ M$
    b. $[C_6H_5OH] = 1.00\ M$; $[C_6H_5O^-] = 1.00\ M$
    c. $[C_6H_5OH] = 0.050\ M$; $[C_6H_5O^-] = 0.10\ M$
    d. $[C_6H_5OH] = 0.70\ M$; $[C_6H_5O^-] = 0.45\ M$

Chemical Applications and Practices

23. Physiologically important buffers help maintain proper pH levels within our cells. Although the actual buffer system is a complex mixture, we can focus on one particular system that involves phosphate ions. The pH of human blood must be maintained at approximately 7.40. What would you calculate as the ratio of dihydrogen phosphate ($H_2PO_4^-$) to monohydrogen phosphate (HPO_4^{2-}) at that pH? You will need to consult the acid dissociation table for the appropriate equilibrium value.

24. Another important buffer system for humans is formed between carbonic acid and the bicarbonate ion. Calculate the molar ratio of bicarbonate ion to carbonic acid present at pH 7.40. Obtain the necessary equilibrium constant from the table of acid dissociation constants.

25. When studying bacterial growth, microbiologists must determine the optimum pH range for maximum growth. Then, during subsequent culturing, this range can be maintained through proper application of buffer chemistry. The K_a value of formic acid ($HCOOH$) is 1.8×10^{-4}.
    a. If this acid and its salt, sodium formate ($HCOONa$), were selected as the main buffer in a bacteria growth medium, what would be the resulting pH of the media when 500.0 mL of 0.20 M formic acid was mixed with 0.45 g of sodium formate?
    b. Would this buffer be better equipped to resist changes in an acidic or basic direction? Explain.

26. Referring to the same situation as presented for the microbiologist in Problem 25, calculate the volume of 2.5 M NaOH that would be needed to neutralize the 0.20 M formic acid solution to prepare a formic acid–sodium formate buffer with a pH of 3.85.

27. Dairy products such as yogurt, buttermilk, and sour cream are made with the aid of bacteria that convert lactose (milk sugar) to lactic acid. During production, a yogurt sample may attain a pH of 4.00 as a consequence of the presence of lactic acid. If a lactic acid–potassium lactate buffer were produced with the following amounts, what would be the resulting pH? Lactic acid ($CH_3CH(OH)COOH$) = 0.020 mol; potassium lactate ($CH_3CH(OH)COOK$) = 0.015 mol; in 0.500 L. The K_a value of lactic acid is 1.4×10^{-4}.

28. Assume that the bacteria mentioned in Problem 27 produced an additional 0.010 g of lactic acid in a 0.500-L sample of yogurt that already contained [lactic acid] = 0.050 M and [lactate] = 0.050 M. What would be the resulting pH?

29. Propanoic acid (CH_3CH_2COOH) is naturally produced by *Propionibacter shermanii*, a bacterium responsible for the holes in Swiss cheese. The K_a value of propanoic acid is 1.3×10^{-5}. If propanoic acid and its sodium salt were chosen to prepare a buffer system, what would be the pH at which the buffer would have equal ability to resist acidic and basic changes?

30. If 100.0 mL of a propanoic acid–propanoate buffer solution contained 0.50 mol of acid and 0.50 mol of propanoate, how many milliliters of 0.10 M NaOH would be required to exhaust the buffer capacity?

Section 18.2 Acid–Base Titrations

Skill Review

31. In each of these strong-acid–strong-base titrations, determine the volume of titrant that would effect a neutralization.
  a. 0.045 L of 0.23 M HCl titrated with 0.15 M NaOH
  b. 50.0 mL of 0.50 M NaOH titrated with 0.23 M HCl
  c. 20.0 mL of 0.20 M H_2SO_4 titrated with 0.15 M KOH
  d. 0.050 L of 0.10 M NaOH titrated with 0.23 M H_2SO_4

32. In each of these weak-acid–strong-base titrations, determine the volume of titrant that would effect a neutralization.
  a. 0.055L of 0.13 M CH_3COOH titrated with 0.15 M NaOH
  b. 50.0 mL of 0.50 M HCOOH titrated with 0.23 M NaOH
  c. 25.0 mL of 0.10 M $ClCH_2COOH$ titrated with 0.45 M KOH
  d. 0.045 L of 0.83 M C_6H_5COOH titrated with 0.70 M KOH

33. Determine the pH of the following titration at each of the points indicated. A 75.0 mL solution of 0.137 M NaOH is titrated with 0.2055 M HCl.
  a. initial pH
  b. after addition of 10.0 mL of HCl
  c. after addition of 25.0 mL of HCl
  d. after addition of 50.0 mL of HCl
  e. after addition of 100.0 mL of HCl

34. Determine the pH of the following titration at each of the points indicated. A 175-mL solution of 0.060 M HCl is titrated with 0.10 M NaOH.
  a. initial pH
  b. after addition of 10.0 mL of NaOH
  c. after addition of 50.0 mL of NaOH
  d. after addition of 105.0 mL of NaOH
  e. after addition of 150.0 mL of NaOH

35. Determine the pH of the following titration at each of the points indicated. A 50.0-mL solution of 0.100 M NH_3 is titrated with 0.125 M HCl.
  a. initial pH
  b. after addition of 10.0 mL of HCl
  c. after addition of 20.0 mL of HCl
  d. after addition of 40.0 mL of HCl
  e. after addition of 50.0 mL of HCl

36. Determine the pH of the following titration at each of the points indicated. A 100.0-mL solution of 0.017 M CH_3COOH ($K_a = 1.8 \times 10^{-5}$) is titrated with 0.025 M NaOH.
  a. initial pH
  b. after addition of 10.0 mL of NaOH
  c. after addition of 34.0 mL of NaOH
  d. after addition of 68.0 mL of NaOH
  e. after addition of 100.0 mL of NaOH

37. Perform the necessary calculations and sketch a titration curve diagram for the following strong-acid–strong-base titration: 25.0 mL of 0.250 M KOH using 0.150 M HNO_3 as the titrant.
  a. initial pH
  b. after adding 2.00 mL of HNO_3
  c. after adding 20.0 mL of HNO_3
  d. after adding 40.0 mL of HNO_3
  e. after adding 41.7 mL of HNO_3
  f. after adding 43.0 mL of HNO_3
  g. after adding 50.0 mL of HNO_3

38. Using 0.25 M NaOH as the titrant, calculate the pH of the resulting solution, and sketch the "pH versus volume of titrant" titration curve, for the neutralization of 50.0 mL of 0.10 M formic acid (HCOOH, $K_a = 1.8 \times 10^{-4}$) at each of these points:
  a. initial pH
  b. after adding 2.00 mL of NaOH
  c. after adding 10.0 mL of NaOH
  d. after adding 19.0 mL of NaOH
  e. after adding 20.0 mL of NaOH
  f. after adding 21.0 mL of NaOH
  g. after adding 30.0 mL of NaOH

39. From the list of indicators provided in the chapter, select the best choice for an indicator to use in each of these titrations:
  a. HCl analyte with NH_3 as the titrant
  b. Propanoic acid analyte with KOH as the titrant
  c. Nitric acid analyte with NaOH as the titrant

40. From the list of indicators provided in the chapter, select the best choice for an indicator to use in each of these titrations:
  a. Acetic acid analyte with NaOH as the titrant
  b. Ammonia analyte with HCl as the titrant
  c. Phenol analyte with NaOH as the titrant, K_a (phenol) = 1.28×10^{-10}

41. Determine the color of each of the following indicators in their respective solutions.
  a. phenolphthalein; pH = 2.5
  b. bromthymol blue; distilled water
  c. methyl orange; 0.0056 M HCl
  d. methyl violet; 0.049 M NH_3

42. Determine the color of each of the following indicators in their respective solutions.
  a. alizarin; 0.025 M NaOH
  b. bromthymol blue; 0.15 M NH_3 and 0.15 M HCl
  c. thymol blue; 0.15 M HCOOH
  d. methyl red; 0.15 M acetic acid and 0.15 M acetate

Chemical Applications and Practices

43. Vinegar is a dilute solution of acetic acid in water. A 50.00-mL vinegar sample was found to require 20.0 mL of 0.15 M NaOH in order to change the phenolphthalein indicator to pink.
  a. What is the pH of the sample after the reaction?
  b. What is the molarity of the vinegar sample?
  c. What percent of the original vinegar solution is acetic acid (CH_3COOH, $K_a = 1.8 \times 10^{-5}$)? (Assume the density of the solution is 1.00 g/mL.)

44. A yogurt dessert was found to contain lactic acid by chemical analysis. Say 100.0 mL of the dessert required 22.43 mL of 0.0156 M NaOH in order to react completely with the acid.
  a. What is the pH of the sample after the reaction?
  b. What is the best indicator to use for this titration?
  c. What mass/volume percent of the dessert is lactic acid ($CH_3CH(OH)COOH$, $K_a = 1.4 \times 10^{-4}$)?

45. A chemist has isolated a potential acid–base indicator from a specific type of tealeaf.
    a. Using the following data, determine the approximate pK_a of the indicator. The extracted compound shows a bright red color when in a solution that has a pH of 7.85. At a pH of 9.85, the color has shifted totally to green.
    b. Using your estimated pK_a value, determine the ratio of the red form to the green form at a pH of 9.50.
    c. If you used this new indicator in a titration of HCl with NaOH, would the resulting endpoint be accurately indicated? Explain why or why not.

46. A vinegar solution, which contains acetic acid as the active ingredient (CH_3COOH, $K_a = 1.8 \times 10^{-5}$), was mixed with some sodium acetate. The pH was found to be 4.15, and the concentration of acetic acid was determined to be 0.0125 M at equilibrium.
    a. What is the equilibrium concentration of sodium acetate?
    b. What color is bromthymol blue at this pH?
    c. What is the pH if another 10.0 g of sodium acetate (CH_3COONa) is added to 500 mL of the solution? (Assume the volume of the solution does not change.)

Section 18.3 Solubility Equilibria

Skill Review

47. Write out the reaction that describes the dissolution of each of these sparingly soluble salts. Then write the corresponding mass-action expression for the equilibria.
    a. AgI   b. Ag_2CrO_4 c. Al_2S_3 d. $Ca_3(PO_4)_2$

48. Write out the reaction that describes the dissolution of each of these sparingly soluble salts. Then write the corresponding mass-action expression for the equilibria.
    a. $PbCl_2$ b. $NiCO_3$ c. MnS   d. $Zn(OH)_2$

49. Use the following data to calculate the molar solubility for each of these solids.
    a. CuS, $K_{sp} = 8.5 \times 10^{-45}$
    b. Ag_3PO_4, $K_{sp} = 1.8 \times 10^{-18}$
    c. $FeCO_3$, $K_{sp} = 2.1 \times 10^{-11}$

50. Use the following data to calculate the molar solubility for each of these solids.
    a. Ag_2S, $K_{sp} = 1.6 \times 10^{-49}$
    b. $Fe(OH)_2$, $K_{sp} = 1.8 \times 10^{-15}$
    c. MgF_2, $K_{sp} = 6.4 \times 10^{-9}$

51. Use the following data to calculate the solubility product constant (K_{sp}) for each of these solids.
    a. NiS, $s = 5.5 \times 10^{-11}$ M
    b. $PbCrO_4$, $s = 1.41 \times 10^{-8}$ M
    c. Ag_2CO_3, $s = 2.0 \times 10^{-4}$ M

52. Use the following data to calculate the solubility product constant (K_{sp}) for each of these solids.
    a. CoS, $s = 2.2 \times 10^{-11}$ M
    b. $Zn(OH)_2$, $s = 2.24 \times 10^{-6}$ M
    c. $CaSO_4$, $s = 7.81 \times 10^{-3}$ M

53. Use the table of K_{sp} values in the text to determine which of these salts has the greatest molar solubility.
    a. CaF_2 b. BaF_2 c. MgF_2

54. Use the table of K_{sp} values in the text to determine which of these salts has the greatest molar solubility.
    a. PbI_2 b. AgI   c. Ag_3PO_4

55. Indicate whether a solid will form in each of these mixtures. Start by finding the concentrations of each ion in the resulting solution.
    a. 125 mL of 0.100 M $BaCl_2$ and 10.0 mL of 0.050 M Na_2SO_4
    b. 35 mL of 0.0045 M $Ag(NO_3)$ and 100.0 mL of 0.0038 M NaCl

56. Indicate whether a solid will form in each of these mixtures. Start by finding the concentrations of each ion in the resulting solution.
    a. 100.0 mL of 0.015 M K_2CO_3 and 100.0 mL of 0.0075 M $BaBr_2$
    b. 25 mL of 0.57 M $Ni(NO_3)_2$ and 100.0 mL of 0.150 M NaOH

57. Iron(III) hydroxide has a very low K_{sp} value: 1.6×10^{-39}. Explain the effect of changing the pH of an iron(III) hydroxide solution on the solubility of this salt.

58. Copper(II) carbonate has a K_{sp} value of 2.5×10^{-10}. Explain the effect of changing the pH of a copper(II) carbonate solution on the solubility of this salt.

Chemical Applications and Practices

59. When sources of the fluoride ion were being considered for use in fluoridated toothpastes, compounds such as calcium fluoride (CaF_2) could have been among them. This salt has a K_{sp} value of approximately 4.0×10^{-11}. Write out the mass-action K_{sp} expression, and calculate the concentration of fluoride ion in a saturated solution.

60. To maintain good health, we need to have certain amounts of several dissolved metal ions. Zinc ions are critical for the role they play with several hundred enzymes that function in digestion, immune systems, and fertility. However, some foods bind the zinc ions and prevent them from being absorbed from food.
    a. Write out the mass-action K_{sp} expression for zinc sulfate, the form of zinc in many vitamin supplements.
    b. If phytic acid, which is found in some foods, reacted with zinc ions, how would this affect the solubility of zinc sulfate?

61. Calcium ions can be mineralized to form bones and teeth. Neglecting any other considerations, which of the following solids would provide the greatest number of calcium ions in a saturated solution? Use the mass-action expression for each to calculate the value for each. Explain the impact of alternative equilibria on your answers.
    Calcium carbonate, $K_{sp} = 3.3 \times 10^{-9}$
    Calcium iodate, $K_{sp} = 7.1 \times 10^{-7}$
    Calcium phosphate, $K_{sp} = 1.2 \times 10^{-29}$

62. The cadmium +2 ion, which is considered a toxic heavy metal ion, has been a by-product of several mining operations. One method that could remove it from aqueous systems would be to tie the ions up as a cadmium hydroxide precipitate. The K_{sp} value of cadmium hydroxide is 2.5×10^{-14}.
    a. What is the molar solubility of cadmium hydroxide?
    b. Explain whether you believe that the presence of dissolved Cd^{2+} might be a greater problem at acidic or basic soil pH values.

Section 18.4 Complex-Ion Equilibria

Skill Review

63. Write equilibria equations that describe the stepwise formation of each of these complex ions.
    a. $Ag(NH_3)_2^+$ b. $Ni(NH_3)_6^{2+}$

64. Write equilibria equations that describe the stepwise formation of each of these complex ions.
    a. $CuBr_3^{2-}$ b. $Ag(S_2O_3)_2^{3-}$

65. How many milliliters of a $0.0156\ M$ EDTA^{4-} solution would be needed to completely complex each of these metals in solution?
    a. 100.0 mL of $0.150\ M$ Zn^{2+}
    b. 50.0 mL of $0.740\ M$ Ca^{2+}
    c. 20.0 mL of $0.050\ M$ Mg^{2+}

66. What would be the molar concentration of an EDTA^{4-} solution in each case if it took exactly 25.00 mL to react completely with each of these solutions?
    a. 30.0 mL of $0.250\ M$ Zn^{2+}
    b. 40.0 mL of $0.700\ M$ Ca^{2+}
    c. 20.0 mL of $0.150\ M$ Mg^{2+}

Chemical Applications and Practices

67. As we noted in the chapter, the fraction of species for the EDTA^{4-} ion is critical when we consider EDTA–metal ion titrations. The available metal ion, uncomplexed with other ligands such as ammonia, can also be an important consideration. The formation constant for the Zn^{2+}–EDTA complex was given as 3×10^{16}. What would be the conditional formation constant if the fraction of free zinc ion were 1×10^{-4} and the fraction of EDTA^{4-} species were 0.05?

68. A 25.0-mL sample of water is treated with ammonia buffer and Eriochrome Black T indicator. The sample requires 15.0 mL of $0.0185\ M$ EDTA solution to reach the endpoint. What is the concentration of Ca^{2+} ion in moles per liter and ppm?

69. A dilute solution of hydrated Cu^{2+} ions will appear blue and without a precipitate. However, the addition of some ammonium hydroxide will cause precipitation of some light blue copper(II) hydroxide, often within a deep blue solution. Further addition of ammonium hydroxide will dissolve the precipitate and form a dark blue solution of $Cu(H_2O)_2(NH_3)_4^{2+}$.
    a. What do these observations suggest about the relative value of the formation constant for $Cu(NH_3)_4^{2+}$?
    b. Write out the stepwise formation of the copper–ammonia complex.

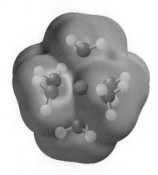

70. Although very toxic, cyanide compounds such as KCN and NaCN can be used to extract gold from ores because the gold will form soluble complexes with cyanide ions. The cumulative formation constant for $Au(CN)_2^-$ is approximately 1.6×10^{38}. In this extraction process, the cyanide extracting solution must be kept very alkaline to prevent the formation of HCN. Very small amounts of gold can be extracted in this manner thanks to the very high value of the formation constant.
    a. Write out the mass-action expression for the formation constant of $Au(CN)_2^-$.
    b. If the concentration of CN^- were maintained at $0.010\ M$ in an extract and the gold complex ion concentration were found to be $8 \times 10^{-5}\ M$, what would you estimate as the concentration of Au^+?

71. Under proper medical supervision, one treatment for lead poisoning may involve reaction with a soluble EDTA salt. This is called chelation therapy. If the following reactions were part of a successful treatment, which complex, the calcium–EDTA ion or the lead–EDTA ion, would you predict to have the higher formation constant?

$$CaEDTA^{2-}(aq) + Pb^{2+}(aq) \rightleftharpoons PbEDTA^{2-}(aq) + Ca^{2+}(aq)$$

72. How many milliliters of a solution of $0.0010\ M$ EDTA^{4-} would be used to titrate the lead in 1000 mL of a $0.0020\ M$ solution of $Pb(NO_3)_2$? (Assume a 1:1 reaction between Pb^{2+} and EDTA.)

Comprehensive Problems

73. Cite three processes in which the use of a buffer would be necessary to maintain the pH within a fixed range.

74. A buffer commonly found in biochemical labs and known as TRIS is $(CH_2OH)_3CNH_2$, $pK_b = 5.70$. If a 1.0-L solution were made with 0.15 mol of TRIS, how many grams of TRISH$^+$ chloride salt, $(CH_2OH)_3CNH_3Cl$, would have to be added to the solution to make a buffer with pH $= 8.1$?

75. a. A compound of highly oxidized iron may be used to break down certain environmental wastes. However, the reactions of the iron compound (K_2FeO_4) are highly pH dependent. In order to do feasibility studies of this compound for possible wastewater treatment, phosphate buffers could be used to maintain a fairly constant pH value. Obtain the K_a values of H_3PO_4, $H_2PO_4^-$, and HPO_4^{2-}. Which two would be the best combination to use if the study were to be done at pH $= 8.20$?
    b. What would be the ratio of the components at that pH?

76. The presence of lead ions in the environment can pose a hazard. One gravimetric method to test for the presence of lead in a sample is to precipitate the lead as lead sulfate. The K_{sp} value for lead sulfate is 1.3×10^{-8}.

   a. Write out the mass-action K_{sp} expression for this compound.

   b. If the sulfate concentration is made sufficiently high, lead ions will be almost completely precipitated from the solution. If a solution had a lead ion concentration of $0.0010\ M$ initially, what concentration of lead would remain after precipitation if the sulfate concentration were maintained at $0.010\ M$?

77. a. Calcium, zinc, and cobalt all form +2 ions. However, from Table 18.4 we can see that the formation constant for calcium–EDTA is considerably less than that for the zinc-EDTA and cobalt–EDTA complexes. Explain why this contrast is logical.

   b. Explain why the formation constant for Fe^{2+}–EDTA is less than that for Fe^{3+}–EDTA.

78. By adjusting solution pH, a biologist may manipulate the charges on side chains of enzymes. A biologist studying the function of an enzyme responsible for a step in the conversion of atmospheric nitrogen to useable forms of nitrogen in a plant finds that the enzyme is neutral when the pH is 6.87.

   a. What is the significance of this pH?

   b. If the enzyme had an acid group with a $pK_a = 7.20$, what should the pH of the enzyme solution be to produce a molar ratio of protonated acid group to unprotonated acid group equal to 3:1?

79. Formic acid (HCOOH, $K_a = 1.77 \times 10^{-4}$) is a weak acid extracted from ants. Suppose that such an extraction resulted in 1.00 mL of volume. This 1.00 mL is then diluted to 50.0 mL with distilled water.

   a. If the resulting solution required 25.0 mL of $0.0010\ M$ NaOH to neutralize, what would you calculate as the molarity of the formic acid solution?

   b. How many moles of formic acid were in the original 1.00-mL extract?

80. A biologist seeks to analyze a sample of lactic acid ($CH_3CH(OH)COOH$, $K_a = 1.4 \times 10^{-4}$) isolated from a tissue sample. The 20.0-mL sample required 12.5 mL of $0.086\ M$ NaOH to neutralize. What was the molarity of the lactic acid sample? What was the initial pH, the pH midway to the equivalence point, and the pH at the equivalence point?

81. An aqueous solution starts as $0.20\ M$ dissolved $Fe(NO_3)_2$. EDTA is added to produce a concentration of $0.10\ M$. Assume that the formation constant for the Fe^{2+}–$EDTA^{4-}$ complex is 2×10^{14}.

   a. Use the mass-action formation constant expression to determine the approximate concentration of Fe^{2+}.

   b. If the solution is now made $0.20\ M$ in hydroxide, is enough Fe^{2+} still present to cause precipitation of $Fe(OH)_2$?

Thinking Beyond the Calculation

82. A researcher has produced an extract from a tropical plant that contains a monoprotic acid.

   a. The researcher titrates 100.0 mL of the plant extract with $0.100\ M$ NaOH. The titration midpoint is reached when 25.6 mL of NaOH has been added. The pH at this point was 3.58. What is the K_a value for the acid?

   b. Graph a titration curve for this titration by determining the pH at each of the following points along the curve: 0 mL, 10.0 mL, 25.6 mL, 50.0 mL, 75.0 mL, and 100.0 mL.

   c. Which indicator would work best in this titration?

   d. By evaporating the extract, the researcher determines that there is only 0.123 g of the acid in every 100.0 mL of plant extract. What is the molecular mass of the acid?

19

Electrochemistry

Contents and Selected Applications

A patient undergoes open-heart surgery. The heart is a muscle that operates by developing a potential across the cell membrane.

"I admit the deed!—tear up the planks!— here, here!—it is the beating of his hideous heart!" (Edgar Allan Poe, "The Telltale Heart"). The heart is an incredible organ. Without it, there is no life. It collects blood from the extremities and pushes it to the lungs, where oxygen and carbon dioxide are exchanged. Then it pulls the blood back and pumps it out to the various regions of the body, where the dissolved oxygen is delivered to the cells. In a normal lifetime, the four chambers of the heart rhythmically contract and relax nearly 3 billion times. The heart is always beating. What causes this fabulous muscle to contract and relax?

Muscle cells contain different concentrations of sodium and potassium cations inside (18 mM Na$^+$, 166 mM K$^+$) and outside (135 mM Na$^+$, 5 mM K$^+$) the cell. This concentration difference arises as the cells work continuously to pump Na$^+$ ions out and K$^+$ ions in. The concentration gradient (a gradually increasing difference) across the cell membrane sets up an electrical potential—*a driving force to perform a reaction that results from a difference in electrical charge between two points*. The potential—in this case, a force to restore the ion concentrations to equality—is measured in volts (V), just as we measure the potential (voltage) of a battery. The muscle cell has a very small potential (~100 mV), but it is enough to prime the cell for contraction.

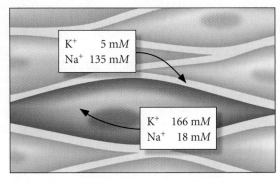

Just prior to a contraction, the muscle cell has changed the concentrations of potassium and sodium to produce a large gradient across its membrane.

Understanding how the concentrations of sodium and potassium ions contribute to the potential inside a heart cell is of interest to the cardiologist, a heart specialist. More broadly, the electron exchanges that occur in chemical reactions are of interest to electrochemists, who create or analyze systems that allow exchanges between chemical and electrical energy. This exchange occurs via *the gain of electrons (reduction) and the loss of electrons (oxidation) in reactions called* redox reactions. Knowing how redox reactions work, how they develop a potential, and how the electrons involved can be harnessed helps scientists understand biological systems (such as muscles and nerves). It also enables them to continue to develop and improve one of the more important inventions that enhances our lives on a daily basis: the battery. The principles behind the exchange between chemical and electrical energy rely on one fact: Chemical reactions can do work. In this chapter, we look at the interplay of electrical and chemical energy, along with some of its interesting and important uses. One of these uses is DNA profiling, the subject of the accompanying How Do We Know? discussion.

19.1 What Is Electrochemistry?

In 2003, over 593 million passengers boarded planes at U.S. airports. On those extremely rare occasions when a jetliner crashes, few may live to tell about it. However, each flight leaves a record of clues, better known as the "black box," for airline officials to decode. Known as a flight data recorder (FDR), the black box, a remarkable combination of engineering, data technology, and chemistry (Figure 19.1), is made rugged enough to survive a crash. So that it too can be found

How do we know?

? DNA Profiling

Ionic compounds move when placed in an electric field. The Swedish chemist Arne Tiselius used this information in the 1930s to develop a separation technique. **Gel electrophoresis**, the use of electric fields to separate ions, is based on the application of an electric field across a gel-filled space. Ions, such as DNA fragments or proteins, are placed at one end of the gel, and a voltage is applied. The molecules with a net negative charge tend to migrate toward the positive pole as the positively charged molecules move toward the negative pole. The average rate of their movement is proportional to the average charge and to the average voltage applied. However, the rate of movement is inversely proportional to the size of the molecules. After a certain amount of time, the apparatus is disassembled and the gel stained to reveal the locations of specific compounds. The molar masses of DNA fragments or proteins can be estimated by comparing their locations with those of reference samples whose molar masses are known.

Gel electrophoresis is widely used in molecular biology for separating DNA, RNA, and proteins by size. After human DNA is broken into small pieces with enzymes, it can be analyzed using gel electrophoresis to provide evidence in criminal cases, to diagnose genetic disorders,

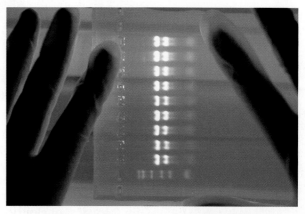

Gel electrophoresis. After staining of the completed gel, each vertical lane contains different-sized fragments of DNA.

and to solve paternity cases. The sizes of the DNA pieces differ among people, so a person's "DNA fingerprint" or "DNA profile" can be constructed. DNA profiling is also used by conservation biologists to determine genetic similarity among populations or individuals. Evolutionary biologists use DNA profile information to construct hypothetical family trees indicating the relationships among species.

after a crash, engineers must invest the same care in the design of the battery that powers the locator beacon. While constructing a battery to the exacting specifications of an FDR is challenging, the principles behind battery construction are nothing new. Like the FDR, for example, the battery in a cardiac pacemaker must also meet tough standards; it is expected to function reliably for up to ten years, to provide a steady supply of power, and not to leak chemicals into the person wearing it. The pacemaker battery is based on the same principles of electrochemistry as the FDR.

What is electrochemistry? Broadly speaking, **electrochemistry** is the study of the reduction and oxidation processes that occur at the interface between different phases of a system. Furthermore, electrochemistry typically involves reactions that take place at the surface of a solid. One important field of study in electrochemistry is called **electrodics**, the study of the interactions that occur between a solution of electrolytes and an electrical conductor, often a metal. Another important field within electrochemistry is **ionics**, the study of the behavior of ions dissolved in liquids.

Electrochemical processes typically take place in an **electrochemical cell**, a device that allows the exchange between chemical and electrical energy. Two types of electrochemical cells are possible. The **voltaic cell** (also called a **galvanic cell**) is named after Alessandro Volta (Figure 19.2). It is a type of electrochemical cell

FIGURE 19.1

The flight data recorder. This "black box" records data about each airline flight. The information it collects can be used to help solve the mysteries of a plane crash.

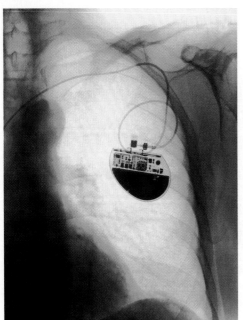

A view of a pacemaker in a patient. Note the battery at the lower portion of the image.

FIGURE 19.2

Count Alessandro Volta (1745–1827) invented the electrophorus, the first well-documented example of a voltaic cell, in 1775. He is also credited with the isolation of methane in 1778.

that *produces* electricity from a chemical reaction. Voltaic cells are commonly known as batteries, although technically speaking, a **battery** is two or more voltaic cells joined together in series. The second type of electrochemical cell is the **electrolytic cell**. This cell *requires* the addition of electrical energy to drive the chemical reaction under study. The industrial production of aluminum (see Section 19.7) is an electrolytic process.

All electrochemical cells require electron exchange that can be characterized in two parts, each known as a **half-reaction**, and the sum of the half-reactions equals the complete reaction observed in the cell. One half-reaction (an **oxidation reaction**) supplies the electrons, and a second (a **reduction reaction**) utilizes these electrons. For this reason, the reactions that take place in electrochemical cells are also known as redox reactions. The oxidation reaction occurs at an **electrode** (typically a metal surface that acts as a collector or distributor for the electrons) known as the **anode**. The reduction reaction takes place at the **cathode**.

How does a redox reaction differ from any other kind of reaction? If we were to place the components for each of the two half-reactions into the same beaker, we wouldn't note any difference. However, the half-reactions do not need intimate contact in order to produce products. As we will see later in this chapter, as long as we make sure that the half-reactions can exchange materials, the overall cell reaction will work. The driving force to complete the reaction—the cell potential—will ensure that the reaction proceeds and that we will be able to harness the power of the electrochemical cell. Our first task in understanding redox reactions and how to make use of the electron exchange is to know a redox reaction when we see it.

19.2 Oxidation States—Electronic Bookkeeping

The space shuttle (Chapter 5) requires electricity for lights, heaters, cameras, communications, and almost every other operation during its orbit of the Earth. In addition, the astronauts need water and oxygen to survive the trip. Electrochemists have discovered a way to provide both water for the crew and electricity for the ship. Their answer is the **fuel cell**, an electrochemical cell that utilizes the reaction of hydrogen with oxygen to produce electricity (Figure 19.3).

$$2H_2(g) + O_2(g) \rightarrow 2H_2O(g)$$

Although we see that this reaction produces water, our first glance at the reaction does not reveal a process that can produce electricity. But it can. Some chemical reactions (the redox reactions), such as this one, involve the shifting or transfer of electrons with one species *losing electrons* (**oxidation**) and another

FIGURE 19.3

Under the hood of a Ford Focus hybrid that utilizes the hydrogen fuel cell to generate electrical power. Hydrogen could be the next big advance in alternative fuels. Many of the world's automobile manufacturers are working toward improving hybrid engines and educating consumers on the benefits of alternative fuels.

species *gaining these electrons* (**reduction**). Examining the **oxidation state** (Section 4.7) of the atoms helps us identify the redox reaction. All we must do is keep track of the electrons. A word of caution: There are times when the oxidation state of an atom has little physical meaning, and it can be misleading if the oxidation state is literally interpreted as an indication of where the electrons are found. For instance, when we determine the oxidation state of the oxygen atoms in formic acid (HCOOH), as we do in Exercise 19.1, we will find that both oxygen atoms have the same oxidation state. This should not be interpreted to mean that the same density of electrons will be found equally on both oxygen atoms. Yet even though that interpretation is wrong, oxidation states can be helpful in identifying the general distribution of the electrons in a substance.

As we discussed in Chapter 4, *the oxidation state of an atom in an element is zero*. In monatomic anions and cations, the oxidation state is written as a superscript to the right of the atom symbol, as is done in Ca^{2+} and Br^-. For compounds, oxidation states of atoms are small integers such as $+2, +7$, and -1 (and occasionally fractions) that indicate how an atom's electrons have shifted relative to the elemental state. In the fuel cell, both O atoms in O_2 and both H atoms in H_2 have an oxidation state of zero because these atoms are found in (neutral) elements. The oxidation state of oxygen in the product is -2, and that of each hydrogen atom is $+1$.

How did we know the oxidation state assignments for each atom in water? Electrochemists are familiar with chemical behavior. For example, they know that the hydrogen atom, which has a relatively low electronegativity, is assigned the oxidation state of $+1$ in all its compounds except metal hydrides such as NaH, in which it is -1 because the Group IA and Group IIA metals have even lower electronegativity values than hydrogen. With rare exceptions, all metals in compounds have positive oxidation states, as can be seen by the values in Figure 19.4. Nonmetals, however, can have either positive or negative oxidation states, depending on the compound in which they are found. Figure 19.5 presents a set of decision rules to assist you in assigning oxidation states.

What does an oxidation state mean? We can think of it as a measure of the electron density distribution in a particular compound. A positive oxidation state indicates that electrons have shifted *away from* that atom. A negative oxidation state means that electrons have shifted *toward* that atom. Because electrons are shared (to varying extents) between adjacent atoms, we generally expect nonzero oxidation states for each of the atoms if they are different elements. For example, in the water molecule, H is assigned as $+1$ and O is assigned as -2. The electrons

FIGURE 19.4

Oxidation states of the metals.

IA	IIA	IIIB	IVB	VB	VIB	VIIB	VIIIB	VIIIB	VIIIB	IB	IIB	IIIA	IVA	VA	VIA	VIIA	VIIIA
Li^+																	
Na^+	Mg^{2+}											Al^{3+}					
K^+	Ca^{2+}	Sc^{3+}	Ti^{2+} Ti^{3+} Ti^{4+}	V^{2+} V^{3+} V^{4+} V^{5+}	Cr^{2+} Cr^{3+} Cr^{6+}	Mn^{2+} Mn^{3+} Mn^{4+} Mn^{7+}	Fe^{2+} Fe^{3+}	Co^{2+} Co^{3+}	Ni^{2+}	Cu^+ Cu^{2+}	Zn^{2+}						
Rb^+	Sr^{2+}									Ag^+	Cd^{2+}		Sn^{2+} Sn^{4+}				
Cs^+	Ba^{2+}									Hg_2^{2+} Hg^{2+}			Pb^{2+} Pb^{4+}				

FIGURE 19.5

Decision rules for assigning oxidation states.

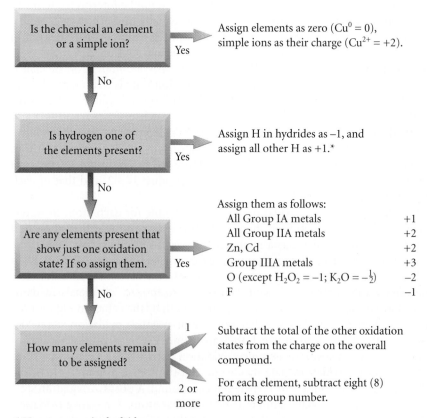

Is the chemical an element or a simple ion? — Yes → Assign elements as zero ($Cu^0 = 0$), simple ions as their charge ($Cu^{2+} = +2$).

No ↓

Is hydrogen one of the elements present? — Yes → Assign H in hydrides as −1, and assign all other H as +1.*

No ↓

Are any elements present that show just one oxidation state? If so assign them. — Yes → Assign them as follows:

All Group IA metals	+1
All Group IIA metals	+2
Zn, Cd	+2
Group IIIA metals	+3
O (except $H_2O_2 = -1$; $K_2O = -\frac{1}{2}$)	−2
F	−1

No ↓

How many elements remain to be assigned? — 1 → Subtract the total of the other oxidation states from the charge on the overall compound.

2 or more → For each element, subtract eight (8) from its group number.

* How to recognize hydrides:

  Hydrides have a metal first in their chemical formula.

    For example: CaH_2, MgH_2, $LiAlH_4$, NaH

  Hydrides contain no nonmetals.

    For example, these are not hydrides: CH_4, $NaHCO_3$, NH_3, HCl

have shifted away from hydrogen toward the oxygen, as shown in the electrostatic density map in Figure 19.6. This is consistent with our understanding of electronegativity (Chapter 7). The oxidation states do not mean that hydrogen has a full +1 charge and oxygen a full −2 charge. Remember from Chapter 7 that water is a covalent molecule. We can talk more comfortably about oxidation states as representations of the charge of atoms in ionic compounds. Whether in covalent or ionic compounds, we will use oxidation state as a bookkeeping tool to see where electrons shift in chemical reactions.

FIGURE 19.6

The electrostatic potential map for water.

EXERCISE 19.1   Oxidation States

Assign an oxidation state to each of the elements in formic acid (HCOOH). Given the Lewis structure shown below, which of the electrostatic density maps that follow represents formic acid?

$$\begin{array}{c} O \\ \parallel \\ H-C-O-H \end{array}$$

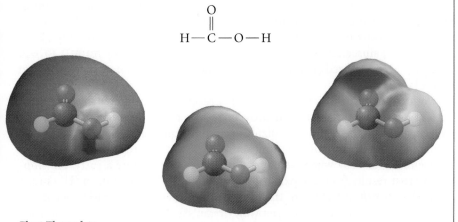

First Thoughts

We have two questions here: a technical one about the oxidation states and a more conceptual one concerning what the oxidation states imply about the electron distribution. In both cases, though, the assignment of the oxidation state and the electrostatic density map should be consistent with our understanding of electronegativity.

Solution

According to our rules for assigning oxidation states in Figure 19.5, each oxygen is assigned an oxidation state of −2, and each hydrogen is +1. For the neutral formic acid molecule, in which the sum of all of the oxidation states must be 0, we have

$$2H = +1 \times 2 = +2$$

$$2O = -2 \times 2 = -4$$

The total is $+2 + (-4) = -2$. The carbon atom must therefore have an oxidation state of +2. This means that the electron density in this molecule is focused more on the oxygen atoms than on the carbon or hydrogen atoms. Given the assignments of the oxidation states, the second electron density map is the most reasonable representation of the molecule. In the other two maps the charge density isn't in the correct location. In the first map, the electron density appears to be opposite of what we'd expect, given that the red color on the map indicates regions of high electron density. The third map again shows electron density that doesn't appear to match where we have predicted the electrons to reside in the molecule.

Further Insights

Carbon can have several oxidation states, depending on the atoms with which it bonds. When we talk about "complete combustion" of carbon, we mean the conversion to its highest possible oxidation state, $+4$, as is true in CO_2. For example, when glucose ($C_6H_{12}O_6$) is burned in air, the carbon atoms can undergo complete combustion to CO_2. However, they can also form partial combustion products, such as carbon monoxide (CO), in which the oxidation state of the carbon atom differs.

PRACTICE 19.1

Determine the oxidation states of carbon in glucose and carbon monoxide, the compounds discussed in the "Further Insights" section just above.

See Problems 5–8 and 44.

We began this section discussing the reaction of hydrogen and oxygen gases in a fuel cell. By comparing the reactants and products, we see that both H and O show a change in their oxidation state. The change indicated that a transfer of electrons from one species to another has occurred. *Any* chemical reaction in which atoms change their oxidation states is classified as an oxidation–reduction reaction, or redox reaction for short. When O_2 and H_2 react to form water, O_2 is reduced (it gains electrons) and its oxidation state decreases from 0 to -2. Similarly, H_2 is oxidized (it loses electrons), and its oxidation state increases from 0 to $+1$:

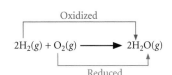

We can look at the compounds in this reaction in a different way. Oxygen (O_2) *causes the oxidation* of the hydrogen (H_2), so it is an **oxidizing agent**. In fact, oxygen stands as the premier oxidizing agent on planet Earth, both because of its abundance and because of its strong ability to accept electrons. We observe oxygen's effect every day when we metabolize glucose or explore a rusty, old shipwreck (rust results from the oxidation of Fe to Fe^{3+}). The hydrogen (H_2) in the fuel cell *causes the reduction* of the oxygen and is therefore a **reducing agent** (see Table 19.1). Looking at this another way, we can say that the oxidizing agent itself is reduced and the reducing agent itself is oxidized.

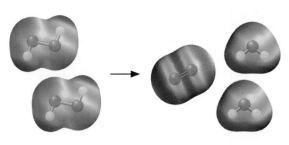

Hydrogen peroxide is sometimes used to bleach hair or disinfect wounds. Is its decomposition into oxygen and water a redox reaction? If so, which species is the oxidizing agent and which is the reducing agent?

$$2H_2O_2(l) \rightarrow O_2(g) + 2H_2O(l)$$

Occasionally, a chemical reaction such as this one employs a single reactant as both the oxidizing and the reducing agent. Such a reaction is known as a **disproportionation**. Using our decision rules in Figure 19.5, we can assign the following oxidation states to each atom.

$$\overset{+1\ -1}{2H_2O_2(l)} \rightarrow \overset{0}{O_2(g)} + \overset{+1\ -2}{2H_2O(l)}$$

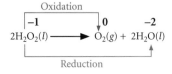

TABLE 19.1	Oxidizing and Reducing Agents	
Reactant	**What Happens**	**Examples**
Oxidizing agent	Gains electrons Is reduced	Element: O_2, O_3, and halogens Compound: H_2O_2 Ionic species (typically with a large positive oxidation state): MnO_4^-
Reducing agent	Loses electrons Is oxidized	Element: H_2 and metals Compound: BH_3 Ionic species: NaH, $LiAlH_4$

In this reaction, the oxygen atoms in hydrogen peroxide (like any peroxide) have an oxidation state of -1. The two products of the reaction contain oxygen atoms with different oxidation states, O_2 with a higher oxidation state (zero) and H_2O with oxygen in a lower oxidation state (-2). We say that the hydrogen peroxide is both the oxidizing agent and the reducing agent.

Not all reactions require the transfer of electrons. Many of the reactions we've discussed in this text thus far are not redox reactions. For example, the neutralization of sodium hydroxide by hydrochloric acid is not a redox reaction. We can tell because the oxidation states for each of the atoms remain the same on both sides of the equation:

$$\overset{+1\,-2\,+1}{NaOH} + \overset{+1\,-1}{HCl} \rightarrow \overset{+1\,-1}{NaCl} + \overset{+1\,-2}{H_2O}$$

Many elements show a variety of oxidation states, depending on the chemical species in which they are found. An example of this can be found in the nonmetal nitrogen, which has a range of possible oxidation states, as shown in Table 19.2 on page 832. The gases found in our atmosphere, both naturally and as pollutants, have different *positive* oxidation states of nitrogen, since the oxygen atom in each compound is more electronegative than nitrogen and is assigned an oxidation state of -2. For the same reason, nitrates (NO_3^-) and nitrites (NO_2^-) have nitrogen with positive oxidation states. However, when combined with a less electronegative element such as hydrogen, nitrogen is assigned a *negative* oxidation state. Accordingly, look for a negative oxidation state of N in ammonia and in compounds containing the ammonium ion, NH_4^+.

The **nitrogen cycle** (Figure 19.7) illustrates how nitrogen moves through its different oxidation states on our planet. You can find similar cycles where the oxidation states of sulfur and carbon change as these elements form different

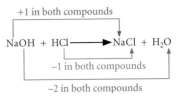

$+1$ in both compounds

$NaOH + HCl \longrightarrow NaCl + H_2O$

-1 in both compounds

-2 in both compounds

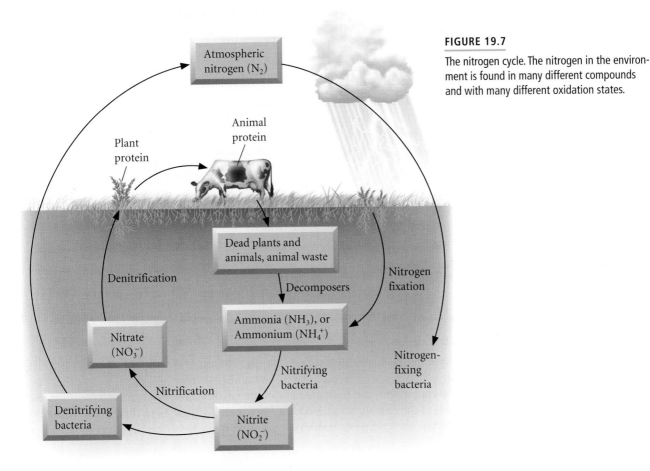

FIGURE 19.7

The nitrogen cycle. The nitrogen in the environment is found in many different compounds and with many different oxidation states.

TABLE 19.2	The Oxidation State of Nitrogen		
Oxidation State	**Formula**	**Name**	**Produced in Nature**
+5	HNO_3 NO_3^-	Nitric acid Nitrate ion	From NO_2^- by nitrifying bacteria
+4	NO_2	Nitrogen dioxide	In air by oxidation of NO
+3	HNO_2 NO_2^-	Nitrous acid Nitrite ion	From NH_3 by nitrifying bacteria
+2	NO	Nitrogen monoxide (nitric oxide)	From N_2 by lightning or volcanoes
+1	N_2O	Nitrous oxide	From NO_2^- by denitrifying bacteria
0	N_2	Nitrogen	From N_2O by denitrifying bacteria
$-\frac{1}{3}$	N_3^-	Azide ion	(not found in nature)
−1	NH_2OH	Hydroxylamine	(not found in nature)
−2	N_2H_4	Hydrazine	(not found in nature)
−3	NH_3 NH_4^+	Ammonia Ammonium ion	From biological decay of proteins
	NH_4OH	Ammonium hydroxide	—

compounds. What is the point? Whereas oxidation states are fixed for a particular compound at a particular moment in time, chemicals in our world constantly undergo change. Oxidation states help us keep track of the changes that involve the important processes of oxidation and reduction.

EXERCISE 19.2 **The Electrochemistry of Smog**

Although oxygen and nitrogen do not react at low temperatures, they combine in a hot automobile engine to form the pollutant NO, with subsequent oxidation by atmospheric oxygen to form the poisonous brown gas NO_2, which is largely responsible for the smog found in urban areas on hot, sunny days:

$$N_2(g) + O_2(g) \rightarrow 2NO(g)$$
$$2NO(g) + O_2(g) \rightarrow 2NO_2(g)$$

Assign oxidation states to all the atoms involved in these two reactions. Which species are oxidized? Which are reduced? Do your answers make sense in terms of the relative electronegativity values of nitrogen and oxygen?

First Thoughts

Which of the two atoms, nitrogen or oxygen, is more likely to be reduced (gain electrons)? Oxygen is the more electronegative, so in this system, nitrogen will be oxidized. That is how we evaluate whether our answers make sense.

Solution

According to Figure 19.5, we may assign all atoms in elements (such as N_2 and O_2) an oxidation state of zero. In the compounds, we may assign oxygen as −2, because the compounds are not peroxides or superoxides. We assign nitrogen so that the sum of the oxidation states is zero, because NO and NO_2, as compounds, carry no charge.

Compound	Oxidation Number of N	Oxidation Number of O
N_2	0	–
O_2	–	0
NO	+2	−2
NO_2	+4	−2

The nitrogen has been successively oxidized going from N_2 to NO to NO_2, and the oxygen has been reduced as it changes from O_2 to its products.

Further Insights

We noted in Figure 19.5 that hydrogen, which is normally assigned an oxidation state of +1 in compounds, is assigned an oxidation state of −1 when combining with Group 1A metals. This can result in a very reactive reducing agent that is quite useful in organic chemical reactions. One example is NaH, mentioned earlier, which is used in the manufacture of many pharmaceuticals, perfumes, and other organic chemicals.

PRACTICE 19.2

Rank these chemicals in order of increasing oxidation state of sulfur: SO_2, H_2SO_4, S_8, and Li_2S.

See Problems 9–12.

19.3   Redox Equations

Ira Remsen (1846–1927), one of the co-discoverers of the artificial sweetener saccharine, was particularly interested in chemistry as a boy. As an adult, he told of a childhood visit to the doctor's office where he, when left alone in the examination room, set out to discover what was meant by something he had read in a chemistry book: "Nitric acid acts upon copper." To discover this for himself, he placed a pure copper penny on the exam table and poured nitric acid from the doctor's bottle onto the penny. Remsen continues,

> But what was this wonderful thing which I beheld? The cent was already changed, and it was no small change either. A greenish blue liquid foamed and fumed over the cent and over the table. The air in the neighborhood of the performance became dark red. A great colored cloud arose. This was disagreeable and suffocating— how should I stop this? I tried to get rid of the objectionable mess by picking it up and throwing it out the window, which I had meanwhile opened. I learned another fact—nitric acid not only acts upon copper but it acts upon fingers. The pain led to another unpremeditated experiment. I drew my fingers across my trousers and another fact was discovered. Nitric acid also acts upon trousers. Taking everything into consideration, that was the most impressive experiment, and, relatively, probably the most costly experiment I have ever performed.

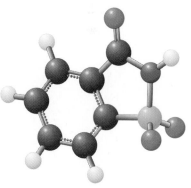

Saccharine

The reaction that Remsen describes, which is illustrated in Figure 19.8 on page 834, is a redox reaction. Shown on the right is the unbalanced equation. How do we know that it is a redox reaction? Examine the oxidation state of copper. Copper metal (oxidation state $= 0$) is being oxidized to the copper(II) ion. Simultaneously, nitrogen in nitric acid is being reduced from +5 to +2 in forming nitrogen monoxide. The NO gas released by the reaction rapidly reacts with O_2 in the air to make $NO_2(g)$, the brown fumes that so alarmed the budding chemist.

$$HNO_3(aq) + Cu(s) \longrightarrow Cu^{2+}(aq) + NO(g)$$

$$2NO(g) + O_2(g) \longrightarrow 2NO_2(g)$$

FIGURE 19.8

Nitric acid acts on copper. The spontaneous reaction is evident from the generation of a blue solution and a cloud of noxious brown gas. The gas results from the reaction of NO with oxygen in the air.

Half-Reactions

Ira Remsen noted that this reaction proceeded spontaneously to generate a cloud of noxious fumes. Can we predict this spontaneity by examining the reaction equation, which tells us whether the driving force (the potential) is favorable for this reaction? To assist us in answering this question, we need to extract the oxidation and reduction reactions from the overall equation. These half-reactions, like so many half-reactions, are so well known that the potential for each has been measured and the results collected into a Table of Standard Reduction Potentials, such as Table 19.3. A more comprehensive table can be found in the Appendix.

What do you notice about these tables? One of the things is that all of the reactions are written as reduction reactions. That is, the reactions show the consumption of electrons to make products with less positive oxidation states. Standard Reduction Potentials tables can be used to determine the potential of a reaction, be it for the silver oxide battery found in a pacemaker or for the action of nitric acid on a copper penny. Moreover, knowing the potential of the half-reactions helps us determine the spontaneity of a redox reaction, as we will see later.

Each half-reaction in the table is balanced both atomically and electrically. Half-reactions are simply what they appear to be: half of an oxidation–reduction reaction that is occurring in aqueous solution. The half-reaction listed in the table for the reduction of copper shows the reactants (copper ions and electrons), the product (copper metal), and the **standard potential ($E°$)** of the half-reaction.

$$Cu^{2+}(aq) + 2e^- \rightarrow Cu(s) \qquad E° = +0.34 \text{ V}$$

The value of $E°$ is a measure of how strongly the reduced species on the right-hand side of the reduction half-reaction pulls electrons toward itself. The standard potential is measured in **volts**, the SI unit of electrical potential. It is sometimes referred to as the **electromotive force (emf)** of the half-cell or, more commonly, as the **voltage**.

The values listed for $E°$ are measured under a specific set of conditions:

■ Any aqueous ion is present at a concentration (technically, activity) of 1.0 M. All gases are at a pressure of 1 bar (approximately 1 atm).

■ The temperature is 25°C (298 K).

These conditions are "standard" for half-reactions and are indicated by the "°" in $E°$. If the conditions are not standard, the voltage will be different from that listed in the table (see Section 19.7), and the potential will be equal to E. Keep in mind that there are several "standards"! For example, standard conditions of temperature and pressure of gases (STP) refer to 0°C (273 K) as the standard temperature.

TABLE 19.3 Selected Standard Reduction Potentials

The selected potentials shown here were obtained under standard conditions (in aqueous solution, 25°C, all solutions 1.0 M, all gases 1.0 atm).

Shorthand Notation	Half-Cell Reaction	Standard Potential, $E°$ (V)
$Li^+(aq) \mid Li(s)$	$Li^+(aq) + e^- \rightarrow Li(s)$	−3.04
$Na^+(aq) \mid Na(s)$	$Na^+(aq) + e^- \rightarrow Na(s)$	−2.71
$Mg^{+2}(aq) \mid Mg(s)$	$Mg^{+2}(aq) + 2e^- \rightarrow Mg(s)$	−2.38
$Al^{3+}(aq) \mid Al(s)$	$Al^{3+}(aq) + 3e^- \rightarrow Al(s)$	−1.66
$H_2O(l) \mid H_2(g)$	$2H_2O(l) + 2e^- \rightarrow H_2(g) + 2OH^-(aq)$	−0.83
$Cd(OH)_2(s) \mid Cd(s)$	$Cd(OH)_2(s) + 2e^- \rightarrow Cd(s) + 2OH^-(aq)$	−0.81
$Fe^{2+}(aq) \mid Fe(s)$	$Fe^{2+}(aq) + 2e^- \rightarrow Fe(s)$	−0.44
$H^+(aq) \mid H_2(g)$	$2H^+(aq) + 2e^- \rightarrow H_2(g)$	0.00
$Fe^{3+}(aq) \mid Fe(s)$	$Fe^{3+}(aq) + 3e^- \rightarrow Fe(s)$	+0.04
$Cu^{2+}(aq) \mid Cu(s)$	$Cu^{2+}(aq) + 2e^- \rightarrow Cu(s)$	+0.34
$O_2(g) \mid OH^-(aq)$	$O_2(g) + 2H_2O(l) + 4e^- \rightarrow 4OH^-(aq)$	+0.40
$NiO_2(s) \mid Ni(OH)_2(s)$	$NiO_2(s) + 2H_2O(l) + 2e^- \rightarrow Ni(OH)_2(s) + 2OH^-(aq)$	+0.49
$Ag^+(aq) \mid Ag(s)$	$Ag^+(aq) + e^- \rightarrow Ag(s)$	+0.80
$HNO_3(aq) \mid NO(g)$	$3H^+(aq) + HNO_3(aq) + 3e^- \rightarrow NO(g) + 2H_2O(l)$	+0.96
$Br_2(l) \mid Br^-(aq)$	$Br_2(g) + 2e^- \rightarrow 2Br^-(aq)$	+1.07
$O_2(g) \mid H_2O(l)$	$O_2(g) + 4H^+(aq) + 4e^- \rightarrow 4H_2O(l)$	+1.23
$Cl_2(g) \mid Cl^-(aq)$	$Cl_2(g) + 2e^- \rightarrow 2Cl^-(aq)$	+1.36
$Au^{3+}(aq) \mid Au(s)$	$Au^{3+}(aq) + 3e^- \rightarrow Au(s)$	+1.50
$F_2(g) \mid F^-(aq)$	$F_2(g) + 2e^- \rightarrow 2F^-(aq)$	+2.87

We speak of standard reduction potential in terms of how strongly the species pulls electrons toward itself. Yet just as in a tug-of-war, *we must consider what we are pulling against.* We need a commonly used reference half-reaction with which to compare our reduction. Our reference is called the **standard hydrogen electrode reaction (SHE)**. This half-reaction, which is assigned the potential of zero volts, is also shown in the table as the reduction of H^+ to H_2. To say that the reduction of Cu^{2+} to Cu^0 has a voltage of +0.34 V, as in Table 19.3, really is to say that it has this voltage *compared to the reduction of H^+ described by the SHE reaction.* All potentials that we use in our discussions will be compared to the SHE reaction.

The potential of a half-reaction can be used to assess the spontaneity of the half-reaction. For instance, fluorine has a strong attraction for electrons. Recalling our discussion of ionization energy and electron affinity from Chapter 7, we might predict that adding electrons to F_2 should be more thermodynamically favorable than adding electrons to a Group IA metal cation such as Li^+. The half-reaction potentials for each reduction bear this out. Fluorine has a large positive reduction potential (+2.87 V), and lithium has a large negative reduction potential (−3.04 V). Michael Faraday (1791−1867), an English electrochemist, worked hard to illustrate how a favorable reaction could be related to the potential. Gibbs later was able to show this relationship mathematically as

$$\Delta G° = -nFE°$$

where n is the number of moles of electrons transferred in the reaction, and F is called Faraday's constant, which we'll discuss in a moment. A key feature of this equation is that the change in free energy, $\Delta G°$, and the cell potential, $E°$, have *opposite* signs (*n* and *F* are always positive). Because a negative value of free energy indicates a spontaneous process, *a positive value of cell potential must also indicate spontaneity.*

Faraday's constant is a unit of electric charge equal to the magnitude of charge on a mole of electrons:

$$1 \text{ faraday} = 1 \text{ F} = 96{,}485 \; \frac{\text{coulombs}}{\text{mol}} = 9.6485 \times 10^4 \frac{\text{C}}{\text{mol}}$$

On the basis of the relationship shown by Faraday, we can determine that 1 joule equals 1 coulomb·volt, and $1 \text{ volt} = 1 \dfrac{\text{joule}}{\text{coulomb}}$:

$$1 \text{ J} = 1 \text{ C} \cdot \text{V}$$

$$1 \text{ V} = \frac{\text{J}}{\text{C}}$$

EXERCISE 19.3 **Spontaneity and Potential**

Copper ions undergo reduction according to the following half-reaction:

$$\text{Cu}^{2+}(aq) + 2\text{e}^- \rightarrow \text{Cu}(s) \qquad E^\circ = +0.34 \text{ V}$$

What is the free energy change associated with this process? Is this a spontaneous half-reaction?

Solution

The free energy change is negative; the half-reaction is spontaneous. However, this is only half of a redox reaction.

$$\Delta G^\circ = -nFE^\circ$$

$$= -(2 \text{ mol e}^-)\left(\frac{96485 \text{ C}}{\text{mol e}^-}\right)\left(\frac{+0.34 \text{ J}}{\text{C}}\right)$$

$$= -65609.8 \text{ J} = -66 \text{ kJ}$$

PRACTICE 19.3

The silver cell battery used in pacemakers utilizes the following reaction with a measured potential of 1.86 V. What is ΔG° for this reaction? Is this reaction spontaneous?

$$\text{Ag}_2\text{O}(s) + \text{Zn}(s) \rightarrow 2\text{Ag}(s) + \text{ZnO}(s)$$

See Problems 25 and 26.

Balancing Redox Reactions

To balance a redox reaction such as the one describing the action of nitric acid on copper, we first determine the identity of the half-reactions. It can be hard (if not seemingly impossible!) to balance a redox equation correctly using a trial-and-error approach (Chapter 3), so we often use a series of steps to accomplish the job (see Figure 19.9). To be fair, this method is just a device to make the balancing go more quickly, rather than a representation of what actually happens at the molecular level. In the nanoworld, electron transfer processes not only occur simultaneously rather than sequentially but also occur in a fairly complex way, with charges building up at the phase changes (the so-called interfaces) in solution. Here we will focus just on the technical aspects of balancing equations.

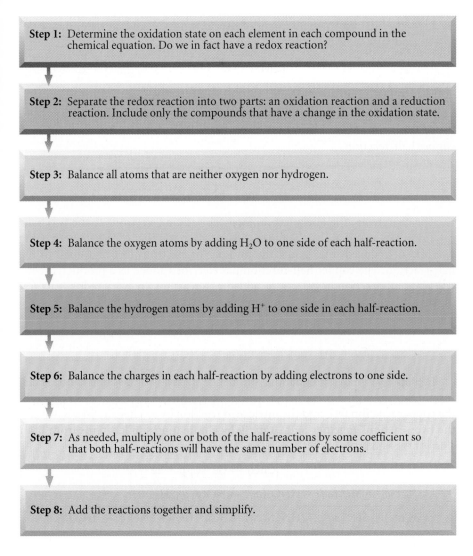

FIGURE 19.9

Algorithm for balancing redox reactions in acidic solution.

Let's follow the algorithm in Figure 19.9 as we balance the copper–nitric acid redox reaction:

$$HNO_3(aq) + Cu(s) \rightarrow Cu^{2+}(aq) + NO(g)$$

Step 1 in Figure 19.9 indicates that we should determine whether we have a redox reaction. That is, does our oxidation state bookkeeping indicate that one species is undergoing oxidation and another is undergoing reduction? We determine that the equation describes a redox process by noting that the oxidation state of copper increases (from 0 to $+2$) while that of nitrogen decreases (from $+5$ to $+2$).

Step 2 indicates that we should separate the redox reaction into the two half-reactions. These half-reactions show the oxidation (copper to copper ion) and the reduction (nitric acid to nitrogen monoxide).

$$Cu(s) \rightarrow Cu^{2+}(aq)$$

$$HNO_3(aq) \rightarrow NO(g)$$

The numbers of atoms (not including H's and O's) are then balanced on both sides of each half-reaction in Step 3. No modification of our reactions is needed for this step.

In Step 4 we balance the number of oxygen atoms by adding water molecules to the product side of the equation.

$$Cu(s) \rightarrow Cu^{2+}(aq)$$

$$HNO_3(aq) \rightarrow NO(g) + 2H_2O(l)$$

In Step 5 the number of hydrogen atoms is then balanced by adding H^+ to the reactant side. Note that in both steps 4 and 5, we did not need to modify the copper half-reaction.

$$Cu(s) \rightarrow Cu^{2+}(aq)$$

$$3H^+(aq) + HNO_3(aq) \rightarrow NO(g) + 2H_2O(l)$$

The charges are then balanced in Step 6 by adding electrons to the two half-reactions. We note that the change in the oxidation number of the element being oxidized or reduced must equal the number of electrons lost or gained in the half-reaction. The copper half-reaction has electrons added as a product; the nitric acid half-reaction has electrons added as a reactant. In every redox reaction, one half-reaction gets the electrons on the right, the other on the left.

$$Cu(s) \rightarrow Cu^{2+}(aq) + 2e^-$$

$$3e^- + 3H^+(aq) + HNO_3(aq) \rightarrow NO(g) + 2H_2O(l)$$

In Step 7 we make sure that the number of electrons is the same in both half-reactions by multiplying the half-reactions by an integer. In this case, we multiply the copper reaction by 3 and the nitric acid reaction by 2. Then, in Step 8, we add the two reactions together and simplify by eliminating similar items from both sides of the equation.

$$3\{Cu(s) \rightarrow Cu^{2+}(aq) + 2e^-\}$$

$$\underline{2\{3e^- + 3H^+(aq) + HNO_3(aq) \rightarrow NO(g) + 2H_2O(l)\}}$$

$$3Cu(s) + 6H^+(aq) + 2HNO_3(aq) \rightarrow 3Cu^{2+}(aq) + 2NO(g) + 4H_2O(l)$$

The result is the balanced redox reaction. One observation and one question can reasonably arise. The observation is that even though the equation is electrically *balanced*, each side is not electrically *neutral*. That is, we have the same +6 charge on each side! Now for the question: Where are the negative charges that would make each side electrically neutral? The answer comes when we remember that we have written *net ionic* equations, rather than complete ionic or molecular equations. In this case, the molecular form comes by adding 6 mol of nitrate ion (NO_3^-) to both sides to give

$$3Cu(s) + 8HNO_3(aq) \rightarrow 3Cu(NO_3)_2(aq) + 2NO(g) + 4H_2O(l)$$

$$3Cu(s) + 6H^+(aq) + 2HNO_3(aq) \rightarrow 3Cu^{2+}(aq) + 2NO(g) + 4H_2O(l)$$
$$\underline{+ 6NO_3^- \qquad\qquad\qquad + 6NO_3^-}$$
$$3Cu(s) + 8HNO_3(aq) \rightarrow 3Cu(NO_3)_2(aq) + 2NO(g) + 4H_2O(l)$$

In other reactions, spectator ions such as Na^+ or Cl^- (if they are actually *in* the solution!) that are not listed in the net ionic equation make the system electrically neutral. The key point is that when we write equations in *net ionic* form, *we expect them to be electrically balanced, not electrically neutral.*

EXERCISE 19.4   **Balancing Redox Equations in Acidic Solutions**

Balance the following equation in acidic solution.

$$Cr_2O_7^{2-}(aq) + NO(g) \rightarrow Cr^{3+}(aq) + NO_3^-(aq)$$

Solution

Step 1: Determine the oxidation state on each element in each compound in the chemical equation. Do we in fact have a redox reaction?

$$Cr_2O_7^{2-}(aq) + NO(g) \rightarrow Cr^{3+}(aq) + NO_3^-(aq)$$

Oxidation states $+6\ -2$ $+2\ -2$ $+3$ $+5\ -2$

Nitrogen is being oxidized from $+2$ to $+5$. Chromium is being reduced from $+6$ to $+3$. This is a redox reaction.

Step 2: Separate the redox reaction into two parts: an oxidation reaction and a reduction reaction. Include just the compounds that have a change in the oxidation state.

$$Cr_2O_7^{2-}(aq) \rightarrow Cr^{3+}(aq) \quad \text{(reduction)}$$

$$NO(g) \rightarrow NO_3^-(aq) \quad \text{(oxidation)}$$

Step 3: Balance all atoms except oxygen and hydrogen.

$$Cr_2O_7^{2-}(aq) \rightarrow 2Cr^{3+}(aq)$$

$$NO(g) \rightarrow NO_3^-(aq)$$

Step 4: Balance the oxygen atoms by adding H_2O to one side in each half-reaction.

$$Cr_2O_7^{2-}(aq) \rightarrow 2Cr^{3+}(aq) + 7H_2O(l)$$

$$2H_2O(l) + NO(g) \rightarrow NO_3^-(aq)$$

Step 5: Balance the hydrogen atoms by adding H^+ to one side in each half-reaction.

$$14H^+(aq) + Cr_2O_7^{2-}(aq) \rightarrow 2Cr^{3+}(aq) + 7H_2O(l)$$

$$2H_2O(l) + NO(g) \rightarrow NO_3^-(aq) + 4H^+(aq)$$

Step 6: Balance the charges in each half-reaction by adding electrons to one side.

$$6e^- + 14H^+(aq) + Cr_2O_7^{2-}(aq) \rightarrow 2Cr^{3+}(aq) + 7H_2O(l)$$

$$2H_2O(l) + NO(g) \rightarrow NO_3^-(aq) + 4H^+(aq) + 3e^-$$

Step 7: As needed, multiply one or both of the half-reactions by some coefficient so that the same number of electrons will appear in both half-reactions.

$$6e^- + 14H^+(aq) + Cr_2O_7^{2-}(aq) \rightarrow 2Cr^{3+}(aq) + 7H_2O(l)$$

$$2\{2H_2O(l) + NO(g) \rightarrow NO_3^-(aq) + 4H^+(aq) + 3e^-\}$$

Step 8: Add the reactions together and simplify. Note that the electrons on each side mathematically cancel, indicating the same number of electrons gained in the reduction as lost in the oxidation.

$$6e^- + 14H^+(aq) + Cr_2O_7^{2-}(aq) \rightarrow 2Cr^{3+}(aq) + 7H_2O(l)$$

$$4H_2O(l) + 2NO(g) \rightarrow 2NO_3^-(aq) + 8H^+(aq) + 6e^-$$

$$\overline{\begin{array}{l} 6e^- + 14H^+(aq) + Cr_2O_7^{2-}(aq) + 4H_2O(l) + 2NO(g) \rightarrow \\ 2Cr^{3+}(aq) + 7H_2O(l) + 2NO_3^-(aq) + 8H^+(aq) + 6e^- \end{array}}$$

$$= 6H^+(aq) + Cr_2O_7^{2-}(aq) + 2NO(g) \rightarrow 2Cr^{3+}(aq) + 2NO_3^-(aq) + 3H_2O(l)$$

The reaction of purple permanganate ion with methanol.

PRACTICE 19.4

Balance the following reaction in acidic solution.

$$ClO^-(aq) + H^+(aq) + Cu(s) \rightarrow Cl^-(aq) + H_2O(l) + Cu^{2+}(aq)$$

See Problems 35–38, 47, 48, and 51. ■

The process we have used to balance the reaction focuses on the use of acidic solutions. Chemical reactions can also occur in basic conditions. The method we present to balance basic reactions requires a little chemical sleight-of-hand but does work effectively. Essentially, we balance the reaction as though it were in an acidic solution (by adding H^+ as necessary) and then add a quantity of hydroxide ion (OH^-) as necessary, to both sides of the equation. Mathematically, we still have our equality. Chemically, we neutralize the H^+, getting water on one side and excess base on the other. *Although this does not depict what goes on in the solution* (we are starting with a base, not doing a titration!) we correctly end up with an excess of OH^- on one side or the other.

We will show the method by looking at the first step in a procedure to analyze methanol (CH_3OH) by reaction with the permanganate ion (MnO_4^-) in base. Before balancing, we have

$$CH_3OH(aq) + MnO_4^-(aq) \rightarrow CO_3^{2-}(aq) + MnO_4^{2-}(aq)$$

To balance the reaction in basic solution, *we first balance it as though it were in acidic solution.* Using our half-reaction technique, we get the following oxidation and reduction half-reactions:

$$2H_2O(l) + CH_3OH(aq) \rightarrow CO_3^{2-}(aq) + 8H^+(aq) + 6e^- \qquad \text{(oxidation)}$$

$$e^- + MnO_4^-(aq) \rightarrow MnO_4^{2-}(aq) \qquad \text{(reduction)}$$

We can multiply the reduction reaction by 6 to balance electrons and add the half-reactions to get the final equation, balanced in acidic solution:

$$2H_2O(l) + CH_3OH(aq) + 6MnO_4^-(aq) \rightarrow CO_3^{2-}(aq) + 8H^+(aq) + 6MnO_4^{2-}(aq)$$

To balance in basic solution, we add an amount of OH^- to each side equal to the amount of H^+.

$$2H_2O(l) + CH_3OH(aq) + 6MnO_4^-(aq) \qquad \rightarrow CO_3^{2-}(aq) + 8H^+(aq) + 6MnO_4^{2-}(aq)$$
$$+ 8OH^-(aq) \qquad\qquad\qquad + 8OH^-(aq)$$

$$8OH^-(aq) + 2H_2O(l) + CH_3OH(aq) + 6MnO_4^-(aq) \rightarrow CO_3^{2-}(aq) + 8H_2O(l) + 6MnO_4^{2-}(aq)$$

We have 8 water molecules on the right and 2 on the left. This leaves an excess of 6 water molecules on the right, to give us our final balanced equation in basic solution:

$$8OH^-(aq) + CH_3OH(aq) + 6MnO_4^-(aq) \rightarrow CO_3^{2-}(aq) + 6H_2O(l) + 6MnO_4^{2-}(aq)$$

EXERCISE 19.5 **Balancing Redox Equations in Basic Solutions**

Balance the following equation in basic solution.

$$I_3^-(aq) + S_2O_3^{2-}(aq) \rightarrow I^-(aq) + SO_4^{2-}(aq)$$

Solution

We may first balance the equation in acidic solution, using our multistep procedure presented in Figure 19.9.

$$I_3^-(aq) + S_2O_3^{2-}(aq) \rightarrow I^-(aq) + SO_4^{2-}(aq)$$

The iodine changes from an oxidation state of $-\frac{1}{3}$ in I_3^- to -1 in I^-. (reduction)

The sulfur changes from an oxidation state of $+2$ in $S_2O_3^{2-}$ to $+6$ in SO_4^{2-}. (oxidation)

The balanced half-reactions in acidic solution are

$$2e^- + I_3^-(aq) \rightarrow 3I^-(aq)$$

$$5H_2O(l) + S_2O_3^{2-}(aq) \rightarrow 2SO_4^{2-}(aq) + 10H^+(aq) + 8e^-$$

We multiply the reduction equation by 4 to equalize the electrons gained and lost in the reduction and oxidation half-reactions

$$4\{2e^- + I_3^-(aq) \rightarrow 3I^-(aq)\} = 8e^- + 4I_3^-(aq) \rightarrow 12I^-(aq)$$

$$5H_2O(l) + S_2O_3^{2-}(aq) \rightarrow 2SO_4^{2-}(aq) + 10H^+(aq) + 8e^-$$

We add the two half-reactions to get the final, balanced equation in acidic solution.

$$5H_2O(l) + S_2O_3^{2-}(aq) + 4I_3^-(aq) \rightarrow 2SO_4^{2-}(aq) + 12I^-(aq) + 10H^+(aq)$$

To balance in base, we add $10OH^-$ to both sides.

$$5H_2O(l) + S_2O_3^{2-}(aq) + 4I_3^-(aq) \rightarrow 2SO_4^{2-}(aq) + 12I^-(aq) + 10H^+(aq)$$
$$+\ 10OH^-(aq) \qquad\qquad\qquad\qquad\qquad\qquad +\ 10OH^-(aq)$$

We cancel our extra waters to give the equation that is now balanced in base.

$$10OH^-(aq) + S_2O_3^{2-}(aq) + 4I_3^-(aq) \rightarrow 2SO_4^{2-}(aq) + 12I^-(aq) + 5H_2O(l)$$

Is the equation electrically and atomically balanced? Check to make sure that the charge is the same on both sides of the equation and that there is the number of atoms on each side. If one or both of these checks do not work, then we've made a mistake balancing the equation.

PRACTICE 19.5

Balance the following equation in basic solution.

$$MnO_4^-(aq) + Mn^{2+}(aq) \rightarrow MnO_2(s)$$

(*Hint*: MnO_2 can be written as the product in both an oxidation and a reduction half-reaction.)

See Problems 39–42 and 52. ∎

Manipulating Half-Cell Reactions

We have learned to balance redox reactions by recognizing that they include electron loss and electron gain. Although calculating the spontaneity of an individual half-reaction may lead to the conclusion that the half-reaction is spontaneous, this is only half of the picture. Because a redox reaction is simply the sum of an oxidation half-reaction and a reduction half-reaction, we determine the spontaneity of the resulting reaction only by including both. Remember that we are using the SHE as our reference point in these calculations.

We can then say that for two half-reactions, the sum of their change in free energy should be equal to the free energy change for the complete redox reaction:

$$\Delta_{rxn}G^\circ = \Delta G_1^\circ + \Delta G_2^\circ$$

If we substitute the equivalent expression $(-nFE^\circ)$ for ΔG°, the equation becomes

$$-n_{rxn}FE_{rxn}^\circ = -n_1FE_1^\circ + -n_2FE_2^\circ$$

Because the value of F is a constant, and because the number of electrons was the same when we balanced the reaction ($n_1 = n_2 = n_{rxn}$), all terms but the cell potentials cancel:

$$E^\circ_{rxn} = E_1^\circ + E_2^\circ$$

This means that if the redox reactions are written so that one is a reduction and one is an oxidation, and the cell potential for the oxidation reaction relative to the SHE has the sign opposite that of its half-reaction potential when written as a reduction, then *the two half-reaction potentials are additive for a balanced redox equation.*

$$E^\circ_{rxn} = E^\circ_{red} + E^\circ_{ox}$$

From that conclusion, we can say, for example, that if copper is oxidized in a reaction, we write it as an oxidation, and just as we reverse the standard free energy value, ΔG°, when we reverse a reaction, we reverse the E°, as follows:

$$Cu^{2+}(aq) + 2e^- \rightarrow Cu(s) \qquad E^\circ = +0.34\,V \text{ (reduction)}$$
$$Cu(aq) \rightarrow Cu^{2+}(aq) + 2e^- \qquad E^\circ = -0.34\,V \text{ (oxidation)}$$

This notion of reversing the cell potential relative to the SHE when we reverse the reaction *gives a consistent picture of the thermodynamic relationship between ΔG° and E°.* In addition, it is a reminder that until 1953, when IUPAC changed its protocol to list half-reaction potentials as reductions, they were formerly listed as oxidations, with opposite signs relative to the SHE.

We know that the nitric acid–copper reaction that we introduced at the beginning of this section is spontaneous, as evidenced by its effect on Ira Remsen's lungs, hands, and pants. Let's see how we can manipulate the half-reactions to confirm this. In Table 19.3, we notice that one of the reactions is the reverse of the desired reaction.

From the balancing process steps 8 and 9:

$$3\{Cu(s) \rightarrow Cu^{2+}(aq) + 2e^-\}$$
$$2\{3e^- + 3H^+(aq) + HNO_3(aq) \rightarrow NO(g) + 2H_2O(l)\}$$
$$\overline{3Cu(s) + 6H^+(aq) + 2HNO_3(aq) \rightarrow 3Cu^{2+}(aq) + 2NO(g) + 4H_2O(l)}$$

From Table 19.3:

$$Cu^{2+}(aq) + 2e^- \rightarrow Cu(s) \qquad E^\circ = +0.34\,V$$
$$3H^+(aq) + HNO_3(aq) + 3e^- \rightarrow NO(g) + 2H_2O(l) \qquad E^\circ = +0.96\,V$$

To make the half-reactions from the table look like the half-reactions in the redox reaction, we need to reverse the copper reduction and write it as an oxidation. As we pointed out above, reversing the reaction also changes the sign on the potential of the reaction, or, in this case, the half-reaction.

$$Cu^{2+}(aq) + 2e^- \rightarrow Cu(s) \qquad E^\circ = +0.34\,V \text{ (reduction)}$$
$$Cu(aq) \rightarrow Cu^{2+}(aq) + 2e^- \qquad E^\circ = -0.34\,V \text{ (oxidation)}$$

However, *no modification of the potential is necessary when we double or triple a half-reaction because the number of electrons involved in the process also doubles or triples.* The free energy, however, does change when we multiply the equation, because $\Delta G^\circ = -nFE^\circ$, and if, as in this case, we triple n, ΔG° will triple as well. This also is consistent with our discussion of thermodynamics in Chapters 5 and 14.

$$Cu(aq) \rightarrow Cu^{2+}(aq) + 2e^- \qquad E^\circ = -0.34\,V \text{ (oxidation)}$$
$$3Cu(s) \rightarrow 3Cu^{2+}(aq) + 6e^- \qquad E^\circ = -0.34\,V \text{ (oxidation)}$$

Table 19.4 lists the key aspects of manipulating half-reactions.

TABLE 19.4	**Important Points for Potentials of Redox Reactions**

- Just as free energies can be combined for chemical reactions, an oxidation and a reduction half-cell potential can be combined to produce a chemical equation.
- Just as you reverse the sign of $\Delta G°$ when you reverse a chemical reaction, you reverse the sign of $E°$ when you reverse a half-cell reaction.
- Although $\Delta G°$ values depend on the coefficients in the chemical equation (that is, when you double the coefficients, you double $\Delta G°$), $E°$ values do not. In a half-reaction, if the coefficients change, the number of electrons, n, will change as well, in essence canceling the effect of the change to the coefficients.
- Because of the negative sign in $\Delta G° = -nFE°$, electrochemical cell reactions with a *positive* voltage are spontaneous. (Recall from Chapter 15 that the rate is not related to the spontaneity of the reaction.)

For the copper–nitric acid reaction, the reaction potential is determined by adding the nitric acid reduction ($+0.96$ V) to the copper oxidation (-0.34 V). The resulting potential is positive ($+0.62$ V), identifying the reaction as a spontaneous process, as is consistent with Ira Remsen's experience.

$$3\{Cu(s) \rightarrow Cu^{2+}(aq) + 2e^-\} \qquad\qquad E° = -0.34 \text{ V}$$

$$\underline{2\{3e^- + 3H^+(aq) + HNO_3(aq) \rightarrow NO(g) + 2H_2O(l)\} \qquad\qquad E° = +0.96 \text{ V}}$$

$$3Cu(s) + 6H^+(aq) + 2HNO_3(aq) \rightarrow 3Cu^{2+}(aq) + 2NO(g) + 4H_2O(l) \quad E°_{cell} = +0.62 \text{ V}$$

EXERCISE 19.6	**Dissolving Gold**

Nitric acid can be used to dissolve copper. Can nitric acid dissolve gold at standard conditions? The unbalanced reaction is shown here.

$$HNO_3(aq) + Au(s) \rightarrow Au^{3+}(aq) + NO(g)$$

First Thoughts

What we're really asking in this problem is "Is the reaction shown spontaneous?" To determine the spontaneity we can use Faraday's equation, which requires us to know the potential of the reaction. We can obtain this by combining properly balanced half-reactions, which have reduction potentials given in Table 19.3.

Solution

The two unbalanced half-reactions of interest are

$$Au(s) \rightarrow Au^{3+}(aq)$$

$$HNO_3(aq) \rightarrow NO(g)$$

We can balance them in acidic solution (because of the presence of nitric acid) and combine them to give

$$Au(s) \rightarrow Au^{3+}(aq) + 3e^- \qquad \text{(oxidation)}$$

$$\underline{3e^- + 3H^+(aq) + HNO_3(aq) \rightarrow NO(g) + 2H_2O(l) \qquad \text{(reduction)}}$$

$$3H^+(aq) + HNO_3(aq) + Au(s) \rightarrow NO(g) + Au^{3+}(aq) + 2H_2O(l)$$

Table 19.3 lists the potential relative to the SHE for each half-reaction written as a reduction. We can reverse the gold reduction reaction because the metal is being oxidized. We can use the potentials of the half-reactions to calculate the cell voltage.

$$Au(s) \rightarrow Au^{3+}(aq) + 3e^- \qquad E° = -1.50 \text{ V}$$

$$\underline{3e^- + 3H^+(aq) + HNO_3(aq) \rightarrow NO(g) + 2H_2O(l) \qquad E° = +0.96 \text{ V}}$$

$$3H^+(aq) + HNO_3(aq) + Au(s) \rightarrow NO(g) + Au^{3+}(aq) + 2H_2O(l) \quad E°_{cell} = -0.54 \text{ V}$$

The negative value for the cell voltage indicates that the reaction of nitric acid and gold is not spontaneous. Nitric acid doesn't dissolve gold.

Further Insights

You've probably noticed that you don't have to balance a redox reaction in order to determine the standard voltage of the reaction. This is because the voltage of a reaction is not dependent on the stoichiometry of the equation. Simply adding the half-reaction potentials (as long as one is an oxidation and the other a reduction) yields the voltage of the resulting reaction. However, it is good practice to balance the equation so that we can tell how many electrons are exchanged. We will need this information if our system is at nonstandard conditions, which is most of the time.

A process for dissolving gold was known during the early days of the alchemists. Because metals like gold and platinum wouldn't react with strong acids, such as nitric acid, they were known as the royal metals. However, there existed a solution that would dissolve gold and platinum. These metals were soluble in a mixture of one part nitric acid and three parts hydrochloric acid known as *aqua regia,* or royal water. Aqua regia is used commercially as a first step in separating platinum from gold that is combined with other metals in their ore mixtures. Both metals are initially dissolved and then selectively precipitated from solution.

PRACTICE 19.6

Determine the cell voltage at standard conditions for the following redox reactions:

$$CH_4(g) + H_2O(g) \rightarrow CO(g) + H_2(g)$$

$$Ag(s) + H_2O_2(aq) \rightarrow H_2O(l) + Ag^+(aq)$$

See Problems 27 and 28.

Application

CHEMICAL
ENCOUNTERS:
The Electric Eel

19.4 Electrochemical Cells

It may be "shocking" to learn, but it's true: The electric eel is a formidable opponent. When startled, stepped on, or hunting for food, the eel can deliver up to 1 ampere (1 coulomb of charge per second) at 600 V, enough electrical energy to stun or even kill large animals. (To be accurate, the electric eel isn't an eel. It lives in fresh water and is really a fish.) How does the electric eel generate the electricity used in hunting?

The powerful shock that the eel can deliver is produced by 5000 to 10,000 specialized cells, called electroplates, in its tail (see Figure 19.10). Using biochemical processes, the eel charges up the electroplates in much the same manner as muscle and nerve cells are charged. Then, when a nerve impulse is sent to the tail, the electroplates discharge their stored potential. Can you think of an electrical storage device similar to the electric eel's that we use every day? The electrochemical cell seems to fit the definition. We'll explore the electrochemical cell in this section

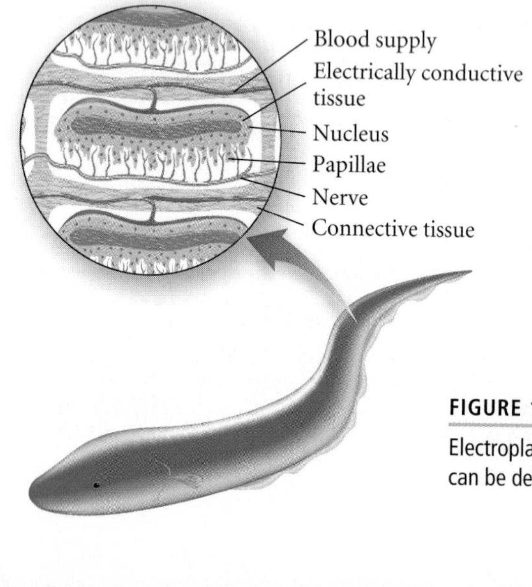

Blood supply
Electrically conductive tissue
Nucleus
Papillae
Nerve
Connective tissue

FIGURE 19.10

Electroplates in the tail of the electric eel develop a potential charge that can be delivered to shock its prey. (Drawing by Rick Simonson.)

and learn how we can make use of the electrical energy of chemical reactions.

Electrochemical Cells in the Laboratory

Redox reactions, such as the dissolving penny, can take place inside a beaker just like other reactions. However, we can harness the energy from the electrons that are exchanged in the redox reaction if we modify the experimental setup. Take a look at what happens when we separate the copper penny from the nitric acid shown in Figure 19.11. The brown fumes produced by the subsequent oxidation of NO to NO_2 by O_2 still waft from the beaker, and the copper ions are still generated. The redox reaction is still working. Examine the experimental setup closely to see why it works. We have

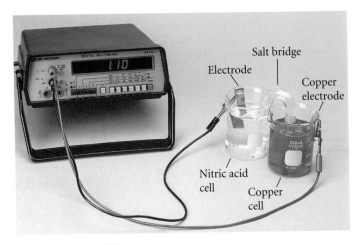

The electrochemical cell. Ira Remsen's observations are still valid in this setup. The nitric acid still acts on the copper. Note the presence of the salt bridge and the electrodes.

$$3Cu(s) + 6H^+(aq) + 2HNO_3(aq) \rightarrow 3Cu^{2+}(aq) + 2NO(g) + 4H_2O(l) \quad E°_{cell} = +0.62 \text{ V}$$

followed by the oxidation of NO to the poisonous NO_2 gas:

$$2NO(g) + O_2(g) \rightarrow 2NO_2(g) \qquad \Delta H° = -112 \text{ kJ}$$

The oxidation half-reaction is in the beaker on the right, and the reduction half-reaction is on the left. The two beakers are connected with a wire that transfers the electrons from beaker to beaker. At both ends of the wire is an electrode. The electrode in the oxidation reaction is called the anode, and the electrode in the reduction reaction is called the cathode. Remember, electrons are one of the products of the copper oxidation. They need someplace to go. Providing a wire for them to travel into the nitric acid reduction reaction keeps the reaction running. If we open the circuit on the wire, the reaction stops. The wire is an essential part of this electrochemical cell.

The tube labeled **salt bridge** in the diagram contains an electrolyte such as potassium chloride or sodium nitrate and *allows ions to pass from beaker to beaker.* The salt bridge is needed because as electrons move from the beaker on the right (the oxidation reaction) to the beaker on the left (the reduction reaction), a strong positive charge will develop at the anode as more of the copper penny becomes Cu^{2+}. A similar thing happens in the other beaker; the H^+ is being removed to make NO and water, and the cathode becomes negatively charged. The developing charges attract the electrons as they move away from the

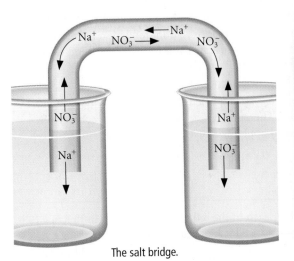

The salt bridge.

FIGURE 19.12

Using the electrochemical cell to light a bulb.

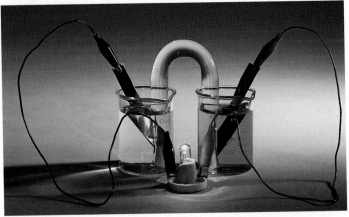

beaker. Without the salt bridge, the electrons would stop this type of movement. We must have a salt bridge in our electrochemical cell design so that the entire system can remain electrically neutral. The finished electrochemical cell produces the same reaction that Ira Remsen observed (nitric acid acts upon copper), but the movement of the electrons through the wire can be used to light a bulb, as shown in Figure 19.12. We have harnessed the electrons as electrical energy.

EXERCISE 19.7   Alkaline Batteries

Some electrochemical cells are constructed using an alkaline electrolyte. Here are two half-cells that can be employed:

$$Cd(OH)_2(s) \rightarrow Cd(s)$$
$$NiO_2(s) \rightarrow Ni(OH)_2(s)$$

a. Based on the information in the standard reduction potentials table (Table 19.3), write the two oxidation–reduction reactions possible from these half-reactions, and calculate their cell potentials.

b. Which could be used as the basis of an electrolytic cell? ... of a galvanic cell? What conditions are required to obtain these specific cell potentials? (Recall our discussion in Section 19.1.)

c. When used as a voltaic cell, this set of reactions makes a useful battery that can power portable appliances and tools. Judging on the basis of the elements that make up the galvanic cell, can you identify the name of this type of battery? What significance does the reverse reaction have?

Solution

a. The two half-cell reactions are

$$Cd(OH)_2(s) + 2e^- \rightarrow Cd(s) + 2OH^-(aq) \qquad E° = -0.81 \text{ V}$$
$$NiO_2(s) + 2H_2O(l) + 2e^- \rightarrow Ni(OH)_2(s) + 2OH^-(aq) \qquad E° = +0.49 \text{ V}$$

If the first reaction is reversed, $E°_{cell} = (+0.81 \text{ V}) + (+0.49 \text{ V}) = +1.30 \text{ V}$.

$$Cd(s) + NiO_2(s) + 2H_2O(l) \rightarrow Cd(OH)_2(s) + Ni(OH)_2(s) \qquad E° = +1.30 \text{ V}$$

If the second reaction is reversed, $E°_{cell} = (-0.81 \text{ V}) + (-0.49 \text{ V}) = -1.30 \text{ V}$.

$$Cd(OH)_2(s) + Ni(OH)_2(s) \rightarrow Cd(s) + NiO_2(s) + 2H_2O(l) \qquad E° = -1.30 \text{ V}$$

In both cases, the $OH^-(aq)$ and the electrons cancel when the half-cell reactions are added.

b. To obtain these voltages, the reactions must be run at 25°C at 1 atm pressure (standard conditions). The concentration of $OH^-(aq)$ must be 1 M (solids have a constant concentration). The first oxidation–reduction reaction could form the basis of a galvanic cell, because $E°_{cell}$ is positive. The second would be electrolytic, because $E°_{cell}$ is negative.

c. This voltaic cell is better known as a NiCad battery. The reverse electrolytic reaction proceeds well, because once formed, the reaction products remain in contact with the electrodes. Therefore NiCad batteries can be recharged by running the cell in reverse by applying a reverse voltage greater than the cell potential.

PRACTICE 19.7

Draw the electrochemical cell for each of the redox reactions given in Practice 19.6. What is the potential of the galvanic cell? ... of the electrolytic cell?

See Problems 57–59.

Cell Notation

Because the balanced chemical equations require a lot of time to write, shorthand notation (called **cell notation**) is often used when describing electrochemical cells. It may look hard to do, but cell notation is as easy as knowing your ABCs—that is, anode, bridge, cathode. Consider the reaction that takes place in the silver oxide cell found in pacemaker batteries:

$$Ag_2O(s) + Zn(s) \rightarrow 2Ag(s) + ZnO(s) \qquad E° = +1.86 \text{ V}$$

A closer look at the half-reactions tells us that silver is being reduced and zinc is being oxidized. The silver metal must be the cathode, and the zinc metal must be the anode. We write each half-reaction, and then, without even balancing them, we construct the overall short-hand notation.

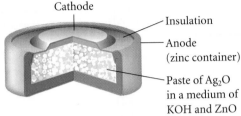

Cutaway view of button battery.

Cathode — Insulation

Anode (zinc container)

Paste of Ag_2O in a medium of KOH and ZnO

$Zn(s) \rightarrow ZnO(s)$ (oxidation, anode) $Zn(s) \mid ZnO(s)$

$Ag_2O(s) \rightarrow Ag(s)$ (reduction, cathode) $Ag_2O(s) \mid Ag(s)$

Bridge

$$Zn(s) \mid ZnO(s) \; \| \; Ag_2O(s) \mid Ag(s)$$

Anode   Cathode

EXERCISE 19.8   Shorthand Notation

Write the shorthand cell notation for the following voltaic cell.

$$Cu^{2+}(aq) + Mg(s) \rightarrow Cu(s) + Mg^{2+}(aq)$$

Solution

Our goal is to write our ABCs—anode, bridge, and cathode. In order to do this, we need to know which half-reaction is the oxidation and which is the reduction. The copper ion gains two electrons, so it is reduced. The copper is the cathode. The magnesium loses two electrons, so it is oxidized. It is the anode. We now have enough information to write the cell notation:

Bridge

$$Mg(s) \mid Mg^{2+}(aq) \; \| \; Cu^{2+}(aq) \mid Cu(s)$$

Anode   Cathode

PRACTICE 19.8

Create a galvanic cell using these half-reactions, and write the cell notation. Check to make sure your reaction is written as a spontaneous redox reaction.

$$Fe^{2+}(aq) + 2e^- \rightarrow Fe(s)$$

$$Al^{3+}(aq) + 3e^- \rightarrow Al(s)$$

See Problems 55 and 56.

Batteries

Commercial batteries come in many shapes and sizes and are based on a wide variety of chemical processes (Table 19.5). The best battery for any application is usually chosen by considering power output, cost, convenience, size, and whether the battery will be rechargeable. The chemistry of commercial batteries is often rather complex compared to the simple electrochemical cells used in the teaching lab to convey the basic principles.

TABLE 19.5	**Selected Batteries**

Zinc–carbon battery Also known as a **standard carbon** battery. Zinc–carbon chemistry is used in all inexpensive AA, C, and D dry-cell batteries. The electrodes are zinc and carbon, with an acidic paste between them that serves as the electrolyte.

Alkaline battery Used in common Duracell and Energizer batteries. The electrodes are zinc and manganese oxide, with an alkaline electrolyte.

Lithium photo battery Lithium, lithium iodide, and lead-iodide are used in cameras because of their ability to supply power surges.

Lead–acid battery (rechargeable) Used in automobiles. The electrodes are made of lead and lead oxide with a strong acidic electrolyte.

Nickel–cadmium battery (rechargeable) The electrodes are nickel hydroxide and cadmium, with potassium hydroxide as the electrolyte.

Nickel–metal hydride battery (rechargeable) This battery is rapidly replacing nickel–cadmium because it does not suffer from the "voltage depression" that nickel-cadmiums do, in which repeated charging after only partial discharges prevents it from fully discharging.

Lithium–ion battery (rechargeable) With a very good power-to-weight ratio, this is often found in high-end laptop computers and cell phones.

Zinc–air battery This battery is lightweight and rechargeable.

Zinc–mercury oxide battery This is often used in hearing aids.

Silver–zinc battery This is used in aeronautical applications because the power-to-weight ratio is good.

Metal–chloride battery Used in electric vehicles.

Hydrogen fuel cell Used in electric vehicles and to power the space shuttle.

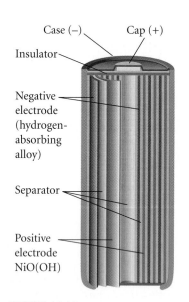

FIGURE 19.13

Nickel metal hydride cell.

The Chemistry of Some Common Batteries

Nickel metal hydride (NiMH) rechargeable batteries are used in many cellular phones (Figure 19.13). During the charging phase, an external source of electricity causes water in the electrolyte (often aqueous potassium hydroxide) to react with a rare earth– or zirconium metal–based alloy at what will be the negative electrode of the battery when it is in operation. This generates hydrogen atoms that are absorbed into the alloy, and releases hydroxide ions:

$$\text{Alloy} + H_2O(l) + e^- \rightarrow \text{Alloy–H}(s) + OH^-(aq) \quad \text{(reduction)}$$

At the other electrode, which will be the positive electrode when the battery is powering the phone, nickel hydroxide reacts with hydroxide ions to form nickel oxyhydroxide, which has nickel in what for it is an unusual +3 oxidation state:

$$Ni(OH)_2(s) + OH^-(aq) \rightarrow NiOOH + H_2O + e^- \quad \text{(oxidation)}$$

When the battery is in use, the hydrogen atoms that were absorbed into the alloy at the negative electrode are released, combining with hydroxide ions to form water and supply the electrons that flow through a circuit to power the phone.

$$\text{Alloy–H}(s) + OH^-(aq) \rightarrow \text{Alloy} + H_2O(l) + e^- \quad \text{(oxidation)}$$

At the positive electrode, nickel oxyhydroxide is reduced back to nickel hydroxide by the electrons that arrive through the circuit, having done their work for us:

$$NiOOH(s) + H_2O(l) + e^- \rightarrow Ni(OH)_2(s) + OH^-(aq) \quad \text{(reduction)}$$

The cycle of charge and discharge can be repeated many times, to power all the talking and text messaging on the move that is such a pervasive part of modern life.

A typical nonrechargeable "alkaline" battery for a flashlight (Figure 19.14) uses the oxidation of zinc metal into zinc ions to generate the electrons for the electric current:

$$Zn(s) \rightarrow Zn^{2+}(aq) + 2e^- \quad \text{(oxidation)}$$

FIGURE 19.14

A common dry cell battery.

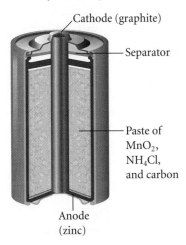

- Cathode (graphite)
- Separator
- Paste of MnO$_2$, NH$_4$Cl, and carbon
- Anode (zinc)

FIGURE 19.15

A lithium ion battery.

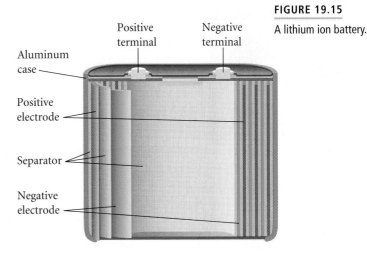

- Positive terminal
- Negative terminal
- Aluminum case
- Positive electrode
- Separator
- Negative electrode

When electrons flow back into the battery at the other electrode, they combine with manganese dioxide:

$$2MnO_2(s) + 2H_2O(l) + 2e^- \rightarrow 2MnO(OH)(s) + 2OH^-(aq) \qquad \text{(reduction)}$$

Therefore, the indirect reaction of zinc with manganese dioxide is the source of the energy that lights the bulb.

Your laptop computer may be powered by a "lithium ion battery" (Figure 19.15). These batteries use lithium oxide mixed with other metal oxides as the positive electrode, and crystalline graphite with lithium ions intercalated within it as the negative electrode. Unlike most conventional batteries, however, the lithium ion battery is not powered by a redox reaction. Instead, lithium ions move back and forth within the battery during the cycle of charging and recharging, accompanied by electrons moving in the external circuit. During charging, the lithium ions are driven into the graphite cathode by application of the external electric current. When the battery is used as a source of power, the ions drift back to the lithium oxide anode. As the ions leave the cathode, electrons must travel around the external circuit, ensuring that there is no overall transfer of electric charge from cathode to anode as the battery is discharged.

19.5   Chemical Reactivity Series

Plumbers often use metal pipes to deliver water from the main water line to your sink faucet. In fact, plumbers used to use lead pipes, but because the lead in the pipe can leach into the water and cause heavy metal poisoning, that practice isn't followed anymore. Even though plastic pipes made from polyvinyl chloride (PVC) are much cheaper than metal pipes, there is still a demand for copper pipes. Why do plumbers use copper for pipes? The demand is mostly due to the durability of copper compared to plastic, but why don't they use iron, lithium, calcium, or magnesium pipes?

The Table of Standard Reduction Potentials (Table 19.3) provides not only cell potentials but also a *ranking* of reducing agents and oxidizing agents. This ranking is called a **reactivity series**. Table 19.6 shows a relative listing of some of the more common metals and includes hydrogen as a reference point. The strongest reducing agents (those elements that are most easily oxidized) are the most reactive metals and can be found at the top of the table: Li, Na, and Mg.

Copper pipes in a home transport water but don't corrode easily.

Sodium reacting with water.

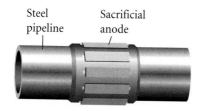

Reaction of copper with water.

TABLE 19.6	Reactivity Series of the Metals		
	Ion	Atom	
Ions difficult to displace	Li^+	Li	**Metals that react with water**
	K^+	K	
	Ca^{2+}	Ca	
	Na^+	Na	
	Mg^{2+}	Mg	
	Al^{3+}	Al	
	Zn^{2+}	Zn	**Metals that react with acid**
	Fe^{2+}	Fe	
	Ni^{2+}	Ni	
	Pb^{2+}	Pb	
Ions easy to displace	H^+	H_2	
	Cu^{2+}	Cu	
	Ag^+	Ag	**Metals that are highly unreactive**
	Au^{3+}	Au	

Steel pipeline   Sacrificial anode

FIGURE 19.16

A sacrificial anode on a steel pipeline.

Because these metals are such good reducing agents, you would not want an earring made out of them; a better choice would be a relatively unreactive metal (and a weak reducing agent) such as gold, copper, or silver, found at the bottom of the table. "Fourteen-carat" gold (which means that $^{14}/_{24}$ of the sample is gold) is an alloy of gold, copper, and silver. "Twenty-four-carat" gold is pure gold. The reactivity series has social importance beyond its significance to earrings. Underwater steel pipelines, which contain substantial amounts of iron, electrochemically corrode (the metal deteriorates via oxidation) as a consequence of the interaction of the iron with water, salt, and oxygen dissolved in the water. This **corrosion** can be minimized by putting, for example, magnesium strips in direct contact with the pipeline, shown in Figure 19.16. The magnesium, which is more chemically active than iron, will preferentially oxidize, ideally leaving the iron in its elemental form. The magnesium, in effect, is sacrificed for the good of the pipeline and therefore is known as a **sacrificial anode**. Other sacrificial anodes include aluminum wrapped around steel in hot water heaters and zinc coating the propellers and rudders of ships.

EXERCISE 19.9	Which Is More Reactive?

Iron, especially in the form of stainless steel, can be used in jewelry, such as in the post of an earring. Where does iron fall on the activity series? Based on the potential for the oxidation of iron to iron(III) ion, why is iron suitable (or not suitable) for jewelry?

Solution

From Table 19.3 we see that the oxidation of metallic iron, Fe(s), has a half-reaction potential of +0.04 V. Metallic copper (−0.34 V), silver (−0.80 V), and gold (−1.50 V) have negative potentials. From this information we can conclude that iron is more reactive than copper, silver, or gold. In this sense *pure* iron would not be suitable, and you may know that iron spontaneously reacts to make rust when in contact with moisture and air. *Stainless steel,* however, is an alloy formulated to inhibit corrosion. Some formulas have as much as 18% chromium and 8% nickel added to the iron. The half-reaction potential for stainless steel is different, and it is difficult to predict reactivity from the $E°$ values for its constituent elements.

PRACTICE 19.9

Arrange the following in decreasing order of reactivity:

Na   Al   Ca   Cu

See Problems 63–66.

19.6 Not-So-Standard Conditions: The Nernst Equation

Native copper and other copper objects can be cleaned with relatively dilute solutions of nitric acid. Concentrated nitric acid is too strong for the job, as Ira Remsen noted, so ancient coins should not be cleaned with concentrated nitric acid. A very dilute solution in the hands of a professional, however, can transform a 1600-year-old coin into a masterpiece that looks as new as the day it was minted. **How does lowering the concentration of nitric acid change the reactivity?** It does reduce the rate of the reaction (see Chapter 15), but is there an effect on the potential of the reaction as well? What about the temperature of the reaction? We know that in general, the rate of a reaction increases as the temperature is raised (also from Chapter 15). Does cold, dilute nitric acid still react with copper? We can understand these relationships, which are at *nonstandard* conditions, by considering a simpler system in which the copper ion reacts with zinc metal.

If we put a zinc strip into a solution of copper(II) chloride, we note that a dark film immediately begins to form on the zinc strip (Figure 19.17a on page 852). Within an hour, the entire zinc strip has oxidized into the solution, and we are left with a brown mass of copper metal (Figure 19.17b). We also note the disappearance of the blue color that is characteristic of Cu^{2+} in water. This is consistent with the following half-reactions and overall cell reaction:

$$Cu^{2+}(aq) + 2e^- \rightarrow Cu(s) \qquad\qquad E° = +0.34\ V$$

$$\underline{Zn(s) \rightarrow Zn^{2+}(aq) + 2e^- \qquad\qquad E° = +0.76\ V}$$

$$Cu^{2+}(aq) + Zn(s) \rightarrow Zn^{2+}(aq) + Cu(s) \qquad E°_{cell} = +1.10\ V$$

We know from Section 19.3 that we can relate the free energy of a system to the cell potential:

$$\Delta G = -nFE$$

We also discussed in Section 14.6 the relationship between free energy change and the standard free energy change:

$$\Delta G = \Delta G° + RT \ln Q$$

in which Q = the reaction quotient, the ratio of the concentrations (more properly, the activities) of the products over the reactants; R is the universal gas constant; and T is the temperature in kelvins. For our current example,

$$\Delta G = \Delta G° + RT \ln \frac{[Zn^{2+}]_0}{[Cu^{2+}]_0}$$

We can substitute for ΔG the expression for the cell potential, $\Delta G = -nFE$:

$$-nFE = -nFE° + RT \ln \frac{[Zn^{2+}]_0}{[Cu^{2+}]_0}$$

Dividing each term by $-nF$ enables us to solve for the cell potential at nonstandard conditions:

$$E = E° - \frac{RT}{nF} \ln \frac{[Zn^{2+}]_0}{[Cu^{2+}]_0}$$

FIGURE 19.17

Zinc metal reacting with copper(II) chloride solution.

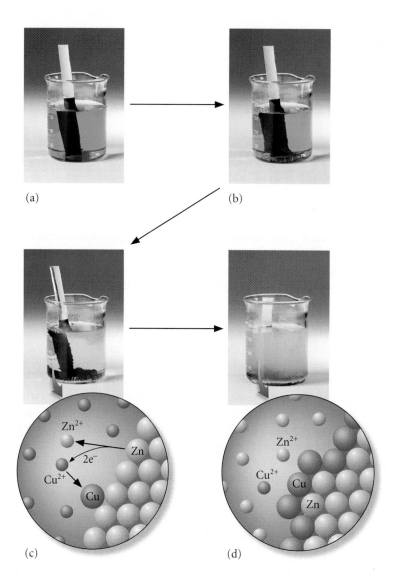

(a)

(b)

(c)

(d)

This is one form of the **Nernst equation**, named after Walther Hermann Nernst (1864–1941), a German chemist who studied the effect of concentration on the potential of an electrochemical cell. We can write a more general form of the equation, taking into account the reaction quotient for any process:

$$E = E° - \frac{RT}{nF} \ln Q$$

Because most reactions are conducted at standard temperature (25 °C, 298 K), we can calculate the term $\frac{RT}{F}$.

$$\frac{RT}{F} = \frac{8.3145 \text{ J·mol}^{-1}\text{·K}^{-1}(298 \text{ K})}{96485 \text{ C·mol}^{-1}} = 0.0257$$

which we can substitute into the Nernst equation in this form:

$$E = E° - \frac{0.0257}{n} \ln Q$$

Although our calculators can easily handle the natural logarithm ("ln") in the equation, we typically convert the equation to the more familiar base 10 "log" by multiplying by 2.3026 (that is, log(10) = 1, and ln 10 = 2.3026, so log = ln/2.3026).

To account for that, we multiply the coefficient, $\dfrac{0.0257}{n}$, by 2.3026, which gives us the *final, common form of the Nernst equation*:

$$E = E° - \frac{0.0592}{n} \log Q$$

Using this equation, we can determine the effect of lowering the concentration of nitric acid on the potential of the copper oxidation.

The Nernst equation can also be used to measure the concentration of a solution if the standard cell potential and the actual potential are known. Electrochemists take advantage of this use of the Nernst equation via ion-selective electrodes, in which the concentration of an ion such as chloride, ammonium, cadmium, nitrate, or hydrogen (in a pH electrode) is determined. And there's something else that's interesting about the Nernst equation. For example, let's consider the hypothetical redox reaction between copper metal and copper ions in solution. The potential of the reduction half-reaction and that of the oxidation half-reaction are the same at *standard conditions,* and, as we'd expect, no net potential should be noticed for an electrochemical cell containing these reactions.

$$Cu^{2+}(aq) + 2e^- \rightarrow Cu(s) \qquad\qquad E°_{red} = +0.34\ V$$
$$\underline{\quad Cu \rightarrow Cu^{2+}(aq) + 2e^- \qquad\qquad E°_{ox} = -0.34\ V \quad}$$
$$Cu(s) + Cu^{2+}(aq) \rightarrow Cu^{2+}(aq) + Cu(s) \qquad E°_{cell} = 0.00\ V$$

However, what would happen if we increased the concentration of the reactant copper ions to 2.0 *M* instead of the standard 1.0 *M*? Doing so changes the distribution of the species in the reaction. Using the Nernst equation, we can calculate the result of our modification.

$$E = E° - \frac{0.0592}{n} \log\left(\frac{1.0}{2.0}\right)$$
$$E = 0.00 - \frac{0.0592}{2} \log(0.5)$$
$$E = 0.00 - (-0.0089)$$
$$E = +0.0089\ V$$

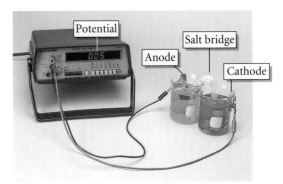

FIGURE 19.18

The concentration cell. The voltage observed in the copper concentration cell is due to the differences in concentration of Cu^{2+} at the anode and cathode.

The electrochemical potential of the reaction is a nonzero value. By adjusting the concentrations of the products and reactants, we have created an electrochemical cell. This type of cell is called a **concentration cell** because the concentrations are driving the potential of the cell (Figure 19.18). This is the same type of potential that develops across the membrane of a muscle cell or nerve cell.

How does our cell notation change to reflect the fact that the conditions are not-so-standard? By indicating the concentrations in parentheses immediately after the species, we can immediately show how the reaction should be written. For example,

$$Cu(s)\ |\ Cu^{2+}(aq)\ (1.0\ M)\ ||\ Cu^{2+}(aq)\ (2.0\ M)\ |\ Cu(s)$$

EXERCISE 19.10   Heart Cell Potential

At the beginning of this chapter, we mentioned the electrical signals in the heart muscle. Given the differing concentrations of potassium ions inside and outside the heart cells, what is the electrochemical potential that corresponds to this concentration gradient? Assume that the electrochemical cell in the body can be represented by the following cell notation. (In truth, no elemental potassium exists in the human body. We use this concentration cell as a model merely to estimate the potential that is obtained in a heart muscle cell.)

$$K(s) \mid K^+(aq)\ (0.005\ M) \parallel K^+(aq)\ (0.166\ M) \mid K(s)$$

Solution

This concentration cell is based on the potassium half-reaction. The complete reaction is

$$K(s) + K^+(aq) \rightarrow K(s) + K^+(aq) \qquad E^\circ_{cell} = 0.00\ V$$

There is one electron involved in the reaction. Using the information from the Nernst equation, we get a potential of +0.090 V.

$$E_{cell} = E^\circ_{cell} - \frac{0.0592}{n} \log\left(\frac{[K^+_{product}]_0}{[K^+_{reactant}]_0}\right)$$

$$E_{cell} = 0.00 - \frac{0.0592}{1}\log\left(\frac{0.005}{0.166}\right)$$

$$E_{cell} = 0.00 - 0.0592\log(0.03012)$$

$$E_{cell} = 0.00 - 0.0592(-1.521)$$

$$E_{cell} = 0.00 - (-0.09005)$$

$$E_{cell} = +0.090\ V$$

In the heart cell, the sodium gradient provides a potential of −0.052 V. The net potential across the membrane of the heart cell is +0.038 V.

PRACTICE 19.10

What is the potential of the following electrochemical cell written in shorthand cell notation? What is the half-reaction listed on the right-hand side? Is this a voltaic cell? (Assume that the pressure of hydrogen gas is 1.0 atm in each half-cell.)

$$H_2(g) \mid H^+(aq)\ (1.0\ M) \parallel H^+(aq)\ (0.10\ M) \mid H_2(g)$$

See Problems 69–72.

When we listen to a battery-powered radio, the sound tends to get softer as the radio is used. What is happening inside the battery that causes this power loss? During the progress of the reaction inside the battery, the reactants are being used up as the products are being formed. According to the Nernst equation, as the value of Q gets larger, the modification to the standard cell potential (E°) gets more and more negative and closer and closer to zero. What is the result? As the reaction proceeds, the potential of the battery decreases as the system inches ever closer to equilibrium, and the music gets softer. At some point, the battery doesn't have enough voltage to run the radio. It has not yet reached equilibrium, but it is below the threshold that will allow the radio to operate. We say that the batteries are dead. As we have pointed out already, some batteries can be recharged, because their discharge reactions can be run in reverse. Rechargeable batteries can be charged only a finite number of times, typically in the range of 500 to 1000 times for household batteries, because the surfaces of the recharged electrodes do not form as cleanly as the original surface, and they eventually become too worn to be useful.

The Nernst Equation and the Equilibrium Constant

Measuring the standard cell potential is a very powerful way to solve for the equilibrium constant of a reaction. Here's how. When a redox reaction proceeds without any intervention, it will inevitably reach equilibrium. At that point the value of E_{cell} must become zero, and the free energy *change* for the process also becomes zero—our thermodynamic definition of equilibrium, introduced in Chapter 16. When this occurs, the Q value in the Nernst equation is equal to the equilibrium constant K. We can show this reasoning by using the following equations:

$$\Delta G = \Delta G° + RT \ln Q$$

At equilibrium, $\Delta G = 0$

so $0 = \Delta G° + RT \ln K$ (note that "Q" has become "K")

$$\Delta G° = -RT \ln K$$

We know that $\Delta G° = -nFE°$

Substituting $-nFE°$ into the previous equation yields

$$-RT \ln K = -nFE°$$

Solving for K, we get $\ln K = \dfrac{nFE°}{RT}$

Calculating $\dfrac{F}{RT}$ at standard conditions (as we did for the Nernst equation), we find that

$$\ln K = 38.92 \, nE°$$

Converting from natural ln to base 10 log (by dividing by 2.3026, as we did in the Nernst equation, yields

$$\log K = 16.9 \, nE°$$

To clearly show the connection to the Nernst equation, we will invert 16.9 and put the result in the denominator.

$$\log K = \dfrac{nE°}{0.0592}$$

We can use the equation in this way. Alternatively, we can take the antilog of both sides and use it in this way:

$$K = 10^{\frac{nE°}{0.0592}}$$

Which form of the equation you use depends mostly on your comfort level. We can solve for the equilibrium constant either way. The key point is that *our understanding of the thermodynamic meaning of equilibrium enables us to relate cell potential to the equilibrium constant.* The rest is just manipulating equations to get where we want to go. Let's see how we use this relationship to determine the equilibrium constant for the copper–nitric acid reaction performed by Ira Remsen. Recall that the reaction is

$$3Cu(s) + 6H^+(aq) + 2HNO_3(aq) \rightarrow 3Cu^{2+}(aq) + 2NO(g) + 4H_2O(l) \quad E°_{cell} = +0.62 \text{ V}$$

$$K = 10^{\frac{nE°}{0.0592}}$$

$$K = 10^{\frac{6(+0.62)}{0.0592}} = 10^{62.8} \approx 10^{63}$$

Alternatively,

$$\log K = \dfrac{nE°}{0.0592} = \dfrac{6(+0.62)}{0.0592} = 62.8$$

Raising both sides to the power of 10 yields

$$K \approx 10^{63}$$

This is yet another confirmation that the reaction does, in fact, proceed toward products. As we have this discussion, however, please keep in mind the difference between thermodynamics and kinetics. Thermodynamics answers the question "Can a process occur spontaneously?" It says absolutely nothing about speed. Kinetics addresses the issues of rates and mechanisms. All that our calculations tell us is that nitric acid *can* react spontaneously with the copper penny. They don't say how fast. That's a question of kinetics.

EXERCISE 19.11   **Equilibrium Constants and Cell Potential**

Vanadium(V) ion can be reduced stepwise (that is, to V^{4+}, V^{3+} and, finally, V^{2+}) by reaction with a "Jones Reductor," a zinc–mercury amalgam. The reaction for the reduction of V^{5+} to V^{4+} ion includes the following two half-reactions:

$$VO_2^+(aq) + H^+(aq) \rightarrow VO^{2+}(aq) + H_2O(l) \qquad E° = +1.00\ V$$

$$Zn^{2+}(aq) \rightarrow Zn(s) \qquad E° = -0.76\ V$$

Calculate the equilibrium constant for this reaction.

First Thoughts

There are a number of steps to solving this problem. One way to figure out what we need to do in working forward is to start by working backward (where do we want to be, and how do we get there?). We want the value for K. In order to get that, we need the value for $E°$. In order to get *that*, we need to have a balanced redox equation for the reduction of VO_2^+ to VO^{2+}, in which V^{5+} is reduced to V^{4+}, and Zn^0 is oxidized to Zn^{2+}. Our order of operations, then, is

1. Balance the redox reaction.
2. Calculate the $E°$ value for the reaction.
3. Calculate the equilibrium constant, knowing the number of electrons exchanged in the reaction, along with the value for $E°$.

How might we assess whether the answer we calculate makes sense? At this point, because we know that the reduction of vanadium ion does occur, our equilibrium constant should be greater than 1. How much greater will depend on the cell voltage and on the number of electrons transferred in the process.

Solution

The balanced half-reactions and overall cell reaction are

$$2VO_2^+(aq) + 4H^+(aq) + 2e^- \rightarrow 2VO^{2+}(aq) + 2H_2O(l) \qquad\qquad E° = +1.00\ V$$

$$Zn(s) \rightarrow Zn^{2+}(aq) + 2e^- \qquad\qquad E° = +0.76\ V$$

$$\overline{2VO_2^+(aq) + 4H^+(aq) + Zn(s) \rightarrow 2VO^{2+}(aq) + Zn^{2+}(aq) + 2H_2O(l) \quad E° = +1.76\ V}$$

$$K = 10^{\frac{nE°}{0.0592}}$$

$$K = 10^{\frac{2(+1.76)}{0.0592}} = 10^{59.5} \approx 10^{60}$$

Alternatively,

$$\log K = \frac{nE°}{0.0592} = \frac{2(+1.76)}{0.0592} = 59.5$$

Raising both sides to the power of 10 yields

$$K \approx 10^{60}$$

Further Insights

Does our answer make sense? The cell voltage is very high and positive in this two-electron transfer, so our equilibrium constant is large, indicating that the reduction of vanadium proceeds essentially to completion.

Here are pictures of the vanadium solutions, showing each ion from V^{5+} (left-most picture) to V^{2+} (rightmost picture). We will discuss the reasons why transition metal ions in solution have color, and often change color when reduced or oxidized, in the next chapter.

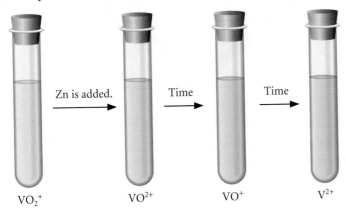

The varying oxidation states of vanadium.

PRACTICE 19.11

What is the equilibrium constant for the reaction of copper metal with zinc ion, discussed at the beginning of this section?

See Problem 68.

19.7   Electrolytic Reactions

Some metals, including copper, gold, and silver, are found in their pure elemental state in the environment. On the other hand, aluminum metal, based on its reactivity (Section 19.5) is found only chemically combined in ores such as bauxite (hydrated aluminum oxide; $Al_2O_3 \cdot H_2O$ or $Al_2O_3 \cdot 3H_2O$). In fact, aluminum, largely in the form of the aluminum oxides and silicates, makes up 8.1% of the Earth's crust. However, we know that pure aluminum can be produced, because it is a major component in so many common products: the can in which we store our soda, the wrap in which we put our fish for freezing, and the lightweight bicycle we ride down the street. How is aluminum metal made from bauxite?

The basic process, called electrolysis, entails passing a current through a solution of metal ions in an electrochemical cell *in the direction opposite to the spontaneous reaction*. Doing so forces the nonspontaneous reaction to occur. This process, also known as **electrowinning**, is responsible for the manufacture and purification not only of aluminum but also of many other metals.

$$Al^{3+} + 3e^- \rightarrow Al$$

$$Cu^{2+} + 2e^- \rightarrow Cu$$

$$Ag^+ + e^- \rightarrow Ag \qquad etc. \dots$$

Electrowinning is the most inexpensive method for making aluminum and magnesium metals. Electrowinning of metals such as aluminum and magnesium

FIGURE 19.19

The Hall–Heroult process. This process is still used today to satisfy the world's demand for aluminum products. The product, molten aluminum, is relatively dense and settles to the bottom of the electrochemical cell, where it is drawn off and poured into castings.

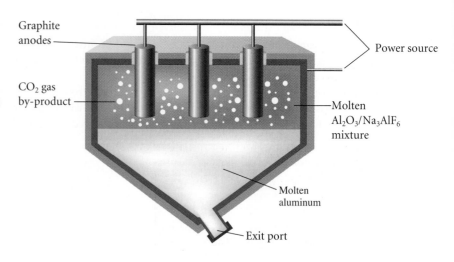

is the isolation of pure metals from a solution of metal ions, and it has been known for quite some time. Humphrey Davey, an English chemist, used this process to isolate metallic sodium from NaCl in 1807. However, the electrowinning of aluminum wasn't invented until 1886. Working independently, Charles M. Hall (an American chemist) and Paul Heroult (a French chemist) discovered that if bauxite ore was purified to alumina (Al_2O_3) and dissolved in molten cryolite (Na_3AlF_6), metallic aluminum could be made. In the **Hall–Heroult process**, an electrical current is passed into a molten mixture of alumina and cryolite to make molten aluminum (Figure 19.19). The overall reaction used in the Hall–Heroult process, shown below, is much simpler than the reactions that take place at the electrodes. Why can't an electric current be applied directly to an aqueous solution of Al^{3+} in order to produce aluminum metal? Because the potential is so large, instead of obtaining aluminum metal from the aqueous solution, the water undergoes electrolysis to form hydrogen and oxygen gases.

$$2Al_2O_3(l) + 3C(s) \rightarrow 4Al(l) + 3CO_2(g) \qquad E° \approx -2.1 \text{ V}$$

The negative potential tells us that this redox reaction is not spontaneous. In fact, the reverse reaction—that is, $4Al(l) + 3CO_2(g) \rightarrow 2Al_2O_3(l) + 3C(s)$—is quite spontaneous ($E° \approx +2.1$ V). Modifying the concentrations and temperatures helps a little to make the potential of the overall reaction less negative, via the Nernst equation, but not enough to make the reaction spontaneous. If we apply a positive potential to the reaction that is larger than the negative potential expressed by the electrochemical cell, we can force the reaction to go forward.

Examination of a simpler redox reaction can be helpful here. For example, in concept, if we wish to make the copper–iron redox reaction spontaneous, we must supply a potential of just over +0.78 V to the reaction to make up for the fact that $E°$ is −0.78 V.

$$Cu(s) + Fe^{2+}(aq) \rightarrow Fe(s) + Cu^{2+}(aq) \qquad E° = -0.78 \text{ V}$$

When we do this, however, we note experimentally that the reaction still doesn't proceed toward products. If we supply a still greater positive potential, the reaction does proceed. The extra voltage required is called the **overpotential** of the reaction. Overpotentials can be fairly high, especially when the products of the reaction are gases. Unfortunately, we can't easily predict what the overpotential for a particular reaction will be. Instead we measure the overpotential experimentally.

The Applications of Electrolysis

The average American uses 142 tin cans each year. From what are tin cans made? That might sound like a silly question, but "tin" cans are actually made of steel coated with a very thin layer of tin (Figure 19.20). Approximately 0.25% of the mass of a tin can is actually tin, and chromium is becoming more common as a coating on the steel. Without the coating, the steel would rust and the contents would spoil. The tin coating on a steel can isn't applied like paint on a house. How is the tin applied to the steel?

The most common use for electrolysis is **electroplating**, or depositing metals onto a conducting surface. The result is a coating that is very tightly integrated into the surface of the metal. Because of this tight integration into the metal surface, the coating resists flaking and peeling. This coating makes the item more attractive and imparts some corrosion resistance or chemical resistance to the surface. Electroplating is used in the manufacture of inexpensive jewelry and chrome bumpers for your car, but most common electroplating today occurs in the manufacture of tin cans.

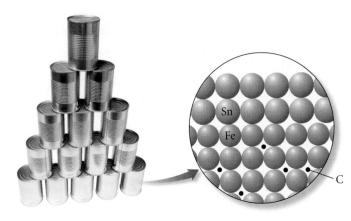

FIGURE 19.20

Tin cans are actually steel cans electroplated with a thin coat of tin. The tin resists corrosion and helps keep the contents fresh.

Application
CHEMICAL
ENCOUNTERS:
Electroplating

Calculations Involving Electrolysis

The process used to coat a steel can with tin is an example of electrolysis. How is it done? The steel can is hooked up to a power supply and dipped into a solution of tin ions (Sn^{2+}). A block of tin metal is also placed in the solution and connected to the power supply. Then a current is applied to the can (Figure 19.21). In the terminology of the electrolytic cell, the block of tin metal becomes the anode and the can becomes the site of reduction (the cathode) for tin ions.

Michael Faraday (remember him from our discussion on potentials and spontaneity) noted that the amount of current applied to a cell is directly proportional to the amount of metal that can be deposited in an electrolytic reaction. We can represent this mathematically as

$$g = \frac{A \cdot s \cdot (\underline{M})}{F} \left(\frac{\text{mol metal}}{\text{mol e}^-} \right)$$

where *A* is the number of amperes applied to the can
    (1 ampere = 1 coulomb of charge per second)
   s is the number of seconds that the current is
    applied
   $\underline{M}$ is the molar mass of the metal
   F is Faraday's constant (96,485 coulombs/mol
    electrons)
   the ratio (mol metal/mol e⁻) is the mole ratio
    of the reduction half-reaction

It is helpful to look at this calculation as an extended unit conversion problem. Exercise 19.12 shows how this is done. Note that the unit conversion problem is the same as the equation shown above.

FIGURE 19.21

Electroplating a tin can. The tin can acts as the cathode in the electrolysis experiment.

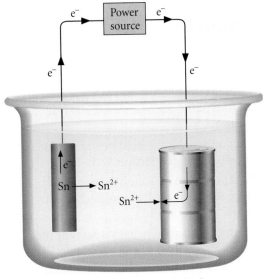

To save money and still have a beautiful set of dinnerware, a chemist decides to electroplate the metal with gold. How many grams of gold will be electroplated on a fork if 2.5 A is applied to the fork for 20 s?

Solution

The number of grams can be calculated by starting with the current and performing a unit conversion. Note that the unit amperes (amps, A) can be written as coulombs/second (C/s). We also need to examine the reduction half-reaction from Table 19.3 to determine the number of electrons involved in the process.

$$Au^{3+}(aq) + 3e^- \rightarrow Au(s)$$

$$\frac{2.5\ C}{s} \times \frac{20\ s}{} \times \frac{1\ mol\ e^-}{96{,}485\ C} \times \frac{1\ mol\ Au}{3\ mol\ e^-} \times \frac{196.97\ g\ Au}{1\ mol\ Au} = 0.034\ g\ Au$$

$$Amperes \times time \times \frac{1}{faraday} \times mole\ ratio \times \underline{M} = grams$$

This means that our chemist would need to make sure to buy at least 0.034 g of gold per fork.

How many grams of tin will be deposited from a solution of tin(II) nitrate on a steel can if 0.45 A are applied to the can for 1.5 h?

See Problems 73–78.

The calculations can also be done in reverse. If we want to coat our steel can with a certain number of grams of tin, we can use either the equation or the unit conversion method to calculate the number of amps that need to be applied.

As we've seen in this chapter, electrochemistry is a very useful topic, especially in today's society. Learning how muscles in our body begin a contraction can help us understand how the heart works and why it is so important to maintain sufficient levels of electrolytes during physical exercise. And as we become increasingly mobile, the demand for longer-lasting batteries will only increase. Batteries power our cell phones, our portable CD players, and even our cars. Electroplating the surfaces of many everyday items makes them appear expensive and confers resistance to corrosion. In fact, everywhere we look, there's electrochemistry!

The Bottom Line

- Redox reactions involve both a reduction and an oxidation half-reaction. (Sections 19.1 and 19.3)
- Redox reactions can be identified by determining the oxidation state of the atoms involved in a reaction. (Section 19.2)
- Redox reactions can be balanced by summation of balanced half-reactions. (Section 19.3)
- Positive cell potentials indicate a spontaneous reaction and are related to the free energy change by $\Delta G° = -nFE°$. (Section 19.3)
- Electrochemical cells require both a path for the electrons and a path for other ions. (Section 19.4)
- The oxidation reaction takes place at the anode. The reduction reaction takes place at the cathode. (Section 19.4)

- The Nernst equation relates the actual potential of a redox reaction to conditions other than the standard conditions. (Section 19.6)
- Half-reaction potentials can be used to determine the relative reactivity of metals. Organization of the metals in this fashion is known as a chemical reactivity series. (Section 19.5)
- Cell potentials enable us to calculate equilibrium constants. (Section 19.6)
- Electrowinning and electroplating are examples of electrolysis reactions. In electrolysis, a positive potential that includes the overpotential is applied to force the reaction to run in reverse. (Section 19.7)

Key Words

anode The electrode at which oxidation takes place. (*p. 826*)

battery Two or more voltaic cells joined in series. (*p. 826*)

cardiologist A heart specialist. (*p. 824*)

cathode The electrode at which reduction takes place. (*p. 826*)

cell notation The chemist's shorthand used to describe electrochemical cells. (*p. 847*)

concentration cell A cell in which different concentrations of identical ions on both sides of the cell provide the driving force for the reaction. (*p. 853*)

corrosion The deterioration of a metal as a consequence of oxidation. (*p. 850*)

disproportionation A reaction in which a single reactant is both the oxidizing and the reducing agent. (*p. 830*)

electrochemical cell A device that allows the exchange between chemical and electrical energy. (*p. 825*)

electrochemistry The study of the reduction and oxidation processes that occur at the meeting point of different phases of a system. (*p. 825*)

electrochemists Scientists who create or analyze systems that allow exchanges between chemical and electrical energy. (*p. 824*)

electrode A metal surface that acts as a collector or distributor for electrons. (*p. 826*)

electrodics The study of the interactions that occur between a solution of electrolytes and an electrical conductor, often a metal. (*p. 825*)

electrolytic cell A cell that requires the addition of electrical energy to drive the chemical reaction under study. (*p. 826*)

electromotive force (emf) A measure of how strongly a species pulls electrons toward itself in a redox process. Also known as voltage. (*p. 834*)

electroplating The process of depositing metals onto a conducting surface. (*p. 859*)

electrowinning The isolation of pure metals from a solution of metal ions. (*p. 857*)

Faraday's constant A unit of electric charge equal to the magnitude of charge on a mole of electrons. (*p. 836*)

fuel cell An electrochemical cell that utilizes continually replaced oxidizing and reducing reagents to produce electricity. (*p. 826*)

galvanic cell A cell that produces electricity from a chemical reaction. Also known as a voltaic cell. (*p. 825*)

gel electrophoresis The use of electric fields to separate ions. (*p. 825*)

half-reaction An equation that describes the reduction or oxidation part of a redox reaction. (*p. 826*)

Hall–Heroult process The most widely used process for the preparation of aluminum from bauxite. (*p. 858*)

ionics The study of the behavior of ions dissolved in liquids. (*p. 825*)

Nernst equation The equation used to determine the cell potential at nonstandard conditions. (*p. 852*)

nitrogen cycle The path that nitrogen follows through its different oxidation states on Earth. (*p. 831*)

overpotential The extra potential needed, above that which is calculated, in order to make an electrochemical process proceed. (*p. 858*)

oxidation The loss of electrons. (*p. 826*)

oxidation reaction In a redox reaction, the half-reaction that supplies electrons. (*p. 826*)

oxidation state A bookkeeping tool that gives us insight into the distribution of electrons in a compound. Also known as oxidation number. (*p. 827*)

oxidizing agent A substance that causes the oxidation of another substance. (*p. 830*)

potential The driving force (to perform a reaction) that results from a difference in electrical charge between two points. (*p. 824*)

reactivity series A ranking of the electrochemical reactivity of some elements. (*p. 849*)

redox reactions Chemical reactions in which reduction and oxidation occur. (*p. 824*)

reducing agent A substance that causes the reduction of another substance. (*p. 830*)

reduction The gain of electrons. (*p. 827*)

reduction reaction In a redox reaction, the half-reaction that acquires electrons. (*p. 826*)

sacrificial anode A material that will oxidize more easily than the one we seek to protect from oxidation. (*p. 850*)

salt bridge A device containing a strong electrolyte that allows ions to pass from beaker to beaker. (*p. 845*)

standard hydrogen electrode reaction (SHE) A reference half-reaction of the reduction of hydrogen ion to hydrogen gas, against which to compare our reduction. (*p. 835*)

standard potential ($E°$) The measure of the potential of a reaction at standard conditions. (*p. 834*)

volt The SI unit of potential. (*p. 834*)

voltage A measure of how strongly a species pulls electrons toward itself. Also known as electromotive force (emf). (*p. 834*)

voltaic cell A cell that produces electricity from a chemical reaction. Also known as a galvanic cell. (*p. 825*)

Focus Your Learning

The answers to the odd-numbered problems appear at the back of the book.

19.1 What Is Electrochemistry?

Skill Review

1. Explain why the descriptive term *battery* is often used, but is technically not correct, to describe these most commonly purchased sources of electricity.

2. Provide two other names for an electrochemical cell.

Chemical Applications and Practices

3. Every electrochemical cell is developed around two types of chemical reactions. Name and describe both of these connected reactions.

4. List three properties of electrochemical cells that are considered when designing an appropriate power source.

Section 19.2 Oxidation States—Electronic Bookkeeping

Skill Review

5. Determine the oxidation number of each atom in the structure of dimethylsulfoxide (DMSO).

6. Determine the oxidation number of each atom in the structure of periodic acid.

7. In which of the following compounds would the chlorine atom have the most positive oxidation number? In which would chlorine have the most negative oxidation number? Cl_2; ClO_2; $NaClO_4$; HCl

8. Which species in the following list shows the nitrogen atom in its most reduced form? Which depicts nitrogen in its most oxidized form? N_2; HNO_3; NH_3

9. Put the following compounds in order from the lowest to the highest oxidation number for nitrogen.
   NO N_2O NO_2 N_2H_4 NH_3

10. Put the following compounds in order from the lowest to the highest oxidation number for carbon.
    $C_6H_{12}O_6$ CO_2 CH_3OH CH_4 C_6H_6

11. Determine the oxidation state for each atom in the following compounds:
    a. $KMnO_4$ b. $LiMnO_2$ c. NH_4ClO_4

12. Determine the oxidation state for each atom in the following compounds:
    a. K_2MnCl_4 b. Cr_2O_3 c. $C_{12}H_{22}O_{11}$

13. Use the following four terms or expressions to identify each of the chemical situations indicated: (*is oxidized; is reduced; is an oxidizing agent; is a reducing agent*). You may use as many terms as apply.
    a. An atom has gained an electron.
    b. An atom increases its oxidation number.
    c. The oxidation number of an atom changes from −2 to −3.

14. Use the following four terms or expressions to identify each of the chemical situations indicated: (*is oxidized; is reduced; is an oxidizing agent; is a reducing agent*). You may use as many terms as apply.
    a. An atom decreases its oxidation number.
    b. An atom loses two electrons.
    c. The oxidation number of an atom changes from +3 to +5.

15. Supply the oxidation number of each atom, on both sides of the reaction arrow, in the equation
$$3Mg(s) + 2H_3PO_4(aq) \rightarrow Mg_3(PO_4)_2(aq) + 3H_2(g)$$

16. Supply the oxidation number of each atom, on both sides of the reaction arrow, in the equation
$$2AgNO_3(aq) + Cu(s) \rightarrow Cu(NO_3)_2(aq) + 2Ag(s)$$

Chemical Applications and Practices

17. The main active ingredient in commercial household bleach is the hypochlorite ion, ClO^-.
    a. What is the oxidation number of the Cl atom in the ion?
    b. Hypochlorite is known as a good oxidizing agent. Would that property indicate that the Cl tends to gain or lose electrons as it reacts? Explain the logic of your response.

18. The combustion of propane in a portable burner is a common redox reaction. Examine each component of the equation. Assign an oxidation number to each atom, and determine which component is acting as the reducing agent.
$$C_3H_8(g) + O_2(g) \rightarrow CO_2(g) + H_2O(g)$$

19. The brilliant red color of many fireworks is due to the presence of strontium. However, strontium metal is not typically found in its pure state. The following redox reaction depicts the isolation of strontium from molten strontium chloride.
$$SrCl_2(l) \rightarrow Sr(s) + Cl_2(g)$$
    a. Assign an oxidation number to each of the atoms in the reaction.
    b. What has been reduced in the reaction?

20. Sodium thiosulfate is familiar to photographers as "hypo." It helps dissolve some of the silver salts used in developing photographs. Aqueous solutions of sodium thiosulfate can undergo disproportionation reactions, as shown here:

$$S_2O_3^{2-}(aq) + H^+(aq) \rightarrow H_2O(l) + S(s) + SO_2(g)$$

   a. What is the change in the oxidation number of S in $S_2O_3^{2-}$ in the oxidation portion of the reaction?
   b. What is the change in the oxidation number of S in $S_2O_3^{2-}$ in the reduction portion of the reaction?

21. Four equations can be written to describe the rusting of iron:

$$O_2(aq) + 2H_2O(l) + 4e^- \rightarrow 4OH^-(aq)$$
$$Fe(s) \rightarrow Fe^{2+}(aq) + 2e^-$$
$$Fe^{2+}(aq) + 2OH^-(aq) \rightarrow Fe(OH)_2(s)$$
$$Fe(OH)_2(s) + OH^-(aq) \rightarrow FeO(OH)(s) + H_2O(l) + e^-$$

   a. Which of these are reduction or oxidation half-reactions?
   b. What other kind of equation is present here?
   c. Combine the equations to give the overall equation that describes the formation of rust, $FeO(OH)(s)$, from iron, $Fe(s)$.

22. In the chapter, we discussed the reaction of hydrogen and oxygen to give water. How is it possible for this reaction to proceed either as an explosion (as in the space shuttle main engines) or as a gentle, readily managed source of electricity?

Section 19.3 Redox Equations

Skill Review

23. The superscript on the symbol $E°$ refers to standard conditions for electrochemical reactions. What specifically does that indicate for the concentrations and pressure of the reacting system?

24. The voltage values (emf) given on a standard reduction table are referenced to a standard called SHE.
   a. To what do the letters refer?
   b. What is the voltage of the reference?

25. Complete each of these statements using the word *positive*, *negative*, *spontaneous*, or *nonspontaneous*.
   a. When $E°$ is negative, the electrochemical reaction is _____.
   b. When $E°$ is positive, the value for $\Delta G°$ is _____.
   c. When a reaction is spontaneous, the values for $\Delta G°$ will be _____, and the values for $E°$ will be_____.
   d. Nonspontaneous redox reactions have a _____ value for $E°$.

26. The typical battery used in a standard flashlight produces approximately 1.5 V. If the value for $\Delta G°$ of the reaction were $-289,500$ J, what would you calculate as the moles of electrons exchanged in the balanced redox reaction?

27. Combine these half-reactions in such a way that a galvanic cell results, and calculate the cell potential.

$$Fe^{3+} + e^- \rightarrow Fe^{2+} \qquad E° = 0.77 \text{ V}$$
$$Fe^{2+} + 2e^- \rightarrow Fe \qquad E° = -0.44 \text{ V}$$

28. Combine these half-reactions in such a way that a galvanic cell results, and calculate the cell potential.

$$Sn^{2+} + 2e^- \rightarrow Sn \qquad E° = -0.14 \text{ V}$$
$$Sn^{4+} + 2e^- \rightarrow Sn^{2+} \qquad E° = +0.15 \text{ V}$$

29. Calculate the free energy change for the cell in Problem 27.

30. Calculate the free energy change for the cell in Problem 28.

31. What is the free energy change for the following reaction at standard conditions?

$$PbO_2 + 4H^+ + 2Hg + 2Cl^- \rightarrow Pb^{2+} + 2H_2O + Hg_2Cl_2$$
$$E°_{cell} = 1.12 \text{ V}$$

32. What is the free energy change for the following reaction at standard conditions?

$$O_2 + 4H^+ + 2Ni \rightarrow 2H_2O + 2Ni^{2+} \qquad E°_{cell} = 1.46 \text{ V}$$

33. What are three considerations or aspects that must be "balanced" in a balanced redox reaction?

34. In this balanced redox reaction, chlorine is shown to replace bromide ions from a solution.

$$Cl_2(aq) + 2Br^-(aq) \rightarrow 2Cl^-(aq) + Br_2(aq)$$

What is the value of n in the overall reaction?

35. Balance these half-reactions in acidic solution. Is each a reduction or an oxidation? Which substance is oxidized and which is reduced?
   a. $CO_2 \rightarrow H_2C_2O_4$ b. $Np^{4+} \rightarrow NpO_2^+$

36. Balance these half-reactions in acidic solution. Is each a reduction or an oxidation? Which substance is oxidized and which is reduced?
   a. $I_2 \rightarrow IO_3^-$ b. $NO_3^- \rightarrow NO$

37. Balance these redox equations in acidic solution:
   a. $Sn^{2+} + Cu^{2+} \rightarrow Sn^{4+} + Cu^+$
   b. $S_2O_3^{2-} + I_3^- \rightarrow S_4O_6^{2-} + 3I^-$
   c. $SO_3^- + Fe^{3+} \rightarrow SO_4^{2-} + Fe^{2+}$

38. Balance these redox equations in acidic solution:
   a. $Al + Cu^{2+} \rightarrow Al^{3+} + Cu$
   b. $UO_2^{2+} + Ag + Cl^- \rightarrow U^{4+} + AgCl$
   c. $H_2SO_4 + HBr \rightarrow SO_2 + Br_2$

39. Balance the redox equation that illustrates the reaction of solid copper and dichromate, first in acidic and then in basic solution.

$$Cu(s) + Cr_2O_7^{2-}(aq) \rightarrow Cu^{2+}(aq) + Cr^{3+}(aq)$$

40. Balance the redox equation that illustrates the reaction of permanganate and methanol, first in acidic and then in basic solution.

$$MnO_4^- + CH_3OH \rightarrow CO_3^{2-} + MnO_4^{2-}$$

41. Balance this redox reaction, first in acidic and then in basic solution.

$$ClO_4^- + I^- \rightarrow ClO^- + IO_3^-$$

42. Balance this redox reaction, first in acidic and then in basic solution.

$$Zn + NO_3^- \rightarrow Zn^{2+} + NH_3$$

Chemical Applications and Practices

43. Using the standard reduction potentials found in the appendix, locate the half-cell reaction for zinc. Zinc is often used in the production of dry cell batteries. It is also used to protect other metals from oxidation.
    a. What is the $E°$ value for this reaction?
    b. What would be the value of $\Delta G°$ for the half-reaction?
    c. What would be the $E°$ value if the reaction stoichiometry were doubled?

44. Splitting water into hydrogen gas and oxygen gas is one technique being investigated as a way to produce hydrogen gas for use in fuel cells. The reaction is shown here as

$$2H_2O \rightarrow 2H_2 + O_2$$

   If the $E°$ value for this nonspontaneous reaction were approximately -2.00 V, what would you calculate as the value for $\Delta G°$?

45. Use the Standard Table of Reduction Potentials to answer the following questions:
    a. Which of the three alkali metal ions Na, K, and Li has the least potential to attract electrons?
    b. Of the three halogens which would be the strongest oxidizing agent, F_2, Cl_2, or Br_2?
    c. If you prepared a battery by connecting two of the following three half-cells, which combination could produce the highest potential? Zn, Cu, Ni

46. Suppose you attempted to build a battery using lead (and Pb^{2+}) with chromium (and Cr^{3+}).
    a. Write out the half-cell reduction reactions and their $E°$ values for each.
    b. Which of the two would provide the reduction reaction, and which would provide the oxidation reaction?
    c. What would be the total $E°$ of the overall redox reaction?
    d. How many moles of electrons would be exchanged in the overall reaction?

47. The oxidation of copper metal gives rise to a beautiful green patina. An equation that illustrates the oxidation of copper is shown here. Balance this redox reaction.

$$Cu(s) + CO_2(g) \rightarrow CuO(s) + C_2O_4{}^{2-}(aq)$$

48. One technique used for the detection of ethanol involves the following redox reaction with dichromate ions. Balance this redox reaction.

$$C_2H_5OH(aq) + Cr_2O_7{}^{2-}(aq) \rightarrow CH_3CO_2H(aq) + Cr^{3+}(aq)$$

49. As with acid–base reactions, careful addition of a solution containing an oxidizing agent to a solution containing a reducing agent can be used for titration analysis. Standardizing a solution of potassium permanganate to be used later in a redox titration often involves reaction with a known amount of sodium oxalate. Balance the redox reaction used in the standardization process.

$$C_2O_4{}^{2-}(aq) + MnO_4{}^-(aq) \rightarrow CO_2(g) + Mn^{2+}(aq) + H_2O(l)$$

50. Once a standard solution of potassium permanganate is prepared, it can be used to determine the concentration of iron in an unknown sample. For example, the iron content of a small steel sample could be obtained through a titration reaction with a standard permanganate solution. The redox reaction that would take place in the analysis is shown here (unbalanced, and after the iron has been prepared as +2 ion). Balance the redox titration and identify the reducing agent.

$$MnO_4{}^-(aq) + Fe^{2+}(aq) \rightarrow Mn^{2+}(aq) + Fe^{3+}(aq) + H_2O(l)$$

51. One step in a common method for the analysis of vitamin C in juice drinks is to oxidize the vitamin C (ascorbic acid) with aqueous I_2. Balance this redox reaction.

$$C_6H_8O_6(aq) + I_2(aq) \rightarrow I^-(aq) + C_6H_6O_6(aq)$$

52. There are many half-cell reaction combinations that could be used to make batteries. One such reaction would be to use system consisting of silver(II) oxide and zinc. The reaction shown below would have to occur in a *basic* environment. Balance this redox reaction.

$$Zn(s) + AgO(s) \rightarrow Zn(OH)_2(s) + Ag(s)$$

Section 19.4 Electrochemical Cells

Skill Review

53. Define the following terms in your own words: cell, half-reaction, galvanic cell, voltaic cell, electromotive force.

54. Compare and contrast an electrolytic cell with a galvanic cell on the basis of sign on the $E°$ value, ability to do work, chemical process taking place at the anode, and spontaneity.

55. The following notation refers to a specific voltaic cell. Identify the species that would serve as the anode and the species that is the oxidizing agent.

$$Zn(s) \mid Zn^{2+}(aq) \parallel Cu^{2+}(aq) \mid Cu(s)$$

56. The following notation refers to a specific voltaic cell. Identify the species that would serve as the anode and the species that is the oxidizing agent.

$$Mg(s) \mid Mg^{2+}(aq) \parallel Co^{2+}(aq) \mid Co(s)$$

57. The following schematic diagram represents two metals and their cations in separate beakers joined by a $NaNO_3$ salt bridge. If the metals were lead and silver (with their respective cations Pb^{2+} and Ag^+), which beaker would require the silver and which the lead if the nitrate ions were moving from left to right through the salt bridge? Justify your answer.

58. The following schematic diagram represents two metals and their cations in separate beakers joined by a $NaNO_3$ salt bridge. If the metals were copper and iron (with their respective cations Cu^{2+} and Fe^{3+}), which beaker would require the copper and which the iron if the nitrate ions were moving from left to right through the salt bridge? Justify your answer.

Chemical Applications and Practices

59. Diagram a battery consisting of two beakers and a salt bridge that makes use of the two half-reactions silver and gold (sort of expensive, but you're worth it).
    a. Predict the $E°$ value for the battery.
    b. What is the value of n for the balanced equation?
    c. Label the cathode.
    d. Exactly what species is acting as the oxidizing agent?
    e. Represent the battery in the ABC notation.

60. Search Internet references using the keywords "hydrogen fuel cell" and report on the basic operation of such a cell. Give particular emphasis to the electrolyte used in such a cell. Be sure to report the necessary URL for your references.

61. Small button-sized batteries can be made using mercury and zinc. If the two half-reactions are as follows, what would you report as the ABC notation for the battery? (Mercury in the batteries is considered a toxic substance and should be carefully recycled.)

$$Zn(s) \rightarrow ZnO(s)$$
$$HgO(s) \rightarrow Hg(l)$$

Note that the reactions are not balanced. The reaction takes place in a basic medium.

62. Write out the standard reduction half-cell reactions and $E°$ values for Zn, Ni, Pb, and $H_2(g)$.
    a. Select the two half-reactions that, when combined, would produce the battery with the greatest theoretical overall $E°$ value, and report that value.
    b. Which, if any, of those represented would have electrons move along an external wire, when connected with the hydrogen half-cell, *toward* the hydrogen electrode?

Section 19.5 Chemical Reactivity Series

Skill Review

63. Use the Standard Table of Reduction Potentials to answer the following questions.
    a. Which is the better reducing agent, Ba or Ca?
    b. Which is the better oxidizing agent, Pb^{2+} or Ni^{2+}?

c. In which direction, to the left or to the right, would the following reaction take place spontaneously? (Assume standard conditions.)

$$Ag + Fe^{3+} \rightarrow Fe^{2+} + Ag^+$$

64. Under standard conditions one of the following two reactions will *not occur* spontaneously. Use the Standard Table of Reduction Potentials to explain how you could correctly predict which one will not take place.

$$Fe + Sn^{2+} \rightarrow Fe^{3+} + Sn$$
$$Cu^{2+} + Fe \rightarrow Fe^{3+} + Cu$$

Chemical Applications and Practices

65. Suppose you have a shiny piece of metal that is unlabeled. It is known to be either aluminum or tin. You also have a solution of $1.0\ M$ nickel(II) nitrate. Suggest a chemical test that you could use to determine the identity of the metal using the solution. Explain your expected results and the basis of your conclusion.

66. One technique to protect against oxidation of structures such as ship hulls and underground iron pipes is to place the structure in contact with a metal that will oxidize more easily than the iron in the structure. The more active metal is then referred to as a sacrificial anode. Neglecting such issues as cost and availability, would copper or zinc make the better sacrificial anode in an attempt to protect an iron-based structure? Explain the basis of your choice.

Section 19.6 Not-So-Standard Conditions: The Nernst Equation

Skill Review

67. The constant used in the Nernst equation, 0.0257, is derived from the combination of three other constants. Obtain the three values, assuming standard temperature, and derive the constant used in the equation. Some texts refer to the Nernst equation using the base 10 logarithmic scale. What would be the value of the constant in that scale?

68. The simplified equation presented here represents the redox reaction taking place inside the typical, nonalkaline flashlight battery. Use the principles described in the Nernst equation to answer the questions that follow.

$$Zn(s) + 2MnO_2(s) + 2NH_4^+(aq) \rightarrow$$
$$Zn^{2+}(aq) + Mn_2O_3(s) + 2NH_3(g) + H_2O(l)$$

a. What would be the effect on the spontaneity of the reaction if the concentration of $NH_4^+(aq)$ were decreased?
b. What would be the effect on the voltage of the cell if the concentration of $NH_4^+(aq)$ were decreased?
c. What is the value of n in the equation?
d. At equilibrium what is the value of E?

69. Calculate the value of E_{cell} for the reaction of iron and copper(II), given the specific concentrations listed.
    a. $Fe(s) \mid Fe^{2+}(0.10\ M) \parallel Cu^{2+}(0.10\ M) \mid Cu(s)$
    b. $Fe(s) \mid Fe^{2+}(1.5\ M) \parallel Cu^{2+}(0.10\ M) \mid Cu(s)$
    c. $Fe(s) \mid Fe^{2+}(0.10\ M) \parallel Cu^{2+}(1.5\ M) \mid Cu(s)$

70. Calculate the value of E_{cell} for the reaction of cobalt(II) chloride and zinc metal, given the specific concentrations listed.
    a. $Zn(s) \mid Zn^{2+}(0.10\ M) \parallel Co^{2+}(0.10\ M) \mid Co(s)$
    b. $Zn(s) \mid Zn^{2+}(2.5\ M) \parallel Co^{2+}(0.050\ M) \mid Co(s)$
    c. $Zn(s) \mid Zn^{2+}(0.010\ M) \parallel Co^{2+}(0.10\ M) \mid Co(s)$

Chemical Applications and Practices

71. Suppose that at night on a campout your flashlight dims and finally stops working. Your friend remarks, "I guess the battery is dead." In what three other chemical ways, using Gibbs free energy, equilibrium, and potential, could you state the same conclusion as your friend?

72. A quick source of hydrogen gas in the lab is to carefully place some solid magnesium in hydrochloric acid.

$$Mg(s) + 2HCl(aq) \rightarrow MgCl_2(aq) + H_2(g)$$

If the Mg^{2+} concentration were 1.0 M and the HCl concentration were 0.10 M (assume completely dissociated HCl), what would you calculate as the E value for the reaction at 25°C?

$$Mg(s) \,|\, Mg^{2+}(aq) \,||\, H^+(0.1\ M) \,|\, H_2(1\ atm)$$

Section 19.7 Electrolytic Reactions

Skill Review

73. Calculate the number of grams of gold electroplated onto a surface given these conditions. (Assume that the solution of Au^{3+} ions is concentrated enough to complete the electrolysis.)
   a. 1.25 A for 60 s   b. 2.11 A for 2.33 h   c. 0.75 A for 1 d

74. Calculate the time required to electroplate 1.0 g of tin metal onto a surface given these conditions. (Assume that the solution of Sn^{2+} ions is concentrated enough to complete the electrolysis.)
   a. 2.25 A   b. 0.11 A   c. 1.38 A

75. Alessandro Volta is given historical precedence in the discovery of the first battery in the sense that we think of batteries today. The "Voltaic pile" consisted of dissimilar metals joined by salt-moistened paper strips. Davy and his assistant Michael Faraday later refined this. At that time, early electroplating businesses began developing in England. If such a business silver-plated a teaspoon, would the teaspoon be the cathode or the anode in such a process? If the spoon received 0.33 g of silver after being plated for 1.0 h, what amperage was used?

76. In addition to isolating sodium, Sir Humphrey Davy isolated potassium, calcium, and magnesium from impure natural ore samples.
   a. If he used a current of 1.00 A for 1.00 h, how many grams of magnesium metal could he obtain from molten $MgCl_2$?
   b. Using the same electrical set up, how many grams of potassium metal could Sir Humphrey isolate from molten KCl?

Chemical Applications and Practices

77. In the typical lead storage battery found in most automobiles, lead is oxidized to Pb^{2+} (in the form of $PbSO_4$). In recharging, the reaction is reversed. If a battery were recharged for 30.0 min at a current of 8.00 A, how many grams of lead would be reduced, from $PbSO_4$ during the process?

78. Germanium has become a valuable metal in semiconductor fields. If a 1.00 A current were used for 1.00 h to plate out 0.677 g of germanium, what would you calculate as the oxidation number of the germanium ions in the plating solution?

Comprehensive Problems

79. Use the illustration below as the starting point to draw the electrolytic cell that would be used to plate copper metal onto a steel saucepan. Be sure to indicate the location of the cathode and the anode, the location of the copper electrode, and the steel saucepan.

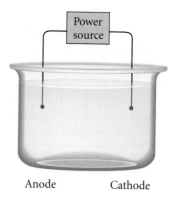

Power source

Anode   Cathode

80. The Nernst equation can be used just as well with half-cell reactions as with balanced redox reactions. An application of this is the use of potential differences in the acid level of solutions compared to a standard when producing the probes for pH meters. Using the half-reaction $2H^+(aq) + 2e^- \rightarrow H_2(g)$ at 1 atm, what would you calculate, using the Nernst equation, as the value for E in these situations?
   a. Pure water, pH = 7.00
   b. An acid solution with pH = 2.00
   c. A 0.10 M solution of nitric acid
   d. A 0.10 M solution of acetic acid, $K_a = 1.8 \times 10^{-5}$

81. Potassium ferrate (K_2FeO_4) is a powerful oxidizing agent ($E° = 2.20$ V relative to SHE in acidic solution) in which the iron(VI) ion is reduced to the iron(III) ion. It oxidizes water to oxygen gas.
   a. Determine the cell potential and equilibrium constant for the reaction at standard conditions for the oxidation of water by ferrate ion in acidic solution.
   b. Balance the reaction in basic solution.
   c. Calculate the cell potential, given the following initial concentrations:
   $$[FeO_4^{2-}] = 1.5 \times 10^{-3}\,M;\ [Fe^{3+}] = 1.1 \times 10^{-3}\,M;$$
   $$P_{O_2} = 8.3 \times 10^{-5}\,atm;\ pH = 2.8$$
   d. The reaction results in the production of a yellow solid that is especially apparent at high pH. Can you suggest what this might be? Further, can you suggest how this solid might help if the ferrate ion were used to treat wastewater contamination?

82. Potassium permanganate ($KMnO_4$) is a useful analytical reagent for determining the percentage of iron in an iron ore. The procedure includes dissolving the iron with HCl and then converting all of the iron in the ore to Fe^{2+} using several reagents. The titration of the resulting Fe^{2+} with MnO_4^- is

$$Fe^{2+} + MnO_4^- \rightarrow Fe^{3+} + Mn^{2+}$$

A sample of the original iron ore weighing 3.852 g was processed for titration in a total volume of 300.0 mL of solution. A 100.0 mL aliquot (accurately measured portion) was removed and titrated with a 0.1025 M $KMnO_4$ solution. A total of 23.14 mL was required to the light pink endpoint. What is the percent of iron in the ore sample?

Thinking Beyond the Calculation

83. A battery designer wishes to prepare a solution-based battery for use in a new automobile. The designer chooses iron and zinc as the two metals for study.

a. Draw the setup (using beakers and a salt bridge) that indicates the location of the iron and zinc electrodes, the iron(II) and zinc(II) solutions, and the flow of electrons.
b. Which half-reaction is the oxidation reaction?
c. What is the cell potential for the reaction if the initial concentrations of iron(II) and zinc(II) are 0.25 M at 25°C?
d. What would be the cell potential if the concentrations of both solutions in part c were increased to 1.0 M? . . . to 2.0 M?
e. If the battery is cooled to 10°C, is there a change in the cell potential? If so, what is the new potential?
f. Describe at least one advantage to using a battery made from these metals.
g. Describe at least one disadvantage to the use of iron in a battery.

20

Coordination Complexes

In 1434, Flemish master Jan van Eyck painted the Arnolfini Wedding. *The pigments that he mixed and applied to the painting bring the scene of a newly married couple to life. The colors we see in this work are a result of the interaction of light with electrons in the d orbitals of transition metals.*

Many of the nutritional supplements we consume on a daily basis contain iron. Why? Iron is an essential nutrient with the U.S. recommended daily allowance of 10 mg for men and 15 mg for women. Even with supplements and recommendations from nutritional scientists, less than 30% of women aged 12–50 meet their daily recommended allowance of iron. Iron isn't a vitamin; rather, it's called a mineral—the term used for any inorganic element important for health. It turns out that few items claiming to be rich in iron actually contain the neutral metal. Instead, they typically contain iron ions in a salt, often iron sulfate. Why is iron so important to good health? Most of the iron in the body is contained in a protein known as hemoglobin within the red blood cells (Chapter 22). Specifically, iron ions are chemically bound in hemoglobin in a form called a coordination complex.

Within hemoglobin, the iron ions are bonded to other atoms in an elegant and complex structure known as a heme (see Figure 20.1). The arrangement of groups attached to the iron enables it to collect an oxygen molecule and later release it at an appropriate time. Close examination of the heme indicates that the conformational changes illustrated in Figure 20.2 occur during oxygen binding. We visited a simpler form of this complex in Chapter 16 when we discussed the

FIGURE 20.1

The iron is bonded to other atoms in an elegant and complex structure known as a heme. The hemoglobin protein uses two amino acid residues to hold the iron within the protein's structure. One of the amino acid residues can move out of the way to allow an oxygen molecule to bind to the iron.

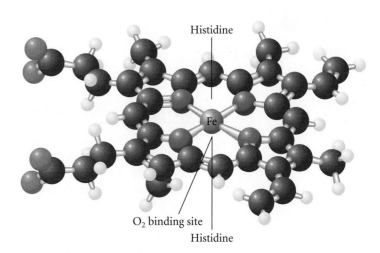

Histidine

O_2 binding site

Histidine

equilibrium involving oxygen and myoglobin. Without this specific complex structure, whether in hemoglobin or myoglobin, iron would be incapable of playing the role of oxygen carrier.

In a typical **coordination complex** (or simply complex), a central metal atom or ion is *chemically bonded* to several other components. For example, natural water often contains iron in the form of a chemical combination of an Fe^{3+} ion and six water molecules, $[Fe(H_2O)_6]^{3+}$, as shown in Figure 20.3. The bonding, the structure, and the many biological, medical, and industrial applications of coordination complexes are the subject of this chapter.

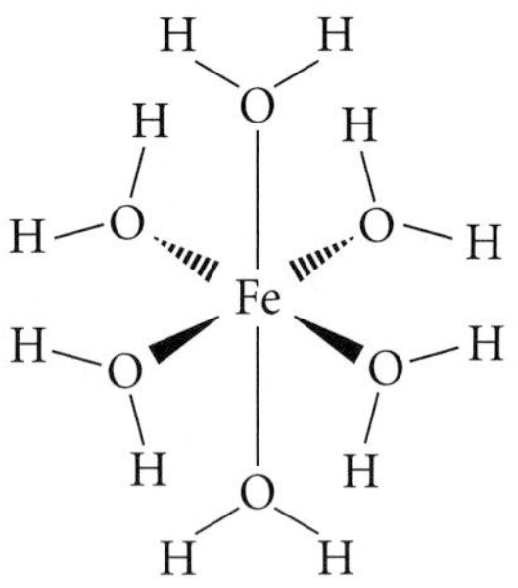

FIGURE 20.3

Natural water often contains iron in the form of a chemical combination of an Fe^{3+} ion and six water molecules, $[Fe(H_2O)_6]^{3+}$.

FIGURE 20.2

Conformational changes take place during the binding of oxygen to the iron ion in hemoglobin. These changes act like a switch in the hemoglobin protein, activating it and increasing its ability to bind to three other molecules of oxygen. In the structure shown here, the oxygen molecule (red) is bound in oxyhemoglobin. When oxygen is not bound to hemoglobin, the protein chains pull the iron so that the heme sits slightly above the center of the iron ion.

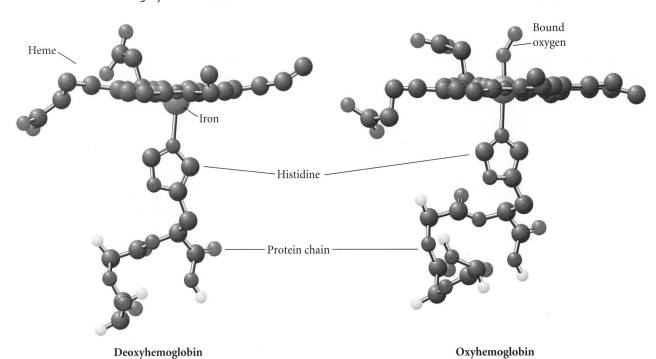

Deoxyhemoglobin   **Oxyhemoglobin**

20.1 Bonding in Coordination Complexes

A common feature of bonding within metal complexes is the **coordinate covalent bond**, which we discussed in Chapter 7. Recall that the coordinate covalent bond forms when *both bonding electrons originate from one atom.* This means that a molecule with a lone electron pair (a Lewis base) could potentially be a component of a coordination complex. Lewis bases that form a coordinate covalent bond with a metal or metal ion are known as **ligands**. In the aqueous iron complex found in natural water that contains iron, each water molecule donates a pair of electrons to the iron(III) ion and is therefore the Lewis base. The iron(III) ion behaves as a Lewis acid, an electron pair acceptor. The resulting bond between the

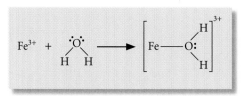

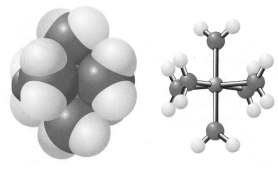

$[Fe(H_2O)_6]^{3+}$

oxygen of water and the iron(III) ion is a coordinate covalent bond. With *six* equivalent water molecules donating electron pairs to create *six* bonds to the central Fe^{3+} ion, the complete complex ion is $[Fe(H_2O)_6]^{3+}$.

In general, we can use the following equation to illustrate the formation of a coordination complex via donation of a lone pair of electrons from a ligand, L, to a metal center, M,

$$M + :L \rightarrow M\text{--}L$$

The chemistry of hemoglobin is an example of the formation of such a coordination complex. The iron ion in the hemoglobin molecule forms a bond with an oxygen molecule and ultimately transports the oxygen molecule from the lungs to cells throughout the body. Using our shorthand, we can represent the bonding with oxygen by the following equation:

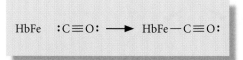

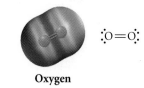
Carbon monoxide

Oxygen

where Hb represents the complex structure of the hemoglobin molecule. Where does the oxygen come from? In the lungs, the oxygen **coordinates** to the hemoglobin in a red blood cell—that is, *forms a coordinate covalent bond to it.* Under slightly different conditions in the cell, the oxygen is released in the reverse process and becomes available for respiration.

Carbon monoxide can also coordinate to hemoglobin. In fact, it does so more strongly than oxygen. A close look at the structure that results indicates that the lone pair of electrons on the carbon forms the coordinate covalent bond with the iron in hemoglobin. Equilibrium principles tell us that because the equilibrium constant for the reaction with CO is much greater (about 200 times greater) than that for the reaction with oxygen, the presence of small amounts of CO in the body limits the amount of O_2 that can be carried by hemoglobin. Excessive amounts of carbon monoxide in the body can result in suffocation. The National Institute of Occupational Safety and Health (NIOSH) cites an immediate danger to life with an exposure of 1200 parts per million of CO in air and specifies an 8-hour exposure limit of 35 ppm in air.

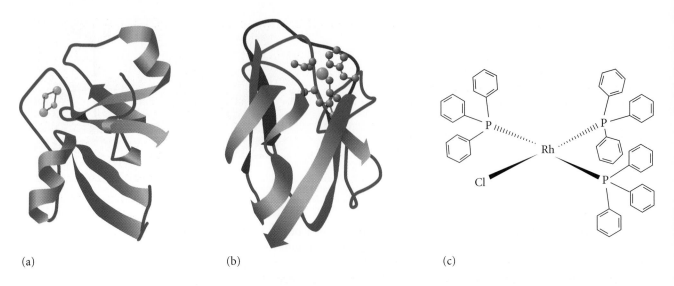

(a) (b) (c)

FIGURE 20.4

Three important coordination complexes: ferrodoxin, plastocyanin, and Wilkinson's catalyst. (a) An illustration of the protein ferrodoxin indicates the location of an Fe_2S_2 cluster—shown in orange. (b) A drawing of the protein plastocyanin contains a copper ion—green—held in place by the amino acids in the structure of the protein. (c) Wilkinson's catalyst contains a rhodium ion surrounded by triphenylphosphine ligands.

The coordinate covalent bond is very common in compounds involving metals and nonmetals. These types of compounds, as shown in Figure 20.4, are often found at critical reaction centers in biological systems and in many industrial processes. For example, cytochromes and ferredoxins are iron-containing coordination complexes in nonanimal biological systems, where they assist in reduction and oxidation reactions (see Chapter 19) during photosynthesis. In some plants, nitrogen is converted into a usable form by coordination of an N_2 molecule to a molybdenum ion in the enzyme nitrogenase. In industrial processes, metal ions can be used to form coordinate covalent bonds with small molecules in order to make the small molecule react in certain ways. Wilkinson's catalyst, shown in Figure 20.5, is a coordination complex of rhodium used to promote reaction of H_2 with alkenes (in polyunsaturated fats) to make margarine. In another industrial process used to make the class of molecules known as aldehydes (which are used in essential oils—volatile compounds that have odors characteristic of plants, polymer formation, and food additives), carbon monoxide forms a coordination

FIGURE 20.5

The reaction of hydrogen with an alkene in the presence of Wilkinson's catalyst. This reaction can be used to convert low-melting-point vegetable oils into semi-solid fats for use in making margarine.

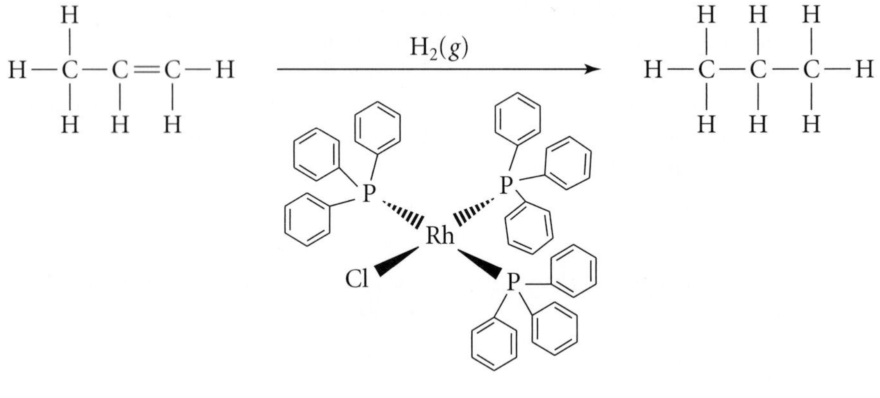

complex with a cobalt atom as it is transformed into the C=O fragment of an aldehyde.

The coordination complexes of transition metals have some particularly interesting properties. The color of the complex, such as that found in rubies, depends on the nature and number of ligands surrounding the metal complex. The magnetism of coordination complexes, such as the magnetism of the iron oxide used in videotape, depends on the nature and number of ligands surrounding the metal. The biochemical reactions that are possible with coordination complexes found in the body are also influenced by the ligands.

Rubies are minerals made of Al_2O_3 containing less than 1% Cr_2O_3 as an impurity.

20.2 Ligands

A coordination complex such as $[Fe(H_2O)_6]^{3+}$ consists of a central Fe^{3+} metal ion and coordinated water molecules. The species, such as the water molecules, that coordinate to the metal are called ligands. Table 20.1 lists some common ligands. Remember that ligands *donate* a lone pair of electrons to the metal or metal ion to form the coordinate covalent bond. A metal ion will tend to form coordinate covalent bonds with a specific number of ligands, often either four or six.

EXERCISE 20.1 | **Identifying Possible Ligands**

Which of the following could act as ligands in forming coordination complexes?

a. CH_4 b. N_3^- c. BH_3 d. CS_2 e. Li^+

Solution

Because each has a nonbonded pair of electrons on one or more atoms, (b) and (d) could be ligands.

PRACTICE 20.1

Indicate the formula of a coordination complex that might result from the combination of these metals and ligands.

a. Fe^{2+} and $6Cl^-$ b. Ni^{2+} and $4NH_3$ c. Zn^{2+} and $6H_2O$

See Problems 3, 4, 9, and 10.

TABLE 20.1 | **Selected Common Ligands and Their Names**

The atoms shown in red donate a lone pair of electrons to form a coordinate covalent bond.

Monodentate ligands

Cl^-	chloro	Br^-	bromo	I^-	iodo
CN^-	cyano	NO_2^-	nitro	NO_3^-	nitrato*
SCN^-	thiocyanato	NO_2^-	nitrito	OSO_3^{2-}	sulfato
SSO_3^{2-}	thiosulfato	O^{2-}	oxido	F^-	fluoro
NH_3	ammine	H_2O	aqua	NO	nitrosyl
CO	carbonyl	OH^-	hydroxo		

Polydentate ligands

$H_2NCH_2CH_2NH_2$	ethylenediamine (en)
$(^-OOCCH_2)_2NCH_2CH_2N(CH_2COO^-)_2$	ethylenediaminetetracetato (EDTA)
$^-OOCCOO^-$	oxalato (ox)

*The nitrato ligand can be monodentate or bidentate.

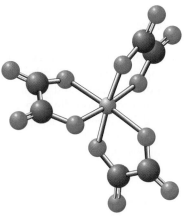

FIGURE 20.6

Examples of ligands.

FIGURE 20.7

The oxalate ion is a bidentate ion. Each oxalate is capable of donating lone pairs of electrons from two different atoms to form two coordinate covalent bonds. Three oxalates can bind to one iron(III) ion.

Some of the molecules and ions that are commonly observed to act as ligands are shown in Figure 20.6. Oxygen, nitrogen, sulfur, and phosphorus atoms in molecules are common donor atoms in ligands because they possess a lone pair of electrons that can be donated to the metal center. Some ligands have non-bonded pairs of electrons in different locations throughout their structure. Often, any of these pairs of electrons can be used to create a coordinate covalent bond. In some cases, only one specific pair of electrons is used to create the bond. For instance, cyanide (CN^-) usually binds via the pair of electrons on the carbon atom. It does so in the "Prussian blue" dye used in dyes and paints, where the complex $[Fe(CN)_6]^{4-}$ is formed.

Ligands can also use more than one nonbonded pair of electrons to bond to a metal center. If more than one atom has a nonbonded pair of electrons, it may use each of those pairs to form independent coordinate covalent bonds to the metal. In such cases, if the ligand forms two bonds to the metal, we say it is **bidentate** ("two-toothed"); we call it **tridentate** ("three-toothed") if it forms three bonds, and so on. For example, the bidentate oxalate ion $C_2O_4^{2-}$ can bind to the iron(III) ion in this fashion, as shown in Figure 20.7. Bathroom stain removers often contain oxalate salts, because the oxalate ion will coordinate to iron ions in rust and help wash the stain away. Another common bidentate ligand that donates more than one pair of electrons is ethylenediamine $H_2NCH_2CH_2NH_2$ (often abbreviated en), in which each nitrogen has a lone pair of electrons that can be donated to the same metal ion.

The **polydentate** ligands (those that form more than one coordinate covalent bond to the metal center) are known as **chelates** (from the Greek *chele* for "claw") because of the way they clamp onto the metal center and bond tightly. For example, the porphyrin ligand is a planar, **tetradentate** ligand found in hemoglobin, vitamin B_{12}, and chlorophyll, as shown in Figure 20.8. The porphyrin chelates to iron in hemoglobin, cobalt in vitamin B_{12}, and magnesium in chlorophyll. The chelates are so good at holding the metal firmly within their grasp that it is difficult to remove the iron from hemoglobin without destroying the hemoglobin molecule itself. Note that the porphyrin leaves two sites on the metal open so that it may bind to other ligands. It is the open locations on the metal within the porphyrin chelate that make chemical reactions possible.

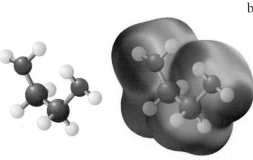

Ethylenediamine

$H_2N — CH_2 — CH_2 — NH_2$

FIGURE 20.8

The basic porphyrin structure, showing a metal at the center coordinated in six different positions. Compare this structure to that found in the hemoglobin protein from Figure 20.1.

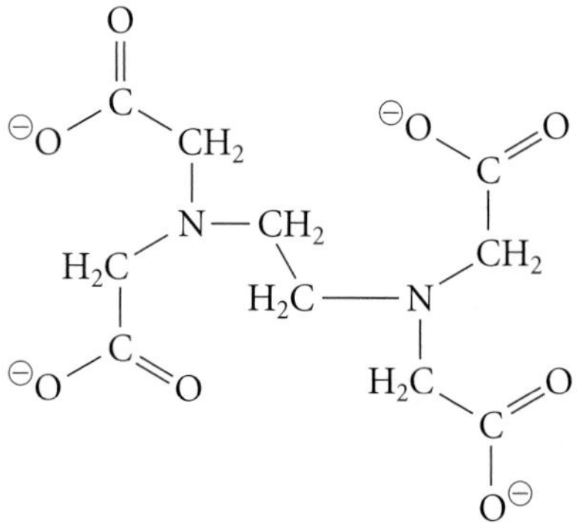

FIGURE 20.9

EDTA^{4-}

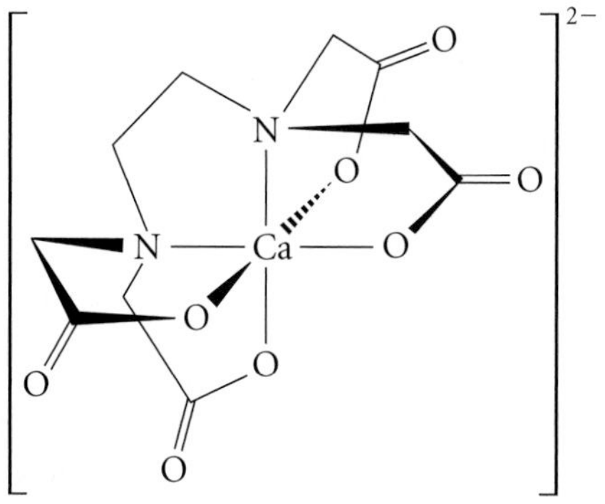

FIGURE 20.10

EDTA^{4-} coordinated to calcium ion.

The most important industrial ligand, discussed in Chapter 17 and 18, is ethylenediaminetetraacetate, which is abbreviated EDTA^{4-}. The structure of this tetraanion, shown in Figure 20.9, illustrates that both nitrogen atoms, and one oxygen atom from each end of the compound, have lone pairs of electrons. It acts as a chelate by forming up to six coordinate covalent bonds to a metal center, depending on the size of the metal ion. For example, EDTA^{4-} forms six bonds to calcium ions, as shown in Figure 20.10. The exceptionally large formation constant for the reaction of EDTA^{4-} with many metal ions illustrates that the formation of these bonds is quite favorable.

20.3 Coordination Number

The number of donor atoms to which a given metal ion bonds is known as its **coordination number**. Coordination numbers of 4 and 6 are most common, but coordination numbers as low as 2 and as large as 8 are not unusual. For example, in the film development process, excess silver ion is removed from photographic film by using the thiosulfate ion ($S_2O_3^{2-}$), which forms a coordination complex with a coordination number of 2 (see Figure 20.11). In another example, cisplatin, a prominent anticancer drug, has at its center a platinum(II) ion with a coordination number of 4, as shown in Figure 20.12. As we discussed earlier, when an Fe^{3+} ion is present in water, it is surrounded by 6 water molecules in a complex, $[Fe(H_2O)_6]^{3+}$. And iron's coordination number is 6. If iron forms a complex with the oxalate ligand, $[Fe(C_2O_4)_3]^{3-}$, its coordination number is still 6, because each oxalate ligand donates two electron pairs.

What makes a metal ion have a certain coordination number? It is primarily a function of the nature of metal ions. Large metal ions have space around them within which more ligands can fit. Not as many ligands can fit around a small metal ion. Other factors, such as the charges on the ligands and metal and the electron configuration of the metal ion, determine the most likely coordination number for a metal ion.

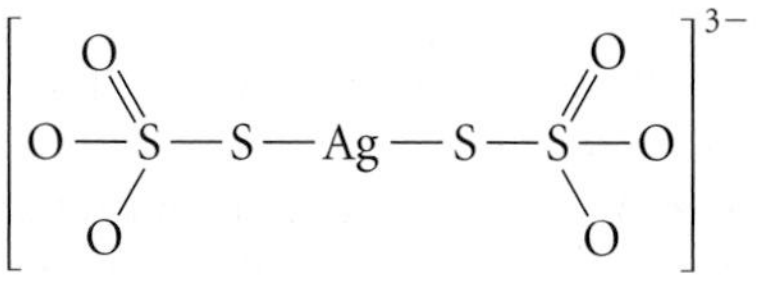

FIGURE 20.11

A two-coordinate complex of silver.

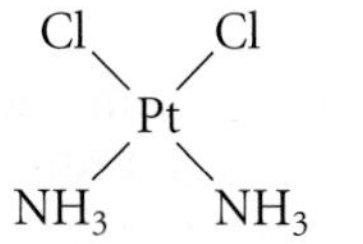

FIGURE 20.12

Four-coordinate cisplatin.

How do we know?

What is the nature of the structure, bonding, and reactivity in cisplatin?

Cancer is an often devastating disease. Research has made significant strides in understanding the disease in its many forms, including advances in detection, treatment, and care that have improved the quality of life for its victims. One prominent drug used in cancer treatment, especially testicular and ovarian cancers, is cisplatin, a coordination complex of platinum(II) that is shown in Figure 20.12. The anticancer activity of cisplatin was discovered as a result careful observation and basic interpretation of an experiment that had nothing to do with fighting cancer. But good science nonetheless led to the discovery.

Dr. Barnett Rosenberg at Michigan State University investigated the effect of an electric current on a culture of *Escherichia coli* bacteria. This bacterium, commonly found in the gastrointestinal tracts of many living creatures, is often used in initial biochemical studies because of its ready availability. Rosenberg observed that when an electric current was applied to solutions of the bacteria, cell division in the vicinity of a platinum electrode was inhibited. Studying this interesting result further, he recognized that it was not due to the electric current, which was the focus of the investigation. Noting that a compound known as *cis*-diamminedichloroplatinum (cisplatin) was being produced in the vicinity of the platinum electrode used for his experiment, Rosenberg reasoned that the cisplatin must be responsible for inhibiting the cell division. It was later determined that this compound, when given to cancer patients, can significantly reduce the size of their tumors and can even cause the disease to go into remission. Since 1970, the survival rate for testicular cancer patients has increased from 10% to over 90%.

How does cisplatin exhibit this remarkable biological activity? Cisplatin is a four-coordinate, square planar complex, as is commonly observed for many metal complexes with eight *d* orbital electrons. The platinum(II) metal center is fairly unreactive, which allows the neutral cisplatin complex to remain largely intact through injection, circulation, and penetration into the nucleus of a cancerous cell. The chloro ligands are eventually replaced by water molecules. This provides an opportunity for the platinum center to coordinate to DNA molecules. Ultimately, the platinum center binds to a nitrogen atom from each of two guanine units in a single DNA strand (see Chapter 22). The geometry of the ligands around the platinum center is vital to this biological activity. In fact, the chloro ligands must be *cis* to each other—on the same side of the complex. Once coordinated to the guanine nitrogens, the inert platinum center remains bound, tying two points on the DNA strand together. Such binding inhibits reproduction of DNA during cell division and restricts use of the DNA for normal cellular functions. Ultimately these effects hinder the growth of the cancer cells.

A drawing of the crystal structure of cisplatin bound to a short piece of DNA.

20.4 Structure

Mercury in the environment poses a particular threat to life, both to aquatic species and to those species that consume them. The most insidious form of mercury is dimethyl mercury, $[Hg(CH_3)_2]$. Transformed from mercury metal in the environment, dimethyl mercury is a very toxic product. The mercury(II) ion in this complex coordinates with the methyl groups, $:CH_3^-$, to form the complex $[H_3C—Hg—CH_3]$. Given the VSEPR rules, the complex is *linear*, with a C—Hg—C bond angle of 180°. This structure is typical of metals with a coordination number of 2.

Dimethylmercury

$CH_3 — Hg — CH_3$

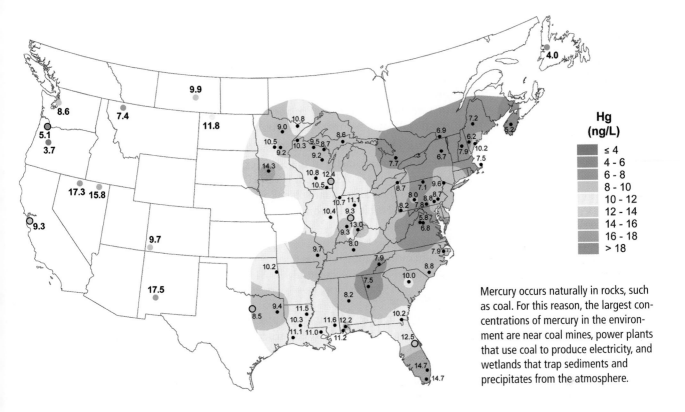

Hg (ng/L)

	≤ 4
	4 - 6
	6 - 8
	8 - 10
	10 - 12
	12 - 14
	14 - 16
	16 - 18
	> 18

Mercury occurs naturally in rocks, such as coal. For this reason, the largest concentrations of mercury in the environment are near coal mines, power plants that use coal to produce electricity, and wetlands that trap sediments and precipitates from the atmosphere.

We observe that two geometries are common for metals that have a coordination number of 4. Those geometries, tetrahedral and square planar, are shown in Figure 20.13. The **tetrahedral** geometry is the one predicted by VSEPR (see Section 8.4) when there are four electron sets around the central atom. In this geometry, the bond angles are close to 109°. The **square planar** geometry arises as a consequence of the electron configuration of the metal ion. Square planar geometry, with bond angles of 90°, is often observed for metal ions such as Ni^{2+} and Pt^{2+} that have an outer nd^8 electron configuration. That is, they have eight electrons in their outermost d orbitals. An example of the square planar geometry is found in the anticancer drug cisplatin, which we introduced in the previous section. The square planar geometry is crucial in the interaction of this drug with DNA.

The final geometry common to the coordination compounds is the **octahedral** complex, an example of which is shown in Figure 20.14. In this geometry, the six ligands occupy equivalent positions around the metal center. For example, hexaaquairon(III), $[Fe(H_2O)_6]^{3+}$, includes six water ligands symmetrically surrounding the central Fe^{3+} ion. We can think of the ligands as sitting at positions on each end of the coordinate x, y, and z axes with bond angles of 90°. The iron in hemoglobin, shown in Figure 20.1, occupies a nearly octahedral coordination environment with four sites occupied by nitrogen atoms from a porphyrin ligand. One site is occupied by a histidine (an amino acid that makes up one part of the hemoglobin molecule), and the final site is occupied by a molecule of oxygen.

90°

Square planar

109.5°

Tetrahedral

Coordination number = 4

FIGURE 20.13

Common geometries with a coordination number of 4.

90°

90°

Octahedral

Coordination number = 6

FIGURE 20.14

The octahedral geometry; all six positions in this geometry are identical.

EXERCISE 20.2 **Coordination Number and Geometry**

Give the coordination number of the central metal and predict the geometry of the following compounds.

a. $[Al(H_2O)_6]^{3+}$ b. $[Ag(CN)_2]^-$ c. $Na_2[PdCl_4]$ d. $[Co(ox)_3]^{3-}$

First Thoughts

Coordination Number: To address this question, we must first identify the ligands and the central metal to which they are attached. In part c, the formula is written as a neutral compound, not only as the coordination complex. The species in brackets represents the coordination complex. It is only the coordination complex that we should consider when answering a question about the coordination number. Remember that oxalate (ox) is a bidentate ligand.

Geometry: Once we know the coordination number of the complex, we can determine the geometry of the complex. For coordination number 2 or 6, the geometry is linear or octahedral, respectively. For four-coordinate complexes, either tetrahedral or square planar geometry is expected. Remember that metals with eight *d* orbital electrons typically form square planar complexes.

Solution

Coordination Number	a. 6	b. 2	c. 4	d. 6
Geometry	a. Octahedral	b. Linear	c. Square planar	d. Octahedral

Further Insights

Remember that the "coordination" of a ligand to a metal is a covalent bond, and the same concepts that you learned earlier for covalent bonds still apply. In short, the metal and ligand mutually attract an electron pair.

PRACTICE 20.2

Determine the coordination number and geometry for each of the following compounds.

a. $[Cr(CO)_6]$ b. $[Fe(H_2O)_6]^{2+}$ c. $K_2[TiCl_4]$ d. $[Cu(NH_3)_4]^+$

See Problems 17, 18, and 23–26. ∎

20.5 Isomers

Organic molecules (Chapter 12) are not unique in their ability to form isomeric structures. Coordination compounds can also form isomers. These types of isomers are divided into two main categories on the basis of whether there is a change in the structure or in the geometry of the complex. Structural differences are observed in the linkage isomers, ionization isomers, and coordination sphere isomers. Differences in geometric isomers arise from the nonspecific nature of the formation of a coordinate covalent bond between a ligand and a metal center.

Some ligands coordinate to a metal through one of several donor atoms. For example, the thiocyanate ion (SCN^-) can coordinate to a chromium(III) ion either through the nonbonded pair of electrons on the nitrogen or through the nonbonded pair of the electrons on the sulfur atom:

$$\left[Cr(H_2O)_5 - SCN\right]^{2+} \qquad \left[Cr(H_2O)_5 - NCS\right]^{2+}$$

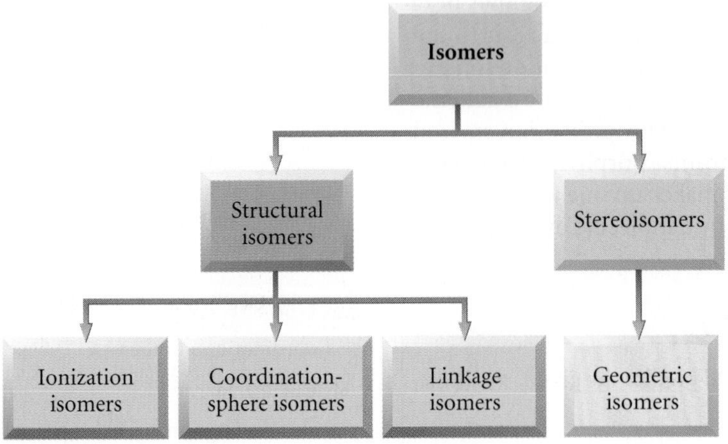

Isomers in coordination compounds.

Isomers → Structural isomers, Stereoisomers
Structural isomers → Ionization isomers, Coordination-sphere isomers, Linkage isomers
Stereoisomers → Geometric isomers

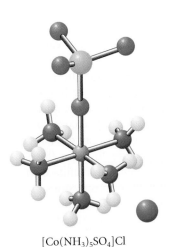

FIGURE 20.15

Ionization isomers.

[Co(NH₃)₅SO₄]Cl   [Co(NH₃)₅Cl]SO₄

These are called linkage isomers. They differ only in the atom that participates in the coordinate covalent bond with the metal.

Another isomer that is common among the coordination compounds is the ionization isomer. These are species in which a ligand and an ion (a counter ion) exchange roles, as with the cobalt complexes shown in Figure 20.15. Note that the counter ion and a ligand have changed positions in the two compounds. It is that change that makes these two compounds ionization isomers.

Coordination sphere isomers contain different ligands in the coordination spheres of cations and anions. In the coordination sphere isomers, both the cation and anion are coordination complexes. Examples are shown in Figure 20.16. Note that each of these complexes includes a cation that is a coordination complex and

FIGURE 20.16

Examples of coordination sphere isomers.

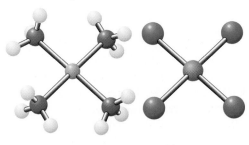

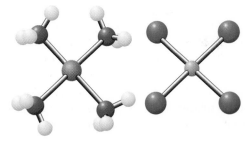

[Pt(NH₃)₄][CuCl₄]   [Cu(NH₃)₄][PtCl₄]

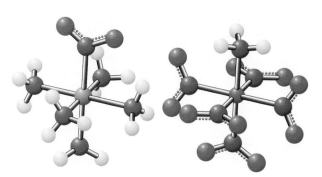

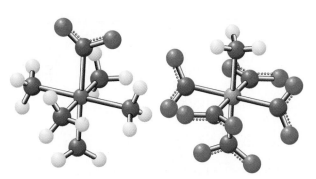

[Co(NH₃)₅NO₂][Cr(NH₃)(NO₂)₅]   [Cr(NH₃)₅(NO₂)][Co(NH₃)(NO₂)₅]

an anion that is a coordination complex. The metal ions in each case have switched location from the cation to the anion.

Geometric isomers, which we first discussed in Section 12.3, are substances in which all of the atoms are attached with the same connectivity, or bonds, but the geometric orientation differs. Square planar four-coordinate complexes of the general composition MA_2B_2 and octahedral complexes of the composition MA_2B_4, where M is the metal and A and B are different ligands, can exist as geometric isomers labeled either *cis* or *trans*. As shown in Figure 20.17 for the platinum complex $[Pt(NH_3)_2Cl_2]$, the *cis* isomer has two identical ligands next to each other. The *trans* isomer has two identical ligands on opposite sides of the metal. Octahedral complexes can exist as *cis* or *trans* isomers in complexes such as $[Co(NH_3)_4Cl_2]^+$ (Figure 20.18). In fact, in the days when Alfred Werner (1866–1919) first defined the nature of coordination complexes (for which he won the 1913 Nobel Prize in chemistry), he noted the two isomers of $[Co(NH_3)_4Cl_2]Cl$. He called one the Praseo complex and the other the Violeo complex. These two isomers were identified easily, and named to reflect their identification, because the difference in their color was quite evident. To be sure, the color of a coordination complex is markedly influenced by the geometric arrangement of the ligands around the metal center. Table 20.2 gives a summary of the various isomers common among coordination compounds.

TABLE 20.2	**Isomers of Coordination Complexes**		
Isomer	**Example**		**Explanation**
Linkage	$\left[Co(NH_3)_5 \!-\! ONO\right]^+$ $\left[Co(NH_3)_5 \!-\! NO_2\right]^+$		Ligand binds through different donor atoms
Ionization	$\left[Pt(NH_3)_3Cl\right]Br$ $\left[Pt(NH_3)_3Br\right]Cl$		Anion and ligand interchanged
Coordination sphere	$\left[Co(en)_3\right]\left[Cr(ox)_3\right]$ $\left[Cr(en)_3\right]\left[Co(ox)_3\right]$		Distribution of coordinating ligands differs
Geometric	*cis*	*trans*	Orientation of ligands around the metal center differs

FIGURE 20.17

Cis and *trans* isomers are geometric isomers. In the *cis* isomer shown here, the two chloro ligands are on the same side of the complex. The chloro ligands are on opposite sides in the *trans* complex.

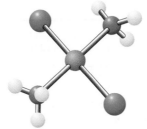

cis-Diamminedichloroplatinum(II)   **trans-Diamminedichloroplatinum(II)**

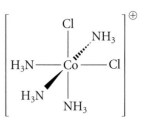

cis

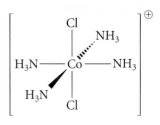

trans

FIGURE 20.18

Cis and *trans* isomers are also possible in octahedral complexes.

HERE'S WHAT WE KNOW SO FAR

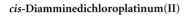

- Coordination complexes are present in simple metal ions in solution and as the reaction center in many biological molecules.
- A Lewis base that donates a lone pair of electrons to a metal to form a coordinate covalent bond forms a coordination complex.
- The coordination numbers of various metal centers are commonly observed to be 2, 4, or 6.
- Common coordination geometries are linear, tetrahedral, square planar, and octahedral.
- A variety of isomer classes are observed for metal complexes.

20.6 Formulas and Names

Coordination compounds are quite varied in their structure, bonding, ability to form isomers, and other features. For this reason, assigning specific names to these compounds must be done with care. Just as in naming binary compounds (Chapter 2) and organic compounds (Chapter 12), IUPAC rules will guide us in constructing the proper name.

Formulas

Coordination complexes (the metal center and the ligands) can be neutral, anionic, or cationic in nature. To ensure continuity from one structure to another, we often write the formula of a coordination compound in accordance with a set of rules. Those rules are outlined in Table 20.3.

Nomenclature

Systematic names for coordination compounds are constructed in accordance with a set of rules. Those rules are outlined in Table 20.4. Let's use these rules to name a few examples. Consider that we are interested in naming the neutral complex $[PtCl_2(NH_3)_2]$. Step 1 from Table 20.4 indicates that we should name the compound using the rules in step 3. The ligands are named alphabetically before

TABLE 20.3	Rules for Writing Formulas for Coordination Compounds

1. The metal is written first, followed by the ligands.
2. Anionic ligands are written before the neutral ligands, each in alphabetical order.
3. The complex is enclosed in brackets.
4. Polyatomic ligands, such as NH_3 or NO_2^-, are enclosed in parentheses.
5. Ionic compounds containing coordination complexes are written in the traditional way: cation on the left, anion on the right.

TABLE 20.4	Rules for Naming Coordination Compounds

1. Name the cation, and then the anion. If the complex is neutral, name it using step 3.
2. Is the cation a complex ion?
3. *Yes* – name it using these rules, and then skip to step 5. *No* – skip to step 4.

   a. Name the ligands first using Table 20.1.

   b. Name the ligands in alphabetical order. Anionic ligands often end in "o," as in bromo, hydroxo, and sulfato.

   c. If more than one ligand of the same type is present, a prefix indicates the number of units. For simple ligands, the prefixes di-, tri-, tetra-, penta-, and hexa- are used. For complex ligands, the prefixes bis-, tris-, tetrakis-, pentakis-, and hexakis- are used.

   d. Name the metal last, with its oxidation number in parentheses in Roman numerals.

      (1) If the complex is negatively charged, the name of the metal ends in *-ate.*

      (2) If the complex is positively charged or neutral, no suffix is added to the metal name.

4. Name the cation using the conventions described in Chapter 3.
5. Is the anion a complex ion?
6. YES – Name it using the rules in step 3, and then stop. NO – Go to step 7.
7. Name the anion using the conventions described in Chapter 3, and then stop.

we name the metal. Thus the ammine ligand is named before the chloro ligand. Moreover, there are two of each of these ligands, so we should write down

diamminedichloro

without any spaces. Then, in step 3d, we write the name of the metal and its charge in parentheses immediately afterward. Because the charge on the entire complex is zero, and the complex is neutral, we do not add a suffix to the name:

diamminedichloroplatinum(II)

The name we have created for the formula indicates the number and type of each ligand, and the metal and its oxidation state. If we knew the three-dimensional arrangement of the atoms in this complex, we could also include that information in the name. For example, if we knew that the structure indicated a *cis* arrangement of the atoms, we could designate that by writing *cis*-diamminedichloroplatinum(II). Without that knowledge, though, we can provide only the name of the formula.

If we wish to name $[Co(NH_3)_6]Cl_3$, we can do so by following the rules. In step 1, we note that the compound is made up of a cationic complex and some anionic counter ions. Step 2 in Table 20.4 directs us to write the name of the complex (the cation). The ligands are named first, like this:

hexaammine

Then in step 3d we name the metal and its charge. Again, we do not add a suffix, because the complex is a cation:

hexaamminecobalt(III)

Finally, steps 6 and 7 tell us to add the counter ions by naming them as we did in Chapter 3. Note that we don't add a prefix to their name.

hexaamminecobalt(III) chloride

An anionic complex is not much different. Suppose we wished to name $K_2[NiCl_4]$. In step 1, we note that the anion is a complex and the cation is a counter ion. Accordingly, we name the cation first.

potassium

The complex anion is named using step 3. The ligands go first (note that there are four of them):

potassium tetrachloro

And the metal is part of an anion, so it gets the suffix -*ate*:

potassium tetrachloronickelate(II)

$K_2[NiCl_4]$ $[Co(NH_3)_6]Cl_3$ $[Co(NO_2)_2(NH_3)_4]_2SO_4$

Examples of coordination compounds. See if you can name them all.

EXERCISE 20.3   Naming Compounds

Give the name for each of these compounds.

a. $[Cr(NH_3)_2(en)_2]SO_4$ b. $(NH_4)_3[Fe(CN)_6]$

First Thoughts

Naming coordination compounds requires us to identify the oxidation states of the metal center in addition to understanding and knowing the charges on the individual ligands and ions. To answer this question accurately, separate the compounds into their two halves (cation and anion). For the half containing the metal ion, determine its oxidation state, and then use the rules in Table 20.4 to name it.

Solution

a. diamminebis(ethylenediamine)chromium(II) sulfate

b. ammonium hexacyanoferrate(III)

Further Insight

The names for these compounds have a different sound to them, compared to the simpler compounds we worked with in Chapter 3. Just remember to follow the rules in Table 20.4, and be sure that you know the names of the ligands from Table 20.1.

PRACTICE 20.3

Name each of these compounds.

a. $[CrCl_2(NH_3)_4]_2SO_4$ b. $Na_2[Ni(CN)_4]$

Draw the formula for each of the following coordination compounds.

c. calcium hexafluoroferrate(II)

d. tetraamminedicarbonylmanganese(II) sulfate

See Problems 37–40.

20.7 Color and Coordination Compounds

Many painters create images that both catch our eye and induce a feeling in our mind. The goal of the painter is often to portray more than just a staged scene. Van Gogh's painting *Starry Night* (see Figure 20.19) evokes a certain sense of wonder. The effect is generated by the brush strokes and the colors applied to the canvas. Are chemical compounds responsible for the color of paint? The answer is a resounding yes. Colors used in paintings are often constructed from ancient

FIGURE 20.19

Van Gogh's *Starry Night* uses the colors of transition metals to evoke the feeling of magic in the night sky.

formulations that include compounds of transition metals. One of the general characteristics of transition metals is the color of their compounds. Compare table salt (NaCl), baking soda ($NaHCO_3$), chalk ($CaCO_3$), and Epsom salts ($MgSO_4$) to ruby (with Cr_2O_3), emerald (with Cr_2O_3), and rust ($Fe_2O_3 \cdot nH_2O$, or hematite). Chromium was so named because of the variety and brilliance of the colors of its compounds. **What causes compounds that contain transition metals to have such striking colors?**

Transition Metals and Color

Application

CHEMICAL ENCOUNTERS: Transition Metals and Color

Because color is a common feature of transition metal compounds, it seems reasonable that there must be some common characteristics that give rise to their colors. The presence of color in most transition metal compounds can be attributed to the presence of partially filled d orbitals in the compounds and to the influence of the coordination environment on the energies of the d orbitals. Let's see how the color of transition metal compounds is related to fundamental atomic structure principles.

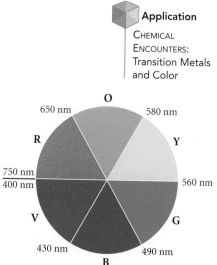

The color wheel indicates the range of wavelengths that corresponds to each color.

We perceive color when our eye detects light rays that differ from the ordinary distribution of those present in white light. For example, a sweater appears blue if white light strikes it, colors complementary to blue are absorbed, and the remaining light is reflected. A glass of fruit punch may appear red if white light strikes it and the colors complementary to red are absorbed. The remaining light, which appears red to our eye, is transmitted through the liquid and gives the liquid its red color. Color, then, is the array of light rays that our eyes observe being reflected from or transmitted through an object.

There are many objects that can absorb or transmit certain wavelengths of light but not be "colored." This occurs when the light being absorbed or transmitted is outside of the visible region (400–700 nm) of the electromagnetic spectrum. Recall from Chapter 6 that ultraviolet (UV) light has shorter wavelengths, typically defined as light in the wavelength range of 200–400 nm. A photon of UV light carries a lot of energy and may be damaging to substances it strikes. Infrared light has longer wavelengths than visible light.

Given our understanding of light (Chapter 6), we can begin to ask questions about how a compound can appear to be colored. **For example, what characteristic change occurs in a substance when light is absorbed?** Answering this question will enable us to understand why lime (CaO) is colorless but rust (Fe_2O_3) is colored. Several fundamental principles are involved.

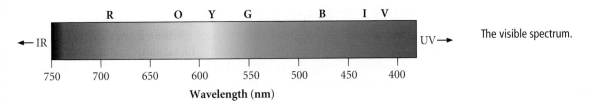

The visible spectrum.

Absorption of a photon of visible light by a compound results in the excitation of an electron from a low energy orbital to a higher energy orbital within the substance. In order for the photon to be absorbed, the difference in orbital energy levels must match the energy of the photon absorbed. Finally, the excited electron must be able to be excited to the higher energy orbital—that is, the higher energy orbital must not be full. For example, when visible light strikes rust, an electron in a lower energy orbital absorbs a photon of blue light. The electron is excited to a higher energy orbital. (Usually the high-energy electron dissipates its energy as heat and relaxes back to its original energy level, ready to absorb again!) Orange light is reflected, and that is what our eyes detect. Rust is orange-colored.

In many transition metal compounds, of which rust is one, the same process occurs. What electronic transitions take place to allow the absorption of visible light? The d orbitals of the transition metal are often arranged such that they have a slight difference in energy. One example is shown in Figure 20.20. This difference in energy is roughly that of a photon in the visible region of the electromagnetic spectrum. If the d orbitals are partially filled, as they are in the transition metal ions, a photon can cause an electron in the lower energy orbitals to jump to an empty (or partially filled) higher energy d orbital.

Let's use this information to compare the colors of rust (Fe_2O_3) and chalk ($CaCO_3$). The iron(III) ion in rust has the electron configuration $[Ar]3d^5$. It contains partially filled d orbitals as its valence orbitals. These d orbitals on the metal, surrounded by a field of oxide ions, are split into different energy levels in ways that we will discuss in the next section. When visible light strikes rust, some wavelengths of light are absorbed, and an electron is excited to a higher empty energy level. The calcium ion in lime is isoelectronic with argon. It does not have partially filled d orbitals, cannot absorb visible light energy, and reflects all of the visible light to our eyes. It appears to be white, as shown in Figure 20.21.

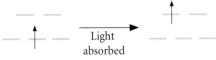

FIGURE 20.20

A slight difference in the energy of the five d orbitals on a transition metal in a complex allows visible light to be absorbed. This causes an electron to be excited to the higher-energy d orbitals.

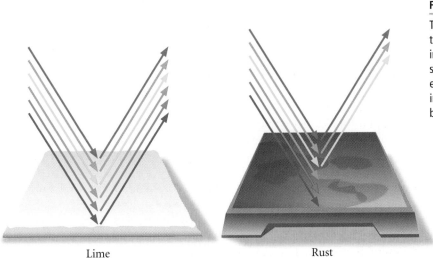

Lime   Rust

FIGURE 20.21

The color of lime and that of rust are a result of the absorption of specific wavelengths of light in the visible region of the electromagnetic spectrum. Calcium ions in lime do not possess electrons in d orbitals and cannot absorb light in the visible region. Iron ions in rust have d orbital electrons and do absorb visible light.

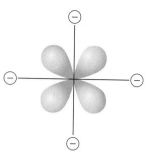

Ligands interacting with a d_{xy} orbital

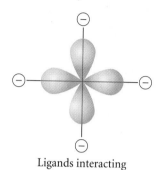

Ligands interacting with a $d_{x^2-y^2}$ orbital

FIGURE 20.22

As ligands approach the d orbitals, they affect the relative energy levels of the $5d$ orbitals. Some, like the $d_{x^2-y^2}$ orbital, have an increased energy due to the repulsion of similar charges.

Crystal Field Theory

We can understand the nature of the d orbital splitting from careful analysis of geometry and d orbital shape. In a free, gaseous metal atom or ion, there is no difference in energy among the orbitals of the same sublevel. We say that these orbitals, such as the $3d$ orbitals on gaseous iron, are degenerate. But something happens when we bring other atoms (such as the negatively charged anions) up close to the metal. They cause distortions in the orbitals of the metal. In a six-coordinate octahedral complex, for example, ions approach the central metal from each end of the three coordinate axes. Their orientation causes the orbitals on the metal to lose their degenerate nature.

Let's look just at the xy plane in an octahedral complex. The octahedral ligands are oriented along the x axis and the y axis. The d orbitals on a metal at the center of our plane are oriented in specific ways. Which electron would have lower energy, an electron in a $d_{x^2-y^2}$ orbital pointed directly at a negatively charged ligand or an electron in a d_{xy} orbital pointed between the negatively charged ligands? Using Figure 20.22 as a graphical guide, we can answer this question. Because like charges repel, an electron in a $d_{x^2-y^2}$ orbital would be higher in energy. We would represent this on an energy-level diagram as follows:

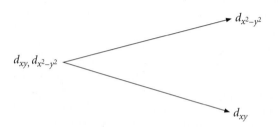

Octahedral Crystal Field Splitting

For a metal center in an octahedral crystal field, an electron in a $d_{x^2-y^2}$ orbital would be at higher energy than an electron in a d_{xy} orbital. We can extend this analysis to three dimensions and include all d orbitals as shown in Figure 20.23. Note that the $d_{x^2-y^2}$ and d_{z^2} orbitals are pointed right at the negatively charged ligands, but the d_{xy}, d_{xz}, and d_{yz} orbitals are pointed between the axes. The d_{xy}, d_{xz}, and d_{yz} orbitals will be at lower energy than the $d_{x^2-y^2}$ and d_{z^2} orbitals. Based on

FIGURE 20.23

d orbitals in an octahedral crystal field.

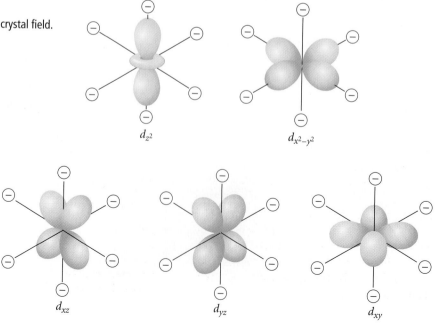

the symmetry of the system, the d_{xz}, d_{yz}, and d_{xy} orbitals are at the same energy level. Although it is less obvious, the $d_{x^2-y^2}$ and d_{z^2} orbitals are at the same energy level, which is higher than that of the d_{xy}, d_{xz}, and d_{yz} orbitals.

In an octahedral array of anions or ligands, the d orbital energies of the central metal are split into a lower energy set (d_{xz}, d_{xy}, d_{yz}) that we label the t_{2g} set and an upper energy set ($d_{x^2-y^2}$, d_{z^2}) that we label the e_g set, as shown in Figure 20.24. The energy difference between the t_{2g} orbitals and the e_g orbitals in the octahedral field, the **crystal field splitting energy**, is given the symbol Δ_o, where the subscript "o" indicates the splitting energy for an octahedral complex. The magnitude of Δ_o, the difference in energy between the t_{2g} and e_g orbitals, depends on the nature of the central metal and the nature of the ligands.

Tetrahedral Crystal Field Splitting

A tetrahedral ligand field can be viewed as one with the metal ion at the center of a cube, with ions at alternate corners of a cube, with the coordinate axes going through the centers of the faces of the cube as shown in Figure 20.25. In this situation, none of the d orbitals of a central atom are pointed at the ions. The d_{xy}, d_{xz}, and d_{yz} lobes are closer to the ions than the $d_{x^2-y^2}$ and d_{z^2} lobes. Thus the d_{xy}, d_{xz}, and d_{yz} orbitals are at a higher energy than the $d_{x^2-y^2}$ and d_{z^2} orbitals. As shown in Figure 20.25, the tetrahedral crystal field splitting energy, Δ_t, where the subscript "t" indicates a tetrahedral complex, is qualitatively the inverse of the octahedral field splitting diagram. We label the lower orbital set "e" and the upper orbital set "t". As the comparison in Figure 20.26 shows, the magnitude of the splitting, Δ_t, is estimated to be 4/9 the size of Δ_o, so the magnitude of tetrahedral crystal field splitting is smaller than that of octahedral field splitting.

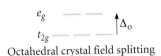

FIGURE 20.24

Crystal field splitting of metal d orbitals for octahedral and tetrahedral geometries.

FIGURE 20.26

The value of Δ_t is 4/9 that of Δ_o, the distance in energy from the $d_{x^2-y^2}$ to the d_{xy} orbital.

FIGURE 20.25

Tetrahedral crystal field splitting (arrows show the distance from orbital lobe to ions).

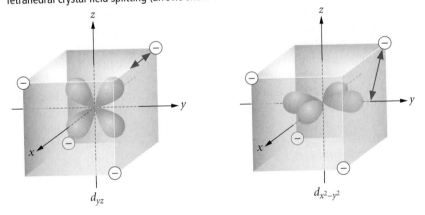

Square Planar Crystal Field Splitting

We can define the square planar geometry as one with the four ligands in the xy plane as in an octahedral complex, but with the two opposing ligands on the z axis completely removed. The crystal field effect in the xy plane remains the same, but the effect in the z direction is removed. This results in stabilization of the d orbitals with z axis components. The resulting crystal field splitting diagram is shown in Figure 20.27. The difference in energy between d_{xy} and $d_{x^2-y^2}$ is still Δ_o. The other energy differences are considerably smaller.

FIGURE 20.27

Square planar coordination complex.

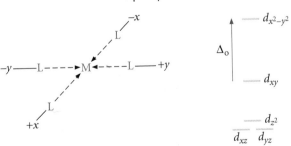

Ligand arrangement of a square planar complex

d Orbital energies in a square planar complex

Orbital Occupancy

The crystal field energy-level diagrams are the basis for understanding both physical and chemical properties of transition metal coordination complexes. However, as with all other chemicals, these properties are related to the electron configuration of the species. This configuration still follows the Aufbau rule, Pauli's exclusion principle, and Hund's rule of maximum multiplicity (Chapter 6). However, the splitting between the energy levels of the d orbitals becomes similar to the electrostatic repulsion that occurs when two electrons occupy the same orbital. This repulsion is called the **pairing energy** (P). Depending on the values of Δ and P, it may be favorable to place an electron in a higher energy orbital rather than pair it with another electron in one orbital where the negatively charged electrons will repel each other.

Octahedral Complexes

An octahedral coordination complex containing a central metal atom with one d electron, such as Ti^{3+} or V^{4+}, will have one electron occupying one of the t_{2g} orbitals. For a central metal with a d^2 configuration, such as V^{3+}, one electron will occupy each of two t_{2g} orbitals, as shown in Figure 20.28. This configuration can be symbolized t_{2g}^2, where the superscript represents the number of electrons in the orbital set labeled t_{2g}. An octahedral complex with three d electrons would give rise to a t_{2g}^3 orbital occupancy. However, if another electron is added, it may either pair up with one of the electrons already in a t_{2g} orbital at an energy cost of $+P$, or occupy one of the e_g orbitals at an energy cost of $+\Delta_o$. The electron will tend to attain the lowest energy situation and hence will occupy the e_g orbital if Δ_o is less than the pairing energy, P. Therefore, depending on the values of Δ_o and P, the configuration could either be t_{2g}^4 with two unpaired electrons or $t_{2g}^3 e_g^1$ with four unpaired electrons, as shown in Figure 20.29.

These two configurations of electrons in the d orbitals are termed **low-spin**, (containing the minimum number of unpaired electrons, in this case two) or **high-spin** (with the maximum number of unpaired electrons, in this case four), respectively. For example, chromium complexes containing the chromium(II) ion (four d electrons) may be either high-spin with four unpaired electrons, as in $[Cr(H_2O)_6]^{2+}$, or low-spin with two unpaired electrons, as in $[Cr(CN)_6]^{4-}$.

Continuing with our orbital occupancy evaluation, a d^5 configuration could be either t_{2g}^5 (low-spin) or $t_{2g}^3 e_g^2$ (high-spin). At the d^6 configuration, electron pairing must occur, but either low-spin (t_{2g}^6) or high-spin ($t_{2g}^4 e_g^2$) may exist. A d^7 configuration could also be either low-spin ($t_{2g}^6 e_g^1$) or high-spin ($t_{2g}^5 e_g^2$). Like the electron configurations with one, two, or three electrons, only one option is available for occupancy of the t_{2g} and e_g orbital sets for the d^8 ($t_{2g}^6 e_g^2$), d^9 ($t_{2g}^6 e_g^3$), and d^{10} ($t_{2g}^6 e_g^4$) configurations.

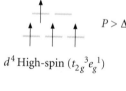

d^4 High-spin ($t_{2g}^3 e_g^1$)

$P > \Delta$

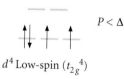

$P < \Delta$

d^4 Low-spin (t_{2g}^4)

FIGURE 20.29

The relative magnitude of the pairing energy and the crystal field energy determine the electron configuration.

FIGURE 20.28

Electron distribution in d^2, d^4, d^6, d^8 octahedral coordination complexes.

d^2 High-spin (t_{2g}^2) d^4 High-spin ($t_{2g}^3 e_g^1$) d^6 High-spin ($t_{2g}^4 e_g^2$) d^8 High-spin ($t_{2g}^6 e_g^2$)

d^4 Low-spin (t_{2g}^4) d^6 Low-spin (t_{2g}^6)

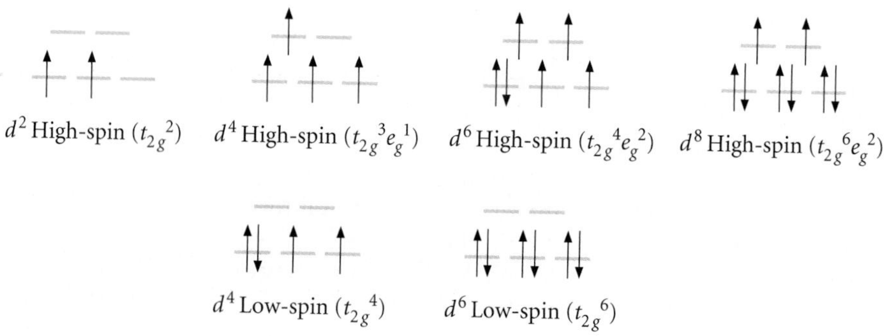

Tetrahedral Complexes

Although it would seem that similar high-spin and low-spin electron configurations would be possible for the $d^3 - d^6$ metals in tetrahedral complexes, such situations are not observed. The magnitude of Δ_t is usually less than the pairing energy P. Recall that Δ_t for a tetrahedral complex is only about ⅘ that of Δ_o for an octahedral complex. Because P is always greater than Δ_t, high-spin complexes are nearly always the only possibility for tetrahedral complexes.

Square Planar Complexes

Similar analyses could be done with square planar complexes. However, it turns out that most square planar complexes occur for metal centers and ligands that generate a low-spin configuration. For example, cisplatin (cis-$[PtCl_2(NH_3)_2]$) has the orbital occupancy shown in Figure 20.30.

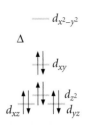

FIGURE 20.30

Electron distribution in square planar cis-$[PtCl_2(NH_3)_2]$.

EXERCISE 20.4   **Drawing Crystal Field Diagrams**

Draw crystal field splitting diagrams with electron occupancy for $[Mn(H_2O)_6]^{2+}$ (high-spin).

Solution

Manganese(II) has a d^5 configuration. With a coordination number of 6, an octahedral crystal field is expected. A high-spin d^5 ($t_{2g}^3 e_g^2$) configuration will result.

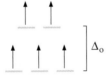

PRACTICE 20.4

How many unpaired electrons would you predict for the low-spin complex $[Fe(CN)_6]^{4-}$? Show the basis of your prediction using the crystal field splitting diagram for the iron metal ion.

See Problems 47–50.

FIGURE 20.31

Absorption of light (arrow) by cobalt complexes. The red solution is a solution of $[Co(H_2O_6)^{2+}]$; the blue solution is the coordination of chloride with cobalt(II) in $[CoCl_4]^{2-}$. Note that different wavelengths of light are absorbed by these complexes.

The Result of d Orbital Splitting

A really dramatic example of color differences occurs in the two complexes of Co^{2+} shown in Figure 20.31. When water is coordinated to Co^{2+} in the $[Co(H_2O)_6]^{2+}$ ion, the color is red. When chloride ligands coordinate to Co^{2+} in $[CoCl_4]^{2-}$, the color is blue. **How does this fit into our understanding of color?** The valence electron configurations of all of these species are shown in Figure 20.32 on page 890. For $[Co(H_2O)_6]^{2+}$ with an octahedral ligand field, the red color arises when an electron is excited from a t_{2g} orbital to an e_g orbital by absorption of a photon of energy Δ_o. For $[CoCl_4]^{2-}$ with a tetrahedral ligand field, the blue color arises when an electron is excited from an e orbital to a t orbital by absorption of a photon of energy Δ_t. Because, in general, Δ_t is smaller than Δ_o, the photon absorbed by $[CoCl_4]^{2-}$ must be lower in energy than the photon absorbed by $[Co(H_2O)_6]^{2+}$. In this case, $[Co(H_2O)_6]^{2+}$ absorbs higher-energy blue light and appears red, and $[CoCl_4]^{2-}$ absorbs lower-energy red light and appears blue.

The absorption spectra in Figure 20.33, which show how much light of various wavelengths is absorbed, exhibit a maximum for $[CoCl_4]^{2-}$ at 660 nm (equivalent to 181 kJ/mol) and a maximum for $[Co(H_2O)_6]^{2+}$ at 510 nm (equivalent to 221 kJ/mol). Recall that longer wavelength corresponds to lower energy, $E = \dfrac{hc}{\lambda}$, so the $[CoCl_4]^{2-}$ complex absorbs lower-energy photons. The key point

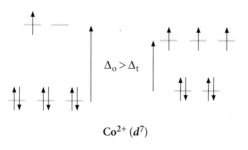

$\Delta_o > \Delta_t$

Co^{2+} (d^7)

FIGURE 20.32

The electron configurations of two cobalt complexes, [Co(H$_2$O)$_6$]$^{2+}$ and [CoCl$_4$]$^{2-}$. The difference in the magnitude of the crystal field energy determines what wavelengths of light they absorb.

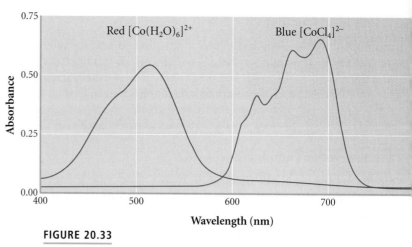

FIGURE 20.33

Absorption spectra of [Co(H$_2$O)$_6$]$^{2+}$ and [CoCl$_4$]$^{2-}$.

is that based on the model and with experimental evidence to support it, *the geometry of the ligand field around a metal center influences the size of* Δ.

The nature of the ligands around the metal center also influences the magnitude of Δ. Figure 20.34 shows solutions of three cobalt(III) complexes with different ligands around the cobalt center. The wavelength of light that is absorbed decreases, as shown in Figure 20.35, as the unique ligand varies from Cl$^-$ to H$_2$O to NH$_3$. As the ligand varies, the value of Δ_o increases and the wavelength of maximum absorbance decreases. Using this type of information from a wide variety of complexes, a **spectrochemical series** was developed that illustrates the effect of a particular ligand on the value of Δ. The series is

$$Cl^- < F^- < OH^- < H_2O < NH_3 < NO_2^- < CN^- < CO$$

Conveniently, this series is generally the same for all metals. Knowing this information, we can predict that the wavelength of light absorbed by [FeF$_6$]$^{3-}$ would be longer (lower in energy) than the wavelength of light absorbed by [Fe(H$_2$O)$_6$]$^{3+}$ because a water ligand produces a larger value of Δ than the fluoride ligand.

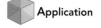 **Application**

Let's use this information to answer a practical question: Why is the blood in your veins dark red, whereas the blood in arteries is bright red? When blood in a vein is exposed to air, its color changes to bright red. Although the exact origin of this color change is fairly complex, it turns out that the *crystal field splitting increases when oxygen binds to the iron center*. When oxygen binds to the Fe^{2+} center, higher-energy light is absorbed, longer-wavelength light is transmitted by the hemoglobin, and the blood changes color. Oxyhemoglobin (with a larger crystal field splitting) absorbs higher-energy blue light and is red in the arteries;

FIGURE 20.34

The influence of coordinated ligands on color of coordination complexes. Each complex of cobalt(III) contains five NH$_3$ ligands and one other ligand. From left to right: [Co(NH$_3$)$_6$]$^{3+}$, [Co(NH$_3$)$_5$(H$_2$O)]$^{3+}$, and [Co(NH$_3$)$_5$Cl]$^{2+}$.

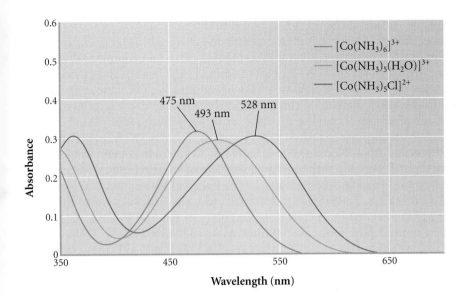

FIGURE 20.35

Absorption spectra of $[Co(NH_3)_6]^{3+}$, $[Co(NH_3)_5(H_2O)]^{3+}$, and $[Co(NH_3)_5Cl]^{2+}$, showing higher-energy, shorter-wavelength absorption in the order $[Co(NH_3)_6]^{3+} < [Co(NH_3)_5(H_2O)]^{3+} < [Co(NH_3)_5Cl]^{2+}$. (Spectra provided by Jerry Walsh.)

deoxyhemoglobin (with a smaller crystal field splitting) absorbs lower energies and appears bluish-red in the veins.

Magnetism

When magnetism is mentioned, it is common to think of bar magnets and their attraction for metal objects. This common form of magnetism shown by iron, nickel, and cobalt is known as **ferromagnetism**. However, there is a more common but also more subtle form of magnetism called **paramagnetism** (Chapter 9). This property exists in any substance that contains unpaired electrons. A substance that is paramagnetic is attracted to a magnetic field, though less strongly than in a ferromagnetic substance. A material that has all of its electrons paired exhibits **diamagnetism**, and these materials are very weakly repelled by a magnetic field.

The origin of paramagnetism is in the spin of the unpaired electrons in a substance. In the absence of a magnetic field, the spins of the unpaired electrons are randomly oriented. When these unpaired electrons are placed in a magnetic field, their spins align with the field and result in a net attraction. The experimental characterization of transition metal coordination complexes was greatly aided by measurement of the paramagnetism of various species. Measurement of the strength of the paramagnetism provides an experimental quantity called the **magnetic moment** (μ). In many cases, μ is related to the number of unpaired electrons, n, and is nearly equal to or slightly greater than the theoretical value given by the formula

$$\mu = [n(n+2)]^{1/2}$$

where n = number of unpaired electrons.

The complex $[Mn(H_2O)_6]^{2+}$ has a magnetic moment of 5.9, whereas the magnetic moment of $[Mn(CN)_6]^{4-}$ is 2.2. Both have five d electrons. Why should they have such different magnetic moments? Using the relationship between magnetic moment and the number of unpaired electrons, $\mu = [n(n+2)]^{1/2}$, we find that if $n = 5$, then μ should be 5.92 for the aqua complex. Thus the $[Mn(H_2O)_6]^{2+}$ complex is a high-spin d^5 complex, as shown in Figure 20.36.

$Mn(OH_2)_6^{2+}$ d^5 High-spin $Mn(CN)_6^{4-}$ d^5 Low-spin

FIGURE 20.36

High-spin and low-spin manganese complexes. In the high-spin case, the crystal field energy is less than the pairing energy. In the low-spin case, the magnitude of Δ is greater than the pairing energy.

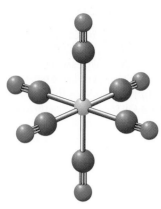

$[Mn(CN)_6]^{4-}$

FIGURE 20.37

Using the same relationship, if $n = 1$ (as it would be in the low-spin case), we expect μ to be 1.73, which is close to the value observed in the cyano complex. Therefore, the $[Mn(CN)_6]^{4-}$ complex must be a low-spin complex. This makes sense when we note that CN^- imparts a strong ligand field (high in the spectrochemical series) and H_2O imparts a weak ligand field. For CN^-, the magnitude of Δ is large enough that the electrons prefer to be paired up in the t_{2g} orbitals rather than unpaired and occupying the higher energy e_g orbitals (Figure 20.37).

A fascinating change related to the paramagnetism of the iron ion in hemoglobin occurs upon binding of oxygen. Deoxyhemoglobin contains a high-spin, paramagnetic Fe^{2+} ion with four unpaired electrons. Upon binding with oxygen, the increased ligand field causes an increase in Δ, and the Fe^{2+} becomes low-spin and diamagnetic. This change in spin state, which can be followed by measurement of its magnetism, is critical to the ability of the iron to bind oxygen and release it under physiological conditions, as we will discuss later.

20.8 Chemical Reactions

Aside from possessing interesting color and magnetism properties, transition metal coordination complexes also undergo useful chemical reactions. Of particular biological importance is a class of reactions known as ligand exchange reactions. This class of reactions includes the coordination of oxygen and its release from an iron ion in hemoglobin. Another class of reactions, known as electron transfer reactions, are also important in biological processes. This class of reactions is quite common in photosynthesis and respiration.

Ligand Exchange Reactions

Why do coordination complexes form? All chemical reactions proceed when the total free energy of the system, ΔG, decreases. Because the free energy change depends on two factors, entropy and enthalpy, these must be considered in a reaction involving the association of a ligand with a metal. Consider the formation of hexaamminenickel(II) from the aqua complex:

$$[Ni(H_2O)_6]^{2+} + 6NH_3 \rightarrow [Ni(NH_3)_6]^{2+} + 6H_2O \qquad K = 4 \times 10^8$$

Because the two different ligands, NH_3 and H_2O, are similar in size and the same number of each are involved in the reaction, the change in entropy for the reaction is small. *The driving force for this reaction must then rely on the stability of the resulting coordinate covalent bonds.* In this example, the Ni^{2+}—N bond is stronger than the Ni^{2+}—O bond, so ΔG is relatively large and negative because of the favorable enthalpy change in nickel—nitrogen bond formation. This translates into a large equilibrium constant for the formation of $[Ni(NH_3)_6]^{2+}$ via the equation $\Delta G = -RT\ln K$.

Consider the following reaction of our nickel complex. Each mole of this complex can react with three moles of ethylenediamine to form $[Ni(en)_3]^{3+}$. Both complexes contain Ni^{2+}—N bonds. Does it make sense that this reaction should also have a very large equilibrium constant?

$$[Ni(NH_3)_6]^{2+} + 3en \rightarrow [Ni(en)_3]^{2+} + 6NH_3 \qquad K = 5 \times 10^9$$

There doesn't appear to be much change in the enthalpy of this reaction (the change in enthalpy is expected to be small because the bonds created in the product are similar to the bonds broken in the reactant), so we must focus on changes in entropy for this reaction. A very favorable entropy change is observed; the reaction produces three more moles of product than moles of reactant. This

$t = 3$ min

$t = 1$ day

FIGURE 20.38

Rates of ligand exchange. $[CoCl_4]^{2-}$ exchanges chloro ligands immediately on mixing.

exceptionally high favorability for forming complexes with polydentate ligands is known as the chelate effect.

Although we can predict the direction of a reaction by using thermodynamics, only an examination of the kinetics of the reaction will determine the rate of the reaction. Some coordination complexes exchange their ligands very rapidly and are referred to as labile; others do so more slowly and are referred to as inert. For example, the blue $[CoCl_4]^-$ complex rapidly exchanges chloro ligands with water to produce the red $[Co(H_2O)_6]^{2+}$ complex, both of which are shown in Figure 20.38. In contrast, the chromium complexes shown in Figure 20.39, green $[CrCl_2(H_2O)_4]^+$ and purple $[Cr(H_2O)_6]^{3+}$, take at least a day to exchange ligands. In the interaction between cisplatin and DNA molecules, it is important for the platinum complex to bond to the DNA and remain bonded long enough for the complex to be toxic to the system. The platinum–DNA complex is inert—and *must* be inert to exhibit the kind of anticancer activity that it does.

The kinetic and thermodynamic factors exhibited in the reactivity of coordination complexes are intriguingly complementary in hemoglobin. The Fe^{2+} metal center is kinetically labile, which is important for the rapid exchange of oxygen ligands:

$$HbFe^{2+} + O_2 \rightleftharpoons HbFeO_2^{2+} \qquad \text{rapid}$$

However, in spite of the fact that Fe^{2+} can exchange its ligands rapidly, the chelate effect of the tetradentate porphyrin ligand maintains stability of the iron–porphyrin portion of the complex.

$$HbFe^{2+} + 6H_2O \rightleftharpoons Hb + [Fe(H_2O)_6]^{2+} \qquad \text{equilibrium lies to the left}$$

The balance of chemical characteristics for molecules in living systems is exquisite. This is why the scientific challenge of generating a chemical substitute for hemoglobin to transport oxygen in the bloodstream has been formidable.

$t = 3$ min

$t = 1$ day

FIGURE 20.39

$[CrCl_2(H_2O)_4]^+$ exchanges ligands slowly, taking a day or more to fully exchange its ligands.

Electron Transfer Reactions

Transition metals typically exhibit several stable oxidation states, and the +2 and +3 states are fairly common. Because many transition metals exhibit stability in two or more oxidation states, transition metal complexes can play important roles in electron transfer processes. For example, cytochromes are electron transfer agents in biological systems. Within a cytochrome protein, an iron ion coordinates to a porphyrin ring. The other sites on the octahedral complex are occupied by ligands that are part of the protein structure, as shown in Figure 20.40. During respiration and photosynthesis, the iron changes oxidation state from Fe^{2+} to Fe^{3+} to Fe^{2+} as the cytochrome shuttles electrons between two biological reaction sites (Figure 20.41).

FIGURE 20.40

Iron coordination in cytochrome electron transfer protein.

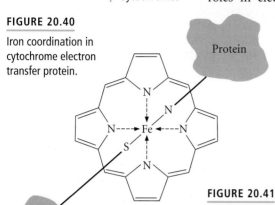

FIGURE 20.41

The role of iron (cytochrome) and copper (plastocyanin) oxidation states in electron transfer reactions in photosynthesis.

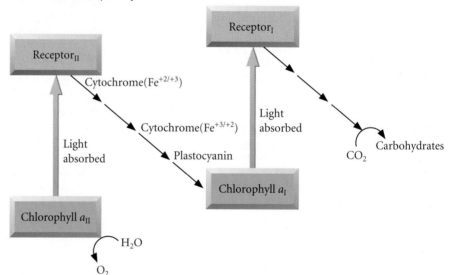

The Bottom Line

- Coordination complexes are present in simple metal ions in solution and as the reaction center in many biological molecules. (Section 20.1)

- A Lewis base that donates a lone pair of electrons to a metal to form a coordinate covalent bond acts as a ligand in producing a coordination complex. (Section 20.2)

- The coordination numbers of various metal centers are commonly observed to be 2, 4, or 6. (Section 20.3)

- Common coordination geometries are linear, tetrahedral, square planar, and octahedral. (Section 20.4)

- A variety of isomer classes are observed for metal complexes. (Section 20.5)

- The proper names and formulas for coordination complexes are specified by IUPAC rules. (Section 20.6)

- In transition metal complexes, the d orbitals are no longer degenerate but split into two or more energy levels, depending on coordination geometry. (Section 20.7)

- The electron configuration for octahedral complexes gives rise to high-spin and low-spin complexes for d^4 to d^7 metal centers. (Section 20.7)

- The color of many transition metal compounds arises when a photon of visible light is absorbed and an electron is excited to a higher energy d orbital. (Section 20.7)

- The order of ligands, in terms of their influence on the magnitude of the *d* orbital splitting and the energy of the photon of light absorbed, is defined as the spectrochemical series. (Section 20.7)

- The number of unpaired electrons determines the magnetic moment of the complex. (Section 20.7)

- Metal centers that exchange ligands rapidly are called labile; those that exchange ligands slowly are called inert. (Section 20.8)

- Chelate complexes have high formation constants because of an entropy effect. (Section 20.8)

- Because transition metal complexes often exhibit several oxidation states, transition metal complexes are good electron transfer (redox) agents. (Section 20.8)

Key Words

bidentate Capable of forming two coordinate covalent bonds to the same metal center. (*p. 874*)

chelate A polydentate ligand that forms strong metal–ligand bonds. (*p. 874*)

chelate effect An unusually large formation constant due to a favorable entropy change for the formation of a complex between a metal center and a polydentate ligand. (*p. 893*)

***cis* isomer** An isomer containing two similar groups on the same side of the compound. (*p. 880*)

coordinate covalent bond A covalent bond that results when one atom donates both electrons to the bond. (*p. 870*)

coordinates Forms a coordinate covalent bond. (*p. 871*)

coordination complex A metal bonded to two or more ligands via coordinate covalent bonds. (*p. 870*)

coordination number The number of coordinate covalent bonds that form in a complex. (*p. 875*)

coordination sphere isomers Substances that contain different ligands in the coordination spheres of complex cations and complex anions. (*p. 879*)

crystal field splitting energy The difference in energy between the *d* orbital sets that arises because of the presence of ligands around a metal; symbolized by Δ. (*p. 887*)

diamagnetism The ability of a substance to be repelled from a magnetic field. This property arises because all of the electrons in the molecule are paired. (*p. 891*)

ferromagnetism Occurs when paramagnetic atoms are close enough to each other (such as in iron) that they reinforce their attraction to the magnetic field, so the whole is, in effect, greater than the sum of its parts. (*p. 891*)

geometric isomers Substances in which all of the atoms are attached with the same connectivity, or bonds, but the geometric orientation differs. (*p. 880*)

high-spin A coordination complex with the maximum number of unpaired electrons. (*p. 888*)

inert The opposite of labile; said of a compound that is very slow to exchange ligands. (*p. 893*)

ionization isomers Isomers that differ in the placement of counter ions and ligands. (*p. 879*)

labile The opposite of inert; said of a compound that exchanges ligands rapidly. (*p. 893*)

ligand A Lewis base that donates a lone pair of electrons to a metal center to form a coordinate covalent bond. (*p. 870*)

linkage isomers Isomers that differ in the point of attachment of a ligand to a metal. (*p. 879*)

low-spin A coordination complex with the minimum number of unpaired electrons. (*p. 888*)

magnetic moment (μ) The strength of the paramagnetism of a compound. Can be used to determine the number of unpaired electrons. (*p. 891*)

octahedral The geometry indicated by six electron groups (lone pairs and/or bonds) positioned symmetrically around a central atom such that the bond angles are 90°. (*p. 877*)

pairing energy (P) The energy required to spin-pair two electrons within a given orbital. (*p. 888*)

paramagnetism The ability of a substance to be attracted into a magnetic field. This attraction arises because of the presence of unpaired electrons within the molecule. (*p. 891*)

polydentate A ligand that contains two or more lone pairs on different atoms, each forming a coordinate covalent bond to a metal center. (*p. 874*)

spectrochemical series The series of ligands organized with respect to their effect on the value of the crystal field splitting energy. (*p. 890*)

square planar The geometry indicated by four electron groups (lone pairs and/or bonds) positioned symmetrically in a plane around a central atom such that the bond angles are 90°. (*p. 877*)

tetradentate Capable of forming four coordinate covalent bonds to the same metal center. (*p. 874*)

tetrahedral The geometry indicated by four electron groups (lone pairs and/or bonds) positioned symmetrically around a central atom such that the bond angles are 109°. (*p. 877*)

***trans* isomer** An isomer containing two similar groups on opposite sides of the compound. (*p. 880*)

tridentate Capable of forming three coordinate covalent bonds to the same metal center. (*p. 874*)

==
Focus Your Learning

The answers to the odd-numbered problems appear at the back of the book.

20.1 Bonding in Coordination Complexes

Skill Review

1. Define each of these terms in your own words:
   a. ligand   b. coordinate covalent bond   c. Lewis acid

2. Define each of these terms in your own words:
   a. Lewis base   b. complex   c. metal center

3. For each of these coordination complexes, state the number of ligands, the oxidation number of the coordinated metal, and the number of coordinate covalent bonds that are formed within the complex.
   a. $[Fe(H_2O)_6]^{2+}$ b. $[Co(NH_3)_6]^{2+}$
   c. $[Zn(NH_3)_4]^{2+}$ d. $[Pt(CO)_4]$

4. For each of these coordination complexes, state the number of ligands, the oxidation number of the coordinated metal, and the number of coordinate covalent bonds that are formed within the complex.
   a. $[Fe(CN)_6]^{3-}$ b. $[CuCl(NH_3)_3]^+$
   c. $[Ni(H_2O)_6]^{2+}$ d. $[Au(NH_3)_2]^{2+}$

5. Diagram a structure that depicts a metal ion (M) surrounded by four symmetrically arranged ligands (L).

6. Diagram a structure that depicts a metal ion (M) surrounded by six symmetrically arranged ligands (L). Why are coordination complexes rarely found with more than six ligands?

20.2 Ligands

Skill Review

7. Diagram the Lewis dot structure for ammonia (NH_3). Explain why this molecule is classified as a Lewis base.

8. Diagram the Lewis dot structure for methylamine (CH_3NH_2). Is this molecule a Lewis base?

9. Would you predict the following molecule to be a ligand? If so, indicate whether it would be monodentate, bidentate, tridentate, or tetradentate.

10. Would you predict the following molecule to be a ligand? If so, indicate whether it would be monodentate, bidentate, tridentate, or tetradentate.

==
11. Which of these are *not* likely act as ligands in forming coordination complexes?
    a. H_2O b. CN^- c. Ca^{2+} d. O_2 e. C_2H_6

12. Which of these can act as a ligand in forming coordination complexes?
    a. CH_4 b. Br_2 c. O^{2-} d. H_2O_2 e. Li^+

Chemical Applications and Practices

13. Explain why the structure of ethylenediamine (en) enables it to act as a bidentate ligand, whereas nitrogen gas, which also contains two nitrogen atoms, cannot act as a bidentate ligand.

14. $EDTA^{4-}$ can coordinate with metal ions at six different sites. $EDTA^{4-}$ is often used as a food preservative in such food products as mayonnaise. Explain how $EDTA^{4-}$ functions in such an effective manner.

15. The formula $Co(A_2B_2)$ represents a coordination complex with two ligands, A and B. The Co ion is coordinated through six sites. If two A ligands occupy two of those sites, what must be true about the bonding for ligand B?

16. Amino acids can act as bidentate ligands. This is due to the presence of both oxygen and nitrogen. For example, alanine (Ala) could form the metal complex $[Fe(ala)_3]^{3+}$. Use the alanine structure to draw a structure of the metal complex.

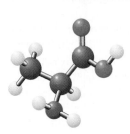

20.3 Coordination Number

Skill Review

17. Determine the oxidation state and the coordination number of the central metal in each of these coordination complexes:
    a. $[Cr(NH_3)_5Br]^{3+}$
    b. $[Mn(NH_2CH_2CH_2NH_2)_3]^{2+}$
    c. $[Cd(NH_2CH_3)_4]^{2+}$

18. Determine the oxidation state and the coordination number of the central metal in each of these coordination complexes:
    a. $[Co(NH_3)_6]^{3+}$ b. $[Pd(en)Cl_2]$ c. $[Mo(ox)_3]^{3-}$

19. Explain how it is possible that the central metals in these two complexes can have the same coordination number even though the number of ligands differs in the complexes.
    $$[Fe(ox)_3]^{3-} \qquad [Co(SCN)_2(H_2O)_4]^+$$

20. Explain how it is possible that the central metal in these two complexes can have the same oxidation state even though the coordination number differs in the complexes.
    $$[Fe(en)_3]^{3+} \qquad [ScI_4]^-$$

Chemical Applications and Practices

21. Many heavy-metal-containing salts are not very water soluble. One way to increase the solubility is to form a complex. Examine the structure of the bidentate oxinate ion shown here. If two of these complexed with a lead ion, what would be the coordination number of the lead?

Oxinate ligand

22. One method used to determine the "hardness" of water samples is to titrate the sample with EDTA. This reaction forms a complex with the calcium ions in the water. Using the structure of EDTA depicted in Figure 20.9, determine what the coordination number of the calcium ion would be if it combined with one disodium EDTA ion. Diagram the structure that justifies your answer.

20.4 Structure

Skill Review

23. Diagram the structures of the complexes listed in Problem 3, and identify the geometry (bond angles and overall shape) of each structure.

24. Diagram the structures of the complexes listed in Problem 4, and identify the geometry (bond angles and overall shape) of each structure.

25. Indicate the oxidation number, coordination number, and geometry for the cobalt ion in the following compound.

$$[CoCl(NO_2)(en)_2]Cl$$

26. Indicate the oxidation number, coordination number, and geometry for the silver ion in the following compound.

$$[Ag(NH_3)_4]Br_2$$

Chemical Applications and Practices

27. When nickel ore is refined, it must be removed from other metals. This can be done by forming a coordination complex between nickel and carbon monoxide. The highly poisonous nickel–carbon monoxide complex $Ni(CO)_4$ evaporates easily and can therefore be used to separate nickel from its impurities. What is the coordination number for nickel, and what two possible geometries could you predict for this structure?

28. The readily available electron pairs found in the oxygen, nitrogen, and some sulfur atoms of amino acids (Chapter 22) provide bonding sites for metals. The metal–amino acid combinations serve as the basis for many important biochemical processes. For example, a certain copper-containing enzyme utilizes an octahedral structure around a Cu^{2+} ion to assist in the transport of electrons within cells. Draw the structure of a copper(II) complex that would form if three glycine amino acids (shown below) formed coordinate covalent bonds with the copper. (Assume that each glycine is bidentate.)

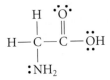

Glycine

20.5 Isomers

Skill Review

29. Define the type of isomer present, if isomerization exists, in each of these pairs of complexes.
    a. *trans*-$[Pt(NH_3)_2Cl_2]$ and *cis*-$[Pt(NH_3)_2Cl_2]$
    b. $[Pt(CN)_2(NH_3)_4]Cl_2$ and $[PtCl_2(NH_3)_4](CN)_2$
    c. $[Fe(H_2O)_6][CuBr_4]$ and $[Cu(H_2O)_6][FeBr_4]$

30. Define the type of isomer present, if isomerization exists, in each of these pairs of complexes.
    a. $[Cu(NH_3)_3(ONO)]$ and $[Cu(NH_3)_3(NO_2)]$
    b. $[Mn(H_2O)_4Cl_2]Br_2$ and $[Mn(H_2O)_4Br_2]Cl_2$
    c. *cis*-$[PdCl_2(NH_3)_2]$ and *trans*-$[PdCl_2(NH_3)_2]$

31. Diagram two square planar geometric isomers with the formula $[PtI_2(NH_3)_2]$. Label the *cis* isomer. It is not possible to diagram two tetrahedral geometric isomers of $[Pt(NH_3)_2I_2]$. Explain why.

32. Diagram all of the possible isomers of $[Co(NH_3)_2(SCN)_2]$.

33. How many different isomers of $[NiCl_3F_3]^{4-}$ can be drawn? Show the structure of each.

34. Show the structures of the coordination sphere isomers for $[Co(NH_3)_6][Cr(NO_2)_6]$.

Chemical Applications and Practices

35. Ethylenediamine (en) is a bidentate ligand, so it forms two attachments to metal ions in coordination complexes. However, the square planar complex $[Pt I_2(en)]$ exhibits only one type of geometric isomer. Draw possible structures for $[Pt I_2(en)]$ and for a complex between iron(III) and en.

36. Diagram the Lewis dot structure for the cyanate ion (OCN^-). Show how this ion would make it possible to have two different forms of the following complex: $[Co(OCN)(NH_3)_5]^{2+}$. What type of isomerism does this example illustrate?

20.6 Formulas and Names

Skill Review

37. Provide names for these complex ions:
    a. $[Co(CN)(en)_2(NH_3)]^{2+}$
    b. $[Cr(C_2O_4)_2(NH_3)_2]^-$
    c. $[Fe(NO_2)_6]^{3-}$
    d. $[CoCl_3(H_2O)_3]$

38. Provide names for these complex ions:
    a. $[Mn(en)_3]^{2+}$
    b. $[Ni(H_2O)_4(NH_3)_2]^{2+}$
    c. $[Cr(NO_2)_6]^{3-}$
    d. $[V(SCN)_2(H_2O)_4]$

39. Write the chemical formula for each of these compounds and complex ions:
    a. tetraammineaquachlorocobalt(III)
    b. *trans*-diaquabis(ethylenediamine)copper(II) chloride
    c. sodium tetrachlorocobaltate(II)
    d. pentacarbonylchloromanganese(I)

40. Write the chemical formula for each of these compounds and complex ions:
    a. tetraaquadichlorocopper(II)
    b. potassium *cis*-dibromooxalatoplatinate(II)
    c. tetraamminenickel(II) sulfate
    d. tetraaquathiosulfatoiron(III) nitrite

41. Which of these species would produce the greater number of ions per mole when dissolved in water?

$$K_2[Cr(C_2O_4)_2(H_2O)_2] \quad \text{or}$$
tetraamminediaquachromium(III) nitrate

42. Which of these species possesses the larger positive charge on the complex ion?

tetraaquacopper(II) nitrate   or
dichlorobis(ethylenediamine)iron(III) bromide

20.7 Color and Coordination Compounds

Skill Review

43. What is the electron configuration for each of these transition metal ions?
    a. Fe^{2+} b. Cr^{2+} c. Zn^{2+}

44. What is the electron configuration for each of these transition metal ions?
    a. Pd^{4+} b. Ag^+ c. Mn^{2+}

45. Consider the following two transition metal ions as free gaseous ions. Which would have the greater number of unpaired d electrons, Fe^{3+} or Cu^{2+}?

46. Which free ion has the greater number of unpaired d electrons, Ti^{2+} or Co^{2+}?

47. Draw the orbital diagram for the d orbitals in an octahedral complex containing each of these metal centers. (Assume that $P < \Delta_o$.)
    a. Fe^{3+} b. Co^{2+} c. Ni^{2+}

48. Draw the orbital diagram for the d orbitals in an octahedral complex containing each of these metal centers. (Assume that $P > \Delta_o$.)
    a. Mn^{2+} b. Fe^{2+} c. Cr^{+2}

49. Repeat Problem 47, but assume that the metal centers are involved in tetrahedral complexes. Although tetrahedral complexes typically have $\Delta_t > P$, what would you draw if the tetrahedral complex existed with $P > \Delta_t$?

50. Repeat Problem 48, but assume that the metal centers are involved in square planar complexes. Assume that $P > \Delta$ in this problem.

51. Draw the orbital diagram for the metal center in each of these complexes. Use the information in the spectrochemical series to assist you in placing the orbitals.
    a. $[FeCl_4]^-$ b. $[Co(CN)_6]^{3-}$ c. $[Mn(CO)_6]^+$

52. Draw the orbital diagram for the metal center in each of these complexes. Use the information in the spectrochemical series to assist you in placing the orbitals.
    a. $[CuF_6]^{4-}$ b. $[Ni(OH)_6]^{4-}$ c. $[Cr(NO_2)_6]^{4-}$

53. Which of the complexes in Problems 47 and 48 is(are) paramagnetic?

54. Calculate the magnetic moment for each of the complexes in Problems 47 and 48.

Chemical Applications and Practices

55. Which one of these complexes would you predict to absorb blue light: $[M(CN)_6^{2-}]$, $[M(H_2O)_6^{4+}]$, $[MCl_6^{2-}]$, or $[M(NH_3)_6^{4+}]$?

56. Which of these complexes would you predict to absorb the longest wavelength of visible light: $[M(CN)_6^{2-}]$, $[M(H_2O)_6^{4+}]$, $[MCl_6^{2-}]$, or $[M(NH_3)_6^{4+}]$?

57. The colors of common gemstones are due to the presence of transition metal ions. The color is produced when the metal ion absorbs visible light. Would you predict the common gemstones to have different "colors" under infrared light?

58. Coordination compounds with Zn^{2+} ions typically are white or colorless. Explain why this particular metal does not form brightly colored compounds the way many other transition metals do.

59. The crystal field theory provides an explanation of color in various coordination complexes. For example, $[Cr(H_2O)_6]^{3+}$ can be detected as a violet color when dissolved.
    a. What colors would the complex be absorbing?
    b. How many unpaired electrons does the central chromium ion have?
    c. The compound $[Cr(NH_3)_6]^{3+}$, when dissolved, appears yellow. Would you expect it to absorb light at a higher or lower frequency than $Cr(H_2O)_6]^{3+}$? Explain.
    d. Which ligand, NH_3 or H_2O, is causing the greater value of Δ_o?

60. Compare the two iron complexes $[Fe(H_2O)_6]^{3+}$ and $[Fe(CN)_6]^{3-}$.
    a. Which is more likely to be paramagnetic?
    b. Which is more likely to absorb light of greater energy?
    c. Which is more likely to be "high-spin"?

20.8 Chemical Reactions

Skill Review

61. Explain why the chelate effect typically provides for a very favorable entropy change when a ligand exchange reaction involves a complex going from a nonchelated complex to a chelate complex.

62. If a ligand exchange reaction produced a large positive ΔG value, would you expect the reaction to have a large or a small equilibrium constant? Justify your choice.

63. A common chemical demonstration is to change a light blue solution containing $[Cu(H_2O)_4]^{2+}$ quickly to a deep purple solution by changing $[Cu(H_2O)_4]^{2+}$ into $[Cu(NH_3)_4]^{2+}$ with the addition of ammonia to the solution. Would you consider the first compound labile or inert? Is the exchange of oxygen in hemoglobin considered to be representative of a labile or an inert complex?

64. Except through loss of blood, the level of iron in humans is fairly constant. One way that iron is moved throughout the body, particularly from the liver, is within a molecule known as ferritin. The iron(III) is held in a six-coordinate system through bonds to oxygen and nitrogen that are part of several amino acids. Would it be more logical for this molecule's iron site to be labile or inert with respect to other metals? Explain. (Remember, the terms *inert* and *labile* refer to kinetic considerations, not to equilibrium predictions.)

Comprehensive Problems

65. In addition to the coordination complexes of rhodium, cobalt, and molybdenum described at the start of the chapter, use other resources (the Internet or journals) to select another transition metal that has a catalytic role in a chemical reaction.

66. Visit the pharmacy section of a grocery store and list the metals found in a mineral supplement. Use a reference (the Internet or journals) to determine the primary biochemical function of two of the metals from your list.

67. If a complex were assembled from a Co^{3+} ion, four NH_3, and two Cl^-, would you expect to see a neutral compound, an anion, or a cation? Show a formula that justifies your answer.

68. The following complex contains an iron ion in the +3 state. However, the resulting charge has been omitted from the complex. Assign the charge for the complex, and indicate how many counter ions (either Na^+ or Cl^-) would have to be ionically bonded to the complex to form a neutral compound.
$$[FeBr_4(H_2O)_2]$$

69. The appearance of a visible color from a compound is associated with three fundamental phenomena. Describe a color-producing compound's properties associated with:
   a. electron excitation
   b. the energy of the photon of light being absorbed
   c. the relative occupancy of lower and higher level orbitals

70. If 35.7 g of the complex $Ca_3[Fe(C_2O_4)_3]_2$ formed as a result of using an oxalate-containing rust remover, how many grams of iron would be removed?

71. Polydentate ligands have been very effective in applications of soil chemistry. EDTA has been added to soil near citrus trees to concentrate iron. Some polydentates have been used to extract heavy metals from soil samples for further analysis. Some internal digestive functions use polydentate ligands to extract metals from foods we eat. Does this indicate that the relative equilibrium constant for these reactions is larger or smaller than one?

Thinking Beyond the Calculation

72. A new ligand is developed for use in a study to mimic the electron transport reactions of copper metal.

$HS-CH_2-CH_2-SH$

Ethanedithiol Cu^+–ligand $[Cu(NH_3)_6]^+$

   a. Draw the octahedral complex that would result from the use of this ligand and copper(II) ions.
   b. Draw the *d* orbital diagram for an octahedral complex of this ligand.
   c. Compare the color of this octahedral complex to that of $[Cu(NH_3)_6]^{2+}$. Where does this ligand most likely fall in the spectrochemical series?
   d. Under certain conditions, 1.00 g of copper(II) produces 3.96 g of the copper–ligand complex. What is the coordination number of the complex under these conditions?
   e. The equilibrium constant for the ligand exchange of this new ligand and chloride ions is 1.45×10^{-4}. What does this indicate about the new ligand?

21

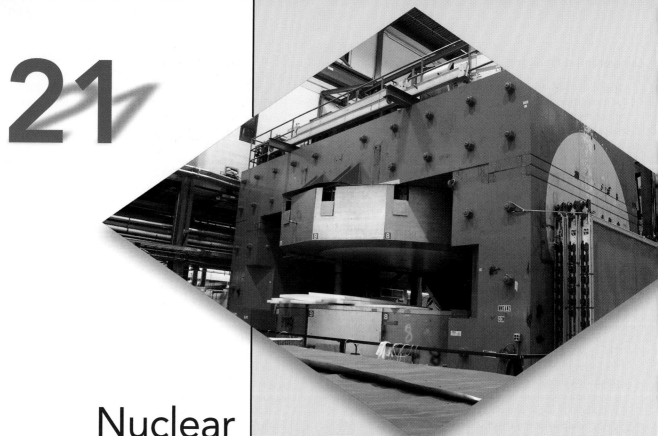

Nuclear Chemistry

Contents and Selected Applications

Enrico Fermi used this very large cyclotron at the University of Chicago in the 1950s. The cyclotron can be used to prepare radioactive isotopes for medical imaging. The cyclotron generates fast-moving subatomic particles that can be directed at nonradioactive nuclei. The resulting collision produces radioactive nuclei such as fluorine-18, which can be used to help doctors observe a particular biological function within a patient's body.

The odds are that you know somebody who has fought cancer. If you have talked with a friend or relative who is a cancer patient, you may have heard that radioactive substances are used in the process of producing images of internal organs. You may know that radiation can shrink a tumor or kill cancer cells. You may even be aware of the dramatic procedure using full-body radiation that is given before a bone marrow transplant. These applications illustrate how a health care team can use nuclear radiation for the benefit of a cancer patient.

Although radiation can save lives, it can also damage and kill. Back in the early 1900s, early radiologists held film plates in an X-ray beam to get pictures of their patients. These radiologists often developed sores on their hands that would not heal, and some eventually lost parts of their fingers. In August 1945, people in the Japanese cities of Hiroshima and Nagasaki were exposed to huge bursts of radiation from the only use of atomic bombs in warfare. Some died immediately, and others succumbed a few weeks later from a then-unknown disease that we now call radiation sickness. In the United States, those who worked in the nuclear weapons industry are now disproportionately contracting lung, stomach, lymphatic, and other cancers.

How can nuclear radiation both cure and cause cancer? The answer to this seeming paradox rests on our understanding of radioactivity (the release of particles and energy accompanying a nuclear change) and how it is produced from nuclear processes. In this chapter we will examine types of radioactive decay, touching on the mathematics of half-lives, the relationship between mass and energy, and the interactions of ionizing radiation with matter. We also will examine nuclear fission, a process that helps produce a whole host of substances useful in nuclear medicine. The story of radioactivity begins, however, at the tiny center of the atom—its nucleus.

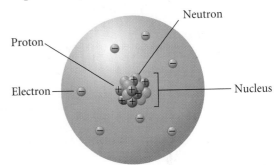

21.1 Isotopes and More Isotopes

Nuclei that occur naturally on Earth can be as small as the nucleus of a hydrogen atom (a single proton) or as large as uranium (92 protons plus 146 neutrons). All of these naturally occurring atoms, and all those that are human-made, are represented by writing their element symbol in the manner described in Chapter 2. The symbol is placed next to a superscripted mass number and a subscripted atomic number. Some of these nuclei are stable—that is, they do not spontaneously decompose—and others are radioactive, decomposing to other nuclei. As we will soon see, the size and makeup of the nucleus determine whether it is stable or radioactive.

Recall from Chapter 2 that we can use nuclide notation, in which we list the symbol for the element, accompanied by its atomic number and the mass number, to indicate the isotope of the element that we wish to describe. For example, consider the element potassium, whose atomic number (Z) is 19. As we know from the periodic table, this element has 19 protons. If the nucleus of a potassium atom has 21 neutrons, we represent this in nuclide notation as $^{40}_{19}K$. The number 40, the mass number, is the sum of 19 protons and 21 neutrons. Because "19 protons" is always potassium, we can more simply represent $^{40}_{19}K$ as ^{40}K, K-40 or

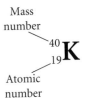

901

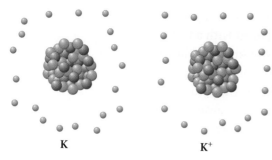

K   K⁺

potassium-40. In nuclear chemistry, we are often not concerned with the number of electrons around a particular nucleus. We are interested only in the nucleus of the atom, so we often omit charges (even though they may exist). This means that in our chemist's shorthand for the discussion of changes in the nucleus, we'll consider $^{40}K^+$ as ^{40}K. The nucleus is our only focus here.

Potassium atoms come in several varieties, shown in Figure 21.1, some with fewer than 21 neutrons and some with more. These varieties are known as isotopes, and each isotope is known as a nuclide of that element, as we learned in Chapter 2.

FIGURE 21.1

Potassium has many isotopes, most of which are listed here. Those colored orange are radioactive. Natural abundances are provided for those isotopes that occur in nature. Note that 99.988% of the potassium atoms on Earth are *not* radioactive.

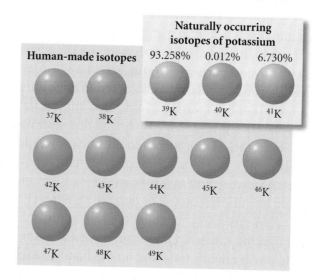

EXERCISE 21.1 | **Decoding Isotopes**

Describe the differences and similarities in nuclear structure among the members of each of these sets:

a. $^{12}_{6}C$, $^{13}_{6}C$, and $^{14}_{6}C$

b. ^{40}Ar, ^{40}K, and ^{40}Ca

c. $^{40}Ca^{2+}$ and ^{40}Ca

First Thoughts

The numbers at the bottom of each representation are simply a restatement of the element symbol. The mass number is the sum of the number of neutrons and protons. To find the number of neutrons in a particular nuclide, just subtract the atomic number from the mass number. Remember from Chapter 2 that numbers written on the upper right-hand side of the nuclide notation indicate a deviation in the number of electrons.

Solution

a. $^{12}_{6}C$, $^{13}_{6}C$, and $^{14}_{6}C$ are isotopes of carbon, each containing six protons. But each has a different mass number and hence a different number of neutrons: 6, 7, and 8, respectively.

b. ^{40}Ar, ^{40}K, and ^{40}Ca have the same mass number but different numbers of protons. Ar has 18p and 22n, K has 19p and 21n, and Ca has 20n and 20p.

c. $^{40}Ca^{2+}$ and ^{40}Ca differ only in the number of electrons, so there is no difference in *nuclear* structure. The ^{40}Ca atom loses two electrons to form the $^{40}Ca^{2+}$ ion.

Further Insights

This exercise, while conceptually important, involves just notation and bookkeeping. The nuclide notations, by themselves, say little about the stability or radioactivity of an isotope. Far more useful and interesting are the topics of natural abundance, radioactivity, and half-life, which we discuss below.

PRACTICE 21.1

Indicate the number of protons and neutrons in each of the following nuclides.

a. ^{32}S c. radon-222

b. $^{23}_{11}Na$ d. Tc-98

See Problems 7 and 8.

Potassium is considered an essential nutrient. Deficiencies in potassium can result in muscle pain, angina, and even heart problems. Eating bananas is one way in which we can ensure a healthy supply of potassium in our bodies. From Figure 21.1 we can see that three isotopes of potassium occur naturally: $^{39}_{19}K$, $^{40}_{19}K$, and $^{41}_{19}K$. However, whereas potassium-39 and potassium-41 possess stable nuclei, $^{40}_{19}K$ is radioactive. This means that when we consume a banana, we get a measurable amount of radioactive potassium-40. How much? The natural abundance of potassium-40 is only 0.012%, or approximately 1 atom in 10,000. A typical banana has approximately 300 mg of potassium. Therefore, with each banana we eat, we ingest approximately 0.036 mg of radioactive potassium-40.

Although potassium has 18 known isotopes, most do not occur in nature and must be produced in a laboratory. Each of these isotopes behaves essentially the same in *chemical* reactions, which involve the interaction of electrons with other atoms. For example, on exposure to oxygen or moisture, potassium metal ionizes to form K^+. *All* isotopes of potassium behave in this manner. Because our planet is wet and blanketed in oxygen, *all* naturally occurring potassium isotopes are found in nature as K^+. Remember, however, that we often omit the charge when writing nuclides, and you are likely to see ^{40}K rather than $^{40}K^+$. The key idea here is that *we differentiate between chemical reactions (electron interactions between atoms) and nuclear processes (changes within the nucleus of an individual atom).* Potassium-39 is a stable nuclide, but potassium metal certainly is not a stable chemical when in the presence of water. On the other hand, argon is chemically inert, but it has isotopes that are radioactive.

Natural isotopic abundances for potassium or for any element can be found in many of the chemistry handbooks in the library. Table 21.1 offers a brief look at what you'll find there. As we just saw, the nuclei of elements present in nature are not necessarily stable. In fact, some elements, such as uranium and radon, exist naturally *only* in radioactive forms. Other elements, such as potassium and carbon, have both stable and radioactive isotopes. Still others, such as aluminum, have only one stable naturally occurring form.

Application

Sources of potassium.

TABLE 21.1	Natural Isotopic Abundances for Selected Elements		
Carbon		Potassium	
^{12}C	98.90%	^{39}K	93.2581%
^{13}C	1.10	^{40}K	0.0117
		^{41}K	6.7302
Oxygen			
^{16}O	99.762%	Iron	
^{17}O	0.038	^{54}Fe	5.8%
^{18}O	0.200	^{56}Fe	91.72
		^{57}Fe	2.2
Magnesium		^{58}Fe	0.28
^{24}Mg	78.99%		
^{25}Mg	10.00	Silver	
^{26}Mg	11.01	^{107}Ag	51.84%
		^{109}Ag	48.16
Aluminum			
^{27}Al	100%		

21.2 Types of Radioactive Decay

There is no way for you hold a potassium atom in your hand and peer into its nucleus. But if you could keep an eye on a few ^{40}K atoms for a period of time (perhaps over a billion years), you would observe that some of the potassium atoms had been replaced by atoms of calcium. **How do we account for this nuclear sleight-of-hand?**

Beta-Particle Emission

The answer in this case is **beta-particle emission**, a type of radioactive decay. In beta emission, the *nucleus* of $^{40}_{19}$K ejects a **beta particle**, $^{0}_{-1}\beta$, that travels at 90% the speed of light. A new nucleus, $^{40}_{20}$Ca, is formed that has one more proton. Because calcium-40 has an energetically stable nucleus (you can verify this in a table of radioisotopes), no further *nuclear* reactions take place. For now, let's write the **nuclear equation** for the beta-minus emission, or "beta emission" for short, as

$$^{40}_{19}K \rightarrow {}^{40}_{20}Ca + {}^{0}_{-1}\beta$$

We note that the sums of the atomic masses, as well as the sums of the atomic numbers, are the same on both sides of our equation. The nuclide that results from the beta emission, $^{40}_{20}$Ca, is comparable in size to potassium. In addition, a tiny product is ejected with mass number zero and a negative charge—an electron. In the context of nuclear decay, this electron is called a beta emission particle. The subscript -1 in $^{0}_{-1}\beta$ may look strange as an atomic number. Interpret it as a "negative one charge" rather than a "minus one proton."

Beta emission, like many other of the nuclear reactions we will study, has the following features:

- A nuclide of one element, through the process of **radioactive decay**, is transformed into a nuclide of another. The resulting **daughter nuclide** may be stable or radioactive.

- The sum of the atomic numbers on one side of the nuclear equation is equal to the sum on the other. For the beta emission of ^{40}K, the sum of the mass numbers on each side of the equation is 40, and the sum of the atomic numbers on each side of the nuclear equation is 19.

- Energy is released in radioactive decay reactions. **Gamma rays** of varying energy nearly always accompany the nuclear reaction.

How can an electron be emitted from a nucleus when there are no electrons in the nucleus? To see how this could happen, let's venture down from the macroworld into the nanoworld to look at the beta emission of a single neutron. Neutrons aren't something you can keep in a bottle in your chemistry lab. But if you had the proper specialized equipment, you could demonstrate that a neutron decays to form a proton, an electron, and an **antineutrino**, $^{0}_{0}\acute{v}$.

$$^{1}_{0}n \rightarrow {}^{1}_{1}p + {}^{0}_{-1}\beta + {}^{0}_{0}\acute{v}$$

The net effect of beta decay is the *transformation of a neutron into a proton* with the release of an electron, an antineutrino, and energy. This is consistent with the beta decay we wrote for $^{40}_{19}$K, where the product nuclide has one more proton.

The antineutrino, $_{0}^{0}\bar{\nu}$, is an example of antimatter. Each antimatter particle has a mate in our world of "real" matter. For the antineutrino, this mate is the neutrino, or "little neutron"—a particle similarly hidden within the neutron. With no charge and probably very little mass, the neutrino required a sophisticated piece of scientific detective work to prove its existence. However, because this ghostly particle and its antimatter mate interact little if at all with matter, neutrinos typically are omitted from nuclear equations.

EXERCISE 21.2	Beta Emissions In and Around Us

A look at the world around us reveals a lot of naturally occurring radiation. Elements responsible for this radiation include carbon-14, potassium-40, and hydrogen-3 (tritium).

a. Write the nuclear equation for a beta emission by carbon-14.

b. If $_{2}^{3}\text{He}$ is formed via a beta emission, what radioisotope produced it?

First Thoughts

Beta emissions follow a set pattern: an increase of $+1$ in Z and no change in A.

Solution

a. $_{6}^{14}\text{C} \rightarrow _{-1}^{0}\beta + _{7}^{14}\text{N}$

b. $_{1}^{3}\text{H} \rightarrow _{-1}^{0}\beta + _{2}^{3}\text{He}$

Further Insights

We discussed the radioactivity of carbon-14 in Chapter 2. Knowing the rate of this nuclear reaction is part of a process that enables us to predict the age of an archaeological artifact.

PRACTICE 21.2

Write the nuclear equation for the beta emission of ^{60}Co.

See Problems 14, 15b, 15c, and 20. ∎

Alpha-Particle Emission

There are two other common forms of radioactivity: alpha-particle emission and gamma-ray emission. To appreciate how these differ, let's revisit potassium-40. Imagine again that you were watching several individual atoms of the nuclide. No matter how long you waited, you would not observe an alpha decay, the emission of a helium nucleus ($_{2}^{4}\text{He}$) from a larger nucleus. Why not? Potassium-40, like many radioisotopes, does not exhibit this form of radioactivity. Why not? The simple answer is that the nucleus is made more energetically stable by beta emission than by alpha decay. Why? The answer to this is a little more complex and will be the focus of Sections 21.5 and 21.6.

Which elements decay by alpha emission? Radon is one example. The nuclear reaction for the alpha decay of radon-222 is

$$_{86}^{222}\text{Rn} \rightarrow _{84}^{218}\text{Po} + _{2}^{4}\text{He}$$

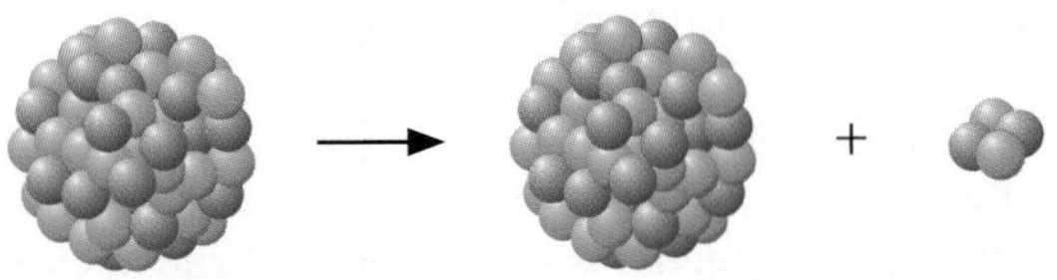

Energy is given off, along with an alpha particle ($_{2}^{4}\text{He}$), which is energetic but travels more slowly than a beta particle, at only about 5–10% of the speed of light.

You also may see $^{4}_{2}He^{2+}, ^{4}_{2}He$ or simply α used to denote the alpha particle. Is alpha emission possible for a hydrogen or helium atom? No, because these atoms are too small to emit an alpha particle and still have any protons left for the remaining nucleus. In fact, alpha emission typically does not occur for small nuclei. It is far more common for elements above bismuth ($Z = 83$).

Gamma-Ray Emission

For both alpha and beta emissions, the nuclear equations we have written so far are not complete, because a gamma ray is usually produced as well. When we include this gamma ray ($^{0}_{0}\gamma$) in the alpha decay of radon, the nuclear equation becomes

$$^{222}_{86}Rn \rightarrow ^{218}_{84}Po + ^{4}_{2}He + ^{0}_{0}\gamma$$

A gamma ray, as indicated in Figure 21.2, is a high-energy photon—a form of electromagnetic radiation with a short wavelength (typically less than a picometer) traveling at the speed of light. Loss of energy from the system, in the form of a gamma ray, is favorable because the products of the reaction would then have less energy than the starting material. In essence, the free energy of the system is lowered.

FIGURE 21.2

Gamma rays are at the high-energy end of the electromagnetic spectrum. They have *very* short wavelengths on the order of ten-trillionths of a meter or less. The energy of cosmic rays is comparable to that of gamma rays, but cosmic rays are particles and are not part of the electromagnetic spectrum.

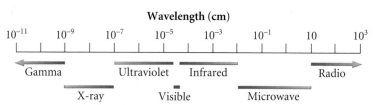

Gamma rays carry off excess energy in an amount depending on the particular nuclide. In some cases, lower-energy gamma rays are identical to X-rays; however, we mentally distinguish between the two by noting that the former originated *inside* the nucleus and the latter *outside* of it. For medical purposes, as we will see in the final section of this chapter, both X-rays and gamma rays can accomplish the same diagnostic and therapeutic tasks.

Few nuclides are pure or almost pure gamma emitters. A notable example is technetium-99m, where the m indicates a **metastable state**. It represents a misarrangement of protons and neutrons in a nucleus after a neutron has become a proton. In beta emitters, this arrangement occurs so rapidly that it appears to be simultaneous with the original beta emission. In some cases, however, it is slow enough to be obvious:

$$^{99m}Tc \rightarrow ^{99}Tc + ^{0}_{0}\gamma$$

Technetium-99m is generated on demand in nuclear medicine imaging.

EXERCISE 21.3   **Alpha Emissions In and Around Us**

Radon, discussed earlier, is present in the atmosphere at a concentration of about 1 part in 10^{21}. In some caves and basements, however, test kits like those shown in Figure 21.3 can detect it at much higher concentrations. Write nuclear equations for the alpha decay of radon-220, radon-222, and radon-219. A gamma ray accompanies each of these processes.

Solution

$$^{222}_{86}\text{Rn} \rightarrow \,^{218}_{84}\text{Po} + \,^{4}_{2}\text{He} + \,^{0}_{0}\gamma$$

$$^{220}_{86}\text{Rn} \rightarrow \,^{216}_{84}\text{Po} + \,^{4}_{2}\text{He} + \,^{0}_{0}\gamma$$

$$^{219}_{86}\text{Rn} \rightarrow \,^{215}_{84}\text{Po} + \,^{4}_{2}\text{He} + \,^{0}_{0}\gamma$$

PRACTICE 21.3

Write nuclear equations for the alpha decay of ^{218}Po and ^{230}Th.

See Problems 15a, 16a, 16c, 17a, and 19.

FIGURE 21.3

Radon test kits can be purchased and used to measure the concentration of radon in a basement.

Other Types of Radioactive Decay

The three types of radioactive decay that we have discussed are the most common, but two other modes of nuclear decay are also important to a comprehensive picture of radioactive processes. **Electron capture (EC)** is the combination of an inner-orbital electron and a proton from the nucleus to form a neutron. The mass of the nuclide doesn't change during the process because a proton and a neutron are similar in mass, but the atomic number decreases by one as the proton is changed to a neutron. Typically, this process is accompanied by the emission of X-rays from the nuclide. The radioactive decay of iodine-125, which is used to diagnose problems with the pancreas and intestines, occurs by the process of electron capture:

$$^{125}_{53}\text{I} + \,^{0}_{-1}\beta \rightarrow \,^{125}_{52}\text{Te}$$

In **positron emission** ($^{0}_{+1}\beta$), a proton decays into a neutron and a positron. A neutrino accompanies this emission, and usually one or more gamma rays as well. A **positron**, or positive electron, is a particle that has the same mass as an electron but carries a charge of +1. Interestingly, the positron typically doesn't have a very long life, because when it comes into contact with an electron, the two particles combine to form two gamma rays. This type of radioactive decay is important in the lighter elements such as aluminum-26.

$$^{26}_{13}\text{Al} \rightarrow \,^{0}_{1}\beta + \,^{26}_{12}\text{Mg}$$

Table 21.2 lists the five types of radioactive decay that are important in understanding nuclear decay processes.

TABLE 21.2	Radioactive Decay Processes		
Type of Decay	**Emission**	**Change in Atomic Number**	**Change in Mass Number**
Alpha-particle emission	$^{4}_{2}\text{He}$	-2	-4
Beta-particle emission	$^{0}_{-1}\beta$	$+1$	0
Gamma-ray emission	$^{0}_{0}\gamma$	0	0
Positron emission	$^{0}_{+1}\beta$	-1	0
Electron capture	X-ray	-1	0

Decay Series

Radon, discussed in Exercise 21.3, is one example in which the products of the nuclear reaction are still radioactive. All isotopes of all elements past bismuth ($Z = 83$) are radioactive. So far we have described nuclear decay as though it were a one-step process. However, a nuclide may decay to form a second *radioactive* nuclide, which in turn may decay more than a dozen times in a stepwise progression toward stability that is called a **decay series**.

Consider the element uranium. Two natural isotopes exist for this element, ^{238}U and ^{235}U, with natural abundances of 99.28% and 0.72%, respectively. These isotopes exhibit a fairly extensive decay series. Both series consist of alpha and beta emissions, as shown in Figure 21.4. The accompanying gamma rays are not shown in these series. Why do the lines in the decay series zig-zag? Alpha decays

Uranium ore (known as yellow cake) can be refined into pellets of uranium metal.

FIGURE 21.4

The four natural decay series. Each decay series begins at the nuclide listed at the top right-hand side of the series and proceeds to the lower left-hand side by nuclear decay. The half-life of many of these transitions are indicated in red numbers. Gamma emissions accompany many of these decays.

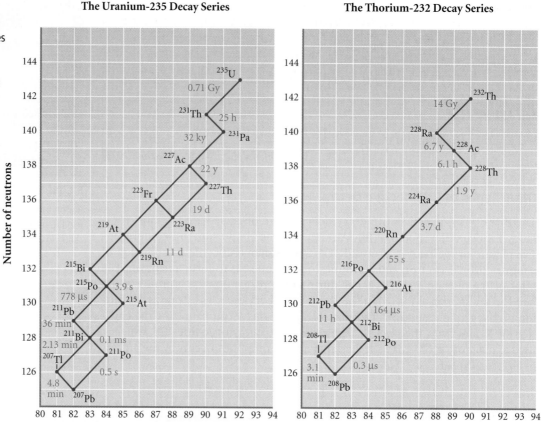

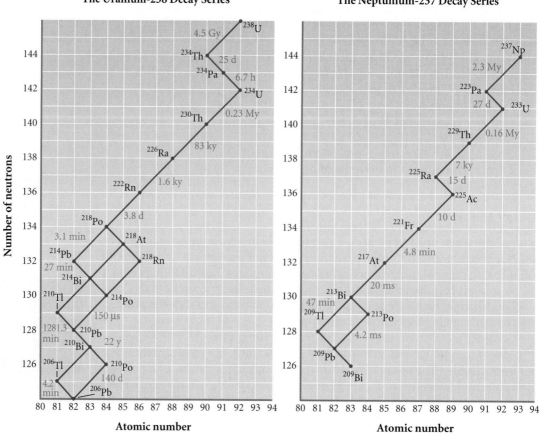

decrease Z by 2, thus moving the line to the left. But a beta-minus emission *increases Z* by 1 unit. If beta emission follows an alpha emission, there is a zag back to the right. The series that begins with ^{235}U ends with the stable lead-207 isotope, and the ^{238}U series forms ^{206}Pb. There are two other naturally occurring decay series, one that begins with ^{237}Np to form ^{209}Bi, and one in which ^{232}Th decays to ultimately form ^{208}Pb. Along the way, these decay chains provide dozens of radioisotopes that we typically find in our biosphere. This is one of the sources of naturally occurring radioactive isotopes. Of particular concern is radon, a radioactive gas that can collect in basements dug into soil that is rich in uranium ores. Is radon harmful to humans? Understanding the relationship between radioactivity and human health will help us answer this question.

Application

HERE'S WHAT WE KNOW SO FAR

- Radioactivity results from the decay of an unstable nucleus.
- There are three main types of radioactive decay and three common forms of radioactivity.
- The alpha particle is a fast-moving helium nucleus.
- The beta particle is an electron ejected from the nucleus of an unstable atom.
- The gamma ray is a burst of high-energy electromagnetic radiation.
- A decay series is a stepwise progression of a radioactive nuclide toward stability.

21.3   Interaction of Radiation with Matter

Taking a walk on a crisp, sunny day is one of the pleasures of autumn. Any cloud that blocks the Sun is easily noticed. Not only does the shade reduce the amount of light hitting your eyes, but your skin also registers the change. The energy exchanges, from the infrared through the ultraviolet regions of the electromagnetic spectrum, are apparent and profound. However, when it comes to detecting the small amounts of alpha particles, beta particles, and gamma rays that bombard you on a daily basis, your senses don't help. For instance, you cannot detect the alpha particles that radioactive radon, an odorless, colorless, and tasteless gas, emits.

Though seemingly invisible, the different types of radiation form quite a nuclear arsenal, as summarized in Figure 21.5. We can envision alpha particles as the cannon balls of the group. With their greater size and +2 charge, they do not travel very far before they smash into other atoms. The typical collision results in the capture of two electrons to form a neutral helium atom. In contrast, beta particles, being smaller and traveling more rapidly, are the equivalent of high-velocity bullets. They are able to travel significantly longer distances before a collision, but they lack the punch of an alpha particle. Gamma rays, with no mass and no charge, are akin to laser weapons. They shoot great distances through matter, now and then searing something in their path. What about the

Collision of an alpha particle and a molecule results in the formation of an atom of helium.

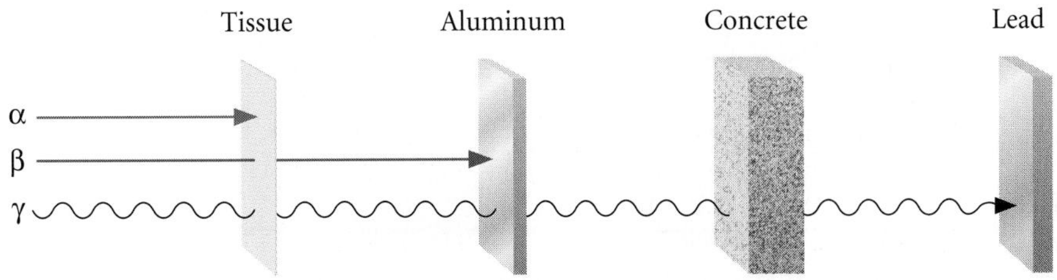

Tissue   Aluminum   Concrete   Lead

FIGURE 21.5

Alpha, beta, and gamma radiation differ in their penetration. Gamma rays are the most highly penetrating, and alpha particles the least.

TABLE 21.3	Differences in Penetration and Shielding for Different Types of Radiation				
Type	Examples	Penetration in Dry Air	Penetration in Skin or Tissue[†]	Shielded by	Q*
Alpha	uranium, plutonium, americium	2–4 cm	0.05 mm	Paper, air, clothing	20
Beta	potassium-40, cesium-137	200–300 cm	4–5 mm	Heavy clothing	~1
Gamma	technetium, cobalt-60	500 m	50 cm	Lead, concrete	~1
Fast neutrons	Accelerators	Several hundred feet	High	Water, plastic concrete	20

*Q is the relative biological effectiveness, a factor that indicates relative amounts of damage to living tissue.
[†]Alpha, beta, and gamma radiation all exhibit a range of energies. The degree of penetration depends on the actual energy.

antineutrinos that accompany beta emissions? Having neither a mass nor a charge, they are not absorbed and are considered harmless.

The type and the energy of the radiation dictate what must be used to shield us to the greatest extent possible (see Table 21.3). Alpha particles penetrate matter the least, being stopped by just a few centimeters of air, by the outer layer of your skin (which is mostly dead cells), or by a piece of paper. Beta particles penetrate more deeply and can pass through several pieces of paper, through a thin sheet of aluminum, or about a centimeter into your skin. In contrast, gamma rays can pass right through you. Shielding your body from them requires several inches of aluminum or lead, and even these may not do the job.

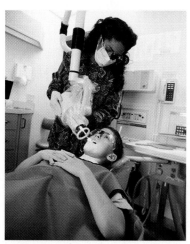

Use of radiation shield on a patient at the dentist's office.

A visit to the dentist reveals an interesting feature of stopping damage from nuclear radiation. Before an X-ray of a patient's teeth is obtained, the patient is typically draped with a sheet of lead. Why is lead one of the materials employed to shield us from high-energy electromagentic radiation, such as X-rays or nuclear radiation? The high density of lead, 11.3g/cm^3, means that only two inches of lead will easily shield you from alpha and beta radiation, as well as from most gamma radiation. However, lead is not unique in this ability. Gold ($d = 19.3 \text{ g/cm}^3$) is more dense than lead and would work even better. Bricks or blocks of a moderately dense material such as concrete also would do the trick. However, no dentist is likely to place an apron of gold or a foot of concrete over your abdomen before taking dental X-rays. Given its density and price, lead is often the shielding medium of choice.

Application
CHEMICAL ENCOUNTERS:
Radiation and Cancer

Although alpha, beta, and gamma radiation differ in penetration, they are alike in the effects they produce on the molecular level. All three are known as **ionizing radiation**; that is, they are capable of forming ions by knocking electrons out of atoms. The damage they cause is the reason for their detection with, for example, a Geiger counter or film badge.

The consequences of ionizing radiation can be negligible or severe, depending on how many molecules are damaged inside the body. Although small amounts of radiation typically lead to only negligible damage that can be repaired by the body, large doses of radiation can be life-threatening. **How does ionizing radiation cause damage?** Because between about 50% and 70% of your body is water, a scenario of particular interest occurs when ionizing radiation strikes a water molecule. The blow can knock off an electron to form a highly reactive species with an unpaired electron:

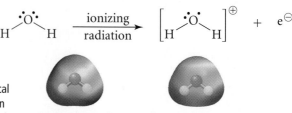

Electron density maps of water and the radical cation of water. Note the decrease in electron density around the oxygen end of the molecule.

Water (neutral)   **Water (cation radical)**

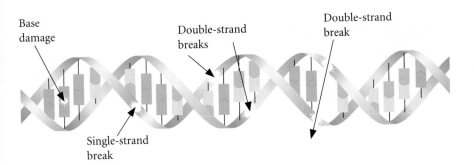

Base damage

Double-strand breaks

Double-strand break

Single-strand break

FIGURE 21.6

Examples of chromosomal damage from radiation.

The resulting radical cation (see Chapter 7) undergoes autoprotolysis to form hydroxyl free radicals:

$$H_2O \cdot^{\oplus} + H_2O \rightleftharpoons H_3O^{\oplus} + \cdot OH$$

The fate of the hydroxyl free radicals is particularly damaging to the cells within your body. If they encounter a molecule of DNA in a dividing cell, they may damage a section of the genetic code (Figure 21.6). The damage could result in death of the cell, triggering the formation of mutant proteins (proteins with a non-natural primary structure; see Chapter 22) or triggering an abnormal function of the cell leading to cancer. In short, nuclear radiation can be carcinogenic. Although we do not know exactly what cellular events ensue after a dose of ionizing radiation, two things seem clear: (1) The more radiation a person is exposed to, the greater the likelihood of that person's developing cancer. (2) These cancers may not show up until decades after the time of exposure.

Is there a threshold below which radiation is safe? Recent studies have convincingly demonstrated that the damage inflicted by low-level radiation upon workers in the nuclear industry and upon World War II nuclear bomb survivors have been greatly underestimated. Similarly, the link between fetal X-rays (an abandoned medical practice) and childhood cancer has been established. Fortunately, because cancer cells grow and divide, they also are susceptible to radiation. Carefully measured doses of radiation directed at cancerous cells can result in their death.

Overall, the biological effects of nuclear radiation depend on the quantity of energy transferred to the cells and tissues. In the United States, the rem or "roentgen equivalent in man" is the unit for estimating the damage. Other units that measure radiation include the becquerel, curie, roentgen, and rad. Of these, only the becquerel (Bq) is an SI unit. Scientists in most parts of the world employ two other SI units, the sievert (Sv) and the gray (Gy), which are related to the rem and the rad, respectively, as shown in Table 21.4.

TABLE 21.4	**Units for Measuring Radiation**		
Measure of	**Name**	**Abbreviation**	**Definition**
Activity	becquerel*	Bq	1 disintegration per second
Activity	curie	Ci	1 curie $= 3.7 \times 10^{10}$ becquerel
Exposure	roentgen	R	1 roentgen $= 2.58 \times 10^{-4}$ couloumbs of charge per kg of air
Absorbed dose	radiation absorbed dose	rad	1 rad $= 1 \times 10^{-2}$ J of energy deposited per kg of tissue
Absorbed dose	gray*	Gy	1 gray $= 100$ rad
Dose equivalent	roentgen equivalent in man	rem	$Q \times$ absorbed dose
Dose equivalent	sievert*	Sv	1 sievert $= 100$ rem

*SI units

TABLE 21.5	Health Effects of Acute Radiation Exposure	
Exposure (rem)	**Health Effect**	**Time to Onset**
10	Burns, changes in blood chemistry	
50	Nausea	Hours
75	Vomiting, hair loss	2–3 weeks
100	Hemorrhage	
400	Death	Within 2 months
1000	Internal bleeding, death	Within 1–2 weeks
2000	Death	Within hours

The quantity of energy absorbed by tissues is directly related to the time of exposure to ionizing radiation. *In fact, time is an important part of the decision-making process in medical diagnosis and treatment.* For example, prostate cancer in elderly men is often treated by the implantation of metal "seeds" coated with ^{125}I or, more recently, ^{103}Pd. Why use these nuclides? They are sufficiently radioactive for only the time needed to control the cancer without creating new cancers. **How do we know how long they will be radioactive?** The most important measure that we use to judge the length of time a substance is radioactive is its half-life.

The U.S. Environmental Protection Agency suggests that the average person receives an annual dose of 0.3 rem of radiation from natural sources. Over the course of a lifetime, this is predicted to result in 5 or 6 deaths due to cancer per 10,000 people. This sounds shocking until we consider that the rate of deaths due to cancer from nonradioactive sources is predicted to be about 2000 people per 10,000. Larger doses received in one exposure have a much more deleterious effect on human health, as shown in Table 21.5. Acute exposures, such as those that result from accidents in nuclear power plants and those that resulted from the U.S. bombing of Japan in World War II, cause severe damage to the human body, often resulting in lifelong health problems and even death.

21.4 The Kinetics of Radioactive Decay

The half-life, $t_{1/2}$, of a radioactive isotope is the period of time it takes for exactly half of the original nuclei in a radioactive sample to decay. We discussed half-life in detail in Chapter 15. Table 21.6 shows that half-lives can vary widely among the radioactive isotopes. They can be as short as a few microseconds and as long as a few billion years.

How can the half-life tell us how much radioactivity remains after a given time? Remember from Chapter 15 that after one half-life, one-half of the sample has reacted and only one-half of the sample remains. After a second half-life, $\frac{1}{2} \times \frac{1}{2} = \frac{1}{4}$ of the sample is left. After 3 half-lives, $\frac{1}{2}$ of $\frac{1}{2}$ of $\frac{1}{2}$, or $(\frac{1}{2})^3 = \frac{1}{8}$, of the sample remains. More generally, then, for n half-lives, the fraction of the original sample remaining is $(\frac{1}{2})^n$. This trend is shown in Figure 21.7 and is valid for all radioactive decay processes.

Palladium-103, used to coat the seeds implanted in the prostate, decays by electron capture, in which an inner-orbital electron is captured by a proton in the nucleus to form a neutron. The half-life of Pd-103 is 16.97 days. How long will it take for the radiation to be diminished to 1.00% of its original value so it is considered safe for radiation workers, the prostate cancer patient, and his family? A look at Figure 21.7 indicates that this will take between 6 and 7 half-lives, or between 102 and

TABLE 21.6	Half-lives of Some Radioactive Elements	
Element	**Nuclide**	**Half-life**
nobelium	^{250}No	250 μs
technetium	^{99m}Tc	6.0 h
thallium	^{201}Tl	21.5 h
radon	^{222}Rn	3.8 d
iodine	^{131}I	8.040 d
palladium	^{103}Pd	16.97 d
cobalt	^{60}Co	5.271 y
hydrogen	^{3}H	12.3 y
carbon	^{14}C	5730 y
radium	^{226}Ra	1.6×10^3 y
uranium	^{238}U	4.5×10^9 y

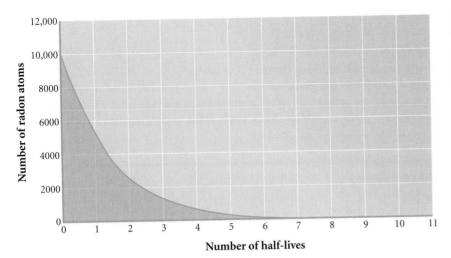

FIGURE 21.7

The kinetics of radioactive decay. The half-life of a radioisotope, such as radon, is the time required for half of the nuclei in the radioactive sample to decompose.

119 days. Such approximations are often sufficient. When necessary, we can also solve explicitly for n.

$$(\tfrac{1}{2})^n = 1/100 = 0.0100$$

Taking the natural logarithm (ln) of both sides yields

$$n[\ln(\tfrac{1}{2})] = \ln(0.0100)$$

$$n(-0.693) = -4.605$$

$$n = 6.645 \text{ half-lives}$$

Solving for the time needed, we find that

$$t = 6.645 \text{ half-lives} \times 16.97 \text{ days/half-life}$$

$$= 113 \text{ days}$$

Three palladium-103 "seeds," which are used for the treatment of prostate cancer, easily fit on the top of a penny.

There is another approach based on the understanding that radioactive isotopes decay via first-order kinetics. Recall from Chapter 15 that the relationship among concentration, time, and half-life for any first-order process is shown by

$$\ln \frac{[A_t]}{[A_i]} = -kt$$

where A_t = the amount of substance remaining
  A_i = the initial amount of substance
  k = the first-order rate constant for the reaction (in this case, the decay)
  t = time

We also know that the rate constant for a first-order reaction can be determined by

$$k = \frac{0.693}{t_{1/2}}$$

This means that we can solve explicitly for the rate constant if we are given the half-life, $t_{1/2}$. In our example,

$$k = \frac{0.693}{t_{1/2}} = \frac{0.693}{16.97 \text{ day}} = 0.04084 \text{ day}^{-1}$$

Assuming that we start with $A_i = 1.000$, we can determine that if we only have 1% remaining, $A_t = 0.0100$. Then

$$\ln \frac{[0.0100]}{[1.00]} = -0.04084t$$

$$-4.605 = -0.04084t$$

$$113 = t$$

so $t = 113$ days, and we obtain the same answer (113 days) by either method.

But when would the *entire* Pd-103 sample be gone? This is a question we cannot *precisely* answer, although we can come very close. Why are we unable to tell when all of the Pd-103 is gone? After each half-life, half of the number of radioactive atoms remaining from a previous half-life are still remaining. Sooner or later, after a very large number (roughly 80) of half-lives have passed, only two radioactive atoms remain for every mole we started with. Half-life is a statistical measure. Probabilities, which don't apply with a sample size of two, will not accurately tell the rate of the reaction.

EXERCISE 21.4   **Half-life Calculations: Here Today, Gone Tomorrow?**

After exercising on a treadmill, a patient was given thallium-201 for a diagnostic scan of his heart (Figure 21.8). How long will it take for 95.0% of the thallium to have decayed? The half-life of thallium-201 is 21.5 hours.

Solution

As discussed previously, we can solve the problem in two ways. Using the first method, we find the number of half-lives that pass until 5.0%, or a fraction of 0.050, of the Tl-201 remains.

$$(\tfrac{1}{2})^n = 0.050$$

$$n[\ln(\tfrac{1}{2})] = \ln(0.050)$$

$$n(-0.693) = -3.00$$

$$n = 4.32 \text{ half-lives}$$

$$t = 4.32 \text{ half-lives} \times 21.5 \text{ hours/half-life} = 93 \text{ hours}$$

Using the second method, we proceed as follows:

$$k = \frac{0.693}{t_{1/2}} = \frac{0.693}{21.5 \text{ h}} = 0.0322 \text{ h}^{-1}$$

$$\ln\frac{[0.050]}{[1.00]} = -0.0322t$$

$$-3.00 = -0.0322t$$

$$93 \text{ hours} = t$$

PRACTICE 21.4

The half-life of ^{198}Au is 2.69 days. How long would it take for 99% of a gold-198 sample to decay?

See Problems 39–42 and 47–48. ■

FIGURE 21.8

The previous problem involved percentages. But you also can work half-life problems given a starting mass or a starting number of atoms. Both are measures of the radioactivity present. Similarly, you can work half-life problems given a unit of activity such as the number of disintegrations per second (becquerels) or curies, because these also measure the amount of radioactivity and are proportional both to the mass and to the number of atoms. Such variations in units reflect the differing needs of real-world situations where you are likely to encounter radioisotopes.

The half-life of a radioactive isotope can also help you to determine how long the radioisotope will be useful or, perhaps, to weigh the hazards associated with that particular isotope. For example, would you rather be around a radioisotope that decayed to 1% of its activity in 10 seconds or one that did so in 10 centuries? For the latter, the rate of decay is much lower, and you would be bombarded with far fewer alpha particles, beta particles, or gamma rays in a given time period. This principle is important in the use of technetium in medical imaging. We have noted that technetium-99m is a gamma emitter. It has a half-life of 6.01 hours, which is long enough for a medical procedure, but short enough that the substance doesn't persist very long.

$$^{99m}_{43}\text{Tc} \rightarrow ^{99}_{43}\text{Tc} + ^{0}_{0}\gamma \qquad t_{1/2} = 6.01 \text{ h}$$

The product nuclide, $^{99}_{43}\text{Tc}$, is still radioactive. However, with its half-life of 213,000 years, the activity of Tc-99 as a beta emitter is low. In the two and a half weeks it takes for the majority of Tc-99 to be completely eliminated from the body, it does little damage.

21.5 Mass and Binding Energy

By now you might be a bit suspicious. Many nuclei are unstable and spontaneously decay. Significant amounts of energy are released during alpha, beta, and gamma emission—enough to ionize molecules or to kill cancer cells—but we haven't talked about the source of the energy. **Where does it come from, and how does this help explain the decay processes that nuclei undergo?**

The place to start to find an answer is with Einstein's famous equation,

$$E = mc^2$$

in which the constant, c, is equal to the speed of light. This relationship illustrates that a particular mass, when completely converted, is equivalent to a surprisingly large quantity of energy. Any chemical reaction that is accompanied by a loss in energy, such as in an exothermic reaction, actually also has a corresponding loss in mass. However, the mass losses are so minuscule that we cannot detect them using conventional instruments. In contrast, the changes in mass due to a nuclear reaction, though tiny, are quite measurable.

Let's explore this connection by examining the formation of nitrogen-14 from its individual nuclear particles:

$$7\text{p} + 7\text{n} \rightarrow ^{14}\text{N nucleus}$$

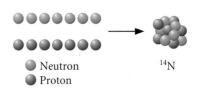

Neutron
Proton
^{14}N

Seven protons and seven neutrons form the nucleus of nitrogen-14.

A mole of nitrogen-14 nuclei (without any electrons) weighs 13.99540 g. What is the mass of 7 separate moles of protons (1.00727 g/mol) and 7 mol of neutrons (1.008665 g/mol)?

$$7 \text{ mol of protons} \times 1.00727 \text{ g/mol} = 7.05089 \text{ g}$$

$$7 \text{ mol of neutrons} \times 1.008665 \text{ g/mol} = 7.060655 \text{ g}$$

$$\text{Total mass} = 7.05089 \text{ g} + 7.060655 \text{ g} = 14.11154 \text{ g}$$

This *exceeds* the mass of a mole of nitrogen-14 nuclei by $(14.11154 \text{ g} - 13.99540 \text{ g}) = 0.11614$ g. This **mass defect**, the mass difference between the individual protons and neutrons and the composite nucleus, was used in binding the protons and neutrons together within the nucleus. The **binding energy**, expressed as a positive number, is the energy required to dismantle the nucleus into its individual protons and neutrons. To ensure that our calculations give us positive numbers for binding energy, we typically use Einstein's equation in a different form:

$$\Delta E = |\Delta m|c^2$$

where ΔE is the binding energy and $|\Delta m|$ is the absolute value of the change in mass *in kilograms*. We use kilograms because our SI unit of energy, the joule, is defined as kg·m/s². For nitrogen-14, using our mass defect of 0.11614 g ($= 1.1614 \times 10^{-4}$ kg), the binding energy can be calculated as

$$\Delta E = |\Delta m|c^2 = |-1.1614 \times 10^{-4} \text{ kg}| \times (2.9979 \times 10^8 \text{ m/s})^2 = 1.04 \times 10^{13} \text{ J}$$

EXERCISE 21.5 **The Energy Advantage of Nuclear Reactions**

When bombarded with neutrons, uranium-235 can split to form bromine-87, lanthanum-146, and three neutrons. The masses reported here are those of the bare nuclei.

$$^{235}_{92}\text{U} + ^{1}_{0}\text{n} \rightarrow ^{87}_{35}\text{Br} + ^{146}_{57}\text{La} + 3^{1}_{0}\text{n}$$

grams/mole 234.9936 1.008665 86.90156 145.8944 3.0260

Calculate the mass defect and the energy released in kJ/mol.

Solution

The mass defect is the difference in mass between the ending and starting materials.

$$\Delta m = (86.90156 + 145.8944 + 3.0260) - (234.9936 + 1.008665)$$
$$= -0.1803 \text{ g/mol} = -1.803 \times 10^{-4} \text{ kg/mol}$$

The energy equivalent to this mass is $\Delta E = |\Delta m|c^2$.

$$\Delta E = |\Delta m|c^2 = |-1.803 \times 10^{-4} \text{ kg/mol}| \times (2.9979 \times 10^8 \text{ m/s})^2$$
$$= 1.621 \times 10^{13} \text{ J/mol} = 1.621 \times 10^{10} \text{ kJ/mol}$$

This is many orders of magnitude greater than the energy released by an equivalent mass of materials in a combustion reaction.

Even though this problem uses the masses of the bare nuclei, the problem could have been solved using the atomic masses, because the number of electrons on each side of the equation remains constant. In radioactive decay processes that involve a change in the number of protons, the mass of the electrons must also be considered in the calculation of the mass defect, when atomic masses are used.

PRACTICE 21.5

Calculate the energy released in the following process.

$$^{224}_{88}\text{Ra} \rightarrow ^{220}_{86}\text{Rn} + ^{4}_{2}\text{He}$$

See Problems 53 and 54. ∎

Some atoms are more thermodynamically stable than others. A table of binding energies shows only that the values generally increase as the atoms get heavier. However, if you recalculate the binding energy for each atom and report the values *per nucleon* (proton or neutron), the stabilities pop right out at you. Nuclei with greater binding energies per nucleon are more stable. Note in Figure 21.9 that the lightest elements, those with mass numbers of 20 or less, have the lowest binding energies per nucleon. In comparison with iron, helium simply does not have enough nucleons to be as strongly glued together. The process that liberates energy on the sun, fusion (or nuclear fusion), is energetically favorable because lighter elements such as helium are joined to form heavier ones that have a more favorable binding energy per nucleon.

Nuclear fusion.

Deuteron

Triton

Fusion reaction

Energetic neutron

Helium nucleus

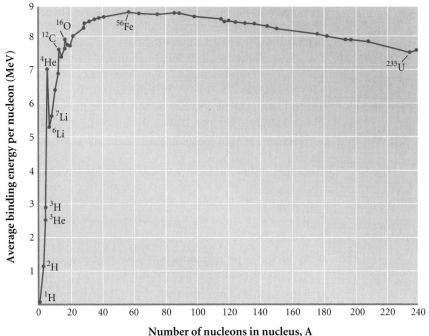

FIGURE 21.9

The binding energy per nucleon reaches a maximum near iron, atomic number 26.

The heaviest elements also have somewhat lower stability. Uranium, with so many protons and neutrons packed into its nucleus, has a lower binding energy per nucleon than iron or cobalt. As we will see in Section 21.7, it is energetically favorable to split heavier nuclei into smaller ones via **fission** (or nuclear fission) to form nuclei with a more favorable binding energy per nucleon.

Finally, look at the maximum of the curve and you will find elements with the most stable nuclei—those with mass numbers around 60, such as iron and nickel. Other elements also have surprisingly high binding energies given their mass number, such as ^{4}He (an alpha particle), ^{12}C, and ^{16}O. Alternatively, one might argue that the values for ^{6}Li and ^{14}N are surprisingly low.

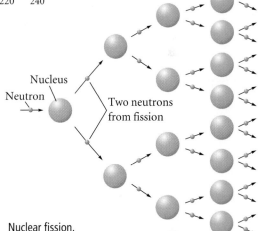

Nuclear fission.

21.6 Nuclear Stability and Human-made Radioactive Nuclides

"Here today, gone tomorrow" doesn't apply to most of the atoms that make up our world. That is fortunate for us. In fact, the majority of the atoms on our planet that are here today can be expected to be here tomorrow. Although it may be hard to locate a specific atom from one day to the next, you can be reasonably sure that it is still here. Why? Most atoms on Earth are *not* radioactive.

Which factors seem to affect nuclear stability? Measurements indicate that nature favors *even* numbers of protons. Elements such as helium, oxygen, iron, and lead that have even atomic numbers tend to be more abundant than their odd neighbors. For example, of the eight elements that make up over 99% of Earth's total mass, only one (aluminum) has an odd atomic number. Still more favored are nuclei that have even numbers of *both* protons and neutrons. Perhaps the most dramatic case is $^4_2$He, the alpha particle. Given this stability, it is not surprising that helium is the second most abundant element in the universe.

Experimental data confirm that certain *numbers* of either protons or neutrons (called "magic numbers") are favored: 2, 8, 20, 28, 50, 82, and 114. The elements helium ($Z = 2$), oxygen ($Z = 8$), calcium ($Z = 20$), and nickel ($Z = 28$) have

Oxygen (shown here in liquid form), calcium, and nickel have magic numbers of nucleons.

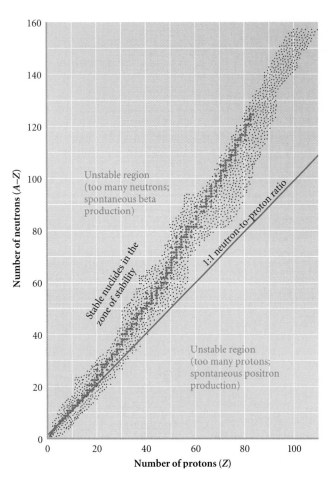

FIGURE 21.10

The band of known isotopes for each element with at least one stable isotope. n/p is the neutron-to-proton ratio. Note that the n/p ratio is greater than 1 for most stable isotopes.

more stable nuclei than their neighbors. Check the graph of binding energy per **nucleon** (proton or neutron in the nucleus) versus the mass number shown in Figure 21.9 to see that these elements sit at local maxima. The nuclides $^{16}_{8}O$ and $^{40}_{20}Ca$ are "doubly magic"; they have magic numbers for both protons and neutrons. In February 2000, a French research team created another doubly magic nucleus, Ni-48, which contains 28 protons and 20 neutrons.

When you examine a larger set of nuclides, other trends appear. There are 279 stable isotopes, a few naturally occurring radioactive elements, and hundreds of synthetic isotopes. Many of these find application in nuclear medicine. Figure 21.10 sketches the band of stable isotopes for each element with at least one stable isotope. Note the following points:

■ At higher atomic numbers, stable nuclei have increasingly more neutrons than protons.

■ Some radioactive elements have *too many neutrons* relative to the stable isotopes. These tend to decay by beta emission, where a neutron changes into a proton and an electron.

■ Some radioactive elements have *too few neutrons* relative to the stable isotopes. These tend to decay by positron emission, where a proton changes into a neutron and a positron.

The plot ends at bismuth, $Z = 83$, for no elements beyond this have stable isotopes. Alpha emission is typical for heavier elements that are unstable, simply because too many nucleons are present, be they protons *or* neutrons. Table 21.7 lists some guidelines that are helpful in determining the type of decay for a particular nucleus.

The radioactive decay can occur by the process of positron emission, or **beta-plus emission**, $^{0}_{+1}\beta$. This process does not occur naturally on Earth and was not discovered until scientists began creating new isotopes in the laboratory. Physically this is done by slamming high-energy particles, ranging from protons and neutrons to atomic nuclei, into a target nucleus. This can result in changing the nucleus's mass number and giving it additional energy. In general, the laboratory process is

$$\text{Nucleus} + \text{small particle} \rightarrow \text{bigger nucleus}$$

The product nucleus that is formed may undergo radioactive decay.

For example, in 1930 phosphorus-30 was synthesized in the laboratory by the bombardment of an aluminum target with alpha particles, $^{4}_{2}He$:

$$^{27}_{13}Al + ^{4}_{2}He \rightarrow ^{30}_{15}P + ^{1}_{0}n$$

More modern work includes the formation of tiny amounts of superheavy elements, which we will define as those beyond atomic number 106. Recent (1999 and 2000) reactions include

$$^{208}_{82}Pb + ^{86}_{36}Kr \rightarrow ^{293}_{118}Uuo + ^{1}_{0}n \qquad (t_{1/2} < 1 \text{ msec})$$

$$^{249}_{97}Bk + ^{22}_{10}Ne \rightarrow ^{267}_{107}Bh + 4^{1}_{0}n \qquad (t_{1/2} = 17 \text{ seconds})$$

TABLE 21.7	Predicting Nuclear Decay	
Type of Decay	Reason for Instability	Change in n/p Ratio
Alpha emission	Nucleus too heavy	Increase (small for heavy nuclides)
Beta emission	n/p too high (*)	Decrease
Positron emission	n/p too low (*)	Increase
Gamma	Too much energy Nucleus energetically excited	None
Electron capture	n/p too low (*)	Increase

*n/p represents the neutron-to-proton ratio.

Some nuclides are expected to be quite stable, others not so. The nature of the nucleus becomes clearer when we study the half-lives of these nuclides.

EXERCISE 21.6   Ten Tin Isotopes

Tin has more stable isotopes than any other element. Explain why you might expect this to be the case. Then examine the radioisotopes of tin and discuss their decay modes.

Stable isotopes	^{112}Sn, ^{114}Sn, ^{115}Sn, ^{116}Sn, ^{117}Sn, ^{118}Sn, ^{119}Sn, ^{122}Sn, ^{124}Sn (^{120}Sn, ^{118}Sn, and ^{116}Sn are the most abundant.)
Radioisotopes that decay by β^-	^{121}Sn, ^{123}Sn, ^{125}Sn, ^{126}Sn, ^{127}Sn (plus others with higher mass and short half-life)
Radioisotopes that decay by β^+ or by electron capture	^{110}Sn, ^{111}Sn, ^{113}Sn (plus others with lower mass and short half-life)

First Thoughts

Data like these exist for every element; in general, they are most conveniently accessed on the Web or in a chemistry handbook. You cannot reason out which isotopes actually exist. Although tin's location provides some guidance, you must still look them up.

Solution

For several reasons, tin would be expected to have a number of stable isotopes. First, tin is in the middle of the periodic table where nuclei are more stable and where a few extra neutrons do little to upset the balance of nuclear forces. Second, it has an atomic number of 50, one of the "magic numbers." Finally, 8 of the 10 isotopes have even numbers of protons and neutrons, and the even isotopes are the most abundant—another indication of their stability.

Further Insights

Isotopic stabilities hold some surprises. For example, a radioisotope may fall between a pair of stable isotopes. We noted this above for tin. It also happens for chlorine, where Cl-35 and Cl-37 are stable, but Cl-36, which has an odd number of both protons (17) and neutrons (19), is radioactive. Again, nuclear stability (or instability) arises from a combination of several factors and is therefore difficult to predict.

PRACTICE 21.6

Predict whether each of the following isotopes might be stable or radioactive.

a. ^{79}Br b. ^{101}Ru c. ^{136}Ba d. ^{180}Ta

See Problems 59–62.

21.7 Splitting the Atom: Nuclear Fission

With the discovery of fission came the birth of new radioisotopes and of a new consciousness that the nuclear age was upon us. Nuclear fission was discovered in the 1930s through the work of scientists such as Enrico Fermi, Fritz Strassman, Otto Hahn, and Lise Meitner. Work on fission continued in the early 1940s in both Germany and the United States, culminating in the deployment by the United States of the first atomic bomb used in war, fueled by uranium-235, on the town of Hiroshima, Japan, on August 6, 1945, and of a second combat-based atomic bomb, fueled by plutonium-239, on Nagasaki, Japan, on August 9, 1945. The war ended shortly after the second bomb was dropped, but the nuclear age had just begun.

Why do ^{235}U and ^{239}Pu split and release energy? The answer lies in part in the thermodynamics of nuclear stability. Refer to Figure 21.9. Uranium nuclei are not so thermodynamically stable as iron, bromine, and other elements in the region of greatest stability near the top of the curve. The answer also lies in considering the precarious balance that exists in large nuclei such as uranium and plutonium. These nuclei are very heavy and are held together by the strong force between nucleons. However, opposing the strong force are the many proton–proton repulsions in an atom of this size. For some atoms, the injection of extra mass into the nucleus can tip the balance in favor of the proton repulsions and send the nucleus flying apart into two or more pieces. This is what happens with ^{235}U and ^{239}Pu. A neutron, with no charge, is an ideal particle to shoot into a nucleus. Once it slips into the nucleus, a heavier nuclide is formed that fragments in a matter of nanoseconds. Figure 21.11 illustrates the process for the fission of uranium-235.

Lise Meitner (1878–1968) and Otto Hahn (1879–1968). As a woman in the male-dominated world of the early 1900s, Meitner worked as a physicist with Otto Hahn. She was responsible for the discovery of protactinium and was the first to explain nuclear fission correctly. Despite her contributions, Otto Hahn did not acknowledge her work when he received the 1944 Nobel Prize. In belated recognition of her work on radioisotopes, element 109 is named meitnerium.

$$^{239}_{94}\text{Pu} + ^{1}_{0}\text{n} \rightarrow [^{240}\text{Pu}] \rightarrow ^{70}_{30}\text{Zn} + ^{167}_{64}\text{Gd} + 3^{1}_{0}\text{n} + \text{energy}$$

$$^{235}_{92}\text{U} + ^{1}_{0}\text{n} \rightarrow [^{236}\text{U}] \rightarrow ^{139}_{56}\text{Ba} + ^{94}_{36}\text{Kr} + 3^{1}_{0}\text{n} + \text{energy}$$

Nuclear reactions such as these were initially of interest because the tremendous energy they released could be unleashed in a weapon. Since the violent birth of fission in 1945, these reactions have found a variety of other, more humanitarian

FIGURE 21.11

A nucleus of ^{235}U undergoing nuclear fission.

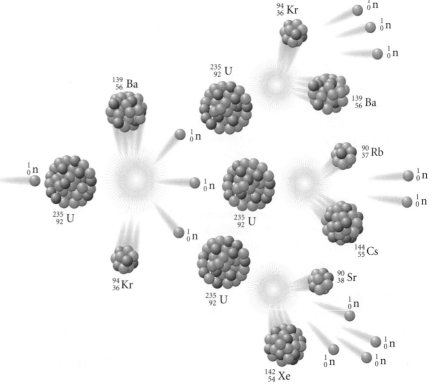

uses. Today, using non-weapons-grade fissionable fuel, they provide the energy in nuclear power plants worldwide, they power spacecraft and submarines, and they are the source of many isotopes used in nuclear medicine.

Nuclear Reactors as a Vital Source of Electricity

The 442 nuclear reactors currently in operation worldwide are alternatives to the pollution and greenhouse gas emissions caused by coal-burning and oil-burning power generation. The world's first nuclear power plant went on line in 1954 in the Russian city of Obninsk. This was immediately followed by the construction of a nuclear facility in Sellafield, England. It wasn't until 1957 that the first full-scale power plant in the United States began operation in Shippingport, Pennsylvania. Municipal power generation by nuclear fission is not new. However, the use of nuclear fission has been controversial because of safety concerns, the two most important being the possible accidental release of radiation, and the disposal and long-term (thousands, and perhaps millions, of years!) safeguarding of radioactive wastes. Accidental releases of radiation occurred on a relatively small scale at the Three Mile Island nuclear facility in Pennsylvania in 1979 and on a much larger scale just outside the Ukrainian town of Chernobyl, in 1986. Still, much of the world uses nuclear power to meet its energy needs, as shown in Figure 21.12.

The goal of any large power plant is to generate electricity by turning a turbine, which converts the mechanical energy into electricity. Steam, resulting from

Application

CHEMICAL ENCOUNTERS:
Nuclear Reactors
as a Vital Source
of Electricity

FIGURE 21.12

Nuclear power plants are located in many countries of the world. The United States, France, Japan, and the Russian Federation possess the majority of the plants, with the capability to produce over 230,000 MW of energy annually.

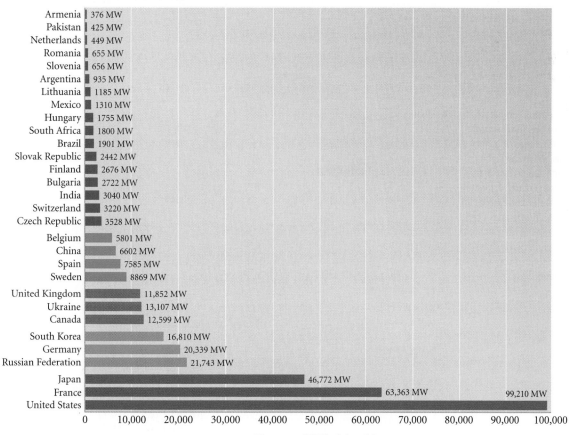

the heating of water, supplies the energy to turn the turbine. *The essential differ-ence among the different types of power plants is the fuel source that creates the steam from water.* In conventional nuclear reactors, this energy is supplied by the controlled fission of ^{235}U (we say that the fission "goes critical").

Conventional nuclear reactors have three essential parts, as shown in Figure 21.13. The nuclear reactor part comprises 100 to 200 fuel rods that contain the fissionable uranium. A series of movable control rods, typically made of boron or cadmium, absorb neutrons as a way of controlling the rate of fission. The rods are located at the bottom of a pool of water, which acts as a moderator to slow these neutrons so that they can be captured by the uranium in the fuel rods. The other two parts of the system, the steam generator and the turbine and condenser, are common to many types of conventional power plants. Other types of nuclear reactors also exist. Breeder reactors, for example, are so named because they produce more fissionable fuel than they consume. In these reactors, rela-tively abundant ^{238}U is bombarded with neutrons to "breed" ^{239}Pu, along with the emission of β-particles.

$$^{238}_{92}U + {}^{1}_{0}n \rightarrow {}^{239}_{92}U \xrightarrow{\beta} {}^{239}_{93}Np \xrightarrow{\beta} {}^{239}_{94}Pu$$

Prototype large breeder reactors either have been built or are being built in China, France, Scotland, the United States, India, Japan, and the former Soviet Union. Breeder reactors are not currently used in the commercial production of energy because of the exceptionally long (24,400 years) half-life of ^{239}Pu. In these reactors, sodium metal is used as a coolant because it can transfer heat away from the reactor core much better than water and has a much higher boiling point, allowing it to remain liquid without being pressurized. Because of the high oper-ating temperature of the liquid sodium, along with sodium's capacity to absorb neutrons (becoming radioactive after it travels by the core), sodium is viewed as particularly hazardous. The future of breeder reactors is, at the very least, uncertain.

FIGURE 21.13

The essential parts of a nuclear power plant. The nuclear reactor, submersed in a pool of water, contains the uranium-based fuel rods and a series of control rods to slow the fission process. The high-pressure water, heated by the fis-sion, travels to a steam generator where the heat vaporizes water and creates high-pressure steam. The steam is used to turn a turbine and generate electricity. The steam is then condensed by passing large amounts of water in a cooling pond through the condenser.

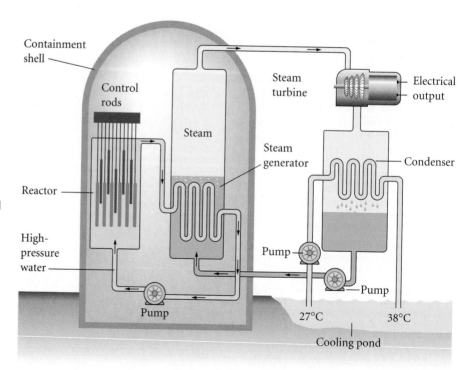

Here are the details of fission as we understand it today:

- Fission reactions release energy. The masses of the product nuclei are less than those of the starting nuclei, and the source of the energy is this mass difference. The energy released is orders of magnitude higher than that of "ordinary" chemical reactions.

- With rare exception, fission is not a naturally occurring process. We initiate it in some nuclei by brute force—that is, by smashing them with a high-energy neutron. The impact simply drives the nucleus apart. A few nuclei can be induced to undergo fission after they capture lower-energy neutrons. Furthermore, the only *naturally occurring* fissionable nucleus is ^{235}U, which is present in only 0.72% of all uranium atoms. The low availability of fissionable fuels slowed the development of fission. It also spurred the breeding of human-made fissionable fuels such as ^{233}U and ^{239}Pu.

- Once induced, fission releases more neutrons, typically 2 to 3 neutrons, per event. These daughter neutrons usually are traveling fast and may escape without further interaction with a fissionable nucleus. In this instance, we have a condition known as a **subcritical mass**. But if enough fissionable nuclei are nearby (a **critical mass**) or if the neutrons are slowed, these neutrons can continue the fission process in the absence of a neutron source. A self-sustaining **chain reaction** is possible. If too much fissionable material (a **supercritical mass**) is present, the reaction goes out of control.

- Nuclei can split in more than one way, forming a whole host of fission products. The split is usually into two or sometimes three fragments. This means that fission is "messy" because of the many products.

- Fission is also messy because the products are usually radioactive. They tend to be neutron-rich and beta emitters. In the case of nuclear reactors, the radioactive products end up in high-level and low-level nuclear waste—in other words, storage. In the case of weapons testing above ground, they result in nuclear fallout.

Most radioactive particles escape the reaction.

Nucleus

Few radioactive particles escape the reaction.

Subcritical mass   **Supercritical mass**

The conditions needed to sustain a chain reaction.

EXERCISE 21.7   Fission: A Chain Reaction

Draw a sketch to show why the fission of ^{235}U can be called a chain reaction. What factors do you think will influence whether the fission chain reaction will merely sustain itself or will be explosive?

First Thoughts

Fission of ^{235}U is initiated by neutrons and produces neutrons. This can result in a chain reaction if enough of the neutrons released are able to interact with more ^{235}U.

Solution

As shown here, the fission events quickly multiply, and the reaction becomes explosive. But if each fission event simply produced one more fission (instead of three), the chain reaction would simply sustain itself.

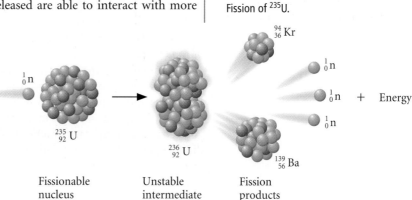

Fission of ^{235}U.

$^{94}_{36}Kr$

$^1_0 n$

$^1_0 n$ +   Energy

$^1_0 n$

$^1_0 n$

$^{235}_{92}U$

$^{236}_{92}U$

$^{139}_{56}Ba$

Fissionable nucleus

Unstable intermediate

Fission products

Further Insights

For a chain reaction to be explosive, two conditions must be met: (1) The fission reaction must produce more than one neutron, and (2) these neutrons must efficiently produce more fission events. ^{235}U produces 2 to 3 neutrons per event, so the first condition is met. The second is a bit tricky. First, you need a critical mass of ^{235}U if you want each fission event to induce one additional event. For ^{235}U, this is a fairly large (on the order of kilograms) amount. To be explosive, you need to have a mass of ^{235}U that is even greater. Second, you need to minimize the presence of substances such as ^{238}U that absorb neutrons and stop the reaction. Finally, you need to keep the ^{235}U in one place, which is difficult because the energy released tends to blow it apart. What are the implications? Although the principles of building a nuclear weapon are fairly simple, engineering one can be very difficult.

PRACTICE 21.7

Draw a sketch that would illustrate the fission reaction of ^{235}U that is just sustainable. (*Hint:* A sustainable reaction is not a supercritical chain reaction.)

See Problems 67 and 68. ■

21.8 Medical Uses of Radioisotopes

Now used almost routinely for diagnosis, radioisotopes enable us to image internal organs, bone, and tissue structures. We can watch biological processes such as oxygen uptake and brain activity. Radioisotopes also make possible the treatment of tumors without anesthesia or invasive surgery. There are more than 40,000 such procedures are carried out in the United States each day.

Application

CHEMICAL
ENCOUNTERS:
Tracer Isotopes
for Diagnosis

Tracer Isotopes for Diagnosis

We have already mentioned that you can image certain internal structures such as bones (or bullets or swallowed coins) using X-rays. The bones, by absorbing the incoming radiation, show up as shadows on the X-ray films or detectors. However, the heart, liver, and thyroid gland do not show up very well on X-ray films because they absorb so little of the X-rays.

Imaging these organs is the job of radioactive tracers, more technically called diagnostic **radiopharmaceuticals**. Radiopharmaceuticals are used in small amounts, so they release only low amounts of radiation into the body. They are considered safe to use for diagnostic purposes. Through introduction into the body by mouth, inhalation, or injection, the radiopharmaceutical can be used to outline the organs of interest. This imaging occurs by measuring the emitted radiation outside the patient. Either a "hot spot" (a tumor that preferentially absorbs the radioisotope) or a "cold spot" (a place where the surrounding tissues preferentially absorb the radioisotope) will produce the desired result. Using an alpha or beta emitter as a radioactive source would *not* work, because *these particles would be absorbed by the tissues inside the body before they could be detected outside the body.*

To understand imaging, we no longer can ignore the chemical form of the nuclide, as we have done throughout most of this chapter. The art of getting a good image lies in understanding the chemical behavior of the nuclide in the body. For example, although you can make elemental iodine, ^{131}I$_2$, from radioactive ^{131}I, you cannot feed this chemical to a patient to image the thyroid gland, because iodine is chemically reactive and would damage the mouth and stomach. Similarly, an organic fat-soluble compound containing iodine would tend to concentrate in the lymph system rather than travel via the bloodstream to the thyroid. The chemical form of choice for thyroid studies is the iodide ion, $^{131}I^-$, in the water-soluble form of sodium iodide, $Na^{131}I$, which can be swallowed in a salty "cocktail." Each radioactive substance must be prepared in a carefully tailored chemical form, because each organ in the body has a different chemical profile.

EXERCISE 21.8 ^{123}I and ^{131}I : Cousins But Not Twins

Radioactive ^{131}I is used for both treatment and diagnostic scans, whereas radioactive ^{123}I is used only for diagnosis. Account for this difference after looking up the decay mode for each nuclide.

Solution

Both of these isotopes of iodine behave the same *chemically* in the body (they both are taken up by a normal thyroid gland), so the difference must lie in their *nuclear* properties. A table of radioactive decay shows that both ^{131}I and ^{123}I release gamma rays. Because gamma rays easily penetrate matter, they can be detected outside the body. Therefore, both can be used for diagnosis. For destruction of a tumor, you need alpha or beta particles that damage tissue at short distances. ^{131}I is a beta emitter; ^{123}I is not.

PRACTICE 21.8

Understanding the biological action of salicylic acid can be enhanced by imaging a patient fed with a radiopharmaceutical. Which of the following salicylic acid derivatives would *not* be a suitable choice for such a study?

See Problems 73–76.

In many cases, technetium-99m is the nuclide of choice. The existence of technetium was predicted by Mendeleev as "eka-manganese," and it is the only non-rare-Earth element he foresaw that was not discovered in his lifetime. Although it was first produced in 1939 by Glen Seaborg and Emilio Segrè, it was not used in nuclear medicine until the 1960s. Technetium has a versatile chemistry and is dispensed in dozens of chemical compounds for imaging different parts of the body. Furthermore, technetium-99m emits only gamma rays, which are little absorbed by the body and therefore expose the patient to only a small radiation dose. Because it has such a short half-life, Tc-99m cannot be stored in a flask on a shelf. Rather, it usually is generated in the hospital from a source of molybdenum called a "molybdenum (or sometimes technetium) cow":

$$^{99}Mo \rightarrow {}^{99m}Tc + {}_{-1}^{0}\beta + {}_{0}^{0}\gamma$$

$$^{99m}Tc \rightarrow {}^{99}Tc + {}_{0}^{0}\gamma$$

The molybdenum-99 isotope used in the cow is not naturally occurring on Earth. It is generated as a fission product of uranium in nuclear reactors and shipped to hospitals worldwide. The ^{99m}Tc nuclide is separated from the molybdenum as it is needed in a process called "milking the cow." Figure 21.14 shows the earliest chromatographic column used to do a hands-on separation of ^{99m}Tc from ^{99}Mo.

FIGURE 21.14

This photograph shows the early column chromatography apparatus used to separate Tc-99m from the parent isotope (Mo-99). The molybdenum remains on the column, and the technetium passes through. The early work on technetium-99m was done at Brookhaven National Lab.

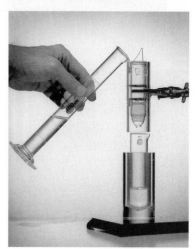

How do we know?

Imaging with Positron Emission Tomography (PET)

Why does nuclear medicine employ such exotic nuclei as technetium and palladium yet seemingly ignore the elements that make up most of our body, including hydrogen, oxygen, carbon, nitrogen, sulfur, and potassium? All of these elements play biochemical roles in the development of cells and tissues, yet none has been mentioned as a diagnostic or therapeutic tool. Why the omission?

Think back on what is needed to do imaging. First is a source of radiation that penetrates well enough to be detected outside the body. Gamma emitters usually are the nuclides of choice. Second, you need availability of the nuclide in sufficient quantity to do a study. Third, you need a half-life that is reasonably short, and if it is very short, the nuclide must be generated on site. Finally, you need to create a chemical form of the nuclide that will give either a "hot spot" or a "cold spot" in the area of medical interest.

Carbon-14, though biologically active, has too long a half-life and is a pure beta-minus emitter (see Figure 21.15). However, ^{11}C, with a n/p that is lower than those of the stable isotopes, is a positron emitter. Other positron emitters include ^{15}O, ^{13}N, and ^{30}S. Positrons themselves do not penetrate very far. But when a positron encounters an electron, which happens almost immediately, an annihilation occurs whereby the particle (positron) and antiparticle (electron) are converted into energy:

$$_{+1}^{0}\beta + e^- \rightarrow 2\,_0^0\gamma$$

A burst of energy is released as a positron and an electron collide.

The photons from the two gamma rays are emitted in exactly opposite directions. When a gamma detector is positioned both above and below the patient, if each one simultaneously records an event, then a positron was annihilated. By feeding the data from the detectors into a computer, it is possible to reconstruct an image of where the positron emission took place.

Positron emission imaging is better known as a PET scan, short for **positron emission tomography**. It is a

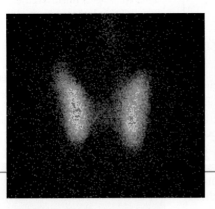

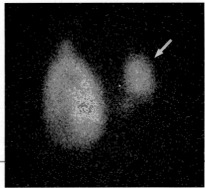

These thyroid scans were taken using radioactive iodine (I-123). The normal scan on the left shows uniform iodine uptake; the two thyroid lobes are similar in size. The lobe marked with an arrow in the photo on the right is not functioning properly, as is typical in thyroid cancer. A biopsy would follow to confirm the presence of cancer.

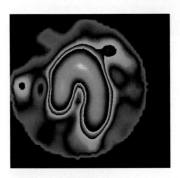

Tc image of heart muscle.

Today such processes are automated. The half-life of ^{99}Mo is a brief 67 hours, so it is shipped to medical suppliers for immediate distribution to hospitals.

One of the more widely used technetium compounds is sodium pertechnetate, $NaTcO_4$. The pertechnetate ion, TcO_4^-, has properties similar to those of the chloride ion, Cl^-, and concentrates in brain tumors, in the thyroid and salivary glands, and in areas of the body where blood is pooling (as happens in internal bleeding). Similarly, technetium pyrophosphate, TcP_2O_7, can be used to image the heart to see the extent of damage to heart muscle after a heart attack.

Although it is well developed, nuclear medicine is still a relatively young field; radioisotope tracers were developed in the 1930s and put into widespread much trickier procedure than other types of nuclear imaging, largely because positron emitters tend to have half-lives on the order of minutes. To have enough radioactive material present, they must be produced nearby or on site at a hospital. In either case, technicians are needed to maintain the production equipment. PET scans also require the injection of radioactive material, which is not the case for MRI or CT scans.

The payoff with PET, though, is impressive. It produces "functional imaging"—that is, images of chemical processes in action. For example, it can record the brain in action during a seizure or when the patient is hearing music, thus decoding the neural pathways. Using glucose labeled with ^{11}C or with ^{18}F (see Figure 21.16), PET can reveal brain metabolism. Similarly, ^{18}F-labeled estrogen can be used within a patient to show how tumors grow. The color-enhanced real-time images are far more dramatic than the black-and-white slices produced by other means.

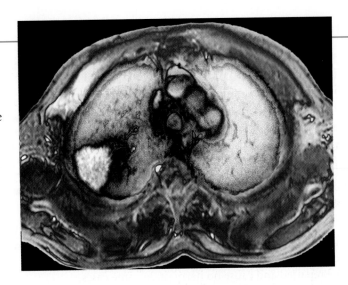

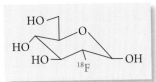

FIGURE 21.16

^{18}F-labeled 2-deoxyglucose, or FDG, is used to study glucose metabolism in the body. It can be used to differentiate benign tumors from cancerous ones, because the latter use glucose at a higher rate. After a patient consumes this radiopharmaceutical, tumors within her or his body show up as white spots where glucose metabolism is higher.

FIGURE 21.15

The isotopes of carbon.

	^{9}C	^{10}C	^{11}C	^{12}C	^{13}C	^{14}C	^{15}C	^{16}C	^{17}C
Type of decay	EC	EC	$+\beta$ or EC	Stable	Stable	$-\beta$	$-\beta$	$-\beta$	$-\beta$
Half-life	0.127 s	19.3 s	20.3 min			5715 years	2.45 s	0.75 s	0.19 s

n/p ratio too low   n/p ratio too high

use in the 1950s and 1960s. In the 1980s, the ready availability of computers to help process images led to explosive growth in the field that continues today. There are announcements of new techniques, new types of images, or methods that require lower amounts of radiation almost daily. (There are also cautions that costly scans are being used too routinely to warrant either the risks or the costs involved.) The odds are that you know somebody who has waged battle with cancer. Nuclear medicine is undoubtedly a part of that person's health history.

The Bottom Line

- Each element is composed of atoms containing the same number of protons. These may contain isotopes with differing numbers of neutrons. (Section 21.1)

- Some nuclear configurations are unstable. They decay in a stepwise progression toward stable nuclei. (Section 21.2)

- There are three main types of radioactive decay: alpha-particle emission, beta-particle emission, and gamma-ray emission. (Section 21.2)

- Ionizing radiation can interact with living tissue and cause damage to the DNA of a cell. This damage may be repaired and cause no harm or, in some cases, may lead to cancer. (Section 21.3)

- Radioactive decay occurs via first-order kinetics. (Section 21.4)

- Energy is released in radioactive decay processes as a consequence of the mass defect in nuclei. (Section 21.5)

- Nuclei with a "magic" number of protons and/or neutrons (2, 8, 20, 28, 50, or 82) are stable. Nuclei with even numbers of protons and/or neutrons are also more likely to be stable. (Section 21.6)

- Nuclear fission is the splitting of heavier nuclei into lighter ones. Nuclear fusion results when smaller nuclei combine into heavier nuclei. (Section 21.7)

- Radioisotopes can be used in medicine for imaging the body and for treating and eliminating cancerous tissues. (Section 21.8)

Key Words

alpha decay A type of radioactive decay wherein an alpha particle is emitted from the nucleus of a radioactive nuclide. Common for elements whose nuclei are larger than bismuth, alpha decay is often accompanied by the release of a gamma ray. (*p. 905*)

alpha particles (α particles) Particles emitted from the nucleus of a radioactive element during the process of alpha decay. They are helium nuclei (2 protons, 2 neutrons), with a +2 charge. (*p. 905*)

antimatter Particles that have the same mass as, but charges opposite to, corresponding matter. Antimatter particles such as the positron and anti-neutrino are similar to the electron and neutrino, respectively, but have opposite characteristics. (*p. 905*)

antineutrino A subatomic particle produced in beta-minus decay that has no charge, has essentially no mass, and interacts only rarely with matter. (*p. 904*)

becquerel (Bq) An SI unit of activity equivalent to one nuclear disintegration per second. (*p. 911*)

beta particles (β particles) Particles emitted from the nucleus of a radioactive atom during the process of beta decay. These particles are high-speed electrons. (*p. 904*)

beta-particle emission A naturally occurring type of radioactive decay wherein an electron is ejected at high speed from the nucleus, typical of nuclei that have too many neutrons to be energetically stable. An antineutrino accompanies this emission, and sometimes one or more gamma rays as well. Also known as beta emission. (*p. 904*)

beta-plus emission A type of radioactive decay wherein a positron is ejected at high speed from the nucleus, typical of nuclides that have too few neutrons. A neutrino accompanies this emission, and usually one or more gamma rays as well. Also known as positron emission. (*p. 918*)

binding energy The energy released when a nucleus is formed from protons and neutrons. Binding energies are expressed as a positive number. (*p. 915*)

chain reaction In nuclear chemistry, a reaction that is self-sustaining as one event in turn causes more events. (*p. 923*)

critical mass The amount of fissionable fuel needed to sustain a chain reaction. (*p. 923*)

curie (Ci) A larger unit of activity than the becquerel, equivalent to 3.7×10^{10} Bq. (*p. 911*)

daughter nuclide An isotope that is the product of a nuclear reaction. (*p. 904*)

decay series A series of nuclear reactions that a large nuclide undergoes as it changes from an unstable and radioactive nucleus to a stable nucleus. (*p. 907*)

electron capture (EC) A type of radioactive decay that occurs when an inner-core electron is captured by a proton from the nucleus to form a neutron. The process is usually accompanied by the emission of X-rays. (*p. 907*)

fission (or nuclear fission) A type of nuclear reaction wherein a large nucleus splits into two or three smaller nuclei with the release of energy. (*p. 917*)

fusion (or nuclear fusion) A type of nuclear reaction wherein small nuclei are joined to form a larger nucleus with the release of energy. Nuclear fusion powers the stars. (*p. 916*)

gamma rays (γ rays) A high-energy form of electromagnetic radiation that is emitted from the nucleus. Gamma rays sometimes accompany alpha and beta decays. (*p. 904*)

gray (Gy) A measure of absorbed radiation equal to 100 rad. (*p. 911*)

ionizing radiation Radiation such as alpha and beta particles, gamma rays, or X-rays that is capable of removing an electron from an atom or a bond when it interacts with matter. (*p. 910*)

mass defect (Section 21.5) The loss in mass that occurs when a nucleus is formed from its protons and neutrons. (*p. 915*)

metastable state An energetically unstable arrangement of protons and neutrons in a nucleus after a neutron has become a proton. (*p. 906*)

neutrino A subatomic particle that is produced in beta-plus decay and that has no charge, has essentially no mass, and interacts only rarely with matter. (*p. 905*)

nuclear equation An equation showing a nuclear transformation, where the atomic and mass numbers are provided. (*p. 904*)

nuclear radiation The particles and/or energy emitted during radioactive decay. (*p. 901*)

nucleon The name given to a particle (proton or neutron) that is part of a nucleus. For example, ^{13}C contains 13 nucleons, 6 protons, and 7 neutrons. (*p. 918*)

positron The antimatter equivalent of an electron. Positrons have a positive charge and the same mass as an electron. (*p. 907*)

positron emission See *beta-plus emission*. (*p. 907*)

positron emission tomography A medical imaging technique that images metabolic processes within the body. Also known as a PET scan. (*p. 926*)

rad A unit of energy absorbed by irradiated material equal to 0.01 J/kg of exposed material. (*p. 911*)

radioactive decay The process by which an unstable nucleus becomes more stable via the emission or absorption of particles and energy. (*p. 904*)

radioactivity The emission of radioactive particles and/or energy. (*p. 901*)

radiopharmaceuticals Compounds containing radioactive nuclides that are used for imaging studies in nuclear medicine. (*p. 924*)

rem A unit that measures the "equivalent dose" of radiation; that is, it takes into account the interaction of radiation with human tissue. The word stands for "roentgen equivalent in man." The rem is not an SI unit but is related to the SI unit, the sievert. (*p. 911*)

roentgen A unit used to measure exposure to radiation. One roentgen is equal to 2.58×10^{-4} C/kg of dry air at STP. (*p. 911*)

sievert (Sv) A unit that measures the "equivalent dose" of radiation; that is, it takes into account the interaction of radiation with human tissue. One sievert equals 100 rem. (*p. 911*)

subcritical mass A mass of a radioactive isotope that is too small to sustain a chain reaction. (*p. 923*)

supercritical mass A mass of a radioactive isotope that not only supports a chain reaction but causes the majority of the nuclei to undergo unfettered radioactive decay within a very short period of time, releasing huge amounts of energy. (*p. 923*)

Focus Your Learning

The answers to the odd-numbered problems appear at the back of the book.

Section 21.1 Isotopes and More Isotopes

Skill Review

1. What is the atom with smallest atomic number? The smallest mass number?

2. Can different elements both have the same number of protons? The same number of neutrons? Explain.

3. Can an atom have no neutrons? Explain.

4. Can an atom have no protons? No electrons? Explain.

5. Can a helium nuclide have a smaller mass number than a hydrogen nuclide? Explain.

6. Can a carbon nuclide have a smaller mass number than a nitrogen nuclide? Explain.

7. Identify the number of protons, neutrons, and electrons in each of the following isotopes.
   a. ^{12}N b. ^{124}Sb c. ^{152}Eu d. ^{9}Be

8. Identify the number of protons, neutrons, and electrons in each of the following isotopes.
   a. ^{7}Li b. ^{122}Cs c. ^{17}O d. ^{18}F

Chemical Applications and Practices

9. A person who weighs 60 kg (132 lb) has about 120 g of potassium in his or her body. How many grams of K-40 does this include? K-40 has a natural abundance of 0.0118%.

10. No isotopes of potassium are chemically *stable* in the presence of water and/or oxygen. Potassium-39 and potassium-41 are *stable* isotopes. Explain these different meanings of the word *stable*.

11. Fallout from a nuclear weapon includes the radioactive nuclide Sr-90.
   a. In the biosphere, which chemical form for Sr-90 is more likely, Sr^{2+} or Sr?
   b. Once Sr-90 lands downwind, it is extremely difficult to separate from the plants and soils. Suggest reasons why.

12. Strontium-90 from fallout gets into the food chain and eventually can end up in cows' milk. Can you remove the radioactivity from cows' milk by boiling it? Why or why not?

Section 21.2 Types of Radioactive Decay

Skill Review

13. Both gamma rays and infrared radiation are forms of electromagnetic radiation. How do they differ?

14. Beta decay involves the emission of a high-speed electron from an atom, yet the overall charge on the atom does not become less negative. Explain why.

15. Write nuclear equations for the following processes:
    a. An alpha particle (along with a gamma ray) is emitted from plutonium-239.
    b. Carbon-14 undergoes beta decay.
    c. Cesium-137 emits a beta particle with an accompanying gamma ray.

16. Write nuclear equations for the following processes:
    a. Plutonium-238 emits an alpha particle with an accompanying gamma ray.
    b. Radon-222 is produced from the decay of a radium isotope with the emission of a gamma ray.
    c. Radium-225 emits a gamma ray followed by an alpha particle.

17. Write nuclear equations for the following processes:
    a. Polonium-215 (with a gamma ray) is produced by an alpha emission.
    b. Strontium-90 decays by beta emission. Little or no gamma radiation is released.
    c. Tc-99 decays by beta-minus emission.

18. Write nuclear equations for the following processes:
    a. Nitrogen-14 is formed from a radioisotope of carbon.
    b. Cadmium-110 is formed from a radioisotope of silver.
    c. Technetium-99 is formed from Technetium-99m.

Chemical Applications and Practices

19. Samarium-146 is the lightest element found naturally on our planet to undergo alpha emission. Write the equation for this alpha decay. There is no accompanying gamma ray.

20. Iodine-131, used in medical imaging, undergoes beta decay. Write the nuclear equation for this reaction.

21. Darlene Hoffman, an award-winning nuclear chemist, postulated the existence of Pu-244 before it was discovered. Into which of the four natural decay series does it fit?

22. A chemistry source states that radon-219 is produced in the actinium-227 radioactive decay series. Into which of the four decay series mentioned in Section 21.2 does actinium-227 fit?

Section 21.3 Interaction of Radiation with Matter

Skill Review

23. Classify the following as ionizing or nonionizing radiation: cosmic rays, infrared radiation, gamma rays, visible light, microwaves, X-rays.

24. You can cook food using microwaves, and you can sterilize food using gamma rays. Why do these two types of radiation produce such different results?

25. Suppose that you had administered a gamma emitter to a patient in order to diagnose how well his or her heart was functioning. Name three things you could do to minimize your exposure to the radiation.

26. Which cells in your body are most susceptible to radiation? Why?

27. Explain the similarities and differences between:
    a. a curie and a becquerel
    b. a rad and a rem

28. Explain the similarities and differences between:
    a. a rem and a sievert
    b. a curie and a rem

29. Smoke detectors use only a small quantity of americium, less than 35 kBq. How many disintegrations per second is this?

30. Using the information in Problem 29, show that the result is comparable to 1 microcurie.

Chemical Applications and Practices

31. In the mid-1990s, a watch was advertised that glowed in the dark. The source of the glow was the radioisotope tritium interacting with a luminous paint. The annual dose for a person wearing the watch as estimated at 4.0 microsieverts.
    a. How many rem is this?
    b. Do you think this amount of radiation warrants concern?

Note the radiation symbol between the hour and minute hands and the H3 (^{3}H, or tritium) on the face of this watch.

32. In the previous problem, we noted that tritium, a radioisotope of hydrogen, was used in some watches.
    a. What mode of decay would you predict for tritium?
    b. Given that radiation escapes from the watch case, does this evidence support your prediction?

33. Three metals—aluminum, iron, and cadmium—are proposed as materials that could be used to shield nuclear radiation.
    a. What property of these materials would you need to look up to determine which one would have to be used in the greatest thickness?
    b. What else might you need to know about a substance before you use it in shielding?

34. If radon-222 gas decays in your lungs to produce solid polonium, which is then trapped there, how many decays does the polonium progress through before reaching the stable isotope of lead-206? How many alpha and beta particles are emitted in the process?

Section 21.4 The Kinetics of Radioactive Decay

Skill Review

35. Here are the decay plots for two different hypothetical radioactive nuclei. The plot denoted by the red line is A; that denoted by the blue line is B. From these graphs, determine:
    a. Which nuclide has the longer half-life?
    b. What is the half-life of the nuclide indicated by the red line?
    c. Which one has the higher activity?
    d. Which one would be more dangerous if swallowed?

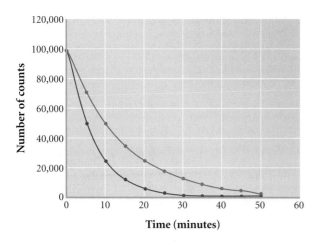

36. Using the plot in Problem 35, estimate the half-life of each nucleus. What does a shorter half-life imply?

37. If 75% of a radioactive sample is gone after 30 days, what is the half-life of the nuclide?

38. If 50% of a radioactive sample remains after 30 days, what is the half-life of the nuclide?

39. Tritium has a half-life of 12.3 years. What fraction of a sample of tritium will remain after 12.3 years? After 24.6 years?

40. What percent of the original sample of strontium-90 (half-life = 28.9 years) will remain
   a. after 14 years?   b. after 49.6 years?   c. after 1000 years?

41. The half-life of strontium-90 is 28.9 years. How long would it take for the activity of a Sr-90 sample to diminish by 87.5%?

42. The half-life of strontium-85 (about 64 days) is considerably shorter than that of strontium-90. How long would it take for the activity of a sample of Sr-85 to diminish by 93.75%? Why do you think that Sr-85 is used diagnostically for bone scans, but Sr-90 is not?

Chemical Applications and Practices

43. A 10-mCi sample of a tracer isotope is used to diagnose blood flow from the heart. If it is desirable that nearly all of the radioactivity (99%) be gone after 3 days, approximately what half-life should the isotope have?

44. It is estimated that the nuclear accident at Chernobyl released 1.85×10^{18} becquerels, a large amount of radiation. How many curies is this? Why is it not easy to translate either of these values into the number of radioactive atoms present?

Chernobyl nuclear power plant.

45. A 0.1-microcurie sample of polonium-210 is used to demonstrate alpha decay in the lecture hall, because there is little accompanying gamma radiation. The half-life of this isotope is 138 days. About how often does an instructor need to buy a new source? State any assumptions you made in arriving at your answer.

46. The world uranium reserves are currently estimated at 3.4 million tonnes, where a tonne is a metric ton, or 1000 kg. Current knowledge places Earth at 4.5 billion years old. How much uranium was present at the time our world formed?

47. The half-life of plutonium-239 is about 24,000 years. After approximately how much time will over 99% of a sample of plutonium-239 have decayed? How can this element exist on our planet if its half-life is so short?

48. Plutonium oxide, used to power the Cassini space-probe to Saturn, was stored in corrosion-resistant materials designed to contain the fuel for 10 half-lives, or 870 years.
   a. What is the half-life of Pu-238?
   b. Why do you think the figure 10 half-lives was selected?
   c. The Cassini batteries contained 72 lb (33 kg) of Pu-238 in the form of plutonium dioxide. How much Pu-238 (in kilograms and in grams) will remain after 870 years?

Section 21.5 Mass and Binding Energy

Skill Review

49. a. Why don't the masses of the neutrons and protons that make up an oxygen-16 atom add up to the mass of the oxygen nucleus?
   b. Is this true for all isotopes of oxygen?

50. a. Is an atom of carbon likely ever to fall apart into its component protons, electrons, and neutrons?
   b. Explain why or why not.

51. Explain how the mass defect and the binding energy are related.

52. Is mass conserved in nuclear reactions, such as alpha decay, that proceed spontaneously? Why or why not?

53. Calculate the mass defect and the resulting energy for the following nuclear reaction:
   ($^1_0$n = 1.008665 g/mol; ^{4}He = 4.002603 g/mol)
   ^{170}Ir (169.974970 g/mol) decays to ^{166}Re (165.965740 g/mol)

54. Calculate the mass defect and the resulting energy for the following nuclear reaction:
   $^{40}_{19}$K (39.963999 g/mol) $\rightarrow$ $^{40}_{20}$Ca (39.962591 g/mol) + $^{0}_{-1}\beta$

Chemical Applications and Practices

55. The masses of the neutral atoms involved for an alpha emission from U-238 are shown below. These values include the masses of the electrons.
   a. Would you expect the U-238 or its decay products to have more mass?
   b. What is the source/result of any difference in these masses?

$^4_2$He	4.002603 u
$^{238}_{92}$U	238.050784 u
$^{234}_{90}$Th	234.040945 u
e^-	0.005485799 u

56. Use the data in Problem 55 to calculate the mass defect for the process. What is the source/result of any difference in these masses?

57. Describe the similarities and differences between beta-minus and beta-plus emission.

58. The stable isotopes of carbon are ^{12}C and ^{13}C. What decay mode would you predict for ^{14}C?

Section 21.6 Nuclear Stability and Human-made Radioactive Nuclides

Skill Review

59. a. What does "doubly magic" mean, in reference to nuclides?
  b. Give two examples of nuclei that are doubly magic and two examples of nuclides that have no magic numbers at all. How would you expect these nuclei to differ?

60. Suggest a reason why the heavier elements have proportionately more neutrons than the lighter ones.

Chemical Applications and Practices

61. Element 114 was recently discovered. Why was this element sought, but not the neighboring elements 115 and 113?

62. Some claims to the discovery of element 118 have been made. Give reasons why this element may be considered to have both nuclear and chemical stability.

Section 21.7 Splitting the Atom: Nuclear Fission

Skill Review

63. Why is alpha emission a better prediction for the mode of radioactive decay for uranium or plutonium than it is for iron, carbon, or hydrogen?

64. Answer the following questions for the fission of plutonium:
$$^{239}_{94}Pu + ^{1}_{0}n \rightarrow [^{240}_{94}Pu] \rightarrow ^{136}_{51}Sb + ^{100}_{43}Tc + 4\,^{1}_{0}n + energy$$
  a. What is the significance of the fact that neutrons are produced?
  b. What is the source of the energy in this equation?

65. Iron and cobalt are not expected to undergo nuclear fission. Why?

66. Would you expect helium to undergo nuclear fission? Will hydrogen-1 undergo fission?

67. Write nuclear reactions for the fission of ^{235}U to form:
  a. ^{94}Kr and ^{139}Ba and neutrons
  b. ^{80}Sr and ^{153}Xe and neutrons

68. An isotope of the element technetium can be produced by bombarding molybdenum-97 with deuterium nuclei. Two neutrons are also formed. Write the nuclear equation.

Chemical Applications and Practices

69. On our planet, both U-235 and U-238 occur naturally.
  a. How do these isotopes differ?
  b. What is the natural abundance of each?
  c. Propose a reason why it is very difficult to separate these two isotopes.

70. Using "conventional" explosives such as TNT, you can make tiny explosive devices as well as huge ones. Is it possible to make a similarly tiny nuclear bomb? Why or why not?

71. When fission of U-235 or Pu-239 occurs, elements such as americium, californium, and berkelium are not found in the fallout. Explain why.

72. One particularly nasty component of nuclear fallout is strontium-90. Explore the reactivity of this particular isotope and explain why it may be harmful to living creatures.

Section 21.8 Medical Uses of Radioisotopes

Skill Review

73. What questions should you ask about a radionuclide to be injected for diagnostic purposes?

74. Why aren't alpha emitters useful for diagnostic scans, such as a scan of the heart or of the thyroid gland?

75. Technetium-99m samples should not be stored overnight but, rather, should be freshly prepared each day for diagnostic scans. Why?

76. Why is molybdenum-99 not used directly as a component of a radiopharmaceutical?

Chemical Applications and Practices

77. A patient was injected with 10 mg of fluorine-18–labeled glucose for a PET scan. Fluorine-18 has a half-life of 110 minutes and disintegrates by positron emission. Write the nuclear equation for the decay.

78. Using the information in Problem 77, determine the amount of time needed to reduce the radioactivity of fluorine-18 to 1/16 of its original activity.

79. In the chapter, it was mentioned that it takes about two and a half weeks for Tc-99 to be eliminated from the body. The Department of Energy reports that it takes approximately 60 hours for the body to eliminate half of the technetium. Are these two figures consistent with each other?

80. Gallium-67 citrate is used as a radiopharmaceutical for diagnosing tumors and infections.
  a. What type of radioactive decay would you predict for this nuclide?
  b. A typical activity of a radionuclide used in the treatment of an adult lymphoma is on the order of 10 mCi. After how many days would radiation levels drop to less than a millicurie?

Comprehensive Problems

81. Use the Internet to research the connection between smoking and exposure to the nuclides polonium-210 and lead-210.

82. For the same dose of radiation, which has a higher dose equivalent, strontium-90 or radon-222?

83. How do you know whether or not a gamma ray accompanies an alpha or a beta emission?

84. Write nuclear equations for the following processes:
  a. A positron is emitted by oxygen-15.
  b. Boron-11 is formed by positron emission.
  c. A positron is emitted by chlorine-35.
  d. Oxygen-18 is formed by positron emission.

85. One of the radioactive decay series is shown below. Identify the mode of radioactive decay at each step.

$$^{232}_{90}Th \rightarrow \, ^{228}_{88}Ra \rightarrow \, ^{228}_{89}Ac \rightarrow \, ^{228}_{90}Th \rightarrow \, ^{224}_{88}Ra \rightarrow \, ^{220}_{86}Rn \rightarrow$$

$$^{216}_{84}Po \rightarrow \, ^{212}_{82}Pb \rightarrow \, ^{212}_{83}Bi \rightarrow \, ^{212}_{84}Po \rightarrow \, ^{208}_{82}Pb$$

86. In the radioactive decay series in the previous problem, lead-212 was formed. Why didn't the decay series stop at lead?

87. In the radioactive decay series given in Problem 85, which elements are represented by the symbols Rn and Ra? Which one is a gas? Which one is a metal? Which one is chemically inert?

88. Radon is produced in three of the naturally occurring decay series. Which three? Which isotopes of radon are formed? How would you expect these isotopes to differ? How would you expect them to be the same?

89. Of the three radon isotopes mentioned in Problem 88, only radon-222 is a health hazard. Propose a reason why, and then research your answer to see whether you are correct.

90. Many tropical islands are volcanic in origin and contain uranium in the rocks and minerals beneath the soils. However, radon is less likely to be a problem in homes built in the tropics. Propose two reasons why (and more if you can).

91. How does the nucleus of a carbon atom compare in density with that of elemental lead ($d = 11.3$ g/cm³)? To answer this question, calculate the volume of a ^{12}C nucleus, assuming that the nucleus is spherical and that the radius is 1.2×10^{-13} cm. The mass of the nucleus in ^{12}C is 11.96709 u, or 1.98718×10^{-23} g.

92. The transformation of elements into other elements also takes place in stars. Write the nuclear equation for the formation of oxygen-16 when carbon-12 is hit with an alpha particle. A gamma ray is also released in this reaction.

93. Does food irradiation make the food radioactive? Find an answer to this question using the resources of the World Wide Web. Cite your sources.

94. Look up on the Internet the current maximum allowed exposure of workers in the nuclear industry. The Department of Energy (DOE) sets this standard. How does this standard vary for some individuals?

95. Irene Curie and her mother Marie are not the only scientists to have won the Nobel Prize for their pioneering work in nuclear chemistry and physics. Others include Ernest Rutherford, Ernest O. Lawrence, and Emilio G. Segrè. Use the Internet to find out why these and/or other prizes for nuclear work were awarded.

Thinking Beyond the Calculation

96. Americium oxide is typically used in household smoke detectors. A document reports that a gram of americium oxide provides enough active material for "more than 5000 household smoke detectors." The particular isotope used in this application is americium-241.

    a. How much americium is present in a typical smoke detector?

    b. Give two reasons why Am-240 and Am-242 would not be appropriate isotopes to use.

    c. Americium-241 decays by alpha emission. Write the nuclear reaction for this process.

    d. The half-life of americium-241 is 432.2 years. How long will it take the reactivity of a sample of this nuclide to drop to 1% of its original activity?

    e. Beta-particle emission by americium-242 is found in 83% of the sample. The rest of an americium-242 sample decays by electron capture. Write nuclear reactions for these processes.

Smoke detectors contain about 150 millionths of a gram of americium-241, which is extracted from spent fuel rods.

Chapter 22:
Chemistry of
Main-Group Elements

taken from

**General Chemistry
Eighth Edition by Ebbing/Gammon**

Chemistry of the Main-Group Elements

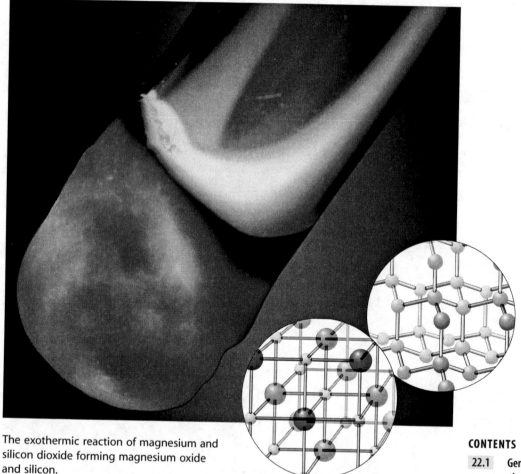

The exothermic reaction of magnesium and silicon dioxide forming magnesium oxide and silicon.

Figure 22.1 is an abridged periodic table showing the main-group elements but omitting the transition elements. Many of these elements are of interest because they are naturally abundant and, when combined with each other, form many of the necessary ingredients for life and living on our planet. For example, consider oxygen, the most abundant element on the surface of the earth: in its elemental form as O_2, it is the airborne fuel for the animal kingdom; when combined with carbon to form CO_2 gas, carbon can be delivered to plants for photosynthesis; and when combined with hydrogen to form water, a substance that is essential for all forms of life results. Many of the other main-group elements play equally important roles. In this chapter you will have the opportunity to explore the properties, chemistry, and commercial applications of several of these elements.

CONTENTS

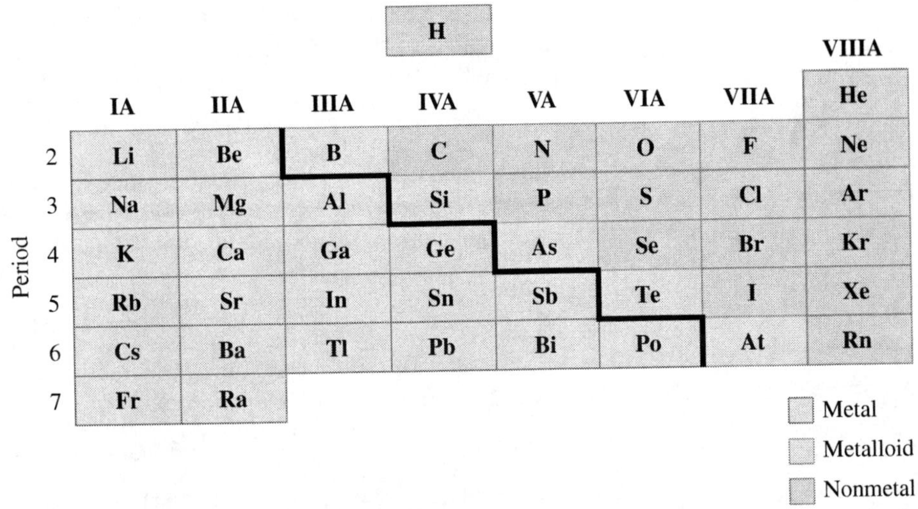

Figure 22.1

An abridged periodic table showing the main-group elements
Elements to the left of the heavy staircase line are largely metallic in character; those to the right are largely nonmetallic.

	IA	IIA	IIIA	IVA	VA	VIA	VIIA	VIIIA
							H	He
2	Li	Be	B	C	N	O	F	Ne
3	Na	Mg	Al	Si	P	S	Cl	Ar
4	K	Ca	Ga	Ge	As	Se	Br	Kr
5	Rb	Sr	In	Sn	Sb	Te	I	Xe
6	Cs	Ba	Tl	Pb	Bi	Po	At	Rn
7	Fr	Ra						

Period

☐ Metal
☐ Metalloid
☐ Nonmetal

22.1 General Observations About the Main-Group Elements

In this section, we want to consider some periodic trends that you will find useful as you study the chemistry of specific elements. The elements on the left side of the periodic table in Figure 22.1 are largely metallic in character; those on the right side are largely nonmetallic. Table 22.1 compares the characteristics of metallic and nonmetallic elements, and the following discussion describes some of these characteristics in greater detail.

The metallic elements generally have low ionization energies and low electronegativities compared with the nonmetallic elements. As a result, the metals tend to lose their valence electrons to form cations (Na^+, Ca^{2+}, Al^{3+}) in compounds or in aqueous solution. Nonmetals, on the other hand, form monatomic anions (O^{2-}, Cl^-) and oxoanions (NO_3^-, SO_4^{2-}).

Table 22.1

Comparison of Metallic and Nonmetallic Elements

Metals	Nonmetals
Lustrous	Nonlustrous
Solids at 20°C (except Hg, which is a liquid)	Solids or gases at 20°C (except Br_2, which is a liquid)
Solids are malleable and ductile	Solids are usually hard and brittle
Conductors of heat and electricity	Nonconductors of heat and electricity (except graphite, an allotrope of C)
Low ionization energies	Moderate to high ionization energies
Low electronegativities	Moderate to high electronegativities
Form cations	Form monatomic anions or oxoanions
Oxides are basic (unless metal is in a high oxidation state)	Oxides are acidic

Also, as noted earlier (Section 8.7), the oxides of the metals are usually basic. The oxides of the most reactive metals react with water to give basic solutions. For example,

$$CaO(s) + H_2O(l) \longrightarrow Ca^{2+}(aq) + 2OH^-(aq)$$

[Oxides of metals in high oxidation states, which you encounter in some transition metals, can be acidic; chromium(VI) oxide, CrO_3, is an acidic oxide.] The oxides of the nonmetals are acidic. Sulfur dioxide, an oxide of a nonmetal, dissolves in water to form an acidic solution.

$$SO_2(g) + 2H_2O(l) \rightleftharpoons H_3O^+(aq) + HSO_3^-(aq)$$

Silicon dioxide (silica sand) does not dissolve in water, but it does react when melted with basic oxides such as calcium oxide to form salts.

$$SiO_2(l) + CaO(s) \longrightarrow CaSiO_3(l)$$

Table 22.2 shows the oxidation states displayed by compounds of the main-group elements. The principal conclusions are as follows: the metallic elements generally have oxidation states equal to the group number (the Roman numeral for a column), representing a loss of the valence electrons in forming compounds. Some of the metallic elements in the fifth and sixth periods also have oxidation states equal to the group number minus two (for example, Pb^{2+}). However, the nonmetals (except for the most electronegative elements fluorine and oxygen) have a variety of oxidation states extending from the group number (the most positive value) to the group number minus eight (the most negative value). For example, chlorine (a Group VIIA element) has the following oxidation states in compounds: $+7, +5, +3, +1, -1$.

The metallic–nonmetallic characteristics of the elements change in definite ways as you move from left to right across a period or down a column of the periodic table. *The metallic characteristics of the main-group elements in the periodic table generally decrease in going across a period from left to right.* Figure 22.1 illustrates this in a broad way. In any period, the elements at the far left are metals and those at the far right are nonmetals. The trend of decreasing metallic character can be seen clearly in the third-period elements. Sodium, magnesium, and aluminum are metals. Silicon is a metalloid, whereas phosphorus, sulfur, and chlorine are nonmetals. The oxides of these elements show the expected trend from basic to acidic. Sodium oxide and magnesium oxide are basic. Aluminum oxide is amphoteric (it has basic and acidic character), as we noted in Section 13.2. The oxides of the elements silicon to chlorine are acidic.

The metallic characteristics of the main-group elements in the periodic table become more important going down any column (group). This trend is more pronounced in the middle groups of the periodic table (Groups IIIA to VA). For example, in Group IVA, carbon is a nonmetal, silicon and germanium are metalloids, and tin and lead are metals. The metallic elements tend to become more reactive as you progress down a column. You can see this most clearly in the Group IIA elements; beryllium is much less reactive than strontium and barium.

A second-period element is often rather different from the remaining elements in its group. The second-period element generally has a small atom that tends to hold electrons strongly, giving rise to a relatively high electronegativity (electron-withdrawing power). For example, nitrogen has an electronegativity of 3.0, but the other Group VA elements have electronegativities between 1.9 and 2.1. Another reason for the difference in behavior between a second-period element and the other elements of the same group has to do with the fact that bonding in the second-period elements involves only s and p orbitals, whereas the other elements may use

Table 22.2

Oxidation States in Compounds of the Main-Group Elements*

Period	IA	IIA	IIIA	IVA	VA	VIA	VIIA
							Group
2	Li +1	Be +2	B +3	C +4 +2 −4	N +5 +4 +3 +2 +1 −3	O −1 −2	F −1
3	Na +1	Mg +2	Al +3	Si +4 −4	P +5 +3 −3	S +6 +4 +2 −2	Cl +7 +5 +3 +1 −1
4	K +1	Ca +2	Ga +3	Ge +4 +2	As +5 +3 −3	Se +6 +4 −2	Br +7 +5 +1 −1
5	Rb +1	Sr +2	In +3 +1	Sn +4 +2	Sb +5 +3 −3	Te +6 +4 −2	I +7 +5 +1 −1
6	Cs +1	Ba +2	Tl +3 +1	Pb +4 +2	Bi +5 +3	Po +4 +2	At +5 −1

*The most common oxidation state is shown in color. Some uncommon oxidation states are not shown.

d orbitals. This places a limit on the types of compounds formed by the second-period elements. For example, although nitrogen forms only the trihalides (such as NCl_3), phosphorus has both trihalides (PCl_3) and pentahalides (PCl_5), which it forms using $3d$ orbitals.

Chemistry of the Main-Group Metals

In the first half of this chapter, we will focus on the chemistry of the Groups IA, IIA, and IIIA metals. The sources and preparation of several of these elements were covered in Sections 13.1 and 13.2 of Chapter 13. Here we will address these questions: What are the chemical and physical properties of some of the main-group metallic elements and their compounds? What are some of the commercial uses of these substances?

22.2 Group IA: The Alkali Metals

IA								VIIIA
H	IIA		IIIA IVA VA VIA VIIA					He
Li	Be			B	C	N	O	F	Ne
Na	Mg	IIIB	IIB	Al	Si	P	S	Cl	Ar
K	Ca	Sc	Zn	Ga	Ge	As	Se	Br	Kr
Rb	Sr	Y	Cd	In	Sn	Sb	Te	I	Xe
Cs	Ba	La	Hg	Tl	Pb	Bi	Po	At	Rn
Fr	Ra	Ac						

The alkali metals, the elements in the first column of the periodic table except hydrogen, are all soft, silvery metals. Figure 22.2 shows sodium metal being cut with a knife. The alkali metals are the most reactive of all metals, reacting readily with air and water. Because the valence configuration of these elements is ns^1, the alkali metals usually react by losing this electron to form the +1 ions, such as Li^+ and Na^+. Most of the compounds of these ions are soluble in water.

Because of their chemical reactivity, the Group IA elements never occur as free metals in nature. They do occur extensively in silicate minerals, which weather to form soluble compounds of the elements (particularly of sodium and potassium). These soluble compounds eventually find their way to landlocked lakes and oceans, where they concentrate. Enormous underground beds of sodium and potassium compounds formed when lakes and seas became isolated by geologic events; the water eventually evaporated, leaving solid deposits of alkali metal compounds. Commercially, sodium and potassium compounds are common, and both sodium and lithium metals are available in quantity.

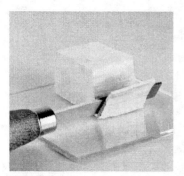

Figure 22.2

Cutting of sodium metal
The metal is easily cut with a sharp knife.

Lithium

In recent years, the commercial importance of lithium metal has risen markedly. Among the alkali metals, only sodium metal is more important.

As you might expect for an alkali metal, lithium is chemically reactive. Like the other alkali metals, it is a relatively soft metal, although the hardest of the Group IA elements. Lithium does exhibit properties that are somewhat different from those of the lower members of the Group IA elements. Many of its ionic compounds are much less soluble than are similar compounds of the other alkali metals. Lithium carbonate, Li_2CO_3, for example, is only slightly soluble in water at room temperature, whereas sodium carbonate, Na_2CO_3, is soluble.

Lithium Metallurgy   The commercial source of lithium metal is the ore spodumene, which is a lithium aluminum silicate mineral, $LiAl(SiO_3)_2$. The ore is heated and then washed with sulfuric acid to obtain a solution of lithium ion, which is precipitated as lithium carbonate. Lithium carbonate from lithium ore is the primary starting substance for the production of lithium metal and lithium compounds. Lithium metal is obtained by electrolysis of the chloride, which was described in Section 13.2.

The use of lithium metal has greatly expanded in recent years (Figure 22.3). A major use is in the production of low-density aluminum alloy for aircraft construction. Batteries with lithium metal anodes have also become common (Figure 22.4). The anode reaction is the oxidation of lithium to the ion:

$$Li(s) \longrightarrow Li^+ + e^-$$

The cathode material varies, but the cathodes in batteries used in cameras, calculators, and similar devices consist of manganese(II) oxide, the same substance used in common dry cells. The electrolyte in this Li/MnO_2 cell is a solution of lithium perchlorate, $LiClO_4$, dissolved in an organic solvent.

Reactions of Lithium Metal   Lithium, like the other alkali metals, reacts readily with water and with moisture in the air to produce lithium hydroxide and hydrogen gas:

$$2Li(s) + 2H_2O(l) \longrightarrow 2LiOH(aq) + H_2(g)$$

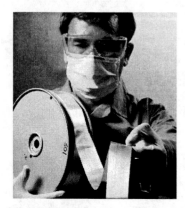

Figure 22.3

A roll of lithium metal for batteries
The metal must be handled in humidity-free rooms to prevent corrosion.

Figure 22.4

Lithium battery
Lithium batteries are used wherever a reliable current is required for a lengthy period. The photograph shows a small pacemaker battery.

When a pellet of lithium is placed in water, the pellet spins around on the surface of the water, evolving bubbles of hydrogen gas. (Lithium floats because it is less dense than water.) The reaction is not as vigorous, however, as the similar reaction of sodium and water.

Lithium burns in air to produce lithium oxide, Li_2O, a white powder.

$$4Li(s) + O_2(g) \longrightarrow 2Li_2O(s)$$

When heated with nitrogen gas, lithium reacts to form lithium nitride, Li_3N, the only stable alkali-metal nitride.

$$6Li(s) + N_2(g) \longrightarrow 2Li_3N(s)$$

Lithium nitride is an ionic compound of the nitride ion, N^{3-}.

Lithium Compounds Lithium carbonate, which is obtained from lithium ore, is the primary source of other lithium compounds. Significant quantities of lithium carbonate are also used in the preparation of porcelain enamels, glazes, and special glass. When purified, the carbonate is used as a source of lithium ion for the treatment of manic-depressive disorders. The physiological action of lithium ion in this treatment is not completely understood, although lithium ion is known to inhibit certain biochemical reactions involved in hormone action.

Lithium hydroxide, LiOH, is a strong base. It is produced by reaction of lithium carbonate with calcium hydroxide in a precipitation reaction. Calcium carbonate is much less soluble than lithium carbonate:

$$Li_2CO_3(aq) + Ca(OH)_2(aq) \longrightarrow 2LiOH(aq) + CaCO_3(s)$$

The calcium carbonate is filtered off, and lithium hydroxide is recovered from the filtrate. Lithium hydroxide is used in the production of lithium soaps, which are used in making lubricating greases from oil. (Lithium soap thickens the oil.) Soaps are salts of fatty acids; they are prepared by heating a fat with a strong base.

Lithium hydroxide is used to remove carbon dioxide from the air in spacecraft and submarines. Humans exhale carbon dioxide that is produced by the normal biochemical reactions of the body. For people to live in a closed space, it is necessary to remove this carbon dioxide. Although carbon dioxide is not normally toxic, increasing concentrations do have a physiological effect by interfering with the blood's capacity to carry oxygen, and high concentrations of carbon dioxide are hazardous. Like the other alkali-metal hydroxides, lithium hydroxide absorbs carbon dioxide from air by forming the carbonate and hydrogen carbonate:

$$2LiOH(s) + CO_2(g) \longrightarrow Li_2CO_3(s) + H_2O(l)$$
$$Li_2CO_3(s) + H_2O(l) + CO_2(g) \longrightarrow 2LiHCO_3(s)$$

Sodium hydroxide could be used to remove carbon dioxide from air, since it undergoes the same reactions. However, the formula weight of LiOH (24 amu) is much lower than that of NaOH (40 amu). Where weight is at a premium, lithium hydroxide is preferred, even though it is more expensive than sodium hydroxide.

Table 22.3 lists some uses of lithium and other alkali metal compounds.

▪ Sodium and Potassium

Sodium compounds are of enormous economic importance. Common table salt, which is sodium chloride, has been an important article of commerce since earliest recorded history. Salt was of such importance in Roman times that a specific allowance of salt

Table 22.3

Uses of Alkali Metal Compounds

Compound	Use
Li_2CO_3	Preparation of porcelain, glazes, special glasses
	Preparation of LiOH
	Treatment of manic-depressive disorders
LiOH	Manufacture of lithium soaps for lubricating greases
	In air-regeneration systems
LiH	Reducing agent in organic syntheses
$LiNH_2$	Preparation of antihistamines and other pharmaceuticals
NaCl	Source of sodium and sodium compounds
	Condiment and food preservative
	Soap manufacture (precipitates soap from reaction mixture)
NaOH	Pulp and paper industry
	Extraction of aluminum oxide from ore
	Manufacture of viscose rayon
	Petroleum refining
	Manufacture of soap
Na_2CO_3	Manufacture of glass
	In detergents and water softeners
Na_2O_2	Textile bleach
$NaNH_2$	Preparation of indigo dye for denim (blue jeans)
KCl	Fertilizer
	Source of other potassium compounds
KOH	Manufacture of soft soap
	Manufacture of other potassium compounds
K_2CO_3	Manufacture of glass
KNO_3	Fertilizers
	Explosives and fireworks

was part of the soldiers' pay. The word *salary* derives from the Latin word for this salt allowance (*salarium,* which comes from the Latin word *sal,* for "salt"). Sodium metal as well as other sodium compounds are produced from sodium chloride.

The economic importance of potassium stems in large part from its role as a plant nutrient. Enormous quantities of potassium chloride from underground deposits are used as fertilizer to increase the world's food supply. In fact, plants were an early source of potassium compounds. Wood and other plant materials were burned in pots to give ashes (potash) that consist primarily of potassium carbonate, from which other potassium compounds could be manufactured. The name potassium has its origin in the word *potash* from this earlier source of the element.

Sodium metal is more reactive than lithium metal, and potassium metal is still more reactive. In general, as you move down the column of alkali metals in Group IA of the periodic table, you find that the metals become more chemically reactive (forming the +1 ions). This is partly a result of the decrease in ionization energy of the atom (from 520 kJ/mol for the first ionization of lithium to 376 kJ/mol for that of cesium). As the atomic size increases going from the top of the column to the bottom, the valence electrons are held less strongly and so are lost more easily.

The Group IA metals also increase in softness going from the top of the column to the bottom. Lithium is a moderately firm metal, whereas potassium is soft enough to be cut with a butter knife. This increasing softness of the metals is in part a result of increasing atomic size, which results in decreasing strength of bonding by the valence-shell s electrons.

Sodium Metallurgy Sodium metal is obtained by the electrolysis of molten, or fused, sodium chloride. Sodium chloride is mined from huge underground deposits. The other source of sodium chloride is seawater, which is a solution of many dissolved substances, but sodium chloride is the principal one. Sodium chloride melts at 801°C, but commercial electrolysis employs a mixture of NaCl and $CaCl_2$, which melts at 580°C. We discussed the electrolysis in some detail in Section 20.9.

Figure 20.20 depicts the commercial Downs cell for the preparation of sodium from molten sodium chloride.

Sodium metal is a strong reducing agent, and this accounts for many of its major uses. For example, it is used to obtain metals such as titanium and zirconium by reduction of their compounds. Titanium is a strong metal used in airplane and spacecraft manufacture. It is produced by reduction of titanium tetrachloride, $TiCl_4$, obtained by chemical processing of titanium ores. The overall process can be written as follows:

$$TiCl_4(g) + 4Na(l) \longrightarrow Ti(s) + 4NaCl(s)$$

Sodium is also employed as a reducing agent in the production of a number of organic compounds, including dyes and pharmaceutical drugs.

Reactions of Sodium Metal Like lithium, sodium metal reacts with water, but with even greater vigor. The reaction is sufficiently exothermic to ignite the hydrogen gas produced in the reaction:

$$2Na(s) + 2H_2O(l) \longrightarrow 2NaOH(aq) + H_2(g)$$

Sodium burns in air, producing some sodium oxide, Na_2O, but mainly sodium peroxide, Na_2O_2, a compound containing the peroxide ion O_2^{2-} (Figure 22.5).

$$2Na(s) + O_2(g) \longrightarrow Na_2O_2(s)$$

The peroxide ion acts as an oxidizing agent (Figure 22.6).

Figure 22.5

Oxygen compounds of alkali metals
Sodium peroxide, Na_2O_2 (yellowish-white, *left*), and potassium superoxide, KO_2 (orange-yellow, *right*). Potassium superoxide is the principal product formed when potassium metal burns in air.

Figure 22.6

Sodium peroxide as an oxidizing agent
Left: A couple of drops of water are added to a mixture of sodium peroxide and sulfur to initiate a reaction. *Right:* During the violent reaction, sulfur is oxidized to sulfur dioxide.

Sodium Compounds   Sodium hydroxide, NaOH, is among the top ten industrial chemicals. It is produced by the electrolysis of aqueous sodium chloride. The overall electrolysis, which was described in Section 20.10, can be written as

$$2NaCl(aq) + 2H_2O(l) \xrightarrow{\text{electrolysis}} H_2(g) + Cl_2(g) + 2NaOH(aq)$$

Figures 20.22 and 20.23 show two different commercial cells for the electrolysis of aqueous sodium chloride.

Both chlorine gas and sodium hydroxide are major products of this electrolysis.

Sodium hydroxide is a strong base, and this property is useful in many applications. It is used in large quantities in aluminum production (which depends on its reaction with the amphoteric aluminum hydroxide) and in the refining of petroleum (where it chemically reacts with acid constituents during the refining process). Large quantities of sodium hydroxide are also used to produce sodium compounds, which occur in a wide variety of commercial products.

For example, soap is made by heating a fat with sodium hydroxide solution. The product is a mixture of sodium salts of fatty acids, obtained from the fat. Fatty acids are chemically similar to acetic acid, but they consist of long chains of carbon atoms. Compare the structure of the acetate ion with that of the stearate ion. (Stearic acid is a typical fatty acid.)

The action of soap in dispersing oil in water is described in Section 12.9.

acetate ion

stearate ion

Soda ash decomposes to sodium oxide when heated. Sodium and calcium oxides, which are basic oxides, react with fused silicon dioxide, SiO_2, an acidic oxide, to produce silicate glass.

Sodium hydroxide is commonly known as lye or caustic soda. You can buy it in a grocery store as a drain opener and as an oven cleaner (Figure 22.7). Both usages depend on the reaction of sodium hydroxide with organic materials, such as fats and hair, to produce soluble materials. Because of these reactions, sodium hydroxide and its solutions require careful handling.

Sodium carbonate is another important compound of sodium. The anhydrous compound, Na_2CO_3, is known commercially as *soda ash*. Large quantities of soda ash are consumed with sand and lime in making glass. The decahydrate, $Na_2CO_3 \cdot 10H_2O$, is added to many detergent preparations and is sold commercially as washing soda. In the United States, most sodium carbonate is produced from the mineral trona, whose chemical formula is approximately $Na_2CO_3 \cdot NaHCO_3 \cdot 2H_2O$. There are large deposits of trona in southwestern Wyoming.

Worldwide, a large fraction of sodium carbonate is still produced by the Solvay process. The **Solvay process** is *an industrial method for obtaining sodium carbonate from sodium chloride and limestone.* In the main step of this process, ammonia is first dissolved in a saturated solution of sodium chloride. Then carbon dioxide is bubbled in, and sodium hydrogen carbonate (baking soda) precipitates. Figure 22.8 shows a laboratory demonstration of this reaction.

$$NH_3(g) + \underbrace{H_2O(l) + CO_2(g)}_{H_2CO_3(aq)} + NaCl(aq) \longrightarrow NaHCO_3(s) + NH_4Cl(aq)$$

You can think of this as an exchange reaction of NH_4HCO_3 (from $NH_3 + H_2CO_3$) with NaCl, to give the products $NaHCO_3$ and NH_4Cl. The sodium hydrogen carbon-

Figure 22.7

Sodium compounds available at the grocery store
Left to right: Salt (NaCl), baking soda ($NaHCO_3$), washing soda ($Na_2CO_3 \cdot 10H_2O$), drain opener (NaOH), and oven cleaner (NaOH).

Figure 22.8

Laboratory demonstration of the Solvay process
Left: A concentrated solution of ammonia is saturated with sodium chloride. When pieces of dry ice (solid CO_2) are added, a cloud of cooled water vapor forms. *Right:* Sodium hydrogen carbonate precipitates from the cold reaction mixture.

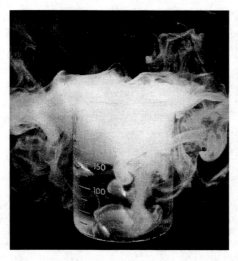

ate is filtered from the solution. When heated to 175°C, it decomposes to sodium carbonate.

$$2NaHCO_3(s) \xrightarrow{\Delta} Na_2CO_3(s) + CO_2(g) + H_2O(g)$$

The reaction to produce sodium hydrogen carbonate uses relatively expensive ammonia. The industrial Solvay process illustrates how you can affect the economics of a process by the ingenious use of raw materials and by recycling intermediate products. Carbon dioxide for the industrial process is obtained by heating limestone ($CaCO_3$):

$$CaCO_3(s) \xrightarrow{\Delta} CaO(s) + CO_2(g)$$

The calcium oxide obtained is used to recycle the ammonia from ammonium chloride for use in the preparation of sodium hydrogen carbonate.

$$CaO(s) + 2NH_4Cl(aq) \xrightarrow{\Delta} 2NH_3(g) + CaCl_2(aq) + H_2O(l)$$

The carbon dioxide obtained when sodium hydrogen carbonate is heated to form sodium carbonate is also recycled to prepare more sodium hydrogen carbonate. The overall result of these steps in the industrial Solvay process is the reaction of limestone ($CaCO_3$) and salt ($NaCl$) to produce sodium carbonate and calcium chloride:

$$CaCO_3 + 2NaCl \longrightarrow Na_2CO_3 + CaCl_2$$

The raw materials (limestone and salt) are cheap, and for many years the Solvay process was the principal source of sodium carbonate. Unfortunately, there is not sufficient demand for the by-product calcium chloride. Some is used for deicing of roads, but much of it has to be disposed of as waste. The environmental cost of this waste disposal has made the Solvay process increasingly less attractive.

Potassium and Potassium Compounds   The principal source of potassium and potassium compounds is potassium chloride, KCl, which is obtained from underground deposits. Small amounts of this salt are used to prepare the metal. Potassium is prepared by the chemical reduction of potassium chloride rather than by electrolysis of the molten chloride, as in the preparation of sodium. In the commercial process, potassium chloride is melted with sodium metal by heating to 870°C.

$$Na(l) + KCl(l) \longrightarrow NaCl(l) + K(g)$$

At this temperature, potassium forms as a vapor. The reaction goes in the direction written because potassium vapor leaves the reaction chamber and is condensed.

Almost all of the potassium metal produced is used in the preparation of potassium superoxide, KO_2, for self-contained breathing apparatus used in situations such as fire fighting where toxic fumes may be present. When potassium burns in air, it produces potassium superoxide:

$$K(s) + O_2(g) \longrightarrow KO_2(s)$$

(The superoxide ion is O_2^-, and the oxidation state of oxygen in this ion is $-\frac{1}{2}$.) In a self-contained breathing apparatus, the potassium superoxide is contained in a canister through which one's breath passes. Moisture in the breath attacks the superoxide, releasing oxygen.

$$4KO_2(s) + 2H_2O(l) \longrightarrow 4KOH(s) + 3O_2(g)$$

The potassium hydroxide produced in this reaction removes the carbon dioxide from the exhaled air. The net effect of the self-contained breathing apparatus is to remove moisture and carbon dioxide from exhaled air and provide oxygen.

More than 90% of the potassium chloride that is mined is used directly as a plant fertilizer. The rest is used in the preparation of potassium compounds. Potassium hydroxide, used in the manufacture of liquid soaps, is obtained by the electrolysis of aqueous potassium chloride. Potassium nitrate is prepared by the reaction of potassium hydroxide and nitric acid. This compound is used in fertilizers and for explosives and fireworks. (Table 22.3 summarizes the major uses of potassium compounds, as well as those of lithium and sodium.)

22.3 Group IIA: The Alkaline Earth Metals

The Group IIA elements are also known as the alkaline earth metals. These metals illustrate the expected periodic trends. If you compare an alkaline earth metal with the alkali metal in the same period, you see that the alkaline earth metal is less reactive and a harder metal. For example, lithium reacts readily with water, but beryllium reacts hardly at all even with steam. Lithium is a soft metal, whereas beryllium is hard enough to scratch glass. You also see the expected trend within the column of alkaline earth metals; the elements at the bottom of the column are more reactive and are softer metals than those at the top of the column (Figure 22.9). Barium, in the sixth period, is a very reactive metal and, when placed in water, reacts much like an alkali metal. It is also a soft metal, much like the alkali metals. Magnesium, in the third period, is much less reactive and a harder metal (comparable to aluminum).

As we noted in Section 22.1, a second-period element is often considerably different from the other elements in its column. Those differences become more pronounced as you progress to the right in the periodic table. We briefly noted differences in properties of lithium from those of the other alkali metals, though those differences are not great. Beryllium, however, shows rather marked differences from the other alkaline earth elements. We have already noted that beryllium differs in its lack of reactivity compared with the other Group IIA metals. Another notable difference is in the properties of the hydroxides. Whereas those of the elements magnesium to barium are basic, beryllium hydroxide is amphoteric, reacting with both acids and bases.

Like the alkali metals, the Group IIA elements occur in nature as silicate rocks. They also occur as carbonates and sulfates, and many of these are commercial sources of alkaline earth metals and compounds.

Calcium and magnesium are the most common and commercially useful of the alkaline earth elements, and we will consider them in some detail in the next two sections. As can be seen from Table 13.1, calcium is the fifth and magnesium the eighth most abundant element in the earth's crust.

Magnesium

The name magnesium comes from the name of the mineral magnesite, which in turn is believed to stem from the name Magnesia, a site in northern Greece where various minerals, including those of magnesium, have been mined since ancient times. The British chemist Humphry Davy discovered the pure element magnesium in 1808. Davy had already discovered the alkali metals potassium and sodium in late 1807. Several months later, he managed to isolate in quick succession the alkaline earth metals barium, strontium, calcium, and finally magnesium. He obtained magnesium by a procedure similar to the one he used for the other alkaline earths. He electrolyzed a moist mixture of magnesium oxide and mercury(II) oxide, from which he obtained magnesium amalgam (an alloy of magnesium dissolved in mercury). To obtain pure magnesium, Davy distilled the mercury from the amalgam.

Magnesium Metallurgy Magnesium has become increasingly important as a structural metal. Its great advantages are its low density (1.74 g/cm^3, which compares with 7.87 g/cm^3 for iron and 2.70 g/cm^3 for aluminum, the other important structural metals) and the relative strength of its alloys.

Some important commercial sources of magnesium are the minerals dolomite, $CaCO_3 \cdot MgCO_3$, and magnesite, $MgCO_3$. However, magnesium ion, Mg^{2+}, is the third most abundant dissolved ion in the oceans, after Cl^- and Na^+. The oceans, therefore, are an essentially inexhaustible supply of the ion, from which the metal can be obtained. ◄

Pure magnesium metal is a relatively reactive element. Its alloys, however, contain aluminum and small quantities of other metals to impart both strength and corrosion resistance. Increasing quantities of magnesium alloy are used to make automobile and aircraft parts, as well as consumer materials such as power-tool and lawn-mower housings (Figure 22.10). Most commercial aluminum metal contains some percentage of magnesium, which improves the hardness and corrosion resistance of the aluminum.

Magnesium metal is also used as a reducing agent in the manufacture of titanium and zirconium from their tetrachlorides. (Sodium is also used as the reducing agent in the production of titanium, as we mentioned earlier.)

$$ZrCl_4(g) + 2Mg(l) \longrightarrow Zr(s) + 2MgCl_2(s)$$

Zirconium metal is used to make containment vessels for uranium-235 fuel rods for nuclear power reactors, because of its low absorption of the neutrons needed in the nuclear fission of uranium-235.

Reactions of Magnesium Metal Once magnesium metal has been ignited, it burns vigorously in air to form the oxide.

$$2Mg(s) + O_2(g) \longrightarrow 2MgO(s)$$

The metal powder and fine wire burn readily. Burning magnesium metal gives off an intense white light; this is the white light you see in the burning of some fireworks and flares.

Figure 22.9

Magnesium and barium metals Magnesium metal turnings are in the beaker (left). Barium metal (right) is much more reactive than magnesium and must be stored in a bottle of kerosene to exclude moisture and oxygen, with which barium reacts.

Magnesium metal is isolated from seawater by the Dow process, which is described in Section 13.2.

Removed due to copyright permissions restrictions.

Figure 22.10

Magnesium in motorcycles Magnesium alloys are used in many motorcycle parts. Shown here is a closeup of the engine area of a Harley-Davidson motorcycle. The V engine (upper right), engine block (lower right), and transmission case (lower left) are made of an aluminum–magnesium alloy.

Magnesium also burns in carbon dioxide, producing magnesium oxide and soot, or carbon (Figure 22.11).

$$2Mg(s) + CO_2(g) \longrightarrow 2MgO(s) + C(s)$$

Many fire extinguishers contain carbon dioxide, which normally smothers a fire by preventing oxygen from air getting to combustible materials. Carbon dioxide, however, cannot be used to extinguish magnesium fires; burning magnesium must be smothered with sand.

The pure metal reacts slowly with water. (Magnesium alloys are even less reactive.) Magnesium does react readily with steam, however.

$$Mg(s) + H_2O(g) \longrightarrow MgO(s) + H_2(g)$$

Magnesium Compounds   When magnesite, a magnesium carbonate mineral, is heated above 350°C, it decomposes to the oxide, a white solid:

$$MgCO_3(s) \xrightarrow{\Delta} MgO(s) + CO_2(g)$$

Careful heating at low temperature results in a powdery form of the oxide that is relatively reactive. It reacts slowly with water to produce magnesium hydroxide but reacts readily with acids to yield the corresponding salts:

$$MgO(s) + H_2O(l) \longrightarrow Mg(OH)_2(s)$$
$$MgO(s) + 2HCl(aq) \longrightarrow MgCl_2(aq) + H_2O(l)$$

Large quantities of magnesium oxide are used in animal feed supplements, because magnesium ion is an important nutrient for animals. (The ion is also important for human nutrition.) Firebricks are produced by strongly heating magnesite (to about 1400°C) to give a hard, relatively inert form of magnesium oxide. Magnesium oxide is quite stable at high temperatures and is a good thermal insulator.

Magnesium hydroxide is only slightly soluble in water. (The solubility product, K_{sp}, is 1.8×10^{-11}.) A suspension of the white compound in water is called *milk of magnesia* (Figure 22.12). This suspension has a pH of about 10, which means the solution is mildly basic. Milk of magnesia is sold as an antacid, because the magnesium hydroxide reacts to neutralize excess hydrochloric acid in the stomach. Table 22.4 gives a summary list of the uses of compounds of magnesium and other Group IIA elements.

Figure 22.11

Reaction of magnesium and carbon dioxide
When a glowing ribbon of magnesium metal is thrust into a beaker of carbon dioxide (from the sublimation of the dry ice at the bottom of the beaker), the metal bursts into a bright flame, producing a smoke of magnesium oxide and carbon.

CONCEPT CHECK 22.1 As discussed in the text, Zr is used as cladding for nuclear fuel rods in power plants. Why wouldn't you want to use a fuel rod cladding material that absorbs neutrons?

Calcium

Calcium is a common element. It is present in the earth's crust as silicates, which weather to give free calcium ion, Ca^{2+}. The ion is about as abundant in seawater as magnesium ion. Calcium ion is an important nutrient for living organisms. As noted in the preceding section, seashells are principally calcium carbonate. Corals are marine organisms that grow in colonies; their calcium carbonate skeletons eventually form enormous coral reefs in warm waters. The Bahamas and the Florida Keys originated as coral reefs. Deposits of limestone (mostly $CaCO_3$) formed in earlier times as sediments of seashells and coral and by the direct precipitation of calcium carbonate from

Figure 22.12

Milk of magnesia

Milk of magnesia is a suspension of $Mg(OH)_2$ in water. It is used as an antacid and a laxative.

Table 22.4

Uses of Alkaline Earth Compounds

Compound	Use
MgO	Refractory bricks (for furnaces)
	Animal feeds
$Mg(OH)_2$	Source of magnesium for the metal and compounds
	Milk of magnesia (antacid and laxative)
$MgSO_4 \cdot 7H_2O$	Fertilizer
	Medicinal uses (laxative and analgesic)
	Mordant (used in dyeing fabrics)
CaO and $Ca(OH)_2$	Manufacture of steel
	Neutralizer for chemical processing
	Water treatment
	Mortar
	Stack-gas scrubber (to remove H_2S and SO_2)
$CaCO_3$	Paper coating and filter
	Antacids, dentifrices
$CaSO_4$	Plaster, wallboard
	Portland cement
$Ca(H_2PO_4)_2$	Soluble phosphate fertilizer
$BaSO_4$	Oil-well drilling mud
	Gastrointestinal x-ray photography
	Paint pigment

seawater. Gypsum, $CaSO_4 \cdot 2H_2O$, is another important mineral of calcium; deposits originated from evaporation of inland lakes and seas.

Calcium Metallurgy Most calcium metal is obtained by the reduction of calcium oxide with aluminum. Calcium metal is used mainly in some alloys. For example, the addition of a small quantity of calcium to the lead used for the electrodes of lead storage batteries substantially reduces the decomposition of water into its elements during the recharging of the battery. Since gases are not produced during recharging, the battery can be sealed so it requires less maintenance.

Reactions of Calcium Metal Calcium is a soft, reactive metal. It reacts with water, like the alkali metals do, to produce the metal hydroxide and hydrogen; the reaction, however, is much less vigorous.

$$Ca(s) + 2H_2O(l) \longrightarrow Ca(OH)_2(aq) + H_2(g)$$

Calcium burns in air to produce the oxide, CaO, and with chlorine to produce calcium chloride. Calcium also reacts directly with hydrogen to give the hydride. Calcium hydride, CaH_2, is a convenient source of hydrogen, because it reacts easily with water to yield H_2.

$$CaH_2(s) + 2H_2O(l) \longrightarrow Ca(OH)_2(aq) + 2H_2(g)$$

Figure 22.13

Raising the pH of a lake with ground limestone
A specially designed barge applies a slurry of finely ground limestone ($CaCO_3$) to a lake to neutralize its acidity, caused by acid-rain pollution. Acid rain results from the burning of sulfur-containing materials (coal and sulfide ores) and from nitrogen oxide pollution from automobiles.

Calcium Compounds   Calcium compounds are extremely important commercially (see Table 22.4). Enormous quantities of them are used in metallurgy, in building materials, in the making of glass and paper, and in other products. Limestone ($CaCO_3$), dolomite ($CaCO_3 \cdot MgCO_3$), anhydrite ($CaSO_4$), and gypsum ($CaSO_4 \cdot 2H_2O$) are all important sources of calcium compounds. An interesting use of ground limestone is shown in Figure 22.13; this application depends on the basic character of the carbonate ion. The mineral gypsum, $CaSO_4 \cdot 2H_2O$, forms plaster of Paris, $CaSO_4 \cdot \frac{1}{2}H_2O$, when heated to 100°C. Plaster of Paris is used to make wallboard.

   Calcium oxide, CaO, is among the top ten industrial chemicals. It is prepared by calcining calcium carbonate. Limestone and seashells are all possible starting materials.

$$CaCO_3(s) \xrightarrow[900°C]{\Delta} CaO(s) + CO_2(g)$$

Calcium oxide is known commercially as *quicklime*, or simply *lime*. Much of the calcium oxide produced is used in the manufacture of iron from its ores. Iron is obtained by reducing iron ore (containing iron oxides with silicate impurities) in a blast furnace. A charge of iron ore, carbon, and calcium oxide is added at the top of the furnace, and a stream of compressed air flows in from the bottom. The purpose of calcium oxide is to combine with silicon dioxide (sand) and silicate impurities in the iron ore to produce a glassy material (called *slag*). The slag is molten at the temperatures of the blast furnace, and it flows to the bottom of the furnace and is withdrawn. The essential reaction is that between a basic oxide (calcium oxide) and an acidic oxide (silicon dioxide). ◄

Iron metallurgy is discussed in Section 13.2.

$$\underset{\substack{\text{basic} \\ \text{oxide}}}{CaO(s)} + \underset{\substack{\text{acidic} \\ \text{oxide}}}{SiO_2(s)} \longrightarrow \underset{\substack{\text{calcium silicate} \\ \text{slag}}}{CaSiO_3(l)}$$

   Calcium oxide reacts exothermically with water to produce calcium hydroxide. The considerable heat released is apparent when you add a few drops of water to a pile of calcium oxide powder; there is a hiss, and puffs of steam rise from the mixture.

$$CaO(s) + H_2O(l) \longrightarrow Ca(OH)_2(s); \ \Delta H° = -65.7 \ \text{kJ}$$

Commercially, calcium hydroxide is referred to as *slaked lime*. Calcium hydroxide is a strong base, and many of its uses depend on this fact. For example, hydrochloric

Figure 22.14

Some antacids contain calcium carbonate
These antacid preparations consist of purified calcium carbonate with flavorings and a binder. Such antacids are sometimes prescribed as a nutrient calcium supplement.

Mortar was used by the ancient Romans for buildings and roads.

A brief discussion of hard water and water softening appears in the essay on water at the end of Chapter 11.

and sulfuric acids are used to remove rust from steel products. After the steel has been cleaned this way, calcium hydroxide is used to neutralize the excess acid.

Calcium hydroxide solutions react with gaseous carbon dioxide (the acid oxide of carbonic acid) to give a white, milky precipitate of calcium carbonate.

$$Ca(OH)_2(aq) + CO_2(g) \longrightarrow CaCO_3(s) + H_2O(l)$$

This reaction, with its formation of a milky precipitate, is the basis of a simple test for carbon dioxide. Commercially, the reaction is important as a method of preparing precipitated calcium carbonate, a pure form of the finely divided compound. An important use of precipitated calcium carbonate is as a filler for paper. (The purpose of a filler is to improve the paper's characteristics, such as brightness and inking ability.) Precipitated calcium carbonate is also used in toothpowders, antacids, and nutritional supplements (Figure 22.14).

Bricklaying mortar is made by mixing slaked lime, $Ca(OH)_2$, with sand and water. The mortar hardens as the mixture dries and calcium hydroxide crystallizes. Over time, however, the mortar sets to a harder solid as calcium hydroxide reacts with carbon dioxide in the air to form calcium carbonate crystals that intertwine with the sand particles. ◄

$$Ca(OH)_2(s) + CO_2(g) \longrightarrow CaCO_3(s) + H_2O(l)$$

Large amounts of quicklime, CaO, and slaked lime, $Ca(OH)_2$, are used to *soften* municipal water supplies. This may seem paradoxical at first, because the process of "softening" water refers to the removal of certain metal ions, particularly calcium ions, from the water. Water that is "hard" contains these metal ions. When soap, which is a sodium salt of a fatty acid, is added to hard water, a curdy precipitate of the calcium salt of the fatty acid forms. (When this precipitate adheres to the tub, it is called bathtub ring.) The calcium ion in hard water results when water containing carbon dioxide from air (and from rotting leaves and other organic matter) passes through limestone ($CaCO_3$). The calcium carbonate dissolves in this water to produce soluble calcium hydrogen carbonate. ◄

$$CaCO_3(s) + H_2O(l) + CO_2(g) \longrightarrow Ca^{2+}(aq) + 2HCO_3^-(aq)$$
limestone   calcium hydrogen carbonate

Figure 22.15 illustrates the dissolution of calcium carbonate by carbon dioxide. The apparent paradox is solved when we observe that the addition of a stoichiometric

Figure 22.15

Reaction of carbon dioxide with calcium hydroxide solution
Left: Calcium hydroxide solution with bromthymol-blue indicator. *Center:* Carbon dioxide from dry ice reacts with calcium ion to precipitate calcium carbonate. *Right:* In an excess of carbon dioxide, the calcium carbonate dissolves to form a solution of calcium ion and hydrogen carbonate ion, HCO_3^-. In this acidic solution, bromthymol blue changes to a yellow color.

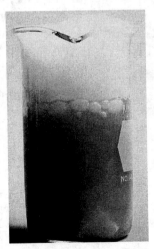
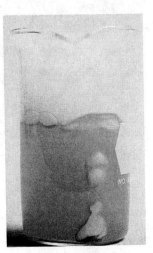

amount of calcium hydroxide to hard water containing calcium hydrogen carbonate can precipitate all of the calcium ions as calcium carbonate.

$$Ca^{2+}(aq) + 2HCO_3{}^-(aq) + Ca(OH)_2(aq) \longrightarrow 2CaCO_3(s) + 2H_2O(l)$$

22.4   Group IIIA and Group IVA Metals

The Group IIIA elements clearly show the trend of increasing metallic character in going down any column of elements in the periodic table. Boron, at the top of Group IIIA, is a metalloid, and its chemistry is typical of a nonmetal. The compound $B(OH)_3$ is actually acidic (boric acid). The rest of the elements (aluminum, gallium, indium, and thallium) are metals, but their hydroxides change from amphoteric (acidic and basic) for aluminum and gallium to basic for indium and thallium.

Bonding to boron is covalent; the atom shares its $2s^2 2p^1$ valence electrons to give the $+3$ oxidation state. Although aluminum has many covalent compounds, it also has definitely ionic ones, such as AlF_3. The cation $Al^{3+}(aq)$ is present in aqueous solutions of aluminum salts. Gallium, indium, and thallium also have ionic compounds and give cations in aqueous solution. The $+3$ oxidation state is the only important one for aluminum, but some $+1$ compounds are known for gallium and indium, and in the case of thallium, both $+1$ and $+3$ states are important.

The Group IVA elements also show the trend of greater metallic character in going down the column of elements. The last two elements of the column, tin and lead, are well-known metals, and we will discuss them in this section. Tin and lead, in their compounds, exist in the $+2$ and $+4$ oxidation states. In tin, both oxidation states are common. In most lead compounds, lead is in the $+2$ oxidation state. Lead(IV) compounds, such as PbO_2, are strong oxidizing agents, indicating their tendency to revert to lead(II).

Aluminum

Aluminum is the third most abundant element in the earth's crust (after oxygen and silicon). It occurs primarily in aluminosilicate minerals. The weathering of these rocks results in aluminum-containing clays, which are an essential part of most soils. Further weathering of clay yields bauxite, the principal ore of aluminum, which contains aluminum hydroxide, $Al(OH)_3$, and aluminum oxide hydroxide, $AlO(OH)$. Deposits of bauxite occur throughout the world but are particularly common in tropical and subtropical regions. Corundum is a hard mineral of aluminum oxide, Al_2O_3. The pure oxide is colorless, but the presence of impurities can give various colors to it. Sapphire (usually blue) and ruby (deep red) are gem-quality corundum (Figure 22.16).

Aluminum Metallurgy   We discussed the details of aluminum metallurgy in Section 13.2. Bauxite, the ore of aluminum, is treated chemically in the Bayer process to obtain aluminum hydroxide, which when calcined yields aluminum oxide, Al_2O_3 (referred to commercially as *alumina*). Aluminum metal is obtained by electrolysis of aluminum oxide dissolved in fused cryolite, Na_3AlF_6.

Aluminum is the most important commercial metal after iron. Despite the fact that pure aluminum is soft and chemically reactive, the addition of a small quantity of other metals, such as copper and magnesium, yields hard, corrosion-resistant alloys. The corrosion resistance of these alloys, together with their relatively low densities, allows their use in structural applications and for containers and packaging (Figure 22.17).

Figure 22.16

Gem-quality corundum
This is the Logan sapphire, on exhibit at the Smithsonian Institution in Washington, D.C. It is the largest sapphire on public display in the United States.

Figure 22.17

Aluminum products
Common items made from aluminum metal.

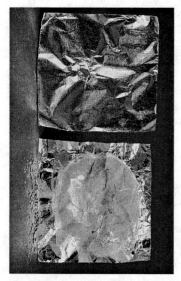

Figure 22.18

Protective oxide coating on aluminum
In air, aluminum metal forms an adherent coating of aluminum oxide that protects the metal from further oxidation. Note the shiny surface of the foil (*top*). When a similar sheet of aluminum (*bottom*) is coated with mercury, however, needle-like crystals of aluminum oxide form at the aluminum–mercury surface. Instead of adhering to the metal, the aluminum oxide flakes away from the metal, and the aluminum continuously oxidizes in air.

The ruby laser is described in the essay at the end of Section 7.3.

Aluminum is also a very good conductor of electricity. Because of this property and its low density, aluminum is used to make electrical transmission wire.

Reactions of Aluminum Metal Aluminum is a chemically reactive metal, although much less reactive than the alkali metals and alkaline earth metals. It does not react at an appreciable rate with water at room temperature. In air, aluminum metal reacts readily with oxygen, but the aluminum oxide that forms gives an adherent coat, which protects the underlying metal from further reaction. (The metal will burn vigorously once started, however.) Thus, unlike iron, which is chemically less reactive than aluminum but corrodes quickly in a moist environment, aluminum is corrosion resistant. The demonstration depicted in Figure 22.18 shows that aluminum does corrode quickly in air in the absence of an oxide coating. That aluminum metal does not normally corrode, or rust, makes the metal extremely useful in many practical applications. However, this property is also the source of an environmental problem. Tin cans (nowadays mostly steel) disintegrate quickly in the environment through rusting, but aluminum cans remain intact for decades. The solution to this problem is to recycle aluminum cans, which also saves on the energy otherwise required in the electrolytic production of the metal.

Aluminum metal is also used to produce other metals. The **Goldschmidt process** is *a method of preparing a metal by reduction of its oxide with powdered aluminum.* Chromium metal is obtained this way; the reaction is highly exothermic, because of the large negative heat of formation of Al_2O_3:

$$Cr_2O_3(s) + 2Al(s) \longrightarrow Al_2O_3(l) + 2Cr(l); \Delta H° = -536 \text{ kJ}$$

A similar reaction with a mixture of iron(III) oxide and aluminum powder (called *thermite*) produces iron for certain kinds of welding. Once the thermite powder is ignited, the reaction is self-sustaining and gives a spectacular incandescent shower. The reaction is also the basis of certain kinds of incendiary bombs.

Aluminum Compounds The most important compound of aluminum is aluminum oxide, Al_2O_3, or alumina. It is prepared by heating aluminum hydroxide, obtained from bauxite, at low temperature (550°C). Alumina is a white powder or porous solid. Although most alumina is used to make aluminum metal, large quantities are used for other purposes. For example, alumina is used as a carrier, or support, for many of the heterogeneous catalysts required in chemical processes, including those used in the production of gasoline (Figure 22.19).

When aluminum oxide is fused (melted) at high temperature (2045°C), it forms corundum, one of the hardest materials known. Corundum is used as an abrasive for grinding tools. When aluminum oxide is fused with small quantities of other metal oxides, synthetic sapphires and rubies are obtained. Synthetic ruby, for example, contains about 2.5% chromium oxide, Cr_2O_3. Ruby is used in fine instrument bearings ("jewel" bearings) and to make lasers. ◄

Aluminum oxide is used in the manufacture of industrial ceramics. Industrial ceramics are materials made by high-temperature firing (heating) of minerals or inorganic substances. (The term *ceramics* derives from the Greek word *kerimikos*, which means "of pottery," referring to objects made by firing clay.) Ceramics made from aluminum oxide are used to line metallurgical furnaces, and the white ceramic material in automobile spark plugs is made from aluminum oxide. Ceramic fibers composed of aluminum oxide with other metal oxides have been developed for special applications, including ceramic-fiber-reinforced aluminum.

Aluminum sulfate octadecahydrate, $Al_2(SO_4)_3 \cdot 18H_2O$, is the most common soluble salt of aluminum. It is prepared by dissolving bauxite in sulfuric acid. The salt

Figure 22.19

Heterogeneous catalysts
Many heterogeneous catalysts use aluminum oxide as a carrier, or support.

> Coagulation of colloids by multiply charged ions is discussed in Section 12.9.

is acidic in aqueous solution. In water, aluminum ion forms a strong hydration complex, $Al(H_2O)_6^{3+}$, and this ion in turn hydrolyzes.

$$Al(H_2O)_6^{3+}(aq) + H_2O(l) \rightleftharpoons Al(H_2O)_5OH^{2+}(aq) + H_3O^+(aq)$$

Large quantities of aluminum sulfate are used in the paper industry. Printing papers require the addition of various materials, such as clay and rosin (a tree resin), to improve the capacity of the paper to hold ink without spreading. Colloidal suspensions (suspensions of extremely fine particles) of clay and rosin in water are coagulated, or aggregated, onto the paper fibers with aluminum sulfate. The aluminum ion does make the papers acidic, however, so paper made by this process deteriorates over time (Figure 22.20).

Aluminum sulfate is also used to treat the wastewater obtained from the process of making paper pulp, a water slurry of fibers obtained from wood. Aluminum sulfate and a base, such as calcium hydroxide, are added to the wastewater, and a gelatinous precipitate of aluminum hydroxide forms.

$$Al^{3+}(aq) + 3OH^-(aq) \longrightarrow Al(OH)_3(s)$$

Colloidal particles of clay and other substances adhere to the precipitate, which is then filtered from the water. The same procedure is one of the steps in the purification of municipal water supplies. The process removes colloidal particles of clay and some bacteria.

Aluminum hydroxide is amphoteric. With acids, aluminum hydroxide acts as a base, as most metal hydroxides do. The reaction is simply a neutralization.

$$Al(OH)_3(s) + 3H_3O^+(aq) \longrightarrow Al^{3+}(aq) + 6H_2O(l)$$

With bases, aluminum hydroxide forms a hydroxo ion (tetrahydroxoaluminate ion, often simply called the aluminate ion). The acidic behavior of the hydroxide is expected of a nonmetal hydroxide.

$$Al(OH)_3(s) + OH^-(aq) \longrightarrow Al(OH)_4^-(aq)$$

The amphoteric character of aluminum hydroxide is a reflection of the partial non-metallic character of aluminum. Table 22.5 lists the major uses of aluminum compounds.

Removed due to copyright permissions restrictions.

Figure 22.20

Deterioration of paper in books
Aluminum sulfate and similar acidic compounds mixed with materials such as clay and rosin are added to paper to improve its printing characteristics. However, the acids decompose the cellulose fibers in paper, causing the paper to deteriorate over time. The Library of Congress estimates that 25% of its collection is brittle from such deteriorating paper. Calcium carbonate, a basic substance, has been suggested as an alternative in preparing paper.

Table 22.5

Uses of Aluminum Compounds

Compound	Use
Al_2O_3	Source of aluminum and its compounds
	Abrasive
	Refractory bricks and furnace linings
	Synthetic sapphires and rubies
$Al_2(SO_4)_3 \cdot 18H_2O$	Making of paper
	Water purification
$AlCl_3$	Preparation of aluminum
	Catalyst in organic reactions
$AlCl_3 \cdot 6H_2O$	Antiperspirant

Tin and Lead

Figure 22.21

Allotropes of tin

A bar of metallic tin (white tin) was cooled to $-45°C$ in a solution of tin(IV) ion catalyst. After several hours, an area of gray tin formed on the bar, then grew rapidly until the bar broke apart.

Tin and lead were both known in ancient times. The Egyptians used lead coins and made lead sculptures perhaps as early as 5000 B.C. The use of tin in the form of bronze, an alloy of copper and tin, dates from about 3500 B.C.

Tin is a relatively rare element (ranking 50th or so in abundance in the earth's crust). However, the element occurs in localized deposits of the tin ore cassiterite (SnO_2), so the metal is much more common than you might expect from its abundance in the earth's crust. Lead is more abundant than tin. Its most important ore is galena, a lead(II) sulfide mineral (PbS). Galena is a common mineral and often occurs in association with other important metallic elements, such as silver.

As noted earlier, metallic character increases in moving down a group of elements. Tin, which is between the metalloid germanium and the metal lead in Group IVA, illustrates this periodic trend in a very interesting way: it has two different forms, or allotropes; one is a metal and the other is a nonmetal.

The nonmetallic form of tin, called *gray tin*, is a brittle, gray powder. The metallic form of tin is called *white tin*. White tin is stable above 13°C, but at lower temperatures white tin slowly undergoes a transition to gray tin.

$$\text{White tin} \overset{13°C}{\rightleftharpoons} \text{gray tin}$$

The transition from white tin to gray tin becomes more rapid if the temperature is much lower than 13°C. During a cold winter in the 1850s, the tin pipes of some church organs in Russia and other parts of Europe began crumbling from what was described then as "tin disease." Tin disease, as we now know, is simply the transition from white to gray tin (Figure 22.21).

Metallurgy of Tin and Lead   Tin metal is obtained from cassiterite. Purified tin(IV) oxide, SnO_2, from tin ore is reduced to the metal by heating with carbon in a furnace.

$$SnO_2(s) + 2C(s) \overset{\Delta}{\longrightarrow} Sn(l) + 2CO(g)$$

Lead metal is obtained from ores containing galena. The ore is first concentrated in the lead(II) sulfide mineral using flotation. The concentrated ore is then roasted; that is, the sulfide ore is burned in air to yield lead(II) oxide.

$$2PbS(s) + 3O_2(g) \longrightarrow 2PbO(s) + 2SO_2(g)$$

The fused mass from the roasting is broken up, mixed with coke (carbon), and fed into a blast furnace. Here the lead(II) oxide is reduced with carbon monoxide produced in the blast furnace by partial oxidation of the carbon.

$$PbO(s) + CO(g) \longrightarrow Pb(l) + CO_2(g)$$

Figure 22.22

Tin alloys

Shown here are solder (and a soldering iron) and bronze.

❙ Lead storage batteries are discussed in Section 20.8.

Tin is used to make tin plate, which is steel (iron alloy) sheeting with a thin coating of tin. Tin plate is used for food containers ("tin cans"). The tin coating protects the iron from reaction with air and food acids. Tin is also used to make a number of alloys. Solder is a low-melting alloy of tin and lead; bronze is an alloy of copper and tin (Figure 22.22).

More than half of the lead produced is used to make electrodes for lead storage batteries. ◀ The manufacture of military and sporting ammunition also consumes a significant fraction of the lead produced. Because lead resists attack from many corrosive substances, the metal is also used to make chemical plant equipment.

Table 22.6	
Uses of Tin and Lead Compounds	
Compound	**Use**
SnO_2	Manufacture of tin compounds
	Glazes and enamels
$SnCl_2$	Reducing agent in preparing organic compounds
PbO	Lead storage batteries
	Lead glass
PbO_2	Cathode in lead storage batteries
Pb_3O_4	Pigment for painting structural steel

Reactions of Tin and Lead Metals Tin and lead are much less reactive than the metals of Groups IA, IIA, and IIIA. Whereas aluminum reacts vigorously with dilute hydrochloric and sulfuric acids, tin reacts only slowly with these acids. Tin reacts more rapidly with the concentrated acids. The products are tin(II) ion and hydrogen:

$$Sn(s) + 2HCl(aq) \longrightarrow SnCl_2(aq) + H_2(g)$$

$$Sn(s) + H_2SO_4(aq) \longrightarrow SnSO_4(aq) + H_2(g)$$

Lead metal reacts with these acids, but the products $PbCl_2$ and $PbSO_4$ are insoluble and adhere to the metal. As a result, the reaction soon stops.

$$Pb(s) + 2HCl(aq) \longrightarrow PbCl_2(s) + H_2(g)$$

$$Pb(s) + H_2SO_4(aq) \longrightarrow PbSO_4(s) + H_2(g)$$

Tin and Lead Compounds Tin(II) chloride, $SnCl_2$, is used as a reducing agent in the preparation of dyes and other organic compounds. In reactions where tin(II) ion acts as a reducing agent, tin(II) ion oxidizes to tin(IV) species. Tin(II) compounds are commonly referred to as *stannous compounds,* using an older naming system. Thus, tin(II) chloride is commonly called stannous chloride. Tin also has a number of tin(IV), or stannic, compounds. Tin(IV) oxide, SnO_2, is, as we have seen, the chemical substance in the mineral cassiterite. Tin(IV) chloride, $SnCl_4$, is a liquid; it freezes at $-33°C$. (These properties indicate that the substance is molecular, rather than ionic.)

Lead also exists in compounds in the $+2$ and $+4$ oxidation states, although lead(II) compounds are the more common. The starting compound for preparing most lead compounds is lead(II) oxide, PbO. This is a reddish-yellow solid, commercially called *litharge.* Lead(II) oxide is prepared by exposing molten lead to air. Lead(IV) oxide, PbO_2, is a dark brown or black powder; it forms the cathode of lead storage batteries. The cathode is made by packing a paste of lead(II) oxide (litharge) into a lead metal grid. When the battery is charged, the lead(II) oxide is oxidized to lead(IV) oxide. Table 22.6 gives a summary list of the uses of tin and lead compounds.

Chemistry of the Nonmetals

The nonmetals are elements that do not exhibit the characteristics of a metal. Nearly half of them are colorless gases; and until the eighteenth century, gases were referred to as "airs" and were not well differentiated. In contrast, the special characteristics of

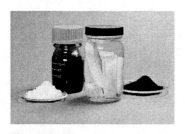

Figure 22.23

Some nonmetals
Left to right: Sulfur, bromine, white phosphorus, and carbon.

metals held special fascination for early humans—only fire was more fascinating. And of the two nonmetals known to the ancients, carbon and sulfur, both are associated with fire.

Carbon was known in the form of charcoal and lampblack, or soot, which are products of fire. Charcoal may have been so common that it was hardly noticed at first, until its role in the reduction of metal ores was discovered. Lampblack was used by the ancient Egyptians to produce ink for writing on papyrus.

Free sulfur was less widely available than carbon, although it was probably well known because of its ready occurrence in volcanic areas. No doubt its yellow color made it stand out among other rocks. That sulfur also burned with a beautiful blue flame made it especially distinctive. The old English name of sulfur was *brimstone*, which means "a stone that burns." This term survives today in the expression "fire and brimstone."

These two nonmetals have rather distinctive physical characteristics, as do some of the nonmetals discovered later. For example, white phosphorus is a waxy, white solid; bromine is a reddish-brown liquid; chlorine is a greenish-yellow gas. Some nonmetallic elements are shown in Figure 22.23.

In the remainder of this chapter, we look at the chemistry of the nonmetals. Some questions we will address are these: What are the chemical and physical properties of the more important nonmetallic elements? What are some of the commercial uses of these substances and their compounds?

22.5 Hydrogen

Hydrogen is the most abundant element in the universe, comprising nearly 90% of all atoms and is the third most abundant element on the surface of the earth. (Oxygen and silicon are the most abundant.) Most stars, including our sun, consist primarily of hydrogen. The hydrogen in our sun is the fuel for the fusion reactions that produce the life-sustaining energy that reaches our planet. On earth, the majority of hydrogen is found in oceans combined with oxygen as water. Hydrogen occurs in a variety of compounds that you have had the opportunity to study as a part of your general chemistry course. These include the organic compounds (Chapter 24), biologically important compounds (Chapter 25), and acids and bases (Chapters 4 and 15).

Properties and Preparation of Hydrogen

Hydrogen was first isolated and identified by Henry Cavendish in 1766. His experiments consisted of reacting iron, zinc, and tin with several different binary acids. For example, $H_2(g)$ can easily be produced on a small scale according to the reaction

$$2HCl(g) + Zn(s) \longrightarrow ZnCl_2(aq) + H_2(g)$$

Hydrogen is a colorless, odorless gas that is less dense than air. Even though hydrogen is often placed in Group IA of the periodic table, aside from its valence electron configuration, it has little in common with the alkali metals that make up the rest of Group IA. It is much less likely to form a cation than any of the alkali metals, with a first ionization energy of 1312 kJ/mol versus 520 kJ/mol for lithium. Because of this, hydrogen generally combines with nonmetallic elements to form covalent compounds such as CH_4, H_2S, and PH_3.

There are three isotopes of hydrogen: *protium*, ^1_1H or H, which is the most abundant; *deuterium*, ^2_1H or D; and *tritium*, ^3_1H or T. All three isotopes are naturally occurring; however, only 0.0156% is D and a trace is T. Because an atom of D has about twice the mass of protium, compounds that contain deuterium often have different properties than those that contain only protium. For example, the normal boiling point of D_2O is 101.42°C versus 100.00°C for H_2O. Tritium is hydrogen produced naturally in the upper atmosphere by nuclear reactions that are induced by cosmic rays or in a nuclear reactor by bombarding lithium-6 with neutrons:

$$^6_3Li + ^1_0n \longrightarrow ^3_1H + ^4_2He$$

Tritium is radioactive with a half-life of 12.3 years, hence very little of what is naturally produced in the upper atmosphere reaches the surface of the earth.

The isotopes of hydrogen find many applications. They are used as markers or labels that can be followed during chemical reactions. For example, if a chemist were interested in determining if hydrogen atoms move between water molecules, he could make a solution that contains DOD and HOH. If hydrogen atom transfer takes place (which is the case in this example), then the solution, after a period of time, would be expected to contain DOD, HOH, and the new compound DOH. Information about the exchange rate of H with D can also be obtained from the experiment by measuring the rate at which the DOH forms. Because so many compounds contain hydrogen, the hydrogen isotopes are widely used in this manner.

The elemental form of hydrogen is a diatomic molecule having a bond dissociation energy of 432 kJ/mol. This is a large value when compared to chlorine at 240 kJ/mol. This relatively high bond dissociation energy indicates why hydrogen is less reactive than its halogen counterparts. However, with the addition of heat or light, or in the presence of a suitable catalyst, hydrogen can be induced to react.

Hydrogen is currently produced on a massive industrial scale, with an annual U.S. production on the order of 10^{10} m^3. Approximately 40% of this production is used to manufacture ammonia via the following chemical reaction with nitrogen at high temperature and pressure:

$$N_2(g) + 3H_2(g) \longrightarrow 2NH_3(g)$$

The hydrogen for this reaction is generally prepared using the **steam-reforming process** *where steam and hydrocarbons from natural gas or petroleum react at high temperature and pressure in the presence of a catalyst to form carbon monoxide and hydrogen.* For example:

$$C_3H_8(g) + 3H_2O(g) \xrightarrow[\Delta]{Ni} 3CO(g) + 7H_2(g)$$

Another viable route for hydrogen production is the *water–gas reaction,* which is no longer used commercially but may become important in the future as natural gas and petroleum become more expensive and scarce. In this reaction, steam is passed over red-hot coke or coal.

$$C(s) + H_2O(g) \longrightarrow CO(g) + H_2(g)$$

Both of these reactions produce a mixture of hydrogen and carbon monoxide. Such mixtures are used to produce various organic compounds, but to obtain pure hydrogen the carbon monoxide must be removed. First the carbon monoxide is reacted with steam in the presence of a catalyst to give carbon dioxide and more hydrogen.

$$CO(g) + H_2O(g) \xrightarrow[\Delta]{catalyst} CO_2(g) + H_2(g)$$

The carbon dioxide is then removed by passing the mixture of gases through a basic aqueous solution.

Hydrogen can also be produced via the electrolysis of water. Water that contains a small amount of an acid can undergo the following reaction with an $E°_{cell} = -1.23$ V.

$$2H_2O(l) \longrightarrow 2H_2(g) + O_2(g)$$

Due to the cost of electricity, this reaction is not economically feasible when more than a very small amount of hydrogen is required. However, electrolysis does become economically viable on an industrial scale when the hydrogen is produced as a by-product of the electrolysis of concentrated aqueous NaCl solutions during the production of NaOH and chlorine. ◄

See Section 20.10 for a discussion of the electrolysis of sodium chloride solutions.

Hydrogen Reactions and Compounds

In addition to the preparation of ammonia, the other major use of hydrogen is in the petrochemical industry. In many cases the reaction is one where hydrogen is added to hydrocarbon compounds containing carbon–carbon double bonds to produce compounds that contain carbon–carbon single bonds. For example, 1-butene can be reacted with hydrogen using a platinum or palladium catalyst to produce butane.

$$CH_3CH_2CH{=}CH_2 + H_2 \xrightarrow{\text{Pt}} CH_3CH_2CH_2CH_3$$

This process, called *hydrogenation,* is used in the food processing industry where oils (liquids) that contain many carbon–carbon double bonds are converted to fats (solids) that contain few or no carbon–carbon double bonds. Another important process that requires hydrogen is the cobalt-catalyzed *synthesis gas* reaction with carbon monoxide to produce methyl alcohol.

$$CO(g) + 2H_2(g) \xrightarrow{\text{cobalt catalyst}} CH_3OH(g)$$

Hydrogen is also used to reduce metal oxides to extract pure metals. For example, molybdenum and tungsten oxides can be reduced at high temperatures via the reaction

$$MO_3(s) + 3H_2(g) \longrightarrow M(s) + 3H_2O(g)$$

Industrial processes are emerging that allow this reaction to be used for iron oxides as well.

When hydrogen combines with another element it forms a **binary hydride**—that is, *a compound that contains hydrogen and one other element.* There are three categories of binary hydrides: ionic hydrides, covalent hydrides, and metallic hydrides.

Ionic hydrides, which contain the hydride ion, H^-, can be directly formed via the reaction of an alkali metal or the larger Group IIA metals (Ca, Sr, and Ba) with hydrogen gas near 400°C.

$$2Li(s) + H_2(g) \longrightarrow 2LiH(s)$$
$$Ba(s) + H_2(g) \longrightarrow BaH_2(s)$$

These hydrides are white crystalline compounds in which the H atoms have an oxidation state of -1. Ionic hydrides can undergo an oxidation–reduction reaction with water to produce hydrogen and a basic solution. For example:

$$LiH(s) + H_2O(l) \longrightarrow H_2(g) + LiOH(aq)$$

Because of this, hydrides can be used as a source of hydrogen gas where transportation of $H_2(g)$ is impractical, such as for inflating weather balloons. Ionic hydrides are also used as reducing agents (a source of electrons) during chemical reactions.

Figure 22.24

A liquid-hydrogen storage tank
Liquid hydrogen is used as a rocket fuel.

Covalent hydrides are molecular compounds in which hydrogen is covalently bonded to another element. Examples of these compounds are NH_3, H_2O, H_2O_2, and HF. Some of these compounds often can be formed from the direct reaction of the elements. If the nonmetal reacting with hydrogen is reactive, the reaction will readily occur without the need for elevated temperatures or a catalyst:

$$F_2(g) + H_2(g) \longrightarrow 2HF(g)$$

The reaction of hydrogen with oxygen to form water is an example of a reaction that requires the input of energy to get started; however, once it does, the reaction is rapid and exothermic.

$$2H_2(g) + O_2(g) \longrightarrow 2H_2O(g) \qquad \Delta H = -484 \text{ kJ}$$

Because it is such an exothermic reaction and the product is a gas, it is an ideal rocket fuel (Figure 22.24).

The combustion of hydrogen produces more heat per gram than any other fuel (120 kJ/g). Unlike hydrocarbons, it is a "clean fuel" because the product (water) is environmentally benign. These features, in the face of a dwindling supply of hydrocarbons, indicate that hydrogen gas may become the favorite fuel of the twenty-first century.

Metallic hydrides are compounds containing a transition metal and hydrogen. Generally, the formula of these compounds is MH_x, where x is often not an integer. These compounds contain hydrogen atoms that are spread throughout a metal crystal occupying the holes in the crystal lattice. Often, hydrogen atoms enter the holes in nonstoichiometric amounts. The result is that the composition of the metallic hydride is variable. For example, under one pressure of H_2 the composition of the metallic hydride MH_x might be $MH_{0.4}$, whereas at a higher pressure of H_2 it might be $MH_{0.5}$. One way to think about these compounds is to consider the metal crystal to be similar to an apartment building with the lattice holes representing the individual apartments. The occupancy of an apartment building is not fixed; it is instead a function of factors like the rent, the condition of the building, and so on. Examples of these compounds are $TiH_{1.7}$ and $ZrH_{1.9}$.

22.6 Group IVA: The Carbon Family

The elements of Group IVA show in more striking fashion than the previous groups the normal periodic trend of greater metallic character going down a column. Carbon, the first element in the group, is distinctly nonmetallic. Silicon and germanium are metalloids, or semimetals, although their chemical properties are primarily those of nonmetals. Tin and lead, the last two elements in the group, are metals.

In the following subsections, we will look at carbon and silicon. Both elements have many important compounds that exhibit tetrahedral (sp^3) bonding. Carbon, however, also has many compounds that contain multiple bonds in which sp and sp^2 bonding occurs; silicon has very few such compounds. Another difference in the bonding characteristics of these elements is silicon's ability to use sp^3d^2 hybrid orbitals in octahedral bonding, which is not possible with carbon. The hexafluorosilicate ion, SiF_6^{2-}, is an example of such bonding.

Carbon

One of the most important features of the carbon atom is its ability to bond to other carbon atoms to form chains and rings of enormous variety. *The covalent bonding of two or more atoms of the same element to one another* is referred to as **catenation**.

Although other elements display catenation, none show it to the same degree as carbon. Millions of carbon compounds are known, most classified as *organic*. These can be thought of as derivatives of hydrocarbons, each consisting of a chain (or more complicated arrangement) of carbon atoms to which hydrogen atoms are bonded. In this section, we will confine ourselves to the element and its oxides and carbonates.

Allotropes of Carbon   Until recently, carbon was thought to occur in only two principal allotropic forms: diamond and graphite. Both allotropes are covalent network solids, whose structures we discussed in detail in Section 11.8. In diamond, each carbon atom is tetrahedrally (sp^3) bonded to four other carbon atoms. To move one plane of atoms in the diamond crystal relative to another requires the breaking of many strong carbon–carbon bonds. Because of this, diamond is one of the hardest substances known. As a pure substance, diamond is colorless, although natural diamond may be colored by impurities.

Graphite is a black substance having a layer structure. Each layer consists of carbon atoms bonded to three other carbon atoms to give a hexagonal pattern of carbon atoms arranged in a plane. The bonding involves sp^2 hybridization of the carbon atoms with delocalized π electrons. You can also describe the bonding in terms of resonance formulas with alternating single and double bonds. One layer of carbon atoms in graphite is held to another layer only by van der Waals forces. Because of the relative weakness of these forces, the layers in graphite easily slide over one another, resulting in a substance that is soft and slippery. Graphite, unlike diamond, is a good electrical conductor, because of the delocalized bonding within layers.

In 1985 a third allotropic form of carbon, known as buckminsterfullerene (C_{60}), was discovered. This molecular form of carbon has been studied intensively. The molecule has a stable "soccer-ball" structure, described in Chapter 13.

Carbon Black   The form of carbon known as *carbon black* is composed of extremely small crystals of carbon having an amorphous, or imperfect, graphite structure. It is produced in large quantities by burning natural gas (CH_4) or petroleum hydrocarbons in a limited supply of air so that heat "cracks" (or breaks bonds in) the hydrocarbon. Lampblack, mentioned earlier, is a form of carbon black.

$$CH_4(g) \xrightarrow{\Delta} \underset{\text{carbon black}}{C(s)} + 2H_2(g)$$

Carbon black is used in the manufacture of rubber tires (to increase wear) and as a pigment in black printing inks. Coke is an amorphous carbon obtained by heating coal in the absence of air; it is used in large quantities in the making of iron.

Oxides of Carbon   Carbon has two principal oxides: carbon monoxide, CO, and carbon dioxide, CO_2. Carbon and organic compounds burn in an excess of oxygen to give carbon dioxide, CO_2. However, an equilibrium exists among carbon, carbon monoxide, and carbon dioxide that favors carbon monoxide above 700°C.

$$CO_2(g) + C(s) \rightleftharpoons 2CO(g)$$

For this reason, carbon monoxide is almost always one of the products of combustion of carbon and organic compounds, unless an excess of oxygen is present, in which case the carbon monoxide burns to carbon dioxide.

These two oxides of carbon are quite different in their chemical and physiological properties. Carbon monoxide is a colorless, odorless gas that burns in air with a blue flame. It is a toxic gas, which poisons by attaching strongly to iron atoms in the hemoglobin of red blood cells, preventing them from carrying out their normal oxygen-carrying function. As a result, the cells of the body become starved for oxygen.

Carbon monoxide is manufactured industrially from natural gas (CH_4) and petroleum hydrocarbons, either by reaction with steam or by partial oxidation. For example,

$$CH_4(g) + H_2O(g) \xrightarrow{Ni} CO(g) + 3H_2(g)$$
$$2CH_4(g) + O_2(g) \longrightarrow 2CO(g) + 4H_2(g)$$

The product in these reactions is a mixture of carbon monoxide and hydrogen, which is called *synthesis gas.* Synthesis gas can yield any of a number of organic products depending on the reaction conditions and catalyst. Methanol (CH_3OH), for example, is produced in large quantities from synthesis gas.

$$CO(g) + 2H_2(g) \xrightarrow{catalyst} CH_3OH(l)$$

Carbon dioxide is a colorless, odorless gas with a faint acid taste. Under normal circumstances, the gas is nontoxic, although at high concentrations it interferes with respiration. Carbon dioxide does not support most combustions, which is why CO_2 fire extinguishers are used in many fire-fighting situations.

Carbon dioxide is produced whenever carbon or organic materials are burned. For example,

$$CH_4(g) + 2O_2(g) \longrightarrow CO_2(g) + 2H_2O(g)$$
$$CS_2(l) + 3O_2(g) \longrightarrow CO_2(g) + 2SO_2(g)$$
$$C_2H_5OH(l) + 3O_2(g) \longrightarrow 2CO_2(g) + 3H_2O(g)$$

Carbon dioxide is obtained commercially as a by-product in the production of ammonia (see Section 22.7) and in the calcining (strong heating) of limestone to give calcium oxide. Liquid carbon dioxide and solid carbon dioxide (dry ice) are used in large quantities as refrigerants. Carbonated beverages are made by dissolving carbon dioxide gas under pressure in an aqueous solution of sugar and flavorings. Carbonated water is acidic as the result of the formation of carbonic acid, although carbonated beverages frequently also contain fruit acids and phosphoric acid.

Carbonates   Carbon dioxide dissolves in water to form an aqueous solution of carbonic acid.

$$CO_2(g) + H_2O(l) \rightleftharpoons H_2CO_3(aq)$$

The acid is diprotic (has two acidic H atoms per molecule) and dissociates to form hydrogen carbonate ion and carbonate ion.

$$H_2CO_3(aq) + H_2O(l) \rightleftharpoons H_3O^+(aq) + HCO_3^-(aq)$$
$$HCO_3^-(aq) + H_2O(l) \rightleftharpoons H_3O^+(aq) + CO_3^{2-}(aq)$$

Carbonic acid has never been isolated from solution, but its salts, hydrogen carbonates and carbonates, are well known. When you bubble carbon dioxide gas into an aqueous solution of calcium hydroxide, a milky white precipitate of calcium carbonate forms (Figure 22.25).

$$CO_2(g) + Ca(OH)_2(aq) \longrightarrow CaCO_3(s) + H_2O(l)$$

This is a standard test for carbon dioxide. The reaction is also used to manufacture a pure calcium carbonate for antacids and other products.

Carbonate minerals are very common and many are of commercial importance. Limestone contains the mineral calcite, which is calcium carbonate, $CaCO_3$. Much of

Figure 22.25

Test for carbon dioxide
When carbon dioxide is bubbled into a solution of calcium hydroxide (limewater), a milky white precipitate of calcium carbonate forms. This is the basis of a test for carbon dioxide. The reaction is also used to manufacture pure calcium carbonate. (The needle at the right is to provide an escape for excess gas.)

Table 22.7

Uses of Some Compounds of Carbon and of Silicon

Compound	Use
CO	Fuel; reducing agent
	Synthesis of methanol, CH_3OH
CO_2	Refrigerant
	Carbonation of beverages
SiO_2	Source of silicon and its compounds
	Abrasives
	Glass
$(CH_3)_2SiCl_2$	Manufacture of silicones
	(used as lubricants, hydraulic fluids, caulking
	compounds, and medical implants)

this was formed by marine organisms, although some limestone was also formed by direct precipitation from water solution.

Table 22.7 lists uses of some compounds of carbon (and of silicon, discussed in the next section).

Silicon

Silicon is the second most abundant element in the earth's crust, following only oxygen. Almost 95% of the crustal rocks and materials that make up the earth contain silicon. It has been important to humans ever since flint, a silicon dioxide mineral, was first used to fashion tools and weapons by early civilizations. The Romans took advantage of silicon-containing minerals when they discovered how to use them to make concrete. Today, our computer industry depends on obtaining pure silicon for the manufacture of integrated circuits and semiconductors.

Compounds That Contain Silicon and Oxygen   The variety and complexity of silicon-containing compounds are immense. However, unlike carbon, which involves a profusion of compounds with atoms of the element bonding to one another, compounds containing chains and networks of silicon–oxygen bonds dominate silicon chemistry. Chapter 13 contains a discussion of the element and many of the important Si—O compounds, which include silica and the silicates. The chemical and physical stability of these compounds can be attributed to the strong Si—O bonds, which have an average bond dissociation energy of 460 kJ/mol. In contrast, a single C—O bond is about 20% weaker.

An important class of compounds that contain silicon and oxygen are the **silicones,** which are *synthetic compounds that contain chains or rings of Si—O bonds with one or more of the bonding positions on each Si atom occupied by an organic group.* Typically, silicones are large molecules that consist of a chain of alternating Si—O bonds with two organic groups bonded to each silicon atom in the chain. This structure is similar to the structure of the silicates where two Si—O silicate bonds of each SiO_4 unit are replaced by two Si—C bonds. Figure 22.26 depicts a portion of a silicone chain. The preparation of many silicone compounds begins with the

Figure 22.26

Molecular model of a silicone
This model shows a fragment of the polydimethylsiloxane molecule. Note how the chain structure is created by linking $(CH_3)_2SiO_2$ tetrahedra through Si—O bonds.

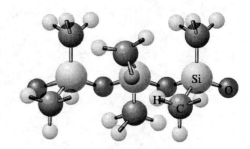

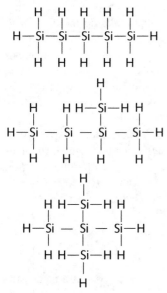

Figure 22.27

Products that contain silicone

reaction of Si with methyl chloride at elevated temperature in the presence of a copper catalyst.

$$Si(s) + 2CH_3Cl(g) \xrightarrow[300°C]{catalyst} (CH_3)_2SiCl_2(g)$$

If a long chain of Si—O bonds is desired, the product of this reaction is reacted with water.

$$(CH_3)_2SiCl_2(l) + 2H_2O(l) \longrightarrow (CH_3)_2Si(OH)_2(l) + 2HCl(g)$$

The silicon-containing product of this reaction then undergoes a condensation reaction to form a silicone oil (polydimethylsiloxane) and water.

$$n(CH_3)Si(OH)_2 \longrightarrow \begin{bmatrix} & CH_3 & \\ & | & \\ & Si-O- & \\ & | & \\ & CH_3 & \end{bmatrix}_n + nH_2O$$

Depending on the application for the silicone, the chain length can be varied to make different weight oils, or the chains can be linked together to form *elastomers* (rubbers). The methyl group, CH_3, can also be replaced by a different organic group, which can lead to the formation of hard materials called resins.

Silicones have a wide variety of applications (Figure 22.27). Due to the strong Si—O and Si—C bonds, silicones are generally unreactive and can be synthesized to perform in temperature ranges of −75°F to 400°F. Silicone oils can be found in cosmetics, car wax, and hydraulic fluids. The silicone elastomers are used for medical tubing, heart valve implants, electrical tape, caulk, and gaskets. Silicone resins are used to insulate electrical equipment and in the molding process of electronic circuit boards. These examples represent only a small portion of the uses for silicone compounds. Because of this extensive use, several hundred thousand tons of silicones are manufactured each year.

Silicon Hydrides (Silanes) and Silicon Halides Silicon hydrides and silicon halides are synthetic silicon compounds that have the distinction of not containing Si—O bonds. Like carbon, which forms hydrocarbons, silicon can be made to form compounds with hydrogen called *silanes*. Silanes are straight chain and branched chain compounds with the general formula Si_nH_{2n+2} with n being a number in the range of 1 to 8. Figure 22.28 illustrates the bonding arrangements in these compounds. Silanes can also form rings, making Si_5H_{10} and Si_6H_{12}. All of the silanes are colorless gases or liquids that explode or ignite when they come in contact with air. This is in contrast to the hydrocarbons, which only combust in air if ignited. In all cases, the silanes are much more reactive than their carbon analogs.

Figure 22.28

Silane bonding
The Lewis structures of three different compounds with the formula Si_5H_{12}, each with a different bonding arrangement of the silicon atoms.

Silicon reacts with all of the halogens to form silicon halides. For example, $SiCl_4$ can be formed by the reaction

$$Si(s) + 2Cl_2(g) \longrightarrow SiCl_4(g)$$

This reaction is of particular use to the semiconductor industry because the $SiCl_4$ product can be used as a source of ultrapure silicon. All of the silicon halides are very reactive and volatile.

22.7 Group VA: Nitrogen and the Phosphorus Family

Like the carbon family of elements, the Group VA elements show the distinct trend of increasing metallic character as you go from top to bottom of the column. The first members, nitrogen and phosphorus, are nonmetallic; arsenic and antimony are metalloids; bismuth is a metal.

As expected for a second-period element, nitrogen is in many respects different from the other elements in its group. You can see this in the formulas of the elements and compounds. Elementary nitrogen is N_2, while white phosphorus is P_4. Similarly, the common $+5$ oxoacid of nitrogen is HNO_3, that of phosphorus is H_3PO_4, and that of arsenic is H_3AsO_4. [Nitrogen exists in many molecular compounds in a variety of oxidation states. Phosphorus exists in many compounds in the $+5$ and $+3$ oxidation states. Many phosphorus compounds have P—O—P bonding.]

Nitrogen

The element nitrogen is crucial to life: it is a component of all proteins, which are involved in almost every biochemical process that occurs in living organisms. Most of the available nitrogen on earth, however, is present as nitrogen gas (dinitrogen, N_2) in the atmosphere, which consists of 78.1% N_2, by mass. Dinitrogen, also simply called "nitrogen," has collected in the atmosphere because of its relative chemical unreactivity. Most organisms cannot use dinitrogen from the atmosphere as their source of the element. However, certain soil bacteria, as well as bacteria that live in nodules on the roots of beans, clover, and similar plants, can "fix" nitrogen; that is, they convert dinitrogen to ammonium and nitrate compounds. Plants use these simple nitrogen compounds to make proteins and other complex nitrogen compounds. Animals eat these plants, and other animals eat those animals. Finally, bacteria in decaying organic matter convert the nitrogen compounds back to dinitrogen. In this way, nitrogen in our environment continually cycles from dinitrogen to living organisms and back. Figure 22.29 depicts this *nitrogen cycle*.

Properties and Uses of Nitrogen Daniel Rutherford, a chemist and physician, discovered nitrogen, N_2, in air in 1772. In his experiments, he removed the oxygen from air by burning a substance in it. When burning carbon-containing substances, he removed the carbon dioxide that formed by reacting it with aqueous potassium hydroxide. He then showed that the residual gas would no longer support either combustion or living organisms. Although this residual gas is mostly N_2, it does contain small amounts of noble gases.

Nitrogen, N_2, is a relatively unreactive element because of the stability of the nitrogen–nitrogen triple bond. (The N≡N bond energy is 942 kJ/mol, compared with 167 kJ/mol for the N—N bond energy.) When substances burn in air, they generally react with oxygen, leaving the nitrogen unreacted. Some very reactive metals do react

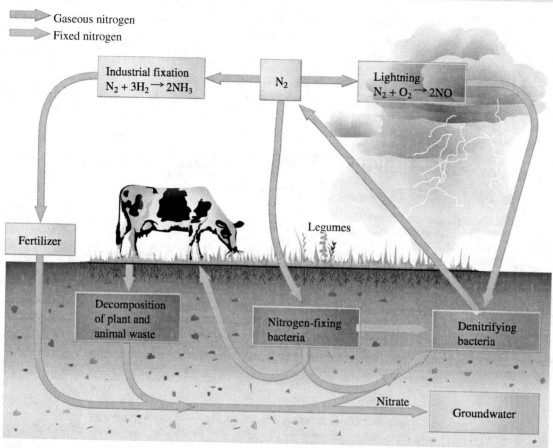

Gaseous nitrogen
Fixed nitrogen

Industrial fixation
$N_2 + 3H_2 \longrightarrow 2NH_3$

N_2

Lightning
$N_2 + O_2 \longrightarrow 2NO$

Fertilizer

Legumes

Decomposition of plant and animal waste

Nitrogen-fixing bacteria

Denitrifying bacteria

Nitrate

Groundwater

Figure 22.29

The nitrogen cycle
Nitrogen, N_2, is fixed (converted to compounds) by bacteria, by lightning, and by the industrial synthesis of ammonia. Fixed nitrogen is used by plants and enters the food chain of animals. Later, plant and animal wastes decompose. Denitrifying bacteria complete the cycle by producing free nitrogen again.

directly with nitrogen, however. For example, when magnesium metal burns in air, it forms the nitride, as well as the oxide.

$$3Mg(s) + N_2(g) \longrightarrow Mg_3N_2(s)$$

Because the nitride ion, N^{3-}, is a very strong base, ionic nitrides react with water, producing ammonia.

$$N^{3-}(aq) + 3H_2O(l) \longrightarrow NH_3(g) + 3OH^-(aq)$$

Magnesium nitride reacts with water to give magnesium hydroxide and ammonia.

$$Mg_3N_2(s) + 6H_2O(l) \longrightarrow 3Mg(OH)_2(s) + 2NH_3(g)$$

Air is the major commercial source of nitrogen. The components of air are separated by liquefaction, followed by distillation. Nitrogen is the most volatile component in liquid air, so it is the first to distill off, leaving behind a liquid that is primarily oxygen with a small amount of noble gases (mostly argon).

Liquid nitrogen is used as a refrigerant to freeze foods, to freeze soft or rubbery materials prior to grinding them, and to freeze biological materials (Figure 22.30). Large quantities of nitrogen are also used as a *blanketing gas,* whose purpose is to protect a material from oxygen during processing or storage. Thus, electronic components are often made under a nitrogen atmosphere. The other principal use of nitrogen is to prepare nitrogen compounds.

Nitrogen Compounds   Ammonia, NH_3, is the most important commercial compound of nitrogen. A colorless gas with a characteristic irritating or pungent odor, it is prepared commercially from N_2 and H_2 by the *Haber process*. Figure 22.31 shows a flowchart of the industrial preparation of ammonia from natural gas, steam, and air. Small amounts can be prepared in the laboratory by heating a solution of an ammonium salt with a strong base, such as NaOH or $Ca(OH)_2$ (Figure 22.32).

$$NH_4Cl(aq) + NaOH(aq) \xrightarrow{\Delta} NH_3(g) + H_2O(l) + NaCl(aq)$$

Ammonia is easily liquefied, and the liquid is used as a nitrogen fertilizer. Ammonium salts, such as the sulfate and nitrate, are also sold as fertilizers. Large quantities of ammonia are converted to urea, NH_2CONH_2, which is used as a fertilizer, as a livestock feed supplement, and in the manufacture of urea–formaldehyde plastics. Ammonia is also the starting compound for the preparation of most other nitrogen compounds.

Nitrous oxide, N_2O, is a colorless gas with a sweet odor. It can be prepared by careful heating of molten ammonium nitrate. (If heated strongly, it explodes.)

$$NH_4NO_3(s) \xrightarrow{\Delta} N_2O(g) + 2H_2O(g)$$

Nitrous oxide, or laughing gas, is used as a dental anesthetic. It is also useful as a propellant in whipped-cream dispensers. The gas dissolves in cream under pressure. When the cream is dispensed, the gas bubbles out, forming a foam.

Nitric oxide, NO, is a colorless gas that is of great industrial and biological importance. ◄ Although it can be prepared by the direct combination of the elements at elevated temperatures, large amounts are prepared from ammonia as the first step

Figure 22.30

Liquid nitrogen
When liquid nitrogen is poured on a table (which, although at room temperature, is about 220°C above the boiling point of nitrogen), the liquid sizzles and boils away violently.

The biological importance of NO was discussed in an essay in Chapter 5.

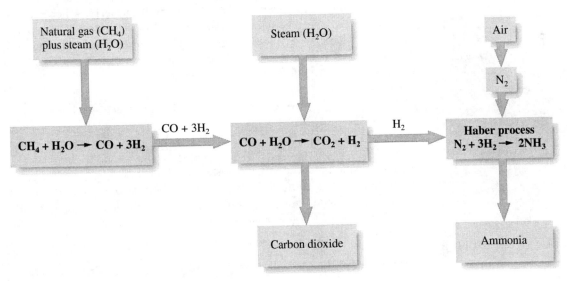

Figure 22.31

Industrial preparation of ammonia (flowchart)
The raw materials are natural gas, water, and air. Hydrogen for the Haber process is obtained by reacting natural gas with steam to give carbon monoxide and hydrogen. In the next step, carbon monoxide is reacted with steam to give carbon dioxide and additional hydrogen. The carbon dioxide is removed by dissolving it in water solution.

Figure 22.32

Preparation of ammonia from an ammonium salt
Sodium hydroxide solution was added to ammonium chloride. Ammonia gas, formed in the reaction, turns colorless phenolphthalein in the moist paper to a bright pink.

Figure 22.33

Reaction of copper metal with dilute nitric acid
Left: Copper metal is oxidized by nitric acid to $Cu^{2+}(aq)$ ion, which has a blue color. The principal reduction product from dilute nitric acid is nitric oxide, NO, a colorless gas. *Right:* When the stopper is lifted from the flask, air enters, and the NO reacts with O_2 to produce NO_2, a colored gas.

in the commercial preparation of nitric acid. The ammonia is oxidized in the presence of a platinum catalyst.

$$4NH_3(g) + 5O_2(g) \xrightarrow{Pt} 4NO(g) + 6H_2O(g)$$

Nitric acid, HNO_3, is the third most important industrial acid (after sulfuric and phosphoric acids). It is used to prepare explosives, nylon, and polyurethane plastics. Nitric acid is produced commercially by the **Ostwald process,** which is *an industrial preparation of nitric acid starting from the catalytic oxidation of ammonia to nitric oxide.* In this process, ammonia is burned in the presence of a platinum catalyst to give NO, which is then reacted with oxygen to form NO_2. The NO_2 is dissolved in water, where it reacts to form nitric acid and nitric oxide.

$$4NH_3(g) + 5O_2(g) \xrightarrow{Pt} 4NO(g) + 6H_2O(g)$$
$$2NO(g) + O_2(g) \longrightarrow 2NO_2(g)$$
$$3NO_2(g) + H_2O(l) \longrightarrow 2HNO_3(aq) + NO(g)$$

The nitric oxide produced in the last step is recycled for use in the second step.

Nitric acid is a strong oxidizing agent. Although copper metal is unreactive to most acids, it is oxidized by the nitrate ion in acid solution. In dilute acid, nitric oxide is the principal reduction product (Figure 22.33).

$$3Cu(s) + 8H_3O^+(aq) + 2NO_3^-(aq) \longrightarrow 3Cu^{2+}(aq) + 2NO(g) + 12H_2O(l)$$

With concentrated nitric acid, nitrogen dioxide is obtained (Figure 22.34).

$$Cu(s) + 4H_3O^+(aq) + 2NO_3^-(aq) \longrightarrow Cu^{2+}(aq) + 2NO_2(g) + 6H_2O(l)$$

When certain nitrates, such as sodium nitrate, are heated, they decompose to the nitrites.

$$2NaNO_3(s) \xrightarrow{\Delta} 2NaNO_2(s) + O_2(g)$$

Figure 22.34

Reaction of copper metal with concentrated nitric acid
The principal reduction product from concentrated nitric acid is nitrogen dioxide, NO_2 (reddish-brown gas).

Table 22.8

Uses of Some Compounds of Nitrogen and of Phosphorus

Compound	Use
NH_3	Nitrogen fertilizer
	Manufacture of nitrogen compounds
N_2H_4	Blowing agent for foamed plastics
	Water treatment
HNO_3	Explosives
	Polyurethane plastics
$Ca(H_2PO_4)_2 \cdot H_2O$	Phosphate fertilizer
	Baking powder
$CaHPO_4 \cdot 2H_2O$	Animal feed additive
	Toothpowder
H_3PO_4	Manufacture of phosphate fertilizers
	Soft drinks
PCl_3	Manufacture of $POCl_3$
	Manufacture of pesticides
$POCl_3$	Manufacture of plasticizers (substances that keep plastics pliable)
	Manufacture of flame retardants
$Na_5P_3O_{10}$	Detergent additive

The corresponding acid, nitrous acid, is unstable and is usually prepared when needed as an aqueous solution. By adding the stoichiometric amount of sulfuric acid to an aqueous solution of barium nitrite, $Ba(NO_2)_2$, barium sulfate precipitates, leaving a solution of nitrous acid.

$$Ba(NO_2)_2(aq) + H_2SO_4(aq) \longrightarrow BaSO_4(s) + 2HNO_2(aq)$$

Table 22.8 lists uses of some compounds of nitrogen (and of phosphorus, discussed in the next section).

CONCEPT CHECK 22.2 Considering the fact that N_2 makes up about 80% of the atmosphere, why don't animals use the abundant N_2 instead of O_2 for biological reactions?

Phosphorus

Phosphorus, the most abundant of the Group VA elements, occurs in phosphate minerals, such as fluorapatite, whose formula is written either $Ca_5(PO_4)_3F$ or $3Ca_3(PO_4)_2 \cdot CaF_2$. Unlike nitrogen, which exists in important compounds with oxidation states between -3 and $+5$, the most important oxidation states of phosphorus are $+3$ and $+5$. Like nitrogen, however, phosphorus is an important element in living organisms. DNA (deoxyribonucleic acid), a chainlike biological molecule in which information about inheritable traits resides, contains phosphate groups along the length of its chain.

Figure 22.35

Allotropes of phosphorus
Left: White phosphorus. *Right:* Red phosphorus.

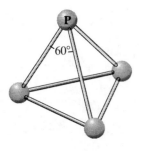

Figure 22.36

Structure of the P₄ molecule
Top: The reactivity of white phosphorus results from the small P—P—P angle (60°). *Bottom:* Space-filling molecular model.

Similarly, ATP (adenosine triphosphate), the energy-containing molecule of living organisms, contains phosphate groups.

Allotropes of Phosphorus   Phosphorus has two common allotropes: white phosphorus and red phosphorus (Figure 22.35). White phosphorus, a waxy, white solid, is very poisonous and very reactive. If white phosphorus is left exposed to air, it bursts spontaneously into flame. Because of its reactivity with oxygen, white phosphorus is stored under water, in which it is insoluble. As you might expect from its low melting point (44°C), white phosphorus is a molecular solid, with the formula P_4.

The phosphorus atoms in the P_4 molecule are arranged at the corners of a regular tetrahedron such that each atom is single-bonded to the other three (Figure 22.36). The experimentally determined P—P—P bond angle is 60°. Because this is considerably smaller than the normal bond angle, the bonding in P_4 is strained and therefore weaker. This accounts for the reactivity seen in this phosphorus allotrope; chemical reactions of P_4 replace its weak bonds by stronger ones.

White phosphorus is a major industrial chemical and is prepared by heating phosphate rock with coke (C) and quartz sand (SiO_2) in an electric furnace. The overall reaction is

$$2Ca_3(PO_4)_2(s) + 6SiO_2(s) + 10C(s) \xrightarrow{1500°C} \underset{\text{calcium silicate}}{6CaSiO_3(l)} + 10CO(g) + P_4(g)$$

The gases from the furnace are cooled by water to condense the phosphorus vapor to the liquid; the carbon monoxide gas is used as a fuel. The other product, calcium silicate glass (called *slag*), is drained periodically from the bottom of the furnace.

Most of the white phosphorus produced is used to manufacture phosphoric acid, H_3PO_4. Some white phosphorus is converted to red phosphorus, which has a chain structure (Figure 22.37). Red phosphorus is much less reactive than white phosphorus and can be stored in the presence of air. This phosphorus allotrope is relatively

Figure 22.37

Chain structure of red phosphorus
The structure is obtained by linking P₄ tetrahedra together after breaking a bond in each tetrahedron.

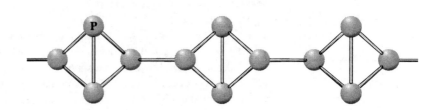

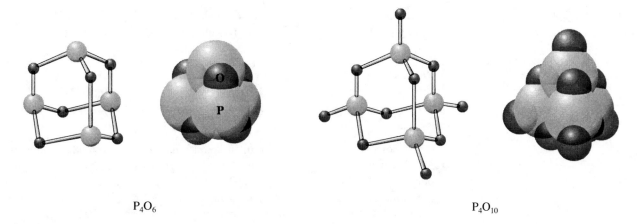

P_4O_6 P_4O_{10}

Figure 22.38

Structures of the phosphorus oxides

Left: The phosphorus atoms in P_4O_6 have tetrahedral positions, as in P_4; however, the phosphorus atoms are bonded to oxygen atoms, forming P—O—P bridges between each pair of phosphorus atoms. *Right:* The P_4O_{10} molecule is similar, except that an additional oxygen atom is bonded to each phosphorus atom. Both ball-and-stick and space-filling models are shown.

nontoxic and is used in the striking surface for safety matches. Red phosphorus is made by heating white phosphorus at about 400°C for several hours.

Phosphorus Oxides   Phosphorus has two common oxides, P_4O_6 and P_4O_{10}. Their common names are phosphorus trioxide and phosphorus pentoxide, respectively. The names are at odds with present rules of nomenclature but stem from their empirical formulas, P_2O_3 and P_2O_5. We will refer to these compounds as phosphorus(III) oxide (P_4O_6) and phosphorus(V) oxide (P_4O_{10}), using the Stock system of nomenclature, in which the oxidation states are given by Roman numerals.

These oxides have interesting structures (Figure 22.38). Phosphorus(III) oxide has a tetrahedron of phosphorus atoms, as in P_4, but with oxygen atoms between each pair of phosphorus atoms. Phosphorus(V) oxide is similar, except that each phosphorus atom has an additional oxygen atom bonded to it. These phosphorus–oxygen bonds are much shorter than the ones in the P—O—P bridges (139 pm versus 162 pm); hence, they are best represented as double bonds.

Phosphorus(III) oxide is a low-melting solid (m.p. 23°C) and the anhydride of phosphorous acid, H_3PO_3. Phosphorus(V) oxide is the most important oxide; it is a white solid that sublimes at 360°C. This oxide is the anhydride of phosphoric acid, H_3PO_4. The reaction with water is quite vigorous, making phosphorus(V) oxide useful in the laboratory as a drying agent. It is prepared by burning white phosphorus in air.

$$P_4(s) + 5O_2(g) \longrightarrow P_4O_{10}(s)$$

Phosphorus(V) oxide is used to manufacture phosphoric acid, an oxoacid.

Oxoacids of Phosphorus   Phosphorus has many oxoacids, but the most important of these can be thought of as derivatives of orthophosphoric acid (often called simply phosphoric acid), H_3PO_4. Orthophosphoric acid is a colorless solid, melting at 42°C when pure. It is usually sold as an aqueous solution, however. Orthophosphoric acid is triprotic (three acidic H atoms per molecule); possible sodium salts are sodium dihydrogen phosphate (NaH_2PO_4), disodium hydrogen phosphate (Na_2HPO_4), and trisodium phosphate (Na_3PO_4). The acid has the following electron-dot formula:

$$H-\overset{\cdot\cdot}{\underset{\cdot\cdot}{O}}-\overset{\overset{:O:}{\|}}{\underset{\underset{H}{|}}{\underset{:O:}{|}}{P}}-\overset{\cdot\cdot}{\underset{\cdot\cdot}{O}}-H$$

Orthophosphoric acid is produced in enormous quantity either directly from phosphate rock or from phosphorus(V) oxide, which in turn is obtained by burning white phosphorus. In the direct process, phosphate rock is treated with sulfuric acid, from which a solution of phosphoric acid is obtained by filtering off the calcium sulfate and other solid materials. The product is an impure phosphoric acid, which is used in the manufacture of phosphate fertilizers. ◄

> Because phosphate rock contains CaF_2, hydrofluoric acid is a by-product in the preparation of phosphoric acid. HF is used in aluminum production.

$$Ca_3(PO_4)_2(s) + 3H_2SO_4(aq) \longrightarrow 3CaSO_4(s) + 2H_3PO_4(aq)$$

A purer grade of orthophosphoric acid is obtained by reacting phosphorus(V) oxide with water. It is used in soft drinks for tartness and also in making phosphates for detergent formulations.

Orthophosphoric acid, H_3PO_4, undergoes condensation reactions to form other phosphoric acids. For example, two orthophosphoric acid molecules condense to form diphosphoric acid (also called pyrophosphoric acid). ◄

> Condensation reactions are discussed in Section 13.6.

$$.\; H-O-\overset{\overset{O}{\|}}{\underset{\underset{H}{|}}{\underset{O}{|}}{P}}-O-H\; +\; H-O-\overset{\overset{O}{\|}}{\underset{\underset{H}{|}}{\underset{O}{|}}{P}}-O-H\; \longrightarrow\; H-O-\overset{\overset{O}{\|}}{\underset{\underset{H}{|}}{\underset{O}{|}}{P}}-O-\overset{\overset{O}{\|}}{\underset{\underset{H}{|}}{\underset{O}{|}}{P}}-O-H\; +\; H_2O$$

Two series of these phosphoric acids exist (all having phosphorus in the +5 oxidation state). One series consists of the linear **polyphosphoric acids,** which are *acids with the general formula $H_{n+2}P_nO_{3n+1}$ formed from linear chains of P—O bonds.*

$$H-O-\overset{\overset{O}{\|}}{\underset{\underset{H}{|}}{\underset{O}{|}}{P}}-O-\overset{\overset{O}{\|}}{\underset{\underset{H}{|}}{\underset{O}{|}}{P}}-O-H \qquad H-O-\overset{\overset{O}{\|}}{\underset{\underset{H}{|}}{\underset{O}{|}}{P}}-O-\overset{\overset{O}{\|}}{\underset{\underset{H}{|}}{\underset{O}{|}}{P}}-O-\overset{\overset{O}{\|}}{\underset{\underset{H}{|}}{\underset{O}{|}}{P}}-O-H$$

diphosphoric acid   triphosphoric acid

The other series consists of the **metaphosphoric acids,** which are *acids with the general formula $(HPO_3)_n$.* Figure 22.39 shows the structure of a cyclic, or ring, metaphosphate anion. When a linear polyphosphoric acid chain is very long, the formula becomes $(HPO_3)_n$, with n very large, and the acid is called *polymetaphosphoric acid.*

The polyphosphates and metaphosphates are used in detergents, where they act as water softeners by complexing with metal ions in the water. Sodium triphosphate, $Na_5P_3O_{10}$, one of the most commonly used polyphosphates, is manufactured by adding sufficient sodium carbonate to orthophosphoric acid to give a solution of the salts NaH_2PO_4 and Na_2HPO_4. When this solution is sprayed into a hot kiln, the orthophosphate ions condense to give sodium triphosphate.

The use of phosphates in detergents has been criticized for contributing to the overfertilization of plants and algae in lakes (a process referred to as *eutrophication*).

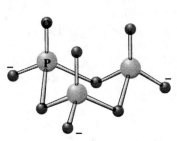

Figure 22.39

The structure of trimetaphosphate ion, $P_3O_9^{3-}$

A cyclic metaphosphate ion; the general formula of the metaphosphate ions is $(PO_3^-)_n$.

Such lakes become oxygen-deficient from decomposing plants and algae, and the fish die. In the United States, the use of phosphates in laundry detergents has been banned in some states.

Table 22.8 lists some uses of compounds of phosphorus.

22.8   Group VIA: Oxygen and the Sulfur Family

IA								VIIIA
H	IIA		IIIA	IVA	VA	VIA	VIIA	He
Li	Be		B	C	N	O	F	Ne
Na	Mg	IIIB IIB	Al	Si	P	S	Cl	Ar
K	Ca	Sc〉〈Zn	Ga	Ge	As	Se	Br	Kr
Rb	Sr	Y 〉〈Cd	In	Sn	Sb	Te	I	Xe
Cs	Ba	La〉〈Hg	Tl	Pb	Bi	Po	At	Rn
Fr	Ra	Ac〉						

Group VIA, like the preceding groups, shows the trend from nonmetallic to metallic as you proceed from top to bottom of the column of elements. Oxygen and sulfur are strictly nonmetallic. Although the chemical properties of selenium and tellurium are predominantly those of nonmetals, they do have semiconducting allotropes as expected of metalloids. Polonium is a radioactive metal.

Oxygen, a second-period element, has rather different properties from those of the other members of Group VIA. It is very electronegative and bonding involves only s and p orbitals. For the other members of Group VIA, d orbitals become a factor in bonding. Oxygen exists in compounds mainly in the -2 oxidation state. The other Group VIA elements exist in compounds in this state also, but the $+4$ and $+6$ states are common. (Oxygen is the most abundant element on earth, making up 48% by mass of the earth's crust. Sulfur, although not as abundant as oxygen, is a common element. Both oxygen and sulfur are important to living organisms.)

Oxygen

Oxygen in the form of dioxygen, O_2, makes up 20.9 mole percent of the atmosphere. Although this might seem to constitute a considerable quantity of the element, most of the oxygen on earth is present as oxide and oxoanion minerals (in silicates, carbonates, sulfates, and so forth). Indeed, oxygen combines with almost every element—only the noble gases helium, neon, and argon have no known compounds. The chemistry of oxygen is therefore very important, though we frequently discuss it in the context of other elements. In fact, much of the chemistry of the elements discussed in this chapter concerns either their reactions with oxygen or the properties of their oxides and oxoacids.

Properties and Preparation of Oxygen   The common form of the element oxygen is dioxygen, O_2. (The element also exists as the allotrope ozone, O_3.) Dioxygen, usually called simply oxygen, is a colorless, odorless gas under standard conditions. The critical temperature is $-118°C$. Therefore, you can liquefy oxygen if you first cool the gas below this temperature and then compress it. Both liquid and solid O_2 have a pale blue color. The melting point of the solid is $-218°C$, and the boiling point at 1 atm is $-183°C$. ◀

Ozone and its presence in the atmosphere are discussed in an essay at the end of Chapter 10.

Oxygen is produced in enormous quantity from air. As described in the discussion of nitrogen, air is first liquefied, then distilled. Nitrogen and argon are more volatile components of air and distill off, leaving liquid oxygen behind.

Oxygen can be prepared in small quantities by decomposing certain oxygen-containing compounds. Both the Swedish chemist Karl Wilhelm Scheele and the British chemist Joseph Priestley are credited with the discovery of oxygen. Priestley obtained the gas in 1774 by heating mercury(II) oxide.

$$2HgO(s) \xrightarrow{\Delta} 2Hg(l) + O_2(g)$$

Figure 22.40

Chromium oxides
Left: Chromium(III) oxide, a basic oxide. *Right:* Chromium(VI) oxide, an acidic oxide.

In one laboratory preparation, potassium chlorate, $KClO_3$, is heated with pure manganese(IV) oxide, MnO_2, as a catalyst.

$$2KClO_3(s) \xrightarrow[MnO_2]{\Delta} 2KCl(s) + 3O_2(g)$$

Reactions of Oxygen Molecular oxygen is a very reactive gas and combines directly with many substances. The products are usually oxides. An **oxide** is *a binary compound with oxygen in the −2 oxidation state.*

Most metals react readily with oxygen to form oxides, especially if the metal is in a form that exposes sufficient surface area. For example, magnesium wire and iron wool burn brightly in air to yield the oxides.

$$2Mg(s) + O_2(g) \longrightarrow 2MgO(s)$$
$$3Fe(s) + 2O_2(g) \longrightarrow Fe_3O_4(s)$$

The resulting oxides MgO and Fe_3O_4 are basic oxides, as is true of most metal oxides. If the metal is in a high oxidation state, however, the oxide may be acidic. For example, chromium(III) oxide, Cr_2O_3, is a basic oxide, but chromium(VI) oxide, CrO_3, is an acidic oxide (Figure 22.40).

The alkali metals form an interesting series of binary compounds with oxygen. When an alkali metal burns in air, the principal product with oxygen depends on the metal. With lithium, the product is the basic oxide, Li_2O. With the other alkali metals, the product is predominantly the peroxide and superoxide. A **peroxide** is *a compound with oxygen in the −1 oxidation state.* (Peroxides contain either the O_2^{2-} ion or the covalently bonded group —O—O—.) A **superoxide** is *a binary compound with oxygen in the $-\frac{1}{2}$ oxidation state;* superoxides contain the superoxide ion, O_2^-. Sodium metal burns in air to give mainly the peroxide.

$$2Na(s) + O_2(g) \longrightarrow Na_2O_2(s)$$

Potassium and the other alkali metals form mainly the superoxides.

$$K(s) + O_2(g) \longrightarrow KO_2(s)$$

Nonmetals react with oxygen to form covalent oxides, most of which are acidic. For example, carbon burns in an excess of oxygen to give carbon dioxide, which is the acid anhydride of carbonic acid (that is, carbon dioxide produces carbonic acid when it reacts with water). Sulfur, S_8, burns in oxygen to give sulfur dioxide, SO_2, the acid anhydride of sulfurous acid.

$$S_8(s) + 8O_2(g) \longrightarrow 8SO_2(g)$$

Sulfur forms another oxide, sulfur trioxide, SO_3, but only small amounts are obtained during the burning of sulfur in air. Sulfur trioxide is the acid anhydride of sulfuric acid.

Compounds in which at least one element is in a reduced state are oxidized by oxygen, giving compounds that would be expected to form when the individual elements are burned in oxygen. For example, a hydrocarbon such as octane, C_8H_{18}, burns to give carbon dioxide and water.

$$2C_8H_{18}(l) + 25O_2(g) \longrightarrow 16CO_2(g) + 18H_2O(g)$$

Some other examples are given in the following equations:

$$2H_2S(g) + 3O_2(g) \longrightarrow 2H_2O(g) + 2SO_2(g)$$
$$CS_2(l) + 3O_2(g) \longrightarrow CO_2(g) + 2SO_2(g)$$
$$2ZnS(s) + 3O_2(g) \longrightarrow 2ZnO(s) + 2SO_2(g)$$

Note the products that are formed; sulfur compounds usually form SO_2.

Why do we need such low temperatures to liquefy gases such as nitrogen, oxygen, and helium?

Sulfur

Sulfur occurs in sulfate minerals, such as gypsum ($CaSO_4 \cdot 2H_2O$), and in sulfide and disulfide minerals, many of which are important metal ores. Pyrite is iron(II) disulfide, FeS_2; it consists of Fe^{2+} and S_2^{2-} ions. This mineral is sometimes called "fool's gold," because its golden color often fooled novice miners into thinking they had found gold. Sulfur is also present in coal and petroleum as organic sulfur compounds and in natural gas as hydrogen sulfide, H_2S. Free sulfur occurs in some volcanic areas, perhaps formed by the reaction of hydrogen sulfide and sulfur dioxide, which are present in volcanic gases.

$$16H_2S(g) + 8SO_2(g) \longrightarrow 16H_2O(l) + 3S_8(s)$$

Commercial deposits of free sulfur also occur in the rock at the top of salt domes, which are massive columns of salt embedded in rock a hundred meters or more below the earth's surface. These deposits are believed to have formed by bacterial action involving calcium sulfate minerals. Figure 22.41 shows free sulfur obtained from such deposits that occur in the United States along the Gulf of Mexico.

Sulfur also occurs in several amino acids, which are the building blocks of the proteins in living organisms. Plants are able to use sulfate ion as a source of sulfur for the synthesis of amino acids. Animals and decay bacteria derive most of their nutritional sulfur from organic sources.

Allotropes of Sulfur Sulfur has a fascinating array of allotropes, including two common crystal forms, rhombic sulfur and monoclinic sulfur (see Figure 6.14). *Rhombic sulfur* is the stablest form of the element under normal conditions; natural sulfur is rhombic sulfur. It is a yellow, crystalline solid with a lattice consisting of crown-shaped S_8 molecules (Figure 22.42). The relative stability of this molecule results in part from the ability of sulfur atoms to undergo catenation—that is, to form stable bonds to other sulfur atoms. Rhombic sulfur melts at 113°C to give an orange-colored liquid.

When this liquid is cooled, it crystallizes to give *monoclinic sulfur.* This allotrope also consists of S_8 molecules; it differs from rhombic sulfur only in the way the molecules are packed to form crystals. Monoclinic sulfur melts at 119°C. It is unstable below 96°C, and in a few weeks at room temperature it reverts to rhombic sulfur.

If, instead of cooling the liquid sulfur, you raise its temperature above 160°C, the sulfur begins to darken and at somewhat higher temperatures changes to a dark reddish-brown, viscous liquid. The original melt consists of S_8 molecules, but these rings of sulfur atoms open up, and the fragments join to give long spiral chains of sulfur atoms. The spiral chains have unpaired electrons at their ends, and these unpaired electrons are responsible for the color. The viscosity of the liquid increases as compact S_8 molecules are replaced by long spiral chains that can intertwine. At temperatures greater than 200°C, the chains begin to break apart and the viscosity decreases. Figure 22.43 shows the appearance of sulfur at various temperatures.

When molten sulfur above 160°C (but below 200°C) is poured into water, the liquid changes to a rubbery mass, called *plastic sulfur.* Plastic sulfur is an amorphous mixture of sulfur chains. The rubberiness of this sulfur results from the ability of the

Figure 22.41

Sulfur obtained from underground deposits
Sulfur is obtained from these deposits by pumping in superheated water; molten sulfur is then pumped to the earth's surface. (Details of this *Frasch process* are described later.) Here, molten sulfur from a well is being directed to an area where it can cool and solidify.

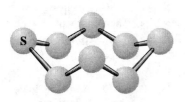

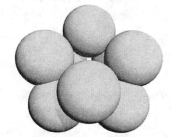

Figure 22.42

Structure of the S_8 molecule
Top: Each molecule consists of eight S atoms arranged in a ring (in the shape of a crown). *Bottom:* Space-filling molecular model.

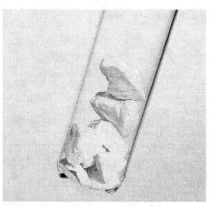

Figure 22.43

Sulfur at various temperatures

Left: Solid rhombic sulfur at 20°C. *Center:* Orange-colored liquid sulfur at 120°C. *Right:* Viscous liquid sulfur at 200°C.

spiral chains of sulfur atoms to stretch and then relax to their original length. Plastic sulfur reverts to rhombic sulfur after a period of time.

Sulfur boils at 445°C, giving a vapor of S_8, S_6, S_4, and S_2 molecules. Measurements of vapor density depend on the temperature, as a result of these different species of molecular sulfur in the vapor. (The relationship between gas density and molecular weight is described in Section 5.3.)

Production of Sulfur Free sulfur that occurs in deep underground deposits is mined by the **Frasch process,** *a mining procedure in which underground deposits of solid sulfur are melted in place with superheated water, and the molten sulfur is forced upward as a froth using air under pressure* (see Figure 22.44). A sulfur well is similar to an oil well but consists of three concentric pipes. Superheated water flows down the outer pipe, and compressed air flows down the inner pipe. The superheated water melts the sulfur, which is then pushed up the middle pipe by the compressed air. Molten sulfur spews from the well and solidifies in large storage areas. Sulfur obtained this way is 99.6% pure.

Hydrogen sulfide, H_2S, recovered from natural gas and petroleum is also a source of free sulfur. The sulfur is obtained from the hydrogen sulfide gas by the **Claus process,** *a method of obtaining free sulfur by the partial burning of hydrogen sulfide.* The partial burning of hydrogen sulfide produces some sulfur, as well as sulfur dioxide.

$$8H_2S(g) + 4O_2(g) \longrightarrow S_8(s) + 8H_2O(g)$$
$$2H_2S(g) + 3O_2(g) \longrightarrow 2SO_2(g) + 2H_2O(g)$$

The sulfur dioxide that forms reacts with the hydrogen sulfide to produce more sulfur.

$$16H_2S(g) + 8SO_2(g) \longrightarrow 3S_8(s) + 16H_2O(g)$$

Most of the sulfur produced (almost 90%) is used to make sulfuric acid. The remainder has a wide variety of uses, including the vulcanization of rubber (sulfur converts the initially tacky material into useful rubber), the production of carbon disulfide (to make cellophane), and the preparation of sulfur dioxide for bleaching.

Figure 22.44

The Frasch process for mining sulfur
The well consists of concentric pipes. Superheated water passing down the outer pipe exits into the sulfur deposit, melting it. Compressed air from the inner pipe pushes the molten sulfur up the middle pipe. Molten sulfur flows from the top of the well onto the ground to cool.

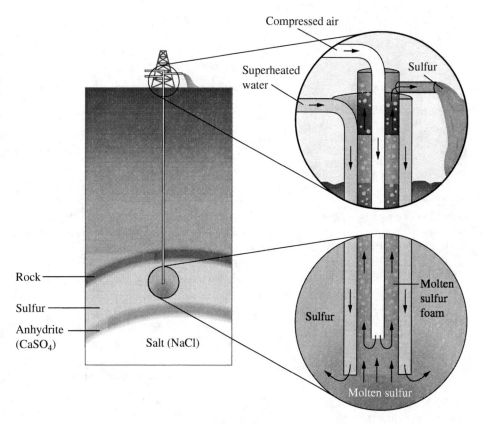

Sulfur Oxides and Oxoacids Sulfur dioxide, SO_2, is a colorless, toxic gas with a characteristic suffocating odor. Its presence in polluted air (from the burning of fossil fuels) is known to cause respiratory ailments. The SO_2 molecule has a bent geometry with a bond angle of 119.5°, very close to that predicted by the VSEPR model (Figure 22.45).

Sulfur dioxide gas is very soluble in water, producing acidic solutions. Although these solutions are often referred to as solutions of *sulfurous acid,* they appear to be composed primarily of hydrated species of SO_2; the acid H_2SO_3 has never been isolated. An aqueous solution of sulfur dioxide, $SO_2(aq)$, does apparently contain small amounts of the ions HSO_3^- and SO_3^{2-}, which would be expected to be produced by the ionization of H_2SO_3.

$$H_2O(l) + SO_2(g) \rightleftharpoons H_2SO_3(aq)$$
$$H_2SO_3(aq) + H_2O(l) \rightleftharpoons H_3O^+(aq) + HSO_3^-(aq)$$
$$HSO_3^-(aq) + H_2O(l) \rightleftharpoons H_3O^+(aq) + SO_3^{2-}(aq)$$

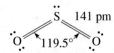

Figure 22.45

Structure of the SO₂ molecule
The molecule has a bent geometry.

When an appropriate amount of base is added to an aqueous solution of sulfur dioxide, the corresponding hydrogen sulfite salt or sulfite salt is obtained. Sodium hydrogen sulfite (also called sodium bisulfite) and sodium sulfite are produced this way commercially using sodium carbonate as the base:

$$Na_2CO_3(aq) + 2SO_2(aq) + H_2O(l) \longrightarrow 2NaHSO_3(aq) + CO_2(g)$$
$$Na_2CO_3(aq) + SO_2(aq) \longrightarrow Na_2SO_3(aq) + CO_2(g)$$

Figure 22.46

Bleaching of a rose by sulfur dioxide

The dye in the rose is reduced by sulfur dioxide (contained in the beaker) to a colorless substance.

Sulfites and hydrogen sulfites decompose when treated with acid to give sulfur dioxide. For example,

$$NaHSO_3(aq) + HCl(aq) \longrightarrow NaCl(aq) + H_2O(l) + SO_2(g)$$

This reaction can be used to prepare small amounts of sulfur dioxide in the laboratory.

Sulfur dioxide is produced on a large scale by burning sulfur, S_8. It is also obtained as a by-product of the roasting of sulfide ores (such as FeS_2, CuS, ZnS, and PbS). Most of this sulfur dioxide is used to prepare sulfuric acid. Some is used as a bleach for wood pulp and textiles (Figure 22.46) and as a disinfectant and food preservative (for example, in wine and dried fruit). Its use as a food preservative depends on the fact that sulfur dioxide is especially toxic to yeasts, molds, and certain bacteria. Because some people are allergic to sulfur dioxide, foods containing it must be properly labeled.

Sulfur trioxide is a liquid at room temperature. The liquid actually consists of S_3O_9 molecules in equilibrium with SO_3 molecules (Figure 22.47). The vapor-phase molecule is SO_3, which has a planar triangular geometry.

Sulfur trioxide is formed in small amounts when sulfur is burned in air, although the principal product is sulfur dioxide. Thermodynamically, sulfur trioxide is the preferred product of sulfur and oxygen. Sulfur dioxide does react slowly with oxygen in air to produce sulfur trioxide, but the reaction is much faster in the presence of a catalyst, such as platinum. Sulfur trioxide is produced commercially by the oxidation of sulfur dioxide in the presence of vanadium(V) oxide catalyst.

$$2SO_2(g) + O_2(g) \xrightarrow{V_2O_5} 2SO_3(g)$$

Sulfur trioxide reacts vigorously and exothermically with water to produce sulfuric acid.

$$SO_3(g) + H_2O(l) \longrightarrow H_2SO_4(aq)$$

The **contact process** is *an industrial method for the manufacture of sulfuric acid. It consists of the reaction of sulfur dioxide with oxygen to form sulfur trioxide using a catalyst of vanadium(V) oxide, followed by the reaction of sulfur trioxide with water.* Because the direct reaction of sulfur trioxide with water produces mists that are unmanageable, the sulfur trioxide is actually dissolved in concentrated sulfuric acid, which is then diluted with water. ◄

Sulfuric acid is a component of acid rain and forms in air from sulfur dioxide, following reactions that are similar to those involved in the contact process. Atmospheric sulfur dioxide has both natural and human origins. Natural sources include plant and animal decomposition and volcanic emissions. However, the burning of coal, oil, and natural gas has been identified as a major source of acid rain pollution. After persisting in the atmosphere for some time, sulfur dioxide is oxidized to sulfur trioxide, which dissolves in rain to give $H_2SO_4(aq)$.

Concentrated sulfuric acid is a viscous liquid and a powerful dehydrating agent. The concentrated acid is also an oxidizing agent. Copper is not dissolved by most acids. $E°$ for $Cu^{2+}|Cu$ is positive, so Cu is not oxidized by $H^+(H_3O^+)$. It is, however, dissolved by hot, concentrated sulfuric acid. In this reaction, sulfate ion in acid solution is reduced to sulfur dioxide:

$$\overset{0}{Cu}(s) + 2H_2\overset{+6}{S}O_4(l) \longrightarrow \overset{+2}{Cu}SO_4(aq) + 2H_2O(l) + \overset{+4}{S}O_2(g)$$

More sulfuric acid is made than any other industrial chemical. Most of this acid is used to make soluble phosphate and ammonium sulfate fertilizers. Sulfuric acid is

Sulfuric acid and acid rain are discussed in an essay in Section 17.2.

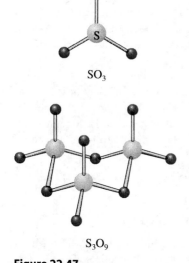

Figure 22.47

Structures of SO₃ and S₃O₉ molecules

These molecules are in equilibrium in liquid sulfur trioxide. The vapor consists mostly of SO_3.

Table 22.9

Uses of Some Sulfur Compounds

Compound	Use
CS_2	Manufacture of rayon and cellophane
	Manufacture of CCl_4
SO_2	Manufacture of H_2SO_4
	Food preservative
	Textile bleach
H_2SO_4	Manufacture of phosphate fertilizers
	Petroleum refining
	Manufacture of various chemicals
$Na_2S_2O_3$	Photographic fixer

also used in petroleum refining and in the manufacture of many chemicals. Table 22.9 lists uses of some sulfur compounds.

22.9 Group VIIA: The Halogens

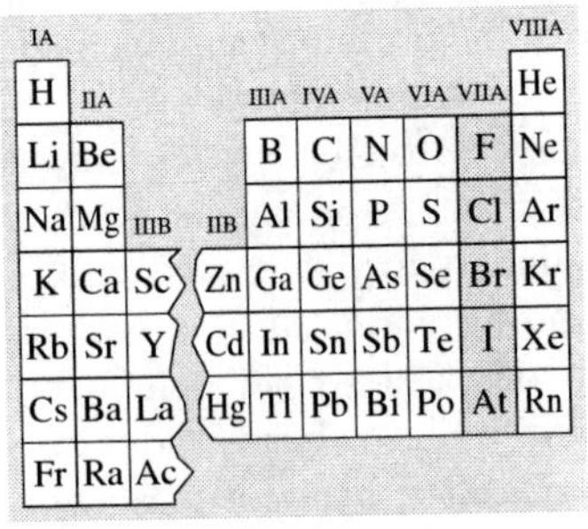

The Group VIIA elements, called the halogens, have very similar properties, or at least they have properties that change smoothly in progressing down the column. All are reactive nonmetals, except perhaps for astatine, whose chemistry is not well known.

As a second-period element, fluorine does exhibit some differences from the other elements of Group VIIA, although these are not so pronounced as those of the second-period elements in Groups IIIA to VIA. The solubilities of the fluorides in water, for example, are often quite different from those of the chlorides, bromides, and iodides. Calcium chloride, bromide, and iodide are very soluble in water. Calcium fluoride, however, is insoluble. Silver chloride, bromide, and iodide are insoluble, but silver fluoride is soluble.

All of the halogens form stable compounds in which the element is in the -1 oxidation state. In fluorine compounds, this is the only oxidation state. Chlorine, bromine, and iodine also have compounds in which the halogen is in one of the positive oxidation states $+1$, $+3$, $+5$, or $+7$. The higher positive oxidation states ($> +1$) are due to the involvement of d orbitals in bonding.

Chlorine

Chlorine gas, Cl_2, was discovered in 1774 by the Swedish chemist Karl Wilhelm Scheele by heating hydrochloric acid with manganese dioxide.

$$4HCl(aq) + MnO_2(s) \longrightarrow MnCl_2(aq) + Cl_2(g) + 2H_2O(l)$$

He immediately noted the suffocating odor of the gas. Scheele also discovered that chlorine solutions could bleach cotton cloth. Within a few decades, chlorine-based bleaches became major items of commerce. Currently, chlorine is the most commercially important halogen.

See the introduction to Chapter 2.

Properties of Chlorine

Properties of Chlorine   Chlorine gas has a pale greenish-yellow color. It is a very reactive oxidizing agent and supports the combustion of many substances in a manner similar to oxygen. We discussed the reactions of chlorine with sodium and antimony in Chapter 2.

All of the halogens are oxidizing agents, though the oxidizing power decreases from fluorine to iodine. Thus, chlorine is a stronger oxidizing agent than either bromine or iodine. When chlorine gas is bubbled into a bromide solution, free bromine is obtained. Similarly, chlorine oxidizes iodide ion to iodine.

$$Cl_2(g) + 2KBr(aq) \longrightarrow 2KCl(aq) + Br_2(aq)$$
$$Cl_2(g) + 2KI(aq) \longrightarrow 2KCl(aq) + I_2(aq)$$

These reactions can be used as a test for bromide and iodide ions. Suppose an aqueous solution of chlorine is added to a test tube containing either bromide or iodide ion. The corresponding free halogen is formed in the water solution. It is readily identified by adding the organic solvent methylene chloride, CH_2Cl_2, which dissolves the halogen, forming a colored layer at the bottom of the test tube. Bromide ion gives an orange layer; iodide ion gives a violet layer. Of course, neither bromine nor iodine is strong enough to oxidize chloride ion.

Chlorine reacts with water by being both oxidized and reduced:

$$\overset{0}{Cl_2}(g) + H_2O(l) \rightleftharpoons \overset{+1}{HClO}(aq) + \overset{-1}{HCl}(aq)$$

In an aqueous solution of chlorine at 25°C, about two-thirds of the chlorine is present as $Cl_2(aq)$; the rest is HClO and HCl.

The electrolysis of aqueous sodium chloride is discussed in Section 20.10.

Preparation and Uses of Chlorine

Preparation and Uses of Chlorine   Chlorine is a major industrial chemical. It is prepared commercially by the electrolysis of aqueous sodium chloride. Chlorine can be prepared in small amounts for laboratory use by the reaction of chloride ion with a strong oxidizing agent, such as potassium dichromate or manganese dioxide. However, chlorine is readily available in steel cylinders for laboratory work.

The principal use of chlorine is in the preparation of chlorinated hydrocarbons, such as vinyl chloride, $CH_2{=}CHCl$ (for polyvinyl chloride plastics), and methyl chloride, CH_3Cl (for the manufacture of silicones, polymers with Si—O bonds and organic groups). Various insecticides are also chlorinated hydrocarbons; many of these (such as DDT) are now restricted in their use because of possible environmental damage.

Other major uses of chlorine are as a bleaching agent for textiles and paper pulp and as a disinfectant. Not long after the discovery of chlorine, chlorine bleaches became available commercially. Chlorine solutions were used as disinfectants early in the nineteenth century. Today, chlorine gas is commonly used for disinfecting municipal water supplies.

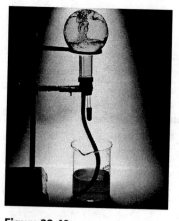

Figure 22.48

The hydrogen chloride fountain
The flask contains hydrogen chloride gas. When water is added to the flask from the dropper, the hydrogen chloride dissolves in it, reducing the pressure in the flask. Atmospheric pressure pushes the water in the beaker into the flask, forming a stream or fountain. Water in the beaker has bromthymol-blue indicator in it. The indicator solution in the flask is yellow because it is acidic.

Hydrogen Chloride

Hydrogen Chloride   Hydrogen chloride, HCl, is a colorless gas with a sharp, penetrating odor. The gas is very soluble in water (Figure 22.48), and the water solution is commonly referred to as hydrochloric acid. The molecular species HCl ionizes nearly completely in aqueous solution:

$$HCl(g) + H_2O(l) \longrightarrow H_3O^+(aq) + Cl^-(aq)$$

Hydrogen chloride can be produced by heating sodium chloride with concentrated sulfuric acid.

$$NaCl(s) + H_2SO_4(l) \xrightarrow{\Delta} NaHSO_4(s) + HCl(g)$$

Figure 22.49

The action of concentrated sulfuric acid on halide salts
Concentrated sulfuric acid was added to watch glasses containing, from left to right, NaCl, NaBr, and NaI. Note the formation of some Br_2 in the center watch glass (brown) and the formation of I_2 vapor (purple) over the watch glass on the right. These halogens form when concentrated sulfuric acid oxidizes the corresponding halide ions. Chloride ion is not oxidized by H_2SO_4.

On stronger heating, the sodium hydrogen sulfate reacts with sodium chloride to produce additional hydrogen chloride.

$$NaCl(s) + NaHSO_4(s) \xrightarrow{\Delta} Na_2SO_4(s) + HCl(g)$$

Hydrogen bromide and hydrogen iodide can also be produced from their salts by a similar replacement reaction, but in these cases phosphoric acid is used instead of sulfuric acid, which tends to oxidize the bromide and iodide ions to the respective elements (Figure 22.49).

Most of the hydrogen chloride available commercially is obtained as a by-product in the manufacture of chlorinated hydrocarbons. In these reactions, hydrogen bonded to carbon is replaced by chlorine, forming the chlorinated compound and HCl. An example is the preparation of methyl chloride, CH_3Cl, from methane.

$$CH_4(g) + Cl_2(g) \longrightarrow CH_3Cl(g) + HCl(g)$$

Hydrochloric acid is the fourth most important industrial acid (after sulfuric, phosphoric, and nitric acids). It is used to clean metal surfaces of oxides (a process called *pickling*) and to extract certain metal ores, such as those of tungsten.

Oxoacids of Chlorine The halogens form a variety of oxoacids (Table 22.10). Figure 22.50 shows the structures of the chlorine oxoacids. The acidic character of these

Table 22.10					
Halogen Oxoacids					
Oxidation State	Fluorine Oxoacids	Chlorine Oxoacids	Bromine Oxoacids	Iodine Oxoacids	General Name
+1	HFO*	HClO†	HBrO†	HIO†	Hypohalous acid
+3	—	HClO$_2$†	HBrO$_2$†	—	Halous acid
+5	—	HClO$_3$†	HBrO$_3$†	HIO$_3$	Halic acid
+7	—	HClO$_4$	HBrO$_4$†	HIO$_4$	Perhalic acid
				H$_5$IO$_6$	

*The oxidation state of F in HFO is -1.
†These acids are known only in aqueous solution.

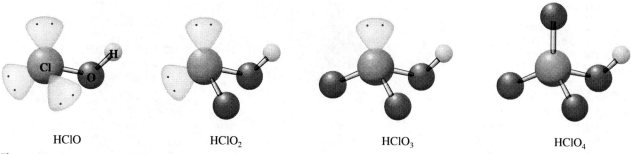

HClO HClO$_2$ HClO$_3$ HClO$_4$

Figure 22.50

Structures of the chlorine oxoacids
The models of the oxoacids also include lone pairs on the Cl atom.

acids increases with the number of oxygen atoms bonded to the halogen atom—that is, in the order HClO, HClO$_2$, HClO$_3$, HClO$_4$. (See Section 16.5 for a discussion of molecular structure and acid strength.) Perchloric acid, HClO$_4$, is the strongest of the common acids. Of the chlorine oxoacids, only perchloric acid is stable; the other oxoacids have never been isolated and are known only in aqueous solution.

Hypochlorous acid, HClO, is produced when chlorine disproportionates (is oxidized and reduced) in water. In basic solution, the equilibrium is very far toward the acid anions:

$$Cl_2(g) + 2OH^-(aq) \longrightarrow Cl^-(aq) + ClO^-(aq) + H_2O(l)$$

Solutions of sodium hypochlorite are manufactured by allowing the chlorine gas released by the electrolysis of aqueous sodium chloride to mix with the cold solution of sodium hydroxide that is also obtained in the electrolysis. These solutions are sold as a bleach (Figure 22.51).

Hypochlorite ion itself is unstable, disproportionating into chlorate ion, ClO$_3$$^-$, and chloride ion.

$$3ClO^-(aq) \longrightarrow ClO_3^-(aq) + 2Cl^-(aq)$$

At room temperature the reaction is slow; but in hot solution in the presence of base, the reaction is fast. Therefore, when chlorine reacts with hot sodium hydroxide solution, sodium chlorate is the product instead of sodium hypochlorite.

$$3Cl_2(g) + 6NaOH(aq) \longrightarrow NaClO_3(aq) + 5NaCl(aq) + 3H_2O(l)$$

Sodium chlorate can be crystallized from the solution. Solutions of chloric acid, HClO$_3$, can be prepared, although the pure acid cannot be isolated.

Sodium perchlorate and potassium perchlorate are produced commercially by the electrolysis of a saturated solution of the corresponding chlorate. The anode reaction is

$$ClO_3^-(aq) + 3H_2O(l) \longrightarrow ClO_4^-(aq) + 2H_3O^+(aq) + 2e^-$$

Hydrogen evolves at the cathode. Perchloric acid can be prepared by treating a perchlorate salt with sulfuric acid.

$$KClO_4(s) + H_2SO_4(l) \longrightarrow KHSO_4(s) + HClO_4(l)$$

The perchloric acid is distilled from the mixture at reduced pressure (to keep the temperature below 92°C, where perchloric acid decomposes explosively).

Table 22.11 lists uses of some halogen compounds.

Figure 22.51

Solution of sodium hypochlorite bleach
The solution is manufactured by allowing chlorine and sodium hydroxide solution (from the electrolysis of aqueous sodium chloride) to react.

Table 22.11

Uses of Some Halogen Compounds

Compound	Use
AgBr, AgI	Photographic film
CCl$_4$	Manufacture of fluorocarbons
CH$_3$Br	Pesticide
C$_2$H$_4$Cl$_2$	Manufacture of vinyl chloride (plastics)
HCl	Metal treating
	Food processing
NaClO	Household bleach
	Manufacture of hydrazine for rocket fuel
NaClO$_3$	Paper pulp bleaching (with ClO$_2$)
KI	Human nutritional and animal feed supplement

22.10 Group VIIIA: The Noble Gases

In our discussions of bonding, we pointed out the relative stability of the electron configurations of the Group VIIIA noble gases. For many years, it was thought that because the atoms of these elements had completed octets, the noble gases would be completely unreactive. Consequently, these elements were known as *inert gases*. Compounds of krypton, xenon, and radon have since been prepared, however, so the term is not quite appropriate.

Helium and the Other Noble Gases

The noble gases were not known until 1894. A couple of years earlier, the English physicist Lord Rayleigh discovered that the density of nitrogen gas obtained from air (1.2561 g/L at STP) was noticeably greater than the density of nitrogen obtained by decomposition of nitrogen compounds (1.2498 g/L at STP). He concluded that one of these two nitrogen sources was contaminated with another substance.

Soon after this, Rayleigh began collaborating with the Scottish chemist William Ramsay. Ramsay passed atmospheric nitrogen over hot magnesium to remove the nitrogen as magnesium nitride, Mg$_3$N$_2$, and obtained a nonreactive residual gas. He placed this gas in a sealed glass tube and passed a high-voltage electrical discharge through it to observe its emission spectrum. The spectrum showed a series of red and green lines and was unlike that of any known element. Ramsay and Rayleigh concluded that they had discovered a new element, which they called argon (from the Greek word *argos,* meaning "lazy"—referring to argon's lack of chemical reactivity). They also surmised that argon was a member of a new column of elements in the periodic table.

Before the discovery of argon, some lines in the spectrum of the sun were ascribed to an element not yet known on earth. This element was called helium (from the Greek *helios,* meaning "sun"). In 1895, Ramsay and the Swedish chemist Per Theodor Cleve (working independently) announced the discovery of helium gas in the mineral cleveite (a uranium ore) by identifying the spectrum of helium.

Several years later, Ramsay discovered neon, krypton, and xenon by fractional distillation of liquid air. Radon was discovered in 1900 as a gaseous decay product of radium.

Preparation and Uses of the Noble Gases   Commercially, all the noble gases except helium and radon are obtained by the distillation of liquid air. The principal sources of helium are certain natural-gas wells. Helium has the lowest boiling point ($-268.9°C$) of any substance and is very important in low-temperature research. The major use of argon is as a blanketing gas (inert gas) in metallurgical processes. It is also used as a mixture with nitrogen to fill incandescent lightbulbs. In these bulbs the gas mixture conducts heat away from the hot tungsten filament, without reacting with it. All the noble gases are used in gas discharge tubes (containing gas through which a high-voltage electric current can be discharged, giving light from atomic emission). Neon gives a highly visible red-orange emission and has long been used in advertising signs. The noble gases are also used in a number of lasers. The helium–neon laser was the first continuously operating gas laser. It emits red light at a wavelength of 632.8 nm.

Compounds of the Noble Gases   Neil Bartlett, working at the University of British Columbia, prepared the first noble-gas compound after he discovered that molecular oxygen reacts with platinum hexafluoride, PtF_6, to form the ionic solid $[O_2^+][PtF_6^-]$. Because the ionization energy of xenon (1.17×10^3 kJ/mol) is close to that of molecular oxygen (1.21×10^3 kJ/mol), Bartlett reasoned that xenon should also react with platinum hexafluoride. In 1962 he reported the synthesis of an orange-yellow compound with the approximate formula $XePtF_6$. ◄ Later in the same year, chemists from Argonne National Laboratory near Chicago reported that xenon reacts directly with fluorine at 400°C to give the tetrafluoride. The elements react even at room temperature when exposed to sunlight.

$$Xe(g) + 2F_2(g) \longrightarrow XeF_4(s)$$

The product is a volatile, colorless solid (Figure 22.52). Since then, a number of noble-gas compounds have been prepared that typically involve bonds to the highly electronegative elements fluorine and oxygen. Most of these are compounds of xenon (see Table 22.12), but a few are compounds of krypton and radon. Recently, an argon compound, HArF, was synthesized as well as compounds of CUO bonded to Ne, Ar, Kr, and Xe. All of these recent compounds were synthesized at very low temperatures.

The product actually has variable composition and can be represented by the formula $Xe(PtF_6)_n$, where n is between 1 and 2.

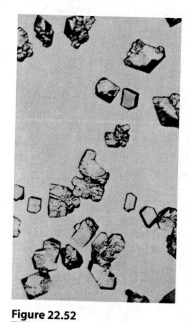

Figure 22.52

Crystals of xenon tetrafluoride This photomicrograph shows crystals obtained in the experiment that first produced a binary compound of xenon.

Table 22.12		
Some Compounds of Xenon		
Compound	**Formula**	**Description**
Xenon difluoride	XeF_2	Colorless crystals
Xenon tetrafluoride	XeF_4	Colorless crystals
Xenon hexafluoride	XeF_6	Colorless crystals
Xenon trioxide	XeO_3	Colorless crystals, explosive
Xenon tetroxide	XeO_4	Colorless gas, explosive

A Checklist for Review

Important Terms

Solvay process (22.2)

Goldschmidt process (22.4)

steam-reforming
  process (22.5)

binary hydride (22.5)

catenation (22.6)

silicones (22.6)

Ostwald process (22.7)

polyphosphoric acids (22.7)

metaphosphoric acids (22.7)

oxide (22.8)

peroxide (22.8)

superoxide (22.8)

Frasch process (22.8)

Claus process (22.8)

contact process (22.8)

Summary of Facts and Concepts

Several general observations can be made about the main-group elements. First, the metallic characteristics of these elements generally decrease across a period from left to right in the periodic table. Second, metallic characteristics of the main-group elements become more pronounced going down any column (group). Finally, a second-period element is usually rather different from the other elements in its group.

The Group IA metals (alkali metals) are soft, chemically reactive elements. Lithium, sodium, and potassium are important alkali metals. In recent years, the commercial uses of lithium have grown markedly. The metal is obtained by the electrolysis of molten lithium chloride and is used in the production of low-density alloys and as a battery anode. Lithium hydroxide is used to make lithium soap for lubricating greases; it is produced by the reaction of lithium carbonate and calcium hydroxide.

Sodium metal is prepared in large quantities. It is used as a reducing agent in the preparation of other metals, such as titanium and zirconium, and in the preparation of dyes and pharmaceuticals. Sodium compounds are of enormous economic importance. Sodium chloride is the source of sodium and most of its compounds. Sodium hydroxide is prepared by the electrolysis of aqueous sodium chloride; as a strong base, it has many useful commercial applications, including aluminum production and petroleum refining. Sodium carbonate is obtained from the mineral trona, which contains sodium carbonate and sodium hydrogen carbonate, and by the *Solvay process* from salt (NaCl) and limestone ($CaCO_3$). Sodium carbonate is used to make glass. Potassium metal is produced in relatively small quantities, but potassium compounds are important. Large quantities of potassium chloride are used as a plant fertilizer.

Magnesium and calcium are the most important of the Group IIA (alkaline earth) metals. Magnesium and its alloys are important structural metals. Calcium is important primarily as its compounds, which are prepared from natural carbonates, such as limestone, and the sulfates, such as gypsum. When limestone is heated strongly, it decomposes to calcium oxide (lime). Enormous quantities of lime are used in the production of iron from its ores.

Of the Group IIIA and Group IVA metals, aluminum, tin, and lead are especially important. Aluminum is the third most abundant element in the earth's crust. It is obtained commercially from bauxite; through chemical processing bauxite

yields pure aluminum oxide. Most of this aluminum oxide is used in the production of aluminum by electrolysis. Some aluminum oxide is used as a carrier for heterogeneous catalysts and in manufacturing industrial ceramic materials.

Tin is normally a metal (called white tin) but does undergo a low-temperature conversion to a nonmetallic form (called gray tin). Tin is obtained by reduction of cassiterite, a mineral form of SnO_2. Tin is used to make tin plate, bronze, and solder. Lead is obtained from galena, which is a sulfide ore, PbS. More than half of the lead produced is used to make electrodes for lead storage batteries. Litharge, or lead(II) oxide, is an important lead compound from which other lead compounds are prepared.

Carbon and tin are the least metallic of the Group IVA elements. *Catenation* is an important feature of carbon chemistry and is responsible for the enormous number of organic compounds. Carbon has several allotropes, the principal ones being diamond and graphite, which are covalent-network solids, and buckminsterfullerene, which is molecular (C_{60}). The element has important industrial uses, including carbon black for rubber tires. The principal oxides of carbon are CO and CO_2. Mixtures of carbon monoxide and hydrogen (synthesis gas) are used to prepare various organic compounds. Liquid and solid carbon dioxide are used as refrigerants, and the gas is used to make carbonated beverages.

Hydrogen is the most abundant element in the universe and is the third most abundant element on the surface of the earth. Most of the hydrogen on earth is found in water. Hydrogen has three isotopes: *protium, deuterium,* and *tritium.* Protium is the most abundant, with less than 0.02% being deuterium and only a trace being radioactive tritium. Deuterium and tritium isotopes can be substituted for protium in chemical compounds in order to provide markers that can be followed during a chemical reaction, or to change the chemical and physical properties of the compound. Elemental hydrogen is produced on an industrial scale by the *steam-reforming process* in which a hydrocarbon is reacted with water in the presence of a catalyst at high temperature. The bulk of the hydrogen produced in this manner is used to make organic compounds including methanol. Hydrogen forms three classes of binary compounds called binary hydrides: ionic hydrides, covalent hydrides, and metallic hydrides. The *ionic hydrides* are reactive solids formed either by the reaction of hydrogen with an alkali metal to form compounds with the general formula MH, or with larger alkaline earth metals to form MH_2. The *covalent hydrides* are compounds in which hydrogen is covalently bonded to another element. The *metallic hydrides* contain a transition metal element and hydrogen. In these compounds, the lattice of metal atoms forms a porous structure that allows hydrogen atoms to enter and bond. Metallic hydrides are often nonstoichiometric, meaning that the ratio of hydrogen atoms to metal atoms is not a whole number.

Silicon is the second most abundant element in the crust of the earth. The majority of silicon-containing compounds consist of chains and networks of silicon–oxygen bonds. Sharing some of the structural attributes of the network solids discussed in Chapter 13 are the *silicones:* materials that contain chains or rings of Si—O bonds with organic groups bonded to the silicon atoms. Depending on the amount and type of bonding between the rings or chains, the silicones can be formulated to be oils, *elastomers,* or resins. Due to their low reactivity and thermal stability, the silicones find many commercial and industrial applications ranging from cosmetics to hydraulic fluids. The *silicon hydrides* (also known as *silanes*) and *silicon halides* are silicon-containing compounds that do not contain Si—O bonds. The silanes consist of straight chains or branched chains of silicon atoms combined with hydrogen atoms with the general formula Si_nH_{n+2} or as rings with the formula Si_5H_{10} or Si_6H_{12}. The silicon halides can be formed by the direct reaction of Si with a halogen. Both the silanes and silicon halides are very reactive.

Of the Group VA elements, nitrogen and phosphorus are particularly important. Nitrogen, N_2, is obtained from liquid air by fractional distillation; liquid nitrogen is used as a refrigerant. Ammonia, NH_3, is the most important compound of nitrogen. It is prepared from the elements and is used as a fertilizer. Ammonia is also the starting compound for the manufacture of other nitrogen compounds. For example, in the *Ostwald process* for the preparation of nitric acid, ammonia is burned in the presence of a catalyst to nitric oxide, NO. The nitric oxide reacts with oxygen to give nitrogen dioxide, which reacts with water to give nitric acid.

Phosphorus has two common allotropes, white phosphorus (P_4) and red phosphorus (chain structure). White phosphorus is obtained by heating a phosphate mineral with sand and coke in an electric furnace. When phosphorus burns in air, it forms phosphorus(V) oxide, P_4O_{10}. This oxide reacts with water to give orthophosphoric acid, H_3PO_4. Phosphorus has many oxoacids; most are obtained by condensation reactions with orthophosphoric acid. One series is called the *polyphosphoric acids;* they have the general formula $H_{n+2}P_nO_{3n+1}$. Triphosphoric acid is an example; sodium triphosphate, $Na_5P_3O_{10}$, is used in detergents. The *metaphosphoric acids* have the general formula $(HPO_3)_n$.

Oxygen, a Group VIA element, occurs in the atmosphere (as O_2), but mostly it is present on earth as oxide and oxoanion minerals. Oxygen has two allotropes: dioxygen, O_2, and ozone, O_3. Dioxygen, usually called simply oxygen, is obtained commercially from liquid air. Oxygen reacts with almost all elements to give *oxides* or, in some cases, *peroxides* or *super-oxides.*

Sulfur, another Group VIA element, occurs in sulfate and sulfide minerals. Free sulfur, S_8, occurring in deep underground deposits is mined by the *Frasch process.* Sulfur is also produced by the *Claus process,* in which hydrogen sulfide (obtained from natural gas and petroleum) is partially burned. Most of the sulfur is used to prepare sulfuric acid by the *contact process.* In this process, sulfur is burned to sulfur dioxide, SO_2, which in the presence of a catalyst and oxygen forms sulfur trioxide, SO_3. This oxide dissolves in concentrated sulfuric acid, which when diluted with water gives additional sulfuric acid. Sulfuric acid is the most important compound of sulfur.

The Group VIIA elements, or halogens, are reactive. Chlorine (Cl_2), a pale greenish-yellow gas, is prepared commercially by the electrolysis of aqueous sodium chloride. Its principal uses are in the preparation of chlorinated hydrocarbons and as a bleaching agent and disinfectant. Hydrogen chloride, HCl, is one of the most important compounds of chlorine; aqueous solutions of HCl are known as hydrochloric acid.

The Group VIIIA elements, the noble gases, were discovered at the end of the nineteenth century. Although the noble gases were at first thought to be unreactive, compounds of these gases are now known.

Operational Skills

Note: The problem-solving skills used in this chapter are discussed in previous chapters.

Review Questions

22.1 Give the commercial source of each of the following metals: Li, Na, Mg, Ca, Al, Sn, Pb.

22.2 Give equations for the reactions of lithium and sodium metals with water and with oxygen in air.

22.3 Write the equation for the reaction of lithium carbonate with barium hydroxide.

22.4 Which do you expect to be more reactive, lithium or potassium? Explain.

22.5   Ethanol, C_2H_5OH, reacts with sodium metal because the hydrogen atom attached to the oxygen atom is slightly acidic. Write a balanced equation for the reaction of sodium with ethanol to give the salt sodium ethoxide, $NaOC_2H_5$.

22.6   (a) Write electrode half-reactions for the electrolysis of fused sodium chloride. (b) Do the same for fused sodium hydroxide. The hydroxide ion is oxidized to oxygen and water.

22.7   How is sodium hydroxide manufactured? What is another product in this process?

22.8   Describe common uses of the following sodium compounds: sodium chloride, sodium hydroxide, and sodium carbonate.

22.9   Describe the main step in the Solvay process. Give the balanced equation for this reaction.

22.10   Because magnesium reacts with oxygen, steam, and carbon dioxide, magnesium fires are extinguished only by smothering the fire with sand. Write balanced equations for the reactions of magnesium with O_2, $H_2O(g)$, and CO_2.

22.11   (a) Calcium oxide is prepared industrially from what calcium compound? Write the chemical equation for the reaction. (b) Write the equation for the preparation of calcium hydroxide.

22.12   Calcium carbonate is used in some antacid preparations to neutralize the hydrochloric acid in the stomach. Write the equation for this neutralization.

22.13   Purified calcium carbonate is prepared by precipitation. Write the equation for the commercial process using carbon dioxide. You can also prepare calcium carbonate by precipitation using sodium carbonate. Write the equation.

22.14   Write the chemical equation of the thermite reaction, in which iron(III) oxide is reduced by aluminum.

22.15   What are some major uses of aluminum oxide?

22.16   How is aluminum sulfate used to purify municipal water supplies?

22.17   Lead(IV) oxide forms the cathode of lead storage batteries. How is this substance produced for these batteries?

22.18   Why are lead pigments no longer used in house paints?

22.19   The yellow paint pigment chrome yellow is produced by a precipitation reaction. Write an equation in which chrome yellow is produced from lead(II) nitrate.

22.20   Describe the reactions that are used in the steam-reforming process for the production of hydrogen.

22.21   Give the names and symbols for the three isotopes of hydrogen. Which isotope is radioactive?

22.22   Explain why hydrogen has the potential to be widely used as a fuel.

22.23   Give an example of a compound of each of the binary hydrides.

22.24   What is meant by the term *catenation*? Give an example of a carbon compound that displays catenation.

22.25   Carbon monoxide is a poisonous gas. What is the mechanism of this poisoning?

22.26   Write equations for the equilibria involving carbon dioxide in water.

22.27   Describe some of the desirable properties of silicones that have led to their widespread use.

22.28   Give the molecular formula for two *silanes* and two hydrocarbon analogs for these compounds.

22.29   Write the balanced equation for the reaction of a halogen with silicon to form a *silicon halide*.

22.30   Describe the natural cycle of nitrogen from the atmosphere to biological organisms and back to the atmosphere.

22.31   Describe Rutherford's preparation of nitrogen from air. Was the gas he obtained pure nitrogen? Explain.

22.32   List the different nitrogen oxides. What is the oxidation number of nitrogen in each?

22.33   In your own words, describe the manufacture of ammonia from natural gas, steam, and air.

22.34   Describe the steps in the Ostwald process for the manufacture of nitric acid from ammonia.

22.35   Describe the structure of white phosphorus. How does the structure account for the reactivity of this substance?

22.36   Give chemical equations for the reaction of white phosphorus in an excess of air and for the reaction of the product with water.

22.37   Describe two different methods used to manufacture phosphoric acid, H_3PO_4, starting from $Ca_3(PO_4)_2$.

22.38   By means of an equation, show how triphosphoric acid could be formed from orthophosphoric acid and diphosphoric acid.

22.39   What is the purpose of adding polyphosphates to a detergent?

22.40   What reaction was used by Priestley in preparing pure oxygen?

22.41   What is the most important commercial means of producing oxygen?

22.42   Define *oxide, peroxide,* and *superoxide*. Give an example of each.

22.43   Give an example of an acidic oxide and a basic oxide.

22.44   List three natural sources of sulfur or sulfur compounds.

22.45   Describe the structure of the rhombic sulfur molecule.

22.46   Discuss the various allotropes of sulfur and describe how they can be prepared from rhombic sulfur.

22.47   Describe the Frasch process for mining sulfur.

22.48   With the aid of chemical equations, describe the Claus process for the production of sulfur from hydrogen sulfide.

22.49   Give equations for preparing each of the following:
a. H_2S b. SO_2

22.50   Give equations for the steps in the contact process for the manufacture of sulfuric acid from sulfur.

22.51   Write equations for each of the following.
a. reaction of H_2S with SO_2
b. oxidation of SO_2 with $Cr_2O_7^{2-}(aq)$ to SO_4^{2-}
c. reaction of hot, concentrated H_2SO_4 with Cu
d. reaction of sulfur with Na_2SO_3

22.52   Give the equation for the reaction used by the Swedish chemist Scheele to prepare chlorine.

22.53 Complete and balance the following equations. Write *NR* if no reaction occurs.

a. $I_2(aq) + Cl^-(aq) \longrightarrow$

b. $Cl_2(aq) + Br^-(aq) \longrightarrow$

c. $Br_2(aq) + I^-(aq) \longrightarrow$

d. $Br_2(aq) + Cl^-(aq) \longrightarrow$

22.54 A test tube contains a solution of one of the following salts: NaCl, NaBr, NaI. Describe a single test that can distinguish among these possibilities.

22.55 What are some major commercial uses of chlorine?

22.56 How is sodium hypochlorite prepared? Give the balanced chemical equation.

22.57 Describe the preparation of perchloric acid from sodium chloride.

22.58 What was the argument used by Bartlett that led him to the first synthesis of a noble-gas compound?

Conceptual Problems

22.59 When producing coke, why is the coal heated in the absence of air? Write the chemical reaction for what would happen if it were to be heated in air.

22.60 Even though hydrogen isn't a metal, why is it in Group IA of most periodic tables?

22.61 What happens to the metallic character of the main-group elements as you move left to right across any row of the periodic table? What happens to the metallic character of the main-group elements as you move down a column (group)?

22.62 Lithium hydroxide, like sodium hydroxide, becomes contaminated when exposed to air. What is the source of this contamination? What reactions take place?

22.63 Aluminum hydroxide is an amphoteric substance. What does this mean? Write equations to illustrate.

22.64 Tin metal would not make a very good structural metal in cold climates. Why?

22.65 Oxygen, like other second-period elements, is somewhat different from the other elements in its group. List some of these differences.

22.66 Given that the reaction $Cl_2(g) + 2KBr(aq) \longrightarrow 2KCl(aq) + Br_2(aq)$ readily occurs, would you expect the reaction $I_2(s) + 2KCl(aq) \longrightarrow 2KI(aq) + Cl_2(aq)$ to occur?

22.67 Hydrogen chloride can be prepared by heating NaCl with concentrated sulfuric acid. Why is substituting NaBr for NaCl in this reaction not a satisfactory way to prepare HBr?

22.68 Do you expect an aqueous solution of sodium hypochlorite to be acidic, neutral, or basic? What about an aqueous solution of sodium perchlorate?

Practice Problems

Group IA: The Alkali Metals

22.69 Caustic soda, NaOH, can be manufactured from sodium carbonate in a manner similar to the preparation of lithium hydroxide. Write balanced equations (in three steps) for the preparation of NaOH from slaked lime, $Ca(OH)_2$, salt (NaCl), carbon dioxide, ammonia, and water.

22.70 Sodium phosphate, Na_3PO_4, is produced by the neutralization reaction. Phosphoric acid, H_3PO_4, is obtained by burning phosphorus to P_4O_{10}, then reacting the oxide with water to give the acid. Write balanced equations (in four steps) for the preparation of Na_3PO_4 from P_4, H_2O, air, and NaCl.

22.71 Complete and balance the following equations.

a. $K(s) + Br_2(l) \longrightarrow$

b. $K(s) + H_2O(l) \longrightarrow$

c. $NaOH(s) + CO_2(g) \longrightarrow$

d. $Li_2CO_3(aq) + HNO_3(aq) \longrightarrow$

e. $K_2SO_4(aq) + Pb(NO_3)_2(aq) \longrightarrow$

22.72 Complete and balance the following equations.

a. $LiHCO_3(s) \xrightarrow{\Delta}$

b. $Na_2SO_4(aq) + BaCl_2(aq) \longrightarrow$

c. $K_2CO_3(aq) + Ca(OH)_2(aq) \longrightarrow$

d. $Li(s) + HCl(aq) \longrightarrow$

e. $Na(s) + ZrCl_4(g) \longrightarrow$

22.73 Francium was discovered as a minor decay product of actinium-227. Write the nuclear equation for the decay of actinium-227 by alpha emission.

22.74 Francium-223 is a radioactive alkali metal that decays by beta emission. Write the nuclear equation for this decay process.

Group IIA: The Alkaline Earth Metals

22.75 Sodium hydroxide and calcium hydroxide are strong bases. What simple chemical test could you use to distinguish between solutions of these two bases?

22.76 Potassium hydroxide and barium hydroxide are strong bases. What simple chemical test could you use to distinguish between solutions of these two bases?

22.77 Devise a chemical method for separating a solution containing $MgCl_2$ and $BaCl_2$ to give two solutions or compounds each containing only one of the metal ions.

22.78   Devise a chemical method for separating a solution containing NaCl and $MgCl_2$ to give two solutions or compounds each containing only one of the metal ions.

22.79   Thorium-230, which occurs in uranium minerals, decays by alpha emission to radium. Write the nuclear equation for this decay process.

22.80   A short-lived isotope of radium decays by alpha emission to radon-219. Write the nuclear equation for this decay process.

22.81   Complete and balance the following equations.
a. $BaCO_3(s) \xrightarrow{\Delta}$
b. $Ba(s) + H_2O(l) \longrightarrow$
c. $Mg(OH)_2(s) + HNO_3(aq) \longrightarrow$
d. $Mg(s) + NiCl_2(aq) \longrightarrow$
e. $NaOH(aq) + MgSO_4(aq) \longrightarrow$

22.82   Complete and balance the following equations.
a. $KOH(aq) + MgCl_2(aq) \longrightarrow$
b. $Mg(s) + CuSO_4(aq) \longrightarrow$
c. $Sr(s) + H_2O(l) \longrightarrow$
d. $SrCO_3(s) + HCl(aq) \longrightarrow$
e. $Ba(OH)_2(aq) + CO_2(g) \longrightarrow$

22.83   You have a 0.12 M solution of calcium hydrogen carbonate. How many grams of calcium hydroxide must be added to 25.0 mL of the solution to precipitate all of the calcium?

22.84   You have a 0.21 M solution of magnesium ion. How many grams of calcium hydroxide must be added to 50.0 mL of the solution to precipitate all of the magnesium ion?

Group IIIA and Group IVA Metals

22.85   Baking powders contain sodium (or potassium) hydrogen carbonate and an acidic substance. When water is added to a baking powder, carbon dioxide is released. One kind of baking powder contains $NaHCO_3$ and sodium aluminum sulfate, $NaAl(SO_4)_2$. Write the net ionic equation for the reaction that occurs in water solution.

22.86   When aluminum sulfate is dissolved in water, it produces an acidic solution. Suppose the pH of this solution is raised by the dropwise addition of aqueous sodium hydroxide. (a) Describe what you would observe as the pH continues to rise. (b) Write balanced equations for any reactions that occur.

22.87   The following solid substances are in separate but unlabeled test tubes: $Al_2(SO_4)_3 \cdot 18H_2O$, $BaCl_2 \cdot 2H_2O$, KOH. Describe how you could identify the compounds by chemical tests using only these substances and water.

22.88   Unlabeled test tubes contain solid $AlCl_3 \cdot 6H_2O$ in one, $Ba(OH)_2 \cdot 8H_2O$ in another, and $MgSO_4 \cdot 7H_2O$ in the other. How could you find out what is in each test tube, using chemical tests that involve only these compounds plus water?

22.89   The $Sn^{2+}(aq)$ ion can be written in more detail as $Sn(H_2O)_6^{2+}$. This ion is acidic by hydrolysis. Write a possible equation for this hydrolysis.

22.90   Lead(II) nitrate, one of the few soluble lead salts, gives a solution with a pH of about 3 to 4. Write a chemical equation to explain why the solution is acidic.

22.91   Lead(IV) oxide is a strong oxidizing agent. For example, lead(IV) oxide will oxidize hydrochloric acid to chlorine, Cl_2. Write the balanced equation for this reaction.

22.92   Lead(IV) oxide can be prepared by oxidizing plumbite ion, $Pb(OH)_3^{-}$, which exists in a basic solution of Pb^{2+}. Write the balanced equation for this oxidation by OCl^{-} in basic solution.

22.93   Complete and balance the following equations.
a. $Al_2O_3(s) + H_2SO_4(aq) \longrightarrow$
b. $Al(s) + AgNO_3(aq) \longrightarrow$
c. $Pb(NO_3)_2(aq) + NaI(aq) \longrightarrow$
d. $Al(s) + Mn_3O_4(s) \longrightarrow$
e. $Ga(OH)_3(s) \xrightarrow{\Delta}$

22.94   Complete and balance the following equations.
a. $Pb(NO_3)_2(aq) + Al(s) \longrightarrow$
b. $Pb(NO_3)_2(aq) + Na_2CrO_4(aq) \longrightarrow$
c. $Al_2(SO_4)_3(aq) + $ dilute $LiOH(aq) \longrightarrow$
d. $Al(s) + HCl(aq) \longrightarrow$
e. $Sn(s) + HBr(aq) \longrightarrow$

Hydrogen

22.95   Calculate the amount of heat evolved when 3.5×10^4 kg of hydrogen is combusted.

$$2H_2(g) + O_2(g) \longrightarrow 2H_2O(g) \qquad \Delta H = -484 \text{ kJ}$$

22.96   How much heat will be evolved when 20.0 grams of the binary covalent hydride HF is produced via the following reaction?

$$F_2(g) + H_2(g) \longrightarrow 2HF(g) \qquad \Delta H = -545 \text{ kJ}$$

22.97   Indicate the oxidation state for the element noted in each of the following:
a. H in CaH_2 b. H in H_2O
c. C in CH_4 d. S in H_2SO_4

22.98   Indicate the oxidation state for the element noted in each of the following:
a. H in H_2 c. Si in SiH_4
b. H in C_2H_4 d. N in HNO_3

Group IVA: The Carbon Family

22.99 Describe the bonding (using valence bond theory) of the Group IVA atoms in each of the following:
a. C_2H_6
b. SiF_6^{2-}
c. $CH_3CH=CH_2$
d. SiH_4

22.100 Describe the bonding (using valence bond theory) of the Group IVA atoms in each of the following:
a. CCl_4
b. HCN
c. SiF_4
d. CH_3COOH (acetic acid)

22.101 Calculate the standard enthalpy change for the following "cracking" reactions.
a. $CH_4(g) \longrightarrow C(graphite) + 2H_2(g)$
b. $C_2H_6(g) \longrightarrow C_2H_4(g) + H_2(g)$

22.102 Calculate the standard enthalpy change for the following reactions involving synthesis gas.
a. $CO(g) + 2H_2(g) \longrightarrow CH_3OH(g)$
b. $CO(g) + 3H_2(g) \longrightarrow CH_4(g) + H_2O(g)$

22.103 Complete and balance the following equations.
a. $CO_2(g) + Ba(OH)_2(aq) \longrightarrow$
b. $MgCO_3(s) + HBr(aq) \longrightarrow$

22.104 Complete and balance the following equations.
a. $NaHCO_3(aq) + HC_2H_3O_2(aq) \longrightarrow$
b. $Ca(HCO_3)_2(aq) + Ca(OH)_2(aq) \longrightarrow$

22.105 Use balanced equations to show how you could prepare Na_2CO_3 from carbon, NaOH, air, and H_2O.

22.106 Use balanced equations to show how you could prepare methanol, CH_3OH, from ethane, C_2H_6, and water.

Group VA: Nitrogen and the Phosphorus Family

22.107 Magnesium nitride, Mg_3N_2, reacts with water to produce magnesium hydroxide and ammonia. How many grams of ammonia can you obtain from 7.50 g of magnesium nitride?

22.108 Ammonia reacts with oxygen in the presence of a platinum catalyst to give nitric oxide, NO. How many grams of oxygen are required in this reaction to give 3.00 g NO?

22.109 You have the following substances: NH_3, O_2, Pt, and H_2O. Write equations for the preparation of N_2O from these substances.

22.110 Give equations for the preparation of N_2O. You can use NaOH, $NaNO_3$, H_2SO_4, and $(NH_4)_2SO_4$ (plus H_2O). Several steps are required.

22.111 Zinc metal reacts with concentrated nitric acid to give zinc ion and ammonium ion. Write the balanced equation for this reaction.

22.112 Silver metal reacts with nitric acid to give silver ion and nitric oxide. Write the balanced equation for this reaction.

22.113 Although phosphorus pentabromide exists in the vapor phase as PBr_5 molecules, in the solid phase the substance is ionic and has the structure $[PBr_4^+]Br^-$. What is the expected geometry of PBr_4^+? Describe the bonding to phosphorus in PBr_4^+.

22.114 Although phosphorus pentachloride exists in the vapor phase as PCl_5 molecules, in the solid phase the substance is ionic and has the structure $[PCl_4^+][PCl_6^-]$. What is the expected geometry of PCl_6^-? Describe the bonding to phosphorus in PCl_6^-.

22.115 Phosphorous acid, H_3PO_3, is oxidized to phosphoric acid, H_3PO_4, by hot, concentrated sulfuric acid, which is reduced to SO_2. Write the balanced equation for this reaction.

22.116 Phosphorous acid, H_3PO_3, is oxidized to phosphoric acid, H_3PO_4, by nitric acid, which is reduced to nitric oxide, NO. Write the balanced equation for this reaction.

22.117 According to an analysis, a sample of phosphate rock contains 74.6% $Ca_3(PO_4)_2$, by mass. How many grams of phosphoric acid, H_3PO_4, can be obtained from 30.0 g of the phosphate rock according to the following reaction?

$$Ca_3(PO_4)_2(s) + 3H_2SO_4(aq) \longrightarrow 3CaSO_4(s) + 2H_3PO_4(aq)$$

22.118 According to an analysis, a sample of phosphate rock contains 71.2% $Ca_3(PO_4)_2$, by mass. How many grams of calcium dihydrogen phosphate, $Ca(H_2PO_4)_2$, can be obtained from 10.0 g of phosphate rock from the following reaction?

$$Ca_3(PO_4)_2(s) + 4H_3PO_4(aq) \longrightarrow 3Ca(H_2PO_4)_2(aq)$$

Group VIA: Oxygen and the Sulfur Family

22.119 Write an equation for each of the following.
a. burning of lithium metal in oxygen
b. burning of methylamine, CH_3NH_2, in excess oxygen (N ends up as N_2)
c. burning of diethyl sulfide, $(C_2H_5)_2S$, in excess oxygen

22.120 Write an equation for each of the following.
a. burning of calcium metal in oxygen
b. burning of phosphine, PH_3, in excess oxygen
c. burning of ethanolamine, $HOCH_2CH_2NH_2$, in excess oxygen (N ends up as N_2)

22.121 What are the oxidation numbers of sulfur in each of the following?
a. SF_6
b. SO_3
c. H_2S
d. $CaSO_3$

22.122 What are the oxidation numbers of sulfur in each of the following?
a. S_8
b. CaS
c. $CaSO_4$
d. SCl_4

22.123 Selenous acid, H_2SeO_3, is reduced by H_2S to sulfur, S_8, and selenium, Se_8. Write the balanced equation for this reaction.

22.124 Concentrated sulfuric acid oxidizes iodide ion to iodine, I_2. Write the balanced equation for this reaction.

22.125 Sodium hydrogen sulfite is prepared from sodium carbonate and sulfur dioxide:

$$Na_2CO_3(s) + 2SO_2(g) + H_2O(l) \longrightarrow$$
$$2NaHSO_3(aq) + CO_2(g)$$

How many grams of $NaHSO_3$ can be obtained from 25.0 g of Na_2CO_3?

22.126 Sodium thiosulfate, $Na_2S_2O_3$, is prepared from sodium sulfite and sulfur:

$$8Na_2SO_3(aq) + S_8(s) \longrightarrow 8Na_2S_2O_3(aq)$$

How many grams of $Na_2S_2O_3$ can be obtained from 50.0 g of sulfur?

Group VIIA: The Halogens

22.127 A solution of chloric acid may be prepared by reacting a solution of barium chlorate with sulfuric acid. Barium sulfate precipitates. Write the balanced equation for the reaction.

22.128 A solution of chlorous acid may be prepared by reacting a solution of barium chlorite with sulfuric acid. Barium sulfate precipitates. Write the balanced equation for the reaction.

22.129 Chlorine can be prepared by oxidizing chloride ion (from hydrochloric acid) with potassium dichromate, $K_2Cr_2O_7$, which is reduced to Cr^{3+}. Write the balanced equation for the reaction.

22.130 Iodic acid, HIO_3, can be prepared by oxidizing elemental iodine with concentrated nitric acid, which is reduced to nitrogen dioxide, $NO_2(g)$. Write the balanced equation for the reaction.

22.131 Discuss the bonding in each of the following molecules or ions. What is the expected molecular geometry?
a. Cl_2O b. BrO_3^- c. BrF_3

22.132 Discuss the bonding in each of the following molecules or ions. What is the expected molecular geometry?
a. $HClO$ b. ClO_4^- c. ClF_5

22.133 Write balanced equations for each of the following.
a. Bromine reacts with aqueous sodium hydroxide to give hypobromite and bromide ions.
b. Hydrogen bromide gas forms when sodium bromide is heated with phosphoric acid.

22.134 Write balanced equations for each of the following.
a. Solid calcium fluoride is heated with sulfuric acid to give hydrogen fluoride vapor.
b. Solid potassium chlorate is carefully heated to yield potassium chloride and potassium perchlorate.

22.135 By calculating the standard emf, decide whether aqueous sodium hypochlorite solution will oxidize $Fe^{2+}(aq)$ to $Fe^{3+}(aq)$ in basic solution under standard conditions. See Appendix I for data.

22.136 Using standard electrode potentials, decide whether aqueous sodium hypochlorite solution will oxidize Br^- to Br_2 in basic solution under standard conditions. See Appendix I for data.

Group VIIIA: The Noble Gases

22.137 Xenon tetrafluoride, XeF_4, is a colorless solid. Give the Lewis formula for the XeF_4 molecule. What is the hybridization of the xenon atom in this compound? What geometry is predicted by the VSEPR model for this molecule?

22.138 Xenon tetroxide, XeO_4, is a colorless, unstable gas. Give the Lewis formula for the XeO_4 molecule. What is the hybridization of the xenon atom in this compound? What geometry would you expect for this molecule?

22.139 Xenon difluoride, XeF_2, is hydrolyzed (broken up by water) in basic solution to give xenon, fluoride ion, and O_2 as products. Write a balanced equation for the reaction.

22.140 Xenon trioxide, XeO_3, is reduced to xenon in acidic solution by iodide ion. Iodide ion is oxidized to iodine, I_2. Write a balanced chemical equation for the reaction.

General Problems

22.141 A 50.00-mL volume of 0.4987 M HCl was added to a 5.436-g sample of milk of magnesia. This solution was then titrated with 0.2456 M NaOH. If it required 39.42 mL of NaOH to reach the endpoint, what was the mass percentage of $Mg(OH)_2$ in the milk of magnesia?

22.142 An antacid tablet consists of calcium carbonate with other ingredients. The calcium carbonate in a 0.9863-g sample of the antacid was dissolved in 50.00 mL of 0.5068 M HCl,

then titrated with 41.23 mL of 0.2590 M NaOH. What was the mass percentage of $CaCO_3$ in the antacid?

22.143 Calculate the standard enthalpy change, $\Delta H°$, for the following reaction at 25°C.

$$Fe_2O_3(s) + 2Al(s) \longrightarrow 2Fe(s) + Al_2O_3(s)$$

What is the enthalpy change per mole of iron?

22.144 Calculate the standard enthalpy change, $\Delta H°$, for the following reaction at 25°C.

$$3CaO(s) + 2Al(s) \longrightarrow 3Ca(s) + Al_2O_3(s)$$

What is the enthalpy change per mole of calcium?

22.145 A sample of limestone was dissolved in hydrochloric acid, and the carbon dioxide gas that evolved was collected. If a 0.1662-g sample of limestone gave 34.56 mL of dry carbon dioxide gas at 745 mmHg and 21°C, what was the mass percentage of $CaCO_3$ in the limestone?

22.146 A sample of rock containing magnesite, $MgCO_3$, was dissolved in hydrochloric acid, and the carbon dioxide gas that evolved was collected. If a 0.1504-g sample of the rock gave 37.71 mL of dry carbon dioxide gas at 758 mmHg and 22°C, what was the mass percentage of $MgCO_3$ in the rock?

22.147 How many grams of sodium chloride are required to produce 10.00 g of $NaHCO_3$ by the Solvay process?

22.148 How many grams of aluminum are required to react with 15.00 g of chromium(III) oxide by the Goldschmidt process for the production of chromium metal?

22.149 Estimate the temperature at which strontium carbonate begins to decompose to strontium oxide and CO_2 at 1 atm.

$$SrCO_3(s) \longrightarrow SrO(s) + CO_2(g)$$

Use thermodynamic data in Appendix C.

22.150 Estimate the temperature at which barium carbonate decomposes to barium oxide and CO_2 at 1 atm.

$$BaCO_3(s) \longrightarrow BaO(s) + CO_2(g)$$

Use thermodynamic data in Appendix C.

22.151 Calculate $E°$ for the disproportionation of $In^+(aq)$.

$$3In^+(aq) \rightleftharpoons 2In(s) + In^{3+}(aq)$$

(*Disproportionation* is a reaction in which a species undergoes both oxidation and reduction.) Use the following standard potentials:

$$In^+(aq) + e^- \rightleftharpoons In(s); E° = -0.21 \text{ V}$$
$$In^{3+}(aq) + 2e^- \rightleftharpoons In^+(aq); E° = -0.40 \text{ V}$$

From $E°$, calculate $\Delta G°$ for the disproportionation (in kilojoules). Does this reaction occur spontaneously?

22.152 Calculate $E°$ for the disproportionation of $Tl^+(aq)$.

$$3Tl^+(aq) \rightleftharpoons 2Tl(s) + Tl^{3+}(aq)$$

(*Disproportionation* is a reaction in which a species undergoes both oxidation and reduction.) Use the following standard potentials:

$$Tl^+(aq) + e^- \rightleftharpoons Tl(s); E° = -0.34 \text{ V}$$
$$Tl^{3+}(aq) + 2e^- \rightleftharpoons Tl^+(aq); E° = 1.25 \text{ V}$$

From $E°$, calculate $\Delta G°$ for the disproportionation (in kilojoules). Does this reaction occur spontaneously?

22.153 Lithium hydroxide has been used in spaceships to absorb carbon dioxide exhaled by astronauts. Assuming that the product is lithium carbonate, determine what mass of lithium hydroxide is needed to absorb the carbon dioxide from 1.00 L of air containing 30.0 mmHg partial pressure of CO_2 at 25°C.

22.154 Potassium chlorate, $KClO_3$, is used in fireworks and explosives. It can be prepared by bubbling chlorine into hot aqueous potassium hydroxide; $KCl(aq)$ and H_2O are the other products in the reaction. How many grams of $KClO_3$ can be obtained from 138 L of Cl_2 whose pressure is 784 mmHg at 25°C?

22.155 The main ingredient in many phosphate fertilizers is $Ca(H_2PO_4)_2 \cdot H_2O$. If a fertilizer is 17.1% P (by mass), and all of this phosphorus is present as $Ca(H_2PO_4)_2 \cdot H_2O$, what is the mass percentage of this salt in the fertilizer?

22.156 A fertilizer contains phosphorus in two compounds, $Ca(H_2PO_4)_2 \cdot H_2O$ and $CaHPO_4$. The fertilizer contains 30.0% $Ca(H_2PO_4)_2 \cdot H_2O$ and 10.0% $CaHPO_4$ (by mass). What is the mass percentage of phosphorus in the fertilizer?

22.157 NaClO solution is made by electrolysis of $NaCl(aq)$ by allowing the products NaOH and Cl_2 to mix. How long must a cell operate to produce 1.00×10^3 L of 5.25% NaClO solution (density = 1.00 g/mL) if the cell current is 3.00×10^3 A?

22.158 Sodium perchlorate, $NaClO_4$, is produced by electrolysis of sodium chlorate, $NaClO_3$. If a current of 2.50×10^3 A passes through an electrolytic cell, how many kilograms of sodium perchlorate are produced per hour?

22.159 The amount of sodium hypochlorite in a bleach solution can be determined by using a given volume of bleach to oxidize excess iodide ion to iodine, because the reaction goes to completion. The amount of iodine produced is then determined by titration with sodium thiosulfate, $Na_2S_2O_3$, which is oxidized to sodium tetrathionate, $Na_2S_4O_6$. Potassium iodide was added in excess to 5.00 mL of bleach (density = 1.00 g/mL). This solution, containing the iodine released in the reaction, was titrated with 0.100 M $Na_2S_2O_3$. If 34.6 mL of sodium thiosulfate was required to reach the endpoint (detected by disappearance of the blue color of the starch–iodine complex), what was the mass percentage of NaClO in the bleach?

22.160 Ascorbic acid, $C_6H_8O_6$ (vitamin C), is a reducing agent. The amount of this acid in solution can be determined quantitatively by a titration procedure involving iodine, I_2, in which ascorbic acid is oxidized to dehydroascorbic acid, $C_6H_6O_6$.

$$C_6H_8O_6(aq) + I_2(aq) \longrightarrow C_6H_6O_6(aq) + 2HI(aq)$$

A 30.0-g sample of an orange-flavored beverage mix was placed in a flask to which 10.00 mL of 0.0500 M KIO_3 and excess KI were added. The IO_3^- and I^- ions react in acid solution to give I_2, which then reacts with ascorbic acid. Excess iodine is titrated with sodium thiosulfate (see Problem 22.159). If 31.2 mL of 0.0300 M $Na_2S_2O_3$ is required to titrate the excess I_2, how many grams of ascorbic acid are there in 100.0 g of beverage mix?

Media Activities

Key: The media activities are designed to direct you to electronic resources that will help you master important concepts or serve as a reference. All resources needed to complete these activities are available on both the student CD and the student web site (select Ebbing/Gammon General Chemistry from www.college.hmco.com/chemistry), with the exception of the ACE practice tests and the Molecule Library, which are available on the student web site.

22.161   Watch the Reaction of Potassium in Water *Visualization.*

a. If cesium metal were reacted with water, how would it compare with the reaction shown in the *Visualization?* Write the balanced equation for the reaction of Cs(s) with water; be sure to include all state symbols in your equation.

b. What are the signs of: ΔH, ΔS, and ΔG for the reaction of sodium with water?

22.162   Watch the Barking Dogs (White Phosphorus) *Visualization.*

a. Using the tabulated values from Appendix C, calculate $\Delta G°$ for the reaction of white phosphorus, P_4, with oxygen, O_2, to produce $P_4O_{10}(s)$. (Don't forget to balance the equation.) Do the results of this calculation agree with what you observed in the *Visualization?*

b. Using the tabulated values from Appendix C, calculate $\Delta S°$ and $\Delta H°$ for the reaction: $N_2(g) + 2O_2(g) \longrightarrow 2NO_2(g)$. Based on the results of these calculations, would you expect this reaction to be spontaneous?

c. Why do you think N_2 is much less reactive than P_4?

22.163   For review, take the ACE practice test for Chapter 22 on the student web site.

Appendixes

Appendix 1

Mathematical Operations

In this discussion, we work with four mathematical tools that are essential parts of the chemist's toolbox: exponents, logarithms, the quadratic equation, and graphing linear functions. This is not intended to be a complete treatment. Rather, it is an introduction upon which you can build as you study chemistry.

A1.1 Working with Exponents

Numbers tell us how much we have. In chemistry, the numbers can be remarkably small, as in the mass of a single sodium atom (0.000 000 000 000 000 000 000 04 gram). They can also be very large, as in the total number of atoms of the universe. For instance, the number of atoms in the universe is estimated by the National Solar Observatory at Sacramento Peak to be, perhaps, 10 000 000 000 000 000 000 000 000 000 000 000 000 000 000 000 000 000 000 000 000 000 000 000 atoms.

These numbers are unwieldy to work with, so we convert them into *exponential notation*, a way of expressing numbers that uses the powers of 10. The key to exponential notation is to know what happens when we multiply 10 by itself any number of times. For example, when we multiply 10 by itself 3 times, what do we get?

$$10 \times 10 \times 10 = 1000$$

When we use exponential notation, we put the number of times we multiply 10 by itself as a superscript immediately after the 10. That is,

$$10 \times 10 \times 10 = 10^3 = 1000$$

We can expand this list indefinitely:

10	$10^1 = 10$
10×10	$10^2 = 100$
$10 \times 10 \times 10$	$10^3 = 1000$
$10 \times 10 \times 10 \times 10$	$10^4 = 10000$
$10 \times 10 \times 10 \times 10 \times 10 \times 10 \times 10 \times 10$	$10^8 = 100000000$
and so on	

Note that the number of zeros after the 1 is equal to the number of the superscript, which is called the *power* of 10. The number 10,000 is equal to 10^4, or, in words, "ten to the fourth power."

What would our number of atoms in the universe look like in scientific notation?

10 000 000 000 000 000 000 000 000 000 000 000 000 000 000 000 000 000 000 000 000 000 000 000 000 000 000 atoms $= 10^{79}$ atoms, or "ten to the 79th power" atoms

What if we have a number such as 60,000? We can split this into two numbers in such a way that one of the numbers is a power of 10. Thus 60,000 becomes $6 \times 10,000$. This is the same as 6×10^4. The number 6 is known as a *pre-exponential*. Using the pre-exponential and the exponential terms, we can express the number 823,000,000 in exponential notation as 8.23×10^8. It may also be expressed as

$$82.3 \times 10^7$$

$$823 \times 10^6$$

or even 8230×10^5 ($8230 \times 100,000$), although that is fairly awkward. In each case, however, we have reduced the exponent by 1 (a power of 10) as we increased the pre-exponential term by a factor of 10. The number remains the same—823,000,000—in each case.

We can also go from the large to the small:

1 $10^0 \; = 1$
1/10 $10^{-1} = 0.1$
$1/(10 \times 10)$ $10^{-2} = 0.01$
$1/(10 \times 10 \times 10)$ $10^{-3} = 0.001$
$1/(10 \times 10 \times 10 \times 10)$ $10^{-4} = 0.0001$
$1/(10 \times 10 \times 10 \times 10 \times 10 \times 10 \times 10 \times 10)$ $10^{-8} = 0.00000001$
and so on

We note that the number of zeros after the decimal point is equal to the negative subscript minus 1. There are seven zeros after the decimal point in 10^{-8}.

Addition and Subtraction

If we wish to add or subtract numbers that are in exponential notation without using an electronic calculator, the numbers must be raised to the same power of 10. We can achieve this prior to the addition or calculation by moving the decimal place as appropriate. For example,

$$(3.11 \times 10^4) + (2.07 \times 10^5) = (3.11 \times 10^4) + (20.7 \times 10^4) = 23.8 \times 10^4 = 2.38 \times 10^5$$

$$(3.11 \times 10^4) - (9.50 \times 10^3) = (31.1 \times 10^3) - (9.50 \times 10^3) = 21.6 \times 10^3 = 2.16 \times 10^4$$

If we are using a calculator, we can just enter the numbers without any adjustment. We do this with the key labeled EXP or EE on most calculators. For example, to enter 3.11×10^4, we key in the following sequence:

$$\boxed{3}\,\boxed{\cdot}\,\boxed{1}\,\boxed{1}\;\boxed{\text{EXP}}\,\boxed{4}$$

To enter a number with a negative exponent, such as 3.11×10^{-4}, we follow the sequence

Multiplication and Division

When numbers expressed in exponential notation are to be multiplied, the exponent parts of the numbers must be added together:

$$(7.20 \times 10^4) \times (2.10 \times 10^3) = (7.20 \times 2.10) \times 10^{3+4} = 15.1 \times 10^7 = 1.51 \times 10^8$$

When numbers expressed in exponential notation are to be divided, the exponent of the denominator is subtracted from the exponent of the numerator:

$$3.70 \times 10^2/2.20 \times 10^3 = (3.70/2.20) \times 10^{\,2-3} = 1.68 \times 10^{-1}$$

PRACTICE

a. Convert 345 000 000 into exponential form.   (Ans: 3.45×10^8)

b. Convert 1.43×10^{-3} into nonexponential form.   (Ans: 0.00143)

c. Calculate: $(2.56 \times 10^2) + (3.41 \times 10^3)$ (Ans: 3.67×10^3)

d. Calculate: $(7.11 \times 10^6) - (2.50 \times 10^5)$ (Ans: 6.86×10^6)

e. Calculate: $(8.26 \times 10^2) \times (1.70 \times 10^4)$ (Ans: 1.40×10^7)

f. Calculate: $(6.32 \times 10^7)/(7.70 \times 10^4)$ (Ans: 8.21×10^2)

A1.2   Working with Logarithms

Logarithms to the Base 10

As we saw in the previous section, we can use exponential notation to indicate the conversion of 10 into 1000 by raising 10 to the third power:

$$10^3 = 1000$$

Here 3 is referred to as the *logarithm* of 1000 to the base 10, because it is the exponent of the base number 10 that is needed to raise 10 to equal 1000. We can indicate this by writing $\log_{10} 1000 = 3$, which is read, "the logarithm to the base 10 of the number 1000 is 3."

Logarithms to the base 10 are known as *common* logarithms, and use of the base 10 is so common that it is not always explicitly stated. When you see a reference to the logarithm, or *log*, of a number without the base being specified, you should assume the base is 10.

Logarithms can be negative as well as positive. Here are some other examples:

logarithm of 10 000 to base 10 = 4 $\log_{10} 10\,000 = 4$

logarithm of 100 to base 10 = 2 $\log_{10} 100 = 2$

logarithm of 1 to base 10 = 0 (because $10^0 = 1$) $\log_{10} 1 = 0$

logarithm of 0.01 to base 10 = -2 $\log_{10} 0.01 = -2$

logarithm of 0.0001 to base 10 = -4 $\log_{10} 0.0001 = -4$

Most numbers are not the simple multiples of 10 used in our examples above. For more awkward numbers, such as 73.5, we use the LOG key on a calculator to find the value of the logarithm to the base 10. Get a scientific calculator, press the LOG key, and then enter 73.5 followed by the equals key. You will find that

$$\log_{10} 73.5 = 1.866$$

which tells us that $10^{1.866} = 73.5$.

This answer makes sense, because 73.5 is between 10 (which has a logarithm of 1, because $10^1 = 10$) and 100 (which has a logarithm of 2, because $10^2 = 100$). Accordingly, we expect the logarithm of 73.5 to be between 1 and 2 and to be closer to 2 than to 1. Because the integers to the left of the decimal in a logarithm only set the location of the decimal point, the number of digits after the decimal point in the logarithm should equal the number of significant figures in the original number. Hence the logarithm 1.866 only has three significant figures.

Now let's consider working in the opposite direction. Finding the number that corresponds to a given logarithm is known as obtaining an *antilogarithm* (or antilog). The calculator will do this for us when we either use the 10^x key or press the inverse function key (labeled INV or SHIFT) followed by the LOG key. Determine which method your calculator uses, and then confirm that

$$\text{antilog } 2 = 100$$
$$\text{antilog } 1.866 = 73.5$$

Natural Logarithms

The mathematical equations that describe the behavior of many natural phenomena frequently involve the constant e, which has a value of 2.71828.... Logarithms that have the number e as the base are referred to as *natural logarithms*. The natural logarithm (or natural log) of a number is the power to which e must be raised to equal that number. The natural logarithm is often symbolized ln to distinguish it from the log or $\log_{10}$ used for logarithms to the base 10.

You can use the LN key of your calculator to find the natural logarithm of any number. For example,

$$\ln 10.0 = 2.303 \text{ because } e^{2.303} = 10$$
$$\ln 73.5 = 4.297 \text{ because } e^{4.297} = 73.5$$

Natural antilogarithms can be obtained by either using the e^x key or pressing the inverse function key followed by the LN key. Use whichever system your calculator employs to confirm that

$$\text{natural antilogarithm of } 2.303 = 10$$
$$\text{natural antilogarithm of } 4.297 = 73.5$$

Mathematical Operations with Logarithms

The logarithm of a product equals the *sum* of the logarithms of the individual numbers being multiplied. This follows from the fact that logarithms are exponents, which we looked at in the previous section.

$$\text{logarithm}(a \times b) = \text{logarithm } a + \text{logarithm } b$$

By the same logic, the logarithm of the result of dividing a number by another is obtained by subtracting the logarithm of the denominator from that of the numerator:

$$\log(a/b) = \log a - \log b$$

And if we wish to raise a logarithm to a certain power, we use the following rules:

$$\log(a^n) = n \log a$$
$$\log(a^{1/n}) = (1/n) \log a$$

These rules apply no matter what base is used.

PRACTICE

Use your calculator to find the numerical answer to the following operations.

a. $\log_{10} 55.2$ (Ans: 1.742)
b. $\ln 27.6$ (Ans: 3.318)
c. antilog 1.522 (Ans: 33.3)
d. natural antilog 3.233 (Ans: 25.4)

A1.3 Solving the Quadratic Equation

A quadratic equation has the variable raised to the second power, and no higher. It has the general form

$$ax^2 + bx + c = 0$$

In this textbook, we use quadratic equations to solve some problems related to chemical equilibrium, including acid–base chemistry, solubility chemistry, and complex-ion chemistry (Chapters 16–18).

Although there are several ways to solve quadratic equations, we will use the *quadratic formula* in this text. The formula will always yield two answers (because second-order polynomial equations describe a parabola that has two y-axis values for every x-axis value), yet only one of these answers will be chemically reasonable. Whenever we use the quadratic equation, we will explain how you will know which of the two answers is reasonable. The quadratic formula is used to solve for the variable x and has the form

$$x = \frac{-b \pm \sqrt{b^2 - 4ac}}{2a}$$

where the constants a, b, and c are the numbers in the quadratic equation when it is written in general form.

For example, if we are solving the following equation, we need to determine the values of a, b, and c in order to use the quadratic formula.

$$x^2 + 0.0500x - 0.0300 = 0$$
$$ax^2 + \quad bx + c \quad = 0$$

Comparing this to the general form for a quadratic equation reveals that the values for the constants a, b, and c are

$$a = 1; \quad b = +0.0500; \quad c = -0.0300$$

Next, we insert our values for a, b, and c into the equadratic equation and solve. We obtain two values for x:

$$x = \frac{-b \pm \sqrt{b^2 - 4ac}}{2a}$$

$$x = \frac{-0.0500 \pm \sqrt{(0.0500)^2 - 4(1)(-0.0300)}}{2(1)}$$

$$x = \frac{-0.0500 \pm \sqrt{0.00250 + 0.120}}{2(1)}$$

$$x = \frac{-0.0500 \pm 0.350}{2(1)}$$

$$x = 0.150, -0.200$$

Just remember: Although we get two answers when we solve the quadratic equation, we will find in our chemistry work that only one of them will be chemically valid.

PRACTICE

What is the value of x in this quadratic equation?

$$x^2 + 0.0505x - 0.0435 = 0 \qquad \text{(Ans: } +0.184, -0.235\text{)}$$

A1.4   Graphing

In your study of chemistry and other aspects of science, you will frequently need to interpret or draw graphs that show the relationship between variables. For any value of one variable, the graph shows the corresponding value of the other variable. The variable whose value we monitor rather than control during an experiment is called the *dependent variable* and is usually displayed along the vertical axis, which is called the *y*-axis. The other variable, which we may be purposely varying during the course of an experiment, is called the *independent variable* and is displayed along the horizontal axis, which is called the *x*-axis. If we are monitoring the production of some chemical product with time, for example, the increasing concentration of the product would be plotted on the vertical *y*-axis, and time would be plotted on the horizontal *x*-axis.

Graphs can be linear (consisting of straight lines), can be made up of curves, or can consist of mixtures of linear and curved portions. Any straight-line graph is described by the general equation

$$y = mx + b$$

where m is the slope of the line and b is the value at the intercept of the line with the *y*-axis.

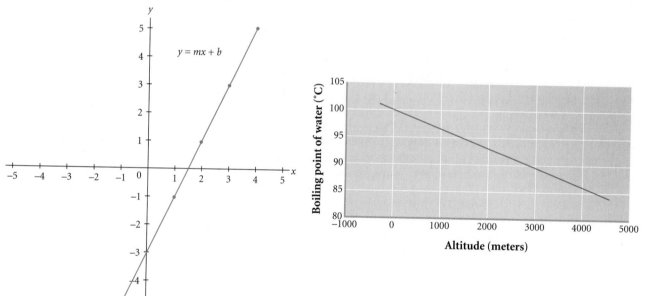

Consider, for example, the two graphs above. The one on the left illustrates the general principles, and on the right we show a real-world example. In the graph on the left, we can calculate the slope m as $(y_2-y_1)/(x_2-x_1) = 4/2 = 2$. And we can see that the intercept occurs at −3 on the *y*-axis. Therefore, the equation of the straight line is $y = 2x - 3$.

PRACTICE

The real world is rarely as neat and tidy as general principles. Calculate the equation of the straight line in the real-world example on the right, above. Note that in this case the slope has a negative value, and the *x*-axis does not cut across the *y*-axis at the zero level. These are both features you may encounter in graphs, but the equation can be readily calculated by using the method illustrated in the example above. (Ans: $y = -0.0033x + 100$)

Appendix 2

Calculating Uncertainties in Measurements

Error in measurements is an obstinate inevitability that all scientists (and everyone else, for that matter) must contend with. When we measure the distance to the store, or the mass of a raisin, we encounter a certain amount of variability. As we learned in Chapter 1, this variability is due not only to random error but also to systematic error. Even during the perfect measurement, where the systematic error is negligible, our measurement still contains some random error. Therefore, when scientists report a measurement, they make sure to include a statement about the level of confidence that they place in that number.

The statement of how *precise* a set of measurements are can be reported as the standard deviation(s) of the measurements. The mathematical definition of *standard deviation* is

$$s = \sqrt{\frac{\sum_{i=1}^{n}(x_i - \bar{x})^2}{n - 1}}$$

where x_i = each individual measurement
$\bar{x}$ = the mean (average) of the measurements
n = number of measurements taken

The equation indicates that we take the difference between each measurement and the mean, square it, and then add all these results together. The total is then divided by one less than the total number of measurements, and the square root of the result is taken.

The standard deviation can be used to determine how well the measurements agree with the literature value. This is typically established by calculating a *confidence limit* or a *confidence interval*. The confidence limit (C.L.) consists of a range of numbers that describes the precision of our set of measurements. The confidence interval (C.I.) describes the mean value and the confidence limit employed to generate a range of numbers surrounding the mean value of our measurements. This number is called a confidence interval because we have a great deal of confidence that the actual number lies within this range. As we increase our confidence in the measurement, the confidence limit increases in size. Conversely, as the confidence limit decreases in size with a set confidence level, our precision increases.

$$\text{C.L.} = \frac{ts}{\sqrt{n}}$$

$$\text{C.I.} = \bar{x} \pm \frac{ts}{\sqrt{n}}$$

where t is a measure of the confidence we place in the measurement.

The levels of confidence that are most commonly used in determining a confidence interval are the 90% and 95% levels. A 90% level of confidence means that in 10% of cases, the accepted value will lie outside our confidence interval. A 95% level of confidence indicates that the accepted value will lie outside our interval in only 5% of cases. For example, say an experiment produces three measurements such that the mean is 2.31 and the standard deviation is 0.48. The value of

TABLE A2.1 Values of *t* for Various Levels of Probability

Number of Measurements	50%	90%	95%	99%	99.9%
2	1.000	6.314	12.706	63.657	636.619
3	0.816	2.920	4.303	9.925	31.98
4	0.765	2.353	3.182	5.841	12.924
5	0.741	2.132	2.776	4.604	8.610
6	0.727	2.015	2.571	4.032	6.869
7	0.718	1.943	2.447	3.707	5.959
8	0.711	1.895	2.365	3.500	5.408
9	0.706	1.860	2.306	3.355	5.041
10	0.703	1.833	2.262	3.250	4.781

t at the 90% confidence level for three measurements is 2.920 (see Table A2.1). Therefore, the confidence interval can be determined to be

$$\text{C.I.} = \bar{x} \pm \frac{ts}{\sqrt{n}}$$

$$= 2.31 \pm \frac{2.920 \times 0.48}{\sqrt{3}}$$

$$= 2.31 \pm 0.82$$

The researcher would report the result of the experiment as 2.31 ± 0.82. This means that in 90% of the cases, the accepted value should lie somewhere between 3.13 and 1.49. In 10% of the cases, the accepted value will lie outside these limits.

Occasionally, a set of measurements are collected for an experiment and one of the values appears to be erroneous. For example, measuring the distance from one town to another could give these data:

21.5 mi, 21.2 mi, 21.6 mi, 21.5 mi, 22.8 mi

Examination of the data leads us to believe that the last measurement is probably not a good measurement. But can we ignore it? No, we can't just throw it away without mathematically showing that it is an outlier.

This is accomplished by using a method known as the *Q-test*. In this method, a value of *Q* is calculated and compared to a *Q* value from a table based on our confidence level (see Table A2.2). Typically, the 90% confidence level is chosen

TABLE A2.2 Critical Values for the Rejection Quotient *Q*

Number of Measurements	90% Confidence	95% Confidence	99% Confidence
3	0.941	0.970	0.994
4	0.765	0.829	0.926
5	0.642	0.710	0.821
6	0.560	0.625	0.740
7	0.507	0.568	0.680
8	0.468	0.526	0.634
9	0.437	0.493	0.598
10	0.412	0.466	0.568

(giving us only a 10% chance of being wrong). The rejection quotient, Q, is determined by solving

$$Q = \frac{d}{r} = \frac{gap}{range}$$

where the gap is the difference between the outlier and the next closest measurement, and the range is the difference between the largest and smallest measurements.

For our hypothetical set of distances, we could determine the value of Q and compare it to the tabulated value of Q for five measurements (0.642). If our calculation of Q is larger than this, we can safely discard the point.

$$Q = \frac{d}{r} = \frac{(22.8 - 21.6)}{(22.8 - 21.2)} = \frac{1.2}{1.6} = 0.75$$

Our calculation is larger than the value of Q from the table (Q at 90% is 0.642), and we have demonstrated the point to be an outlier. However, if the calculated Q is only slightly larger than the table value, it may be statistically safer *not* to reject the point.

Appendix 3

Thermodynamic Data for Selected Compounds at 298 K

The signs of the values for $\Delta_f H^\circ$ and $\Delta_f G^\circ$ are explicitly shown. The sign on all S° values is positive unless otherwise noted. All values are rounded to the nearest whole number.

	$\Delta_f H^\circ$ (kJ·mol^{-1})	$\Delta_f G^\circ$ (kJ·mol^{-1})	S° (J·K^{-1}·mol^{-1})		$\Delta_f H^\circ$ (kJ·mol^{-1})	$\Delta_f G^\circ$ (kJ·mol^{-1})	S° (J·K^{-1}·mol^{-1})
				Ba(OH)$_2$(s)	-946		
Aluminum				BaSO$_4$(s)	-1465	-1353	132
Al(s)	0	0	28	**Beryllium**			
Al(l)	$+11$	$+7$	40	Be(s)	0	0	10
Al(g)	$+326$	$+286$	164	Be(g)	$+324$	$+287$	136
Al$_2$O$_3$(s)	-1676	-1582	51	BeO(s)	-599	-569	14
Al(OH)$_3$(s)	-1277			Be(OH)$_2$(s)	-904	-815	47
AlCl$_3$(s)	-704	-629	111	**Bismuth**			
Antimony				Bi(s)	0	0	57
Sb(s)	0	0	46	Bi(g)	$+207$	$+168$	187
SbH$_3$(g)	$+145$	$+148$	233	**Bromine**			
Argon				Br$_2$(l)	0	0	152
Ar(g)	0	0	155	Br$_2$(g)	$+31$	$+3$	245
Arsenic				Br$_2$(aq)	-3	$+4$	130
As(s)	0	0	35	Br(g)	$+112$	$+82$	175
As(g)	$+302$	-261	174	Br$^-$(aq)	-121	-104	82
As$_4$(g)	$+144$	$+92$	314	HBr(g)	-36	-53	199
AsH$_3$(g)	$+66$	$+69$	223	**Cadmium**			
Barium				Cd(s)	0	0	52
Ba(s)	0	0	67	Cd(g)	$+112$	$+77$	168
Ba(g)	$+180$	$+146$	170	CdO(s)	-258	-228	55
BaO(s)	-582	-552	70	CdCO$_3$(s)	-751	-669	92
BaCl$_2$(s)	-859	-810	124	Cd(OH)$_2$(s)	-561	-474	96
BaCO$_3$(s)	-1219	-1139	112				

(Continued)

	$\Delta_f H°$ (kJ·mol^{-1})	$\Delta_f G°$ (kJ·mol^{-1})	$S°$ (J·K^{-1}·mol^{-1})
CdS(s)	−162	−156	65
CdSO$_4$(s)	−953	−823	123
Calcium			
Ca(s)	0	0	41
Ca(g)	+178	+144	155
CaC$_2$(s)	−63	−68	70
CaO(s)	−635	−604	40
CaCO$_3$(s)	−1207	−1129	93
CaF$_2$(s)	−1220	−1167	69
CaCl$_2$(s)	−796	−748	105
CaBr$_2$(s)	−683	−664	130
Ca(OH)$_2$(s)	−987	−899	83
Ca$_3$(PO)$_4$(s)	−4126	−3890	241
CaSO$_4$(s)	−1433	−1320	107
CaSiO$_3$(s)	−1630	−1550	84
Carbon			
C(s) (graphite)	0	0	6
C(s) (diamond)	+2	+3	2
C(g)	+717	+671	158
C$_2$(g)	+832	+776	119
CO(g)	−111	−137	198
CO$_2$(g)	−394	−394	214
CO$_2$(aq)	−414	−386	118
H$_2$CO$_3$(aq)	−700	−623	187
CCl$_4$(l)	−135	−65	216
CH$_3$Cl(g)	−84	−60	234
CS$_2$(l)	+90	+65	151
HCN(g)	+135	+125	202
HCN(l)	+109	+125	113
CH$_4$(g)	−75	−50	186
C$_2$H$_2$(g)	+227	+209	201
C$_2$H$_4$(g)	+52	+68	220
C$_2$H$_6$(g)	−85	−33	230
C$_3$H$_6$(g)	+21	+63	267
C$_3$H$_8$(g)	−104	−24	270
C$_4$H$_8$(g) (1-butene)	−0.1	+71	306
C$_4$H$_{10}$(g)	−126	−17	310
C$_5$H$_{12}$(g)	−146	−8	348
C$_5$H$_{12}$(l)	−173	−251	263
C$_6$H$_6$(l)	+49	+124	173
C$_6$H$_6$(g)	+83	+130	269
C$_6$H$_{12}$(l)	−156	+27	204
C$_6$H$_{14}$(l)	−199		204
C$_7$H$_{16}$(l) (heptane)	−224	+1	329
C$_8$H$_{18}$(l) (octane)	−250	+6	361
C$_8$H$_{18}$(l) (iso-octane)	−255		328
CH$_3$OH(l)	−239	−166	127
CH$_3$OH(g)	−201	−162	240
C$_2$H$_5$OH(l)	−278	−175	161

	$\Delta_f H°$ (kJ·mol^{-1})	$\Delta_f G°$ (kJ·mol^{-1})	$S°$ (J·K^{-1}·mol^{-1})
C$_2$H$_5$OH(g)	−235	−168	283
C$_6$H$_5$OH(s) (phenol)	−165	−51	146
HCOOH(l) (formic acid)	−425	−361	129
CH$_3$COOH(l) (acetic acid)	−484	−389	160
CH$_3$COOH(aq) (acetic acid)	−486	−396	179
H$_2$C$_2$O$_4$(s) (oxalic acid)	−827		115
C$_6$H$_5$COOH(s) (benzoic acid)	−385	−245	168
HCHO(g) (formaldehyde)	−109	−103	219
CH$_3$CHO(l) (acetaldehyde)	−192	−128	160
CH$_3$CHO(g) (acetaldehyde)	−166	−129	250
CH$_3$COCH$_3$(l) (acetone)	−248	−155	200
C$_6$H$_{12}$O$_6$(s) (glucose)	−1268	−911	212
C$_{12}$H$_{22}$O$_{11}$(s) (sucrose)	−2222	−1543	360
Cesium			
Cs(s)	0	0	85
Cs(g)	+76	+49	176
Chlorine			
Cl$_2$(g)	0	0	223
Cl$_2$(aq)	−23	7	121
Cl$^-$(aq)	−167	−131	57
HCl(g)	−92	−95	187
Chromium			
Cr(s)	0	0	24
Cr$_2$O$_3$(s)	−1128	−1047	81
CrO$_3$(s)	−579	−502	72
Copper			
Cu(s)	0	0	33
CuCO$_3$(s)	−595	−518	88
Cu$_2$O(s)	−170	−148	93
CuO(s)	−156	−128	43
Cu(OH)$_2$(s)	−450	−372	108
CuS(s)	−49	−49	67
Fluorine			
F$_2$(g)	0	0	203
F$^-$(aq)	−333	−279	−14
HF(g)	−271	−273	174
Hydrogen			
H$_2$(g)	0	0	131
H(g)	+217	+203	115
H$^+$(aq)	0	0	0
OH$^-$(aq)	−230	−157	−11
H$_2$O(l)	−286	−237	70
H$_2$O(g)	−242	−229	189
Iodine			
I$_2$(s)	0	0	116
I$_2$(g)	+62	+19	261
I$_2$(aq)	+23	+16	137
I$^-$(aq)	−55	−52	106

	$\Delta_f H°$ (kJ·mol^{-1})	$\Delta_f G°$ (kJ·mol^{-1})	$S°$ (J·K^{-1}·mol^{-1})
Iron			
Fe(s)	0	0	27
Fe$_3$C(s)	+21	+15	108
Fe$_{0.95}$O(s) (wustite)	−264	−240	59
FeO	−272	−255	61
Fe$_3$O$_4$(s) (magnetite)	−1117	−1013	146
Fe$_2$O$_3$(s) (hematite)	−826	−740	90
FeS(s)	−95	−97	67
FeS$_2$(s)	−178	−166	53
FeSO$_4$(s)	−929	−825	121
Lead			
Pb(s)	0	0	65
Pb(g)	+195	+162	175
PbO(s, yellow)	−217	−188	69
PbO(s, red)	−219	−189	66
PbO$_2$(s)	−277	−217	69
PbS(s)	−100	−99	91
PbSO$_4$(s)	−920	−813	149
Lithium			
Li(s)	0	0	29
Li(g)	+159	+127	139
Magnesium			
Mg(s)	0	0	33
Mg(g)	+148	+113	149
MgO(s)	−602	−570	27
MgCO$_3$(s)	−1096	−1012	65
MgCl$_2$(s)	−641	−592	90
Mg(OH)$_2$(s)	−925	−834	64
Mg$_3$N$_2$(s)	−461	−401	89
Manganese			
Mn(s)	0	0	32
MnO(s)	−385	−363	60
Mn$_3$O$_4$(s)	−1387	−1280	149
Mn$_2$O$_3$(s)	−971	−893	110
MnO$_2$(s)	−521	−466	53
MnO$_4^-$(aq)	−543	−449	190
Mercury			
Hg(l)	0	0	76
Hg(g)	+61	+32	175
Hg$_2$Cl$_2$(s)	−265	−211	193
HgCl$_2$(s)	−230	−184	144
HgO(s)	−91	−59	70
HgS(s, black)	−54	−48	88
Neon			
Ne(g)	0	0	146
Nickel			
Ni(s)	0	0	30

	$\Delta_f H°$ (kJ·mol^{-1})	$\Delta_f G°$ (kJ·mol^{-1})	$S°$ (J·K^{-1}·mol^{-1})
NiCl$_2$(s)	−316	−272	107
NiO(s)	−241	−213	38
Ni(OH)$_2$(s)	−538	−453	79
NiS(s)	−93	−90	53
Nitrogen			
N$_2$(g)	0	0	192
N(g)	+473	+456	153
NH$_3$(g)	−46	−16	192
NH$_3$(aq)	−80	−27	111
NH$_4^+$(aq)	−132	−79	113
HN$_3$(l)	264	327	141
HN$_3$(g)	294	328	239
NH$_4$NO$_3$(s)	−366	−184	151
NH$_4$Cl(s)	−314	−203	95
NH$_4$ClO$_4$(s)	−295	−89	186
NH$_4$Cl(s)	−314	−203	96
HNO$_3$(l)	−174	−81	156
HNO$_3$(aq)	−207	−111	146
NH$_2$OH(s)	−114		
NO(g)	+90	+87	211
NO$_2$(g)	+33	+51	240
N$_2$O(g)	+82	+104	220
N$_2$O$_4$(g)	+9	+98	304
N$_2$O$_5$(s)	−43	+114	178
N$_2$O$_5$(g)	+11	+115	356
N$_2$H$_4$(l)	+51	+149	121
N$_2$H$_3$CH$_3$(l)	+54	+180	166
Oxygen			
O$_2$(g)	0	0	205
O(g)	+249	+232	161
O$_3$(g)	+143	+163	239
Phosphorus			
P(s) (white)	0	0	41
P(s) (red)	−18	−12	23
P(s) (black)	−39	−33	23
P(g)	+315	+278	163
P$_2$(g)	+144	+104	218
P$_4$(g)	+59	+24	280
PH$_3$(g)	+5	+13	210
PF$_5$(g)	−1578	−1509	296
PCl$_3$(g)	−287	−268	312
PCl$_3$(l)	−320	−272	217
PCl$_5$(g)	−375	−305	365
PCl$_5$(s)	−444		
H$_3$PO$_3$(s)	−964		
H$_3$PO$_3$(aq)	−965		
H$_3$PO$_4$(s)	−1279	−1119	111
H$_3$PO$_4$(l)	−1267		

(Continued)

	$\Delta_f H°$ (kJ·mol^{-1})	$\Delta_f G°$ (kJ·mol^{-1})	$S°$ (J·K^{-1}·mol^{-1})
$H_3PO_4(aq)$	-1277	-1019	-222
$P_4O_{10}(s)$	-2984	-2697	229
Potassium			
$K(s)$	0	0	64
$K(g)$	$+89$	$+61$	160
$KF(s)$	-576	-538	67
$KCl(s)$	-437	-409	83
$KBr(s)$	-394	-381	96
$KI(s)$	-328	-325	106
$KClO_3(s)$	-391	-290	143
$KClO_4(s)$	-433	-304	151
$KOH(s)$	-425	-379	79
$KOH(aq)$	-481	-440	9
$KO_2(s)$	-283	-238	117
$K_2O(s)$	-361	-322	98
$K_2O_2(s)$	-496	-430	113
Silicon			
$Si(s)$	0	0	19
$Si(g)$	$+456$	$+411$	168
$SiO_2(s)$	$+911$	-857	42
$SiCl_4(l)$	-687	-620	240
Silver			
$Ag(s)$	0	0	43
$Ag(g)$	$+285$	$+246$	173
$Ag^+(aq)$	$+105$	$+77$	73
$AgBr(s)$	-100	-97	107
$AgCN(s)$	$+146$	$+164$	84
$AgCl(s)$	-127	-110	96
$Ag_2CrO_4(s)$	-712	-622	217
$AgI(s)$	-62	-66	115
$Ag_2O(s)$	-31	-11	121
$AgNO_3(s)$	-129	-33	141
$Ag_2S(s)$	-32	-40	146
Sodium			
$Na(s)$	0	0	51
$Na(g)$	$+107$	$+77$	153
$Na^+(aq)$	-240	-262	59
$NaH(s)$	-56	-33	40
$NaHCO_3(s)$	-948	-852	102
$NaCl(s)$	-411	-384	72
$NaBr(s)$	-361	-349	87
$NaI(s)$	-288	-286	99
$NaNO_2(s)$	-359		
$NaNO_3(aq)$	-467	-366	116
$NaOH(s)$	-426	-379	64
$NaOH(aq)$	-470	-419	50
$Na_2CO_3(s)$	-1131	-1048	136

	$\Delta_f H°$ (kJ·mol^{-1})	$\Delta_f G°$ (kJ·mol^{-1})	$S°$ (J·K^{-1}·mol^{-1})
$Na_2O(s)$	-416	-377	73
$Na_2O_2(s)$	-515	-451	95
Sulfur			
$S(s)$	0	0	32
$S(g)$	$+279$	$+238$	168
$S^{2-}(aq)$	$+42$	$+86$	$+22$
$S_2(g)$	$+128$	$+79$	228
$S_8(s)$	$+102$	$+50$	431
$H_2S(g)$	-21	-34	206
$H_2S(aq)$	-40	-28	121
$SF_6(g)$	-1209	-1105	292
$SO_2(g)$	-297	-300	248
$SO_3(g)$	-396	-371	257
$SO_4^{2-}(aq)$	-909	-745	20
$H_2SO_4(l)$	-814	-690	157
$H_2SO_4(aq)$	-909	-745	20
Tin			
$Sn(s)$ (white)	0	0	52
$Sn(s)$ (grey)	-2	$+0.1$	44
$Sn(g)$	$+302$	$+267$	168
$SnO(s)$	-286	-257	57
$SnO_2(s)$	-581	-520	52
$Sn(OH)_2(s)$	-561	-492	155
Titanium			
$TiCl_4(g)$	-763	-727	355
$TiO_2(s)$	-945	-890	50
Uranium			
$U(s)$	0	0	50
$UF_6(s)$	-2137	-2008	228
$UF_6(g)$	-2113	-2029	380
$UO_2(s)$	-1084	-1029	78
$UO_3(s)$	-1230	-1150	99
$U_3O_8(s)$	-3575	-3393	282
Xenon			
$Xe(g)$	0	0	170
$XeF_2(g)$	-108	-48	254
$XeF_4(s)$	-251	-121	146
$XeF_6(g)$	-294		
$XeO_3(s)$	402		
Zinc			
$Zn(s)$	0	0	42
$Zn(g)$	$+131$	$+95$	161
$ZnO(s)$	-348	-318	44
$Zn(OH)_2(s)$	-642		
$ZnS(s)$ (wurtzite)	-193		
$ZnS(s)$ (zinc blende)	-206	-201	58
$ZnSO_4(s)$	-983	-874	120

Appendix 4

Colligative Property Constants for Selected Compounds

	K_f (°C/m)	T_f (°C)	K_b (°C/m)	T_b (°C)
Acetic acid	3.9	16.2	3.1	117.9
Acetone	2.4	−94.8	1.7	56.5
Benzene	5.1	5.5	2.6	80.1
Camphor	40	175	5.6	204
Carbon disulfide	3.8	−112	2.4	46
Carbon tetrachloride	30	−23	5.0	76.7
Chloroform	4.7	−63.5	3.6	61.2
Cyclohexane	20.0	6.5	2.8	80.7
Cyclohexanol	40.8	20	3.5	161
Diethyl ether	1.8	−116.3	2.0	34.6
1,4-Dioxane	4.6	11.8	3.3	101.5
Ethanol	2.0	−117.3	1.2	78.5
Ethylene glycol	3.1	−13	2.3	197.3
Formic acid	2.8	8.4	2.4	100
Methanol		−98	0.80	64.7
Naphthalene	6.9	80	5.8	217.7
Phenol	7.4	43	3.0	182
Toluene	3.6	−94.5	3.3	110.7
Water	1.86	0.0	0.51	100.0

Appendix 5

Selected Equilibrium Constants at 298 K

TABLE A5.1   **Acid Ionization Constants (K_a) at 298 K**

All values except those of the strong acids (HI, HBr, HCl, H_2SO_4, $HClO_4$, HNO_3, and H_3O^+) are reported to two significant figures.

Name	Formula	K_a	Name	Formula	K_a
Acetic acid	CH_3COOH	1.8×10^{-5}	Hydronium ion	H_3O^+	1
Benzoic acid	C_6H_5COOH	6.5×10^{-5}	Hypobromous acid	HBrO	2.8×10^{-9}
Boric acid (K_{a_1})	H_3BO_3	5.8×10^{-10}	Hypochlorous acid	HClO	3.5×10^{-8}
Butanoic acid	$CH_3CH_2CH_2COOH$	1.5×10^{-5}	Hypoiodous acid	HIO	2.0×10^{-11}
Chlorous acid	$HClO_2$	1.2×10^{-2}	Iodic acid	HIO_3	1.7×10^{-1}
Formic acid	HCOOH	1.8×10^{-4}	Lactic acid	$CH_3CH(OH)COOH$	1.3×10^{-4}
Hydroazoic acid	HN_3	2.2×10^{-5}	Nitric acid	HNO_3	1×10^1
Hydrobromic acid	HBr	1×10^9	Nitrous acid	HNO_2	7.0×10^{-4}
Hydrochloric acid	HCl	1×10^7	Perchloric acid	$HClO_4$	4×10^1
Hydrofluoric acid	HF	7.2×10^{-4}	Phenol	C_6H_5OH	1.6×10^{-10}
Hydrogen cyanide	HCN	6.2×10^{-10}	Propanic acid	CH_3CH_2COOH	1.3×10^{-5}
Hydrogen peroxide	H_2O_2	2.4×10^{-12}	Sulfuric acid (K_{a_1})	H_2SO_4	1×10^2
Hydroiodic acid	HI	1×10^{11}	Thiocyanic acid	HSCN	1.3×10^{-1}

TABLE A5.2	Base Ionization Constants (K_b) at 298 K	

All values are reported to two significant figures.

Name	Formula	K_b
Ammonia	NH_3	1.8×10^{-5}
Aniline	$C_6H_5NH_2$	3.8×10^{-8}
Diethylamine	$(CH_3CH_2)_2NH$	7.1×10^{-4}
Dimethylamine	$(CH_3)_2NH$	5.9×10^{-4}
Ethylamine	$CH_3CH_2NH_2$	6.4×10^{-4}
Hydrazine	H_2NNH_2	1.3×10^{-6}
Hydroxylamine	$HONH_2$	1.1×10^{-8}
Methylamine	CH_3NH_2	5.9×10^{-4}
Pyridine	C_5H_5N	1.7×10^{-9}
Triethylamine	$(CH_3CH_2)_3N$	5.6×10^{-4}
Trimethylamine	$(CH_3)_3N$	6.4×10^{-5}

TABLE A5.3	Polyprotic Acid Ionization Constants (K_{a1}, K_{a2}, and K_{a3}) at 298 K		

The formula of the acid (HA) and that of its conjugate base (A^-) are indicated.

Acid	HA	A^-	K_a
Arsenic acid	H_3AsO_4	$H_2AsO_4^-$	5.0×10^{-3}
dihydrogen arsenate	$H_2AsO_4^-$	$HAsO_4^{2-}$	8.0×10^{-8}
hydrogen arsenate	$HAsO_4^{2-}$	AsO_4^{3-}	6.0×10^{-10}
Ascorbic acid (vitamin C)	$H_2C_6H_6O_6$	$HC_6H_6O_6^-$	7.9×10^{-5}
ascorbate	$HC_6H_6O_6^-$	$C_6H_6O_6^{2-}$	1.6×10^{-12}
Carbonic acid	H_2CO_3	HCO_3^-	4.3×10^{-7}
hydrogen carbonate	HCO_3^-	CO_3^{2-}	5.6×10^{-11}
Citric acid	$H_3C_6H_5O_7$	$H_2C_6H_5O_7^-$	8.4×10^{-4}
dihydrogen citrate	$H_2C_6H_5O_7^-$	$HC_6H_5O_7^{2-}$	1.8×10^{-5}
hydrogen citrate	$HC_6H_5O_7^{2-}$	$C_6H_5O_7^{3-}$	4.0×10^{-6}
Hydrogen sulfide	H_2S	HS^-	1.0×10^{-7}
hydrogen sulfide ion	HS^-	S^{2-}	1.0×10^{-15}
Oxalic acid	$H_2C_2O_4$	$HC_2O_4^-$	6.5×10^{-2}
hydrogen oxalate	$HC_2O_4^-$	$C_2O_4^{2-}$	6.1×10^{-5}
Phosphoric acid	H_3PO_4	$H_2PO_4^-$	7.4×10^{-3}
dihydrogen phosphate	$H_2PO_4^-$	HPO_4^{2-}	6.2×10^{-8}
hydrogen phosphate	HPO_4^{2-}	PO_4^{3-}	4.8×10^{-13}
Sulfuric acid	H_2SO_4	HSO_4^-	1.0×10^2
hydrogen sulfate	HSO_4^-	SO_4^{2-}	1.0×10^{-2}
Sulfurous acid	H_2SO_3	HSO_3^-	1.5×10^{-2}
hydrogen sulfite	HSO_3^-	SO_3^{2-}	1.0×10^{-7}

TABLE A5.4	Solubility Product Constants (K_{sp}) at 298 K						

Name	Formula	K_{sp}		Name	Formula	K_{sp}
Aluminium hydroxide	$Al(OH)_3$	2.0×10^{-32}		Iron(II) carbonate	$FeCO_3$	2.1×10^{-11}
Aluminium phosphate	$AlPO_4$	9.8×10^{-21}		Iron(II) fluoride	FeF_2	2.4×10^{-6}
Barium carbonate	$BaCO_3$	1.6×10^{-9}		Iron(II) hydroxide	$Fe(OH)_2$	1.8×10^{-15}
Barium chromate	$BaCrO_4$	8.5×10^{-10}		Iron(II) sulfide	FeS	3.7×10^{-19}
Barium fluoride	BaF_2	2.4×10^{-5}		Iron(III) hydroxide	$Fe(OH)_3$	1.6×10^{-39}
Barium hydroxide	$Ba(OH)_2$	5.0×10^{-4}		Iron(III) phosphate	$FePO_4$	9.9×10^{-16}
Barium iodate	$Ba(IO_3)_2$	4.0×10^{-9}		Lead(II) bromide	$PbBr_2$	4.6×10^{-6}
Barium molybdate	$BaMoO_4$	3.5×10^{-8}		Lead(II) carbonate	$PbCO_3$	1.5×10^{-15}
Barium phosphate	$Ba_3(PO_4)_2$	6.0×10^{-39}		Lead(II) chloride	$PbCl_2$	1.6×10^{-5}
Barium selenate	$BaSeO_4$	3.4×10^{-8}		Lead(II) chromate	$PbCrO_4$	2.0×10^{-16}
Barium sulfate	$BaSO_4$	1.5×10^{-9}		Lead(II) fluoride	PbF_2	4.0×10^{-8}
Barium sulfite	$BaSO_3$	5.0×10^{-10}		Lead(II) hydroxide	$Pb(OH)_2$	1.2×10^{-15}
Beryllium hydroxide	$Be(OH)_2$	6.9×10^{-22}		Lead(II) iodide	PbI_2	1.4×10^{-8}
Bismuth arsenate	$BiAsO_4$	4.4×10^{-10}		Lead(II) phosphate	$Pb_3(PO_4)_2$	1.0×10^{-54}
Bismuth iodide	BiI	7.7×10^{-19}		Lead(II) sulfate	$PbSO_4$	1.3×10^{-8}
Cadmium carbonate	$CdCO_3$	5.2×10^{-12}		Lead(II) sulfide	PbS	7.0×10^{-29}
Cadmium fluoride	CdF_2	6.4×10^{-3}		Lithium carbonate	Li_2CO_3	8.2×10^{-4}
Cadmium hydroxide	$Cd(OH)_2$	2.5×10^{-14}		Magnesium carbonate	$MgCO_3$	1.0×10^{-5}
Cadmium oxalate	CdC_2O_4	1.4×10^{-8}		Magnesium hydroxide	$Mg(OH)_2$	8.9×10^{-12}
Cadmium phosphate	$Cd_3(PO_4)_2$	2.5×10^{-33}		Magnesium oxalate	MgC_2O_4	4.8×10^{-6}
Cadmium sulfide	CdS	1.0×10^{-28}		Magnesium phosphate	$Mg_3(PO_4)_2$	1.0×10^{-24}
Calcium carbonate	$CaCO_3$	8.7×10^{-9}		Magnesium fluoride	MgF_2	6.4×10^{-9}
Calcium fluoride	CaF_2	4.0×10^{-11}		Manganese(II) carbonate	$MnCO_3$	8.8×10^{-11}
Calcium hydroxide	$Ca(OH)_2$	1.3×10^{-6}		Manganese(II) hydroxide	$Mn(OH)_2$	2.0×10^{-13}
Calcium iodate	$Ca(IO_3)_2$	7.1×10^{-7}		Manganese(II) oxalate	MnC_2O_4	1.7×10^{-7}
Calcium oxalate	CaC_2O_4	2.3×10^{-9}		Manganese(II) sulfide	MnS	2.3×10^{-13}
Calcium phosphate	$Ca_3(PO_4)_2$	1.3×10^{-32}		Mercury(I) bromide	Hg_2Br_2	1.3×10^{-22}
Calcium sulfate	$CaSO_4$	6.1×10^{-5}		Mercury(I) carbonate	Hg_2CO_3	9.0×10^{-15}
Cesium perchlorate	$CsClO_4$	4.0×10^{-3}		Mercury(I) chloride	Hg_2Cl_2	1.1×10^{-18}
Cesium periodate	$CsIO_4$	5.2×10^{-6}		Mercury(I) chromate	Hg_2CrO_4	2.0×10^{-9}
Chromium(III) hydroxide	$Cr(OH)_3$	6.7×10^{-31}		Mercury(I) fluoride	Hg_2F_2	3.1×10^{-6}
Cobalt(II) arsenate	$Co_3(AsO_4)_2$	6.8×10^{-29}		Mercury(I) iodide	Hg_2I_2	4.5×10^{-29}
Cobalt(II) carbonate	$CoCO_3$	1.0×10^{-10}		Mercury(I) oxalate	$Hg_2C_2O_4$	1.8×10^{-13}
Cobalt(II) hydroxide	$Co(OH)_2$	2.5×10^{-16}		Mercury(I) sulfate	Hg_2SO_4	6.5×10^{-7}
Cobalt(II) phosphate	$Co_3(PO_4)_2$	2.1×10^{-35}		Mercury(I) thiocyanate	$Hg_2(SCN)_2$	3.2×10^{-20}
Cobalt(II) sulfide	CoS	5.0×10^{-22}		Mercury(II) bromide	$HgBr_2$	6.2×10^{-20}
Cobalt(III) hydroxide	$Co(OH)_3$	2.5×10^{-43}		Mercury(II) iodide	HgI_2	2.9×10^{-29}
Copper(I) bromide	$CuBr$	6.3×10^{-9}		Mercury(II) hydroxide	$Hg(OH)_2$	3.0×10^{-26}
Copper(I) chloride	$CuCl$	1.7×10^{-7}		Mercury(II) oxide	HgO	3.6×10^{-26}
Copper(I) cyanide	$CuCN$	3.5×10^{-20}		Mercury(II) sulfide	HgS	1.6×10^{-54}
Copper(I) oxide	Cu_2O	2.0×10^{-15}		Neodymium carbonate	$Nd_2(CO_3)_3$	1.1×10^{-33}
Copper(I) iodide	CuI	1.3×10^{-12}		Nickel(II) carbonate	$NiCO_3$	1.4×10^{-7}
Copper(I) thiocyanate	$CuSCN$	1.8×10^{-13}		Nickel(II) hydroxide	$Ni(OH)_2$	1.6×10^{-16}
Copper(II) carbonate	$CuCO_3$	2.5×10^{-10}		Nickel(II) phosphate	$Ni_3(PO_4)_2$	4.7×10^{-32}
Copper(II) hydroxide	$Cu(OH)_2$	1.6×10^{-19}		Nickel(II) sulfide	NiS	3.0×10^{-21}
Copper(II) oxalate	CuC_2O_4	4.4×10^{-10}		Palladium(II) thiocyanate	$Pd(SCN)_2$	4.4×10^{-23}
Copper(II) phosphate	$Cu_3(PO_4)_2$	1.4×10^{-37}		Praseodymium hydroxide	$Pr(OH)_3$	3.4×10^{-24}
Copper(II) sulfide	CuS	8.5×10^{-45}		Radium sulfate	$RaSO_4$	3.7×10^{-11}
Europium(III) hydroxide	$Eu(OH)_3$	9.4×10^{-27}		Scandium fluoride	ScF_3	5.8×10^{-24}
Gallium(III) hydroxide	$Ga(OH)_3$	7.3×10^{-36}		Scandium hydroxide	$Sc(OH)_3$	2.2×10^{-31}

(Continued)

TABLE A5.4 (*Continued*)

Name	Formula	K_{sp}	Name	Formula	K_{sp}
Silver(I) acetate	$AgCH_3COO$	1.9×10^{-3}	Strontium phosphate	$Sr_3(PO_4)_2$	1.0×10^{-31}
Silver(I) arsenate	Ag_3AsO_4	1.0×10^{-22}	Strontium sulfate	$SrSO_4$	3.2×10^{-7}
Silver(I) bromide	$AgBr$	5.0×10^{-13}	Thallium(I) bromide	$TlBr$	3.7×10^{-6}
Silver(I) carbonate	Ag_2CO_3	8.1×10^{-12}	Thallium(I) chloride	$TlCl$	1.9×10^{-4}
Silver(I) chloride	$AgCl$	1.6×10^{-10}	Thallium(I) chromate	Tl_2CrO_4	8.7×10^{-13}
Silver(I) chromate	Ag_2CrO_4	9.0×10^{-12}	Thallium(I) hydroxide	$Tl(OH)_3$	1.7×10^{-44}
Silver(I) cyanide	$AgCN$	6.0×10^{-17}	Thallium(I) iodide	TlI	5.5×10^{-8}
Silver(I) hydroxide	$AgOH$	2.0×10^{-8}	Thallium(I) sulfide	Tl_2S	6.0×10^{-22}
Silver(I) iodide	AgI	1.5×10^{-16}	Tin(II) hydroxide	$Sn(OH)_2$	3.0×10^{-27}
Silver(I) oxalate	$Ag_2C_2O_4$	5.4×10^{-12}	Tin(II) sulfide	SnS	1.0×10^{-26}
Silver(I) phosphate	Ag_3PO_4	1.8×10^{-18}	Yttrium carbonate	$Y_2(CO_3)_3$	1.0×10^{-31}
Silver(I) sulfate	Ag_2SO_4	1.2×10^{-5}	Yttrium hydroxide	$Y(OH)_3$	1.0×10^{-22}
Silver(I) sulfite	Ag_2SO_3	1.5×10^{-14}	Zinc carbonate	$ZnCO_3$	2.0×10^{-10}
Silver(I) sulfide	Ag_2S	1.6×10^{-49}	Zinc fluoride	ZnF	3.0×10^{-2}
Strontium carbonate	$SrCO_3$	7×10^{-10}	Zinc hydroxide	$Zn(OH)_2$	4.5×10^{-17}
Strontium chromate	$SrCrO_4$	3.6×10^{-5}	Zinc oxalate	ZnC_2O_4	1.4×10^{-9}
Strontium fluoride	SrF_2	7.9×10^{-10}	Zinc selenide	$ZnSe$	3.6×10^{-26}
Strontium hydroxide	$Sr(OH)_2$	3.2×10^{-4}	Zinc sulfide	ZnS	2.5×10^{-22}
Strontium oxalate	SrC_2O_4	5.0×10^{-8}			

TABLE A5.5 Complex Ion Formation Constants (K_f) at 298 K

Complex Ion	K_f	Complex Ion	K_f	Complex Ion	K_f
$[Ag(CN)_2]^-$	5.6×10^{18}	$[Co(ox)_3]^{3-}$	1.0×10^{20}	$[HgI_4]^{2-}$	6.8×10^{29}
$[Ag(EDTA)]^{3-}$	2.1×10^{7}	$[Cr(EDTA)]^-$	1.0×10^{23}	$[Hg(ox)_2]^{2-}$	9.5×10^{6}
$[Ag(en)_2]^+$	5.0×10^{7}	$[Cr(OH)_4]^-$	8.0×10^{29}	$[Ni(CN)_4]^{2-}$	2.0×10^{31}
$[Ag(NH_3)_2]^+$	1.6×10^{7}	$[CuCl_3]^{2-}$	5.0×10^{5}	$[Ni(EDTA)]^{2-}$	3.6×10^{18}
$[Ag(SCN)_4]^{3-}$	1.2×10^{10}	$[Cu(CN)_2]^-$	1.0×10^{16}	$[Ni(en)_3]^{2+}$	2.1×10^{18}
$[Ag(S_2O_3)_2]^{3-}$	1.7×10^{13}	$[Cu(CN)_4]^{3-}$	2.0×10^{30}	$[Ni(NH_3)_6]^{2+}$	5.5×10^{8}
$[Al(EDTA)]^-$	1.3×10^{16}	$[Cu(EDTA)]^{2-}$	5.0×10^{18}	$[Ni(ox)_3]^{4-}$	3.0×10^{8}
$[Al(OH)_4]^-$	1.1×10^{33}	$[Cu(en)_2]^{2+}$	1.0×10^{20}	$[PbCl_3]^-$	2.4×10^{1}
$[Al(ox)_3]^{3-}$	2.0×10^{16}	$[Cu(CN)_4]^{2-}$	1.0×10^{25}	$[Pb(EDTA)]^{2-}$	2.0×10^{18}
$[Au(CN)_2]$	1.6×10^{38}	$[Cu(NH_3)_4]^{2+}$	1.1×10^{13}	$[PbI_4]^{2-}$	3.0×10^{4}
$[Bi(EDTA)]^{2-}$	8.0×10^{27}	$[Cu(ox)_2]^{2-}$	3.0×10^{8}	$[Pb(OH)_3]^-$	3.8×10^{14}
$[Ca(EDTA)]^{2-}$	5.0×10^{10}	$[Fe(CN)_6]^{4-}$	1.0×10^{37}	$[Pb(ox)_2]^{2-}$	3.5×10^{6}
$[Cd(CN)_4]^{2-}$	6.0×10^{18}	$[Fe(EDTA)]^{2-}$	2.1×10^{14}	$[Pb(S_2O_3)_3]^{4-}$	2.2×10^{6}
$[Cd(en)_3]^{2+}$	1.2×10^{12}	$[Fe(en)_3]^{2+}$	5.0×10^{9}	$[PtCl_4]^{2-}$	1.0×10^{16}
$[Cd(NH_3)_4]^{2+}$	1.3×10^{7}	$[Fe(ox)_3]^{4-}$	1.7×10^{5}	$[Pt(NH_3)_6]^{2+}$	2.0×10^{35}
$[Co(EDTA)]^{2-}$	2.0×10^{16}	$[Fe(CN)_6]^{3-}$	1.0×10^{42}	$[V(EDTA)]^-$	8.0×10^{25}
$[Co(en)_3]^{2+}$	8.7×10^{13}	$[Fe(EDTA)]^-$	1.7×10^{24}	$[Zn(CN)_4]^{2-}$	1.0×10^{18}
$[Co(NH_3)_6]^{2+}$	1.3×10^{5}	$[Fe(ox)_3]^{3-}$	2.0×10^{20}	$[Zn(EDTA)]^{2-}$	3.0×10^{16}
$[Co(ox)_3]^{4-}$	5.0×10^{9}	$[Fe(SCN)]^{2+}$	8.9×10^{2}	$[Zn(en)_3]^{2+}$	1.3×10^{14}
$[Co(SCN)_4]^{2-}$	1.0×10^{3}	$[HgCl_4]^{2-}$	1.2×10^{15}	$[Zn(NH_3)_4]^{2+}$	4.1×10^{8}
$[Co(EDTA)]^-$	1.0×10^{36}	$[Hg(CN)_4]^{2-}$	3.0×10^{41}	$[Zn(OH)_4]^{2-}$	4.6×10^{17}
$[Co(en)_3]^{3+}$	4.9×10^{48}	$[Hg(EDTA)]^{2-}$	6.3×10^{21}	$[Zn(ox)_3]^{4-}$	1.4×10^{8}
$[Co(NH_3)_6]^{3+}$	4.5×10^{33}	$[Hg(en)_2]^{2+}$	2.0×10^{23}		

Appendix 6

Water Vapor Pressure Table

T (°C)	Vapor Pressure (mm Hg)	T (°C)	Vapor Pressure (mm Hg)	T (°C)	Vapor Pressure (mm Hg)
0	4.58	22	19.80	50	92.57
5	6.54	23	21.05	60	149.4
10	9.21	24	22.36	70	233.7
11	9.84	25	23.74	80	355.1
12	10.52	26	25.20	90	525.7
13	11.23	28	28.34	95	634.0
14	11.99	30	31.82	96	657.7
15	12.79	33	37.74	97	682.2
20	17.54	37	47.09	98	707.4
21	18.62	40	55.35	99	733.4
				100	760.0

Appendix 7

Standard Reduction Potentials at 298 K

All half-reaction potentials are reported to two decimal places.

$E°$ (V)	Reduction Half-reaction
+2.87	$F_2(g) + 2e^- \rightarrow 2F^-(aq)$
+2.07	$O_3(g) + 2H^+(aq) + 2e^- \rightarrow O_2(g) + H_2O(l)$
+2.05	$S_2O_8^{2-}(aq) + 2e^- \rightarrow SO_4^{2-}(aq)$
+1.99	$Ag^{2+}(aq) + e^- \rightarrow Ag^+(aq)$
+1.82	$Co^{3+}(aq) + e^- \rightarrow Co^{2+}(aq)$
+1.78	$H_2O_2(aq) + 2H^+(aq) + 2e^- \rightarrow 2H_2O(l)$
+1.70	$Ce^{4+}(aq) + e^- \rightarrow Ce^{3+}(aq)$
+1.69	$Au^+(aq) + e^- \rightarrow Au(s)$
+1.69	$PbO_2(s) + 4H^+(aq) + SO_4^{2-}(aq) + 2e^- \rightarrow PbSO_4(s) + 2H_2O(l)$
+1.68	$MnO_4^-(aq) + 4H^+(aq) + 3e^- \rightarrow MnO_2(s) + 2H_2O(l)$
+1.67	$Pb^{4+}(aq) + 2e^- \rightarrow Pb^{2+}(aq)$
+1.63	$2HClO(aq) + 2H^+(aq) + 2e^- \rightarrow Cl_2(g) + 2H_2O(l)$
+1.60	$2HBrO(aq) + 2H^+(aq) + 2e^- \rightarrow Br_2(l) + 2H_2O(l)$
+1.60	$IO_4^-(aq) + 2H^+(aq) + 2e^- \rightarrow IO_3^-(aq) + H_2O(l)$
+1.51	$MnO_4^-(aq) + 8H^+(aq) + 5e^- \rightarrow Mn^{2+}(aq) + 4H_2O(l)$
+1.51	$Mn^{3+}(aq) + e^- \rightarrow Mn^{2+}(aq)$
+1.50	$Au^{3+}(aq) + 3e^- \rightarrow Au(s)$
+1.46	$PbO_2(s) + 4H^+(aq) + 2e^- \rightarrow Pb^{2+}(aq) + 2H_2O(l)$
+1.36	$Cl_2(g) + 2e^- \rightarrow 2Cl^-(aq)$
+1.33	$CrO_7^{2-}(aq) + 14H^+(aq) + 6e^- \rightarrow 2Cr^{3+}(aq) + 7H_2O(l)$
+1.24	$O_3(g) + H_2O(l) + 2e^- \rightarrow O_2(g) + 2OH^-(aq)$
+1.23	$O_2(g) + 4H^+(aq) + 4e^- \rightarrow 2H_2O(l)$
+1.21	$MnO_2(s) + 4H^+(aq) + 2e^- \rightarrow Mn^{2+}(aq) + 2H_2O(l)$
+1.20	$IO_3^-(aq) + 6H^+(aq) + 5e^- \rightarrow \frac{1}{2}I_2(s) + 3H_2O(l)$
+1.09	$Br_2(l) + 2e^- \rightarrow 2Br^-(aq)$
+1.00	$VO_2^+(aq) + 2H^+(aq) + e^- \rightarrow VO^{2+}(aq) + H_2O(l)$

(Continued)

$E°$ (V)	Reduction Half-reaction
+0.99	$AuCl_4^-(aq) + 3e^- \rightarrow Au(s) + 4Cl^-(aq)$
+0.97	$Pu^{4+}(aq) + e^- \rightarrow Pu^{3+}(aq)$
+0.96	$NO_3^-(aq) + 4H^+(aq) + e^- \rightarrow NO(g) + 2H_2O(l)$
+0.91	$2Hg^{2+}(aq) + 2e^- \rightarrow Hg_2^{2+}(aq)$
+0.89	$ClO^-(aq) + H_2O(l) + e^- \rightarrow Cl^-(aq) + 2OH^-(aq)$
+0.86	$Hg^{2+}(aq) + 2e^- \rightarrow Hg(l)$
+0.80	$NO_3^-(aq) + 2H^+(aq) + e^- \rightarrow NO_2(g) + H_2O(l)$
+0.80	$Ag^+(aq) + e^- \rightarrow Ag(s)$
+0.80	$Hg_2^{2+}(aq) + 2e^- \rightarrow 2Hg(l)$
+0.77	$Fe^{3+}(aq) + e^- \rightarrow Fe^{2+}(aq)$
+0.76	$BrO^-(aq) + H_2O(l) + 2e^- \rightarrow Br^-(aq) + 2OH^-(aq)$
+0.68	$O_2(g) + 2H^+(aq) + 2e^- \rightarrow H_2O_2(aq)$
+0.62	$Hg_2SO_4(s) + 2e^- \rightarrow 2Hg(l) + SO_4^{2-}(aq)$
+0.60	$MnO_4^{2-}(aq) + 2H_2O(l) + 2e^- \rightarrow MnO_2(s) + 4OH^-(aq)$
+0.56	$MnO_4^-(aq) + e^- \rightarrow MnO_4^{2-}(aq)$
+0.54	$I_2(s) + 2e^- \rightarrow 2I^-(aq)$
+0.52	$Cu^+(aq) + e^- \rightarrow Cu(s)$
+0.53	$I_3^-(aq) + 2e^- \rightarrow 3I^-(aq)$
+0.49	$NiOOH(aq) + H_2O(l) + e^- \rightarrow Ni(OH)_2(aq) + OH^-(aq)$
+0.45	$Ag_2CrO_4(s) + 2e^- \rightarrow 2Ag(s) + CrO_4^{2-}(aq)$
+0.40	$O_2(g) + 2H_2O(l) + 4e^- \rightarrow 4OH^-(aq)$
+0.36	$ClO_4^-(aq) + H_2O(l) + 2e^- \rightarrow ClO_3^-(aq) + 2OH^-(aq)$
+0.36	$[Fe(CN)_6]^{3-}(aq) + e^- \rightarrow [Fe(CN)_6]^{4-}(aq)$
+0.34	$Cu^{2+}(aq) + 2e^- \rightarrow Cu(s)$
+0.34	$Hg_2Cl_2(s) + 2e^- \rightarrow 2Hg(l) + 2Cl^-(aq)$
+0.25	$CO(g) + 6H^+(aq) + 6e^- \rightarrow H_2O(g) + CH_4(g)$
+0.22	$AgCl(s) + e^- \rightarrow Ag(s) + Cl^-(aq)$
+0.20	$SO_4^{2-}(aq) + 4H^+(aq) + 2e^- \rightarrow H_2SO_3(aq) + H_2O(l)$
+0.20	$Bi^{3+}(aq) + 3e^- \rightarrow Bi(s)$
+0.16	$Cu^{2+}(aq) + e^- \rightarrow Cu^+(aq)$
+0.15	$Sn^{4+}(aq) + 2e^- \rightarrow Sn^{2+}(aq)$
+0.07	$AgBr(s) + e^- \rightarrow Ag(s) + Br^-(aq)$
0.00	$Ti^{4+}(aq) + e^- \rightarrow Ti^{3+}(aq)$
0.00	$2H^+(aq) + 2e^- \rightarrow H_2(g)$
−0.04	$Fe^{3+}(aq) + 3e^- \rightarrow Fe(s)$
−0.08	$O_2(g) + H_2O(l) + 2e^- \rightarrow HO_2^-(aq) + OH^-(aq)$
−0.13	$Pb^{2+}(aq) + 2e^- \rightarrow Pb(s)$
−0.14	$In^+(aq) + e^- \rightarrow In(s)$
−0.14	$Sn^{2+}(aq) + 2e^- \rightarrow Sn(s)$
−0.15	$AgI(s) + e^- \rightarrow Ag(s) + I^-(aq)$
−0.23	$Ni^{2+}(aq) + 2e^- \rightarrow Ni(s)$
−0.28	$Co^{2+}(aq) + 2e^- \rightarrow Co(s)$
−0.34	$In^{3+}(aq) + 3e^- \rightarrow In(s)$
−0.34	$Tl^+(aq) + e^- \rightarrow Tl(s)$
−0.35	$PbSO_4(s) + 2e^- \rightarrow Pb(s) + SO_4^{2-}(aq)$
−0.37	$Tl^{3+}(aq) + e^- \rightarrow Tl^{2+}(aq)$
−0.40	$Cd^{2+}(aq) + 2e^- \rightarrow Cd(s)$
−0.40	$In^{2+}(aq) + e^- \rightarrow In^+(aq)$
−0.44	$Fe^{2+}(aq) + 2e^- \rightarrow Fe(s)$
−0.44	$In^{3+}(aq) + 2e^- \rightarrow In^+(aq)$
−0.48	$S(s) + 2e^- \rightarrow S^{2-}(aq)$
−0.49	$In^{3+}(aq) + e^- \rightarrow In^{2+}(aq)$
−0.50	$Cr^{3+}(aq) + e^- \rightarrow Cr^{2+}(aq)$

Appendix 8 Common Radioactive Nuclei   A19

$E°$ (V)	Reduction Half-reaction
−0.61	$U^{4+}(aq) + e^- \rightarrow U^{3+}(aq)$
−0.73	$Cr^{3+}(aq) + 3e^- \rightarrow Cr(s)$
−0.76	$Zn^{2+}(aq) + 2e^- \rightarrow Zn(s)$
−0.81	$Cd(OH)_2(aq) + 2e^- \rightarrow Cd(s) + 2OH^-(aq)$
−0.83	$2H_2O(l) + 2e^- \rightarrow H_2(g) + 2OH^-(aq)$
−0.91	$Cr^{2+}(aq) + 2e^- \rightarrow Cr(s)$
−1.18	$Mn^{2+}(aq) + 2e^- \rightarrow Mn(s)$
−1.19	$V^{2+}(aq) + 2e^- \rightarrow V(s)$
−1.63	$Ti^{2+}(aq) + 2e^- \rightarrow Ti(s)$
−1.66	$Al^{3+}(aq) + 3e^- \rightarrow Al(s)$
−1.79	$U^{3+}(aq) + 3e^- \rightarrow U(s)$
−2.09	$Sc^{3+}(aq) + 3e^- \rightarrow Sc(s)$
−2.23	$H_2(g) + 2e^- \rightarrow 2H^-(aq)$
−2.37	$Mg^{2+}(aq) + 2e^- \rightarrow Mg(s)$
−2.37	$La^{3+}(aq) + 3e^- \rightarrow La(s)$
−2.48	$Ce^{3+}(aq) + 3e^- \rightarrow Ce(s)$
−2.71	$Na^+(aq) + e^- \rightarrow Na(s)$
−2.76	$Ca^{2+}(aq) + 2e^- \rightarrow Ca(s)$
−2.89	$Sr^{2+}(aq) + 2e^- \rightarrow Sr(s)$
−2.90	$Ba^{2+}(aq) + 2e^- \rightarrow Ba(s)$
−2.92	$Ra^{2+}(aq) + 2e^- \rightarrow Ra(s)$
−2.92	$Cs^+(aq) + e^- \rightarrow Cs(s)$
−2.92	$K^+(aq) + e^- \rightarrow K(s)$
−2.93	$Rb^+(aq) + e^- \rightarrow Rb(s)$
−3.05	$Li^+(aq) + e^- \rightarrow Li(s)$

Appendix 8

Common Radioactive Nuclei

More information can be found at the following websites:
http://www.epa.gov/radiation/radionuclides/index.html (accessed November 2005)
http://www.ndc.tokai.jaeri.go.jp/CN04/ (accessed November 2005)

Element	Nuclide	Half-life	Element	Nuclide	Half-life
Americium	^{240}Am	51 h	Plutonium	^{238}Pu	87.7 y
Americium	^{241}Am	432.2 y	Plutonium	^{239}Pu	2.44×10^5 y
Americium	^{242}Am	16 h	Plutonium	^{240}Pu	6.56×10^3 y
Carbon	^{14}C	5730 y	Polonium	^{210}Po	138 d
Cesium	^{137}Cs	30 y	Radium	^{226}Ra	1.6×10^3 y
Cobalt	^{58}Co	71 d	Radon	^{220}Rn	54.5 s
Cobalt	^{60}Co	5.271 y	Radon	^{222}Rn	3.8 d
Fluorine	^{18}F	110 min	Strontium	^{85}Sr	64 d
Gallium	^{67}Ga	78.25 h	Strontium	^{90}Sr	28.9 y
Gold	^{198}Au	2.69 d	Technetium	^{99}Tc	2.13×10^5 y
Hydrogen	^{3}H	12.3 y	Technetium	^{99m}Tc	6.0 h
Iodine	^{129}I	1.57×10^7 y	Thallium	^{201}Tl	21.5 h
Iodine	^{131}I	8.040 d	Thorium	^{232}Th	1.4×10^{10} y
Lead	^{210}Pb	22.3 y	Uranium	^{234}U	2.46×10^5 y
Molybdenum	^{99}Mo	67 h	Uranium	^{235}U	7.0×10^8 y
Nobelium	^{250}No	250 μs	Uranium	^{238}U	4.5×10^9 y
Palladium	^{103}Pd	16.97 d			

Answers to Practice Exercises and Selected Exercises

Chapter 1

P1.1 a. chemical; **b.** chemical; **c.** physical; **d.** physical; **e.** physical; **f.** chemical   **P1.2 a.** homogeneous; **b.** heterogeneous; **c.** heterogeneous; **d.** homogeneous; **e.** homogeneous; **f.** heterogeneous   **P1.3** Answers to this problem may vary. The following solution is only one possibility.

Step 1: *Formulating a question:* The question is provided: "There is a dark liquid in my cup. What is the liquid and how did it get there?" Step 2: *Finding out what is already known about your question.* You could ask people nearby if they knew what was in your cup, or if they had themselves poured the liquid in the cup. You may have your answer to the question after completing this step. Similar findings occur in scientific investigations in that a specific problem may have already been solved. Step 3: *Making observations.* Your first observations may be the odor you smell from the cup, the actual color and deepness of color of the liquid, and the thickness of the liquid in the cup. As a final step, you may wish to taste the liquid, which should provide the true identity of the liquid. Step 4: *Creating a hypothesis:* Here you would begin to posit an explanation of how the liquid got into your cup: "My friend Anne poured the coffee into my cup." Or "My nephew emptied his juice cup into my cup." To pose the proper question you need to both identify what is in the cup and how it got there. Step 5: *Designing and performing experiments.* You could create several experiments that could range from asking everyone around if they had seen what had happened to checking for fingerprints. If this is a repeated occurrence, you could hold a "stakeout."

Depending on what you find, you may need to change your hypothesis. For example, Anne might not have been to school or work that day and couldn't have done it. If it is a repeated occurrence and the same thing happened each time, you might have a reasonable theory that stated: "My nephew empties his grape juice into my cup each time he is here." Otherwise, if a reasonable explanation cannot be found, you might be limited to stating a law such as "Each Tuesday, coffee appears in my cup."   **P1.4** 104°C, 377 K   **P1.5** intensive   **P1.6** 3.0×10^1 cm³   **P1.7 a.** 24600 g; **b.** 15.5 gal; **c.** $19.51CN   **P1.8** 1003 m², 1,555,200 in²   **P1.9 a.** five; **b.** three or four; **c.** two; **d.** four; problem: two

1. "Chemistry is concerned with the systematic study of the matter of our universe. This study involves the composition, structure, and properties of matter." Because chemistry is a systematic study (following the scientific method) of our surroundings, it is a science. **3.** Some possible answers include carpet, plastic soda bottles, computers, foods, inks, building materials, ceramic tile, sunglasses, *anything!* **5.** The recipe will work only if we add 1 cup of water (no more, no less) to the mix. Too much water and the batter will be thin and watery; too little water and there might not be enough liquid to fully mix and bind the ingredients. Likewise, precise amounts are required for chemical reactions and processes to ensure that the correct products or processes are achieved. **7.** An element is composed of only a single type of atom and cannot be further simplified by chemical or physical processes, whereas a compound is composed of more than one type of atom (or element) and can be separated into its component elements. Oxygen, carbon, and sodium are three examples of elements. Water, salt, and rust (iron oxide) are three examples of compounds. **9.** Elemental oxygen exists as a diatomic molecule (it contains two atoms of oxygen). It is an element because there is only one type of atom involved. It is a molecule because more than one atom constitutes this natural form. It is not a compound because there are not two or more different types of atoms involved. **11.** Both can be separated into simpler substances: the mixture by mechanical means into its component parts and the compound by chemical means into its component elements. **13. a.** element; **b.** compound: sodium and chlorine; **c.** compound: carbon, hydrogen, oxygen; **d.** element; **e.** compound: sulfur, copper, oxygen; **f.** element   **15. a.** both possible; **b.** heterogeneous; **c.** heterogeneous; **d.** homogeneous; **e.** heterogeneous; **f.** heterogeneous   **17.** distillation, reverse osmosis, electrodialysis, boiling/freezing   **19. a.** physical; **b.** chemical; **c.** physical; **d.** physical   **21.** It is a mixture of several gases: oxygen, nitrogen, argon, and others.   **23.** By stating that we should "Eat natural food, not chemicals," the writer implies that natural food is not made up of chemicals. All the food we eat is exactly that—chemicals. All everyday matter is composed of chemicals! What the writer was trying to convey is that we should eat natural food, not synthetically or artificially produced chemicals (or additives) or those foods produced with pesticides, artificial fertilizers, etc. **25.** You would make *observations* to gather data about what is not working or why it is not working. Based on those observations you could develop a working *hypothesis* that was consistent with your observations that might explain what had happened. You would then *develop experiments* that would test your hypothesis. Depending on the outcome of the tests, you will have either solved the problem or ruled out your hypothesis, which would make a new hypothesis and experiments necessary. **27.** Anything that involves observation or analysis of experimental data can be open to interpretation and can influence what hypotheses or further experiments might be developed. To some extent, finding out what is already known and what well-established theories exist should be the least ambiguous because they have been the most extensively tested and refined. **29.** A hypothesis is a possible explanation for some observations, usually with little or no testing. With much testing, a hypothesis may eventually become a theory, which carries much more weight scientifically than a hypothesis. **31.** Conflicting results can often be attributed to the fact that some variable is not the same in the two studies. **33.** Some of the important questions: Are the fishes dying only in town? Are there places in the river where they are not dying? Are there contaminants in the water known to be lethal to fish? How do the levels of the contaminants vary with proximity to the industrial area, to the farmland, and to the town? Chemical analysis of the water at various locations, surveys of fish populations, and analysis of contaminants in the fish themselves are all tests that should be conducted. **35.** 1 terameter > 1 kilometer > 1 millimeter > 1 nanometer   **37. a.** 1×10^5 g; **b.** 2.59×10^{-2} km; **c.** 77°F; **d.** 3.20×10^{-3} g; **e.** 9.11×10^3 pm; **f.** 37.0°C   **39. a.** 8.7×10^6 mg; **b.** 2.59 m; **c.** 374°F; **d.** 3.20×10^{-4} kL; **e.** 9.11×10^9 ns; **f.** 177°C   **41.** 20 containers   **43. a.** 3.27×10^5 m; **b.** 3.27×10^8 mm; **c.** 3.27×10^{11} μm; **d.** 3.27×10^{14} nm   **45.** 13.6 g/mL   **47.** 1.36 g/mL   **49. a.** m s⁻¹; **b.** m s⁻²; **c.** m³; **d.** J kg⁻¹ K⁻¹   **51.** ruler with four divisions between each number   **53.** 172°F, 162°F   **55.** 6.5×10^7 atoms   **57. a.** 7×10^1 ms; **b.** 2.8×10^5 μs;   **59.** The red tomato is denser. Two tomatoes with the same mass can have different densities because they have different volumes; the red tomato must have a smaller volume than the green tomato, even though they have the same mass.   **61.** The density of the water would decrease. We can write the formula Density = mass/volume. As the volume increases with no change in the mass, the density goes down.

63. 4 "just a bits"

65.

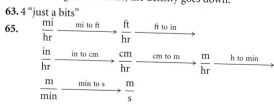

A20

67. 22.6 g/cm³; 11 kg   **69. a.** 56 kph; **b.** 2.24 × 10⁴ cm³/s; **c.** 312 km/L; **d.** 5.125 × 10⁻³ lb/°F   **71. a.** 1.12 × 10⁷ mi/min; **b.** 1.61 × 10¹⁰ mi/day; **c.** 5.87 × 10¹² mi/gr   **73. a.** 0.12 lb; **b.** 3.8 L; **c.** 72.6 kg; **d.** 2.4 m; **e.** 4.0 × 10² cm; **f.** 51 km   **75.** 95 μ yr; 0.95 μcentury; 9.5 μdecade   **77.** 3.27 ×10⁻²² g/atom; 327 yg/atom **79.** $1.27/s; $13,700/game   **81.** 51.4 kg   **83.** Neither accurate nor precise.   **85. a.** 18.170g; 15.412g; 13.871g; **b.** student 3; **c.** student 2; **d.** human error   **87. a.** 8; **b.** exact; **c.** 3; **d.** 2; **e.** 1; **f.** exact **89. a.** 0.700 cm; **b.** 0.101 kg; **c.** 100.0 cm; **d.** 100 m (ambiguous); **e.** 0.01010 g   **91. a.** three; **b.** four; **c.** four; **d.** one; **e.** seven; **f.** six; **g.** one; **h.** five; **i.** six; **j.** four   **93. a.** 9.6; **b.** 8.57; **c.** 5.81; **d.** 63; **e.** 8 × 10³; **f.** 19; **g.** 5.8 × 10²; **h.** 71; **i.** 2.81   **95.** 105 cm   **97.** 10.2 g/cm³ **99. a.** The prefix *nano-* refers to the metric multiplier 10⁻⁹, implying technology on very small scales. **b.** 1 × 10⁻⁶ cm   **101.** One advantage is that genetic engineering of corn has greatly increased the yield per acre, and the disadvantages of some engineering include the decrease in genetic diversity of the corn and the risk of the development of pesticide-resistant insects or herbicide-resistant weeds as a consequence of the use of the corn. The genetic selection of crops is as old as agriculture.   **103.** Possible answers could include improved materials, clean water, and life-saving drugs.   **105.** One of the main energy problems that the United States faces is continuing growth of energy demands while oil, gas, and coal reserves are nearing depletion. Because these reserves influence the global energy market, this problem affects developing countries as well. The United States is in a much better position, with its resources, to tackle the problem than poorer countries are.   **107.** All aspects of daily life are likely to be affected.   **109.** Chemical changes: the incorporation of carbon dioxide and oxygen to form glucose in photosynthesis and the intake of nitrogen (from nitrates or other nitrogen-containing molecules) for protein and DNA formation. Physical changes: evaporation and condensation of water in the water cycle that provides moisture to the plants are two important physical changes.   **111.** Observationally, the sugar appears to break up and disappear into the water as it dissolves, while chemically, the molecules in the sugar crystal disperse among the molecules of the water.   **113. a.** Any measurement has some uncertainty, whereas an exact number is infinitely precise; **b.** 36 cans; **c.** 7,200 mL—not exact, 36 cans—exact.   **115.** Two extensive properties of seawater are its volume and mass. Two intensive properties of seawater are its density and temperature.   **117.** The original sources are Miller, S., 1953. "A production of amino acids under possible primitive earth conditions." *Science 117*: 528–529, and Miller, S., and H. Urey, 1959. "Organic compound synthesis on the primitive earth." *Science 130*: 245–251. You should be very careful when conducting Internet searches for this material. Much of what is posted is biased and often patently wrong in that the scientific method has not been properly used. This topic is very "controversial" and both sides are very passionate in the arguments. Although minor parts of the evolutionary theory are still being actively researched and scientists are still working to explain all the details, this is not an indication that the theory itself is wrong. The vast scientific consensus is that biological evolution is real and deserves its status as a theory in the strictest scientific sense.

Chapter 2

P2.1 196 g oxygen; 220 g water   **P2.2** nitrogen-14: 7p, 7n, 7e; neon-20: 10p, 10n, 10e; titanium-48: 22p, 26n, 22e; carbon-11: 6p, 5n, 6e; lithium-11: 3p, 4n, 3e; phosphorus-31: 15p, 16n, 15e   **P2.3** 65.40 amu

P2.4

Symbol	Protons	Neutrons	Electrons	Charge
$^{52}_{24}Cr^{6+}$	24	28	18	+6
$^{39}_{19}K^{1+}$	19	20	18	+1
$^{79}_{35}Br^{1-}$	35	44	36	−1

P2.5 CsCl   **P2.6** SF_4; CCl_4; P_2O_5; phosphorus trichloride; dinitrogen monoxide; oxygen difluoride   **P2.7** $MgCl_2$; LiF; sodium bromide; lithium oxide   **P2.8** copper(II) chloride; chromium(VI) oxide; NiO; PdS_2 **P2.9** potassium permanganate; $(NH_4)_2Cr_2O_7$

1. The slow formation of the crystals on the branches from apparently clear air must indicate the presence of very small particles that are slowing adding to the crystal until their numbers are great enough to be seen.   **3.** Taking the word *dormitory* apart yields the following letters: d, i, m, o, o, r, r, t, y. These letters could be recombined to form the words *dim, dorm, door, toy, dot, rot, trim, try, moor, or, it,* and others. Each of these new words has a different meaning and function than the original word *dormitory*.   **5.** The law of conservation of mass means that atoms can't spontaneously appear or disappear in a chemical reaction; they have to go somewhere. **7.** Just like Democritus, the researcher trying to discover the age of the earth has to ask what processes are occurring and whether these processes have always been the same. The researcher must look for similarities in current and past processes to discover a common theme that can explain a way to determine the age of the earth. **9.** 5.7 g water; law of definite composition and law of conservation of mass   **11. a.** The law of conservation of mass; **b.** 247.8 g   **13.** 4.28 g O; 45.7 g Cu   **15.** If the ratio of 65 g Cu to 16 g O (4.1:1.0) represents a 1:1 ratio of atoms, you would expect a mass ratio of 8.1:1.0 for a 2 Cu : 1 O compound or a 2.0:1.0 mass ratio for a 1 Cu: 2 O compound.   **17.** $CaCO_3$ ($CaCO_3$ is 40% Ca; CaCl is 36% Ca)   **19.** The ratio of the amount of oxygen that combines with 2 g of hydrogen in water to the amount that combines with 2 g of hydrogen in hydrogen peroxide is 16:32, which is 1:2. This ratio is a small whole-number ratio, which agrees with the law of multiple proportions. **21.** Proton = +2; neutron = 0
23.

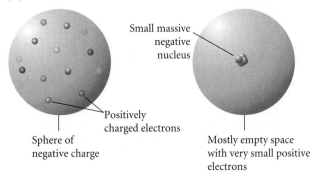

J. J. Thomson's Model — Rutherford's Model

Small massive negative nucleus

Positively charged electrons

Sphere of negative charge

Mostly empty space with very small positive electrons

25.

Isotope	Protons	Neutrons	Electrons	Charge
carbon-12	6	6	6	0
aluminum-27	13	14	10	+3
chlorine-35	17	18	18	−1

27. a. proton; **b.** neutron; **c.** neutrons or electrons   **29.** 1.6735 × 10⁻²⁴ g; 3.3484 × 10⁻²⁴ g   **31.** 0; 0   **33.** 0.54%   **35. a.** Fe; **b.** Te; **c.** Co; **d.** Ne   **37.** ₁H, ₅B, ₉F, ₁₃Al, ₂₀Ca, ₂₆Fe   **39.** ₁H, ₅B, ₐF, ₁₃Al,

$_{20}$Ca, $_{26}$Fe   **41.** H   **43.** +2, cation
45.

Symbol	Protons	Electrons	Neutrons
$^{24}_{11}$Na	11	11	13
$^{131}_{53}$I	53	53	78
$^{60}_{27}$Co	27	27	33
$^{51}_{24}$Cr	24	24	27
$^{32}_{15}$P	15	15	17

47. 8.000000 amu; 0.5000000 amu   **49.** 1.9926×10^{-23} g;
3.3247×10^{-23} g; 3.1550×10^{-23} g   **51.** Indium-113 = 4.2%;
indium-115 = 95.8%   **53.** 32.06 amu

Mass Spectrum of Sulfur

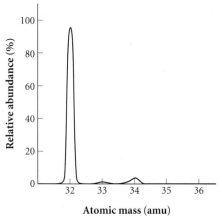

55. 140.1 amu

Mass Spectrum of Cerium

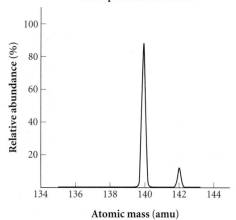

57. a. Be; **b.** Mn; **c.** Kr   **59.** 5;(F, Cl, Br, I, At)   **61.** sulfur – chalco-
gens (Group VIA); iodine – halogens (Group VIIA); helium – noble
gases (Group VIIIA); beryllium – alkaline earth metals (Group IIA);
francium – alkali metals (Group IA)   **63.** Metals are the elements
that are usually shiny; gold, silver, and lead are metals. Additionally,
silicon, as a metalloid, may be shiny.   **65.** Ca; Al; Al; Sr; Be
67. LiCl; BeCl$_2$; NaCl; CaCl$_2$; AlCl$_3$ **69.** MgBr$_2$, Mg^{2+} and Br$^-$;
FeCl$_3$, Fe^{3+} and Cl$^-$; KI, K$^+$ and I$^-$; Na$_2$S, Na$^+$ and S^{2-} **71. a.** ionic
compounds; **b.** molecules; **c.** ionic compounds   **73.** K$_2$O; WO$_2$
75. a. HO; **b.** C$_2$H$_5$; **c.** CF$_2$; **d.** CH$_2$O   **77.** SO$_2$ – sulfur dioxide;

N$_2$O$_5$ – dinitrogen pentoxide; Cl$_2$O – dichlorine monoxide; PCl$_3$ –
phosphorus trichloride; CCl$_4$ – carbon tetrachloride   **79.** K$_2$O –
potassium oxide; CaBr$_2$ – calcium bromide; Li$_3$N – lithium nitride;
AlCl$_3$ – aluminum chloride; BaS – barium sílfide   **81.** CaBr$_2$ –
calcium bromide; Fe(NO$_3$)$_3$ – iron(III) nitrate; CaSO$_4$ – calcium sulfate; NH$_4$Cl – ammonium chloride; NaCl – sodium chloride
83. copper(II) hydroxide – Cu(OH)$_2$; magnesium sulfate – MgSO$_4$;
chromium(III) oxide – Cr$_2$O$_3$; sodium sulfite – Na$_2$SO$_3$; sulfur
hexachloride – SCl$_6$; ammonium hydroxide – NH$_4$OH; carbon
tetraiodide – CI$_4$; boron tribromide – BBr$_3$; aluminum hydroxide –
Al(OH)$_3$; sodium acetate – NaCH$_3$COO   **85.** Mn$_2$(SO$_4$)$_5$; MnCl$_5$;
Mn(NO$_2$)$_5$; Mn$_2$(CO$_3$)$_5$; Mn(HSO$_3$)$_5$ **87.** MnC$_2$O$_4$; Cu$_2$C$_2$O$_4$;
Fe$_2$(C$_2$O$_4$)$_3$; Mn$_2$(C$_2$O$_4$)$_5$; Ti(C$_2$O$_4$)$_2$ **89.** (NH$_4$)$_2$CO$_3$ – ammonium
carbonate; NaHCO$_3$ – sodium bicarbonate; Cu(HSO$_3$)$_2$ – copper
(II) bisulfite; Ca(OH)$_2$ – calcium hydroxide; KMnO$_4$ – potassium
permanganate; Na$_3$PO$_4$ – sodium phosphate; Mg(CN)$_2$ – magnesium cyanide; LiClO$_3$ – lithium chlorate   **91.** V = +5; Ti = +2;
W = +6; Ag = +1; Ru = +3   **93.** The formula Fe(NO$_3$) does not
give enough information to identify the salt, because it could be either Fe(NO$_3$)$_2$ or Fe(NO$_3$)$_3$. By using the compound in a chemical
reaction, you should be able to determine its identity. The two forms
of iron nitrate also have different physical properties that could be
used to identify the salt.   **95.** The major objections to Dalton's original atomic theory have been that atoms do appear to be divisible
(they can emit radiation) and there do appear to be atoms of the
same element that are not identical (isotopes). Dalton's atomic theory would serve most of chemistry if we rewrote it as follows: Every
substance is made of atoms.

- Atoms are divisible and consist of electrons, protons, and neutrons. The protons and neutrons occupy the center of the atom
(the nucleus), and the electrons occupy the space around the
nucleus.
- All atoms of any one element have the same number of protons
and have the same chemical properties.
- The average atomic masses of different elements are different, and
the masses of individual isotopes are related to the total number
of protons, neutrons, and electrons in the atom.
- A chemical reaction rearranges the attachments between atoms in
a compound.

97. The law of combining volumes would apply in both cases, in that
both predict small whole-number ratios. The law of definite composition applies to both cases for the same reason. The important fact
that Dalton did not account for was that elemental hydrogen and
chlorine exist as diatomic molecules. Because hydrogen chloride
contains one atom of each, two molecules of hydrogen chloride
are formed from one molecule each of hydrogen and chlorine.
99. The number of balls per box and the total price of the box
101. 9.81×10^{-28} kg. This mass was lost as energy.   **103.** One condition that might have changed that would affect radiocarbon dating is
the relative amount of carbon-13 available to be incorporated into
the plants. If the amount in the past was greater than what is measured now, the amount of carbon-13 still present would be higher
than expected, making the artifact appear not to be as old as it is.
On the other hand, if the amount of carbon-13 in the past was
lower than the current amount, the artifact would appear to be older
than it is.

Chapter 3

P3.1 a. 299.4 amu; **b.** 120.38 amu; **c.** 227.14 amu
P3.2 3.06×10^{23} atoms   **P3.3** 4.78×10^{-4} mol; 9.0×10^{23} molecules   **P3.4** NaCl: 1.5×10^3 g, 0.15 g; H$_2$O: 4.7×10^2 g, 0.045 g; aspartame: 7.7×10^3 g; 0.74 g   **P3.5** C$_3$H$_6$O$_3$: 0.059 mol, 2.4×10^{-5} mol;
H$_2$SO$_4$: 0.054 mol, 2.2×10^{-5} mol   **P3.6** 5.01×10^{22} molecules,

1.59×10^7 g, swimming pool   **P3.7** 52.45% K   **P3.8** CH, C_6H_6
P3.9 $C_2H_4O_2$ **P3.10** $Ca_3(PO_4)_2 + 3H_2SO_4 \rightarrow 3CaSO_4 + 2H_3PO_4$
P3.11 72.04 g   **P3.12** 678 kg   **P3.13** 71 g   **P3.14** 18.47 g
P3.15. 88.6 g

1. a. 28.01 amu; **b.** 60.09 amu; **c.** 17.03 amu; **d.** 158.12 amu;
e. 891.5 amu   **3.** $H_2O < CO < C_2H_4OH < C_6H_6 < CaCl_2$
5. a. saccharin = 183.19 amu; aspartame = 294.3 amu;
b. 1.607: 1.000; **c.** 26.1 g   **7.** $\$3 \times 10^{-21}$/atom   **9. a.** 10.8 g;
b. 3.271×10^{-10} g; **c.** 7.181×10^{-22} g; **d.** 7.321×10^{-23} g
11. a. 4.014×10^{23}; **b.** 4.896×10^{23}; **c.** 4×10^{24}; **d.** 7.7×10^{18}
13. a. 60.06 amu; **b.** 60.06 g; **c.** 6.006 g   **15.** 1.99×10^{21} molecules
17. 4.2×10^{23} units   **19. a.** 1.48 mol; **b.** 0.025 mol; **c.** 0.57 mol;
d. 7.5 mol   **21.** 245 g C   **23. a.** 8.14×10^{22} units; **b.** 9.03×10^{24}
units; **c.** 3.8×10^{21} units   **25. a.** 3.0×10^4 g; **b.** 287 g; **c.** 12 g
27. 3.1×10^{22} atoms   **29. a.** 9.274×10^{-23} g; **b.** 1.6×10^{20} atoms;
c. 2.7×10^{-4} mol   **31. a.** 2.5×10^{-5} mol; **b.** 1.5×10^{19} atoms
33. a. 1.30×10^3 g; **b.** 1.77 mol   **35.** 9.22×10^{-4} mol; 5.55×10^{20}
molecules; 4.44×10^{21} atoms   **37. a.** 85.63%; **b.** 37.48%; **c.** 92.26%;
d. 42.10%   **39.** $H_2S > SO_2 > H_2SO_3 > Na_2S_2O_4$ **41.** 85.40%,
23.14%, 61.81%   **43. a.** Na_2SO_4; **b.** $KMnO_4$; **c.** HNO_3 **45.** 18.75%
C, 31.29% Ca, 49.96% C   **47.** The mass percent of carbon in the saturated hydrocarbon would decrease relative to the unsaturated hydrocarbon. The percentage of carbon decreases because the total
mass of the compound increases while the mass of carbon is un-
changed; when we divide by the larger total mass, the percentage
decreases   **49.** 8 violinists, 6 brasses, 2 cellos, 1 percussionist
51. CH_2 **53. a.** C_2H_2O; **b.** 84   **55.** $KAgC_2N_2$ **57.** $C_{18}H_{32}O_2$
59. a. 2,1,3,4; **b.** 1,2,1,2; **c.** 1,4,1,5; **d.** 1,6,3,2   **61.** $3CaCl_2 + 2Na_3PO_4$
$\rightarrow Ca_3(PO_4)_2 + 6NaCl$ **63.** $TiCl_4 + 2H_2O \rightarrow TiO_2 + 4HCl$
65. a. 2,1,1,1; **b.** 70.9 g   **67.** 0.639 g   **69. a.** 4,5,4,6; **b.** 59.9 g;
c. 54.0 g; **d.** 21.0 g   **71. a.** 3,2,1,6; **b.** 0.406 g; **c.** 0.358 g
73. a. 50 sandwiches, pickles   **75. a.** 129 g; **b.** 24%   **77.** 6.65 g
79. 11.2 g   **81.** 25.6%   **83.** $4Fe(s) + 3O_2(g) \rightarrow 2Fe_2O_3(s)$, 136 g O_2,
318 g Fe   **85.** $C_6H_{12}O_6 \rightarrow 2C_2H_5OH + 2CO_2$, 0.278 mol
87. The effect of a chemical on the body is often purely an effect of
the amount with one dose having a beneficial effect while another
dose having a detrimental effect. In the case of vitamin C, there is
strong evidence that small amounts are crucial for a healthy life;
however, large doses, while promoted by some, may possibly be
harmful   **89.** The atomic masses given on the periodic table can be
thought of in two ways: First, it is the total mass of 1 mole ($6.022 \times$
10^{23} atoms) of a substance (with all isotopes present), or second, it is
the weighted average mass of all that element's isotopes. In either
case, a single atom's mass is not the same as the average mass (unless
there is only one possible isotope of that element)   **91.** 19.8 g
93. 5.99×10^4 g   **95.** 83.2% C, 16.8% H, C_5H_{12} **97.** Since different
compounds will contain differing numbers of atoms of each ele-
ment, there is no reason that the coefficients should add up to equal
numbers on each side of a reaction. It is important that there be the
same number of atoms of each element on each side of the equation
98. a. C_4H_5; **b.** C_8H_{10}; **c.** $2C_8H_{10} + 13O_2 \rightarrow 16CO + 10H_2O$;
d. 24.5 g; **e.** O_2, 33.4 g CO; **f.** 4.19%

Chapter 4

P4.1 a. 0.17 M; **b.** 0.0202 M; **c.** 33.17 g   **P4.2** 3.8 mol, 12 mol
P4.3 a. 1.40 L; **b.** 2.4 L, 1.2 L   **P4.4** 7.69×10^{-6} M   **P4.5** 19 mL
P4.6 0.0445 M   **P4.7** $K_2CO_4(aq) + 2HNO_3(aq) \rightarrow H_2C_2O_4(aq) +$
$2KNO_3(aq)$; $2K^+(aq) + C_2O_4{}^{2-}(aq) + 2H^+(aq) + 2NO_3{}^-(aq) \rightarrow$
$H_2C_2O_4(aq) + 2K^+(aq) + 2NO_3{}^-(aq)$; $C_2O_4{}^{2-}(aq) + 2H^+(aq) \rightarrow$
$H_2C_2O_4(aq)$ **P4.8** $AgNO_3 + NaCl$ (forms $AgCl(s)$); $AgNO_3 + Na_2S$
(forms $Ag_2S(s)$); $AgNO_3 + ZnSO_4$ (forms $Ag_2SO_4(aq)$); $Na_2S +$
$ZnSO_4$ (forms $ZnS(s)$)   **P4.9** 17 g   **P4.10** 7.58 mL   **P4.11** K(+1),
Cl(−1); Fe(+3), O(−2); P(0); C(0), H(+1), Cl(−1); Al(0); P(+3),
Br(−1); H(+1), C(+2), N(−3)   **P4.12** No

1. Because the water molecule contains both partial positive charges
(on the hydrogens) and partial negative charges (on the oxygen), it
can interact favorably with both cations and anions.   **3.** The hydration sphere is the cage of water molecules that surrounds a charged
particle as it dissolves in water.   **5.** Water tends to dissolve those
compounds that have some type of charge on the molecule or ion;
however, oil molecules have very little, if any, charges on the molecule that water can attract. Oil, then, doesn't dissolve because it cannot interact favorably with water.   **7.** When some compounds dissolve, they form anions and cations in the water. Even though the
particles formed a neutral compound before dissolving, these ions
exist separately in the water and are free to move. Since the current
requires freely moving charges, the new ions in the water can carry
the current.   **9.** The apparatus could identify a strong electrolyte
with a brightly lit bulb, but could not distinguish between weak electrolyte and nonelectrolyte solutions that will not light the bulb.
11. c.   13. 0.300 mol   **15. a.** 5.68×10^{-4} M; **b.** 2.84×10^{-3} M;
c. 9.9×10^{-3} M   **17. a.** 0.11 g; **b.** 0.136 g; **c.** 8.06 g   **19. a.** 0.221 M;
b. 0.442 M; **c.** 55.5 M   **21.** 1.2×10^3 L   **23. a.** 0.80 L; **b.** 0.80 L;
c. 9.32 L   **25. a.** 2.5 ppm; **b.** 10.5 ppm; **c.** 41.7 ppm   **27. a.** 7.01 ppm;
b. 5.33×10^3 ppb; **c.** 0.0170%   **29.** Both have the same molarity.
31. 9.93 kg   **33.** 2.34 M   **35.** 3.0×10^{-6} g; 1.4×10^{-8} M
37. 0.010 mol   **39. a.** 0.217 M; **b.** 0.0140 M; **c.** 0.22 M
41. 0.10 M $CuCl_2$
43. In words: Potassium hydroxide + hydrochloric acid →
potassium chloride + water

Molecular equation: $KOH(aq) + HCl(aq) \rightarrow KCl(aq) + H_2O(l)$

Ionic equation: $K^+(aq) + OH^-(aq) + H^+(aq) + Cl^-(aq) \rightarrow$
$K^+(aq) + Cl^-(aq) + H_2O(l)$

Net ionic equation: $OH^-(aq) + H^+(aq) \rightarrow H_2O(l)$

45. Molecular equation: $2NaCl(aq) + Ca(NO_3)_2(aq) \rightarrow$
$2NaNO_3(aq) + CaCl_2(aq)$

Ionic equation: $2Na^+(aq) + 2Cl^-(aq) + Ca^{2+}(aq) + 2NO_3{}^-(aq) \rightarrow$
$2Na^+(aq) + 2NO_3{}^-(aq) + Ca^{2+}(aq) + 2Cl^-(aq)$

Net ionic equation: none

47. Brand A has higher conc.; Brand B has more vitamin C.
49. 0.05899 M   **51.** $H^+ + OH^- \rightarrow H_2O$, 4.499 M   **53. a.** $CaCO_3 +$
$2HCl \rightarrow CaCl_2 + H_2O + CO_2$; **b.** 0.125 g
55. a. $2C_4H_{10}(g) + 13O_2(g) \rightarrow 8CO_2(g) + 10H_2O(l)$, Redox
(Combustion); **b.** $Ca(OH)_2(aq) + 2HNO_3(aq) \rightarrow$
$Ca(NO_3)_2(aq) + 2H_2O(l)$, acid–base; Net ionic equation:
$H^+(aq) + OH^-(aq) \rightarrow H_2O(l)$; **c.** $Pb(NO_3)_2(aq) + 2NaCl(aq) \rightarrow$
$PbCl_2(s) + 2NaNO_3(aq)$, precipitation; Net ionic equation:
$Pb^{2+}(aq) + 2Cl^-(aq) \rightarrow PbCl_2(s)$ **57. c., d.,** and **e.**
59. a. $BaCl_2(aq) + 2NaNO_3(aq) \rightarrow Ba(NO_3)_2(aq) + 2NaCl(aq)$;
Net ionic equation: none; **b.** $2Fe(NO_3)_3(aq) + 3(NH_4)_2SO_4(aq) \rightarrow$
$Fe_2(SO_4)_3(aq) + 6NH_4NO_3$; Net ionic equation: none;
c. $CaCl_2(aq) + K_2SO_4(aq) \rightarrow CaSO_4(s) + 2KCl(aq)$;
Net ionic equation: $Ca^{2+}(aq) + SO_4{}^{2-}(aq) \rightarrow CaSO_4(s)$
61. a. $Cu(NO_3)_2(aq) + 2KOH(aq) \rightarrow Cu(OH)_2(s) + 2KNO_3(aq)$;
Net ionic equation: $Cu^{2+}(aq) + 2OH^-(aq) \rightarrow Cu(OH)_2(s)$;
b. $3Na_2CO_3(aq) + 2AlCl_3(aq) \rightarrow 6NaCl(aq) + Al_2(CO_3)_3(s)$;
Net ionic equation: $3CO_3{}^{2-}(aq) + 2Al^{3+}(aq) \rightarrow Al_2(CO_3)_3(s)$;
c. $2(NH_4)_3PO_4(aq) + 3ZnCl_2(aq) \rightarrow 6NH_4Cl(aq) + Zn_3(PO_4)_2(s)$;
Net ionic equation: $2PO_4{}^{3-}(aq) + 3Zn^{2+}(aq) \rightarrow Zn_3(PO_4)_2(s)$
63. Answers may vary. **a.** $Ba(NO_3)_2 + Na_2S$; **b.** $Cu(NO_3)_2 + NaOH$;
c. $Pb(NO_3)_2 + Na_2SO_4$ **65.** First NaCl, next Na_2SO_4, then Na_2S
67. a. $AgNO_3(aq) + NaCl(aq) \rightarrow NaNO_3(aq) + AgCl(s)$; $Ag^+(aq)$
$+ Cl^-(aq) \rightarrow AgCl(s)$; **b.** 0.867 g AgCl; 0.653 g Ag^+ **69.** $H^+(aq) +$
$OH^-(aq) \rightarrow H_2O(l)$ **71. a.** 0.770 M; **b.** 17.2 mL   **73.** 0.220 M
75. a. $H_2CO_3 + 2NaOH \rightarrow 2H_2O + Na_2CO_3$; $H^+ + OH^- \rightarrow H_2O$;
b. 0.05633 M   **77. a.** 0.0130 g; **b.** 0.0146 g; **c.** 0.0250 g   **79. a.** C;
b. F; **c.** O; **d.** P; **e.** O   **81. a.** O(−2), N(+5); **b.** O(−2), P(+5);

c. $Cu(+2)$, $C(+4)$, $O(-2)$; **d.** $N(0)$; **e.** $H(+1)$, $S(+4)$, $O(-2)$
83. Yes, Fe $(+2$ to $+3)$ and Cr $(+6$ to $+3)$ **85.** Water is called the universal solvent because it dissolves so many molecules of varying sizes from small ionic compounds to very large proteins and DNA.
87. 43.4 mL **89.** $CuOH$, $BaCO_3$, and Cu_2CO_3 **91.** $Ba(NO_3)_2(aq)$ $+ Na_2SO_4(aq) \rightarrow BaSO_4(s) + 2NaNO_3(aq); Ba^{2+}(aq) + 2\ NO_3^-(aq)$ $+ 2Na^+(aq) + SO_4^{2-}(aq) \rightarrow BaSO_4(s) + 2Na^+(aq) + 2NO_3^-(aq)$; 13.8 g **92. a.** soluble; **b.** $H_2C_2O_4(s) \rightarrow H_2C_2O_4(aq) \rightarrow 2H^+(aq)$ $+ C_2O_4^{2-}(aq)$; **c.** CO_2; **d.** MnO_4^-; **e.** 10; **f.** MnO_4^- reduced, $C_2O_4^{2-}$ oxidized; **g.** 0.0736 g

Chapter 5

P5.1 Plants use energy in the environment (from the Sun, in the chemical bonds of water, carbon dioxide, minerals) to create sugars and starches. These sugars and starches, along with everything else that makes up a plant, are storage systems for chemical energy, which is the total of the kinetic and potential energies due to the motion and position of the atoms of the chemicals. Thus plants serve as storage depots of chemical energy for animals that eat them—and even for future fossil fuels as the plant material is converted into coal or oil. **P5.2** -270 L·atm, -2.70×10^4 J **P5.3** $+44.8$ J **P5.4** 2.9 **P5.5** -3220 kJ/mol **P5.6** -6.03×10^2 kJ **P5.7 a.** 0.494 mol; **b.** 1.52 mol **P5.8** $+1973$ kJ **P5.9** -1532 kJ

1. At the top of one side, the skateboarder has only potential energy. As the skater begins down one side of the half-pipe, the potential energy begins to decrease as it is converted to the kinetic energy of the skater. As the skater hits the bottom of the half pipe, the kinetic energy is at a maximum and the potential energy is at a minimum. As the skater begins to climb the opposite wall of the half-pipe, the kinetic energy decreases and some of it is converted into potential energy. At the top of the wall, the kinetic energy reaches zero and the potential energy is at a maximum. **3. a.** 5.4×10^2 J; **b.** 1.3×10^{-2} J; **c.** 1.1×10^{-20} J **5. a.** potential; **b.** potential and kinetic; **c.** kinetic **7.** Some of the kinetic energy in the particles is what is transferred between the system and the surroundings. The transfer is completed as the more energetic (higher-temperature) particles collide and transfer energy to the less energetic (lower-temperature) particles. **9.** system: chemicals in combustion; surroundings: everything else; system is losing; $w = $ "$-$" **11.** 36 J, lose **13. a.** 90 J, lose; **b.** 930 J, lose; **c.** 9 kJ, lose; **d.** 44 kJ, lose **15.** CO_2 is fully combusted (digested) and can release no further heat in these processes. **17.** Less force is required because of lower gravity and less atmospheric drag. **19.** $q = $ "$+$"; $w = $ "$-$" **21.** 19 m/s **23.** 4.1×10^{-21} J **25.** 2.6 Cal/g; 2.6 kcal/g; 11 kJ/g **27.** 2.93 kJ **29.** 1.06 kJ **31. a.** 71.0°C; **b.** 71.0°C **33.** 1.23×10^3 kJ **35.** The size of a temperature *change* is the same in kelvins as in degrees Celsius. **37.** part b **39.** 0.239 g; 5.8 J, 0.0243 J·g^{-1}·°C^{-1} **41.** 0.444 J·g^{-1}·°C^{-1} **43.** 26.72 kJ/°C **45. a.** 49.3 kJ/g; **b.** molar mass of sugar **47.** 6.5 g **49.** CH_4 **51.** 30.3°C **53.** Any gases that are generated as a result of the chemical process will expand (or contract) until the pressure of the gas matches the atmospheric pressure. Because the entire process begins and ends at the same pressure, we can consider the process to be a constant-pressure process. **55.** Enthalpy is equivalent to the amount of heat energy transferred in a constant-pressure process. **57.** surroundings **59.** 1 atm pressure; 1 M concentrations (25°C is common, but not standard) **61. b.** forms 2 moles (not 1) of NH_3; **c.** describes phase change not formation; **d.** nonstandard state for H_2; **e.** and **f.** more than one product and nonelemental reactants **63.** ΔH and ΔU differ by the term $P\Delta V$. Because there are 29 more moles of gas as products, ΔV and $P\Delta V$ are large, making ΔH and ΔU different. **65. a.** $C(s) + \frac{1}{2}O_2(g) \rightarrow CO(g)$; **b.** exothermic; **c.** $+110.5$ kJ/mol **67.** $C_4H_{10}(g) + \frac{13}{2}O_2(g) \rightarrow 4CO_2(g) + 5H_2O(l)$ **69.** $10\ C(s, \text{graphite}) + \frac{15}{2}H_2(g) + \frac{5}{2}N_2(g) + \frac{13}{2}O_2(g) +$ $3P(s, \alpha \text{ white}) \rightarrow C_{10}H_{15}N_5O_{13}P_3(s)$ **71. a.** $+1012$ kJ; **b.** -506 kJ;

c. -2024 kJ **73.** Arrange the reactions such that $\Delta H(\text{total}) =$ $\Delta H_f(\text{propane}) = -\Delta H_c(\text{propane}) + 4\ \Delta H_c(\text{hydrogen})$ $+ 3\ \Delta H_c(\text{carbon})$ **75.** -1273 kJ **77. a.** -1367 kJ/mol; **b.** -2967 kJ **79.** -5472 kJ/mol **81.** -413 kJ **83.** There are many possible answers for each type: solar cells, solar thermal systems, biomass conversion, hydroelectric systems, wind power, and geothermal systems. In addition to being renewable: several of these (solar, solar thermal, geothermal, wind, and biomass) can generate power on-site; biomass can use unwanted by-products of agriculture or even boost the prices of the commodities that are used; and all would probably reduce the overall production of pollution due to greenhouse gases or combustion by-products. **85.** 5.62×10^{-21} J; less because the mass is lower. **87.** It gets the reaction "over the hill" (that is, it gets the reaction started). Yes. Most reactions require more energy to get started. Then some energy is released, making the activation energy larger than the energy change. **89. a.** exothermic, the heat that you feel is heat that has been released; **b.** surroundings; **c.** out; **d.** raised; **e.** no work except minor expansion of materials **91.** 4.36 Cal/g; 1.82×10^4 J/g; 18.2 kJ/g; 231 m/s **93. a.** 78.1 kJ; **b.** heat capacity of the mug or total heat absorbed by water and mug **95.** 4.35 kJ/°C **97.** 38 kJ/g **99. a.** $+453$ kJ; **b.** -11.6 kJ; **c.** exothermic; **d.** 2.07 g; **e.** -2.39 kJ; **f.** 28.8°C

Chapter 6

P6.1 403 nm; The wavelength should be shorter because of higher frequency. **P6.2** 2.48×10^{-23} J **P6.3** 1875.6 nm, 2625.8 nm, 7459.7 nm **P6.4** 91.9 nm **P6.5** 3.6×10^{-38} m **P6.6** 2.00×10^{-3} kg·m·s^{-1}·mol^{-1}; 5.70×10^{-4} kg·m·s^{-1}·mol^{-1}; 3.99×10^{-4} kg·m·s^{-1}·mol^{-1}; Because the momentum is inversely proportional to the wavelength, there is a marked difference.
P6.7 $2p$ **P6.8** Ga: $1s^2 2s^2 2p^6 3s^2 3p^6 4s^2 3d^{10} 4p^1$, or $[Ar]4s^2 3d^{10} 4p^1$; Sr: $1s^2 2s^2 2p^6 3s^2 3p^6 4s^2 3d^{10} 4p^6 5s^2$, or $[Kr]5s^2$

3. red tomato, yellow squash, green squash, and finally purple eggplant **5. a.** 2.0×10^{19}/s; **b.** 1.3×10^{-14} J; **c.** 8.0×10^9 J/mol **7.** infrared, 1.2×10^{13}/s, 8.0×10^{-21} J **9.** based on 5 ft 6 in: 1.68 m, 1.68×10^9 nm, 1.77×10^{-16} light-years, meters are most convenient. **11.** 0.364 m to 0.336 m, radio **13.** 3.05 m **15.** 2.94×10^{-19} J, 4.52×10^{-19} J **17.** 177 kJ/mol, 272 kJ/mol **19. a.** 3.52×10^{-19} J; **b.** 2.81×10^{-18} J **21.** 6.85×10^{-19} J per photon, 1.03×10^{15}/s **23.** 1.2×10^{-17} m, 2.5×10^{25}/s **25.** 1.95×10^{18}/s, X-ray **27.** 5.00×10^{-7} m, 5.00×10^3 Å, 5.00×10^{-5} cm, 1.97×10^{-5} in **29.** While the whole number difference between the level is only one in each case, the emitted wavelengths are proportional to the difference in the inverse squares of the numbers. When using the inverse squares, the values come out much different. **31.** for $n_i = 5$: 4341.6 Å, 6.91×10^{14}/s, 4.58×10^{-19} J; for $n_i = 6$: 4102.8 Å, 7.31×10^{14}/s, 4.84×10^{-19} J; for $n_i = 7$: 3971.1 Å, 7.55×10^{14}/s, 5.01×10^{-19} J **33. a.** 1.40×10^{15}/s; **b.** UV **c.** Zinc **35. a.** -2.1786×10^{-18} J; **b.** -2.4207×10^{-19} J; **c.** -8.7144×10^{-20} J; **d.** -4.4461×10^{-20} J **37. a.** 2.0424×10^{-18} J; **b.** 1.9365×10^{-18} J; **c.** 4.9018×10^{-20} J; **d.** 5.0019×10^{-19} J **39. a.** 121.57 nm; **b.** 1282.1 nm; **c.** 486.26 nm; **d.** 93.779 nm; **e.** 94.973 nm; **f.** 1875.6 nm **41.** shortest (with $n_i = \infty$) is 1458 nm; longest (with $n_i = 5$) is 4052.2 nm **43.** yes ($n = 6$ to $n = 2$) **45.** 2.1786×10^{-18} J **47.** Classically, matter has mass in discrete particles and can therefore have momentum; further, any possible value of energy (and momentum) or position is allowed. Both position and momentum can be measured (at the same time) to infinite precision. Waves can have specific but infinitely variable energies and amplitudes, but they do not have a specific location because they are spread out over space and time. **49.** 1.9×10^{-22} kg·m·s^{-1} **51.** 8.4×10^6 kg·m·s^{-1} **53.** 1.23×10^{-27} kg·m·s^{-1} **55.** Electrons have mass and can have discrete position. **57.** 0.6648 nm **59.** 3.8×10^{-33} m; A softball moving at the same speed, with its higher mass, would have a smaller wavelength. **61.** Here p represents the momentum of the particle, whereas x

represents its position. Because the uncertainties are multiplied, the more certain the measurement of one, the more *uncertain* the value for the other.   **63.** $\Delta x \geq 5.5 \times 10^{-10}$ m; $\Delta x \geq 2.8 \times 10^{-10}$ m; Both are larger than the first Bohr radius.   **65.** 1.0×10^{-24} kg·m·s^{-1} **67.** 0.60 kg·m·s^{-1}·mol^{-1} **69.** 1.1×10^2 kg·m·s^{-1} **71.** The electron orbital describes the energy state and relative position in space of the electron within the atom. Since the position is described based on a probability, we cannot specify exactly where the electron is, but we can in some cases say where it is not and where it is most likely (but not required) to be.   **73.** It is easier to start thinking about this problem in terms of the Bohr model. The Bohr orbits are stable because the wavelengths perfectly overlap with themselves after completing the orbit. In other words, they constructively interfere and become stable standing waves. At any other radius the electron wavelengths will not overlap correctly after completing the orbit and will destructively interfere. No stable orbit is possible. Since there are no stable orbits possible between two adjacent states, the transition from one state to another is abrupt and not gradual. The same thinking applies to the more complicated Schrödinger equation.   **75.** Only sequence (e) is valid. Sequences (a), (b), and (d) are not possible because *l* can have only *positive* integer values that *must be less than n.* Sequence (c) is also not allowed because m_l must have a magnitude less than or equal to *l*.   **77.** 5 sublevels, 25 orbitals   **79.** 7   **81.** 50   **83.** Usually, the "shape" of an orbital refers to the surface within which 90% of the total probability of finding an electron is found. Very little of the electron probability occurs exactly on the surface, and the electron probability is spread throughout much of that space. By specifying these "shapes," we can better visualize where the most probable places for finding the electron are.   **85.** A radial node exists at all angles at a given distance from the nuclear center. For example, the 2s orbital has a probability of 0 at a given distance from the nucleus. A planar node exists for a particular angle at all radial distances and usually passes through the nucleus. For example, the 2p orbitals (x, y, and z) have a node passing through the nucleus, separating the two parts of the orbital.   **87. a.** Nothing actually touches in the conventional sense. When the atomic-sized needle tip comes close enough to the sample material, the wavefunction of the atom at the very tip of the needle overlaps the wavefunction of the nearest atoms in the material. With sufficient overlap, the electrons from the tip can move to the sample. This movement of electrons produces a current that is detected by the STM. **b.** Tunneling is the movement of a particle between two allowed spaces (or orbitals) through a space where it could not be classically. Classically, this current could not flow until the two physically touched. The closer the tip to the surface or an atom, the greater is the overlap of the orbitals and the greater the current that arises as the electrons move through space from one allowed orbital to the other.   **89.** $m_s = +\frac{1}{2}$; electron spin quantum number   **91.** C, O   **93.** In the extreme example, we could place all electrons in the 1s orbital, choosing half with spin up and half with spin down. (However, we could also choose to have every electron spin up and to have all unpaired if the Pauli exclusion principle did not apply.) Other possibilities also exist.   **95.** In multielectron atoms, the shapes of the orbitals are still very similar, the quantum numbers for the orbitals and the rules for using them remain the same, and the behavior of the nodes within the orbitals remain the same. The energies of the orbitals are changed!   **97.** He is easier. Because the attraction will be higher in removing the second electron (+2 ion and −1 electron), ionizing He$^+$ is more difficult.   **99. a.** $1s^2 2s^2 2p_x^1 2p_y^1 2p_z^1$ or $1s^2 2s^2 2p^3$; **b.** $1s^2 2s^2 2p^6$ **101. a.** Si; **b.** Cl; **c.** K; **d.** Sr   **103.** $1s^2 2s^2 2p^6 3s^2 3p^6 4s^2 3d^1$. Because of the effects of shielding on the orbital energies, the 4s orbitals lie at lower energy than the 3d orbitals and fill first.   **105.** K, Fe   **107.** $1s^2 2s^2 2p^6 3s^2 3p^6 4s^1 3d^{10}$ **109. a.** 8.70×10^5; **b.** 6.71×10^8 mi/h   **111.** 121.56 nm   **113.** $\Delta r_{1,2} = 0.15875$ nm; $\Delta r_{3,4} = 0.37042$ nm; $\Delta r_{5,6} = 0.5821$ nm; The distances between

successive levels continues to increase; the shells are becoming increasingly farther apart.   **115.** In order to be stable, the electron must create a standing wave by perfectly overlapping itself after a single circumference. Perfect overlap occurs only if an integer number of waves lie on the circumference; therefore, *n* must be a positive integer.   **117.** *n, l, m_l*: **a.** 1, 0, 0; **b.** 2, 1, (±1 or 0); **c.** 3, 2, (±2, ±1 or 0)   **119. a.** 9.18×10^{-20} J; 5.53×10^4 J/mol; **b.** 1.39×10^{14}/s; **c.** IR; **d.** $n = 7$; **e.** 371.11 nm; uv; **f.** $2s^1$ or $2p^1$

Chapter 7

P7.1 a. Sn; **b.** Ta; **c.** H   **P7.2** Metals: Li, Ni, Ce, Al, Po, Rb, and Cu; Heavy metals: Ce, Po, Rb, and Cu   **P7.3 a.** Ba; **b.** Na; **c.** O; **d.** C   **P7.4** 119, 168   **P7.5** Ra (lowest ionization energy)   **P7.6** You would expect the energies to be high to start and to get higher with each electron. When atoms have either a filled orbital or a half-filled orbital, it takes more energy to ionize the electron than would otherwise be expected. When electrons are being ionized from a noble gas configuration (10 electrons and 2 electrons), there is a significant jump in the ionization energy, especially when electrons must be removed from the 1s orbital.

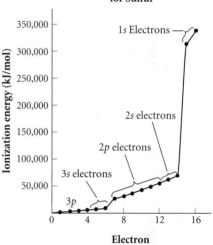

Electron Ionization Energies for Sulfur

P7.7 The trends are opposite one another. Those elements the most willing to part with an electron (lower ionization energy) will be the least willing to gain an electron (smaller electron affinity).   **P7.8** Electronegativity generally increases as an element is closer to fluorine (upper left), so P is more electronegative than Na; Cl is more electronegative than Ne (noble gases generally don't form bonds and therefore have very low electronegativities); N is more electronegative than C.

1. $_{28}$Ni and $_{27}$Co; $_{52}$Te and $_{53}$I (126.9 g/mol); $_{18}$Ar and $_{19}$K; $_{90}$Th and $_{91}$Pa; $_{92}$U and $_{93}$Np.   **3. a.** s; **b.** d; **c.** p; **d.** p; **e.** p; **f.** f; **g.** p   **5. a.** p; **b.** s; **c.** d; **d.** d; **e.** s; **f.** p; **g.** f   **7.** ~3090°C   **9. a.** Ca; **b.** P; **c.** Br; **d.** Cs   **11. a.** metal; **b.** metal; **c.** metalloid; **d.** metal; **e.** metalloid; **f.** nonmetal; **g.** nonmetal; **h.** metalloid   **13.** Br, Hg   **15. a.** 8.76g Ni, 16.7 g Cr; **b.** 8.99×10^{22} atoms Ni, 1.93×10^{23} atoms Cr   **17.** Metalloid, $Sb_2S_3 + 3Fe \rightarrow 3FeS + 2Sb$, 4.47×10^8 mol Sb   **19.** Li_2O; BeO; B_2O_3; CO_2; N_2O_5; O_2; and OF_2 **21.** Except for Po, the Group VIA elements are nonmetals forming anions and will form compounds with metals.   **23.** 1, 0   **25.** New order: H, O, C after converting masses to moles.   **27.** Many transition elements play a critical role as the "active site" within enzymes.   **29.** It has a *completely* filled shell (a duet).   **31.** Removing an electron from the filled s subshell in Ca is more difficult than removing an electron from the unfilled shell in K.   **33.** When placed in the proper groups, both Te and I have the same number of valence electrons as their groups. **35.** From left to right: Na, S, Mg. **37.** 77 pm **39.** 94 pm **41.** K; Because K is lower in the same group, it has an additional filled shell, which makes it larger. **43.** 2.01 g **45. a.** From lowest to highest: Al, Si, P. For the second ionization energy, you would expect Al to be higher than Si or P because it would have to remove an electron from a filled 3s orbital, whereas Si and P continue to remove electrons from the unfilled 3p orbitals. (Rank: Si, P, Al); **b.** From lowest to highest: Kr, Ar, Ne. No change in order for the ranking by second ionization energy. **47.** A: metal, Group IIA; B: nonmetal, Group VIA or VIIA **49.** Group VIIIA, lower, first ionization energies decrease down the group. **51. a.** +1, +1; **b.** K⁺; **c.** K **53.** Magnesium's first ionization removes an electron from a filled s orbital, which requires more energy than removing sodium's electron from an unfilled s orbital. The second ionization for sodium requires removing an electron from a completely filled shell, which takes even more energy, whereas magnesium's second electron is being removed from the now unfilled s orbital. **55. a.** Magnesium never forms a +3 ion, because removing a third electron would require breaking up a filled shell of electrons; **b.** Fluorine, seeking a filled shell, needs to gain an electron to achieve an octet configuration. A +1 fluorine ion is a move in the opposite direction; **c.** Hydrogen has only one electron to lose; it can never get to a +2 state; **d.** Aluminum, in losing three electrons, achieves an octet (filled shell) configuration; the octet configuration is more stable than other configurations. **57.** S, because Xe is a noble gas and doesn't spontaneously accept electrons. **59.** Cl **61.** Mg, Al, Na. No change. **63.** Fluorine is the smallest ion-forming element in the second period, which means that its electrons are the most tightly packed. Accepting an additional electron is not as favorable as would otherwise be expected because of the greater electron–electron repulsions in the small volume. **65. a.** +146 kJ/mol, endothermic; **b.** −502 kJ/mol, very exothermic and reactive **67.** Na, Li, As, S, F **69. a.** O; **b.** S; **c.** Br; **d.** O **71.** Change is 0.8 from Ga to Se; change is 0.3 from Zn to Sc. If the electronegativity difference were based on the number of protons, you might have expected a difference three times as large (nine protons rather than three protons). Electronegativity cannot be solely dependent on the atomic number. **73.** Mg, Na, Rb **75.** Metal: Lower ionization energy, more reactive; Nonmetal: generally opposite of metals **77. a.** all in Group IB; **b.** bottom; **c.** Yes; given that the most reactive elements are found toward the lower left and upper right of the periodic table (excluding the noble gases) and working to the center from the outside in toward Group IB, the metals in the activity series are found in the order that the periodic table would predict. **79.** O, with its higher electronegativity, will pull shared electrons more toward itself and therefore is the more negative of the two elements. **81.** A possible explanation for the lack of iron in the mantle relative to the crust is that during the early formation of the Earth, the very dense elements, such as iron, were drawn to the core and are therefore missing from the mantle. **83. a.** Ar; **b.** 5.62 × 10²¹ atoms **85.** Cu, Au **87. a.** Johan Dobereiner first identified groups of three elements that shared similar properties. These first "triads" form the basis for the current alkali metals group (Group IA), alkaline earth metals group (Group IIA), and halogens group (Group VIIA); **b.** John Newlands first placed elements in order of increasing mass and found that elements eight places apart share similar properties. He arranged the elements in octaves (periods of eight), a scheme that very much mirrors the s- and p-blocks of current periodic tables; **c.** Dmitri Mendeleev added more elements to his table, generally in mass order, that created vertical groups of elements with similar properties. Mendeleev left holes in his table and predicted elements would be discovered to fill those holes. Mendeleev's use of the table as a predictive tool laid the basis for the modern periodic table. **89. a.** carbon-steel; **b.** Carbon-steel contains iron and carbon only; other steels contain other elements. **91.** 115 pm.

93. With the exception of He (Group VIIIA, two valence electrons), there is very good correspondence between number of valence electrons and group number. The number of valence electrons is a periodic property;

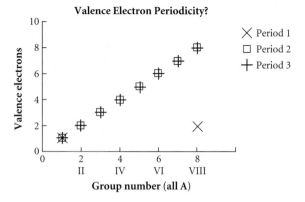

b. The oxidation number for the first 18 elements also appears to be periodic. Even though there is a large break in the trend, the values repeat with successive periods, making the property periodic and predictable.

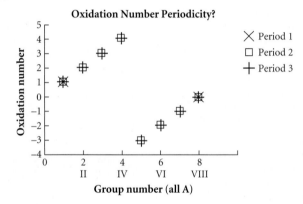

95. There are two competing trends in how the atomic number affects the size of the atom: (1) In a group, size increases with increasing atomic number. (2) In a period, size decreases with increasing atomic number. It is important to account for the relative positions (period and group) of the two atoms to be compared. **97.** The attraction of the increasingly more positive ion is larger, and the energy needed to remove electrons from the lower shells also increases. **99.** A configuration that half-fills the set of orbitals has additional stability. Arsenic has a valence configuration that is $4s^2 4p^3$, half-filling the p orbital set, whereas selenium has $4s^2 4p^4$ and doesn't have the additional stability. **101. a.** exothermic; **b.** Cl + e → Cl⁻ + 350 kJ/mol **103. a.** $NaHCO_3 + HCl \rightarrow H_2CO_3 + NaCl$; **b.** H: Period 1, Group 1A; Na, Period 3, Group 1A; C, Period 2, Group IVA; O: Period 2, Group VIA; Cl: Period 3, Group VIIA; **c.** Na; **d.** $H_2CO_3 \rightarrow H_2O + CO_2$; **e.** 25.3 ppm; **f.** 9.95 ppm; **g.** This reaction generates CO_2, which leavens the bread or pastry.

Chapter 8

P8.1 S^{2-}: $1s^2 2s^2 2p^6 3s^2 3p^6$, $\left[:\ddot{S}:\right]^{2-}$, Ar; F^-: $1s^2 2s^2 2p^6$, $\left[:\ddot{F}:\right]^-$, Ne; Mg^{2+}: $1s^2 2s^2 2p^6$, $[Mg]^{2+}$, Ne; Br^-: $1s^2 2s^2 2p^6 3s^2 3p^6 4s^2 3d^{10} 4p^6$, $\left[:\ddot{Br}:\right]^-$, Kr

P8.2 $\left[Na\cdot\right]\ \left[:\ddot{O}:\right]\ \left[\cdot Na\right] \longrightarrow \left[Na\right]^+\ \left[:\ddot{O}:\right]^{2-}\ \left[Na\right]^+$

P8.3 $Mg^{2+} < Na^+ < Ne < F^- < O^{2-}$.   **P8.4** $FeCl_3$ **P8.5** polar covalent; nonpolar covalent; ionic   **P8.6** OCl: O (F.C. $= -1$), Cl (F.C. $= 0$); CH_3NH_2: all F.C. $= 0$

P8.7 $\left[\begin{array}{c} H \quad H \\ C=C \\ H \quad H \end{array}\right], \left[\begin{array}{c} H \\ C=N-H \\ H \end{array}\right]$ **P8.8** $\Delta H = -22$ kJ/mol

P8.9 HNO_3: trigonal planar, 120°; CCl_4, tetrahedral, 109.5°; NH_3, trigonal pyramidal, 107°   **P8.10** SO_2 **P8.11** N_2: nonpolar bond, no dipole; NH_3, polar bonds, net dipole:

$$\left[\begin{array}{c} \uparrow \\ N \\ H \diagup \; | \; \diagdown H \\ H \end{array}\right]$$

1. a. N; **b.** N; **c.** N   **3.** C^{2+}, N^{3-}, and H^+ **5. a.** Group VIA; **b.** Group IIA; **c.** Group VA   **7. a.** two extra, -2; **b.** three extra, -3; **c.** one extra, -1 **9. a.** $\left[:\overset{\cdot\cdot}{Se}:\right]^{2-}$; **b.** $\left[:\overset{\cdot\cdot}{I}:\right]^-$; **c.** $[Sr]^{2+}$; **d.** $[Sc]^{3+}$; **e.** $[Si:]^{2+}$ **11.** Na^+, F^-, Al^{3+} **13.** Ca^{2+}, Ar, and Cl^- **15.** Group IVA or Group IVB   **17. a.** [Li·], [Na·], [K·]; **b.** Li_2O, Na_2O, and K_2O **19. a.** true; **b.** false; **c.** true; **d.** true   **21.** To reduce its valence to an octet configuration, aluminum goes from the atom to the ion by losing three electrons: $[:\overset{\cdot}{Al}] \rightarrow [Al]^{3+} + 3$ electrons. Oxygen forms oxide (and creates an octet) by gaining two electrons: $\left[:\overset{\cdot\cdot}{O}:\right] + 2$ electrons $\rightarrow \left[:\overset{\cdot\cdot}{O}:\right]^{2-}$. Chlorine forms chloride (and creates an octet) by gaining one electron: $\left[:\overset{\cdot\cdot}{Cl}:\right] + 1$ electrons $\rightarrow \left[:\overset{\cdot\cdot}{Cl}:\right]^-$. When forming a compound with chlorine, aluminum loses three electrons, which allows for the formation of three chlorides. All electrons have been accounted for, and the charges on the ions balance one another—$AlCl_3$ is the stable compound that forms, creating the 1:3 ratio. When forming a compound with oxygen, two aluminum atoms lose three electrons each (six in all), which allows for the formation of three oxides. All electrons have been accounted for, and the charges on the ions balance one another—Al_2O_3 is the stable compound that forms, creating the 2:3 ratio.   **23. a.** $I^{5+} < I < I^-$; **b.** $S^{6+} < S^{4+} < S^{2-}$; **c.** $C^+ < C < C^-$; **d.** $Fe^{3+} < Fe^{2+} < Fe$ **25.** LiCl > NaCl > KCl > RbCl > CsCl

27. $[K\cdot] \; [:\overset{\cdot\cdot}{Cl}:] \longrightarrow [K]^+ \; [:\overset{\cdot\cdot}{Cl}:]^-$

29. Na_2O: $[Na]^+ \left[:\overset{\cdot\cdot}{O}:\right]^{2-} [Na]^+$, NaOH: $[Na]^+ \left[:\overset{\cdot\cdot}{O}:H\right]^-$

31. Mn^{5+} **33.** KBr, the distance between K^+ and Br^-, is smaller than Cs^+ and Br^-, so the attraction and energy are greater.   **35.** Electron affinity gauges how much a particular atom (or molecule) "wants" to wholly gain an electron, with larger electron affinities indicating greater likelihood of gaining an electron. Electronegativity values gauge how much a particular atom will attract electrons from a shared covalent bond to itself. However, both electron affinity and electronegativity tend to increase toward the upper right of the periodic table (excluding the noble gases) and can predict the favorability of forming ionic compounds. Electronegativity is more useful, because its predictive capability extends to polar covalent bonding and dipoles.   **37.** Within your table you should have a vertical arrow pointing up, indicating an increase in electronegativity as you go up a group, and a horizontal arrow pointing to the right, indicating an increase in electronegativity as you go to the right in a period.   **39.** H_2O: $\left[H-\overset{\cdot\cdot}{O}-H\right]$, NO (radical): $\left[:N=\overset{\cdot\cdot}{O}:\right]$, CO: [:C≡O:],

NO$_2$ (radical): $\left[:\overset{\cdot\cdot}{O}-N=\overset{\cdot\cdot}{O}:\right]$, HCl: $\left[H-\overset{\cdot\cdot}{Cl}:\right]$,

PCl_2(radical): $\left[:\overset{\cdot\cdot}{Cl}-\overset{\cdot}{P}-\overset{\cdot\cdot}{Cl}:\right]$, NBr_3: $\left[\begin{array}{c} :\overset{\cdot\cdot}{Br}: \\ | \\ :\overset{\cdot\cdot}{Br}-N: \\ | \\ :\overset{\cdot\cdot}{Br}: \end{array}\right]$

41. OH^-: $\left[:\overset{\cdot\cdot}{O}-H\right]^-$, NO_2^-: $\left[:\overset{\cdot\cdot}{O}-N=\overset{\cdot\cdot}{O}:\right]^-$, Br^-: $\left[:\overset{\cdot\cdot}{Br}:\right]^-$,

PO_4^{3-}: $\left[\begin{array}{c} :\overset{\cdot\cdot}{O}: \\ | \\ \overset{\cdot\cdot}{O}=P-\overset{\cdot\cdot}{O}: \\ | \\ :\overset{\cdot\cdot}{O}: \end{array}\right]^{3-}$, SO_3^{2-}: $\left[\begin{array}{c} :\overset{\cdot\cdot}{O}: \\ | \\ \overset{\cdot\cdot}{O}=S: \\ | \\ :\overset{\cdot\cdot}{O}: \end{array}\right]^{2-}$,

CO_3^{2-}: $\left[\begin{array}{c} :\overset{\cdot\cdot}{O}: \\ | \\ :\overset{\cdot\cdot}{O}=C \\ | \\ :\overset{\cdot\cdot}{O}: \end{array}\right]^{2-}$, BrO_4^-: $\left[\begin{array}{c} :\overset{\cdot\cdot}{O}: \\ | \\ \overset{\cdot\cdot}{O}=Br=\overset{\cdot\cdot}{O} \\ | \\ :\overset{\cdot\cdot}{O}: \end{array}\right]^-$

43. C_2H_6: $\left[\begin{array}{c} H \quad H \\ | \quad\;\; | \\ H-C-C-H \\ | \quad\;\; | \\ H \quad H \end{array}\right]$, C_3H_6: $\left[\begin{array}{c} H \quad\;\; H \\ | \quad\quad | \\ H-C-C=C-H \\ | \quad\quad\quad | \\ H \quad\quad\;\; H \end{array}\right]$,

C_2H_4: $\left[\begin{array}{c} H \quad H \\ | \quad\;\; | \\ C=C \\ | \quad\;\; | \\ H \quad H \end{array}\right]$, C_3H_8: $\left[\begin{array}{c} H \quad H \quad H \\ | \quad\;\; | \quad\;\; | \\ H-C-C-C-H \\ | \quad\;\; | \quad\;\; | \\ H \quad H \quad H \end{array}\right]$,

C_4H_{10}: $\left[\begin{array}{c} H \quad H \quad H \quad H \\ | \quad\;\; | \quad\;\; | \quad\;\; | \\ H-C-C-C-C-H \\ | \quad\;\; | \quad\;\; | \quad\;\; | \\ H \quad H \quad H \quad H \end{array}\right]$

45. $\left[\begin{array}{c} :O: \\ \|\; \\ \overset{\ominus}{:O}-N^{\oplus} \\ \overset{\ominus}{:O}: \end{array}\right]^- \leftrightarrow \left[\begin{array}{c} \overset{\ominus}{:O}: \\ \| \\ :O=N^{\oplus} \\ \ominus:O: \end{array}\right]^- \leftrightharpoons \left[\begin{array}{c} \overset{\ominus}{:O}: \\ | \\ :O-N^{\oplus} \\ \| \\ :O: \end{array}\right]^-$

hybrid structure: $\left[\begin{array}{c} :O: \\ \| \\ \overset{\cdot\cdot}{O}=N \\ \| \\ :O: \end{array}\right]^-$

47. C_4H_4: $\left[\begin{array}{c} H \quad H \\ | \quad\;\; | \\ C=C \\ | \quad\;\; | \\ C=C \\ | \quad\;\; | \\ H \quad H \end{array}\right] \leftrightarrow \left[\begin{array}{c} H \quad H \\ | \quad\;\; | \\ C-C \\ \| \quad\;\; \| \\ C-C \\ | \quad\;\; | \\ H \quad H \end{array}\right]$ C_4H_6: $\left[\begin{array}{c} H \quad H \\ | \quad\;\; | \\ C-C-H \\ \| \quad\;\; | \\ C-C-H \\ | \quad\;\; | \\ H \quad H \end{array}\right]$

C_4H_8: $\left[\begin{array}{c} H \quad H \\ | \quad\;\; | \\ H-C-C-H \\ | \quad\;\; | \\ H-C-C-H \\ | \quad\;\; | \\ H \quad H \end{array}\right]$

49. N_2O: $\left[:N≡N-\overset{\cdot\cdot}{O}:\right] \leftrightarrow \left[:\overset{\cdot\cdot}{N}=N=\overset{\cdot\cdot}{O}:\right]$,

N_2: $\left[:N≡N:\right]$, N_2H_4: $\left[\begin{array}{c} H-\overset{\cdot\cdot}{N}-\overset{\cdot\cdot}{N}-H \\ | \quad\;\; | \\ H \quad H \end{array}\right]$; $N_2 = 946$ kJ/mol;

$N_2O = 418$ kJ/mol; $N_2H_6 = 160$ kJ/mol

51. Na_3PO_4:

$$[Na]^+ \quad \begin{bmatrix} :\ddot{O}: \\ \| \\ \ddot{O}=P-\ddot{O}: \\ | \\ :\underset{\cdot\cdot}{O}: \end{bmatrix}^{3-} \quad [Na]^+$$

$[Na]^+$

Covalent bonding

Ionic bonding

$CaCO_3$:

Covalent bonding

$$[Ca]^{2+} \quad \begin{bmatrix} :\ddot{O}: \\ \| \\ :\ddot{O}=C \\ | \\ :\underset{\cdot\cdot}{O}: \end{bmatrix}^{2-}$$

Ionic bonding

$Fe(NO_3)_2$:

$$\begin{bmatrix} :\ddot{O}: \\ \| \\ :\ddot{O}=N \\ | \\ :\underset{\cdot\cdot}{O}: \end{bmatrix}^- \quad [Fe]^{2+} \quad \begin{bmatrix} :\ddot{O}: \\ \| \\ :\ddot{O}=N \\ | \\ :\underset{\cdot\cdot}{O}: \end{bmatrix}^-$$

Ionic bonding

Covalent bonding

The ionic bonding occurs between the separate ions, whereas the covalent bonding is happening between the atoms of the polyatomic anions. **53.** C—C < H—C < N—O < Ca—H < Ca—N

55. a. 0; **b.** no change; **c.** 0; **d.** −1   **57.**

$$\begin{bmatrix} H \\ | \\ H-N-H \\ | \\ H \end{bmatrix}^+ \quad [:\overset{\cdot\cdot}{\underset{\cdot\cdot}{Cl}}:]^-$$

59. The structure of NO_2 is $\left[\overset{\ominus}{*\overset{**}{\underset{**}{O}}*} : \overset{\oplus}{N} :: \overset{\circ}{\overset{**}{\underset{**}{O}}} \right]$. In this diagram, the (*)

are lone-pair electrons, (:) are bonding electrons, and (°) is a radical electron. The nonzero formal charges are labeled within the

circles.   **61.** $\left[:C \equiv \overset{\circ}{\underset{\ominus}{N}}:\right]^-$ Because the formal charge of −1 is on the carbon, H^+ with its positive charge should attach to carbon and its negative charge.

63.

$$\begin{bmatrix} :\ddot{O}-H \\ | \\ \ddot{O}=\overset{\circ}{\underset{|}{S}:} \\ | \\ :\ddot{O}-H \end{bmatrix}$$ The formal charge on sulfur is 0

(F.C. = 6 − 4 − 2 = 0), and the oxidation number on sulfur is +4. In the calculation of the oxidation number, oxygen is taken at −2 and hydrogen at +1, giving the sulfur a +4 oxidation number, but in the calculation of formal charges, both oxygen and hydrogen have a value of zero.

65.

$$\begin{bmatrix} :\ddot{O}: \\ | \\ :\ddot{O}=\overset{\oplus}{N} \\ | \\ :\underset{\cdot\cdot}{O}: \end{bmatrix}^- , \begin{bmatrix} :\ddot{O}-\overset{\circ}{\overset{\oplus}{N}}=\ddot{O}: \end{bmatrix}^-$$

67.

$$\begin{bmatrix} H & :\ddot{O}: \\ | & | \\ H-\ddot{N}-C-C=\ddot{O} \\ | & | \\ H & H \end{bmatrix} \leftrightarrow \begin{bmatrix} H & \ddot{O}: \\ | & \| \\ H-\ddot{N}-C-C-\ddot{O}: \\ | & | \\ H & H \end{bmatrix}$$

69. C_2H_6: $\begin{bmatrix} H & H \\ | & | \\ H-C-C-H \\ | & | \\ H & H \end{bmatrix}$, C_2H_4: $\begin{bmatrix} H & H \\ | & | \\ C=C \\ | & | \\ H & H \end{bmatrix}$,

C_2H_2: $[H-C\equiv C-H]$ The number of bonds between carbon increases from one to two to three, as shown above. The greater number of bonds between two atoms, the stronger the bond and the shorter the bond length. C_2H_2 will have the strongest (and shortest) bond, and C_2H_6 will have the longest (and weakest) bond.   **71.** $\Delta H =$ −2674 kJ/mol. This value is different from the direct determination because the values for the bond energies are taken from the average of the bond in several molecules and may not be exactly the same as the bond energies in the molecules of this reaction.

73. $\Delta H(H_2O) = $ −254 kJ/mol, $\Delta H(H_2O_2) = $ −153 kJ/mol. Because water releases more energy than hydrogen peroxide in its formation, it will be the more stable of the two molecules.   **75.** H_2O: bent; NO_2: bent; PCl_2: bent; NBR_3: trigonal pyramidal   **77.** NO_2^-, bent; PO_4^{3-}: tetrahedral; SO_3^{2-}: trigonal pyramidal; CO_3^{2-}: trigonal planar; BrO_4^-: tetrahedral   **79.** C_2H_6: tetrahedral at each; C_3H_6: tetrahedral on left, trigonal planar at the other two; C_2H_4: trigonal planar at each, C_3H_8: tetrahedral at each; C_4H_{10}: tetrahedral at each

81. The Lewis structure of ClO_2 is $\left[:\overset{\cdot\cdot}{\underset{\cdot\cdot}{O}}-\overset{\cdot}{\underset{\cdot\cdot}{Cl}}=\ddot{O}:\right]$ (note the radical electron). At Cl, it has four electron groups (tetrahedral) but two lone pairs/radicals, making the molecular geometry bent.
83. $BeCl_2$ > $AlCl_3$ > CCl_4 > NCl_3 > $XeCl_4$

85. $\begin{bmatrix} :\ddot{Cl}-\overset{\cdot\cdot}{Se}-\ddot{Cl}: \\ / \quad \backslash \\ :\ddot{Cl}: \quad :\ddot{Cl}: \end{bmatrix}$, see-saw

87. In N_2H_2, each nitrogen has three electron groups (trigonal planar) but one lone pair, so the molecular geometry is bent. The H—N—N bond angle will be slightly less than the normal 120° because of the additional lone-pair repulsion. In $N_2H_2^{2+}$, each nitrogen has only two electron groups and no lone pairs, making the geometry linear. The bond angle is then expanded from 120° in N_2H_2 to 180° in $N_2H_2^{2+}$.
89. C←H < C→N = C←B = C→Cl < C→O < C←Mg (arrow denote dipoles)

91. The structures are SF_6 $\begin{bmatrix} :\ddot{F}: & :\ddot{F}: \\ | & \diagup \\ :\ddot{F}-S-\ddot{F}: \\ \diagup & | \\ :\ddot{F}: & :\ddot{F}: \end{bmatrix}$ and

SF_5 $\begin{bmatrix} :\ddot{F}: & :\ddot{F}: \\ \diagdown & | \\ S-\ddot{F}: \\ \diagup & | \\ :\ddot{F}: & :\ddot{F}: \end{bmatrix}$. SF_6 is octahedral (six electron groups

around S) and nonpolar because all the S—F dipoles cancel. SF_5 has six electron groups but one lone pair, making the geometry square pyramidal. Removing one S—F dipole that helped make SF_6 nonpolar makes SF_5 polar, because not all the S—F dipoles cancel out.
93. A: ionic, B: nonpolar, C: polar   **95.** The structure of H_2O_2 is

$\left[H-\ddot{O}-\ddot{O}-H\right]$ and is bent (see Problem 76). The O—H

bonds are polar with an electronegativity difference of 1.4. Because the molecule is bent, even though the dipoles point in nearly opposite directions, the dipoles do not cancel and the molecule is polar. If the molecule were linear, the dipoles would cancel out, because they would be aligned and in opposite directions. The linear molecule would be nonpolar.   **97.** From left to right: H^+, H^-, and H
99. Because N_2 has a triple bond, its bond energy is very large

(941 kJ/mol). Breaking this bond in order to cause a reaction is very difficult and therefore unlikely. N_2 will emerge just as it entered. **101.** There is only a single choice for the anion (-2), so our choice will be based on which cation will have a weaker interaction. The weakest lattice attractions will come from ion pairs that are widely separated and have smaller charges. This set of ions (the small $+1$ and the larger $+3$) have these trends in opposition. The ion with the $+3$ charge has roughly twice the diameter, which is not a large enough increase in size to offset the larger charge. The $+3$ ion will have a larger ionic attraction. Therefore, the weakest interaction will be between the -2 anion and $+1$ cation. **103.** $+3$ cation with -2 anion **105. a.** The attraction that two charges particles have for one another is larger as the charges on each become larger, and the attraction is larger as the particles get closer to one another. Large attractive forces lead to high melting points. Neutral molecular species at most have partial charges from the dipoles, limiting the strength of attraction to other molecules. The lower attraction leads to lower melting points; **b.** For a high melting point, we should choose species that are small and have high charges. For a low melting point, we should choose low charges and large radii. By far the highest charge and lowest size belong to B^{3+}. For the anion we could choose N^{3-} or O^{2-}. Nitride has the higher charge but is bigger (171 pm versus 140 pm), but it is less than 1.25 times larger whereas its charge is 1.5 times larger than that of oxide. Highest melting point: BN. The largest ions are I^- and Cs^+; CsI should have the lowest melting point. **107. a.** Very few molecules can be found in only a diatomic form allowing for direct measurement of the bond energy. Inside larger molecules, the strength of the bond can vary depending on the other atoms and on how well the electrons are distributed within the molecule. In these cases, several measurements are made, and the average value of the bond energy is placed in the table; **b.** The presence of the three fluorine atoms with their high electronegativity will tend to shift the electrons from the other bonds toward the fluorine atoms. This has the potential to weaken the carbon–carbon bond.

109. a.

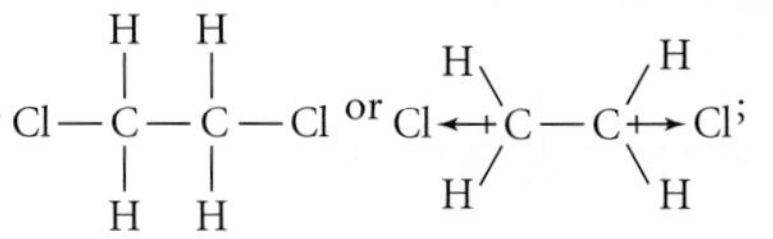

b.

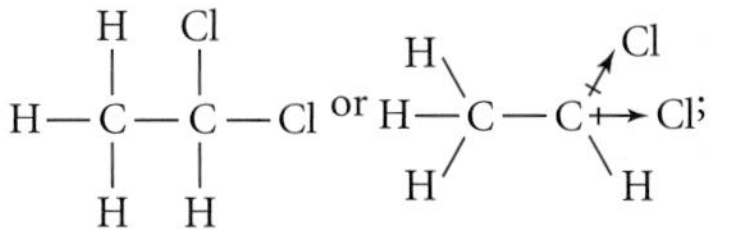

c. Molecule in part a; **d.** 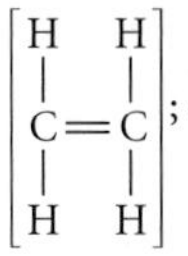 ; **e.** Yes, all bonds are nonpolar.;

f. 0.57 g

Chapter 9

P9.1 The configuration of the valence electrons in fluorine is $2s^2 2p^5$. Overlap of one of the $2p$ orbitals from each fluorine allows the electrons to be shared between the two atoms. The valence bond model of F—F shows a $2p$–$2p$ orbital overlap that constitutes the covalent bond.

P9.2 The bond formed in F_2 is from the overlap of two $2p$ orbitals, in HCl from $1s$ and $3p$ orbitals, and in Cl_2 from two $3p$ orbitals. Because both $2p$ orbitals are smaller than the $3p$ orbitals, the bond in F_2 is shorter than Cl_2 and because the $1s$ orbital is much smaller than the $3p$ orbital, the HCl bond is shorter than the Cl_2 bond. Cl_2 has the longest bond.
P9.3 a. Lewis dot structure model for OF_2, $\left[\ddot{\underset{..}{F}} - \ddot{\underset{..}{O}} - \ddot{\underset{..}{F}} \right]$,

indicates that the central oxygen has two bonds and two lone pairs. Mixing the four orbitals (one $2s$ and three $2p$) on the oxygen atom allows us to have two lone pairs of equal energy and two bonds to the adjacent fluorine atoms. The oxygen atom possesses sp^3 hybridized orbitals. **b.** Lewis dot structure model for H_2S, $\left[H - \ddot{\underset{..}{S}} - H \right]$, indicates that the central sulfur has two bonds and two lone pairs. Mixing the four orbitals (one $3s$ and three $3p$) on the sulfur atom allows us to have two lone pairs of equal energy and two bonds to the adjacent hydrogen atoms. The sulfur atom possesses sp^3 hybridized orbitals. **c.** Lewis dot structure model for

NH_4^+, 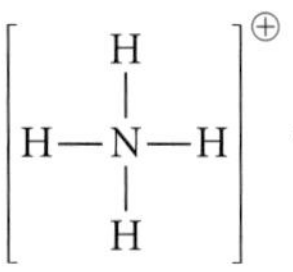 , indicates that the central nitrogen has four

bonds. Mixing the four orbitals (one $2s$ and three $2p$) on the nitrogen atom allows us to have four bonds to the adjacent hydrogen atoms. The nitrogen atom possesses sp^3 hybridized orbitals.
P9.4 a. OF_2 geometry: sp^3 hybridized atoms adopt a tetrahedral geometry. Because two of the sp^3 orbitals contain lone pairs, the VSEPR model indicates that the molecule has an overall bent geometry. The bond angles should be less than $109.5°$ because the lone pairs repel each other more than the bonding pairs. **b.** H_2S geometry: sp^3 hybridized atoms adopt a tetrahedral geometry. Because two of the sp^3 orbitals contain lone pairs, the VSEPR model indicates that the molecule has an overall bent geometry. The bond angles should be less than $109.5°$ because the lone pairs repel each other more than the bonding pairs. **c.** NH_4^+ geometry: sp^3 hybridized atoms adopt a tetrahedral geometry. The bond angles should be $109.5°$.
P9.5 A quick look at the Lewis dot structure for

CH_2O, 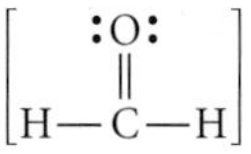 , shows that C will need three sigma bonds

(one to O and two to H) and will use sp^2 hybridization to create the bonds. Oxygen also will be sp^2 hybridized to create the sigma bond to carbon and for the two lone pairs. Both carbon and oxygen have a half-filled p orbital that can be used to create a pi bond to complete the double bond (one sigma bond, one pi bond) between C and O. Formaldehyde has a total of one pi bond and three sigma bonds.
P9.6 To answer the question, a quick look at the Lewis dot structures will help:

CH_2NOH:

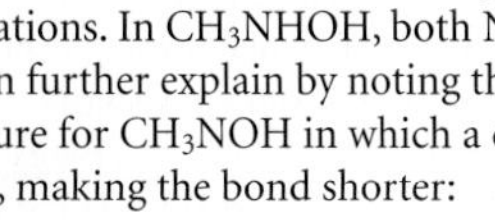

CH_3NHOH:

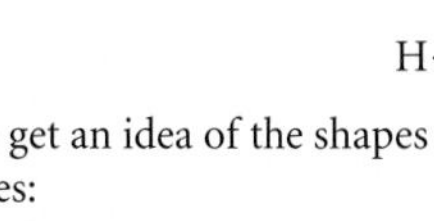

The shorter bond will be found in CH_2NOH as the NO bond is formed from the combination of sp^2 (on N) and sp^3 (on O) hybridizations. In CH_3NHOH, both N and O have sp^3 hydridization. We can further explain by noting that we can write a resonance structure for CH_3NOH in which a double bond exists between N and O, making the bond shorter:

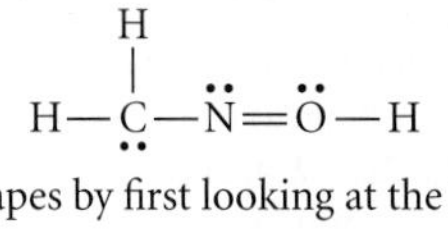

P9.7 We can get an idea of the shapes by first looking at the Lewis dot structures:

a.

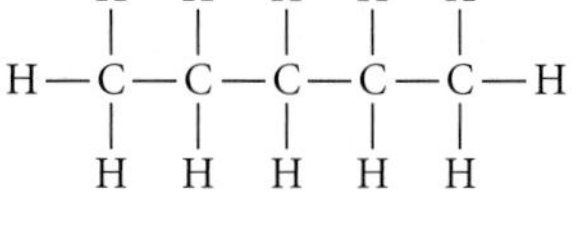

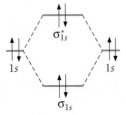

b.

c.

Pentane (structure a) has a straight chain structure and will be able to pack more closely together. It should have the most intermolecular attraction and the highest boiling temperature. The other two molecules are progressively more branched and can pack less tightly. They will boil at lower temperatures.

P9.8 The molecular orbital diagram for He_2 is shown here, including only the valence electrons ($1s^2$) from each He atom. Note that all the molecular orbitals are filled; equal numbers of bonding and antibonding orbitals are filled. The bond order will be zero, and He_2 is not stable.

σ^*_{1s}

$1s$ $1s$

σ_{1s}

P9.9 The molecular configuration for H_2 shows two valence electrons in the bonding σ_{1s} and none in the antibonding σ^*_{1s}. The bond order for H_2 is only 1. Through promotion of a single bonding electron to an antibonding orbital, the bond order would be zero and the molecular bond would be cleaved. The molecular configuration for O_2 (using only the valence $2s$ and $2p$ electrons, like the F_2 diagram) shows eight bonding electrons and four antibonding electrons, giving a bond order of 2. There are several possibilities for single photon absorptions. A transition from the π^* to σ^* MO causes no change in the bond order. A transition from the π to π^* MO decreases the bond order to 1, because this transition moves a bonding electron into an antibonding orbital. In either case, the bond order in oxygen remains higher.

1. a. The dashed line doesn't tell anything about the bond length, strength, or energy; it merely indicates that the connected atoms are bound in some manner. (It also doesn't tell anything about specific bond angles.); **b.** Using better models for bonding allows chemists to understand more fully the interaction between chemicals and how molecular shapes, bond strength, and polarity play a role in those interactions.   **3.** $1s^22s^22p^63s^23p^2$; two bonds, not consistent **5.** Cl: $1s^22s^22p^63s^23p^5$, one; Se: $1s^22s^22p^63s^23p^64s^23d^{10}4p^4$, two; B: $1s^22s^22p^1$, one   **7.** $1s^22s^22p^2$; Carbon has only two unpaired electrons ($2p_x^{1}2p_y^{1}$) to use in the formation of two covalent bonds. With only two electrons to form bonds, carbon cannot form the four bonds in CCl_4.   **9. a.** H: $1s^1$; Br: $1s^22s^22p^63s^23p^64s^23d^{10}4p^5$; **b.** H: $1s$; Br: $4p$; **c.** This bond should be weaker than the H—F bond because the overlap of the much larger Br orbital with the small H orbital

creates a weaker interaction and a weaker bond.   **11.** Because each chlorine atom has a configuration of $1s^22s^22p^63s^23p^5$, one $3p$ orbital from each Cl is involved in creating the covalent bond. These orbitals are exactly the same size and energy, so the amount of overlap in the bond is substantial.   **13.** Cl_2; Br_2; HBr   **15.** The $1s$ orbital on H ($1s^1$), the $3p$ orbital on Cl ($1s^22s^22p^63s^23p^5$), and the $2p$ orbitals on O ($1s^22s^22p^4$) are likely candidates for bonding in HOCl. (Using the hybridization model, we realize that the sp^3 orbitals on oxygen are used in the molecule.) Because the same bonds are used by O in the bonds with H and Cl, the size of the orbitals on H (smaller) and Cl (larger) predict a larger O—Cl bond.   **17.** KH; KH should have the shorter and stronger bond because the $4s$ orbital on K is smaller than the $6s$ orbital on Cs.   **19.** The milk represents the s orbital and is involved in all hybridization schemes. The eggs represent the p orbitals and can be mixed with the milk such that one part milk combines with one, two, or three eggs. The character of the omelet representing the hybrid orbitals is a little different in each case, but all are similar in that each is still an omelet. Also, the size of the omelet increases (as does the size of the hybrid orbital) as the number of eggs (p orbitals) increases.   **21. a.** six; **b.** We will still finish with generally the same shape for the hybrid orbital as for sp^3; however, the presence of more orbitals causes the angles between them to decrease to 90°, with an overall octahedral shape. Additionally, because the d orbitals are larger than the s or p orbitals, the sp^3d^2 hybrid orbitals will tend to be longer than any of the sp hybrid types.   **23. a.** $\left[:\overset{\displaystyle .}{\underset{\displaystyle .}{Si}}\cdot\right]$, sp^3; **b.** tetrahedral   **25.** $H_2O = \sim104.5°$; $NH_3 = \sim107°$; $CH_4 = 109.5°$ **27.** The $3p$ orbitals used in the bonding by Cl are longer and larger than the $1s$ orbitals in H. The lengthening of the three C—Cl bonds relative to the C—H bonds changes the tetrahedral shape. Additionally, the Cl—C—Cl bond angles may increase slightly to accommodate the larger Cl atoms relative to H.   **29.** two   **31.** two, three, four **33. a.** sp^3; **b.** sp^3; **c.** sp^2; **d.** sp **35. a.** linear; **b.** trigonal planar; **c.** tetrahedron; **d.** trigonal bypyramid; **e.** octahedron

37.

sp hybrids
form σ bonds

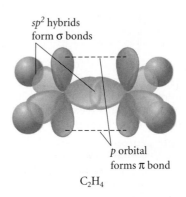

Two p orbitals
form π bonds

C_2H_2

sp^2 hybrids
form σ bonds

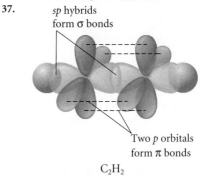

p orbital
forms π bond

C_2H_4

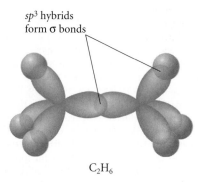

sp³ hybrids
form σ bonds

C_2H_6

The least amount of energy is required to break the bond in C_2H_6 because it has only a single bond between the carbon atoms.
39. a. sp^2, trigonal planar; **b.** sp^3, trigonal pyramidal; **c.** sp^3d^2, octahedral; **d.** sp^3, ring/crown   **41. a.** sp^3, tetrahedral; **b.** sp^3d^2, square planar; **c.** sp^3d, see-saw; **d.** sp^2, bent   **43.** For atoms bound to more than one other atom: O, sp^3; left C, sp^2; right C, sp^3; N, sp^3 **45.** Both Li_2 and K_2 will have the same bonding (because both have the same valence configuration of one *s* electron); however, the orbitals on K are larger. The overlap of the atomic orbitals from K in forming the covalent bond will be less than that on Li. K_2 would have the weaker bond.   **47.** sp^3, <109.5°   **49.** six, sp^2, 120°   **51.** left N: one lone pair, 120°, sp^2; right N: one lone pair, 109.5°, sp^3 **53.** sp^3, 109.5°
55. a.

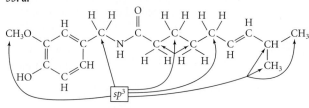

b. two; **c.** five; **d.** two
57.

Model	Scientist	General Summary
VSEPR	G. Lewis	Distribute bonding and nonbonding electron pairs.
VB	L. Pauling	Overlap and hybridization create new orbitals.
MO	E. Schrödinger	Subtract and add overlap to create π and σ bonds.

59. Because the *p* orbitals on sulfur are larger, the bond distance in S_2 is larger. Because the atoms are further apart than oxygen, the *p* orbitals are not able to create a good overlap to create the pi bond.

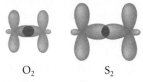

O_2 S_2

61. The greatest difference between bonding and antibonding orbitals is that bonding orbitals do not have a node perpendicular to the bond axis, whereas antibonding orbitals do. The bonding orbitals also have lower energies than antibonding orbitals made from the same atomic orbitals.   **63. a.** LCAO stands for linear combination of atomic orbitals. It is the method by which the molecular orbital theory creates its orbitals. The electron densities of the atomic orbitals

can be added or subtracted to create the new molecular orbitals;
b. HOMO stands for highest-energy occupied molecular orbital. It is the orbital that has the highest energy among those orbitals that contain electrons; **c.** LUMO stands for lowest-energy unoccupied molecular orbital. It is the orbital that has the lowest energy among those orbitals that do not contain electrons.   **65. a.** The bond orders for the molecules shown below are as follows: N_2^-, 2.5; N_2, 3; and N_2^+, 2.5; **b.** N_2^- and N_2^+; **c.** $N_2 < N_2^- \approx N_2^+$

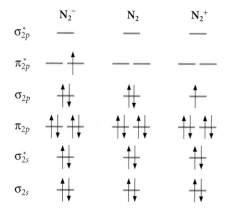

67. a. Ne; **b.** paramagnetic; **c.** 1.5   **69.** seven sigma bonds, two pi bonds   **71. a.** 1; **b.** 1.5; **c.** 1   **73. a.** 3; **b.** none   **75. a.** Orbital overlap occurs when the orbitals on two adjacent atoms share some space in common. When this occurs, the orbitals are free to combine and make bonds (or antibonds);
b.

s–s overlap   *s–p* overlap   *p–p* overlap

77. a. The Lewis dot structures (or skeleton structures) cannot show the single average structure that truly exists for molecules that have resonance structures. Some molecules will have bonds of order 1.5 or 1.33 that are difficult to draw without the resonance structures; **b.** This resonance structure has alternating positions for the double bonds inside the ring.

79. *sp*   **80.** 1-2-3 and 2-3-4 are both 180°.   **81.** 3 pi bonds, thirteen sigma bonds   **82.** carbon atoms 1 and 6   **87. a.** The carbons in the ring and the carbon attached to the ring have delocalized electrons; **b.** sp^2; **c.** *p* orbitals   **89.** All carbon atoms are sp^2.

91. In the minimum-energy states: **a.** two; **b.** none; **c.** two; **d.** four
93. a. sp^3 hybridization, tetrahedral shape for orbitals, molecule has trigonal pyramidal geometry; **b.** sp^3d^2 hybridization, octahedral shape; **c.** sp^3 hybridization, tetrahedral shape for orbitals, molecule has bent geometry; **d.** sp^3d hybridization, trigonal bipyramid shape
95. NO_2^-: Nitrogen in both has sp^2 hybridization. Because nitrite has a lone pair in one of the sp^2 orbitals, the O—N—O bond angle in nitrite is reduced from the normal 120° that is found in the nitrate ion.
97. Each carbon in octane will be sp^3 hybridized with tetrahedral geometry and form a straight chain of carbons. Each C—C bond will be free to rotate, and the separate molecules can arrange themselves to closely associate with each other, making the formation of a solid more likely. 2,2,3,3-Tetramethylbutane has a branched structure. Each carbon is still sp^3 hybridized, but the center two carbons have three additional carbons attached to each. The molecule will be like a large ball, with little possible change in its geometry. This geometry makes close association between different molecules more difficult and the process of boiling easier. Octane will not boil as easily as 2,2,3,3-tetramethylbutane.

99. The structure of NH_2CHO is

$$H-\overset{\overset{\displaystyle ..}{}}{\underset{\displaystyle H}{N}}-\overset{\displaystyle H}{\underset{}{C}}=O$$

. The carbon

is sp^2 hybridized (three sigma bonds, no lone pairs) and will be trigonal planar. Nitrogen is sp^3 hybridized (three sigma bonds, one lone pair) and will be tetrahedral. Because the carbon is sp^2 hybridized, the atoms connected to carbon lie in a single plane, but nitrogen has tetrahedral geometry, so its two hydrogens are not in the same plane as the rest of the molecule. The overall molecule is not planar and will be puckered.

101. a.

$$:\overset{\displaystyle H}{\underset{\displaystyle H}{N}}-\overset{\displaystyle H}{\underset{\displaystyle H}{N}}:$$

b. trigonal pyramidal

around each N; **c.** sp^3; **d.** This compound in unlikely to have a color because it does not have a low-lying orbital to which an electron may make a transition. The sp^3 hybridization scheme has all four orbitals used in bond making or holding an electron pair. No empty pi or pi* are present; **e.** $N_2H_4 + O_2 \rightarrow N_2 + 2H_2O$ $\Delta H = -590$ kJ/mol.

Chapter 10

P10.1 6.7 m/s² **P10.2** 0.979 atm; 744 torr; 0.992 bar; 9.92×10^4 Pa **P10.3** 1.2×10^2 torr **P10.4** 0.75 mol **P10.5** 1.3 L **P10.6** 522 K **P10.7** It is polar and experiences attractive intermolecular forces. **P10.8** 0.34 L **P10.9** 0.036 mol **P10.10** 0.734 atm **P10.11** O_2: ideal, 24.4 atm; van der Waals, 23.9 atm; NH_3: ideal, 24.4 atm, van der Waals, 21.2 atm **P10.12** 46.1 g/mol **P10.13** 53.7 g **P10.14** 18.5 kg **P10.15** If the masses of two particles are different, but the particles have the same kinetic energy, their velocities must be different to offset the difference in mass. As the mass increases, the velocity must decrease in order for the kinetic energy to remain the same. **P10.16** F_2 **P10.17** H_2 effuses 1.4 times as rapidly as He.

1. These forces are collectively known as van der Waals forces and are very small because of the large distances between the molecules and the rapid velocities. **3.** High temperature and low pressure **5.** 8.7 N **7.** 8.4×10^2 N **9.** 1.06×10^5 Pa; 106 kPa; 1.05 atm; 797 torr; 1.06 bar; 31.4 in Hg **11.** 4.9 lb **13.** 3.25×10^3 lb **15.** 32.2 psi, 2.19 atm **17.** 5.5×10^2 mm Hg **19.** N_2: 0.656 atm; O_2: 0.574 atm **21.** 758 mm Hg **23.** Ne: 0.306 mm Hg; He: 3.12 mm Hg **25.** 9.0 mol, 1.8 mol **27.** 5.32 L, 10.1 L **29.** 0.847 L, 1.34 L

31. 10.5 L **33.** 594 K **35.** 0.12 L **37.** 0.144 mL **39. a.** 0.08205 L·atm·mol⁻¹·K⁻¹, 8314 L·Pa·mol⁻¹·K⁻¹; **b.** 62.36 L·mm·Hg·mol⁻¹ K⁻¹; **c.** 1.206 L·psi·mol⁻¹·K⁻¹ **41.** 3.8×10^7 L **43.** 22.4 L, 51.2 L **45.** 0.193 mol **47.** 17.1 g/mol **49.** 0.755 g/L **51.** 2.06×10^{21} molecules **53.** 114 g/mol **55.** 1.41×10^3 g/mol, No **57.** 271×10^4 K **59.** 8.47 L **61.** 12.6 g/L **63.** 0.306 atm **65.** H_2 is the limiting reagent, 1.33 L **67.** 33.9 g/mol **69.** F_2 **71.** 529 L **73.** According to the kinetic-molecular theory, the average kinetic energy of a particle is directly proportional to the temperature. The pressure of a gas inside the cylinder depends on both the number of collisions with the walls of the container and the speed of the molecules. As the temperature increases, the speed increases and both the number and the velocity of the collisions increase; therefore, the pressure is directly proportional to the temperature. **75. a.** same; **b.** $Cl_2 < ClO_2$; **c.** ClO_2; **d.** ClO_2 **77. a.** 4.4×10^{-20} J; **b.** 1.7×10^{-20} J; **c.** 2.0×10^{-20} J **79.** Ar $< C_2H_6 < H_2$ **81.** 411 m/s **83.** CO_2: 376 m/s; H_2O: 588 m/s **85.** Point 1: The marbles do not have negligible size relative either to the container or to the distance between marbles. Point 2: Unless the marbles are dirty and sticky, this should be true because the marbles will not be strongly attracted to each other. Point 3: If the marbles are continuously shaken during the demonstration, this should be true. Point 4: This should also be true during the demonstration if the marbles are continuously shaken. As the piston is moved, the number of particle collisions per surface area will change. A smaller volume will correspond to larger pressures. Point 5: This will be approximately correct. There will be some small energy loss (due to friction and collisional heating) as the marbles move and collide with each other and the container. Point 6: This will not be true in the analogy, but more violent shaking could be applied to show higher temperatures. **87.** Xe $< SO_3 < CO_2 < N_2$ **89.** 72.7 g/mol **91.** Ar **93.** Because the masses are not exactly the same ($CO_2 = 44.01$ g/mol and $C_3H_8 = 44.09$ g/mol), there will be a slight difference in the effusion rates. It would be possible, though impractical, to try to separate these molecules via effusion. **95.** 16 cm from the HCl end **97.** 0.57% faster **99. a.** 1.57×10^{13} L; **b.** 1.97×10^{13} L; **c.** 1.43×10^6 metric tons; **d.** 1.09×10^{12} mol **101.** 4.75×10^{24} molecules **103.** ideal: 21.8 atm; van der Waals: 22.1 atm **105.** $\Delta T = 894$ K; $V_{final} = 0.916 V_{initial}$ **107.** 91.4 g; 338 balloons **109.** One of the considerations is which property is easier to manage: a temperature of only 20 K or a high pressure of 400 atm. Each requires a different infrastructure to handle. High pressures require thick walls with excellent welding, whereas low temperatures require vacuum dewers (like a thermos), and any variation in temperature causes the hydrogen to boil and be lost. **110. a.** dispersion only; **b.** hydrocarbons behave ideally except at high pressures or low temperatures; **c.** 0.0123 mol; **d.** C_3H_8; **e.** 0.453 L

Chapter 11

P11.1 The size of the London dispersion force between the molecules increases as the size of the molecule increases. Therefore, the forces between the molecules of dodecane are much larger than the forces between hexane molecules, which in turn are much larger than the forces between propane molecules. The larger the force, the closer the molecules and the stronger they will be held together. Dodecane is so strongly held that it forms a solid, and hexane is held strongly enough to cause it to condense to a liquid at room temperature. **P11.2** Propylene glycol has a higher boiling point because the intermolecular forces will be higher. **P11.3** Any molecule with greater forces will have a higher boiling point and a lower vapor pressure. Examples include ethylene glycol and propylene glycol. **P11.4** Hexane should have lower overall forces than acetone and is likely to have the higher vapor pressure. **P11.5** 440 kJ **P11.6** 80°C; Yes, lower external pressures make for lower boiling temperatures.   **P11.7** CCl_4 and I_2 **P11.8** 47.1 g KOH, $\chi_{water} = 0.975$ **P11.9** $1.33 \times 10^{-7} M$ **P11.10** No, 6.4 mL   **P11.11** 122.5 torr   **P11.12 a.** 101.0°C; **b.** 100.7°C; **c.** 67.1°C   **P11.13 a.** 2.45 atm; **b.** 27.5 atm; **c.** 91.7 atm

1. Intermolecular forces are between molecules, while intramolecular forces are between atoms in a molecule and are stronger.
3. Intermolecular forces are due to the attraction of positive and negative charges, partial to full in magnitude, between molecules.
5. S—H ═ C—H < N—H < O—H   **7. a.** intermolecular; **b.** intramolecular; **c.** intermolecular; **d.** intramolecular, intermolecular   **9.** 0.101 nm, stronger and intramolecular; 0.175, intermolecular   **11.** Larger forces lead to a higher boiling point. **a.** pentane, less compact and larger dispersion forces; **b.** cyclohexane, larger dispersion forces on rings than on chains; **c.** hexane, larger mass and dispersion forces; **d.** water, stronger forces (hydrogen bonding); **e.** pentane, larger mass and dispersion forces   **13. a.** B → O; **b.** P → Cl; **c.** H → O   **15. a.** dispersion, dipole–dipole, hydrogen bonding; **b.** dispersion; **c.** dispersion; **d.** dispersion, dipole–dipole, hydrogen bonding   **17. a.** CF_4; **b.** H_2O **19. a.** yes; **b.** yes; **c.** no, lacks O, F, or N; **d.** no, lacks H bound to O, F, or N   **21. a.** C—O bonds; **b.** dispersion, dipole–dipole   **23.** hexane, because lower intermolecular forces (only dispersion versus hydrogen bonding in methanol) give a higher vapor pressure   **25.** Kr, because it has the largest mass (and number of electrons) and is most polarizable, giving larger dispersion forces   **27. a.** As the central atom becomes larger and more polarizable, the intermolecular forces increase. Higher forces lead to increasing boiling point, which is the trend seen down the group; **b.** It is the most polar and can hydrogen-bond.
29. The forces in water, including hydrogen bonding, are much larger than in methane, leading to higher energy requirements.
31. 2.5×10^6 J   **33. a.** dispersion; **b.** gas; **c.** It is pressurized.   **35.** The H—Te bond is not polar enough to allow for hydrogen bonding.
37. 48.0 kJ   **39. a.** 231 K; **b.** 0.75 atm, 224 K; **c.** gas   **41.** gas to solid   **43.** liquid to solid   **45.** As the pressure increases, the gas will become a liquid at 1.4 atm.   **47.** See the accompanying diagram; note that the pressure is plotted on a logarithmic scale.

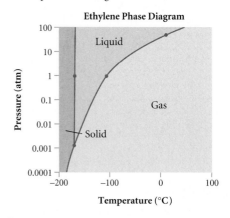

49. Surface tension is a measure of how strongly the molecules of a substance interact and "pull" the surface molecules toward the center. Viscosity is a measure of how strongly the molecules interact and prevent the flowing of one molecule past another. Capillary action is a balance of two interactions: that of the substance with its container and that of the substance with itself. Molecules capable of strong intermolecular interactions often have strong interactions with other surfaces.   **51.** The figure should show a convex surface (curved upward).   **53.** From least to most viscous: gasoline, water, honey. The order is the same as the increase in intermolecular forces—larger forces make for higher viscosity.   **55.** The forces (and viscos-

ity) are high because the molecules are large, with correspondingly large dispersion forces.   **57. a.** positive; **b.** 49 g per100 g water
59. Water is able to dissolve many different sizes and shapes of molecules, from very small salts to very large protein molecules.
61. a. yes; **b.** There is additional stability as a consequence of mixing.
63. A-water; B-heptane   **65. a.** Solubility has limits, whereas miscibility is possible in any combination; **b.** They share type and size of intermolecular forces.   **67. a.** 2.10 M; **b.** 0.222 M; **c.** 4.16 M
69. a. 2.01 m; **b.** 0.310 m; **c.** 0.217 m **71. a.** 0.266; **b.** 0.0555;
c. 0.00318   **73.** NH_4Cl: 0.0424, 2.46 M; KNO_3: 1.96 g, 0.00278;
$C_6H_{12}O_6$: 325 g, 7.21 M **75.** 0.037%, $2.1 \times 10^{-3} M$, $1.9 \times 10^{-3} m$ **77.** 0.873 M **79. a.** 0.0130%; **b.** 1.30×10^5 ppb
81. a. left; **b.** right   **83.** $5.1 \times 10^{-4} M$ **85.** 0.00300 M
87. pentane > water > glycerol   **89. a.** 100.76°C; **b.** 100.02°C;
c. 100.39°C; **d.** 89.1°C   **91. a.** –0.93°C; **b.** –0.20°C; **c.** 42.1°C;
d. –2.23°C   **93. a.** 3.66 torr; **b.** 3.9 torr; **c.** 4.01 torr; **d.** 4.39 torr
95. The vapor pressure is the equilibrium position at a specific temperature and does not depend on the surface area of the liquid. The area of the liquid affects how quickly that equilibrium can be reached, but the final value of the vapor pressure will be the same whether the liquid is in a cup or forms an ocean, as long as the container is closed.   **97.** All these solutions have the same number of particles dissolved, whereas electrolytes may produce more or fewer ions than others.   **99.** 5340 g

101. a.

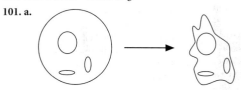

b. If the solution and body fluid do not have the same osmotic pressure, cell damage from shrinkage or rupture will result.   **103.** A hydrogen bond is formed between a hydrogen on O or N and a second O or N without a hydrogen.

105. 0.868 g   **107.** $CHBr_3$ because of its larger dispersion forces and dipole–dipole interactions   **109.** Boiling occurs when the vapor pressure of the liquid matches the external pressure. Turning up the gas will not change the external pressure but only cause the boiling to be more vigorous.

111. 5.73 M

112. a.

$$H-\underset{\underset{H}{|}}{\overset{\overset{H}{|}}{C}}-\underset{\underset{H}{|}}{\overset{\overset{H}{|}}{C}}-\underset{\underset{H}{|}}{\overset{\overset{H}{|}}{C}}-\underset{\underset{H}{|}}{\overset{\overset{H}{|}}{C}}-H$$

b. dispersion forces;
c. yes, because the dispersion forces are small; **d.** no; **e.** 0.301 mol;
f. The gas is under pressure, raising its boiling point; **g.** Pentane boils higher than butane, and propane boils lower than butane.

Chapter 12

P12.1

$CH_3-CH_2-CH_2-CH_2-CH_2-CH_2-CH_3$

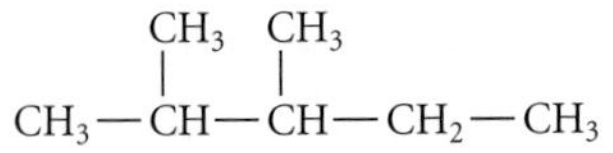

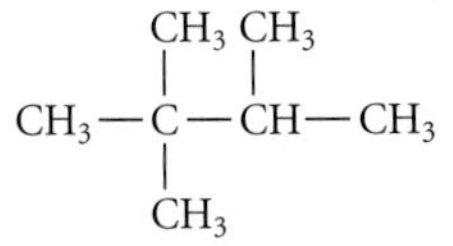

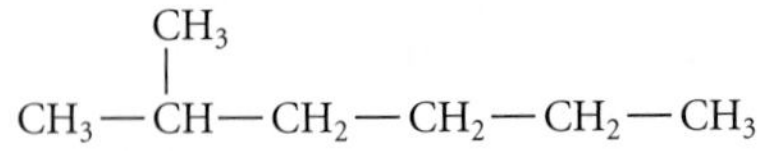

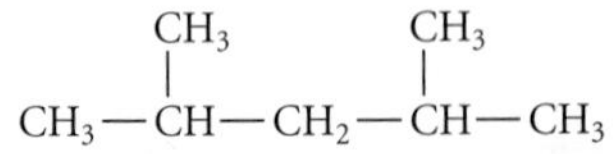

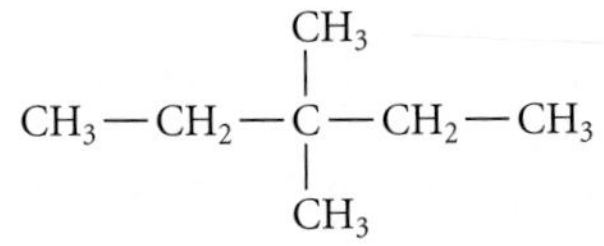

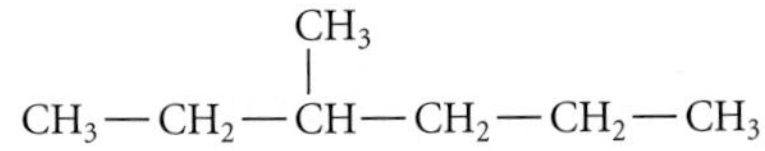

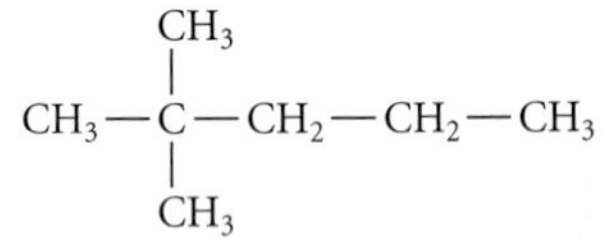

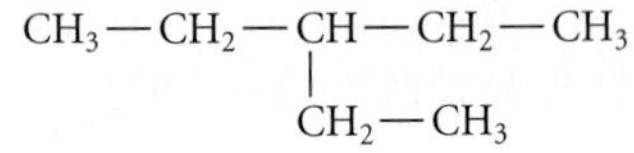

$CH_3-CH(CH_3)-CH(CH_3)-CH_2-CH_3$

$CH_3-C(CH_3)(CH_3)-CH(CH_3)-CH_3$

$CH_3-CH(CH_3)-CH_2-CH_2-CH_2-CH_3$

$CH_3-CH(CH_3)-CH_2-CH(CH_3)-CH_3$

$CH_3-CH_2-C(CH_3)(CH_3)-CH_2-CH_3$

$CH_3-CH_2-CH(CH_3)-CH_2-CH_2-CH_3$

$CH_3-C(CH_3)(CH_3)-CH_2-CH_2-CH_3$

$CH_3-CH_2-CH(CH_2-CH_3)-CH_2-CH_3$

P12.2

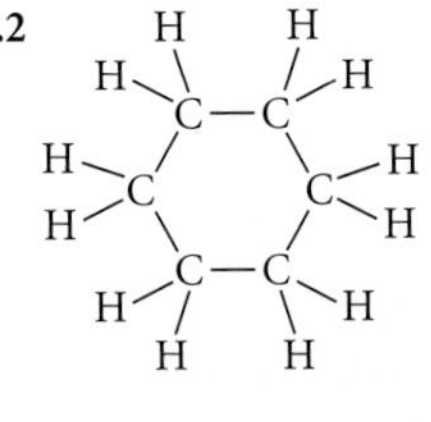

P12.3

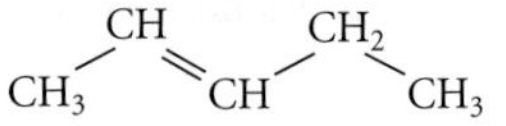

trans

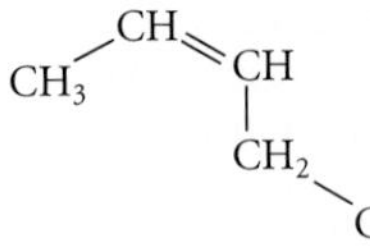

cis

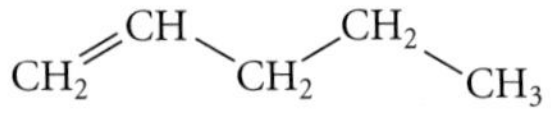

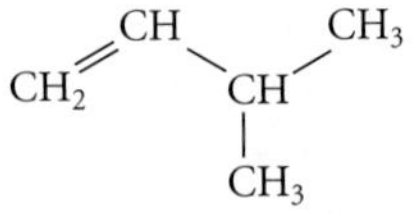

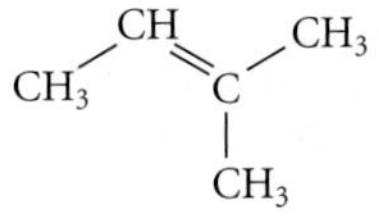

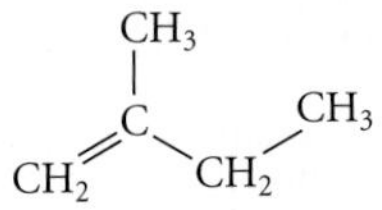

P12.4

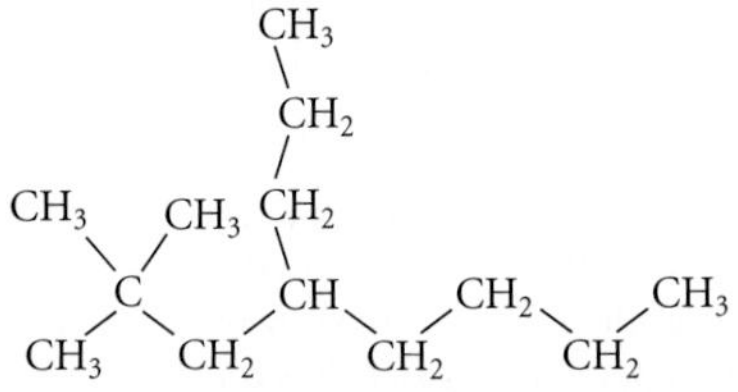

P12.5

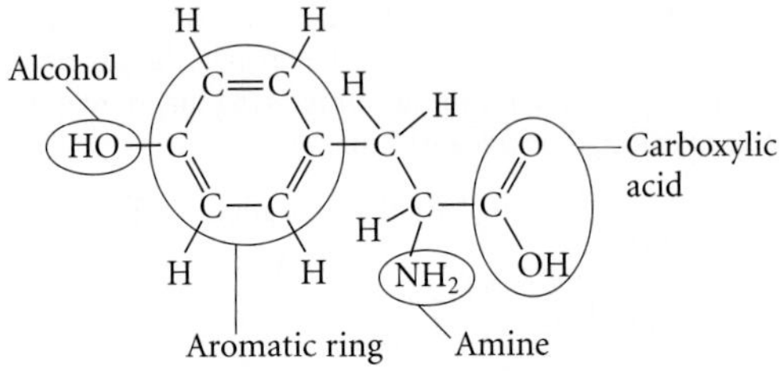

Alcohol, Carboxylic acid, Aromatic ring, Amine

P12.6

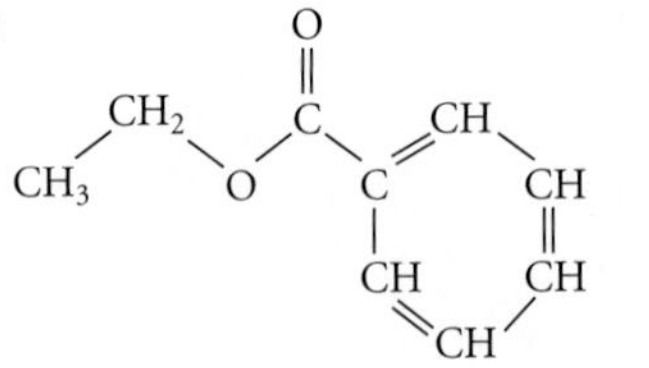

Ethyl benzoate

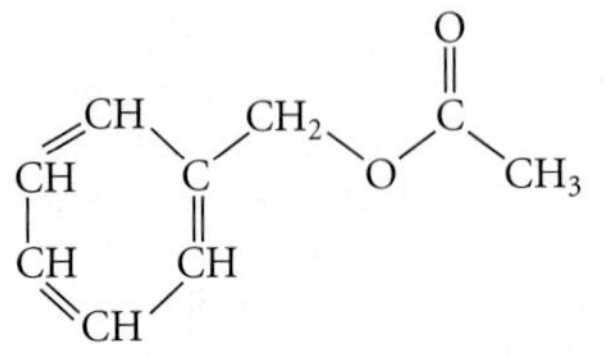

Benzyl ethanoate

P12.7 Left molecule: second carbon from left; right molecule: carbon at the lower right   **P12.8** Yes, m-amsacrine will attack the DNA in healthy cells also.

P12.9

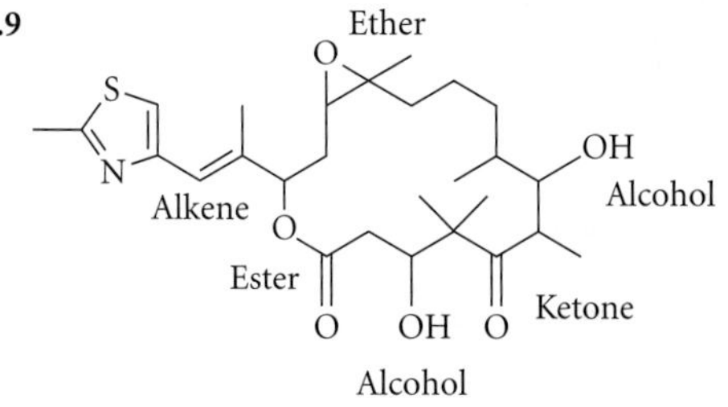

1. diamond (sp^3), graphite (sp^2), fullerenes (sp^2)   **3.** In diamond, all of the carbons are sp^3 hybridized (tetrahedral) and form an extensive three-dimensional network of carbon atoms bound together. The carbon atoms in graphite are all sp^2 (recall that sp^2 atoms form trigonal planes) hybridized and form extended planar surfaces that are only weakly bound via van der Waals forces between the planes.
5. 2.01×10^{22} atoms   **7.** Aliphatic compounds are those with no double or triple bonds, while the aromatics are characterized by structures with several multiple bonds.   **9.** Because many biological compounds (proteins and others) contain sulfur and the source of the crude oil is those biological materials, many compounds resulting from the breakdown of this material also contain sulfur.
11. a. 2-methyloctane; **b.** 2-methylpentane; **c.** 3-ethylpentane; **d.** pentane

13. a.

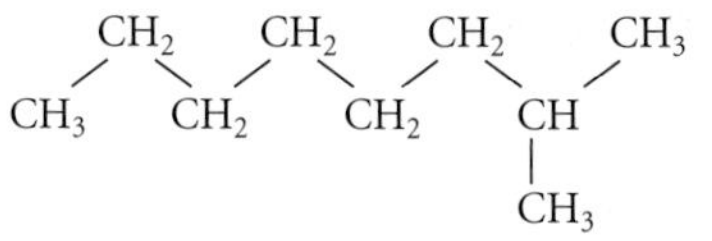

b.

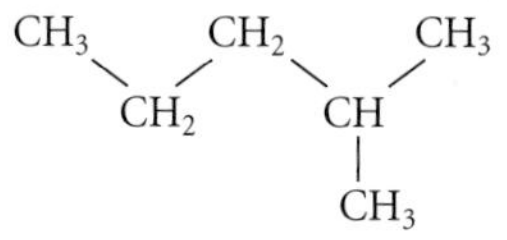

c.

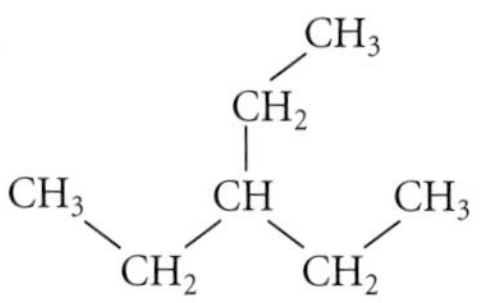

d.

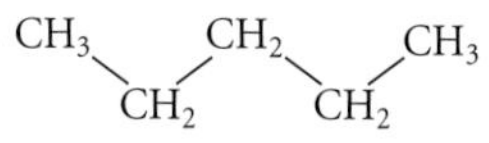

15.

Alkane	Alkene	Alkyne
C—C	C=C	C≡C
sp^3	sp^2	sp

17. a.

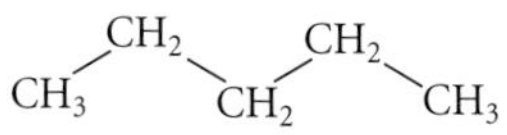

Pentane

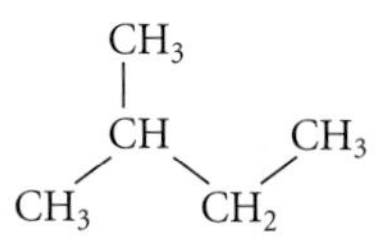

2-Methylbutane

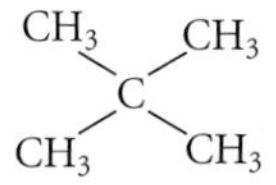

2,2-Dimethylpropane

Each molecule is C_5H_{12}; **b.** pentane (36°C), 2-methylbutane (28°C), 2,2-dimethylpropane (9.5°C)   **19.** $C_{28}H_{58}$

21.

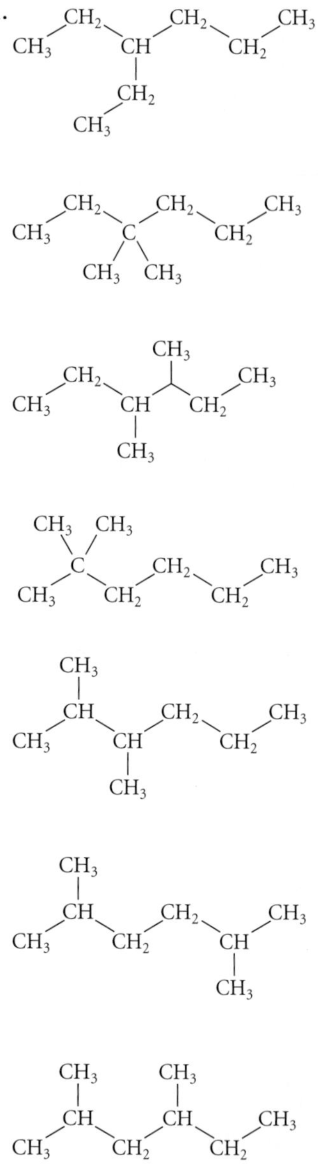

23. C_6H_{12} and C_7H_{14} **25.** left: *trans;* right: *cis*   **27.** $CaC_2 + 2H_2O \rightarrow Ca(OH)_2 + C_2H_2$ **29.** Cyclohexane: **a.** 12 H; **b.** sp^3; **c.** 109.5°; **d.** no double bonds; benzene: **a.** 6 H; **b.** sp^2; **c.** 120°; **d.** three double bonds;
e.

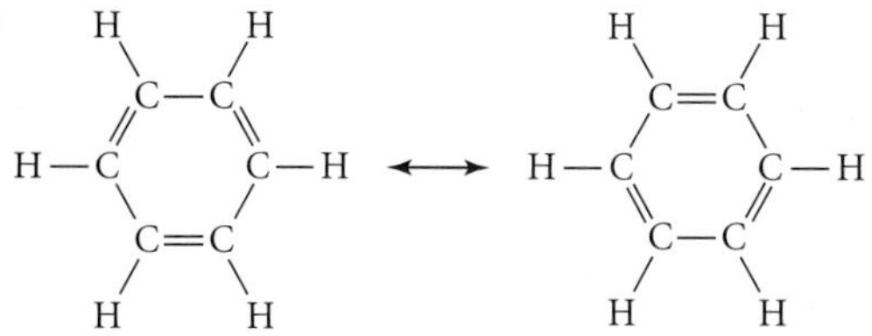

31. During a "run" of the gas chromatograph, a sample is injected into the instruments and heated to vaporize the sample. A carrier gas takes the sample into and through a column. Inside the column, the different molecules interact to varying extents with the materials

inside the column. The greater the interaction, the more slowly the molecules move through the column. The molecules are separated by being selectively slowed on the basis of their properties and are later detected upon exiting the column. **33.** Boiling temperature; Larger and straighter molecules have higher boiling points.
35. C_8H_{18}; $2C_8H_{18} + 25O_2 \rightarrow 16CO_2 + 18H_2O$ **37.** C_7H_{16}
39. 87% isooctane and 13% heptane **41.** $CH_4 + Br_2 \rightarrow CH_2Br_2 + H_2$

43.

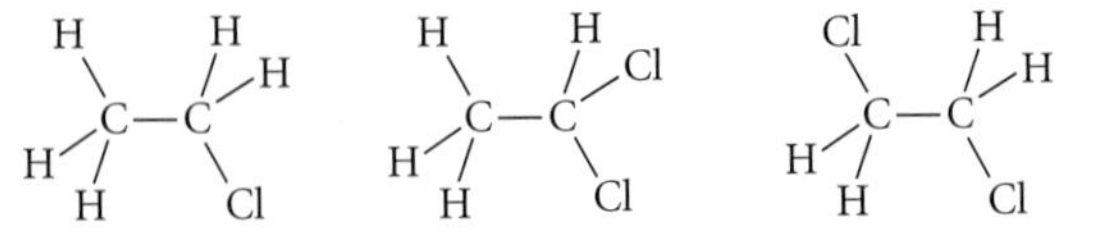

1-Chloroethane 1,1-Dichloroethane 1,2-Dichloroethane

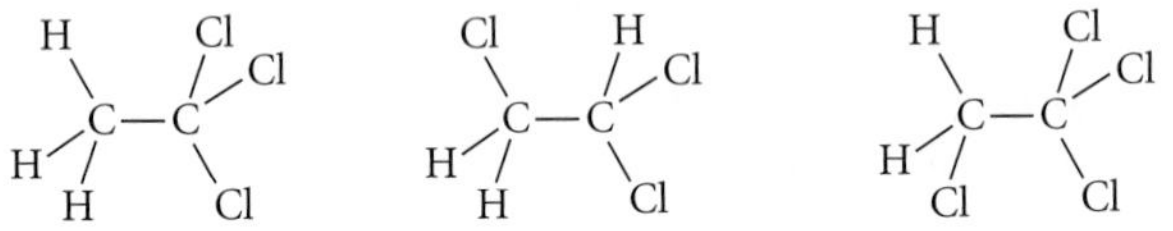

1,1,1-Trichloroethane 1,1,2-Trichloroethane 1,1,1,2-Tetrachloroethane

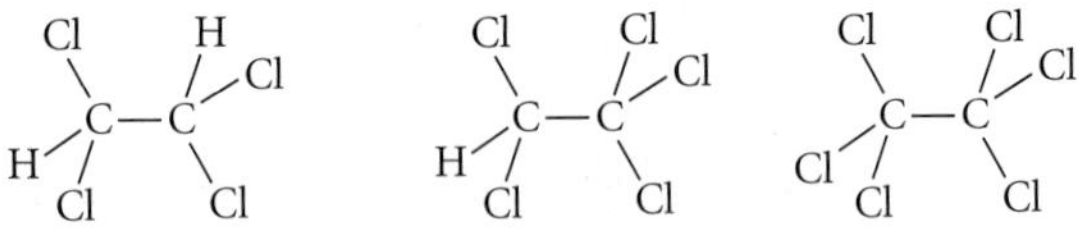

1,1,2,2-Tetrachloroethane Pentachloroethane Hexachloroethane

45. During complete combustion: H_2O and CO_2 **47.** -2.10×10^3 kJ

49. a. CH_3OH,

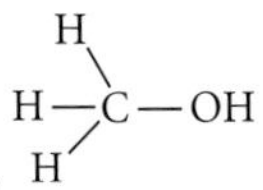

b. CH_2O,

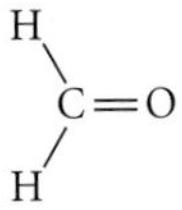

c. C_2H_4,

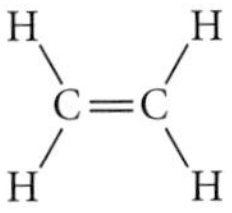

d. CH_3COCH_3,

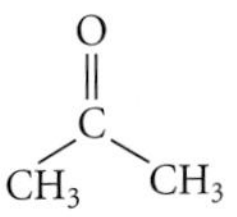

51.

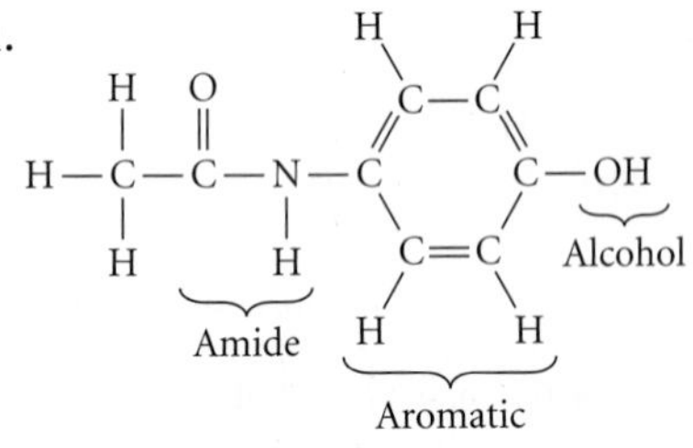

53.

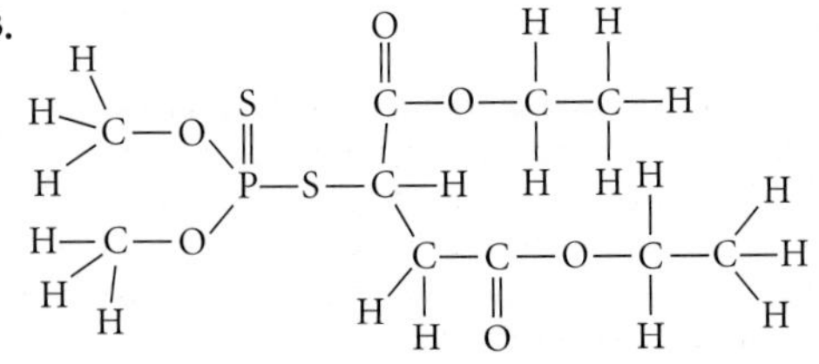

55. a. none; **b.** three; **c.** seven

57. a.

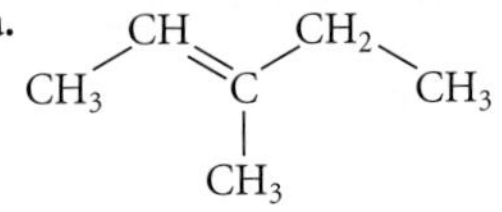

b.

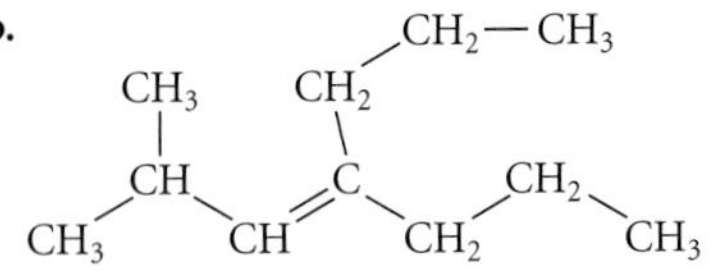

59. Alkane, C_2H_6

61. a.

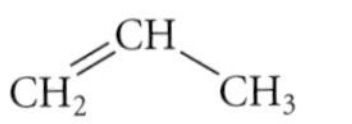

b. $C_3H_6 + H_2O \rightarrow C_3H_7OH$

63. a.

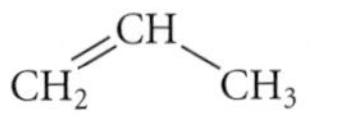

b.

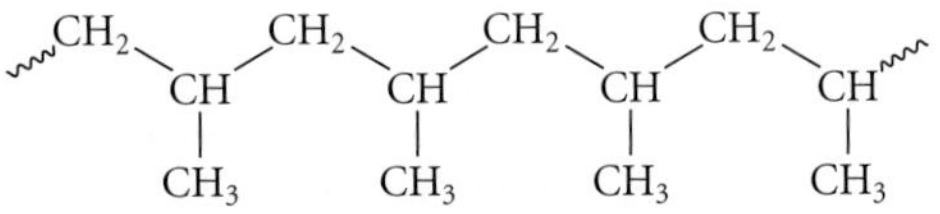

65. The HDPE units are long and unbranched, allowing close packing and high density, whereas the LDPE units are shorter and more branched, leading to loose packing and low density.
67. 1,4-Pentanediol

69.

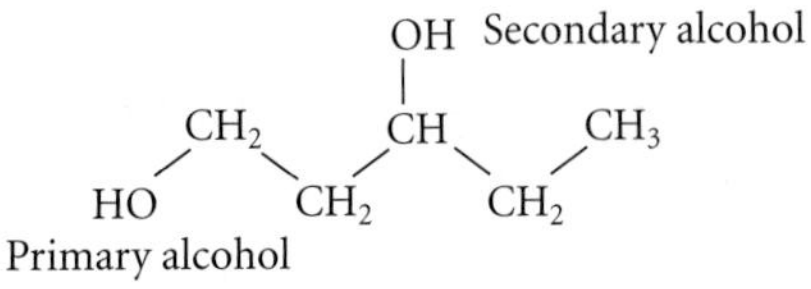

71.

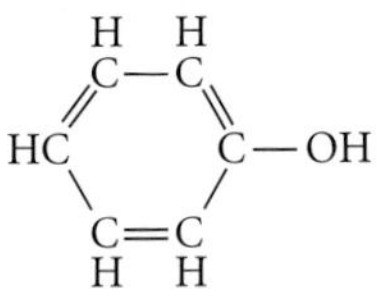

73.

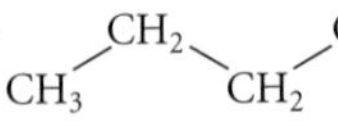

,

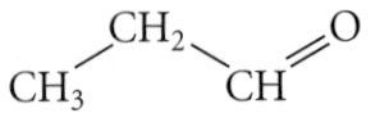

75.

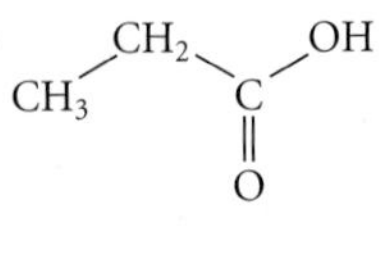

, Propanal:

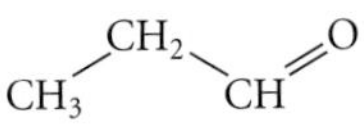

77.

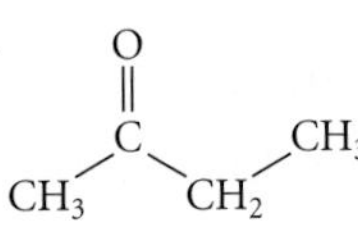

, 2-Butanol:

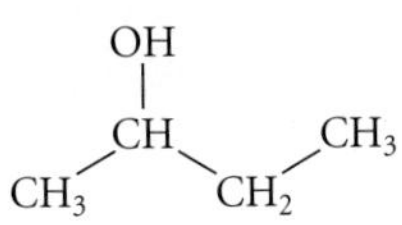

79. $CH_3CH_2COOH + H_2O \rightarrow CH_3CH_2COO^- + H_3O^+$

81.

CH₃–CH(CH₃)–CH₂–CH₂–OH + CH₃–C(=O)–OH → CH₃–CH(CH₃)–CH₂–CH₂–O–C(=O)–CH₃ + H₂O

83.

CH₃–CH₂–CH₂–CH₂–CH₂–OH + CH₃–CH₂–CH₂–C(=O)–OH → CH₃–CH₂–CH₂–CH₂–CH₂–O–C(=O)–CH₂–CH₂–CH₃ + H₂O

85.

CH₃–CH₂–CH₂–CH₂–CH₂–CH=CH–CH₂–CH=CH–CH₂–CH₂–CH₂–CH₂–CH₂–CH₂–C(=O)–OH

87.

H₂N–CH₂–C(=O)–NH–CH₂–C(=O)–NH–CH₂–C(=O)–OH, H₂O

89.

~~~S–CH₂–CH₂–O–CH₂–CH₂–S–S–CH₂–CH₂–O–CH₂–CH₂–S–S–CH₂–CH₂–O–CH₂–CH₂–S~~~, NaCl

91. dimethyl ether and butyl methyl ether   **93. a.** Yes with designs, no without; **b.** yes; **c.** yes; **d.** no   **95.** In each, the carbon bound to the Br is the chiral center.   **97.** 63%   **99.** Because of the different temperatures, the volatility of the different components changes. In order to maintain similar vaporization and combustion characteristics, the components in the winter need to be more volatile. In the summer the volatility is decreased to prevent "vapor lock" problems that could arise if some of the formulation "boiled" in the gas lines.

101. a.

HO–C(=O)–C(=O)–OH

b. Polar molecule, hydrogen bonding, solid, acidic; **c.** 61.6%;

d.

CH₃–CH₂–O–C(=O)–C(=O)–O–CH₂–CH₃ + 2H₂O → CH₃–CH₂–OH + HO–C(=O)–C(=O)–OH + HO–CH₂–CH₃

e.

~~~CH₂–O–C(=O)–C(=O)–O–CH₂–CH₂–O–C(=O)–C(=O)–O–CH₂–CH₂–O–C(=O)–C(=O)–O–CH₂–CH₂–O–C(=O)–C(=O)–O~~~

Chapter 13

P13.1 a.

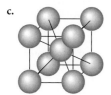

b.

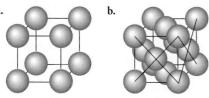

c.

(unit cell illustration)

P13.2 47.6%　**P13.3** 11.35 g/cm³　**P13.4** 1306 nm
P13.5 metal, glass/ceramic, ceramic, metal (or alloy)
P13.6 composite (magnetic media on plastic), plastic, composite (glass and plastic)　**P13.7** 4.11 × 10⁻⁷ mol; 4.15 × 10⁴ layers for 1 g, 8.30 × 10⁵ layers for 20 g; no

1. Crystalline solids have a regular arrangement of particles, whereas amorphous solids exhibit a random arrangement of particles.　**3.** A simple unit cell consists of atoms arranged within a parallelepiped (often at the corners, centered inside or on the faces and edges). The crystal lattice consists of rows and columns of the parallelepiped (unit cells) connected at the corners.

5.

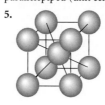

7. four atoms   **9.** A, metal; B, molecular; C, ionic   **11. a.** 4.42×10^{-29} m³; **b.** 2.10×10^{-28} m³; **c.** 6.23×10^{-28} m³   **13.** 0.559 g   **15.** 125 pm   **17.** 142 pm, 32.0%   **19.** 6.1×10^{23} atoms per mole   **21.** Rh   **23.** Na, Al, Ca, Cr, Bi   **25.** one, three   **27.** metal (2.5 kJ/mol), semiconductor (85 kJ/mol), insulator (450 kJ/mol)   **29.** Since the valence electrons from the metals are free to travel in the delocalized orbitals spanning the entire metal (the electron gas), the remaining positive atomic cores are all attracted to the sea of electrons that surrounds them. Because all cores are attracted, it doesn't matter what the specific identity of the metal is; all metals can be accommodated in the metal alloy crystal lattice.   **31.** If one considers a display of apples that is originally all one color (green, for example), alloys can be created in two ways: **a.** Remove some of the green apples and replace each, in that same position, with a red apple. This represents a substitutional alloy; **b.** Place some smaller red crabapples in the open spaces left between the green apples, without rearranging the apples or removing any apples. This represents an interstitial alloy.   **33. a.** one; **b.** Sodium donates one orbital to the metal "molecular" orbitals. The number of molecular orbitals that are created must equal the number of atomic orbitals that were used, with half being bonding and the other half antibonding. Because each orbital can hold two electrons and sodium donates only one per atom, only half of the orbitals are filled. In other words, the lower half, all bonding, are filled. Any transition from the highest occupied molecular orbital to the lowest unoccupied molecular orbital will be a transition from a bonding orbital to an antibonding orbital.   **35.** 2.42×10^{-19} J   **37.** Indium, from Group IIIA, has one fewer valence electron than silicon. For each indium in the semiconductor, there is one fewer electron (one more *positive* hole), making the semiconductor p-type.   **39.** Adding boron to carbon results in fewer electrons than pure carbon would have, creating openings in the valence band and a larger gap to the conduction band than in pure carbon. There are now lower-energy transitions available within the valence band. Because of these transitions, the electrons absorb some visible light, leaving behind the blue color we see.   **41.** Ceramics are characterized by ionic bonding, which has a very large gap between the valence and conduction bands. A large amount of energy is required to bridge the gap, and very few (if any) electrons are promoted into the conduction band. Without electrons in the conduction band, no (or very little) current can be conducted through the ceramic.   **43.** Because the bonding in glass is very disordered and random, different regions within the glass experience different localized bonding strengths. Different amounts of energy will be required to loosen up and melt these interactions, resulting in a range of melting temperatures.   **45.** 1.2 m, 1.66×10^{-25} J

47.

49. 7.51 g   **51. a.** plastic or metal; **b.** plastic; **c.** metal or plastic   **53.** All plastics are formed by the linking of several smaller monomer units that are then thermally molded and hardened in a particular shape. DNA is a polymer, but because it is not thermally molded and hardened, it is not a plastic.   **55. a.** plastic or metal; **b.** glass and metal; **c.** plastic or metal; **d.** plastic, glass, ceramic, or metal   **57.** A composite material used for automobile exteriors should be both strong and lightweight in order to provide protection in crashes and also to enhance the car's performance or economy of operation by reducing its weight. Composites tend to be expensive to produce.   **59.** Most of the bonds in most polymers are sigma bonds and are strongly localized. The electrons are not free to conduct electricity.

61. 8.4×10^{20} atoms   **63.** 7.67×10^{15} atoms   **65.** 1.37×10^{-6} g, 4.12×10^{-6} g   **67.** physical deposition or chemical-vapor deposition, depending on the exact process   **69.** the size of holes within the zeolite   **71.** Televisions are made from many plastics, metals, and glass and sometimes a large portion of lead. The plastics, metals, and lead are often recycled.   **73.** The nucleic acids (DNA and RNA) make up one class of biopolymers; a second class consists of proteins (mostly enzymes); the third class consists of some carbohydrates, including cellulose, chitin, and starches.   **75.** heterogeneous; It limits the formation of waste by-products.   **77.** It is lighter, more insulating, and more flexible.   **79.** Molecular solids do not conduct; ionic solids, when molten or dissolved, do conduct.   **81.** Because so many metal atoms are in the bulk form of a metal, and because each donates an orbital to the overall molecular orbital, there are an extremely large number of bonding and antibonding orbitals produced. Because the molecular orbitals are so plentiful and close together, electrons can absorb and release almost any wavelength of light from the infrared to the ultraviolet. The result is the luster that we associate with metals.   **83.** See http://www.dnr.state.oh.us/recycling/awareness/facts/tires/goodyear.htm   **85.** contamination of groundwater and drinking water
86. a.

b.

c. reacts with water, may be biodegradable; **d.** 0.558 g; **e.** acidic, but does not react with water in ester cleavage

Chapter 14

P14.1 112 splits/256 combinations; 43.8%   **P14.2** All but photosynthesis are spontaneous.   **P14.3 a.** not spontaneous; **b.** spontaneous; **c.** spontaneous   **P14.4** −209 J/K; 136 J/K   **P14.5** The entropy change is positive for the first reaction and negative for the second.   **P14.6** 109 J/K; −137 J/K   **P14.7** 0.224 kJ/mol; −0.986 kJ/mol   **P14.8** spontaneous (−2827 kJ); spontaneous (−2074 kJ); spontaneous (−401 kJ)   **P14.9** 337.2 K; 373.0 K

1. 16   **3.** 37.5%   **5.** A macrostate represents the total properties of the system. A microstate is a representation of a single way to arrange the parts of a system.   **7.** One possibility is all students in one room with one seat between every student and the next. Another possibility is half the students in each room with vacant seats between students.   **9.** $2^{1000} = 1.07 \times 10^{301}$. Because the number of microstates becomes very large, the number of individual microstates that correspond with either exact or very close to exact even distributions is much larger than the number of unequally distributed microstates.   **11.** It has increased. We know that there have to be many more microstates available after mixing, because the process is spontaneous, indicating a final state with more available microstates.   **13.** Water evaporation only   **15. a.** At room temperature, burning a piece of paper requires the intervention of a heater or ignition source. **b.** Hard-boiling an egg requires the addition of heat. **c.** Muscle mass is not added without a lot of work, such as lifting weights.   **17.** The entropy of the universe decreases in a nonspontaneous process.   **19.** The greater the number of microstates, the greater the entropy in a system.   **21.** The number of microstates corresponding to an even dispersal of the aroma-producing molecules is much larger than the number of microstates in which the aroma remains contained in one part of the room. The spontaneous process is then the dispersal of the aroma corresponding to the greater number of microstates.   **23.** If the total entropy of the universe increases, the process is spontaneous. The conversion of the gasoline from a liquid to a gas involves a large increase in entropy, which offsets the small decrease in entropy due to the removal of heat (and therefore available microstates) from your hand.   **25.** The change in entropy of the carbon dioxide is very large and positive as the molecules go from solid to gas. Because the heat to sublime the CO_2 is taken from the environment, the nearby gases are cooled, lowering their entropy, which is a negative entropy change. Because the process is spontaneous, the entropy of the universe increases.   **27.** As the reaction proceeds from left to right, the number of moles of gas is reduced. Removal of a mole of gas corresponds to a large decrease in the entropy; therefore, a reaction from right to left will cause an increase in the entropy of the system.   **29. a.** positive; **b.** need more information; **c.** need more information   **31.** The more ways a molecule can move, the greater the multiplicity in a system.   **33.** The entropy of the surroundings increases.   **35. a.** negative; **b.** positive; **c.** positive   **37.** positive; For the CO_2 the transition from a dissolved species, confined to the liquid, to a gas with a much greater available volume, represents a large increase in entropy.   **39.** $\underline{1}C_3H_8(g) + \underline{5}O_2(g) \rightarrow \underline{3}CO_2(g) + \underline{4}H_2O(g)$; 6 mol of reactants gas; 7 mol of products gas; entropy increases.   **41.** $\underline{1}C_3H_8(l) + \underline{5}O_2(g) \rightarrow \underline{3}CO_2(g) + \underline{4}H_2O(l)$; 5 mol of reactant gas; 3 mol of product gas; entropy decreases.   **43.** Because the number of microstates that become available in a gas rather than a liquid or solid is so large, any conversion to a gas greatly influences the entropy. The change in the number of microstates of liquids and solids is much lower and influences the reaction much less.   **45. a.** negative; **b.** positive; **c.** negative   **46. a.** −284.5 J/K; **b.** 216.5 J/K; **c.** −99.5 J/K   **49.** $\underline{1}C_2H_5OH(l) + \underline{3}O_2(g) \rightarrow \underline{2}CO_2(g) + \underline{3}H_2O(g)$; 219 J/K   **51.** 4 J/K   **53. a.** high temperature; **b.** none   **55. a.** 61.0 kJ/mol; **c.** −1.59 × 10³ kJ/mol   **56. a.** −97.7 kJ/mol; **c.** 507 kJ/mol   **57. a.** 938 J/K·mol; **c.** −2.42 × 10⁴ J/K·mol   **58. a.** 1075 K; **c.** 769 K   **59. a.** spontaneous; **b.** nonspontaneous; **c.** spontaneous   **61.** −1.48 × 10³ kJ   **63.** −71 kJ/mol   **65.** −532 kJ/mol; −122 J/K; −446 kJ/mol   **67. a.** 1681 K; **b.** 138 K; **c.** 420 K   **69.** 1.09 × 10⁻²³ atm   **71.** 6.05 × 10³ J/K   **73.** 1094 K   **75. a.** −802 kJ/mol; **b.** −794 kJ; **c.** The negative value shows that the reaction is spontaneous at room temperature, but it says nothing about the rate at which the reaction proceeds. The additional heat from the spark or flame is necessary to get the reaction to happen at an appreciable rate.   **77.** $\underline{2}C_4H_{10}(g) + \underline{13}O_2(g) \rightarrow \underline{8}CO_2(g) + \underline{10}H_2O(g)$; As the reaction proceeds, 15 mol of gas is converted to 18 mol of gas. The increase of 3 mol of gas will cause an increase in entropy.   **79.** To predict spontaneity, we must calculate if the entropy of the universe increases. To complete this calculation, we must consider both the system and the surroundings. In other words, we need to account for the entire universe. Using Gibb's equation, we need only consider variables related to the system.   **81.** Under these conditions, Q becomes an equilibrium constant.   **83. a.** $\underline{1}C_6H_{12}O_6(s) + \underline{6}O_2(g) \rightarrow \underline{6}CO_2(g) + \underline{6}H_2O(l)$; There should be an increase of entropy on the order of a few hundred J/K·mol; **b.** −2812 kJ; 262 J/K, −2875 kJ; **c.** −2548 kJ, 976 J/K, −2827 kJ; **d.** 4.07 L, the gas is removed via respiration; **e.** −71 kJ; **f.** 13.8 kJ/mol; **g.** If there were no glucose directly available to the organism, it would have to rely on other sources of energy, such as fructose. Fructose is naturally available in many fruits and vegetables; it also is a product in the hydrolysis of table sugar (sucrose).

Chapter 15

P15.1 Rate $= -\dfrac{1}{2}\dfrac{\Delta[HI]}{\Delta t} = \dfrac{\Delta[H_2]}{\Delta t} = \dfrac{\Delta[I_2]}{\Delta t}$

P15.2 4.6 × 10⁻⁴ M/s   **P15.3** Second order with respect to [HI]; second order overall   **P15.4** 8.01 × 10⁴ years; 2.41 × 10⁴ years   **P15.5** 30 days; 60 days; 2.5 × 10² days   **P15.6** Rate = (2.80 × 10⁵ $M^{-1} \cdot s^{-1}$) [CO]¹ [Hb]¹; second order   **P15.7** The second-order plot (inverse concentration versus time) shows a straight line, whereas the others do not. The reaction is second order.   **P15.8** The overall reaction is $2NO(g) + O_2(g) \rightarrow 2NO_2(g)$. The intermediate is $NO_3(g)$, and the rate law for the reaction is rate = $k[NO]^2[O_2]$.   **P15.9** First and second reactions: 10.1 kJ/mol; first and third reactions: 12.6 kJ/mol; second and third reactions: 13.8 kJ/mol. The values vary slightly as a consequence of small variations in experiments and mathematical rounding. When more than two data points are available, the preferred method is graphical (plot ln k versus $1/T$), which gives a value of 12.8 kJ/mol.

1. a. Total distance run = extent of reaction; **b.** average speed (total distance over time) = average rate of reaction; **c.** exact speed the runner is moving at a particular moment (perhaps using a radar gun) = instantaneous rate; **d.** exact speed as the runner started the race (again, with the radar gun) = initial rate   **3.** 2.5 × 10⁻⁸ M/s; Yes, for many reactions, the initial rate of the reaction is fastest and the rate of the reaction slows as the reaction proceeds. In this case, the initial (and instantaneous) rate and others near the start of the reaction would be larger than the average rate.   **5.** C_2H_4 is produced at twice the rate;

Rate $= -\dfrac{\Delta[C_4H_8]}{\Delta t} = \dfrac{1}{2}\dfrac{\Delta[C_2H_4]}{\Delta t}$ **7. a.** 5 × 10⁻⁴ M/s;
b. 1.3 × 10⁻³ M/s; **c.** 1.2 × 10⁻⁹ M/s; **d.** 2.0 × 10⁻⁵ M/s
9. a. −6.8 × 10⁻² M/s; **b.** 2.2 × 10⁻² M/s; **c.** 4.5 × 10⁻² M/s
11. a. 0 mi/h; **b.** 112 mi/h; **c.** 187 mi/h; **d.** 134 mi/h; **e.** This plot is the opposite of most reactions, in which the amount of products is high at first and then levels off as the reaction slows down. Here the distance covered is lowest initially and is larger as the racer speeds up.
13. a. The rate of appearance of water is twice the rate of appearance of oxygen.

b. Rate $= -\dfrac{1}{2}\dfrac{\Delta[H_2O_2]}{\Delta t} = \dfrac{1}{1}\dfrac{\Delta[O_2]}{\Delta t} = \dfrac{1}{2}\dfrac{\Delta[H_2O]}{\Delta t}$

15.

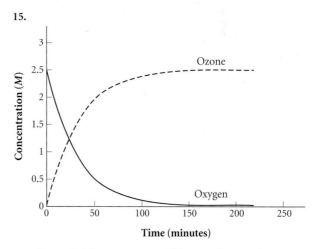

17. a. Increasing the temperature will increase the rate of reaction because that temperature increase (1) increases the number of collisions and (2) increases the speed of the molecules, which increases the energy in those collisions, making reaction more likely. **b.** Will not increase the rate: see part a above. **c.** Increasing the initial concentration of the reactants, will make collisions between those reactants more likely, thereby increasing the rate of the reaction. **d.** Will not increase the rate; lowering the concentration of the reactants will make collisions between those reactants less likely, thereby decreasing the rate of the reaction.   **19. a.** Third order; **b.** k is the rate constant of the reaction. **c.** The reaction rate quadruples. **d.** no effect **21.** 2.01×10^{-4} M/s **23.** Rate laws are experimentally determined, so there is no way, without additional information, to know what order the reaction is. Further, we cannot merely look at a reaction to determine the order of the reaction.   **25. a.** 3.61×10^{-4} s^{-1}; **b.** 1.32×10^{-3} /min; **c.** 5.55×10^{-10}/year; **d.** 1.21×10^{-4}/year **27. a.** 43 min; **b.** 86 min; **c.** 143 min   **29. a.** 0.0916 M; **b.** 0.0839 M; **c.** 0.183 M; **d.** 0.193 M **31.** 0.195 M **33. a.** $[A]_0 = 0.100$ M cannot be correct because the initial concentration cannot be lower than the later concentration. **b.** The time values here are reversed—that is, the initial time should be lower than the later time.   **35.** 409 s for $[A]_0 =$ 0.0333 M.   **37.** 0.0141 M/h **39.** 8.65 $M^{-1}\cdot min^{-1}$ **41. a.** 0.0999 M; **b.** 0.499 M; **c.** 0.327 M; **d.** 7.82×10^{-4} M **43.** Because collisions between the reactants must occur for a reaction to take place, and the number of reactants is decreasing with time, the number of collisions between reactants becomes rarer with time. A slower rate of collision results in a slower reaction rate.   **45.** The half-life is constant for a first-order reaction and does not depend on the initial concentration. Pablo's experimental measurement should be consistent. The half-life of a second-order reaction is inversely proportional to the initial concentration. Peter's experiment will be different because the initial concentration, and therefore the half-life, will be different.   **47. a.** 1.71×10^{-3} h^{-1}; **b.** 1.98 $M^{-1}\cdot h^{-1}$; **c.** 1.49×10^{-6} M/h **49.** 0.594 M **51.** 141 years   **53.** The reaction is second order.   **55. a.** rate doubles; **b.** rate doubles; **c.** rate quadruples   **57.** Rate $= (2.2\ s^{-1})\ [B]^1$, first order   **59.** Rate $= (1.0 \times 10^2\ M^{-2}\cdot s^{-1})\ [A]^1\ [B]^2$, third order   **61.** zero order, 0.047 M/min   **63. a.** first-order plot [ln(large dark atoms) versus time]; **b.** The rate at left is double the rate at right. **c.** s^{-1} **65.** first order; 0.229 min^{-1} **67. a.** Rate $= k$ [Stabilizer]$^{0.5}$ $[O_2]^2$; **b.** $3.60 \times 10^{-3}\ M^{-1.5}\cdot s^{-1}$; **c.** $1.20 \times 10^{-3}\ M/s$; **d.** 0.360 M **69.** 84% (458 cpm) **71.** Because each of those values is the y intercept of the graph, each line would be moved vertically until the intercept was at $y = 0$. **73.** negative   **75.** $8.95 \times 10^{-2}\ s^{-1}$ **77.** –1·   **79.** A *reaction mechanism* is a collection of single simple steps called *elementary steps* that represent what is thought to occur in a reaction. The slowest step in the mechanism usually determines the rate of the reaction and is called the *rate-determining step*.   **81.** The answers will vary. One example: (1) Hear phone ring. (2) Decide to answer. (3) Push chair out from table. (4) Stand up. (5) Walk to phone. (6) Pick up phone. (7) Say "Hello," etc. Depending on how agile you are and how far the phone is from the table, you might choose step 3, 4, or 5 as the slow step.   **83.** 8.84 kJ/mol   **85.** Mechanism B, with its first-step slow step has a rate law of Rate $= k[H_2O_2][I^-]$, which does not have the proper hydrogen ion concentration dependence. The rate law for Mechanism A does match and is derived by setting the rates of the forward and reverse reactions in the first step equal, solving for the intermediate concentration, and placing that concentration into the rate law from the second step:

$$\text{Rate} = \frac{k_1}{k_{-1}} k_2\ [H_2O_2][H^+][I^-] = k'[H_2O_2][I^-][H^+]$$

87. a. 97.9 kJ/mol; **b.** $2.4 \times 10^{-3}\ M^{-1}\cdot s^{-1}$ **89. a.** A reaction intermediate is a compound that is formed and then consumed during the course of a reaction. **b.** An activated complex is the species or collection of atoms that exists at the transition state midway between reactants and products in a single elementary step. **c.** A homogeneous catalyst is a species in the same phase as the rest of the reactants and aids in the reaction by lowering the overall activation energy in the process of converting reactants to products. A homogeneous catalyst is destroyed, and then re-created, in the course of the reaction. **d.** A heterogeneous catalyst is a species or material in a different phase from the rest of the reactants; it aids in the reaction by lowering the overall activation energy in the process of converting reactants to products.   **91. a.** $2N_2O \rightarrow 2N_2 + O_2$; **b.** O is an intermediate. There are no catalysts; **c.** first step   **93. a.** Lactose → glucose + galactose; **b.** (Lactase–lactose) and (lactase–glucose–galactose) are

intermediates. Lactase is the catalyst. **c.** Rate $= k$[Lactase][Lactose] **95. a.** $N_2(g) + 3H_2(g) \rightarrow 2NH_3(g)$; **b.** FeH_2 and FeN_2; **c.** $Fe(s)$; **d.** heterogeneous   **97.** 1.7×10^{-3} M/s; 0.10 M/h **99. a.** 0.350 s^{-1}; **b.** 1.98 s   **101.** 200 kJ   **103. a.** $C_2H_4(aq) + HCl(aq) \rightleftharpoons C_2H_5Cl(aq)$; **b.** Rate $= k_1[C_2H_4][HCl]$ **104.** See diagram; the uncatalyzed profile is represented by the solid line. **a.** exothermic ($\Delta H = -92$ kJ); **b.** spontaneous ($\Delta G = -32$ kJ); $T = 458$ K; **c.** See short-dashed line in diagram.

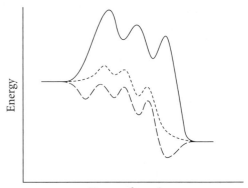

Extent of reaction

d. See long-dashed line in diagram. **e.** 15 g; **f.** 12.2 kg

Chapter 16

P16.1 0.224 M **P16.2** $K = \dfrac{[CO][H_2]^3}{[CH_4][H_2O]}$

P16.3 a. $K = \dfrac{[NO_2][O_2]}{[NO][O_3]}$; **b.** $K = \dfrac{[NH_4Cl]}{[HCl][NH_3]}$;

c. $K = \dfrac{[C_2H_6]}{[C_2H_2][H_2]^2}$

P16.4 a. reactants; **b.** reactants; **c.** reactants; **d.** products **P16.5** 1.1×10^3 **P16.6** 1.5×10^8 **P16.7 a.** left; **b.** right; **c.** right; **d.** left   **P16.8** 0.016 M **P16.9** $[H^+] = 1.8 \times 10^{-5}$ M, $[C_2H_3O_2^-] =$ 0.050 M, $[C_2H_4O_2] = 0.050$ M **P16.10 a.** shift right; **b.** shift left; **c.** no change; **d.** shift left   **P16.11** $K = 0.017$; The difference between the two values may lie in the difference between the activities and concentrations.

1. Even though the concentrations are not changing, the reactants and products are continuously reacting to form each other, making the equilibrium dynamic.   **3.** A reaction that does not go to completion stops reacting before all of the reactants have been converted to products. In other words, the reaction reached equilibrium and a zero Gibbs energy change before all of the reactants were converted.

5. a. $K = \dfrac{[C_2H_5Cl]}{[HCl][C_2H_4]}$; **b.** $K = \dfrac{[CO_2][H_2O]^2}{[CH_4][O_2]^2}$; **c.** $K = \dfrac{1}{[H_2]^2[O_2]}$

7. a. At equilibrium, the forward and reverse reaction rates are equal. **b.** The concentrations are related via the equilibrium expression,

$K = \dfrac{[CaSO_4]^3[H_3PO_4]^2}{[H_2SO_4]^3}$. **c.** At equilibrium, $\Delta G = 0$.

9. $\dfrac{k_1}{k_{-1}} = \dfrac{[HCl]^2}{[H_2][Cl_2]} = K +$

11. If equilibria could not be controlled, the amounts of products could not be maximized for profit.   **13. a.** blue; **b.** yellow

15. a. $K = \dfrac{1}{[O_2]}$; **b.** $K = \dfrac{[H_2SO_4]}{[SO_3]} +$

17. a. 0.10 (any value slightly smaller than 1); **b.** $[CO] > [CO_2]$

19. $C_3H_8(g) + 5O_2(g) \rightleftharpoons 3CO_2(g) + 4 H_2O(g)$,

$K = \dfrac{[CO_2]^3[H_2O]^4}{[C_3H_8][O_2]^5}$

21. $0.050\ M$ **23.** $K = \dfrac{[SO]^4}{[O_2]^5}$

25. Values of $K \gg 1$ are product favored; values of $K \ll 1$ are reactant favored; and values of K near 1 produce mixtures. The ammonia synthesis produces a mixture, the ozone depletion is product favored, and the acid ionization is reactant favored.   **27. a.** In order to get a quantitative 1:1 reaction between EDTA and the metal, the reaction needs to go to completion. If the reaction does not go to completion, we will not have a firm idea of how much metal is in the solution. **b.** A $K = 10^{10}$ ensures complete reaction, whereas a $K = 10$ produces a mixture.

29. a. $K = \dfrac{[H_2O]^2}{[H_2]^2\,[O_2]}$; **b.** 82.8; **c.** 0.0121; **d.** 9.10   **31.** 11

33. a. $K = \dfrac{[C_2H_2]^{1/2}\,[H_2]^{3/2}}{[CH_4]}$; **b.** $2CH_4(g) \rightleftharpoons C_2H_2(g) + 3H_2(g)$;

$K = \dfrac{[C_2H_2]\,[H_2]^3}{[CH_4]^2}$; **c.** $K_b = (K_a)^2$ **35.** 6.6×10^2

37. Adding the two reactions results in a third reaction with $K = 1.3 \times 10^4$, which is a sufficiently large value to ensure the reaction proceeds enough toward the products for the investigators to do the analysis.   **39.** $K = 0.092$, the strategy is not reasonable.
41. 0.76   **43. a.** $3.0 \times 10^{-3}\ M$; **b.** $1.8 \times 10^{-5}\ M$; **c.** $4.2 \times 10^{-4}\ M$
45. a. forward; **b.** reverse   **47. a.** forward; **b.** no change; **c.** reverse;
d. reverse   **49.** $1.05 \times 10^{-5}\ M$ **51.** 1.7×10^{-93} **53. a.** $7.8 \times 10^{-6}M$;
b. $0.76\ M$ **55. a.** $H_2O \rightarrow H^+ + OH^-$ plus the forward and reverse codeine reaction; **b.** Only the forward codeine reaction is important; **c.** forward; **d.** $[OH^-] = [C_{18}H_{21}NO_3H^+] = 4.0 \times 10^{-4}\ M$; $[C_{18}H_{21}NO_3] = 0.10\ M$ **57.** $Q < K$ for the conditions given, so more silver can be extracted.
59. a. $2.72\ M$;

b. Reactants ————————————————— Products

E

61. $0.22\ M$ **63.** $5.0 \times 10^{-13}\ M$
65. $[V^{3+}] = 0.0115\ M$, $[VO^+] = 0.138\ M$, $[H^+] = 0.0770\ M$
67. $[MbO_2] = 1.8 \times 10^{-12}M$, $[Mb] = 0.00102\ M$ $[O_2] = 0.000020\ M$
69. a. right; **b.** left; **c.** no effect; **d.** left; **e.** no effect   **71. a.** CuCl system; **b.** no effect because solids do not appear in K **73.** Because the reaction shifts toward the blue upon heating, we could assume that the reaction would shift in the opposite direction upon cooling—toward the pink.   **75.** A catalyst affects the speed of a reaction but does not affect the equilibrium position.   **77. a.** 1.00; **b.** 1.00; **c.** 0.357; **d.** 52.2   **79.** -6.45 kJ/mol   **81.** 9.69 kJ/mol   **83.** The strongest is formic acid; the weakest is acetic acid.   **85.** The most important calculation would be the total cost per unit of product formed. Although Method A uses more expensive reactants, little would be wasted. With a much smaller equilibrium constant, Method B will produce less product per given amount of reactant. Much more reactant will be needed to produce the same amount of product as Method A, a disadvantage that offsets the lower cost of the reactants. The exact balance of reactant price versus amount of product formed will be the deciding factor.   **87.** 2.6×10^{-29}
89. An equilibrium condition would exist if the total number of people inside the shop remained the same. There would be the same number of people entering the shop as finishing their shopping and leaving. A larger value of K would indicate a greater number of people in the shop, which should be more profitable. If Q were less than K, there would be fewer people in the shop, indicative of a poor business day.   **91.** $[CO] = [H_2] = 24.2$ atm; $[H_2O] = 27.8$ atm
93. 1 min; All frames beginning at 1 min. have the same composition.
94. a. $\Delta G = -24.8$ kJ/mol; spontaneous; **b.** $K = 2.22 \times 10^4$,

product favored; **c.** 4.5×10^{-5}; **d.** $3.56 \times 10^{-12}\ M/s$; **e.** $0.30\ M$;
f. The methanol concentration will increase. **g.** \$301

Chapter 17

P17.1
$H_2NCH_2CH_2NH_2\ (aq)$ + $H_2O\ (l)$ $\rightleftharpoons$ $H_2NCH_2CH_2NH_3{}^{\oplus}\ (aq)$ + $OH^{\ominus}\ (aq)$
Base   Acid   Conjugate Acid   Conjugate Base

P17.2
$CH_3(CH_2)_{10}COOH\ (aq)$ + $H_2O\ (l)$ $\rightleftharpoons$ $CH_3(CH_2)_{10}COO^{\ominus}\ (aq)$ + $H_3O^{\oplus}\ (aq)$
Acid   Base   Conjugate Base   Conjugate Acid

P17.3 Three possible acids weaker than HF ($K_a = 7.2 \times 10^{-4}$) are acetic acid (CH_3COOH, $K_a = 1.8 \times 10^{-5}$), phenol (C_6H_5OH, $K_a = 1.6 \times 10^{-10}$), and hypobromous acid ($HBrO$, $K_a = 2.8 \times 10^{-9}$). Three acids that are stronger than HOCl ($K_a = 2.9 \times 10^{-8}$) are acetic acid (CH_3COOH, $K_a = 1.8 \times 10^{-5}$), hydrofluoric acid (HF, $K_a = 7.2 \times 10^{-4}$), and nitrous acid (HNO_2, $K_a = 4.0 \times 10^{-4}$).
P17.4 Any of these are correct: hydrogen sulfate ion, chlorous acid, hydrofluoric acid, nitrous acid, and lactic acid.   **P17.5** Because bromine is more electronegative than sulfur (2.8 vs. 2.5), more electrons will be pulled away from the hydrogen end of the bond in HBr than in H_2S. HBr should be a stronger acid than H_2S.   **P17.6** $7.55 \times 10^{-5}M$
P17.7 a. 2.336; **b.** 8.558; **c.** 5.492; **d.** $1.2 \times 10^{-4}\ M$; **e.** $3.2 \times 10^{-4}\ M$;
f. $1.2 \times 10^{-10}\ M$ **P17.8** 6.14   **P17.9** 1.65, 0.022 M, $4.5 \times 10^{-13}\ M$
P17.10 3.00, 4.602   **P17.11** 2.92   **P17.12** 14.025   **P17.13** 12.23
P17.14 1.46   **P17.15** 9.07   **P17.16** 6.10

1. In the Arrhenius model, a base produces OH^- in solution, which ammonia does in the reaction $NH_3 + H_2O \rightleftharpoons NH_4^+ + OH^-$. In the Brønsted–Lowry model, a base accepts a proton from another species (the acid), which NH_3 does from water in the formation of NH_4^+ in the reaction.   **3. a.** NO_3^-; **b.** Br^-; **c.** OH^-; **d.** ClO_4^-
5. a. H_2O; **b.** NH_4^+; **c.** H_3O^+; **d.** HF   **7. a.** $2Al(s) + 6HCl(aq) \rightarrow 2AlCl_3(aq) + 3H_2(g)$, aluminum chloride; **b.** $Ca(s) + 2HNO_3(aq) \rightarrow Ca(NO_3)_2(aq) + H_2(g)$, calcium nitrate; **c.** $2Na(s) + 2HCl(aq) \rightarrow 2NaCl(aq) + H_2(g)$, sodium chloride; **d.** $2\ K(s) + 2HNO_3(aq) \rightarrow 2KNO_3(aq) + H_2(g)$, potassium nitrate   **9.** A strong acid is one that dissociates completely in solution to form H^+.

11. a.
$HCl + H_2O \rightarrow Cl^-$ + H_3O^+
Acid   Base   Conj. base   Conj. acid

b.
$NaOH + CH_3COOH \rightarrow CH_3COONa + H_2O$
Base   Acid   Conj. base   Conj. acid

c.
$H_2SO_4 + Mg(OH)_2 \rightarrow MgSO_4 + 2H_2O$
Acid   Base   Conj. base   Conj. acid

13.
$Mg(OH)_2 + 2HCl \rightarrow MgCl_2 + 2H_2O$
Base   Acid   Conj. base   Conj. acid

15. a. $K_a > 1$; **b.** The conjugate base will not regain H^+. **c.** 100%
17. HI; Even though bromine is slightly more electronegative than iodine, the iodide ion is much larger and has a much more diffuse electron density than the bromide ion. The attraction of H^+ for the larger I^- with its lower electron density is less, so the HI bond breaks more easily and HI is the stronger acid.   **19.** Because both acids have an equal number of oxygen atoms that contribute to pulling the electrons from the bond to hydrogen, we must consider the electronegativity of the central halogen atom. Chlorine has a higher electronegativity than bromine and weakens the bond to hydrogen more than in $HBrO_4$; therefore, $HClO_4$ must be the stronger acid.

21. a. acetic acid; **b.** formic acid   **23.** 1.2×10^{-5} **25. a.** 2.342; **b.** 5.485; **c.** 8.091   **27. a.** $3.8 \times 10^{-5}\,M$, $2.6 \times 10^{-10}\,M$, 9.58; **b.** 2.25, $1.8 \times 10^{-12}\,M$, 11.75; **c.** $1.3 \times 10^{-10}\,M$, 9.89, 4.11; **d.** $1.3 \times 10^{-4}\,M$, 3.9, $7.9 \times 10^{-11}\,M$ **29.** The concentration is lowered.   **31.** 12.769   **33. a.** 4.509; **b.** 4.538   **35.** 4.4×10^{-5} mol of OH^- **37. a.** 0.35; **b.** 1.35; **c.** 3.312; **d.** 3.59   **39. a.** 3.90; **b.** 3.17; **c.** 2.00; **d.** 3.47   **41. a.** 4.426; **b.** 1.735; **c.** 7.338   **43.** 1.6×10^{-6} **45.** both ($1.03 \times 10^{-3}\,M$ and $0.0010\,M$)   **47. a.** 513 g; **b.** $[F^-] = [H^+] = 1.3 \times 10^{-2}\,M$, $[OH^-] = 7.7 \times 10^{-13}\,M$ **49.** pH = 3.12; The approximation cannot be used.   **51. a.** 9.79; **b.** 12.00; **c.** 11.32   **53.** $[OH^-] = 1.18 \times 10^{-6}\,M$, pOH = 5.92, pH = 8.07   **55.** 7.1×10^{-4} **57.** $H_3PO_3 + H_2O \rightleftharpoons H_2PO_3^-$ + H_3O^+; $H_2PO_3^- + H_2O \rightleftharpoons HPO_3^{2-} + H_3O^+$; $HPO_3^{2-} + H_2O \rightleftharpoons$ $PO_3^{3-} + H_3O^+$; Phosphorus has an oxidation number of +3 in each of the species.   **59.** $[HPO_4^{2-}] = 6.2 \times 10^{-8}\,M$; pH = 1.08

61. $H_2SO_3 + H_2O \rightleftharpoons H_3O^+ + \boxed{HSO_3^-}$; $HSO_3^- + H_2O \rightleftharpoons H_3O^+ +$ $\boxed{SO_3^{2-}}$ **63.** 10.25   **65.** In order of decreasing pH: $NaC_2H_3O_2$, NaCl, NH_4Cl.   **67.** NaY   **69.** The isoelectric pH is the point where a chemical (usually an amino acid) is in its zwitterionic form (dual positive and negative charges) and is electrically neutral. Each amino acid will have its own isoelectric pH, which enables chemists to separate the amino acids electrically in a medium that has a pH gradient.   **71.** 5.31   **73. a.** 2.34×10^{-10}; **b.** 1.20×10^{-6}; **c.** 1.4×10^{-3} **75.** 8.22   **77. a.** $NH_3 + HCl \rightarrow NH_4Cl$; **b.** acidic because of NH_4^+; **c.** 5.06   **79.** 11.72   **81. a.** $C_6H_5COO^- + H_2O \rightarrow$ $C_6H_5COOH + OH^-$, $K_b = 1.5 \times 10^{-10}$; **b.** 8.09

83.

$$H_3\overset{\oplus}{N}-CH_2-CH_2-CH_2-CH_2-\overset{\overset{\displaystyle H}{|}}{\underset{\underset{\displaystyle COO^{\ominus}}{|}}{C}}-NH_2$$

85.

$$\overset{\overset{\displaystyle O}{\|}}{\underset{\underset{\displaystyle O}{\|}}{S}}=O$$

87. a. Because water is a neutral molecule, the addition of a positive proton to the structure results in a +1 charge. **b.** The hydrogen ion can associate with more than one unit of water to form $H_5O_2^+$, $H_7O_3^+$, etc. **c.** The Lewis structure of H_3O^+ has three bonds and one lone pair on the central oxygen. This molecule would have a tetrahedral electron geometry. Because the lone pair takes one corner of the tetrahedron, the molecular geometry is a trigonal pyramid. **89.** Yes. Even though a strong acid is 100% dissociated, a low enough concentration of the acid could be made to match the acidity of a concentrated weak acid solution.   **91.** Acetic acid is a stronger acid than water and therefore makes a weaker base than water. The strong acids will have a more difficult time dissociating in an acetic acid solution so that the differences in the strong acids can be detected by their varying dissociation in acetic acid.   **93.** The larger positive charge left behind, along with the reduced pull of the electronegative atoms due to the extra electrons left from the first ionization, limits the extent of the second ionization.   **95. a.** Ephedrine alkaloids act as a stimulant, as does caffeine. The combination of two stimulants greatly increases the chance of undesired side effects, including death. **b.** The ephedrine structure:

c. Yes. Alkaloids are natural nitrogen-containing molecules. The nitrogen in the structure is an amine that has basic (alkaline) properties; hence the name *alkaloid*.   **97. a.** Basic;

b. $KC_6H_7O_2(s) \rightarrow K^+(aq) + C_6H_7O_2^-(aq)$ followed by $C_6H_7O_2^- + H_2O \rightleftharpoons HC_6H_7O_2 + OH^-$; **c.** 8.38; **d.** 96.9 g; **e.** 10.63; The pH of the solution is much higher because of the presence of the ammonia.

Chapter 18

P18.1 8.88   **P18.2** acidic, 3.87   **P18.3** 8.2 g   **P18.4** 37 mL **P18.5** 4.44   **P18.6** 9.61, 8.59   **P18.7** 34 mL   **P18.8 a.** (0 mL, 0.6021); **b.** (10.00 mL, 0.9700); **c.** (20.00 mL, 1.5563); **d.** (25.00 mL, 7.000); **e.** (30.00 mL, 12.3565); **f.** (40.00 mL, 12.7611)

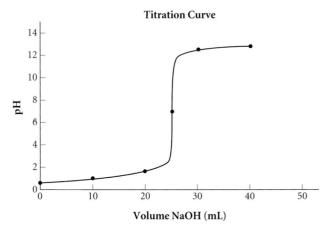

Titration Curve

P18.9 a. (0 mL, 2.67); **b.** (5.00 mL, 4.14); **c.** (12.50 mL, 4.74); **d.** (24.00 mL, 6.12); **e.** (25.00 mL, 8.92); **f.** (40.00 mL, 12.7611)

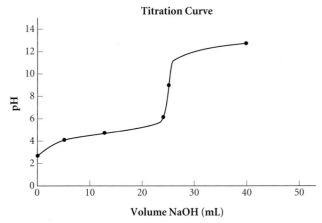

Titration Curve

P18.10 bromothymol blue   **P18.11** 1.82×10^{-2} mol/L **P18.12** 4.6×10^{-6} **P18.13** Yes, $Q_{sp} = 2.71 \times 10^{-14} > K_{sp}$ **P18.14** 6×10^{-5} **P18.15** 7.945 mL

1. a. $NH_3 + H_2O \rightleftharpoons NH_4^+ + OH^-$; $2H_2O \rightleftharpoons H_3O^+ + OH^-$; **b.** $Fe(OH)_3 \rightleftharpoons Fe^{3+} + 3OH^-$; $Fe^{3+} + 6H_2O \rightleftharpoons Fe(H_2O)_6^{3+}$; $Fe(H_2O)_6^{3+} + H_2O \rightleftharpoons Fe(H_2O)_5(OH)^{2+} + H_3O^+$; $2H_2O \rightleftharpoons$ $H_3O^+ + OH^-$; **c.** $HCOO^- + H_2O \rightleftharpoons HCOOH + OH^-$; $2H_2O \rightleftharpoons$ $H_3O^+ + OH^-$ **3. a.** yes; **b.** no; **c.** no; **d.** no; **e.** yes   **5. a.** 9.25; **b.** 8.30; **c.** 4.22   **7. a.** raises pH; **b.** lower pH; **c.** no effect   **9. a.** 10; **b.** 1.0; **c.** 0.10   **11. a.** 62 mL; **b.** 6.7 mL; **c.** 106 mL   **13. a.** 9.25; **b.** 4.74; **c.** 3.74   **15.** The final pH of a buffer is determined by the pK_a of the acid that sets the center of the possible range of pH for the buffer, whereas the exact ratio of the concentration of a conjugate base to its acid determines how far away the final pH is from the pK_a of the acid.

17. a. $K_a = \dfrac{[H^+][ClCH_2COO^-]}{[ClCH_2COOH]}$ and $K_b = \dfrac{[OH^-][ClCH_2COOH]}{[ClCH_2COO^-]}$;

b. 2.91　**19.** The two methods yield the same value: 10.34.　**21. a.** 9.26; **b.** 9.86; **c.** 10.43; **d.** 8.08　**23.** 0.64　**25. a.** 2.56; **b.** The buffer would be more resistant in the basic direction because there is more acid to react with added base.　**27.** 3.73　**29.** 4.88　**31. a.** 0.069 L; **b.** 0.11 L; **c.** 0.053 L; **d.** 0.011 L　**33. a.** 13.137; **b.** 12.99; **c.** 12.71; **d.** 7.00; **e.** 1.231　**35. a.** 11.13; **b.** 9.74; **c.** 9.26; **d.** 5.25; **e.** 1.903　**37. a.** 13.398; **b.** 13.342; **c.** 12.859; **d.** 11.59; **e.** 7.00; **f.** 2.53; **g.** 1.777

Titration Curve (KOH by HNO₃)

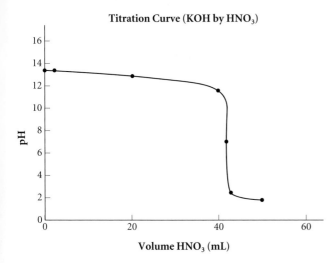

39. a. methyl orange or methyl red; **b.** phenolphthalein; **c.** bromthymol blue　**41. a.** colorless; **b.** green; **c.** red; **d.** blue　**43. a.** 8.69; **b.** 0.060 M; **c.** 0.36%　**45. a.** 8.85; **b.** 0.22; **c.** No, the endpoint will be at pH = 7.00, but the midpoint of color change will not occur until pH = 8.85.　**47. a.** $AgI(s) \rightleftharpoons Ag^+(aq) + I^-(aq)$; $K_{sp} = [Ag^+][I^-]$; **b.** $Ag_2CrO_4(s) \rightleftharpoons 2Ag^+(aq) + CrO_4{}^{2-}(aq)$; $K_{sp} = [Ag^+]^2[CrO_4{}^{2-}]$; **c.** $Al_2S_3(s) \rightleftharpoons 2Al^{3+}(aq) + 3S^{2-}(aq)$; $K_{sp} = [Al^{3+}]^2[S^{2-}]^3$; **d.** $Ca_3(PO_4)_2(s) \rightleftharpoons 3Ca^{2+}(aq) + 2PO_4{}^{3-}(aq)$; $K_{sp} = [Ca^{2+}]^3[PO_4{}^{3-}]^2$　**49. a.** 9.2×10^{-23} mol/L; **b.** 1.6×10^{-5} mol/L; **c.** 4.6×10^{-6} mol/L　**51. a.** 3.0×10^{-21}; **b.** 2.0×10^{-16}; **c.** 3.2×10^{-11}　**53.** BaF_2　**55. a.** A solid forms; **b.** A solid forms.　**57.** Acid reacts with iron (III) hydroxide, increasing its solubility. Additional base lowers the solubility because of to the excess hydroxide ion in solution.　**59.** $K_{sp} = [Ca^{2+}][F^-]^2$, 4.3×10^{-4} mol/L　**61.** $Ca(IO_3)_2$; Acidic solutions enhance the solubility by reacting with the anions, which are weak bases.　**63. a.** $Ag^+(aq) + NH_3(aq) \rightleftharpoons Ag(NH_3)^+$; $Ag(NH_3)^+ + NH_3(aq) \rightleftharpoons Ag(NH_3)_2{}^+$; **b.** $Ni^{2+}(aq) + NH_3(aq) \rightleftharpoons Ni(NH_3)^{2+}(aq)$; $Ni(NH_3)^{2+}(aq) + NH_3(aq) \rightleftharpoons Ni(NH_3)_2{}^{2+}(aq)$; $Ni(NH_3)_2{}^{2+}(aq) + NH_3(aq) \rightleftharpoons Ni(NH_3)_3{}^{2+}(aq)$; $Ni(NH_3)_3{}^{2+}(aq) + NH_3(aq) \rightleftharpoons Ni(NH_3)_4{}^{2+}(aq)$; $Ni(NH_3)_4{}^{2+}(aq) + NH_3(aq) \rightleftharpoons Ni(NH_3)_5{}^{2+}(aq)$; $Ni(NH_3)_5{}^{2+}(aq) + NH_3(aq) \rightleftharpoons Ni(NH_3)_6{}^{2+}(aq)$　**65. a.** 962 mL; **b.** 2370 mL; **c.** 1.5×10^{-11}　**67.** 64 mL　**69. a.** Because the K_{sp} value for $Cu(OH)_2$ is low (1.6×10^{-19}), the formation constant must be quite large to overcome the low solubility of the salt; **b.** $Cu^{2+}(aq) + NH_3(aq) \rightleftharpoons Cu(NH_3)^{2+}(aq)$; $Cu(NH_3)^{2+}(aq) + NH_3(aq) \rightleftharpoons Cu(NH_3)_2{}^{2+}(aq)$; $Cu(NH_3)_2{}^{2+}(aq) + NH_3(aq) \rightleftharpoons Cu(NH_3)_3{}^{2+}(aq)$; $Cu(NH_3)_3{}^{2+}(aq) + NH_3(aq) \rightleftharpoons Cu(NH_3)_4{}^{2+}(aq)$　**71.** lead–EDTA　**73.** blood chemistry, EDTA titrations of certain metals, growth of certain bacteria in a lab culture, and so on.　**75. a.** $H_2PO_4{}^-$ and $HPO_4{}^{2-}$; **b.** $[HPO_4{}^{2-}]/[H_2PO_4{}^-] = 9.8$　**77. a.** The zinc and cobalt ions are smaller than calcium, preventing strong coordination with all six EDTA binding sites. **b.** The higher charge of Fe^{3+} interacts more strongly with the –4 charge on EDTA.　**79. a.** 0.00050 M; **b.** 2.5×10^{-5} mol　**81. a.** 9.5×10^{-15} M; **b.** no　**82. a.** 2.6×10^{-4}; **b.** (0 mL, 2.46); (10.0 mL, 2.97); (25.6 mL, 3.58); (50.0 mL, 5.20); (75.0 mL, 12.134); (100.0 mL, 12.387); **c.** thymol blue; **d.** 24.0 g/mol

Titration Curve (HA by NaOH)

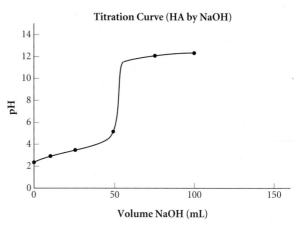

Answer 82b.

Chapter 19

P19.1 In $C_6H_{12}O_6$: H(+1), O(−2), C(0); In CO: O(−2), C(+2)　**P19.2** $Li_2S < S_8 < SO_2 < H_2SO_4$　**P19.3** −359 kJ, spontaneous　**P19.4** $2H^+(aq) + ClO^-(aq) + Cu(s) \rightarrow Cl^-(aq) + H_2O(l) + Cu^{2+}(aq)$　**P19.5** $2MnO_4{}^-(aq) + 3Mn^{2+}(aq) + 4OH^-(aq) \rightarrow 5MnO_2(s) + 2H_2O(l)$　**P19.6** −0.25 V, +0.98 V

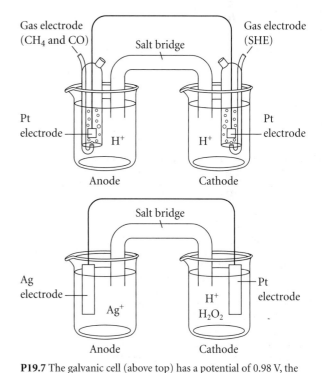

P19.7 The galvanic cell (above top) has a potential of 0.98 V, the electrolytic cell (above bottom) has a potential of −0.25 V.　**P19.8** $Al(s) \mid Al^{3+}(aq) \parallel Fe^{2+}(aq) \mid Fe(s)$　**P19.9** Ca > Na > Al > Cu　**P19.10** −0.0592 V, cathode, no　**P19.11** 1.45×10^{37}　**P19.12** 1.5 g

1. A *battery* is a series of cells, most "batteries" are single cells. **3.** The two reactions are a reduction reaction that involves the gain of electrons and an oxidation reaction that involves the loss of electrons.　**5.** O (−2), H (+1), S (−2), C (−1)　**7.** $NaClO_4$, HCl　**9.** $NH_3 < N_2H_4 < N_2O < NO < NO_2$　**11. a.** K (+1), O (−2), Mn (+7); **b.** Li (+1), O (−2), Mn (+3); **c.** H (+1), O (−2), N (−3), Cl (+7)　**13. a.** is reduced, is an oxidizing agent; **b.** is oxidized, is a reducing agent; **c.** is reduced, is an oxidizing agent　**15.** Reactants: Mg (0), H (+1), P (+5), O (−2); Products: Mg (+2), P (+5), O (−2), H (0)　**17. a.** +1; **b.** If ClO^- is a good oxidizing agent, it must be itself reduced which is a gain of electrons. **19. a.** Reactants: Sr $(+2)$, Cl (-1), Products: Sr (0), Cl (0); **b.** Sr^{2+} **21. a.** reduction: 1st reaction; oxidation: 2nd and 4th reactions; **b.** precipitation; **c.** $4Fe(s) + 3O_2(aq) + 2H_2O(l) \rightarrow 4FeO(OH)(s)$ **23.** concentrations $= 1M$, pressures $= 1$ atm **25. a.** non-spontaneous; **b.** negative; **c.** negative, positive; **d.** negative **27.** $2Fe^{3+} + Fe \rightarrow 3Fe^{2+}$, $E^{\circ}_{cell} = +1.2$ V **29.** -228 kJ **31.** -216 kJ **33.** The redox atoms must be balanced, the non-redox atoms must be balanced, and the electrons (used to balance the charges) involved in the oxidation and reduction half-reactions must cancel. **35. a.** $2CO_2 + 2H^+ + 2e^- \rightarrow H_2C_2O_4$, reduction, CO_2 is reduced; **b.** $Np^{4+} + 2H_2O \rightarrow NpO^{2+} + 4H^+ + e^-$, oxidation, Np^{4+} is oxidized. **37. a.** $Sn^{2+} + 2Cu^{2+} \rightarrow Sn^{4+} + 2Cu^+$; **b.** $I_3^- + 2S_2O_3^{2-} \rightarrow S_4O_6^{2-} + 3I^-$; **c.** $Fe^{3+} + SO_3^- + H_2O \rightarrow SO_4^{2-} + Fe^{2+} + 2H^+$ **39.** acidic: $Cr_2O_7^{2-} + 14H^+ + 3Cu \rightarrow 3Cu^{2+} + 2Cr^{3+} + 7H_2O$; basic: $Cr_2O_7^{2-} + 7H_2O + 3Cu \rightarrow 3Cu^{2+} + 2Cr^{3+} + 14OH^-$ **41.** $ClO_4^- + I^- \rightarrow IO_3^- + ClO^-$ **43. a.** -0.76 V; **b.** 1.5×10^2 kJ; **c.** -0.76 V **45. a.** Li^+; **b.** F_2; **c.** $Zn + Cu^{2+} \rightarrow Cu + Zn^{2+}$, $E^{\circ}_{cell} = 1.10$ V **47.** $2CO_2 + Cu + H_2O \rightarrow CuO + 2H^+ + C_2O_4^{2-}$ **49.** $2MnO_4^- + 16H^+ + 5C_2O_4^{2-} \rightarrow 10CO_2 + 2Mn^{2+} + 8H_2O$ **51.** $I_2 + C_6H_8O_6 \rightarrow C_6H_6O_6 + 2H^+ + 2I^-$ **53.** A *cell* is an electrochemical device consisting of an anode and cathode allowing for the exchange between chemical and electrical energy. A *half reaction* is the equation that describes the reduction or oxidation part of a redox reaction. A *galvanic cell* is a cell that produces electricity from a chemical reaction (also known as a *voltaic cell*). The *electromotive force* is a measure of how strongly a species pulls electrons towards itself in an redox process. **55.** Zn, Cu^{2+} **57.** The reduction potentials for lead ion and silver ion are -0.13 V and 0.80 V respectively. For a spontaneous reaction, the silver ion reaction will remain as a reduction and lead will be oxidized. If the nitrate ions are moving left to right through the salt bridge, the electrons are moving from the right cell to the left cell, which is the opposite of the standard convention. This requires that the left beaker be the cathode (gaining electrons) and the right beaker be the anode (losing electrons). Therefore, the oxidation of lead will occur in the right beaker and reduction of silver in the left beaker.

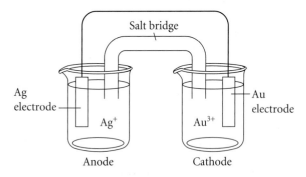

59. a. 0.70 V; **b.** 3; **c.** shown above; **d.** Au^{3+}; **e.** $Ag | Ag^+ \| Au^{3+} | Au$ **61.** $Zn(s) | ZnO(s) \| HgO(s) | Hg(l)$ **63. a.** Ba; **b.** Pb^{2+}; **c.** left **65.** Placing the metal in the solution will reveal its identity. Only the oxidation potential of aluminum in nickel is positive enough to be spontaneous when coupled with the reduction of nickel. The tin will not react.

67. $\dfrac{RT}{F} = \dfrac{(8.3145 \text{ J/mol·K})(298.15 \text{ K})}{\left(96485 \text{ C/mol} \times \frac{1 \text{J/V}}{1 \text{C}}\right)} = 0.0257 \text{ V}$ Natural logarithms and base 10 logarithms are related by $\ln x = 2.303 \log x$, so we must multiply the value of 0.0257 V by 2.303 to give 0.0592 V. **69. a.** 0.78 V; **b.** 0.75 V; **c.** 0.81 V **71.** $\Delta G = 0$, the battery has

reached equilibrium, and $E_{cell} = 0$ V **73. a.** 0.051 g; **b.** 12.0 g; **c.** 44 g **75.** cathode, 0.33 A **77.** 15.5 g **79.** The steel pan is the cathode, copper metal can serve as the anode. **81. a.** $E^{\circ} = 0.97$ V, $K = 3.98 \times 10^{196}$; **b.** $4FeO_4^{2-} + 10H_2O \rightarrow 20OH^- + 4Fe^{3+} + 3O_2$; **c.** 0.76 V; **d.** At high pH, $Fe(OH)_3$ forms. This solid removes Fe^{3+} from the water and forces the reaction to completion. **83. a.**

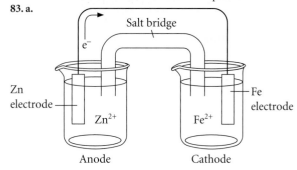

b. $Zn \rightarrow Zn^{2+} + 2e^-$; **c.** 0.32 V; **d.** 0.32 V, 0.32 V; **e.** No. Because the concentrations are equal, the ln term goes to zero and the temperature has no effect. **f.** Avoids use of toxic metals like lead. **g.** Both Zn and Fe corrode in water.

Chapter 20

P20.1 a. $[FeCl_6]^{4-}$; **b.** $[Ni(NH_3)_4]^{2+}$; **c.** $[Zn(H_2O)_6]^{2+}$
P20.2 a. 6, octahedral; **b.** 6, octahedral; **c.** 4, tetrahedral; **d.** 4, tetrahedral **P20.3 a.** tetraamminedichlorochromium(IV) sulfate; **b.** sodium tetracyanonickelate(II); **c.** $Ca_2[FeF_6]$; **d.** $[Mn(NH_3)_4(CO)_2]SO_4$
P20.4 none unpaired

1. a. A ligand is a Lewis base that donates a lone pair of electrons to a metal center to form a coordinate covalent bond; **b.** A coordinate covalent bond is a covalent bond that results when one atom donates both electrons needed to form the bond; **c.** A Lewis acid accepts a pair of electrons from another atom in the formation of a coordinate covalent bond. **3. a.** 6, +2, 6; **b.** 6, +2, 6; **c.** 4, +2, 4; **d.** 4, 0, 4

5.

7. $H-\overset{\displaystyle ..}{\underset{\displaystyle |}{N}}-H$; NH_3 is a Lewis base because it is capable of donating the electron pair to form a bond.

9. Yes; bidentate **11.** Ca^{2+} and C_2H_6 have no lone pairs and would not act as ligands. **13.** The structure of ethylenediamine is $NH_2CH_2CH_2NH_2$. Both NH_2 groups will have a lone pair and be able to act as a Lewis base. The carbon backbone is long enough to allow both nitrogen atoms to form a bond with the same metal atom. While N_2 does have two lone pairs, they are found at opposite ends of a linear molecule. It is not possible for both nitrogen atoms to form separate bonds with the same metal atom. **15.** B is bidentate **17. a.** +4, 6; **b.** +2, 6; **c.** +2, 4 **19.** Some of the ligands are bidentate; there can be more bonds than ligands. **21.** 4

23. a.

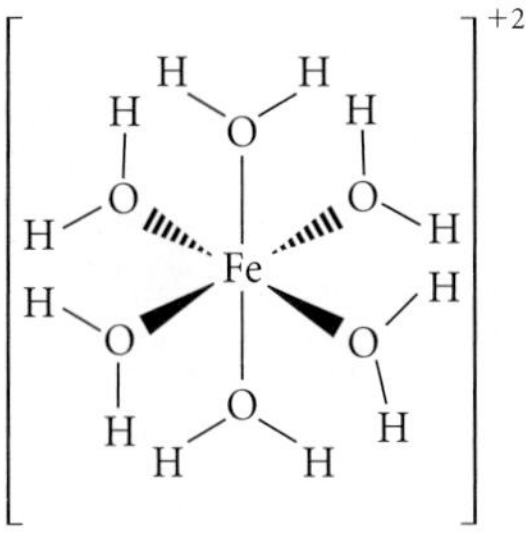

octahedral, all 90°;

b.

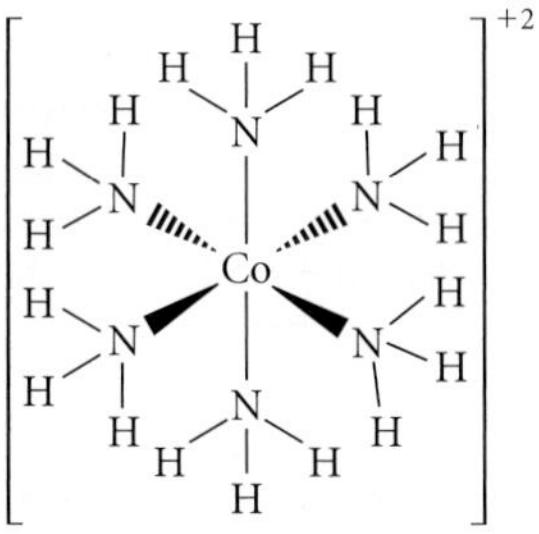

octahedral, all 90°;

c.

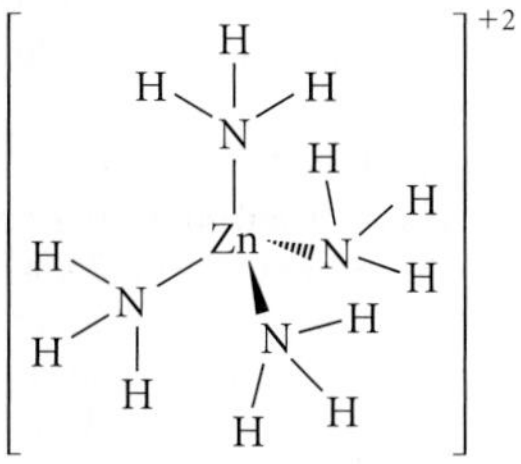

tetrahedral, all 109.5°;

d.

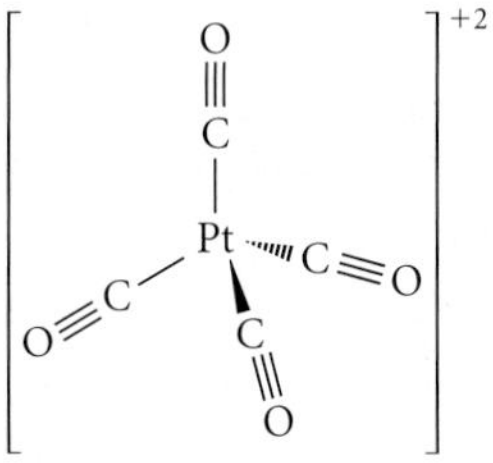

tetrahedral, all 109.5°

25. +3, 6, octahedral **27.** 4, tetrahedral or square planar
29. a. geometric; **b.** ionization; **c.** coordination sphere
31.

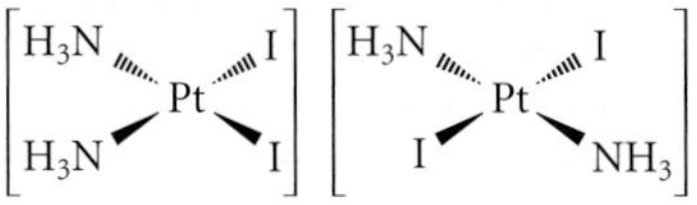

cis   *trans*

If the platinum is placed at the center of a hypothetical tetrahedron, each ligand would reside at one of the vertices. Because each vertex is directly connected to the other three (containing one ligand like itself and two that are different), it is not possible to create more than one unique arrangement. There can be no isomers.

33. Only two:

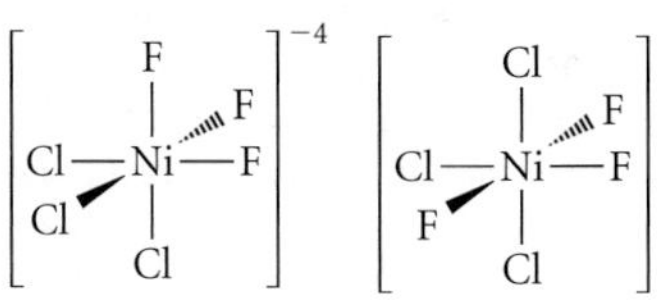

35.

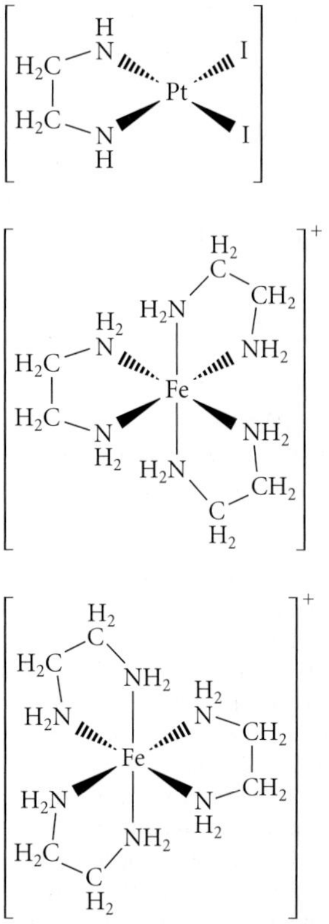

37. a. amminecyanobis(ethylenediamine) cobalt (III);
b. diamminedioxalatochromate(III); **c.** hexanitroferrate(III);
d. triaquatrichlorocobalt(III)
39. a. $[CoCl(NH_3)_4(H_2O)]^{2+}$; **b.** *trans*-$[Cu(H_2O)_2(en)_2]Cl_2$;
c. $Na_2[CoCl_4]$; **d.** $[MnCl(CO)_5]$ **41.** Tetraamminediaquachromium(III) nitrate, $[Cr(NH_3)_4(H_2O)_2](NO_3)_3$ **43. a.** $[Ar]3d^6$;
b. $[Ar]3d^4$; **c.** $[Ar]3d^{10}$ **45.** Fe^{3+}

47. a. Fe^{3+} is d^5: 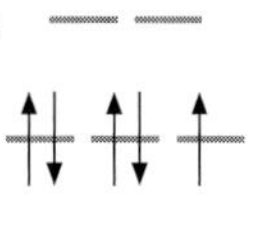   **b.** Co^{2+} is d^7:

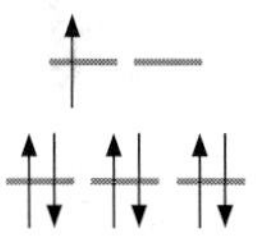

c. Ni^{2+} is d^8:

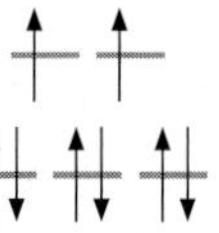

49. a. Fe^{3+} is d^5: 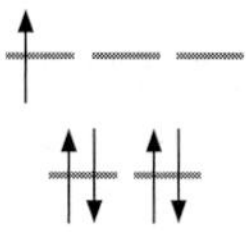   **b.** Co^{2+} is d^7:

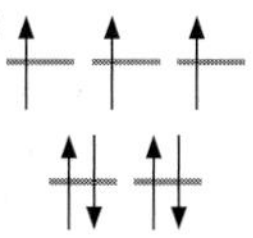

c. Ni^{2+} is d^8:

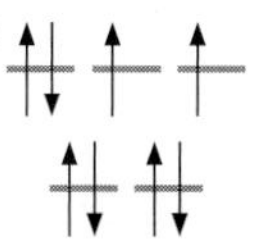

51. a. tetrahedral high spin Fe^{3+} (d^5),

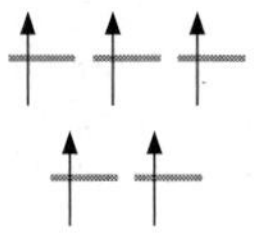

b. octahedral low spin Co^{3+} (d^6)

c. octahedral low spin Mn^+ (d^6)

53. all **55.** $M(CN)_6^{2-}$ **57.** No, The chemical species that form the majority of the common gemstones is the same for most stones and will have the same spectrum. **59. a.** yellow and red; **b.** 3; **c.** higher; According to the electrochemical series, ammine ligands cause larger splits in the d orbitals than does water; therefore, the ammine complex should absorb higher energy visible light; **d.** NH_3 **61.** Replacing two ligands with a single chelating ligand frees more species into solution, raising the entropy. **63.** Labile; labile **65.** Nearly all transition metals have important catalytic properties. **67.** Cation; $[Co(NH_3)_4Cl_2]^+$ is +1 because the total charges are $(+3) + 4 \times (0) + 2 \times (-1) = +1$. **69. a.** If there are some electrons in the d-orbitals of the metal center in a complex, but not enough electrons to fully fill the orbitals, electronic transitions are possible. Any configuration from d^1 to d^9 will be able to have its electrons promoted by light absorption; **b.** The energy of the photon being absorbed is determined by the splitting between the d-orbital levels, which is controlled by the ligands of the complex. The splitting increases in order with the spectrochemical series: $Cl^- < F^- < OH^- < H_2O < NH_3 < NO_2^- < CN^- < CO$; **c.** The intensity of the transition will increase with greater population in the lower states and lower population in the higher states. **71.** Larger K

72. a.

b.

c. Since the ammine complex has a violet color and the ethanedithiol complex is blue, the absorbed colors are green and yellow respectively. Green light lies at a higher energy than yellow; therefore the splitting caused by the ethanedithiol is less than that caused by ammine. The new ligand will fall before NH_3 in the spectrochemical series; **d.** 4; **e.** The ligand is inert.

Chapter 21

P21.1 a. 16, 16; **b.** 11, 12; **c.** 86, 136; **d.** 43, 55 **P21.2** $^{60}_{27}Co \rightarrow$ $^{0}_{-1}\beta + ^{60}_{28}Ni$ **P21.3** $^{218}_{84}Po \rightarrow ^{4}_{2}He + ^{214}_{82}Pb + ^{0}_{0}\gamma$, $^{230}_{90}Th \rightarrow ^{4}_{2}He + ^{226}_{88}Ra + ^{0}_{0}\gamma$ **P21.4** 17.8 days **P21.5** 5.588×10^8 kJ/mol **P21.6 a.** Stable; **b.** Stable; **c.** Stable; **d.** Stable or unstable: The numbers of protons and neutrons are odd, which argues for instability, but the mass is very close to the average periodic table mass, which argues for stability. It is in fact stable.

P21.7

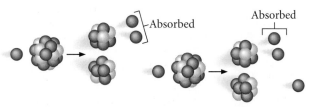

P21.8 The first and third structures are not suitable. This first has a radioactive tritium that is easily removed as an acidic hydrogen ion, and the third is not structurally the same as salicylic acid.

1. ^1_1H for both **3.** Yes, an atom can have no neutrons. Hydrogen, ^1_1H, has no neutrons—only a proton is required. **5.** Yes, ^2_2He has a smaller mass than ^3_1H. **7. a.** 7, 5, 7; **b.** 51, 73, 51; **c.** 63, 89, 63; **d.** 4, 5, 4 **9.** 0.014 g **11. a.** Sr^{2+}; **b.** Its chemical behavior is similar to that of calcium. **13.** Gamma rays have more energy per photon. **15. a.** $^{239}_{94}Pu \rightarrow ^4_2He + ^{235}_{92}U + ^0_0\gamma$; **b.** $^{14}_6C \rightarrow ^{0}_{-1}\beta + ^{14}_7N$; **c.** $^{137}_{55}Cs \rightarrow ^{0}_{-1}\beta + ^{137}_{56}Ba + ^0_0\gamma$ **17. a.** $^{219}_{86}Rn \rightarrow ^4_2He + ^{215}_{84}Po + ^0_0\gamma$; **b.** $^{90}_{38}Sr \rightarrow ^{0}_{-1}\beta + ^{90}_{39}Y$; **c.** $^{99}_{43}Tc \rightarrow ^{0}_{-1}\beta + ^{99}_{44}Ru + ^0_0\gamma$ **19.** $^{146}_{62}Sm \rightarrow ^4_2He + ^{142}_{60}Nd$ **21.** Th-232 **23.** Ionizing: cosmic rays, gamma rays, X-rays; Nonionizing: visible light, microwaves, IR radiation **25.** Use minimum gamma doses, wear protective clothing, apply the dose while in a different room. **27. a.** They differ only in the amount of disintegrations, (1 curie $= 3.7 \times 10^{10}$ Bq); **b.** A rem is the biologically adjusted version of rad. **29.** 3.5×10^4 disintegrations/s **31. a.** 0.40 mrem; **b.** This radiation is not unduly hazardous. **33. a.** Density; **b.** chemical reactivity, radiation hardness (does it weaken with exposure?), secondary radiation reactivity **35. a.** A; **b.** 10 min; **c.** A; **d.** A **37.** 15 days **39.** 50%, 25% **41.** 86.7 yr **43.** 0.45 days **45.** The sample would need to be replaced every other year (assuming that 5% of the original activity is still useful.) **47.** 1.6×10^5 yr; It is continuously generated by the decay of other long-lived radioactive nuclei. **49. a.** Some of the mass is lost as energy in the process of creating the nucleus; **b.** Yes. **51.** The binding energy, ΔE, is related to the mass defect, Δm, via $\Delta E = |\Delta m|c^2$. **53.** -0.006627 g/mol; 5.956×10^8 kJ/mol **55. a.** reactants **b.** The result is the release of energy and creation of binding energy of the products. **57.** Both processes involve the conversion between a neutron and proton. However, the beta-minus decay converts a neutron into proton, whereas the beta-plus decay converts a proton into a neutron. **59. a.** "Doubly magic" means that a nuclide has both a number of protons and a number of neutrons that are among the most stable numbers (2, 8, 20, 28, 50, 82, and 114); **b.** Oxygen-16 has 8 each of protons and neutrons, and 8 is one of the magic numbers. Helium-4 has 2 each of protons and neutrons, matching the magic number of 2. Carbon-12 has 6 each, and nitrogen-14 has 7 each. These two nuclides do not have a magic number of either protons or neutrons. In general, those nuclei without a magic number of protons or neutrons are more likely to be radioactive. **61.** Element 114 would have a magic number of protons and would probably be more stable and have a longer half-life before decaying. **63.** In order to reach the nearest stable nuclide, the heavy radioactive nuclides such as uranium and plutonium need to shed at lot of mass and can do so by emitting alpha particles. For nuclides of lighter elements, there are stable nuclides that can be created by converting protons and neutrons by beta decay and need not lose mass to achieve stability. **65.** Iron and cobalt have the most stable nuclei of all atoms, with the largest binding energy per nucleon. **67. a.** $^{235}_{92}U + ^1_0n \rightarrow ^{139}_{56}Ba + ^{94}_{36}Kr + 3^1_0n$ + energy; **b.** $^{235}_{92}U + ^1_0n \rightarrow ^{80}_{38}Sr + ^{153}_{54}Xe + 3^1_0n$ + energy **69. a.** The number of neutrons differs; **b.** U-235 is 0.72% and U-238 is 99.28% of the total. **c.** They are alike chemically and differ by only 1.3% in their total mass, which makes them difficult to separate using physical methods.   **71.** Fission creates smaller nuclei. Americium, californium, and berkelium are all heavier than uranium.   **73.** Some of the most important questions should be about the total radioactive dose expected, as well as the form of the radiation emitted. What is the half-life of the nuclide, and what is its expected persistence in the body?   **75.** Tc-99m has a half-life of 6 hours. After the night (12 hours) is over, only 1/4 of the original will remain.   **77.** $^{18}_{9}F \rightarrow \, ^{0}_{+1}\beta + \, ^{18}_{8}O$ **79.** Yes, with a half-life of 60 hours, only 0.8% remains after 2.5 weeks.   **81.** The medical reference to see is Winters. T. H., & Franza, J. R., Radioactivity in Cigarette Smoke, *New England Journal of Medicine*, 1982; 306(6): 364–365. The radioactive isotopes lead-210 and polonium-210 are found in the tobacco leaves and cigarettes.   **83.** The gamma ray represents the energy that is given off in the reaction, which is possible only if a mass defect exists.   **85.** alpha, beta, beta, alpha, alpha, alpha, alpha, beta, beta, alpha   **87.** Rn is radon, an inert gas; and Ra is Radium, a reactive metal solid.   **89.** The main reason why Rn-222 is the most dangerous is that it is the only species with a long half-life. The other isotopes decay much more rapidly into solid species. Rn-222 has a half-life of 3.8 days, which is enough time for the gas to seep into houses and be inhaled by people inside.   **91.** The density of the nucleus is much greater: 2.8×10^{15} g/cm^3 compared to 11.3 g/cm^3 for lead.   **93.** Websites may vary. The answer is NO!   **95.** A nice site with clickable names and more information can be found at http://www.slac.stanford.edu/library/nobel/.   **96. a.** <0.2 mg; **b.** Am-240 undergoes electron capture with a half-life of 51 hours. Not only does it not emit a particle, but nearly all would be gone very quickly—not a useful property for a smoke detector, which should last several years. Am-242 does emit beta particles 83% of the time, but it has a half-life of only 16 hours. Again, there would be little left in a very short time, making it also impractical for use in a smoke detector.   **c.** $^{241}_{95}Am \rightarrow \, ^{4}_{2}He + \, ^{237}_{93}Np + \, ^{0}_{0}\gamma$; **d.** 2900 yr; **e.** $^{242}_{95}Am \rightarrow \, ^{0}_{-1}\beta + \, ^{242}_{96}Cm + \, ^{0}_{0}\gamma, \, ^{242}_{95}Am + \, ^{0}_{-1}\beta \rightarrow \, + \, ^{242}_{94}Pu + \, ^{0}_{0}\gamma$

Chapter 22

P22.1 Adenine   **P22.2** The sequence that pairs with our strand is GATACG, *or* we need to reverse the smaller strand (CGTATC), which would then bind with a sequence of GCATAG in the longer strand:

AAAATGCTG GCATAG CGTTCCA GATACG GACTGACTGC . . . .
        CGTATC   CTATGC

P22.3 Methionine–tryptophan–proline–lysine–leucine–aspartic acid–methionine–phenylalanine–aspartic acid   **P22.4** Lyase, transferase, ligase

1. DNA is a huge nucleotide polymer that has a double-helical structure. Each strand of the DNA polymer complements the other by forming base pairs. DNA provides instructions for the synthesis of proteins and enzymes that carry out the biological activities of the cell.   **3.** TAATTTTTCCCTGAT   **5.** Four   **7.** Valine and leucine or glycine and alanine
9.

11. A codon is a three-nucleic-acid sequence on an mRNA that is translated into a particular amino acid during protein synthesis.   **13.** If the wrong nucleotide is used in the production of the mRNA or an extra nucleotide is added to or removed from the mRNA, a different three-nucleotide codon may result that could specify a different amino acid.   **15.** Middle   **17.** Globular   **19.** Oxidoreductase   **21.** By binding to the enzyme and inhibiting further production, the product itself can ensure that its concentration does not rise too high or ensure that it is created only as needed.   **23.** Tetrose   **25.** Aldose   **27.** Glucose   **29.** Fructose is one of the two sugars that results from the hydrolysis of sucrose. Fructose is classified as a hexose, and ketose.   **31.** At room temperature, fats are solids and oils are liquids.   **33.** Fat   **35.** The upper polar region

37.

39. Because the body uses principally a single type of enantiomer, having chiral enzymes ensures that only the proper enantiomer is used in a protein or other product. The cell will not waste resources on a molecule it cannot use.   **41.** Tryptophan, no   **43.** RNA: AUG|UCG|CGA|AUU|UAA|GGC|UGC|UUA|UU; Protein: methionine-serine–arginine–isoleucine   **45.** Each of the molecules is saturated. As the chain length increases, the strength of the dispersion forces increases, requiring more energy and higher temperatures to melt. The longer chains therefore have higher melting points.   **47.** If the receptors that are responsible for detecting the sweetness of a food are sensitive only to a particular enantiomeric form, the other enantiomer is not sensed as sweet. However, if the receptors are *not* specifically sensitive to only the normal enantiomeric form, the other form could also taste sweet. The advantage to being able to taste the opposite enantiomer is that it may not be able to be metabolized—it would have no calories!

49. a.

b. Because both reactions involve the hydrolysis, the enzyme may be able to catalyze the reaction; however, many enzymes have a very specific active site and therefore would not be able to catalyze the reaction; **c.** Lysine can be coded by the AAA or AAG codon on mRNA and by the UUU or UUC anticodon on tRNA; **d.** 9.50 kg; **e.** 8.16 kg; **f.** Nonedible fibers could be converted into edible food.

Credits

Text and Illustrations

Photos

Chapter 1

Chapter 2

Chapter 3

Chapter 4

(**top right**) Photograph by Michele A. Justice. (**center**) Brookhaven National Laboratory. (**bottom**) blinkwinkel/Alamy.

Chapter 5

167: NASA. **168:** NASA. **172: (top)** Achim Sass/Westend61/Alamy. (**bottom**) NASA. **174:** AP/Wide World Photos. **175: (all)** © Houghton Mifflin Company. All rights reserved. **177:** NASA. **178:** NASA. **179: (top)** Douglas Pulsipher/Alamy. (**bottom**) © Houghton Mifflin Company. All rights reserved. **180: (both)** © Houghton Mifflin Company. All rights reserved. **181:** © Houghton Mifflin Company. All rights reserved. **187: (top)** Mark Baker/Reuters/Landov. (**bottom**) © Houghton Mifflin Company. All rights reserved. **188:** Kim Heacox/Peter Arnold Photography. **193:** AP Photo/Dean J. Koepfler. **196:** Archive of the Goldschmidt Gmbh. **197:** Goh Cha Hin/AFP/ Getty Images. **198: (top)** Peter Frischmuth/ Peter Arnold Photography. (**bottom left**) FPL Energy. (**bottom right**) Corbis Royalty-Free. **199: (top)** © Reuters CORBIS (**bottom**) John A. Turner/National Renewable Energy Laboratory.

Chapter 6

209: Courtesy: IBM Research, Almaden Research Center. Unauthorized use prohibited. **210:** Photo 24/Brand X Pictures/Getty Images. **212:** Courtesy of Casio. **213:** Science Photo Library/Photo Researchers, Inc. **214: (bottom)** National Telecommunications and Information Administration Office of Spectrum Management. (**top**) Junko Kimura/Getty Images. **215:** © Alfred Pasieka/Peter Arnold, Inc. **217: (left)** © Houghton Mifflin Company. All rights reserved. (**right**) © Richard Megna/Fundamental Photographs, NYC. **221:** Post Danmark. **224: (top)** Index Stock/Alamy. (**bottom**) © B. Runk/S. Schoenberger/Grant Heilman Photography. **225: (top)** © Peter Beck/CORBIS. (**bottom**) Science Photo Library/Photo Researchers Inc. **226:** © Royalty-Free/Corbis. **228:** © Bettmann/CORBIS. **229:** NIST. **230:** © George D. Lepp/CORBIS. **232: (top)** © Bettmann/CORBIS. (**bottom**) © Hulton-Deutsch Collection/ CORBIS. **233:** © Royalty-Free/Corbis. **237:** Courtesy: IBM Research, Almaden Research Center. Unauthorized use prohibited. **242: (top)** © Bettmann/CORBIS. (**bottom**) © Gabe Palmer/CORBIS. **243:** Science Photo Library/Photo Researchers, Inc. **255:** © Royalty-Free/Corbis.

Chapter 7

259: Getty Images. **260: (top)** © Royalty-Free/Corbis. (**bottom**) Photodisc Green/Getty Images. **261:** © PEMCO-Webster & Stevens Collection; Museum of History and Industry, Seattle/CORBIS. **262: (all)** © Houghton Mifflin Company. All rights reserved. **264: (top)** © Houghton Mifflin Company. All rights reserved. (**bottom left**) University of Chicago Library. (**bottom right**) Edgar Fahs Smith Collection, University of Pennsylvania Library. **265:** © Houghton Mifflin Company. All rights reserved. **266:** © Royalty-Free/Corbis. **267: (left)** The Art Archive/British Library. (**right**) Mark Joseph/Digital Vision/Getty Images. **268: (left right)** © Houghton Mifflin Company. All rights reserved. **270: (left and right)** © Houghton Mifflin Company. All rights reserved. **271: (all photos of metals)** © Houghton Mifflin Company. All rights reserved. (**bottom left**) AP/Wide World Photos. **272: (all)** © Houghton Mifflin Company. All rights reserved. **273: (top left and right)** © Houghton Mifflin Company. All rights reserved. (**bottom**) © Roger Ressmeyer/CORBIS. **274: (top photos, bottom left)** © Houghton Mifflin Company. All rights reserved. (**bottom right**) © 1993 Richard Megna, Fundamental Photographs, NYC. **275: (top)** Photodisc Blue/Getty Images. (**center**) David Buffington/Photodisc Green/Getty Images. (**bottom**) © Houghton Mifflin Company. All rights reserved. **276: (top)** Modified from the protein data bank structure, 1AG6. Primary reference: Xue, Y., Okvist, M., Hansson, O., Young, S. "Crystal structure of spinach plastocyanin at 1.7 A resolution," *Protein Sci.,*

1998, *7,* 2099. (**bottom left and right**) © Houghton Mifflin Company. All rights reserved. **277:** Elementree © Fernando Dufour. Photographer Joseph Donahue, Montreal, Quebec, Canada. **278:** Scott Camazine/Photo Researchers, Inc. **283: (all)** © Houghton Mifflin Company. All rights reserved. **289:** Wonderfile. **291:** Modified from the protein data bank structure, 1A3N and 1GZX. Primary reference: Paoli, M., Liddington, R., Tame, J., Wilkinson, A., Dodson, G. "Crystal Structure of T State Haemoglobin with Oxygen Bound at All Four Haems," *J. Mol. Biol.*, 1996, *256,* 775. **292: (left)** Chuck Pefley/Alamy. (**right**) David Toase/Photodisc Green/Getty Images. **293:** © Houghton Mifflin Company. All rights reserved. **299:** © Royalty-Free/Corbis. **301:** © Houghton Mifflin Company. All rights reserved.

Chapter 8

302: © Houghton Mifflin Company. All rights reserved. **304:** Lewis, Gilbert Newton. *Valence and the Structure of Atoms and Molecules.* New York: The Chemical Catalog Company, Inc., 1923. Othmer Library of Chemical History, Chemical Heritage Foundation, Philadelphia, PA. **307: (top)** Wonderfile. (**chalk**) Stockbyte Gold/Alamy. (**salt**) © Houghton Mifflin Company. All rights reserved. (**pigment**) Photograph by James Scherer. © Houghton Mifflin Company. All rights reserved. (**Milk of Magnesia**) Photograph by James Scherer. © Houghton Mifflin Company. All rights reserved. (**glass**) Ragnar Schmuck/fStop/Getty Images. (**baking soda**) © Houghton Mifflin Company. All rights reserved. (**salt**) © Royalty-Free/Corbis. (**toothpaste**) Ingram Publishing/Alamy. **310:** Science Photo Library/Photo Researchers, Inc. **316: (top)** Stockfood. (**bottom**) © Houghton Mifflin Company. All rights reserved. **317: (left)** © Houghton Mifflin Company. All rights reserved. (**top center**) Don Farrall/Photodisc Green/Getty Images. (**bottom center**) Robert Sullivan/Getty Images. (**right**) © Houghton Mifflin Company. All rights reserved. **318:** Bryan Mullennix/Getty Images. **323:** Collection of The Corning Museum of Glass, Corning, NY, gift of Mr. and Mrs. Richard Barons. **329:** © Houghton Mifflin Company. All rights reserved. **338:** © Houghton Mifflin Company. All rights reserved.

Chapter 9

355: Omikron/Photo Researchers, Inc. **363: (left)** Andrew Lawson Photography/Alamy. (**center**) Andrew Cowin/Alamy. (**right**) © Eric Crichton/CORBIS. **364:** © Houghton Mifflin Company. All rights reserved. **380:** © Richard Megna/Fundamental Photographs, NYC. **382: (left)** Library of Congress. (**right**) Courtesy of Eastman Kodak Company.

Chapter 10

394: Kevin Kelley/Getty Images. **396:** © Air Products and Chemicals, Inc. **400:** © Houghton Mifflin Company. All rights reserved. **401: (left)** © Houghton Mifflin Company. All rights reserved. (**right**) Courtesy of Cryovac, Inc. **402:** © Houghton Mifflin Company. All rights reserved. **403:** © Shepard Sherbell/CORBIS SABA. **404: (all)** © Houghton Mifflin Company. All rights reserved. **406: (left)** Courtesy of the Chemical Heritage Foundation Image Archives. *The Shannon Portrait of Hon. Robert Boyle F.R.S. (1627–1691),* 1689, Johann Kerseboom, oil on canvas. Chemical Heritage Foundation Collections, Philadelphia, Pennsylvania, U.S.A. Photo by Will Brown. (**center**) Courtesy of Carlos Castro-Acuna. (**left**) Michael Mosher. **407:** Michael Mosher. **408:** © Houghton Mifflin Company. All rights reserved. **409: (top)** Musee Lambinet, Versailles, France/Bridgeman Art Library. (**bottom**) Edgar Fahs Smith Collection, University of Pennsylvania Library. **419:** Patti McConville/Getty Images. **421: (left)** Bert Hardy/Getty Images. (**right**) © SSPL/The Image Works. **427:** © Houghton Mifflin Company. All rights reserved. **429:** NASA. **430:** BananaStock/Alamy. **431: (left)** © Royalty-Free/Corbis. (**right**) The source of this material is the Cooperative

Program for Operational Meteorology, Education, and Training (COMET®) Website at http://meted.ucar.edu/ of the University Corporation for Atmospheric Research (UCAR) pursuant to a Cooperative Agreement with National Oceanic and Atmospheric Administration. © 2000 University Corporation for Atmospheric Research. All Rights Reserved. **432:** New York Times Graphics. **436:** © Houghton Mifflin Company. All rights reserved. **439:** © Houghton Mifflin Company. All rights reserved.

Chapter 11

440: © Julio Etchart/Peter Arnold, Inc. **442:** Map entitled "Freshwater Withdrawal by Sector in 2000," from *World Resources 2000–2001, People and Ecosystems: The Fraying Web of Life,* WRI, 2000. **443:** USGS; aquaculture photo courtesy of Clear Springs Foods, Inc. **445, 452, 455, 456:** © Houghton Mifflin Company. All rights reserved. **459:** NASA/JPL-Caltech. **462:** (**top center**) © Houghton Mifflin Company. All rights reserved. (**bottom**) imagebroker/Alamy. **463:** (**top**) © Royalty-Free/Corbis. (**bottom left and right**) © Houghton Mifflin Company. All rights reserved. **465:** © Houghton Mifflin Company. All rights reserved. **472:** (**top**) DigitalVues/Alamy. (**bottom**) © Houghton Mifflin Company. All rights reserved. **473:** Art Vandalay/Photodisc Red/Getty Images. **476:** Edgar Fahs Smith Collection, University of Pennsylvania Library. **477:** © Houghton Mifflin Company. All rights reserved. **480:** © Leonard Lessin/Peter Arnold, Inc. **481:** (**top**) Mark Richards/PhotoEdit. (**center**) David Young Wolff/PhotoEdit. (**bottom**) Christine Osborne Pictures/Alamy.

Chapter 12

491: © Karen Kasmauski/CORBIS. **492:** (**top**) ZEE/Alamy. (**bottom**) Hugh Threlfall/Alamy. **493:** © Royalty-Free/Corbis. **494:** AP/Wide World Photos. **495:** Andrew Lambert/Photo Researchers, Inc. **496:** (**left**) © Amos Nachoum/CORBIS. (**center**) Shape'n'color/Alamy. (**right**) B.A.E. Inc./Alamy. **501:** Stockbyte Platinum/Alamy. **506:** © Royalty-Free/Corbis. **507:** Courtesy of Agilent. **515:** © Houghton Mifflin Company. All rights reserved. **524:** © Houghton Mifflin Company. All rights reserved.

Chapter 13

539: Don Tremain/Photodisc Green/Getty Images. **540:** © Ari J. Bauman/Phototake. **541:** © Royalty-Free/Corbis. **545:** (**left**) Edward Kinsman/Photo Researchers, Inc. (**right**) Courtesy of CCLRC. **546:** N. Vogelaar, Virginia Tech Cyrstallography Lab. **555:** © Reuters/CORBIS. **557:** (**top**) Mauro Fermariello/Photo Researchers, Inc. (**bottom**) Mauro Fermariello/Photo Researchers, Inc. **558:** (**left**) Winfred Evers/Getty Images. (**right**) Courtesy of Lehigh Northwest Cement Ltd. **559:** © James L. Amos/CORBIS. **560:** Phanie/Photo Researchers, Inc. **561:** © Gabe Palmer/CORBIS. **562:** (**left**) Courtesy of Bruker. (**right**) Courtesy of Bruker. **567:** AP/Wide World Photos. **568:** Scott Camazine/Photo Researchers, Inc. **569:** © Houghton Mifflin Company. All rights reserved. **570:** AP/Wide World Photos. **572:** (**top**) Clive Freeman/Biosym Technologies/Photo Researchers, Inc. (**bottom**) Lawrence Berkeley National Lab.

Chapter 14

579: © Houghton Mifflin Company. All rights reserved. **582:** John Noel Photographic Collection. **586:** (**top**) © Houghton Mifflin Company. All rights reserved. (**bottom**) © David G. Houser/Post-Houserstock/Corbis. **591:** imagebroker/Alamy. **593:** (**left**) Panoramic Images/Getty Images. (**right**) V. Tunicliffe, University of Victoria. **594:** Philip & Karen Smith/Getty Images. **608:** © Galen Rowell/CORBIS. **614:** © Houghton Mifflin Company. All rights reserved.

Chapter 15

619: Photolibrarycom/Getty Images. **622:** © Reuters/CORBIS. **623:** AP/Wide World Photos. **631:** © Nicole Duplaix/CORBIS. **632:** Courtesy of Brookhaven National Laboratory. **639:** Courtesy of Delphi. **642:** © Still Pictures/Peter Arnold, Inc. **656:** Courtesy of Engelhard. **657:** (**top**) © Houghton Mifflin Company. All rights reserved. (**bottom**) PDB ID: 1W2T; F. Alberto, B. Henrissat, M. Czjzek, 2004.

Chapter 16

668: K-Photos/Alamy. **669:** (**top**) AP/Wide World Photos. (**bottom**) Modified from the protein data bank structure, 1A3N and 1GZX. Primary reference: Paoli, M., Liddington, R., Tame, J., Wilkinson, A., Dodson, G. "Crystal Structure of T State Haemoglobin with Oxygen Bound at All Four Haems," *J. Mol. Biol.,* 1996, *256,* 775. **676:** (**left**) Steve Dunwell/Getty Images. (**right**) Photolink/Photodisc Green/Getty Images. **679:** Science Photo Library/Photo Researchers, Inc. **700:** Edgar Fahs Smith Collection, University of Pennsylvania Library. **701:** AP/Wide World Photos. **704:** Image courtesy Altair Nanotechnologies. **709:** Photograph by James Scherer. © Houghton Mifflin Company. All rights reserved. **714:** © Houghton Mifflin Company. All rights reserved.

Chapter 17

717: © Bob Daemmrich. **719:** © Houghton Mifflin Company. All rights reserved. **720:** Edgar Fahs Smith Collection, University of Pennsylvania Library. **723:** © Todd Gipstein/CORBIS. **727:** © Pete Stone/CORBIS. **748:** (**both**) © Houghton Mifflin Company. All rights reserved. **756:** Photograph of isoelectrically focused barley proteins is by permission of the Department of Primary Industries and Fisheries, Queensland, Australia. **757:** David Woodfall/Getty Images. **758:** National Atmospheric Deposition Program.

Chapter 18

765: © Peticolas/Megna/Fundamental Photographs, NYC. **766:** © Houghton Mifflin Company. All rights reserved. **767:** © Houghton Mifflin Company. All rights reserved. **772:** (**both**) © Houghton Mifflin Company. All rights reserved. **787:** (**left**) © Houghton Mifflin Company. All rights reserved. (**right**) Courtesy of Dispersion Technology, Inc. **799:** (**all**) © Houghton Mifflin Company. All rights reserved. **802:** © Jonathan Blair/CORBIS. **807:** © Houghton Mifflin Company. All rights reserved. **809:** Jonathan A. Meyers/Photo Researchers, Inc.

Chapter 19

823: Maximilian Stock Ltd./Photo Researchers, Inc. **825:** (**top**) Siman Fraser/Photo Researchers, Inc. (**bottom**) AP/Wide World Photos. **826:** (**left**) © Charles O'Rear/CORBIS. (**right**) Edgar Fahs Smith Collection, University of Pennsylvania Library. **827:** Joe Raedle/Getty Images. **834:** (**all**) © Houghton Mifflin Company. All rights reserved. **840:** (**both**) © Houghton Mifflin Company. All rights reserved. **845:** (**both**) © Houghton Mifflin Company. All rights reserved. **849:** © Royalty-Free/Corbis. **850:** (**both**) © Houghton Mifflin Company. All rights reserved. **852:** (**all**) © Houghton Mifflin Company. All rights reserved. **853:** © Houghton Mifflin Company. All rights reserved. **859:** Stockdisc Classic/Getty Images. **860:** © Houghton Mifflin Company. All rights reserved.

Chapter 20

868: Erich Lessing/Art Resource, NY. **873:** © E. R. Degginger/Color-Pic, Inc. **876:** From Coste et al., "Crystal structure of a double-stranded

Index/Glossary

Page numbers followed by *f* refer to figures. Page numbers followed by *t* refer to tables.

Degree Celsius (°C) *The unit of temperature on the Celsius scale,* 19
Degree Fahrenheit (°F) *The unit of temperature on the Fahrenheit scale,* 18–19
Dehydrogenation *The removal of hydrogen,* 510–511
Delocalized *Term used to describe a π system wherein the electron density in a molecule can be distributed among more than two atoms,* 233, 384–385
Democritus, 46–47
Denature *To destroy the biochemical activity of a protein,* 946
Density *The mass of a substance that is present in a given volume of the substance. The SI unit for measuring density is kilograms per cubic meter (kg/m^3),* 8, 22, 682
  of crystalline solids, 548–549
  as derived unit, 22–23
  as intensive property, 23–24
  of metals, 25
  and molar mass of gases, 419
Dental amalgams, 557
Deoxyhemoglobin, 870f, 892
Deoxyribonucleic acid (DNA) *A huge nucleotide polymer that has a double-helical structure. Each strand of the DNA polymer complements the other by forming base pairs. DNA provides instructions for the synthesis of proteins and enzymes that carry out the biological activities of the cell,* 935–939
  basic structure of, 70, 935–939
  compared with RNA, 941–942
  composition of, 47, 65
  DNA profiling, 825
  effects of radiation on, 911
  impact of damage to, 945
  location of, 939
  as multi-charged ion, 938
  nucleotide sequence of, 941
  replication process, 938–939
Deoxyribose *A dehydrated carbohydrate used in the construction of DNA,* 935, 937f, 941
Dependent variable, A6
Deposition *The process of a gas undergoing a phase transition to a solid; the opposite of sublimation,* 452
Derived units *Units formed by the combination of SI base units,* 21–23
Desalination *The process that removes dissolved salts from seawater to make potable water,* 10–11, 480–481
Desorbed *Released from a surface,* 656
Deuterium, 57, 58t, 244
Diamagnetism *The ability of a substance to be repelled from a magnetic field. This property arises because all of the electrons in the molecule are paired,* 380, 891
Diamminedichloroplatinum(II), 881–882

Diamond
  band gap of, 554
  structure of, 493
Diatomic elements *Elements whose normal state is in the form of molecules composed of two atoms attached together (most notably H_2, N_2, O_2, F_2, Cl_2, Br_2, and I_2),* 51f, 70, 71
  MO diagrams for, 378–380
Diazinon, 638
Dibasic salt *A salt that can accept two hydrogen ions,* 748
Dichloroethane, 514
Dichloromethane, 385t, 510
Diet
  organic foods, 62–63
  power of peanuts, 180–181
  quantitative chemistry and, 116
  units of Calories, 179–181
  vitamins, 116, 950–952
Diethylenetriaminepentaacetic acid (DTPA), 811t
Diethyl ether, 512t, 524
Diffraction pattern *A pattern of constructive and destructive interference after EMR passes through a solid material,* 546
Diffusion *The process by which two or more substances mix,* 424–427
  entropy and, 588
Dilithium, 362, 378, 551
Dilution
  ideal solutions and, 474
  of solutions, 137–139
Dimensional analysis *An extremely useful method for performing calculations by using appropriate conversion factors and allowing units (dimensions) to cancel out, leaving only the desired answer in the desired units,* 26–28
2,2-Dimethylbutane, 446–447
2,3-Dimethylbutane, 446–447
Dimethyl mercury, 876
2,4-Dimethylpentane, 498f
2,2-Dimethylpropane, 498
2,5-Dimethylpyrazine, formulas for, 99–101
Dinitrogen tetroxide, reaction with methylhydrazine, 195–196
Diode lasers, 224t
Dipole–dipole forces, 448
Dipole moment *The polarization of electrons in a molecule that results in a net unequal distribution of charges throughout the molecule,* 344–345, 444
Diprotic *Can produce 2 mol of H^+ when it dissolves,* 151
Diprotic acid *An acid that contains two acidic protons,* 736
Disaccharide *A carbohydrate made from the condensation of two simple sugars,* 955f, 956
Disorder, vs. entropy, 588
Disproportionation *A reaction in which a single reactant is both the oxidizing and reducing agent,* 830–831

Dissociation constant, 683
Distribution constant *The equilibrium constant that describes the partitioning of a solute between two immiscible phases,* 678
DNA. *See* Deoxyribonucleic acid
Dobereiner, Johan, 263
Dodecane, boiling point of, 447–448
Dopamine, 963
Dope *To add an impurity to a pure semiconductor to alter its conductive properties,* 554
Double bond *A covalent bond consisting of two individual bonding pairs of electrons,* 326, 327
Double helix, 936–937
"Dover Boat," 51–52
Drug testing
  chromatography for, 678, 679f
  mass spectrometer for, 61, 62f
Ductile *Able to be pulled or drawn into a wire,* 552–553, 556
Duet rule *The exception to the octet rule involving the atoms H and He. A full valence shell for the atoms H and He,* 306, 323, 359
Dynamic equilibrium *A term sometimes used in chemistry as synonymous with equilibrium to emphasize that molecular-level equilibrium is not static,* 453

Earth
  gravitational force of, 398
  structure of, 292–294
EDTA. *See* Ethylenediaminetetraacetic acid
Effusion *The process by which a gas escapes through a small hole,* 424–427
Einstein, Albert, 47, 215, 222
Ekasilicon, 264
Electric current, 17t, 20
Electric eel, 844
Electrochemical cells *A device that allows the exchange between chemical and electrical energy,* 825–826, 844–849
  cell notation, 847
  commercial batteries, 846, 847–849
  concentration cell, 853–854
  electrolytic cells, 826
  fuel cells, 826, 827f, 830
  heart cells, 853–854
  in laboratory, 845–846
  voltaic cells, 825–826
Electrochemistry *The study of the reduction and oxidation processes that occur at the meeting point of different phases of a system,* 824–860
  balancing redox reactions, 836–841
  chemical reactivity series and, 849–850
  defined, 824–826
  determining standard voltage, 844
  electrochemical cells, 825–826, 844–849
  electrolytic reactions, 857–860

Valence shell electron-pair repulsion model *A model that proposes the three-dimensional shapes of molecules on the basis of the number of electron groups attached to a central atom. Also known as VSEPR,* 335–343
  bond angles and electron pairs in, 341–343
  description of, 337
  examples of, 337–341
  limitations of, 357
Valine, 755*f*, 940*f*
Valium, 747*t*
Vanadium
  electron configuration of, 249
  reduction of, 856–857
  in steel, 267
Vanadium oxide, 704
van der Waals, Johannes Diderik, 416–417, 445
van der Waals equation *The equation that corrects the gas laws for gases that deviate from ideal behavior,* 416–417
van der Waals forces *The intermolecular forces of attraction that result in associations of adjacent substances,* 445
Vanilla, GC/MS analysis of, 62–63
van't Hoff, Jacobus Henricus, 336, 476, 479
van't Hoff factor *A factor that modifies the colligative properties on the basis of their ability to dissociate in solution,* 476, 477*t*
Vaporization, heat of, 457–458
Vapor pressure *The pressure of vapor above a liquid in a closed system,* 452–455, A17
Vapor pressure lowering, 474–475
Velocity
  as derived unit, 22*t*
  kinetic energy and, 170
Venable, Francis, 420
Vinyl chloride, 420, 516*t*
Violeo complex, 880
Viscosity *A measure of resistance to flow,* 462
Visible spectrum, 213, 885*f*
Vitamins *Small molecules that we need for proper health. Normally, vitamins either are not synthesized in our bodies or are made in insufficient amounts,* 950–952
Vitamin A (retinol), 287–288, 950–951
Vitamin B1 (thiamine), 949*f*, 950*t*, 952
Vitamin B2 (riboflavin), 950*t*
Vitamin B6, 950*t*
Vitamin B12, 951*t*
Vitamin C (ascorbic acid), 89, 723, 951*t*
  in human body, 116, 952
  molecular formula of, 140*f*
  titration of, in solution, 140–141
  water solubility of, 287–288
Vitamin D (calciferol), 950, 951*t*
Vitamin E (alpha-tocopherol), 951–952
Vitamin K, 951*t*
Volt *The SI unit of potential,* 834

Volta, Alessandro, 825, 826*f*
Voltage *A measure of how strongly a species pulls electrons toward itself. Also known as electromotive force (emf),* 834
Voltaic cell *A cell that produces electricity from a chemical reaction. Also known as a galvanic cell,* 825–826. *See also* Electrochemical cells
Volume
  conversion factors for, 26
  as derived unit, 22
  deviations of real gases, 416–417
  as extensive property, 23*t*
  law of combining, 50–51
  in pressure–volume work, 176–177, 186
  relationship with amount, 404–405, 423
  relationship with pressure, 15–16, 405–408, 422
  relationship with temperature, 408–411, 423
  of unit cells, 547–548
  using molarity to calculate, 134–135
Volumetric glassware, 138
VSEPR model *A model that proposes the three-dimensional shapes of molecules on the basis of the number of electron groups attached to a central atom. See* Valence shell electron-pair repulsion model

Walker, John E., 545
Warner, John, 571
Water
  autoprotolysis of, 733, 737, 738
  boiling-point elevation of, 476*t*
  boiling point of, 19, 445
  different names for, 71
  dipole–dipole forces in, 448
  dipole moment in, 345, 444
  dissolution of salt in, 465–466
  electrolysis of, 397
  electron density map of, 127*f*, 829*f*
  enthalpy of formation of, 188
  formation of, 6, 7*f*, 10, 50–51, 150–151
  formula for, 70
  freezing-point depression for, 478*t*
  heating curve for, 456–458
  hybrid orbitals in, 367
  hydrogen bonds in, 448–450
  impact of radiation on, 910–911
  intermolecular forces in, 444–445
  iron in, 870–871
  meniscus of, 463–464
  molecular shape of, 336–337, 340, 357, 368, 444
  oxidation numbers for, 154, 827–829
  phase changes of, 451–452
  phase diagram for, 459–460, 461
  pH scale and, 733–735
  polar covalent bonds in, 321
  properties of, 465, 766
  protecting fresh water, 157–159
  reaction with phosgene, 333

  simultaneous detection of elements in, 219–220
  specific heat of, 181*t*, 456, 457
  stability as liquid, 444, 445, 449
  standard state of, 187
  structure of ice, 459, 461
  surface tension of, 462–463
  testing for small amounts of, 142
  as universal solvent, 126–131, 465–468
  vapor pressure of, 452–453, 474, A17
Water consumption, 441–443
Water treatment and standards
  chlorine usage, 157–158
  desalination process, 10–11, 480–481
  with fluoride ion, 137–139, 313
  for hard water, 309–310, 767, 814
  industrial wastewater, 145–146, 148, 158, 807
  measuring contaminants, 135–136, 157–159
  sedimentation, 808–809
  use of chelates, 812*t*
Watson, James, 936–937
Wave energy, 172–174
Wave function *The mathematical equation describing a system, such as an electron, atom, or molecule, that contains all physical information that can be obtained for the system by quantum mechanics,* 232–234
Wavelength *A descriptor of electromagnetic radiation. Defined as the distance from the top of one crest to the top of the next crest of the electromagnetic wave,* 211–215
Wave–particle duality *The quantum mechanical theorem that states that all things have both wave and particle natures simultaneously and that both of these natures can be observed on the atomic scale,* 225–227
  of electrons, 227–229
  of protons, 230–231
Waves
  classical mechanics view of, 226–227
  quantization and, 227–229
  standing, 226
Weak acids *An acid that only partially dissociates in water,* 150, 724–730
  equilibrium constants for, 725*t*
  pH of, 738–742
Weak bases *A base that partially dissociates in solution,* 150
Weak electrolyte *Any substance that only partially dissociates in solution,* 129–131
Weight *A measure of the gravitational force exerted on a body,* 17–18
  counting by, 89–92
Weight percent *A concentration unit based on the mass of the solute per total mass of solution, reported in percent,* 470
Werner, Alfred, 880
Whole-number ratios, 100
Wilkinson's catalyst, 872

SI Units

Physical Quantity	Name of Unit	Symbol
Amount of substance	mole	mol
Electric current	ampere	A
Length	meter	m
Luminous intensity	candela	cd
Mass	kilogram	kg
Temperature	kelvin	K
Time	second	s

SI Unit Prefixes

Multiple	Prefix	Name
10^{24}	Y	yotta
10^{21}	Z	zetta
10^{18}	E	exa
10^{15}	P	peta
10^{12}	T	tera
10^{9}	G	giga
10^{6}	M	mega
10^{3}	k	kilo
10^{-1}	d	deci
10^{-2}	c	centi
10^{-3}	m	milli
10^{-6}	μ	micro
10^{-9}	n	nano
10^{-12}	p	pico
10^{-15}	f	femto
10^{-18}	a	atto
10^{-21}	z	zepto
10^{-24}	y	yocto